PRACTICAL BUSINESS FORECASTING

Michael K. Evans

Blackwell Publishers

© Michael K. Evans 2003

Editorial Offices:
108 Cowley Road, Oxford OX4 1JF, UK
  Tel: +44 (0)1865 791100
350 Main Street, Malden, MA 02148-5018, USA
  Tel: +1 781 388 8250

First published 2002 by Blackwell Publishers Ltd, a Blackwell Publishing company

Library of Congress Cataloging-in-Publication Data has been applied for

ISBN 0-631-22065-8 (hbk)
ISBN 0-631-22066-6 (pbk)

A catalogue record for this title is available from the British Library.

Set in 10.5 in 12.5 pt Plantin
by SNP Best-set Typesetter Ltd., Hong Kong
Printed and bound in MPG Books, Bodmin, Cornwall

For further information on
Blackwell Publishers, visit our website:
www.blackwellpublishers.co.uk

PRACTICAL BUSINESS FORECASTING

DATE DUE

Demco, Inc. 38-293

To Sophie Evans Brill

CONTENTS

ACKNOWLEDGMENTS

I would first like to thank Donald P. Jacobs, the "legendary Dean" at the Kellogg Graduate School of Management at Northwestern University, who provided the opportunity for me to teach this course at Kellogg. I would also like to thank Dipak Jain, who was Professor of Marketing and has now replaced Don Jacobs as Dean, for many helpful comments and suggestions.

Al Bruckner, the former Executive Editor at Blackwell Publishing, has been most helpful in guiding me through the writing and publishing process, sticking with me "through thick and thin" to develop this textbook in its present form. In a day and age when editors often seem to change at the drop of a hat, it has indeed been a pleasure to have someone of Al's experience and expertise to work on the book from start to finish.

This book has also benefited from numerous conversations with my son, David, who has built several credit scoring models for a major financial institution – which, I am proud to report, had continued increases in earnings throughout the recent recession even as competitors posted sharply lower earnings or actual losses.

It has become pro forma in these pages to thank one's wife, but in this case, I owe an extraordinary debt of gratitude to my wife, Susan. For more than 30 of the past 40 years, she has worked with me in my various companies, has heard the good, the bad, and the crazy, and has always served as an invaluable sounding board. Without her encouragement this book never would have been completed.

PREFACE

Practical Business Forecasting is designed to appeal to a wide range of academic, corporate, and consulting economists who have interest or responsibilities in forecasting at the macroeconomic, industry, or individual company level.

The text first discusses various methods of forecasting and alternative goals that might be desired. It then turns to a discussion of econometric and regression analysis, followed by material on time-series forecasting, and concludes with a wide variety of practical forecasting applications for both single-equation and simultaneous-equation models.

The material in this text is written at a level for those who have some familiarity with basic statistics, but is not designed to be a theoretical treatment. Proofs are not given in the text, and no matrix algebra is used, although references are provided for those with further interest.

The emphasis of this book, as shown by the title, is in building practical forecasting models that produce optimal results. Sometimes, robust theories cannot be empirically implemented because of data limitations. Often, standard tests will tell the practitioner little or nothing about whether the equation can forecast accurately. The text is not intended to be an encyclopedia or long review article. Hence references are quoted only when clearly relevant. Practical hints about how to build a forecasting equation that works are given much higher priority than extended discussion about properties of normal distributions.

In the 1960s and the early 1970s, most economists and practical business forecasters alike thought that econometric models would provide the most accurate forecasts, both at the macroeconomic level and for individual industries and product lines. However, the results were particularly disappointing in the late 1970s and the early 1980s. As a result, several other methods of forecasting moved to the forefront: statistical methods that did not involve economic theory but were based on lagged variables and previous error terms; surveys of consumer and business sentiment; consensus forecasts; and informed judgment. Several economists suggested that forecasting accuracy could be significantly improved by combining these methods. Currently, there is no general agreement among economists and forecasters about which methods are most likely to generate forecasts with the smallest error.

Interpreting forecast records will always be a subjective undertaking. Unlike, say, the stock market, where a 20% increase or decrease in the S&P 500 index is an immutable record once it happens, data on which forecasts are based are often subject to revision. There is also the question of being "right for the wrong reasons"; if someone forecasts continued growth next year because they miss the signs of emerging weakness, but the economy begins to soften and the monetary authorities manage to avert a downturn by timely easing, is that a good forecast or not? At the company level, who is the better forecaster: the analyst who predicts that sales and earnings will rise next quarter, which is what the company initially reports, or the analyst who predicts that sales and earnings will drop, which is what finally emerges after the SEC investigates the company for fraudulent accounting practices?

For these reasons, it is unlikely that anyone will ever establish a definitive method for benchmarking true ex ante forecasts. Nonetheless, it is usually possible to determine, for any given time frame, whether forecaster A provided more accurate results than forecaster B, and to identify the methods used by each forecaster. Over time, as the evidence accumulates, it should be possible to identify which methods work better than others.

This author has been generating macroeconomic, industry, and company forecasts for almost 40 years; obviously not all of these forecasts have been successful. Nonetheless, this experience has provided a clear picture of what works and what does not work. A fairly extensive track record of alternative methods of forecasting at the macro level also provides additional information about which methods work best.

Based on this information, this text takes the following position. Most of the time, the best forecasts are generated using properly specified and properly estimated econometric models, adjusted for recent developments and structural shifts in the underlying functions. That may appear to be a broad generalization, but in fact leads to some very specific conclusions. Mechanical methods of forecasting, such as correlating the current variable with its own lagged values and previous error terms, generate inferior forecasts. At the macro level, surveys of consumer and business sentiment usually generate larger forecasting errors than do econometric models. Combining various forecasting methods that individually provide inferior results does not usually improve the forecasting record.

There are a few exceptions, notably short-term forecasting in the financial sector, where econometric models have so far proven to be inferior. Because the impact of human interaction and reaction is so great in these areas, short-term forecasts based on econometric models are no better than naive models that assume the change next period will be the same as the change this period, or the average change in the past. Over the longer term, though, underlying economic relationships become more important and can be helpful in gauging changes in market behavior.

The weight of the evidence this author has been able to accumulate strongly suggests that the proper use of econometric models will generate the most accurate forecasts. Hence most of the book focuses on the methods that should be used to estimate these models. Some material is included on time-series models – generally known as ARIMA models – and on sentiment and judgment, but the evidence suggests they have not improved forecasting accuracy over the past years and decades.

Having said this, it should be emphasized that forecasting is an art, not a science, and even the best econometric model needs to be adjusted regularly to generate optimal forecasts. That will indeed raise the cry in some quarters that it is really judgment, rather than econometrics, that is driving the forecast, and those complicated multiple regression equations are merely an attempt to distract the unwary client into believing that a tremendous amount of intellectual effort went into building this sophisticated model structure, whereas in fact the equations are largely extraneous and the real forecasts are based on judgmental factors.

Once again, it is virtually impossible to provide an unbiased answer to that charge; the consultant will claim that "of course" the econometrics are the key ingredient, while the critic will answer "nonsense." However, it is not necessary to engage in a battle of histrionic proportions to provide an intelligent framework in which to evaluate this claim. Consider three alternative and competing hypotheses.

1   Underlying structural relationships remain stable over time, although they are sometimes jolted by exogenous forces.
2   Because people learn from past mistakes, behavioral patterns of the past will not be repeated in the future, and hence any attempt to project the future from these past patterns is doomed to failure.
3   No underlying structural relations are really stable, but they change slowly.

If researchers and forecasters believe that (1) most accurately describes the state of the real world, then the classical postulates of statistics and econometric would apply. If they believe that (2) is most accurate, which is essentially the view postulated by the rational-expectations critics of models, than econometric and statistical methodology are inept and inaccurate methods to use for forecasting. If they believe that (3) is most accurate, which is the hypothesis advanced by Charles Bischoff in a recent article on forecasting discussed in detail in chapter 12, then one ought to proceed by estimating econometric models but adjusting them frequently.

The underlying focus and purpose of this book is based on the hypothesis that (3) most accurately describes the underlying economic forces in the real world, and hence concentrates on this approach.

The material in this text is divided into five parts. Part I provides some basic background information about the forecasting process. Chapter 1 discusses the general concepts of forecasting accuracy and describes alternative types of forecasts. Since no model is any better than its data, chapter 2 discusses where to find useful data and how to check for possible errors. A brief statistical review of goodness-of-fit statistics is also included. Since the examples in this book are based on the EViews statistical package for the PC, this program is briefly described.

Part II focuses on estimating and forecasting with econometric models that consist of a single equation. Chapter 3 provides a brief review of the standard classical linear model; a detailed statistical treatment is not included, since that is available in many other textbooks. Also, most of the underlying assumptions are not applicable to practical business forecasting. Hence after setting the stage, the remainder of chapter 3 discusses how forecasters should treat auto-correlation and heteroscedasticity. Chapter 4 covers the topics of eliminating or reducing spurious trends, and determining the optimal lag structure, issues that are not often treated within the confines of the classical linear model but are of great importance for practical business forecasting. This chapter also explains the proper use of dummy variables and estimation of nonlinear regressions. Chapter 5 presents and analyzes a battery of tests designed to determine the structural stability of the equation, and also discusses methods for adjusting the constant terms in forecasting equations. Most of this material in this part focused on the econometric approach; the contributions of judgment are not discussed here.

Part III covers the standard material for univariate time-series modeling and forecasting. Chapter 6 shows how a time series can be decomposed into the trend, cyclical, seasonal, and irregular components, with particular emphasis given to smoothing data and methods of seasonal adjustment. Chapter 7 presents the development and rationale for ARIMA models – regressing a variable on its lagged values and previous error terms. The issue of trend removal and integration is also discussed in this chapter. While these methods can be useful for tracking models containing thousands of equations, several examples are introduced to show that, most of the time, these methods do not generate very accurate forecasts compared with econometric models.

Part IV focuses on the forecasting accuracy for single-equation models, as opposed to the underlying econometric and statistical methodology. Chapter 8 discusses the situations under which combining forecasts is likely to provide more accurate results, and when it probably will not. In general, combining forecasts will not improve forecasting accuracy if the forecasts are all based on the same underlying data set, assumptions, or methodology. In contrast, fore-casting accuracy can be significantly improved by adjusting the constant terms in the regression equations. Chapter 9 provides several examples of actual short-term sales forecasting models, including the key steps that are important in presenting these forecasts to management or consulting clients. Chapter 10 turns to a variety of statistical and judgmental methods for long-term forecast-ing, where it is generally assumed that the underlying structural relationship will shift over time.

Part V covers additional forecasting issues associated with multi-equation models. Chapter 11 discusses the issues associated with simultaneous equation bias, which is shown to be a much smaller contributor to forecasting error than improperly specified equations. Chapter 12 presents the results of a small prototype macro model, and shows how forecasting accuracy is affected by adjusting the constant terms of the model, using an autoregressive adjustment, and combining these results with surveys, consensus forecasts, and informed judgment.

Throughout the book, case studies are used to illustrate how these models are actually estimated and adjusted to generate true ex ante forecasts. An old story has it that, in the old days of secretaries and Dictaphones, one novice transcribed "econometrics" as "economist's tricks." In the minds of many economists and business executives, that aroma still lingers. This book attempts to dispel that concern, to erase the "black box" image, and explicitly present the actual methods and adjustment procedures that are used. It is clear that in many cases, the choice of variables that are used, the form in which they enter the equations, the lag structures, and the adjustment of the constant terms, are all matters of judgment. However, after reading this book, it is also hoped that the reasons behind these choices will become clearer, and students and readers will have a firmer foundation to use in estimating econometric models used for practical business forecasting.

PART I

CHAPTER 1

CHOOSING THE RIGHT TYPE OF FORECASTING MODEL

INTRODUCTION

Practical business forecasting is both a science and an art. It is a science in the sense that correct use of sophisticated statistical tools will invariably improve forecasting accuracy. It is an art in the sense that empirical data seldom if ever provide an unequivocal answer, so the user must choose between alternative relationships to select those equations that will provide the most accurate forecasts.

There are no perfect forecasts; they always contain some error. While perhaps that is obvious, it is nonetheless important to emphasize this fact at the outset. The point of this book is to show how to minimize forecast error, not to pretend that it can be eliminated completely. To accomplish this goal, a variety of forecasting methods may be used. In many cases, these methods will be complementary, not competitive.

Forecasts can be used for many purposes. Sometimes, predicting the direction of change is sufficient. For example, a model that could accurately predict the direction of the stock market the following day – even without providing any information about how much it would rise or fall – would be extremely valuable and profitable. No such model has ever been successfully constructed, although many have tried, and the goal will presumably remain elusive. At the other extreme, a model that predicted the direction of change in the consumer price index (CPI) the following month without forecasting the magnitude would be virtually useless, since over the past 40 years the monthly changes in the CPI have been negative only about 1 percent of the time.

There are many ways of forecasting, not all of which are based on rigorous statistical techniques. In some cases, informed judgment can provide the best forecasts, such as when "insiders" have company information that is not available to anyone else. Surveys may provide useful information about forecasts for the overall economy, specific sectors, or individual industries and firms. To the extent that these methods improve forecasting accuracy, they should be utilized.

Nonetheless, there is no rigorous way of testing how much informed judgments or survey techniques have boosted forecast accuracy, so they are mentioned only peripherally in this text. Instead, this text concentrates on illustrating how statistical and econometric methods can be used to construct forecasting models and minimize forecast errors. Initially, most economic forecasts were generated with structural equations; more recently, time-series analysis has been utilized more effectively. The benefits and shortcomings of both methods for generating optimal forecasts are identified.

This book is not a theoretical text; the emphasis is placed on practical business forecasting. As a result, theorems and proofs, which can be found in many other texts, will be kept to a minimum, with most of the material related to actual forecasting examples. In particular, this text will illustrate how statistical theory often needs to be adjusted to take into account those problems that recur in actual empirical estimation. Methods of adjusting the models to increase predictive accuracy are not to be denigrated or dismissed; they are an integral part of practical business forecasting.

1.1 STATISTICS, ECONOMETRICS, AND FORECASTING

Statistics is the application of probability theory and other mathematical methods to improve decision making where uncertainty is involved. Statistical theory and results are used widely in economics, but also apply to a large and diverse number of other disciplines, including sociology, agriculture, astronomy, biology, and physics.

The use of statistics is designed to provide answers where uncertainty exists, whether the uncertainty is due to randomness, or ignorance about the true underlying relationship that is to be tested. To illustrate the first case, we know the underlying probability distribution and hence the proportion of straights that will be dealt in a poker hand over the long run, but not what the next hand will show. To illustrate the second case, we probably do not know the true underlying relationship between capital spending and the rate of interest, or between the rate of inflation and the rate of unemployment, or changes in the value of the dollar and net exports. Cases where the underlying probability distribution is known are rare in economics.

Econometrics is the application of statistical and mathematical methods to the analysis of economic data to verify or refute economic theories. When structural equations are used, a specific theory is being tested for verification or rejection. By comparison, statistical methods are increasingly used with economic data to obtain parameter estimates without specifying any particular theory. Those models are usually known as time-series analysis; one standard technique is integrated autoregressive moving-average (ARIMA) models. Those models consist of correlating a given economic variable with its own lagged values, adjusted for trend and seasonal factors; no attempt is made to postulate an underlying theory.

Economic forecasting often relies on statistical or econometric methods, but even that need not be the case. Some types of forecasts do not involve mathematical techniques at all; for example, surveys or polls may produce valuable forecasts without utilizing any econometric methods. However, these types of forecasts are not featured in this book. Most of the examples will be confined to those types of forecasts that use statistical methods.

1.2 THE CONCEPT OF FORECASTING ACCURACY: COMPARED TO WHAT?

No forecast is ever perfect; opinions about what will happen in the future invariably contain errors. Anyone who has ever attempted to predict anything knows that. On the other hand, forecasting can be quite useful if it provides better answers than alternative methods of guessing about the future. The relevant test for any forecast, then, is never whether the results contain errors, but how accurate they are compared to the alternatives. Like that old Henny Youngman one-liner "How's your wife?" the appropriate answer is always "Compared to what?"

Throughout this book, the difference between the *science* of statistics and econometrics and the *art* of forecasting is emphasized. Most of the sophisticated theorems and proofs in those fields are based on highly unlikely assumptions about the distribution of the error terms, and furthermore assume that the data generating process remains the same in the sample and the forecast periods. Adjusting models to generate better forecasts when these assumptions are not satisfied has often been disdainfully called ad hoc adjustment, unworthy of the name of econometrics. Yet it plays a vital role in improving forecast accuracy.

From 1940 through 1970, primary emphasis was placed on theoretical refinements of statistical and econometric procedures, with scant attention paid to systematic methods of adjusting forecasts to improve their accuracy. When macroeconomic models proved unable to predict any of the major changes in the economy in the 1970s, the emphasis gradually shifted to developing methods that produced useful forecasts even if they did not follow the theoretical procedures developed in earlier decades.

In *Forecasting Economic Time Series*, a reference book recommended for those with more advanced mathematical skills, Clements and Hendry[1] have classified the basic issues in forecasting, as opposed to econometrics. They state that "The

---

[1] Clements, Michael P., and David F. Hendry, *Forecasting Economic Time Series* (Cambridge University Press, Cambridge, UK), 1998.

features of the real-world forecasting venture that give rise to the sources of forecast error . . . induce a fairly radical departure from the literature on 'optimal' forecasting . . . and at the same time help to explain why some apparently ad hoc procedures work in practice" (p. 3).

The approach used here is much less mathematically rigorous than Clements and Hendry's. Also, the discussion of forecasting accuracy begins with structural models and then moves to time-series analysis, contrary to the procedure that they (and others) use. Yet the methodology in which real-world practical forecasting is approached is very much in the spirit of their approach. While the method of least squares is used for the vast majority of the examples, the reader should always keep in mind that the assumptions of the classical linear model seldom hold in practical business forecasting.

In many cases, the underlying data generating function has shifted, the variables are not normally distributed, the residuals are not independent, and the independent variables are not known at the time of the forecast. Even more important, repeated rerunning of regression equations, and the substitution of different empirical data series that measure the same theoretical concept, often help to improve forecasting accuracy but are outside the constructs of the classical linear model. For this reason, the statistical estimates generated under those assumptions must be interpreted carefully, and often with a degree of skepticism.

It is too crude to say that what makes the best forecasts is "whatever works," but that is closer to the spirit of the present approach than the method of choosing rigorous statistical techniques that minimize the root mean square error or other similar measures in the sample period but generate suboptimal forecasts. Sometimes structural econometric models provide better forecasts, and sometimes the results from ARIMA models with no economic structure are better. In certain cases, the *combination* of these methods will generate better forecasts than either method separately. Far from being relegated to the criticism of ad hoc adjustments, changing the model during the forecast period will invariably produce better results than a "pure" unadjusted model, provided it is done properly.

As Newbold and Granger have written,[2] "the evaluation criteria employed should be as demanding as possible since the object ought to be self-criticism rather than self-congratulation" (p. 266). The principal aim should be to build a forecasting model that will generate the smallest forecasting error, not necessarily maximize the goodness-of-fit statistics over the sample period.

The reader should always keep in mind that any forecasting model, no matter how sophisticated the underlying statistical techniques, must perform better than forecasts generated by random variables or naive methods. That means

---

[2] Granger, C. W. J., and Paul Newbold, *Forecasting Economic Time Series* (Academic Press, San Diego, CA), 1986.

always checking whether the model provides better results than other methods that are available – including naive models, surveys, and qualitative judgments.

A naive model generally assumes that the level or rate of change of the variable to be predicted this period will be the same as last period, or the change this period will be the same as the average change over an extended time period. For a time series without any significant trend, such as the Treasury bill rate, a naive model might state that the bill rate this month will be the same as it was last month. For a time series with a significant trend, the naive model would usually be couched in terms of percentage changes. For example, a naive model might state that the percentage change in the S&P 500 stock prices index next month will equal the percentage change last month, or it might equal the average percentage change over the past 480 months. A more sophisticated type of non-structural model incorporates regression equations using lagged values of the variable that is to be predicted. If more complicated modeling techniques cannot generate forecasts that beat these naive models, the model building attempt is presumably not worthwhile.

For people engaged in industry and finance, where having more accurate forecasts than your competitors will materially improve profitability, forecasts are useful if they provide results that are more accurate than the competition's. A model that accurately predicted the direction of change in the stock market the next day 60 percent of the time would be tremendously valuable – even though it would be wrong almost half the time – regardless of the methodology used to develop those predictions. In a similar vein, calculations by this author have shown, in some semi-annual polls of economists published in the *Wall Street Journal*, over 50 percent of the forecasts incorrectly predicted the *direction* interest rates would change over the next six months. Hence any model that could even predict the direction in which interest rates would move over the next several months would significantly improve the current status of forecasting financial markets.

Yet the decision not to forecast at all means throwing in the towel and claiming that any deviations from past trends can never be predicted. That would be the case only if the variable in question always grew at the same rate and was never subject to exogenous shocks. For even if changes are truly unexpected (an oil shock, a war, a wildcat strike, a plant explosion) forecasting models can still offer useful guidance indicating how to get back on track. Virtually everyone in a management or executive role in business or finance makes guesses about what will happen in the future. While these guesses will never be perfect, they are likely to be much improved if the practitioner combines robust statistical techniques with the ability to adjust the forecasts when actual events do diverge from predicted values.

Forecasting makes practitioners humble. That does not mean people who choose forecasting as a profession are necessarily humble; the opposite is more likely to be true. But unlike economic theories, which can often persist for decades without anyone ever being able to verify whether they are accurate or useful, forecasters generally find out quickly whether or not their opinions are correct.

Since highly visible forecasts of the overall economy or financial markets have compiled a very unimpressive track record over the past 30 years, it is sometimes argued that predicting economic variables is not a useful exercise. Indeed, most consensus forecasts of real growth, inflation, and interest rates have not been much better than from a naive model. In view of these results, some have concluded that forecasting models do not work very well.

Before reaching that conclusion, however, we should try to determine what causes these forecasting errors. For example, suppose the majority of forecasters thought interest rates would rise because inflation was about to increase. The Federal Reserve, also expecting that to happen, tightened policy enough that inflation decreased and, by the time six months had elapsed, interest rates actually fell. I am not suggesting this always occurs, but it is a reasonable hypothesis. Thus before beginning our analysis of how to reduce forecasting errors, it is useful to categorize the major sources of these errors. Some may be intractable, but others can be reduced by a variety of methods that will be explored in this book.

When the econometric model and the mechanism generating the model both coincide in an unchanging world, and when the underlying data are accurate and robust, the theory of economic forecasting is relatively well developed. In such cases, the root mean square forecasting error in the forecast period ought not to be any larger than indicated by the sample period statistics.

This does not happen very often; in the majority of forecasts, the actual error is significantly larger than expected from sample period statistics. In some cases that is because the model builder has used inappropriate statistical techniques or misspecified the model through ignorance. Most of the time, however, unexpectedly large forecasting errors are due to some combination of the following causes:

- structural shifts in parameters
- model misspecification
- missing, smoothed, preliminary, or inaccurate data
- changing expectations by economic agents
- policy shifts
- unexpected changes in exogenous variables
- incorrect assumptions about exogeneity
- error buildup in multi-period forecasts.

1.2.1 STRUCTURAL SHIFTS IN PARAMETERS

Of the factors listed above, structural shifts in parameters are probably the most common. These may occur either within or outside the sample period. For example, sales at Ace Hardware will drop dramatically when Home Depot opens a store three blocks away. At the macroeconomic level, a recession used to be accompanied by a stronger dollar; now it is accompanied by a weaker dollar. Company profits of American Can were influenced by completely different factors after it became a financial services company.

Perhaps stated in such stark terms, structural shifts are obvious, but most of the time the changes are more subtle. For 1997 through 1999, macroeconomists thought the growth rate of the US economy would slow down from about 4% to the 2–2½% range; yet each year, real growth remained near 4%. Forecasters thought that with the economy at full employment, inflation would increase, causing higher interest rates, lower stock prices, and slower growth, yet it did not happen. At least in retrospect, there were some structural shifts in the economy. For one thing, full employment no longer produced higher inflation. Also, the technological revolution boosted capital spending and productivity growth more rapidly. Yet even after several years, the consensus forecast failed to recognize this shift.

1.2.2 MODEL MISSPECIFICATION

Model misspecification could be due to the ignorance of the model builder; but even in the case where the best possible model has been estimated, some terms might be omitted. In many cases these might be expectational variables for which data do not exist. For example, economists agree that bond yields depend on the expected rate of inflation, a variable that cannot be measured directly. A company might find that cutting prices 5% would not invoke any competitive response, but cutting them 10% means competitors would match those lower prices. The missing variable in this case would be the trigger point at which competitors would respond – which itself is likely to change over time.

It is also possible that the underlying model is nonlinear. In one fairly straightforward and frequently documented case, purchases of capital goods with long lives (as opposed to computers and motor vehicles) generally increase faster when the rate of capacity utilization is high than when it is low. At the beginning of a business cycle upturn, capital spending for long-lived assets is often sluggish even though interest rates are low, credit is easily available, stock prices are rising rapidly, sales are booming, and profits are soaring. Once firms reach full capacity, they are more likely to increase this type of capital spending even if interest rates are higher and growth is slower.

To a certain extent this problem can be finessed by including variables that make the equation nonlinear, and I will discuss just such an example later. For example, investment might grow more rapidly when the rate of capacity utilization is above a certain level (say 85%) than when it is below that level. However, the situation is not that simple because a given level of capacity utilization will affect investment differently depending on the average age of the capital stock, so using a simple rule of thumb will generally result in model misspecification. An attempt to pinpoint the exact rate at which capital spending accelerates is likely to result in data mining and the resultant penalty of relatively large forecast errors.

1.2.3 MISSING, SMOOTHED, PRELIMINARY, OR INACCURATE DATA

The data used in estimating forecasting models generally comes from one of three major sources. Most macroeconomic data are prepared by agencies of the Federal government, including the Bureau of Economic Analysis (BEA), the Bureau of the Census, and the Federal Reserve Board of Governors. Financial market data on individual company sales and earnings are prepared by individual corporations. In an intermediate category, many industry associations and private sector institutions prepare indexes of consumer and business sentiment, and measures of economic activity for specific industries or sectors; perhaps the best known of these are the Conference Board index of consumer attitudes and the National Association of Purchasing Managers index of business conditions in the manufacturing sector.

Except for specific data based on prices given in financial markets, virtually all macroeconomic or industry data are gathered by sampling, which means only a relatively small percentage of the total transactions is measured. Even when an attempt is made to count all participants, data collection methods are sometimes incomplete. The decennial census is supposed to count every person in the US, but statisticians generally agree the reported number of people in large cities is significantly less than the actual number; many of the uncounted are assumed to be undocumented aliens. Thus even in this most comprehensive data collection effort, which is supposed to count everyone, some errors remain. It is reasonable to assume that errors from smaller samples are relatively larger.

Virtually all macroeconomic and industry data series collected and provided by the government are revised. The issuing agencies named above make an attempt to provide monthly or quarterly data as quickly as possible after the period has ended. These releases are generally known as "advance" or "preliminary" data. In general, these data are then revised over the next several months. They are then revised again using annual benchmarks; these revisions usually incorporate changing seasonal factors. Finally, they are revised again using five-year censuses of the agricultural, manufacturing, and service sectors. In addition, some of the more comprehensive series, such as GDP and the CPI, may be revised because of methodological changes.

The revisions in the data prepared and released by the Federal government are often quite large. Sometimes this is because preliminary data, which appears shortly after the time period in question has ended, are based on a relatively small sample and then revised when more comprehensive data become available. In other cases, seasonal factors shift over time. Data revisions quite properly reflect this additional information.

Most government data are collected from surveys. From time to time, respondents do not send their forms back. What is to be done? The sensible solution is to interpolate the data based on those firms that did return their forms. The problem with this approach is that, in many cases, it is precisely those firms that failed to return their forms that faced unusual circumstances, which would have substantially modified the data. Eventually the problem is solved when more complete numbers are available, but the initial data are seriously flawed.

Sometimes, the methodology is changed. In October 1999, a comprehensive data revision boosted the average growth rate of the past decade by an average of 0.4% because the Bureau of Economic Analysis (BEA) – the agency that prepares GDP and related figures – decided to include software purchased by businesses as part of investment; previously it had been treated as an intermediate good and excluded from GDP. Since software had become an increasingly important part of the overall economy, this change was appropriate and timely.

In another important example, the methodology for computing the rate of inflation was changed in the mid-1990s. As a result, the same changes in all individual components of the CPI would result in an overall inflation rate that was 0.7% lower. These changes reflected the improved quality of many consumer durables, shopping at discount malls instead of department stores, and changes in market baskets that included a higher proportion of less expensive goods. Most economists agreed these changes were warranted, and many thought they were overdue. A commission headed by former Chairman of the Council of Economic Advisers Michael Boskin calculated that the rate of inflation had been overstated by an average of 1.1% per year.[3]

The Federal government statisticians cannot reasonably be criticized for including improved information and methodology in their data releases when they become available. Indeed, failure to include these changes would be a serious error. Nonetheless, the appearance of preliminary data that are later revised substantially raises significant issues in both building and evaluating forecasting models. At least in the past, it has sometimes had a major impact on policy decisions.

For example, one of the major examples of misleading preliminary data occurred in the 1990–1 recession. During that downturn, BEA initially indicated the recession was quite mild, with a dip in real GDP of only about 2%. Subsequent revisions revealed that the drop was much more severe, about 4%.[4] Acting on the data that were originally reported, the Fed assumed the slump was not very severe and hence eased cautiously. If it had known how much real

[3]   Boskin, Michael J., E. R. Dulberger, R. J. Gordon, and Z. Griliches, "The CPI Commission: Findings and Recommendations," *American Economic Review Papers and Proceedings*, 87 (1997), 78–83.
[4]   This result was not entirely a surprise. Joseph Carson, an economist at Chemical Bank who had previously worked at the Commerce Department, stated at the time that he thought real GDP was declining at a 4% annual rate in late 1990.

GDP had really fallen, it probably would have eased much more quickly. Indeed, when the recovery failed to develop on schedule in 1991, the Fed did reduce short-term interest rates to unusually low levels by the end of 1992, and the economy finally did recover. However, that boosted inflationary pressures, causing the Fed to tighten so much in 1994 that real growth plunged to 1% in the first half of 1995. Not until the latter half of that year did the economic effects of those incorrect data completely disappear.

The most accurate forecast would have said the economy is in worse shape than the government reports indicate, so initially the Fed will not ease enough and hence the economy will be slow to rebound, which means the Fed will eventually have to ease more than usual, so two years from now interest rates will be much lower than anyone else expects, in which case inflationary expectations will rise and the Fed will have to tighten again. Of course no one said that, nor could anyone have reasonably been expected to predict such a sequence of events.

This example clearly indicates how inaccurate data can cause poor forecasts. Yet economists were roundly criticized for underpredicting the severity of the recession, overpredicting the initial size of the rebound, and failing to gauge the decline change in interest rates accurately. No forecaster won plaudits following that recession, but it is not unreasonable to suggest that forecast errors would have been smaller with more accurate data.

In May 1974, the wage and price controls imposed by the Nixon Administration ended. As a result, the producer price index (PPI) rose by a record amount that month. For the next few years, the seasonal adjustment program used by the Bureau of Labor Statistics (BLS) assumed the PPI always rose sharply in May, so the seasonally adjusted data for the May PPI showed a big dip, while the unseasonally adjusted data were virtually unchanged. In this case perhaps the obvious solution would have been to ignore those data, but it is not clear what method the forecaster should use. Running regression equations without any data for May? Using seasonally unadjusted data? Treating May 1974 with a dummy variable – e.g., 1 in that period and 0 elsewhere? All these are possible, but none is optimal.

Of course, it is not only the Federal government that revises their data. Companies often restate their earnings for a variety of reasons. They book sales when they ship the goods, but if they aren't paid for, writeoffs must be taken. Sometimes reorganizations, or sales of divisions, result in huge one-quarter writeoffs. Other times, accounting errors are at fault. Analysts try to take these anomalies into account, but most if not all attempts to predict stock prices based on reported company earnings suffer from the changes and inconsistencies in these data.

There will never be any perfect solution to the issue of data revisions. Nor does it make any sense to castigate government statisticians for providing the most accurate estimates possible based on incomplete data and the changing nature of the economy. Nonetheless, a few observations relating to data revisions are appropriate at this point.

1   Evaluation of forecast accuracy should take into account the data at the time when the forecasts were issued, rather than the most recently revised data. This means, for example, that an attempt to evaluate forecasting accuracy of macroeconomic forecasts made many years ago provides far different results depending on which set of "actual" data are used.

2   Some, although certainly not all, forecast error stems from the assumptions of changes in fiscal and monetary policy that are based on the preliminary data issued by the government. Later revisions of these data sometimes make it appear that those assumptions were unwarranted.

3   When estimating a structural model over an extended period of time, it is useful and appropriate to use dummy or truncated variables in the regression equation. For example, the methodological changes in the CPI that began in 1994 can be entered explicitly as an additional variable; before 1994, any such variable would have the value of zero.

1.2.4   CHANGING EXPECTATIONS BY ECONOMIC AGENTS

This is often cited as one of the major reasons given for the failure of macroeconomic modeling in the 1970s and the 1980s. It has been argued that economic forecasts based on past historical evidence cannot be accurate because people adjust their behavior based on previous events, and thus react differently to the same phenomena in the future. This concept is generally known as the Lucas Critique;[5] however, it was formulated by Oskar Morgenstern in 1928,[6] so it is hardly a recent idea. Formally, we can express this concept by saying that the data generation process underlying the model has changed during the sample period, or between the sample and the forecast periods. I mention the roots of this concept to emphasize that it far predates the idea that mismanaged monetary policy in the 1950s and 1960s was the primary factor that caused the short-term tradeoff between inflation and unemployment.

Indeed, the Lucas Critique is just a special case, although an extremely well-known one, of changing expectations. Economic agents often change their behavior patterns based on what has happened in the past. That is not only true at the macro level. Growth in individual company sales will be significantly affected as competitors enter and exit the industry. Firms will raise or lower prices depending on how their competitors react. Borrowers may have a higher or lower rate of default on loans depending on recent changes in the bankruptcy laws.

Lucas and others, and Morgenstern before them, claimed that econometric models would not work whenever economic agents learned from previous

[5]   Lucas, Robert E., "Some International Evidence on Output–Inflation Tradeoffs," *American Economic Review*, 63 (1973), 326–34.

[6]   Morgenstern, Oskar, *Wirtschaftsprognose: eine Ubtersuchung ihrer Vorussetzungen und Moglichkeiten* (Julius Springer, Vienna), 1928.

experience and adjusted their behavior accordingly in the future. Yet many economic links continue to hold over a wide variety of different experiences. On a ceteris paribus basis, consumers will spend more if income rises, although admittedly their increase in consumption will be greater if they think the change is permanent rather than temporary. If interest rates rise, capital spending will decline. If the value of the currency increases, the volume of net exports will decline. If the growth rate for profits of an individual firm accelerates, the stock price will rise. There are many similar examples where structural relationships continue to hold in spite of changing expectations.

Sometimes, a change in expectations in one area of the economy will generate changes in other sectors that are consistent with past experience. One major example of this occurred in the US economy in the second half of the 1990s. Expectations about future profit growth shifted significantly, so that the price/earnings ratio of the stock market doubled even though bond yields were at just about the same level in 1995 and 2000. Few forecasters were able to predict that change. On the other hand, the rise in stock prices and the decline in the cost of equity capital impacted consumer and capital spending in a manner consistent with previous historical experience. In addition, the more rapid growth in capital stock stemming from an increase in the ratio of capital spending to GDP boosted productivity growth, which reduced the rate of inflation and lowered interest rates further. That in turn boosted real growth enough that the Federal budget position moved from a deficit to a surplus, which further boosted equity prices. Predicting the change in the stock market was difficult; but given that change, predicting more robust growth in the overall economy was more straightforward. Conversely, when the stock market plunged, all of the reverse factors occurred – lower capital spending, a slowdown in productivity, and a return to deficit financing.

1.2.5 POLICY SHIFTS

Anyone who tries to estimate an equation to predict short-term interest rates will soon find that, during the mid-1970s, Fed Chairman Arthur Burns used monetary policy to offset the recessionary impact of higher oil prices, leading to unusually low real interest rates; whereas in the early 1980s, Chairman Paul Volcker refused to accommodate the further increase in oil prices, leading to unusually high real interest rates. The real Federal funds rate equals the nominal rate minus the change in inflation over the past year. Its pattern is shown in figure 1.1.

No model estimated on data through 1979 would have predicted the massive increase in real interest rates that started in late 1980. With hindsight, of course, one can include a well-chosen set of economic variables that track this pattern, but that is not the point. In July 1980, the Blue Chip consensus forecast of the six-month commercial paper rate for 1981 was 8.7%; the actual figure was 14.8%. This is one of the clearest policy shifts that ever occurred in the US economy.

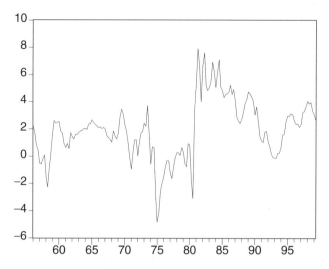

Figure 1.1   The real Federal funds rate.

What lessons can forecasters learn from this experience? In the short run, fluctuations in short-term interest rates are determined primarily if not exclusively by the action of the Federal Open Market Committee. That is why short-term interest rate forecasting today is reduced to a series of guesses about what the Fed will do next. In the long run, however, we learn another lesson. If the Fed holds short-term rates at below equilibrium for an extended period, eventually both inflation and interest rates will rise; whereas if it holds short-term rates above equilibrium, eventually both inflation and interest rates will decline. In this case, a model that captured this underlying relationship would provide very little guidance in predicting interest rates in the short run, but would be useful in the long run. In particular, a forecast that interest rates and inflation would start to decline in 1982, hence setting in motion the biggest bull market in history, would have been particularly valuable. Yet hardly anyone believed the few forecasters who accurately predicted that development.

Even the best econometric model is not designed to predict the impact of unexpected policy or exogenous changes in the short run. However, once these changes have occurred, correctly structured models should be able to offer valuable insights into what will happen in the longer run.

1.2.6 UNEXPECTED CHANGES IN EXOGENOUS VARIABLES

The change in Fed policy under Paul Volcker is a classic example of a policy change initiated by the government. As seen by forecasts made at the time, it was a major surprise. Another major example of an unexpected policy change, although it occurred over several years, was the decision by senior officials in the Clinton Administration to reduce the level of real per capita government spending during his tenure as President.[7] That changed the budget deficit to a budget surplus, which (as already noted above) was one of the factors causing an almost unprecedented increase in the price/earnings ratio of the stock market.

Changes of this sort are undertaken by government officials. However, other shocks that affect the economy have nothing to do with policy, such as energy shocks, wars, and natural disasters. Unless foreseen, they will not be incorporated in any forecasts. Yet if they were predicted, vigorous action would be taken to offset or eliminate these developments.

I have already noted how the Fed acted quite differently to the first and second energy shocks in 1973–4 and 1979–80 respectively. However, that was not the only change; private sector economic agents also reacted differently. The first energy shock was viewed by most consumers and businesses as a once-in-a-lifetime event, so they did not alter their behavior patterns very much. As a result, oil imports continued to increase, and eventually oil prices rose again. After the second energy shock, attitudes changed significantly. Most people now expected that massive price increases would continue on a regular basis, and forecasts were common that oil prices would rise to $100/bbl by the end of the twentieth century. As a result, both consumers and businesses started using less energy, buying more fuel-efficient motor vehicles, and constructing more fuel-efficient buildings. Those plans were successful enough to reduce oil imports, so in 1986 energy prices plunged by more than half. In 1998 they were lower in real terms than in 1972, before the first energy shock occurred.

Any forecast of the economy in the 1980s – whether right or wrong – was influenced by the assumption about energy prices. However, this example indicates the value of some of the alternative types of forecasts discussed in section 1.3: conditional vs unconditional, point vs interval, and alternative scenarios weighted by probabilities. An appropriate way for many businesses to proceed would have been to generate alternative forecasts based on different scenarios about oil prices: higher, steady, or lower. When prices gradually started to decline in the mid-1980s as the worldwide energy glut increased, more weight would have been given to the lower-price scenario, so businesses would have been better prepared when crude oil prices suddenly fell by more than half in 1986.

There is little to be gained by pointing out that forecasts are inaccurate when they fail to predict unexpected exogenous shocks, many of which would never have occurred if they had been accurately predicted. However, models that correctly analyze the impact of these shocks when they do happen can still be quite useful in indicating what lies ahead.

---

[7]   Most of these changes were suggested by Treasury Undersecretary, and then Secretary, Robert Rubin.

1.2.7 INCORRECT ASSUMPTIONS ABOUT EXOGENEITY

In some cases, models designed for forecasting generate much larger errors than would be indicated by the sample period statistics because some of the independent variables are assumed to be exogenous when they really are not. Technically, an exogenous variable is one whose value is not determined within an economic model, but which plays a role in the determination of the endogenous variables. However, as a practical matter, there are degrees of exogeneity. Only a relative handful of variables, such as weather conditions and defense expenditures, are exogenous in all circumstances. Most of the time, policy variables have some endogenous components as well.

For example, foreign currency values are often considered to be exogenous. After the collapse of the Thai baht, Korean won, Indonesian rupiah, and Malaysian ringgit in the latter half of 1997, US net exports declined dramatically in 1998 and the first half of 1999. As a result, manufacturing production rose much more slowly than total GDP; whereas during boom years, production usually rises faster than overall GDP. North Carolina has the highest proportion of workers in manufacturing, so its growth rate fell sharply after the collapse of those currencies.

A model that linked growth in North Carolina employment to the value of the dollar (among other variables) would show a high correlation. However, a forecast made in 1997 would have been inaccurate if it had assumed the values of those currencies would remain stable. In such a case, the model would appear to work well, but forecasts of the North Carolina economy would be far off the mark. In this case, the equations might have continued to work well in the sense of high correlations and low standard errors, but the forecasts would have been poor because of the inability to predict the exogenous variables.

In the past, monetary policy used to be treated as exogenous, although this error is made far less often today. Even in the days before Paul Volcker, the Fed routinely tightened monetary policy as inflation increased. Thus assuming that monetary policy variables were exogenous and would not change invariably led to forecast errors that were much larger than expected from the sample period statistics.

1.2.8 ERROR BUILDUP IN MULTI-PERIOD FORECASTS

Analyses of macroeconomic models undertaken many years ago by this author showed that the single biggest source of error in multi-period forecasting was caused by using the lagged dependent variable on the right-hand side of the equation. If current consumption were estimated as a function of lagged consumption, for example, an error made one quarter could distort all the forecasts from that point forward. I will discuss a variety of methods to overcome that difficulty; now that this error has been well documented, it does not occur so much in multi-period forecasting models. Nonetheless, it is an error that beginning modelers often commit.

1.3 ALTERNATIVE TYPES OF FORECASTS

When most people think of forecasts, they think of point estimates. For example, sales will rise 12% next year, the Dow will climb to 12,000 a year from now, the Federal Open Market Committee will vote to boost the Federal funds rate 25 basis points at its next meeting, the price of oil will climb 20% over the next six months, and so on.

While it is true that point estimates are the most common type of forecasts, there are many other ways in which forecast results can be presented. Sometimes a range for the predicted variable is more appropriate; other times, different probabilities are assigned to alternative scenarios. Sometimes the penalties associated with being too high or too low are equal; at other times, the loss function is asymmetric. In this section, I discuss some of the more common types of alternative forecasts.

1.3.1 POINT OR INTERVAL

Suppose a company has a limited amount of excess manufacturing capacity. If sales grow less than 5% per year, the company will be better off using its existing facilities. If sales grow more than 5% per year, it will be better off building a new plant. In this case, the point estimate for sales growth is not as important as the probability that sales growth will exceed 5%.

A similar case might be made for advertising budgets. If a firm thinks a $1 million expenditure on advertising will boost sales by at least $5 million, it will decide to go ahead and spend the money. It doesn't matter so much whether the increase in sales is $6 or $10 million, but if it is $4 million, the expenditure will not be made.

At the macro level, suppose the Fed decides that 3% is the highest level of inflation that is tolerable. If inflation rises 1%, $1\frac{1}{2}$%, or 2%, there will be no change in monetary policy. If it exceeds 3% – or if it appears likely it will soon exceed 3% if policy is not changed – the Fed will boost short-term interest rates.

A company may have a loan covenant with the bank stating that if cash reserves drop below a certain level, the loan will be called. That level might be correlated with the assumption of increased profitability, so a decline in profits would trigger the loan call. In that case, the key forecast is whether company profits have risen or not, rather than the precise amount they would increase.

1.3.2 ABSOLUTE OR CONDITIONAL

Forecasts can be either absolute or conditional. Some examples of absolute, or unconditional forecasts are: real GDP will grow 4% next year, the Republicans will retain (or regain) majority control of Congress, and company sales will rise at least 15% per year over the next decade. However, many forecasts are issued on a conditional basis: real GDP will grow 4% next year if the Fed does not tighten, the Republicans will be the majority party in Congress if they also capture the Presidency, and sales will grow if competitors do not double their capital spending and advertising budgets.

The choice of which type of forecast is appropriate will depend largely on how the results are to be used. A speculator in financial markets wants to know whether prices will rise or fall, not whether they will rise or fall under certain circumstances. An automobile dealer wants to know what lines of vehicles will sell most quickly, so he can optimize his ordering procedure. A pharmaceutical company wants to know how rapidly a new drug will be adopted.

Conversely, conditional forecasts can often be quite useful. Firms might want to determine how fast sales are likely to grow under normal business conditions, using those results as guidelines for rewarding superior performance. If sales are then affected by some exogenous event, guidelines can be adjusted accordingly. Forecasts of production planning might be determined based on the assumption that materials are delivered on time, compared with what might happen if a strike occurred. The most common way of delivering conditional forecasts is by using alternative scenarios, as discussed next.

1.3.3 ALTERNATIVE SCENARIOS WEIGHED BY PROBABILITIES

A forecast that sales will rise 8% if the economy booms, rise 6% if real growth remains sluggish, and fall 2% if there is a recession may appear to be an excuse to avoid offering a firm forecast at all. However, that is not always true. In many cases, firms need to be prepared to take appropriate action if the economy falters even if the probability of that occurring is relatively low.

Based on the historical forecasting record of macroeconomists, it would appear that recessions were not predictable. Consider the case of a lending institution involved in sub-prime auto loans. As long as the economy remains healthy, the vast majority of these loans will be repaid; if a recession strikes, the loss rate will rise enough to put the company out of business. Prudence might dictate less risky loans; but if the company is too picky, it will lose business to competitors and won't make enough loans to stay in business.

In this case the most appropriate procedure would be to assess the probability of a recession occurring next year. If it were only 5%, then the lending institution would continue to expand its sub-prime loan portfolio. On the other hand, if it were to rise to 25%, some trimming would be in order. Note that in this case the probability of an actual downturn the following year is well below 50%, yet some adjustment in corporate strategy is warranted.

The alternative-scenario method of forecasting can also be used for long-range planning, since long-term economic forecasts are generally little more than trend extrapolations in any case. The company might discover that the probability of meeting its stated goal of a 15% annual gain in sales and earnings would occur only if the most optimistic macroeconomic forecast, with a probability of only 10%, were met. The company could then make plans to move into faster-growing areas of the economy or, alternatively, trim its ambitious long-term goals to more realistic levels.

1.3.4 ASYMMETRIC GAINS AND LOSSES

So far we have been assuming that a forecast error of +8% carries the same penalty as an error of –8%. Often, however, that is not the case. For many companies, if sales increase faster than expected, that is fine; but if they don't, disaster strikes. I have already described such a situation for a sub-prime auto lending company. The same general type of argument could be applied to municipal bonds; as long as the community tax base grows above a certain rate, the interest and principal will be repaid, but if it dips below that rate, the issuing authority will default on the bonds.

In many companies, the rewards for exceeding the plan are substantial: bonuses, promotions, and larger budgets for next year. Similarly, the penalties for failing to meet planned targets are severe, including loss of employment. In a situation of that sort, many planners will set targets below their predicted level, so they will appear to have exceeded their goals. Eventually, management may catch on to this trick and fire all the planners, which is another risk. Nonetheless, the percentage of plans that are exceeded compared with the percentage that are not met strongly suggests that corporate planners are well aware of the asymmetric loss function.

Money managers may face a similar dilemma. If they beat the benchmark averages – Dow Jones Industrials, S&P 500, or Nasdaq composite index – they are handsomely rewarded; investors will switch their assets into those funds, and salaries and bonuses rise. If their performance falls short of the gains posted by the major averages, they will lose customers and possibly their own jobs.

This is not just a hypothetical example. The so-called January effect occurs because many money managers aggressively buy growth stocks early in the year (or the previous December) and, if they can show substantial gains, lock in those gains and buy the equivalent of index funds for the rest of the year. In the same vein, very few money managers who are already ahead of the average for the first three quarters of the year would take risks in the fourth quarter that would jeopardize their hefty year-end bonuses.

1.3.5 SINGLE-PERIOD OR MULTI-PERIOD

So far we have not specified how many time periods in the future are being predicted. That can make a great deal of difference in the way a model is formulated. In models used to forecast only one period ahead, it might well be appropriate to use the lagged value of the variable that is being predicted. Interest rates in the next period might very well depend on rates this period, as well as on other variables such as the inflation rate, growth rate, unemployment rate, value of the currency, budget surplus or deficit, and other relevant variables.

However, suppose the model is used to predict interest rates on a monthly basis for the next 12 months. In this case, the forecasts for interest rates later in the year would depend on "lagged" values of interest rates that were not known at the time of forecast. For example, suppose the forecast made at the beginning of March for interest rates depends on the level of interest rates in January and February. As the year progresses, the forecast for interest rates in June would depend on their level in April and May, which are not yet known.

For this reason, using the lagged dependent variable for multi-period forecasts causes serious difficulties that do not exist for the single-period forecast. That does not rule out the use of lagged dependent variables on an a-priori basis, but it does raise a red flag. One of the tenets of the classical linear model, as will be shown in the next chapter, is that the values of all the independent variables are known at the time of forecast. Obviously that is not the case when the lagged dependent variable is used in multi-period forecasting. Hence it is advisable to use a different approach when multi-period forecasts are required.

1.3.6 SHORT RUN OR LONG RANGE

To a certain extent, the difference between short- and long-run forecasts can be viewed as the difference between single- and multi-period forecasting. However, whereas short-term forecasts are more generally concerned with deviations from trends, long-run forecasts are often designed to predict the trend itself. As a result, different methods should be used.

One of the principal goals of short-term forecasting, and one that has been emphasized by time-series analysis, is to remove the trend from time-series variables so the underlying properties of the series may be properly examined. If company sales have been growing an average of 12% per year, the challenge in short-term forecasting is to indicate how much sales next year will deviate from that trend. Long-range forecasters, on the other hand, might want to determine how many years it will take for the trend growth in sales to diverge from that 12% average gain. The difference is analogous to the split responsibilities of the COO, who asks "How are we doing?", and the CEO, who asks "Where are we heading?"

In large part, then, the method of building forecasting models will be different depending on whether the primary goal is short-term or long-range forecasting. In general, the same model will not be optimal for attempting both goals.

1.3.7 FORECASTING SINGLE OR MULTIPLE VARIABLES

In the models discussed above, it has been implicitly assumed that the independent variables – the variables on the right-hand side of the equation – are either known in advance or are truly exogenous. In the case of financial decision or qualitative choice models, actual information is entered for economic and demographic data. In the case of sales forecasting models, the variables are either exogenous to the firm or are determined by management decisions.

In the case of macroeconomic and financial forecasting models, however, that assumption is not generally valid. Interest rates depend on expected inflation, which is generally not known. Net exports depend on the value of the currency, which also is not known. In cases of this sort, it is necessary to build multi-equation models in order to explain all the endogenous variables in the system. In the case of macro models, some variables are generally treated as exogenous, such as changes in fiscal and monetary policy, but even these are often related to the state of the economy. Only variables such as wartime expenditures, energy shocks, or weather conditions are truly exogenous.

1.4 SOME COMMON PITFALLS IN BUILDING FORECASTING EQUATIONS

Before turning to a brief review of statistics, I will illustrate some of the most common pitfalls that occur in estimating regression models for forecasting. These topics will be treated in a more rigorous fashion after the statistical groundwork has been prepared, but it is useful to introduce them initially so they can be kept in mind as the statistical and econometric exposition unfolds.

I have already noted that there is no such thing as a perfect forecast. Even if all of the statistical methods are applied correctly, some random error will occur. This error can be quantified and measured for any existing data set, and can be used as an estimate of the forecast error that can be expected. In the vast majority of cases, though, the actual forecasting error is larger than is indicated by the regression equation or econometric model. Some of the major reasons for unexpectedly large forecast error are discussed next.

The residuals in any stochastic equation, which are supposed to be independent, may be correlated with each other. As a result, there are far fewer independent observations than indicated by the statistical program. Hence the goodness-of-fit statistics are overstated, and the forecasting errors are understated. Structural relationships estimated with time-series data – consumption as a function of income, prices as a function of unit labor costs, or interest rates as a function of the inflation – are all likely to have serially correlated residuals. Because consumer spending patterns, for example, change slowly over time, the number of independent observations is probably far less than the sample period data would indicate. Consequently, the standard errors are significantly understated.

Virtually all statistical and econometric tests are based on the underlying assumption that the residuals are normally distributed. Often, however, that is not the case. That is another reason why the calculated goodness-of-fit statistics overstate the robustness of the equation.

The "law of large numbers" indicates that as the sample size increases, all distributions with a finite variance tend to approach the normal distribution. However, that is scant comfort to those who must deal with relatively small samples. Furthermore, some financial market data do not have bounded data; in particular, percentage changes in daily stock prices are not normally distributed. Every once in a while, an unexpected event will cause a much larger change than could be expected from past history – especially in financial markets. Such distributions are colloquially referred to as "fat tails." Estimates based on the assumption of a normal distribution when that is not the case are likely to generate disappointing forecasts.

Spurious correlation may destroy the usefulness of any model for forecasting, even if the sample period statistics appear to provide a remarkably accurate fit. Many studies have shown that series that actually have no correlation – because they were generated from random number series – can provide highly significant goodness-of-fit statistics if enough alternative regressions are calculated. This problem has become particularly virulent in the PC era, where it is a simple matter to run hundreds if not thousands of regression equations very quickly.

The problem of "data mining" has also run rampant because of quick and inexpensive computing power. This issue always represents somewhat of a dilemma. One does not want to test only one or two versions of any given equation. After all, the theory may not be precisely specified; and even if the long-run determinants are well determined, the lag structure and adjustment process may not be known. Empirical approximations of theoretical concepts may not be precise, so it is logical to try several different measures of the concept in question. Also, research results are often improved when alternative specifications were tried because the first attempt did not produce reasonable results. Yet having provided all these reasons for diligent research, it is much more likely that econometricians and statisticians will "torture the data until they confess" instead of failing to calculate the necessary minimum number of regressions. Such attempts at curve fitting seldom produce useful forecasting equations.

Sometimes the equation fits very well during the sample period, and the goodness-of-fit statistics hold even in the forecast period, yet the equation generates very poor forecasts because the values of the independent variables are not known. For example, sales growth for a particular company or individual product line is likely to change if competitors react to an erosion of their market share. At the macroeconomic level, financial markets certainly will react differently to anticipated and unanticipated changes in policy. Consumers are likely to alter their spending patterns based on what they think will happen in the future as well as changes in current and lagged income and monetary conditions.

It is not very helpful to develop theories that produce optimal forecasts under severely stylized sets of assumptions that are rarely encountered in the real world. Practical business forecasting invariably consists of two interrelated steps: use of standard statistical theory that has been developed based on restrictive assumptions, followed by modification of that theory to improve actual forecasting accuracy. These two steps cannot be considered in isolation. Thus even in this introductory chapter, I have pointed out some of the major pitfalls that commonly occur in forecasting models. Further details will be provided throughout the text.

The following examples are indicative of many cases where robust economic theories, which have been verified by sophisticated econometric methods, do not generate accurate forecasts unless they are further modified.

- *Example 1.* Economic theory says that the riskless long-term interest rate is related to the underlying growth rate of the economy, the Federal budget deficit ratio, and the expected rate of inflation. Econometrics can be used to test this theory. However, it cannot be used for forecasting unless, in addition, we can find an accurate way to predict the expected rate of inflation. Essentially the same comments could be made for forecasting the stock market, foreign exchange rates, or commodity prices. Since inflationary expectations are not formed in a vacuum, they could presumably be tied to changes in economic and political variables that have already occurred. So far, no one has been very successful at this.
- *Example 2.* The price of oil is tied to the world demand and supply for oil, which can perhaps be predicted accurately by econometric methods, using the geopolitical situation of Saudi Arabia *vis-à-vis* the US and other major powers as a major factor in the forecast. However, world economic hegemony cannot be predicted econometrically – and probably cannot be predicted very well with any method – so this is not a useful forecasting model. Certainly no one in the early 1980s publicly predicted the fall of the Berlin Wall by the end of the decade.
- *Example 3.* Historically, the growth rate for PCs, modems, and other high-tech equipment can be accurately tracked over the sample period by identifying the time when major innovations were introduced and matching their performance to various growth curves. In the future, since the timing of such innovations is unknown, such a set of regression equations would not serve as a useful forecasting model.
- *Example 4.* Economic theory says that the value of the dollar depends on relative real interest rate differentials; the *higher* the real rate in the US, the more likely it is that the dollar will appreciate. However, economic theory also says

that a stronger dollar will attract capital from abroad, hence resulting in a *lower* interest rate than would otherwise occur. Both of these theories can be verified separately, but unless further adjustments are made they are useless for predicting either the value of the dollar or interest rates, since they lead to opposite conclusions. This is indicative of a larger problem in forecasting, where an individual theory may provide robust empirical results *in isolation* but may be useless for forecasting because the factors that are being held constant in the theory are in fact always changing.

These examples provide a flavor of the problems of building a practical forecasting model. Many of the examples involve interrelationships between several variables that must be predicted simultaneously. However, even in the cases where the independent variables are actually known ahead of time, and in that sense are truly exogenous, model builders often go astray by failing to realize the spurious correlation introduced by common trends in several of the time series.

Using econometrics to build forecasting models is deceptively difficult. As Clive Granger has put it, "econometric modeling is an activity that should not be attempted for the first time."[8] It takes practice to develop useful forecasting models.

Problems and Questions

1. As an economist, you are asked to prepare quarterly forecasts for the next two years for shipments of oil-drilling equipment. Data on company and industry shipments are available back to 1959. Figure 1.2 shows the relationship between constant-dollar shipments of oil-drilling equipment and the relative price of crude oil.

(a) Would you prepare an unconditional or conditional forecast? If the latter, for what variables would you prepare alternative scenarios?
(b) How would you generate forecasts of oil prices?
(c) In general, would you predict that the next time oil prices rise sharply, shipments of oil-drilling equipment would rise rapidly as they did in the 1970s and the 1980s?

2. The loan portfolio of a bank has been growing at an average of 10% per year. The bank officers would like to expand growth to 15% per year,

continued

---

[8] Granger, C.W. J., *Forecasting in Business and Economics*, 2nd edn (Academic Press, San Diego, CA), 1989.

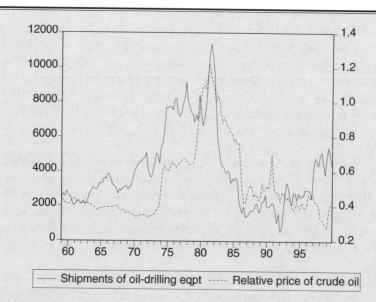

Figure 1.2   Problem 1.

and have asked you to develop a model that would evaluate credit risks on personal loans more accurately. The CEO also points out that the default rate on loans has fallen from 11% in 1990 to 2% in 1999.

(a)   How would your advice to the CEO differ if (i) the consensus forecast called for a continuation of 5% growth and a further decline in the unemployment rate, (ii) a decline in the growth rate to $2\frac{1}{2}\%$ and a gradual rise in the unemployment rate, or (iii) the reemergence of recession next year?

(b)   Suppose your result showed that credit card loans could be doubled by reducing the APR from 13.9% to 6.9%. Under what circumstances would you recommend that move, and under what circumstances would you advise against it?

(c)   The two largest banks in the metropolitan area have merged and have significantly increased the average monthly charge on checking accounts. What information would you need to determine whether it would be advisable to offer "free" checking accounts in an attempt to obtain more customers who would then borrow money from the bank? To what extent would the likely macroeconomic outlook influence this decision?

3.   A hotel chain would like to determine whether to build a major new hotel in Las Vegas or Orlando; essentially its decision will be based on whether the "gambling" market or the "family entertainment" market is

continued

expected to grow faster. Historical data are available on the number of trips to each city, the occupancy rate for hotel rooms, the average amount spent per traveler, the proportion arriving by automobile and airplane, and total available rooms.

(a) What other variables would be useful in making this determination? (Hint: what proportion of the visitors are foreign?)

(b) Suppose one presidential candidate said he thought gambling was sinful, whereas the other said consumers should have freedom of choice. How would that influence your forecast?

(c) In recent years, Florida voters have decided against permitting on-shore casinos in the state, but the issue will be voted on again in the future. How would that affect your forecast?

(d) The recent building boom in Las Vegas could affect the decision either way. On the negative side, there may be excess hotel rooms. On the positive side, more hotel rooms may attract more business conventions and stay for vacations. How would you determine whether the building boom should have a positive or negative impact on the decision?

4. As a financial manager, your client wants you to recommend the purchase of Mutual Fund X, Y, or Z. From 1997 through 1999, Fund X earned a total rate of return of 32% per year, Fund Y has earned 19% per year, and Fund Z has earned 8% per year.

(a) What additional data would you need to make an informed choice of which fund to purchase?

(b) Further analysis shows, not surprisingly, Fund X outperforms the market when it is rising at above-average rates, but underperforms it otherwise, whereas the opposite is true for Fund Z. However, your client has made it clear he does not want a conditional forecast. How would you proceed?

(c) The day before your client calls, the Federal Reserve Board has just voted to raise the funds rate by 50 basis points. How does this influence your decision? (Hint: was the change expected or unexpected?)

5. Your client is a state government, and legislators are debating whether to raise the tax on cigarettes by an additional $1/pack. Proponents of the bill claim that (i) needed revenue will be raised without boosting other taxes, and (ii) higher prices will reduce smoking, which will benefit the general health of society. However, as an economist, you know there is a tradeoff: the more people who quit, the less additional revenue will be raised.

continued

(a) How would you estimate the price elasticity of demand?
(b) Would you expect the price elasticity to be larger for younger or older smokers? How would this affect your overall conclusion?
(c) How would your answer differ if (i) Nevada were the client, and it was planning to raise its tax rate but California was not, or (ii) California were the client, and it was planning to raise its tax rate but Nevada was not?
(d) How would your estimates of tax revenue in the short run and the long run vary?

CHAPTER 2

USEFUL TOOLS FOR PRACTICAL BUSINESS FORECASTING

INTRODUCTION

Statistical theories may provide the necessary base for estimating regression equations, but any modeler immediately faces the following practical questions:

- Where do I find the data?
- How should the data be collected and organized?
- What is the best method for presenting the data graphically?
- What software should be chosen for calculating the regressions and building the model?

There are hundreds if not thousands of data sources, and many graphical packages and econometric software that will perform well. However, this author and his colleagues have found that model builders are not helped by being presented with an encyclopedic list of possible sources. Instead, this text uses an eclectic approach, offering the data sources and software packages that have proven most useful in our own work.

Today, much of the relevant data can be obtained from the Internet. This book provides addresses with the following caveat: they change frequently, and sometimes updated links are not given. Nonetheless, by briefly describing the relevant data sources, it should be straightforward to track them down even if the addresses have changed.

Before using the data for any type of analysis, it is always best to check for errors. Few things are more annoying than spending a great deal of time building and testing a model, only to find the underlying data are flawed. In most cases, the data will be identified as being seasonally adjusted or unadjusted, but different methods of seasonal adjustment could cause a variety of problems when the model is being used for forecasting. In addition, it is always prudent to check for outlying observations, and for missing or incomplete data, which could seriously distort the results of the model.

The software package used to estimate the models given in this text is EViews, a comprehensive program that is useful both for estimating regressions and building models. For those who plan to engage in large-scale data collection and model building, a program with the capacity and power of EViews is essential. On the other hand, many model builders develop equations with relatively few observations, and would prefer to link their models to spreadsheet analysis that has already been developed in Excel. While Excel is not recommended for heavy number-crunching, it can be a very useful tool for small models. However, the examples given in the text are based on EViews.

2.1 TYPES AND SOURCES OF DATA

The data that economic model builders use to generate forecasts can be divided into three principal categories: time-series, cross-section, and panel data. Most forecasting models use time-series data. A time series is a sequence of data at equidistant intervals where each point represents a certain time period (e.g., monthly, quarterly, or annually). Examples include quarterly data for consumption, monthly data for industrial production or housing starts, daily data for the stock market, annual data for capital spending, quarterly data for individual company sales and profits, or monthly levels of production and inventories.

Most econometric and forecasting books cover "regression models" and "time-series models." The first category includes the construction of models based on underlying economic theory; which are generally known as structural models. The second category incorporates models that relate the data to its previous values, time trends, seasonal adjustment factors, and other exogenous variables. Since no attempt is made to provide an underlying theory, these are known as non-structural models. As is shown later, superior forecasts are often generated by combining these two methods.

2.1.1 TIME-SERIES, CROSS-SECTION, AND PANEL DATA

Admittedly, use of the term "time series" to describe two different phenomena can sometimes be confusing. Time-series *data* are used in both regression models and time-series *models*. Time-series data refer to a time sequence of events regardless of the type of model in which they are used. Most of the material in this book will utilize time-series data. Part II of the text covers regression models, while Part III discusses time-series models; both are based on time-series data.

Cross-section data represent a snapshot of many different observations taken at a given time. The decennial census of population data are often used for cross-section analysis; for any given census year, statistical relationships can be used to estimate the correlation between income and education, location, size of family, race, age, sex, and a whole host of other variables.

Internal Revenue Service data are often used by the Congressional Budget Office to determine how various changes in the tax laws would affect individuals at various levels of income distribution; e.g., whether a particular tax cut would mainly benefit the "rich" or the "poor." Consumer survey data reveal the proportion of income that is spent on various goods and services at different levels of income. For example, economists might want to examine the behavior of a group of consumers to determine the level of their income, saving, and pattern of consumption (the relative amounts spent on food, rent, cars, vacations, etc.) at some specific time, say June 1995. Similar surveys can be used to determine the mix of goods purchased by, say, consumers in New York City compared to Denver, Colorado. At a more detailed level, individual companies use cross-section analysis to help determine who buys their products at department stores and supermarkets. Data on personal health collected at a specific time can be used to reveal what type of individual has the greatest risk for various diseases based on age, income, eating habits, use of tobacco and alcohol, parental health history, and other factors.

Much econometric work is based on cross-section data. For example, researchers might be interested in finding out how different types of consumers reacted to a tax change in the past. Economists have used cross-section data to determine whether the overall growth rate in a given country is due to government policies, the saving and investment ratio, education of the population, and many other factors. Financial advisors might be interested in determining the probability that a municipal bond issue would default, based on per capita income of the issuing municipality, age/sex/race characteristics, projects for which the money will be used, existing tax base and growth in that base, and so on. There are many more useful examples of how cross-section data can be used to predict various events, some of which will be used as examples later in this book.

Panel data refers to the reexamination of cross-section data with the same sample at different periods of time. For example, the problem with the June 1995 data might be that individuals buy a new car on average only once every four years (say), so that month might not have been typical. Thus the same people could be asked about their income, saving, and consumption in January 1997, and at other periods. Over a longer period of time, the spending patterns of these individuals could be tracked to help determine how much is saved at different levels of income, whether upper-income people spend a larger proportion of their income on housing, transportation, or medical care, or a host of other items. Panel data could also be used to determine whether individuals who started smoking cigarettes at a young age continued to smoke throughout their lives, whereas those who started smoking later found it easier to quit. These data could also help determine whether an increase in excise taxes on cigarettes has a greater effect in reducing smoking in the long run than in the short run.

2.1.2 BASIC SOURCES OF US GOVERNMENT DATA

Those who build a forecasting model using time-series data generally use government data even if they are predicting individual industry or company sales. Unless these forecasts are entirely driven by technology, they will depend on the level of economic activity both in the US and abroad.

The main US government data search engine (see section 2.2) lists 70 agencies that supply US economic data. However, for most economic forecasting needs, the main data sources are the Bureau of Economic Analysis (BEA), the Bureau of the Census, the Bureau of Labor Statistics (BLS), and the Board of Governors of the Federal Reserve System (Fed). Other important government sources of data include the Statistics of Income Division of the Internal Revenue Service; the Economic Research Service of the Department of Agriculture, and the Energy Information Administration of the Department of Energy. Since this is a brief book on forecasting rather than the sources of government data, the discussion at this point will be limited to the first four agencies.

The National Income and Product Accounts (NIPA) are prepared by BEA, which is part of the Commerce Department. The figures for current dollar and inflation-adjusted GDP,[1] consumption and investment, and personal and corporate income are all calculated and reported by BEA. In addition, BEA offers comprehensive data on state and county personal income and employment by detailed industry classification.

BEA processes and compiles data that are collected by various other government agencies. Most of the series that serve as inputs for NIPA are collected by the Bureau of the Census, which is also part of the Commerce Department. The Census Bureau is perhaps best known for its decennial count of all people in the country, but that is only a small part of its total activity. Most of the monthly reports on economic activity issued by the government are published by Census. These reports include data for manufacturers shipments, orders, and inventories; wholesale and retail sales and inventories; housing starts and construction put in place; and exports and imports. While most of the NIPA figures (except consumption and income) are quarterly data, data in the census publications listed here are all available on a monthly basis. Census also publishes the *Quarterly Report for Manufacturing Corporations*, which provides data for all major income statement and balance sheet items for all major manufacturing industries by asset size.

---

[1] Before 1996, figures were available in current and constant dollars. However, the methodological revisions introduced by BEA in 1996 switched to the use of chain-weighted figures to adjust for inflation, which essentially differ from constant dollars in that the weights are reset each year. The practical impact of this change is that the components of aggregate demand with decreasing prices, notably computer purchases, rise less rapidly than the constant-dollar figures, so the distorting influence on total aggregate demand is smaller.

Data for wages, prices, employment, unemployment, productivity, and labor costs are issued monthly by the BLS, which is part of the Labor Department. The BLS data have the biggest short-term impact on financial markets. The Employment and Earnings Report, which contains data on employment, unemployment, and wage rates; and the producer price index and consumer price index (PPI and CPI) are the most closely watched economic indicators by financial markets. The BLS also compiles monthly data on state and metropolitan area employment and unemployment.

The fourth major source of government data is the Fed. As would be expected, most of its reports cover monetary variables, including the money supply, bank assets and liabilities, interest rates, and foreign exchange rates. However, the Fed also provides figures for industrial production and capacity utilization for the overall economy and by detailed manufacturing industry.

Most of the key numbers that economists use are collected and issued in a monthly release called, appropriately enough, *Economic Indicators*, which is issued by the Council of Economic Advisers. It contains slightly over 500 series of economic data and can be purchased from the Government Printing Office for $55.00 per year (as of 2002). Updated data are also available on the Internet at www.access.gpo.gov/congress.cong002.html.

Economic Indicators is designed to present the most recent data, so it does not contain very much historical data. That can be found in the annual issues of the *Economic Report of the President*, a useful source for annual government data, although monthly and quarterly data are presented only for recent years.

The *Survey of Current Business*, published by the Commerce Department, contains comprehensive NIPA tables and a few other series, but it contains far less data since budget cuts stripped thousands of series from its tables. All the data in that publication can be found by accessing the BEA home page at www.bea.doc.gov and following the directions. Data for GDP by industry, state personal income, and a variety of regional economic data can be obtained by purchasing CD-ROMs at prices ranging from $20.00 to $35.00, and may be purchased from the BEA order desk. This website also allows viewers to access individual tables in the NIPA accounts and data for individual US states.

Those who want to obtain the government data immediately can subscribe to a Commerce Department service known as STAT-USA, which provides all key economic reports within minutes of their release time by the particular government agency. It's not free: having the data available immediately means subscribing for $175 or more per year. It is well worth it for those who follow the data closely and depend on those numbers for making financial market decisions, but for those who are just building a quarterly or annual model, time is generally not of the essence.

For those not familiar with the scope of government data, the best place to start for "one-stop" shopping is the *Statistical Abstract of the United States*, which is issued annually by Census. It contains approximately 1500 tables of data, most of it pertaining to the US economy, and also lists Internet addresses for the 33 major sources of Federal government data. The numbers found in the *Statistical Abstract* are collected from over 200 sources. Census sells a CD-ROM for each annual edition; the major drawback is that most of the series are given for only a few years, so to collect historical time series one must go to the original source or look through back issues of the *Statistical Abstract*. Census also sells CD-ROMs with economic data series for states, metropolitan areas, and individual counties.

2.1.3 MAJOR SOURCES OF INTERNATIONAL GOVERNMENT DATA

So far we have looked at only US government data, whereas many business applications increasingly rely on foreign data. For those who are building a specific model of a foreign country, most other industrialized countries have central sources of data similar to the US. In most cases, however, model builders will want general summary statistics for a wide variety of countries, which might be used (for example) in determining which countries represent the fastest growth potential, the best place for locating new plants, or the biggest risk factor in terms of depreciating currencies.

There are two general sources for international data. The first is the Organization for Economic Cooperation and Development (OECD), which is headquartered in Paris but has an office with most of their statistical documents in Washington, DC. It publishes several volumes of data, mainly NIPA figures and basic data for employment, production, and prices. Most of the data series are monthly or quarterly, but they are available only for the 29 OECD countries.

The International Monetary Fund (IMF), also in Washington, DC, provides data for over 170 countries, but almost all of the series are annual. As might be expected, its series concentrate on monetary data, balance of payments figures, and exchange rates, with relatively little data for real output, production, prices, and employment.

Specific data for Canada can be obtained from Statistics Canada, at www.statcan.ca/. Data for Europe issued by the European Central Bank can be found at www.ecb.int/. Data for Japan are available from the Bank of Japan at www.boj.or.jp/en/. Eurostat has a website with a wide variety of economic indicators for countries that have joined together in the euro; that information can be found at www.europa.eu.int/comm/eurostat.

For those who like to keep up to date on international data at a relatively modest cost, *The Economist* magazine carries key economic series for major countries in each weekly issue, which can be accessed at www.economist.com. Some data are available to all users; most are restricted to those who subscribe to the print version of that publication.

The Census Bureau has a comprehensive database for 227 countries and areas of the world for those interested in demographic and socioeconomic data: population, birth and death rates, literacy, and so on; it also contains statistics for labor force, employment, and income. This can be found at www.census.gov/ipc/www/idbnew.html.

If you are looking for specific economic data that are not found at the above sources, the Dallas Fed has a comprehensive set of links to international data. This can be accessed at www.dallasfed.org/htm/data/interdata.html. One of the most useful links will take you to Statistical Data Locators, a comprehensive list of organizations that is compiled by NTU Library at Singapore.

The Office of Productivity and Technology at BLS also publishes monthly data for the CPI and unemployment rates for major countries, plus figures for unit labor costs in manufacturing and per capita GDP for most OECD countries. As is the case for other BLS series, these can be accessed at www.bls.gov.

Those figures cover recent years; for older data, the standard source is by Robert Summers and Alan Heston, entitled *The Penn World Table Mark 5: An Expanded Set of International Comparisons, 1950–88*. This article originally appeared in the *Quarterly Journal of Economics* in 1991, but the data can also be obtained from the National Bureau of Economic Research (NBER) in New York. Actual data can be downloaded at http://datacentre.chass.utoronto.ca:5680/pwt/index.html. While these data are very comprehensive and are used for many international research studies, most of the series are only available up to 1994 and are not updated very frequently. As of 2001, the latest available version, 5.6, was released in January, 1995.

2.1.4 PRINCIPAL SOURCES OF KEY PRIVATE SECTOR DATA

While there are myriad sources of private sector data, many of them are either available only to members of specific organizations, or are sold at a very high price. This book does not offer a survey of these private sector databases; comments here are restricted to data that are generally available at a zero or modest price. These sources can be divided into the following categories:

*   financial market data
*   individual company data
*   consumer behavior
*   housing surveys
*   manufacturing sector surveys
*   individual industry data.

Except for financial data, the first place to look is often the *Statistical Abstract*, which has recent figures for most series and provides the source for comprehensive historical data. Although most of their data comes from government sources, about 10 percent of the 1,500 tables, each containing several series, are from private sector sources.

FINANCIAL MARKET DATA

The standard source is the Center for Research on Security Prices at the University of Chicago. However, that huge database is likely to be more than is needed by those who are planning to analyze only a few companies, or need data for only a relatively short period of time. Worden Brothers, which can be accessed at www.TC2000.com, will send a CD-ROM with daily stock market data for up to 15 years at no cost. They hope users will update the data at $1.00/day, but even for those who do not choose that option, the CD-ROM will supply a great deal of historical data on individual stocks.

INDIVIDUAL COMPANY DATA

The best bet is to access the Web. Hoover's On-Line is one convenient source that has over 50 databases that offer individual company data. One of those databases is Public Register's Annual Report Service, which provides free annual reports for over 3,600 firms. The Securities and Exchange Commission EDGAR file contains all reports that must be filed by public companies; that would be more than most people need, but it can be a valuable resource.

CONSUMER BEHAVIOR

The two key surveys are undertaken by the Conference Board and University of Michigan. The Conference Board is willing to have their data disseminated, and makes much of it available for free or a modest fee. The University of Michigan, on the other hand, is concerned that if they give out their survey results, hardly anyone will pay to subscribe. Nonetheless, all the wire services carry their reports a few minutes after they are released, so the data can be obtained second-hand from various sources. However, the Conference Board is much more customer-friendly. In empirical testing, this author has found relatively little difference between the two series.

HOUSING SURVEYS

The main surveys are undertaken by the National Association of Home Builders and the National Association of Realtors. These surveys contain data for number of homes sold and average price by state and detailed metropolitan area, characteristics of new homes being built, and attitude surveys about the likelihood of consumer purchases in the near term. In both cases, the overall numbers are available for free, while data in the detailed reports can be purchased.

MANUFACTURING SECTOR SURVEYS

The best-known survey is published by the National Association of Purchasing Managers. It is released monthly, based on questionnaires filled out by approximately 250 purchasing managers about shipments, production, employment, delivery times, and especially prices paid and received. Several regional purchasing managers' indexes are also published, notably for Chicago and New York, but the national survey is generally thought to have a higher level of accuracy and is referenced much more frequently.

INDIVIDUAL INDUSTRY DATA

Some of the major associations that will make their summary data available free or at modest cost include the American Iron & Steel Institute, Association for Manufacturing Technology (formerly Association of Machine Tool Builders), American Petroleum Institute, Electronics Industry Association, Dataquest Gartner (for computer shipments and revenues), and the Semiconductor Industry Association.

2.2 COLLECTING DATA FROM THE INTERNET

Many model builders want to obtain complete historical series of quarterly or monthly data without having to type them in by hand. There are essentially three choices. First, you can pull each series off the Web using the cut and paste routines; the major sources of data from the Internet are discussed in this section. Second, you can order disks or CDs from each of the government agencies. Third, you can pay someone else to do the heavy lifting by purchasing a comprehensive database from some commercial vendor. The databases used in conjunction with EViews are compiled by Haver Analytics. Other commercial vendors offer similar databases, but at somewhat higher prices. Unless otherwise stated, the data referenced in this text were either collected by the author directly or are found in the Haver Analytics database. The basic Haver database covers only US data except for a few foreign interest and exchange rates. Comprehensive foreign data can be purchased from OECD or IMF either in printed form or on CD-ROMs.

The section on collecting data from the Internet could be an entire monograph. However, the purpose is not to list all, or even most, of the sources of economic data available on-line. It is to provide a comprehensive but nonetheless compact directory for finding most of the data that are likely to be useful in building econometric models.

For those who know what data series they want, and know the government or private sector source for that data, the obvious choice is to proceed directly to that website. If you don't know who publishes the data, or aren't sure what series you want, several comprehensive data sites on the Web are recommended. The principal sources of US and international public sector data are as follows (website addresses were current as of 2001). The sites that combine many databases are listed in increasing order of generality.

- Bureau of Economic Analysis: National income and product accounts, international transactions, regional income and employment. www.bea.doc.gov
- Bureau of the Census: Monthly data for manufacturers shipments, orders, inventories; wholesale and retail trade and inventories; housing starts and construction put in place; monthly foreign trade statistics. www.census.gov
- Bureau of Labor Statistics: Employment and unemployment; CPI and PPI; wage rates, productivity, and unit labor costs. www.bls.gov
- Board of Governors of the Federal Reserve System: money supply, bank balance sheets, interest rates, foreign exchange rates, industrial production. www.bog.gov
- Internal Revenue Service: income tax data. www.irs.gov
- Organization for European Cooperation and Development (OECD): Most key economic series for OECD countries, many on a monthly or quarterly basis. www.oecd.org
- International Monetary Fund (IMF): Many of the same series as OECD, but for over 170 countries. Most data are on an annual basis, and most of the series are monetary, as opposed to real sector variables or prices. www.imf.org

If you want US government data but do not know who publishes it, try www.Fedstats.gov. That contains a comprehensive list of all data published by 70 government agencies, and the search engine is quite thorough. It is highly recommended for those who want to use government data. The search engine also includes a long list of articles written about subjects related to economic data.

There are many comprehensive sites for economic data on the Internet. If you are looking for strictly economic data, the best site is the St. Louis Federal Reserve Bank database, appropriately named FRED. It can be found at www.stls.frb.org/fred.

For those who want to cast their "net" wider and look for data that encompass both economic and other social sciences, one good choice is the business and economics database at the University of Michigan. The address is www.lib.umich.edu/libhome/Documents.center/stats.html.

Finally, if you are looking for a broader range of economic and business data, the following website lists literally hundreds of individual Web-based databases, although some of the links are out of date. That is found at www.mnsfld.edu/depts/lib/ecostats.html.

2.3 FORECASTING UNDER UNCERTAINTY

Statisticians generally distinguish between two distinct types of forecasting models: those where the underlying probability distribution is known, and those where it isn't. The first type includes such examples as poker hands, chances at the roulette wheel, or the correlation between height and weight. If one were able to perform enough experiments to include the entire population, the results would be known with certainty. Of course that does not mean the outcome of the next event would be known in advance, only the probability that it would occur. However, if enough experiments were performed, the sample mean and variance would approach the population mean and variance. Even more important, all observations are independent, and the underlying probability distribution does not change. No matter how many times in a row you have won or lost at the roulette wheel, the probability of success on the next spin is independent of what previously happened – assuming that the wheel is not "fixed."

The other type of forecasting model, which is more relevant to business forecasting, occurs when the underlying probability distribution is not known. We think, for example, that consumers spend more when their income rises, and businesses invest more when the real rate of interest declines. Those are certainly reasonable hypotheses and are buttressed by economic theory. However, consider all the factors we don't know: *how much* consumption will change when income changes, the time lag, other factors that affect income, the fact that the observations are not independent (most people are creatures of habit), and the fact that we don't know what income will be in the future. Even more important, the relationship between consumption and income may change for the same individuals depending on the economic environment. They may be more optimistic or more pessimistic; they may have recently moved into a larger home and need more furniture, their children may be approaching college age, and a host of other factors.

Over the past century, a large amount of statistical literature has been devoted to the issue of the "best" methods of estimating empirical relationships. The majority of these articles are related to the method of least squares. However, almost all of the tests and relationships are based on assumptions that do not exist in the typical practical business forecasting environment. The major problems can be briefly summarized as follows:

- The data are not normally distributed.
- The residuals are not all independent (the forecasting error in this period is often closely connected with the error last period).
- The independent variables are supposed to be known at the time of forecast, which is generally not the case.
- The data are sometimes inaccurate and subject to substantial revision.
- Finally, and most important, the underlying data generation function may have shifted during the sample period, or – even more damaging – during the forecast period.

In spite of all these drawbacks, the vast majority of economic forecasting models are estimated using least squares, and the examples given in this book will follow this approach. However, emphasis will be placed on adjusting for the fact that the classical least squares criteria often do not occur. For this reason I will not offer the usual introductory discussion of the statistics, which can be found in many other suitable textbooks. Two texts this author generally uses for supplementary statistical and econometric material when teaching this course are *Econometric Models and Economic Forecasts,* by Robert S. Pindyck and Daniel L. Rubinfeld, and *Econometric Methods* by Jack Johnston and John DiNardo.[2] The following chapters will develop as much of the outline of the general linear model as is needed as a framework to explore where the actual results differ. However, before turning to the general linear model, it is best to discuss some of the more common terms that will be used throughout the text. The treatment that follows is non-technical.

2.4 MEAN AND VARIANCE

Suppose the same experiment is performed several times, and we take a weighted average of all the outcomes, where the weights are the probabilities. That weighted average is known as the *expected value,* or *mean* of the distribution, and is usually denoted in statistics by μ. It can be defined as follows:

$$\mu_x = E(X) = p_1 X_1 + p_2 X_2 + \cdots + p_n X_n = \sum_{i=1}^{N} p_i X_i \qquad (2.1)$$

where the p_i are the probabilities associated with events X_i.

The expected value is closely related to, but not the same as, the *sample mean,* which is the *actual* average value one obtains by performing the experiment a certain number of times. The sample mean is denoted as $\overline{X}$, where

$$\overline{X} = (1/N)\sum_{i=1}^{N} X_i. \qquad (2.2)$$

As the number of experiments increases, the sample mean always approaches its expected value. That is one of the bases of statistical theory. It is a simple matter to show that $E(\overline{X}) = \mu_X$.

In trying to determine the true underlying value of the parameter with sampling, it is also important to measure the *dispersion* around the mean, and determine whether the sample observations are tightly clustered around the mean or are spread out so that they cover almost the entire range of probabilities. The dispersion around the mean is known as the *variance,* which can be defined as

$$\text{Var}(X) = \sigma_x^2 = \sum p_i [X_i - E(X)]^2 \qquad (2.3)$$

---

[2] Pindyck, Robert S., and Daniel L. Rubinfeld, *Econometric Models and Economic Forecasts,* 4th edn (Irwin McGraw-Hill, Boston), 1998. Johnston, Jack, and John DiNardo, *Econometric Methods,* 4th edn (McGraw-Hill, New York), 1997. All page numbers and references are to these editions.

where p_i is the probability of each event X_i occurring, and $E(X)$ is the the expected value of X.

Just as we distinguish between the expected value and the sample mean, we can distinguish between the true variance and its sample estimator. However, whereas the sample mean $\overline{X}$ was an unbiased estimator of the expected value, it turns out that the sample variance $(X - \overline{X})^2$ is *not* an unbiased estimator of the variance. Instead, it must be adjusted for what is known as *degrees of freedom*, which equals the number of observations minus the number of variables in the equation. As a result, an unbiased estimate of the variance of a random variable, S_x, is given by

$$S_x = 1/(N-1)\sum(X_i - \overline{X})^2 . \tag{2.4}$$

A simple example can be used to illustrate this point of why the sample variance must be adjusted by the degrees of freedom. One can always connect two points with a straight line. The mean value is the average of these two points. The variance is supposed to be the dispersion around the line connecting these two points, but there isn't any variance: the line connects the two points exactly, leaving no residual. Similarly, a plane can always be drawn through three points, and so on. The argument is the same as we move into n dimensions. The more variables that are contained in the equation, the more likely it is that the n-dimensional line will connect all the points, even if the relationship doesn't explain anything. Thus an unbiased estimate of the true variance must be calculated by adjusting for the degrees of freedom.

The square root of the sample period variance is known as the *standard deviation*, which is the more common measure used in statistical parlance. The comparison of the estimated mean to its standard deviation indicates whether that mean is statistically significantly different from some preassigned value, usually zero.

The mean and variance are the two sample statistics most often used to describe the characteristics of the underlying probability distributions. They are not the only ones. Statistics books generally refer to the methods of "moments," which show that the mean and variance are only the first and second moments of a long list of characteristics that describe various probability distributions. Sometimes it is useful to find out how much distributions deviate from the normal distribution by looking at the third and fourth moments, known as *skewness* and *kurtosis*. For example, a distribution might be "lopsided" with the peak value far away from the middle, which is skewness. The tails might be too "fat," which is kurtosis. Also, the distribution could have more than one peak. However, for practical purposes in most practical statistical work – including but not limited to economics – the mean and variance are the only tools that are used to describe the shape of the probability distribution. That is because the normal distribution, which is the most important distribution for statistical work, is completely defined by its mean and variance.

2.5 GOODNESS-OF-FIT STATISTICS

One of the major aims of this book is to explain how to build a forecasting model that will minimize forecast error. As will be seen in numerous examples, independent variables that appear to be highly correlated with the dependent variable in the sample period often show a much smaller correlation in the forecast period. Nonetheless, in a brief statistical review it is useful to indicate the tests used to determine which variables are statistically significant, and how well the equation fits, over the sample period. We want to determine if the parameter estimates – the coefficients – in the model are significantly different from zero, and also what proportion of the total variance of the dependent variable is explained by the regression equation. The statistical significance of each coefficient is determined by dividing the value of each coefficient by its standard error. If the residuals are normally distributed, the parameter estimates will generally be statistically significant from zero at the 95% probability level if this ratio is 2 or greater, and at the 99% level if this ratio is 2.7 or greater.

The proportion of the variance of the dependent variable explained by the equation is known as R-squared. It is sometimes thought that the higher the R-squared, the more accurate the forecasts will be; but as will be shown throughout this book, that is often not the case. Nonetheless, virtually every model builder looks at the values of R-squared in determining which equation to choose, and to a certain extent I will follow that general practice.

2.5.1 COVARIANCE AND CORRELATION COEFFICIENTS

We have defined the theoretical and sample mean and variance for each random variable X. However, from the viewpoint of statistics, econometrics, and forecasting, the interesting part is not so much the characteristics of a single random variable X, but its correlation with other random variables Y and Z. At this point we consider only the bivariate case, or the correlation between two random variables X and Y. To determine this correlation, we can calculate the *covariance*, which is defined as

$$\text{Cov}(X, Y) = E(X - E(X))(Y - E(Y))]. \qquad (2.5)$$

Substituting the mean values of X and Y for their expected values, and switching from the true covariance to its sample period estimate, we have

$$\text{Cov}(X, Y) = \sum \frac{(X_i - \overline{X})(Y_i - \overline{Y})}{N - 1}. \qquad (2.6)$$

The *correlation coefficient* is defined as the covariance divided by the product of the standard deviation of X and Y. The point of this transformation is that the size of the covariance depends on the scale factors used (millions, percent changes, square feet, etc.) whereas the correlation coefficient is always between −1 and +1, so one can see at a glance how strong the correlation is. The correlation coefficient is thus given as

$$\rho(X, Y) = \frac{\text{Cov}(X, Y)}{\sigma_X \cdot \sigma_Y} \tag{2.7}$$

where σ_X and σ_Y are the standard deviations of X and Y respectively.

2.5.2 STANDARD ERRORS AND t-RATIOS

After determining the correlation coefficient, the model builder wants to know whether this correlation is significantly different from zero at some designated level, usually the 95% probability level. One could easily test whether the parameter estimate is significantly different from some other value, but most of the time researchers want to determine whether the coefficient is significantly different from zero.

Consider the simple bivariate linear equation

$$Y_t = \alpha + \beta X_t. \tag{2.8}$$

Estimating the regression equation yields an estimate of the intercept α and the slope coefficient β; the least squares algorithm also supplies estimates of the variances of the estimated values of α and β. The significance level is determined by taking the ratio of the coefficient to its standard error, which is the square root of the variance. In everyday terms, this means the standard error serves as a measure of the dispersion of the probability distribution of that coefficient around its mean value. If the standard error is small relative to the coefficient, the probability is high that the actual value will be close to the estimate; if the standard error is large relative to the coefficient, the actual value could be just about anything, and the estimated value is not very useful. If the error term is normally distributed, then we can determine whether the coefficient is significantly different from some desired test value, generally zero.

Some actual numerical examples are provided later. For now, consider the case where the coefficient is 0.70 and the standard error is 0.30. Also assume that the error term is normally distributed. The ratio of the coefficient to the standard error is 2.33. What does that mean?

We have already noted that one rule of thumb – almost taken for granted in most of the empirical articles in economics – states that if this ratio is greater than 2, the variable is significantly different from zero; or, in short, significant. For the practicing econometrician, that is the rule used to show that your results are meaningful. Perhaps a better level of significance could be found, but this result is so ingrained in statistics that we will continue to use it.

As the sample gets smaller, the ratio of the coefficient to its standard error must be somewhat larger for any given level of significance. The ratio of the sample mean to the sample variance – as opposed to the population mean and variance – is known as a t-ratio. The t-distribution is similar to the normal distribution. In general it has fatter tails than the normal distribution, but approaches it as the sample size increases.

Tables for the t-ratio are given in any standard statistics or econometrics textbook. These tables show that as the sample size diminishes, the ratio of the coefficient to its standard error must be increasingly greater than 2 to be significant at the 5% level. Given that the 5% level of the normal distribution is 1.96 times the standard error, below are listed some values of the t-distribution to see how much difference the sample size makes. All these levels of significance are based on what are known as *two-tailed tests*; i.e., no a-priori guess is made about whether the sign ought to be positive or negative. If we knew for sure what the sign was supposed to be, the t-ratios would be about 20% lower for comparable levels of significance (e.g., the 5% level of significance would be 1.64 instead of around 2).

Degrees of freedom	t-ratio for 5% significance
5	2.57
10	2.23
15	2.13
20	2.09
40	2.02
60	2.00
∞	1.96

For practical purposes the difference narrows very quickly. As a general rule of thumb, this author suggests that you should not try to build a forecasting model using less than 20 independent observations. At that level, the difference between a t-ratio of 2.1 and 2.0 will probably be overwhelmed by other statistical difficulties in the data.

2.5.3 F-RATIOS AND ADJUSTED R-SQUARED

The F-ratio, which measures the overall significance of the estimated equation, can be defined as

$$F = \frac{X * (n - k)}{Y * (k - 1)} \tag{2.9}$$

where X is the *explained* part of the variance of the dependent variable, and Y is the *unexplained* part. Also, n is the total number of observations and k is the number of estimated coefficients, so $n - k$ is the number of degrees of freedom in the equation, and $k - 1$ is the number of independent variables. The F-ratio can be used to test whether the explained part of the variance – compared with the unexplained part – is large enough to be significantly different from zero (or whatever other number is selected).

If the F-ratio measures the significance of the entire equation, and the t-ratio measures the significance of an individual coefficient, there ought to be some relationship between the two ratios for the bivariate case, which is

$$t^2 = F. \tag{2.10}$$

An intuitive explanation of this relationship is that the t-ratio measures the explained coefficient relative to its standard error, while the F-ratio measures the explained variance relative to the unexplained variance for the entire equation. In the bivariate case, t is the ratio of the explained part of the equation to the unexplained part, while F is the square of both those terms. Thus the F-ratio is usually considered only in multivariate equations; for the simple bivariate case, the F-ratio does not contain any additional information not already found in the t-ratio.

However, the F-ratio is not particularly easy to interpret without having the F-distribution tables in front of you. Does a value of 8.4 mean the equation is significant or not? (Answer: it depends on the number of degrees of freedom.) Recall that the covariance between two variables could be easy converted into a correlation coefficient that ranged between -1.00 and $+1.00$, which gave us an easy-to-interpret figure without further adjustment.

The F-ratio is amenable to a similar interpretation. The statistic most commonly used is known as R-bar squared, which is the proportion of the total variance of the dependent variable that is explained by the regression equation, adjusted for degrees of freedom. $\overline{R}^2$ is equally suitable for multiple regression equations, as will be seen in chapter 3. It is defined as

$$\overline{R}^2 = 1 - \frac{\text{unexplained variance} * (n - 1)}{\text{total variance} * (n - k)}. \tag{2.11}$$

This is similar to, but not exactly the same as

$$R^2 = \frac{\text{explained variance}}{\text{total variance}}. \tag{2.12}$$

To see the difference, suppose that the explained variance equals 95% of the total variance. Then R^2 would be 0.95. However, suppose there are 50 observations; then $n - 1 = 49$ and $n - k = 48$, so $\overline{R}^2 = 1.00 - 0.05* (49/48)$, which is 0.949.

When n is large, R^2 is large, and k is small, there is very little difference between $\overline{R}^2$ and R^2. However, as R^2 drops, the difference can be substantial, especially for small samples. In extreme cases, $\overline{R}^2$ can be negative. In this book, it is often listed as RSQ.

One word of caution: all these formulas are calculated by taking variables around their mean values. It is possible to calculate a regression equation without any constant term. In that case, the formulas do not apply and often give ridiculous values for R^2 that cannot be used; often the reported results are negative. Most programs will warn if you have inadvertently left out the constant term.

2.6 USING THE EVIEWS STATISTICAL PACKAGE

The graphs shown in this text are produced by the EViews software program, which is used throughout this book. Just as there are hundreds if not thousands of sources of data, there are many different software programs written for the PC that can be used to estimate regressions and build models. However, for our purposes, the list can quickly be narrowed down to a few names.

The program should be primarily designed for economic model building, which means including an efficient simulation capability as well as estimating regression equations. It should be simple to generate transformations of the variables, including lags, percentage changes, and ratios, and it should also be easy to add dummy variables and estimate nonlinear equations. The program should also contain a full battery of standard tests to determine whether the various parameters are statistically significant. It should also permit easy data entry and exit and be compatible with existing large-scale economic databases. Other programs satisfying all these criteria include SAS, SPSS, PCGIVE, and RATS. Minitab and Excel are widely used for spreadsheet forecasting but are not so useful for building models. In this author's experience, the modeling capabilities of EViews are easier to use than those found in competing programs.

The examples and printouts in this text are based on EViews; other programs generally have similar formats and provide essentially the same information. Figure 2.1 shows a typical printout, and the following text identifies some of the standard terms that appear along with each regression equation to show the reader what is expected. For most of the equations in this book, an abbreviated form is used to convey the most important statistical information.

- @PCH(WAGERATE) is the dependent variable. The symbol WAGERATE stands for an index of average annual wage rates. @PCH means percentage changes are being used. In EViews, percentage changes are *not* multiplied by 100, so a change from 1.00 to 1.05 would appear as 0.05 rather than 5.0.
- The sample period is given along with the number of observations, in case any years were skipped because of missing data. In this case, there are 50 years from 1949 through 1998 inclusive, so no data are missing. From time to time it might be advisable to omit one or more observations if it appeared to be far out of line with the rest of the information. Alternatively, data might be missing for one or more observations.

Dependent Variable: @PCH(WAGERATE)
Method: Least Squares

Sample(adjusted): 1949 1998
Included observations: 50 after adjusting endpoints

Variable	Coefficient	Std. Error	t-Statistic	Prob.
C	0.009	0.003	2.94	0.005
@PCH(CPI)	0.613	0.049	12.56	0.000
@PCH(MINWAGE)	0.042	0.008	5.01	0.000
@PCH(POIL)	−0.013	0.005	−2.66	0.011
@PCH(M2,2)	0.078	0.020	4.01	0.000
1/UN(-1)*DBR	0.079	0.010	7.67	0.000
R-squared	0.90	Mean dependent var		0.056
Adjusted R-squared	0.89	S.D. dependent var		0.023
S.E. of regression	0.0076	Akaike info criterion		−6.80
Sum squared resid	0.0027	Schwarz criterion		−6.57
Log likelihood	176	F-statistic		80.3
Durbin-Watson stat	2.07	Prob(F-statistic)		0.000

Figure 2.1 A typical output of EViews. The elements are explained in the text.

- @PCH(CPI) is the percentage change in the consumer price index.
- @PCH(MINWAGE) is the percentage change in the minimum wage.
- @PCH(POIL) is the percentage change in the price of crude oil. This enters with a negative sign to show that when there are major swings in oil prices, wage rates do not adjust as much as when changes occur in the CPI due to other factors.
- @PCH(M2,2) is the percentage change in the M2 measure of the money supply over the past two years.
- UN is the unemployment rate. It used to be thought that when the unemployment rate declined, wage rates increased. However, once Paul Volcker reestablished the credibility of monetary policy in 1982, that term was no longer needed, so it is zeroed out starting in 1982. The reader can verify that adding a term $1/UN(-1)*(1 - DBR)$ – where DBR is 1 before 1981 and 0 afterwards – has a t-ratio that is very close to zero.
- The coefficient for each term (including the constant term) is followed by its standard error. The t-statistic is the ratio of the coefficient to its standard error. The "prob" column shows the probability that the coefficient is not significantly different from zero. For the percentage change of oil term, the probability is 0.011 that the term is zero. The CPI is clearly quite significant; the probability that it is zero is less than 0.00005.

- R-squared is the percentage of the variance of the dependent variable explained by the equation. Adjusted R-squared (often called RSQ in this text) is R^2 adjusted for degrees of freedom; in this case it is 0.89. The standard error of the regression equation is 0.0076, or 0.76%. That means that approximately two times out of three, the sample period error for predicting the wage rate was less than 0.76%, compared with an average change of 5.6% (noted below). The sum of squares residual is the standard error squared multiplied by the degrees of freedom; it does not add very much information.
- The log likelihood ratio is used to test for maximum likelihood estimates, which are not considered in this book, and can be ignored here.
- The Durbin–Watson statistic is discussed in chapter 3. It is a test for the auto-correlation of the residuals. If no autocorrelation is present, the DW statistic is 2. If this statistic is less than about 1.4, the residuals are serially correlated. When that happens, the t-ratios and R^2 are overstated, so the equation will usually not predict as well as indicated by the sample period statistics. The DW of 2.07 indicates there is no autocorrelation in this equation.
- The mean dependent variable is 0.056, which means the average annual change in wage rates over the sample period was 5.6%. The SD dependent variable line show the standard error of the variable around its mean, which is 2.3%.
- The Akaike and Schwarz criteria are designed to show whether an equation would be better by containing fewer terms; those are used for time-series models and are discussed in Chapter 7.
- The F-statistic measures where the overall equation is significant; the probability that the entire relationship is not statistically different from zero is 0.000000. Since several terms are significant, the overall equation must be significant in any case; for this reason, the F-ratio is not used very often. While it is possible to estimate an equation where none of the t-ratios is greater than 2 but the overall F-statistic was significant, that would mean cluttering the equation with individual terms that are not significant, which would ordinarily generate a very poor forecasting equation.

A brief note on the number of significant digits. The actual program for EViews generally shows six or seven numbers. I have reduced this clutter to show two or three significant figures, which makes more sense economically. There is no real difference between, say, $\overline{R}^2$ of 0.8732 and 0.8741, or between t-ratios of 5.88 and 5.84.

A typical graph, showing the actual values, those estimated by the equation, and the residuals, is in figure 2.2. The top half of this figure shows the actual values of changes in wage rates compared with the estimated values calculated by the regression equation in figure 2.1; these are also called simulated or fitted values. The bottom half shows the residuals, defined as the actual minus the fitted values. The largest error occurs in 1989, when wages rose far less than would be predicted by the equation; almost as large a discrepancy occurred in 1992 in the other direction.

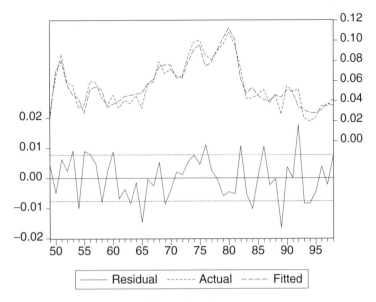

Figure 2.2 A typical output from EViews. See the text.

2.7 UTILIZING GRAPHS AND CHARTS

The construction of econometric models is often based on economic theory. However, in virtually all cases, the researcher looks at the underlying data in order to form some opinion of how the variables are correlated, and whether the correlation is improved when the independent variables are lagged.

There are three principal methods of displaying time-series data. Line graphs usually show two or more series graphed against time. Scatter diagrams have all the sample period points for one variable on the *y*-axis and the other variable on the *x*-axis. Bar graphs are often utilized to describe the characteristics of a single series; the most common use in this text is histograms, where either the original series or the residuals from a regression equation can be checked for normality and other statistical properties. Bar graphs can be used for multiple variables, either on a side-to-side basis or stacked. Sometimes pie charts are used as graphical aids, but these are usually for a snapshot of events at some given time and are not ordinarily utilized with time-series data.

The well-known comment about lies, damn lies, and statistics, variously attributed to Benjamin Disraeli and Mark Twain among others, summarizes how many people view graphical analysis. The same data can tell completely different stories depending on how they are presented. To see this, consider the simple relationship between consumption and disposable income, both in constant dollars. Figure 2.3 shows a line diagram of the difference between actual and simulated consumption. It looks like almost a perfect fit. Figure 2.4 shows

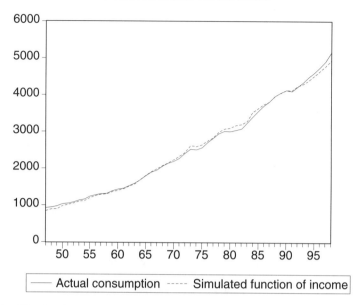

Figure 2.3 The level of real consumer spending appears to follow real disposal income very closely.

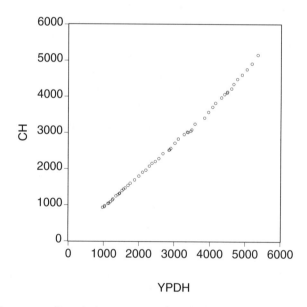

Figure 2.4 The scatter diagram between consumption and income shows almost a perfect fit.

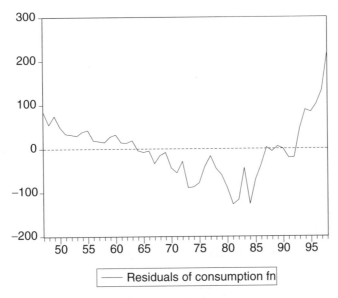

Figure 2.5 The residuals when consumption is regressed on real disposal income are quite large in many years.

the same data in a scatter diagram, which reinforces that conclusion. Yet figure 2.5 shows the residuals of that equation; when put on a different scale, it is more easily seen that the errors in predicting consumption with this simple equation may be as much as $200 billion per year.

One could claim that, without reference to further benchmarks, we don't know whether $200 billion is a "large" error or not. Some further comparison is warranted. In 1999, real consumer spending in the US was about $6,000 billion, and over the past 10 years had grown at an average annual rate of 3.5% per year. Hence a naive model that said the growth rate in 2000 would continue at 3.5% would predict an increase of about $210 billion. In fact the actual increase, based on preliminary data, was $316 billion, for an error of $106 billion. Seen in that light, a $200 billion error is abnormally large, since it is almost double the error generated by a naive model.

Finally, figure 2.6 shows the actual and forecast values for the percentage changes in each of these variables; which makes it obvious that while income is an important determinant of consumption, it is hardly the only one. The lines in the top part of this graph show the actual percentage change in consumption compared with the percentage changes that are estimated by the regression equation, which in this case simply states that percentage changes in consumption are a function of percentage changes in income plus a constant term. The line in the bottom part of this graph, which is on a different scale, plots the residuals, or the differences between the actual and estimated values of the dependent variable.

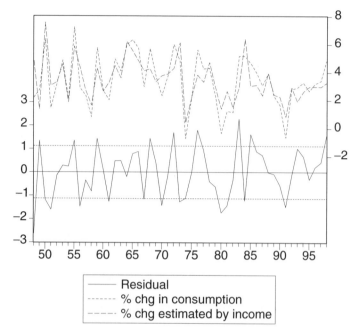

Figure 2.6 The percentage change in income is an important determinant of the percentage change in consumption, but the residuals are still quite large.

In another example, consider the correlation between the Federal funds rate and the rate of inflation, as measured by the consumer price index (CPI), on an annual basis. In general, we see that when the inflation rate changes, the Federal funds rate is likely to change by a similar proportion.

Figure 2.7 shows a scatter diagram with annual data for the funds rate and the inflation rate for the period 1955 through 1998 (no data are available for the funds rate before 1955). It is clear the series are positively correlated, although not perfectly. The solid line represents the regression line as calculated by least squares. Note that the slope of the regression line is slightly less than unity, which means when the inflation rate is zero, the funds rate is slightly positive.

Figure 2.8 shows the same two variables using a line graph. From 1955 through 1980, the funds rate exceeded the inflation rate by only a small amount. From 1981 through 1989, the gap between the funds rate and the inflation rate was much greater, indicating a shift in Federal Reserve policy. The line graph shows this clearly, whereas the scatter diagram does not.

According to the assumptions of the classical linear model, the residuals are supposed to be normally distributed. One simple test is to examine the histogram of the residuals to see whether that is indeed the case. We look at the residuals from the equation shown above, where the Federal funds rate is a function of the inflation rate.

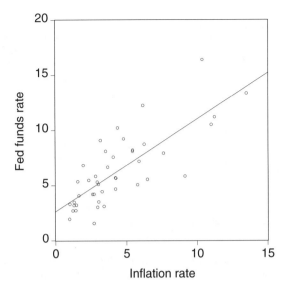

Figure 2.7 When inflation rises, the Fed funds rate also increases, but not quite as rapidly.

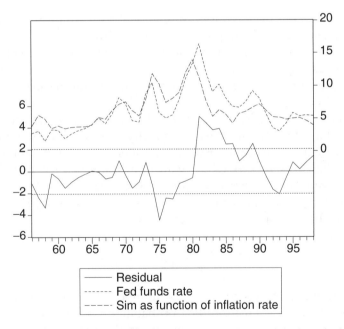

Figure 2.8 After 1980, the Fed funds rate was usually much higher than the inflation rate.

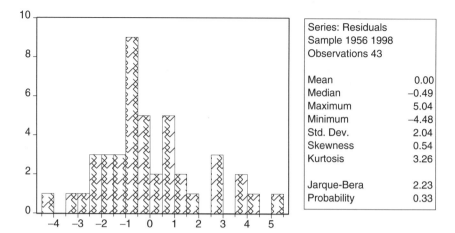

Figure 2.9 When annual data are used, the residuals from the equation where the Fed funds rate is a function of the inflation rate are normally distributed.

The residuals from the equation using annual data are normally distributed, as shown in figure 2.9. The graph, which is taken from EViews, is accompanied by several statistics. By definition the mean is zero. The median is slightly negative, indicating that there are more negative than positive residuals. The maximum and minimum values of the residuals are given next. The standard deviation is 2.03.

The next line measures skewness, which is the measure of how much the distribution is lopsided. If this were a perfectly normal distribution, skewness would be zero. Kurtosis measures the "fatness" of the tails; for the normal distribution, kurtosis is 3. A casual glance indicates the calculated measures of skewness and kurtosis are not very far away from the values of a normal distribution, but we need a formal test. The standard measure is known as the Jarque–Bera (JB) statistic, which is defined as

$$JB = \frac{(N-k)*}{6}\left[S^2 + \frac{(K-3)^2}{4}\right]$$

(2.13)

where N = number of observations, k = number of variables in the equation, S = skewness, and K = kurtosis. The probability 0.33 means that one would observe a JB statistic this high 33 percent of the time under the hypothesis that the residuals are normally distributed. Since that is well above the usual 5% level of significance, in this particular case the residuals are normally distributed.

However, if we run a regression with the same variables using quarterly instead of annual data, a different result emerges for the residuals. As shown in

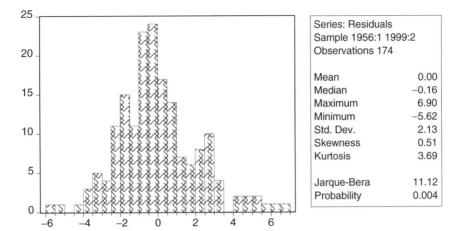

Figure 2.10 When quarterly data are used, the residuals from the equation where the Fed rate is a function of the inflation rate are not normally distributed.

figure 2.10, kurtosis is much higher, as shown by the proliferation of outlying values with both positive and negative signs. As we will see later, the main reason is that, on a quarterly basis, the Federal funds rate depends on the lagged as well as current values of inflation. The point illustrated here is that using annual and quarterly data can give far different statistical results even if the coefficients are quite similar.

2.8 CHECKLIST BEFORE ANALYZING DATA

When teaching courses in forecasting, I have found that one of the most frustrating tasks is to convince students to check the data before they start using them. Even if the data are obtained from reputable sources, mistakes happen. Sometimes the series are corrupted, and sometimes the starting and ending dates are not exactly as listed. Even if the data are error-free, one or two outliers may distort the entire model-building process; unless you check ahead of time, that won't become apparent until your regression estimates provide unrealistic sample period estimates or inadequate forecasts. Sometimes series that are supposed to be in comparable units are not; one series is in millions, while the other is in thousands.

Except for financial markets, most government data are seasonally adjusted, but most company data are not. Thus if you are going to mix the two types of data, some adjustment procedure is required. This topic will be discussed more in Part III, but at this juncture we look briefly at some of the major seasonal adjustment methods, including their plusses and minuses.

2.8.1 ADJUSTING FOR SEASONAL FACTORS

Most economic time-series data have seasonal patterns. For the most part, government data have already been seasonally adjusted, but this is not usually the case for individual company data. Attempts to use these data for modeling efforts without first applying seasonal factors will usually lead to suboptimal results.

Typical examples of seasonal patterns in economic data are the following: sales rise every Christmas, more people visit the beach in the summer, sales of snow shovels rise every winter, broiler (chicken) prices peak in the week of July 4, the unemployment rate for construction workers rises in the winter, and so on. To the extent that these patterns are regular, it is best to remove the common seasonal factors; otherwise one could end up with a correlation based on seasonal factors rather than underlying economic trends. The classic story here is about the economist who correlated seasonally unadjusted consumer spending with unadjusted money supply figures; since both of them rise sharply in the fourth quarter, a spuriously high correlation was obtained. Some wag suggested this economist had "discovered that the money supply causes Christmas."

Suppose one calculated a regression for unseasonally adjusted department store sales on dummy variables for each month of the year (e.g., the variable for December would be 1 for that month and 0 elsewhere, and so on). That regression would produce a very high correlation, but the equation would have explained nothing except that department store sales data rise before Christmas and Easter and fall during February and July. The fit would be high, but an equation of that sort would contain no relevant information. What retailers usually want to know is whether sales this year – or this Christmas season – will be better or worse than usual, adjusted for the overall growth trend.

After removing the trend and seasonal factors, the data series that remain is more likely to resemble a random variable and hence more closely satisfy the basic statistical criteria and tests. As a result, the statistical results that are obtained are more likely to provide a realistic appraisal of how accurate the forecasts will be. Of course that does not guarantee that the results will be useful, but it does improve the odds.

2.8.2 CHECKING FOR OUTLYING VALUES

Once the data have been successfully entered into EViews or a similar program, it is quite simple to create a histogram for each variable and make sure that outlying observations will not dominate any regression equations that might be estimated. Take the time; it's well worth it.

Technically, only the residuals need to be normally distributed to satisfy the usual statistical criteria. However, if there are outliers you should either exclude them or treat them with dummy variables; otherwise they will dominate the regression results. Later I show what happens when outliers are ignored.

Suppose an observation is five standard deviations from the mean. If the variable really is normally distributed, the odds of that occurring are only about one in a million. Yet as a practical matter, since the sum of squares is being minimized, such a residual would have a weight 25 times as great as an observation that is one standard deviation from the mean. In a modest sample size of 20 to 50 observations, that one outlier would dominate the regression equation and in effect the regression would just be fitting that point.

Figure 2.11 shows the histogram of quarterly percentage changes in auto sales. Clearly the changes are not normally distributed. There is substantial kurtosis (fat tails), and the probability that this series is normally distributed is less than 10^{-6}. Given that fact, the next question is whether there is any compelling economic reason for those outliers. To answer that question, we turn to a time-series plot of the data, which is shown in figure 2.12.

It is clear that the major pairs of outlying observations occurred in 1959.4/60.1, 1964.4/65.1, and 1970.4/71.1. The first pair was caused by a major steel strike; the others were major auto strikes. Thus strike periods should be handled differently. In this case a dummy variable for auto strikes is the most appropriate treatment; in other cases, outliers should be omitted entirely.

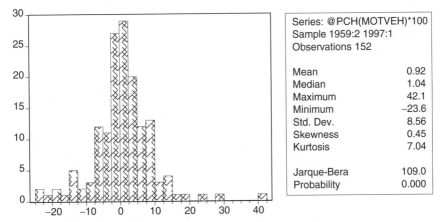

Figure 2.11 Histogram of percentage changes in quarterly motor vehicle sales.

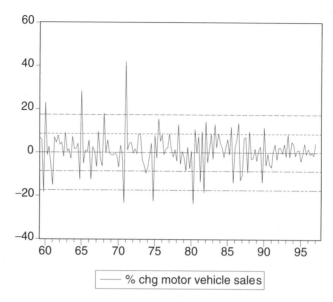

Figure 2.12   Percentage change in quarterly motor vehicle sales. The horizontal lines are 2, 1, 0, −1, and −2 standard deviations from the mean.

2.9 USING LOGARITHMS AND ELASTICITIES

One of the key themes in this book is that model builders should eliminate spurious trends by a variety of methods, including percentage first-difference equations, in equations where two or more variables have strong time trends. Also, there are often many cases where logarithms should be used, particularly if the underlying theory suggests a constant elasticity for the parameter being estimated. The use of logarithms often reduces the spurious effect of common upward trends, while using logarithms instead of percentage changes reduces the chances of one or two extreme values distorting the entire equation. Since the relationship between coefficients and elasticities is sometimes confusing, it is briefly reviewed.

The next two figures show the historical pattern of the S&P 500 stock price index in levels and in logarithms. Figure 2.13 seems to indicate that the market is rising at ever-more rapid rates, but in fact that is not the case. Figure 2.14 shows that from 1947 through 2000, this stock price index has advanced about 7% per year; it rose less rapidly during the period of high interest rates in the late 1970s and early 1980s, and more rapidly in the late 1990s and 2000, when it appeared to some investors that inflation and interest rates had moved to "permanently" lower levels. Except for these diversions, the long-run growth rate of stock prices is seen to be quite steady.

An *elasticity* measures the percentage change of a given variable relative to some other variable. Suppose that a 1% increase in the price of food results in

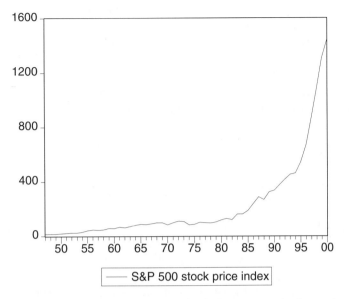

Figure 2.13   Using levels, the S&P 500 stock price index seems to be increasing at an ever-faster rate.

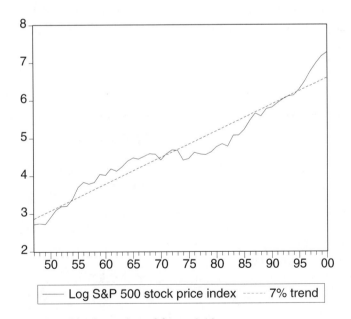

Figure 2.14   The logarithmic version of figure 2.13.

a 0.4% decline in purchases of food, ceteris paribus. In that case, the price elasticity of food is −0.4.

Both logarithms and elasticities measure percentage changes. Furthermore, in the regression equation $\log y = a + b \log x$, the coefficient b is the elasticity of y with respect to x. Hence estimating this equation in logarithms assumes the elasticity remains constant over the sample period. Using logs provides a convenient measure of the elasticity being estimated.

Because of how logarithms are defined, $\log x - \log x_{-1}$ is approximately equal to $(x - x_{-1})/x_{-1}$ and $\log y$ is approximately equal to $(y - y_{-1})/y_{-1}$. That means, as a first approximation:

$$\log y - \log y_{-1} = b(\log x - \log x_{-1}) \tag{2.14}$$

can be written as

$$(y - y_{-1})/y_{-1} = b(x - x_{-1})/x_{-1}. \tag{2.15}$$

If we take the definition of elasticities at their mean value, then

$$\eta_{yx} = \frac{(y - y_{-1})/y_{-1}}{(x - x_{-1})/x_{-1}} \tag{2.16}$$

so that b and η_{yx} are the same. In a similar vein, equations that compare percentage change of levels and first differences of logarithms will give almost identical results.

Problems and Questions

1. Use the data for monthly stock prices as measured by the S&P 500 (all necessary data can be collected from the website).

(a) Calculate the mean and variance for this series.

(b) Now take the first difference of this series and recalculate the mean and variance, and the percentage first difference and recalculate the mean and variance.

(c) Calculate a simple regression where stock prices are a function of a time trend. Calculate the variance of the residuals of this equation.

(d) Which of these four methods has the smallest variance? What meaning, if any, does that have for forecasting the stock market one month from now? Five years from now?

continued

2. Run a least squares regression where constant-dollar (real) consumption is a function of constant-dollar disposable income for the period 1947–92.

(a) Show your results. What is the standard error of estimate for that period?
(b) Now use this equation to "forecast" the values of real consumption for 1993–8 using the same equation. What is the standard error of the forecast for those six years? How does it compare to the standard error during the sample period?
(c) What factors do you think made the standard error so much larger in the forecast period?
(d) Now run a regression where the percentage change in real consumption is a function of the percentage change in real disposable income. Compare the R^2 and standard errors from these two equations.
(e) Use the percentage change equation to predict consumption for the 1993–8 period. Compare the standard error during this period with the standard error from the levels equation. Which equation is better for forecasting?

3. Plot the monthly percentage changes in the PPI-finished goods index.

(a) Test this series for normality, using a histogram. What do the results show?
(b) Use the same series, but use 12-month percentage changes. Using the same histogram analysis, are the residuals now normally distributed? Why or why not?
(c) Calculate a regression of the 12-month percentage changes in the PPI on 12-month percentage changes in the price of oil. Examine the residuals. What does this suggest about the lag structure? Try using lagged values of the percentage changes in oil prices to determine the optimally fitting lag structure, and show your results.
(d) Explain why you would or would not use this equation for forecasting changes in the PPI. Take into account the DW statistic and the normality tests in your answer.

4. Plot a scatter diagram of non-farm payroll employment and real GDP using quarterly data.

(a) Based on this diagram, what would you say about the relationship of these two variables?

continued

(b)   Now plot a scatter diagram of the percentage changes in the same two variables. Do you still think they are closely correlated?

(c)   Calculate a regression of employment on real GDP with no lag. Now expand the equation to include lags of one and two quarters for GDP. How do the coefficients change? Do you think this is a sensible interpretation?

(d)   Rerun this equation using logarithms, with log of real GDP lagged by zero, one, and two quarters. Compare and contrast the coefficients.

(e)   Now calculate a regression where the percentage change in employment is a function of the percentage change in GDP with lags of zero, one, and two quarters. Of these three equations, which one would probably the most useful for forecasting employment? What criteria did you use to make this decision?

5.   Monetarists often claim that the rate of inflation is closely tied to changes in the money supply lagged two years.

(a)   Create a scatter diagram between the inflation rate and changes in M2 lagged two years for the sample period 1947–2001. Do you think that correlation is very strong?

(b)   Now subdivide the sample period into two periods, 1947–81 and 1982–2001. Based on the scatter diagrams, during which period is the correlation with the money supply stronger? What happened in 1982 to change this relationship?

(c)   Now plot a scatter diagram using the rate of inflation and the change in unit labor costs. The correlation is much stronger. Does that necessarily mean the latter equation would provide better forecasts of inflation? (Hint: how difficult is it to predict unlagged unit labor costs?)

6.   Regress the log of constant-dollar tobacco shipments on the relative price of tobacco.

(a)   What is the price elasticity, according to this equation?

(b)   Now add a time trend to that equation. What happens to the elasticity?

(c)   Now regress the percentage change in real tobacco shipments on the percentage change in the relative price of tobacco. What is the coefficient, and how does that compare with the elasticity?

(d)   Several sophisticated studies have shown that the price elasticity of tobacco is approximately −0.45. How do these results compare with the simple calculations in (a)–(c)?

continued

(e)   By shortening the sample period, observe what happens to the elas-
      ticity. Based on that finding, what do you think will happen to the
      demand for cigarettes as the relative price continues to rise?

7.   Calculate a regression of current-dollar purchases of computers on a
time trend.

(a)   Now regress the log of computer purchases on a time trend. Accord-
      ing to this equation, what is the average annual growth rate of
      computer sales?
(b)   Based on this regression, what do you think will happen to the
      average annual growth rate in computer sales over the next decade?

8.   Using the data from the latest *Wall Street Journal*, plot the yield curve
for Treasury securities.

(a)   Using historical quarterly data, plot the three-month Treasury bill
      rate, two-year note rate, 10-year note rate and 30-year bond rate
      (which does not begin until 1977.2). Most of the time, the longer the
      maturity, the higher the rate. However, there are several occasions
      when that does not occur. Identify those time periods.
(b)   Now plot the Federal funds rate and the Aaa corporate bond yield
      (data begin in 1955.1). Note the periods when the funds rate is higher
      than the bond yield. Are they the same as the times when the Trea-
      sury yield curve was inverted?
(c)   Plot the percentage change in real GDP with the *yield spread* between
      the 10-year Treasury note rate and the three-month bill rate lagged
      one year. What happens to real GDP every time the yield spread turns
      negative. Do you think that would be a valuable tool for predicting
      whether there will be a recession next year?
(d)   Now repeat the plot for (c) using annual data. Has your conclusion
      reached in (c) changed?
(e)   As a practical business forecaster, why do you think economists have
      been unable to predict any recessions in the past 40 years including
      the 2001 recession, even though each one has been preceded by an
      inverted yield curve? (Hint: what happens to forecasters who are
      wrong when everyone else is right, compared to those who make the
      "consensus" error?)

PART II

CHAPTER 3

THE GENERAL LINEAR REGRESSION MODEL

INTRODUCTION

One common tendency of many model builders is to calculate a large number of regression equations for a given dependent variable and then choose the equation with the highest $\bar{R}^2$. That is often a suboptimal procedure, for several reasons.

In the first place, changing the form of the dependent variable (e.g., from level to percentage change) may reduce R^2 but may also reduce the standard error. It is important not to compare apples and bicycles. Sometimes an equation with a lower R^2 will provide much more accurate forecasts.

In many forecasting models, the residuals are not normally distributed. When that happens, the goodness-of-fit statistics are invariably overstated. In particular, many models built with time-series data have residuals that are autocorrelated. When that happens, the t-ratios and R^2 statistics are overstated, so forecast errors tend to be much larger than indicated by the equation.

First-order autocorrelation of the residuals is tested using the Durbin–Watson (DW) statistic. DW can range from 0 to 4; if it is near 2, no autocorrelation exists; if it is below 1.4, the residuals are positively autocorrelated. A standard method exists for adjusting for autocorrelation, known as the Cochrane–Orcutt transformation. However, an equation transformed in that manner often generates inferior predictions, especially for multi-period forecasting. If DW is very low, this transformation is almost the same as using a first-difference equation – but the R^2 statistic is based on the levels form of the dependent variable, thus creating a highly unrealistic estimate of how accurate the forecasts will be.

The residuals may also exhibit heteroscedasticity, which often means they are dominated by a few extreme outliers. If heteroscedasticity of the residuals is present, the goodness-of-fit statistics are overstated, but that is not the major problem. Least-squares regressions give the highest weight to extreme observations, which often distorts the coefficients during normal times. Hence such an equation would be suboptimal for forecasting unless the same unusual conditions that created the outlying observations were repeated in the forecast period.

3.1 THE GENERAL LINEAR MODEL

The general linear model outlined below is based on the use of least squares to estimate the parameters, their level of significance, and the goodness of fit of the overall equation. The bivariate case is presented first, followed by a discussion of some of the desirable qualities of the estimated parameters, before moving to the more general case with several independent variables.

3.1.1 THE BIVARIATE CASE

The bivariate linear model can be written as

$$Y_i = \alpha + \beta X_i + \varepsilon_i \tag{3.1}$$

where Y is an observable random variable, X is a fixed or non-stochastic variable (i.e., known at time i), α is the constant term in the equation (to be estimated), β is the slope of the line relating Y and X (to be estimated), ε is a random error term with mean 0 and variance σ^2, and all the ε_i and ε_j are uncorrelated. The i subscript means there are i observations, $i = 1$ to T. (For example, in a time series, that might be 1955.1 through 1999.4.)

We need to explore the concept of X being a "non-stochastic" variable in this context. By definition, it is uncorrelated with the error term ε. But what does that mean?

- X could be a strictly exogenous variable, such as a time trend or a dummy variable.
- X could be a lagged variable. Since it occurred in some previous time period before Y, the error component of X would not be correlated with the error component of Y. To look at this another way, changes in X could influence changes in Y – indeed, that is what we expect to find by using it in the regression equation – but changes in Y could not influence changes in X, because X already happened.
- X could be an exogenous variable in the economic sense, such as defense spending. While the level of defense spending may indeed influence the level of Y (say GDP), the value of Y at any time will not determine defense spending, which is tied to world political considerations. Politicians do not vote to increase defense spending because the economy is in a recession and needs to be stimulated – unless they are planning to start another world war!

In most standard time-series equations, though, this assumption about X is *not true*. For example, income influences consumption, but consumption also influences income because if consumers boost their spending, more output will be produced, hence raising income. Also, current income is not known at the time of forecast. Stock prices are positively correlated with bond prices, but a drop in stock prices may cause a "flight to quality," hence boosting bond prices. The price of gasoline influences the consumption of gasoline, but if consumption of gasoline rises enough, OPEC may decide to boost its prices.

The problem of two-way correlation, which is sometimes known as simultaneity bias and sometimes as the identification problem, is a serious one in building forecasting models and is discussed later in this book. First, however, the theory and operating rules are developed under the simpler assumption that Y does not influence X.

3.1.2 DESIRABLE PROPERTIES OF ESTIMATORS

The previous chapter provided unbiased estimates of the mean and variance, μ and σ^2. It is desirable for these estimates to be consistent and efficient as well.

Unbiasedness means that the expected value of the variable is equal to the population mean. That is certainly one desirable quality of statistical estimators, or parameter estimates. However, it is not the only one.

Consistency means that the error diminishes as the sample size increases. One would certainly expect that a sample size of 100 would have a smaller standard error than a sample size of 10. This term is similar in most cases to asymptotic unbiasedness, which means the bias falls to zero as the size of the sample increases. There are a few odd probability distributions where the two terms are not the same, but for our purposes they may be considered equivalent.

While presumably no researcher wants a "biased" estimate, consistency is actually more important to statisticians than bias. Small sample sizes (often in the range of less than 20 observations) generally do not give robust estimates anyhow, but it is critical that as the sample size grows, the error diminishes. Otherwise there is no reason to suppose that the researcher is zeroing in on the correct value.

Efficiency is the other important criterion; that means the estimate in question has a smaller variance than any other estimate for a given sample size.

Sometimes efficiency is more important than unbiasedness. Consider the case where a mugger has attacked you and there are two witnesses. The actual height of the mugger is 5 ft 10 in. The first witness thinks the mugger was 5 ft 10 in, but isn't sure; his height could have been anywhere between 5 ft 2 in and 6 ft 6 in. That is an unbiased estimate, but not very useful. The other says his height was between 5 ft 8 in and 5 ft 9 in, whereas in fact it turns out to be 5 ft 10 in. That is a biased estimate but more useful.

In the same vein, a biased forecast that the stock market would rise 6% to 8% next year when in fact it rose 10% would be much more useful than an unbiased forecast that the change would be between −10% and +30%.

3.1.3 EXPANDING TO THE MULTIVARIATE CASE

The general regression model can be written in a form analogous to the simple bivariate regression model, as follows:

$$Y_i = \beta_1 + \beta_2 X_{2i} + \beta_3 X_{3i} + \ldots + \beta_k X_{ki} + \varepsilon_i \qquad (3.2)$$

where Y is the dependent variable, the X_k are the independent variables, β_1 is the constant term, or intercept, of the equation, the other β are the parameter estimates for each of the X terms, ε_i is the error term, and there are i observations ($i = 1$ to T).

The assumptions for the general linear model are as follows.

- The underlying equation is linear.
- The X_i are non-stochastic, which means they are uncorrelated with the error term.
- The error term is normally distributed.
- The error term has constant variance (e.g., it does not increase as the size of the dependent variable increases).
- The errors for different observations are independent and therefore uncorrelated (no autocorrelation of residuals).
- None of the X_i is perfectly correlated with any other X_j. If two or more variables were perfectly correlated, the equation could not be solved at all; since that would lead to a singular matrix that could not be inverted. Even if one or more pairwise correlations is very high although not unity, the parameter estimates are less likely to provide reasonable forecasts.

3.2 USES AND MISUSES OF $\overline{R}^2$

As already shown, the formula for $\overline{R}^2$ can be written as

$$\overline{R}^2 = 1 - \frac{\text{unexplained variance} * (n-1)}{\text{total variance} * (n-k)} \qquad (3.3)$$

In the simple bivariate model, $k = 2$; so unless R^2 or n are quite low, there is very little difference between the two measures. However, when k increases as variables are added to the regression, the difference between R^2 and $\overline{R}^2$ can become quite large.

Table 3.1 Examples of R^2 and $\bar{R}^2$ under different circumstances.

R^2	n	k	$\bar{R}^2$
0.99	105	5	0.990
0.60	105	5	0.584
0.25	105	5	0.220
0.99	25	5	0.988
0.60	25	5	0.520
0.25	25	5	0.100
0.99	10	5	0.982
0.60	10	5	0.280
0.25	10	5	−0.350

3.2.1 DIFFERENCES BETWEEN R^2 AND $\bar{R}^2$

The practical significance of this adjustment means that $\bar{R}^2$ can never be increased by adding another variable if its t-ratio is less than unity. As $(n - k)$ becomes small – i.e., as the number of variables increases to the point where it is almost as great as the number of observations – the difference between R^2 and $\bar{R}^2$ increases dramatically; whereas when R^2 is very high and there are many degrees of freedom, the difference between the two measures is minimal. Also note that $\bar{R}^2$ can be negative, whereas that can never be the case for R^2. A few examples show how these two measures compare under different circumstances (table 3.1).

Note that if the t-ratio is greater than 1 for an additional variable, $\bar{R}^2$ will increase when that variable is added; if $t < 1$, it will decrease when it is added.

3.2.2 PITFALLS IN TRYING TO MAXIMIZE $\bar{R}^2$

Most beginning – and even intermediate – model builders often follow the procedure of estimating several different regression equations and then choosing the one with the highest $\bar{R}^2$. What is wrong with that procedure?

To a certain degree, it would not be sensible to choose one equation over another just because it had a lower $\bar{R}^2$. However, there are several good reasons why maximizing $\bar{R}^2$ might not produce the best forecasting equation, some of which are as follows.

1 Adding lagged values of the dependent variable will invariably increase $\bar{R}^2$ for variables with strong trends, but it will almost certainly raise the error in multi-period forecasting.

2   Using what is essentially the same variable on both sides of the equation will also boost the fit, but will invariably result in worse forecasts.

3   Using seasonally unadjusted data will result in a better R^2, but only because you are "explaining" the seasonal factors that are already explained. In an extreme example, this is the "money supply causes Christmas" phenomenon.

4   In general, the stronger the trend, the higher the R^2, and the weaker the trend, the lower the R^2. But equations that merely explain a common trend provide no help in the forecast period.

5   Explaining an "extreme" value (one for which the error term is more than three standard deviations from the mean) by the use of dummy variables will always boost R^2, but will usually not provide any additional accuracy to the forecast.

6   Running hundreds of additional regressions to boost R^2 a little bit – "torturing the data until they confess" – may conceivably improve the forecast, but it is more likely that the slight improvement in the correlation is due to random elements that will not reoccur in the forecast period.

I have already noted that changing the form of the dependent variable may result in a lower $\overline{R}^2$ – but also a lower standard error, and hence a better forecast. That means maximizing $\overline{R}^2$ and minimizing the standard error of the estimate are not necessarily the same thing.

3.2.3 AN EXAMPLE: THE SIMPLE CONSUMPTION FUNCTION

To see this, consider various different estimates of the simple consumption function, where consumption is a function only of disposable income. The following example shows that shifting the dependent variable from consumption to saving reduces the R^2 but keeps the standard error (SE) unchanged. Also, shifting to a percentage first-difference equation sharply reduces the R^2 but also reduces the SE significantly. Clearly, maximizing R^2 is not the same thing as minimizing the standard error of the equation. All these equations are based on annual data.

A simple function in levels yields the result

$$CH = 43.1 + 1.11 * DIH - 0.27 * M2H$$
$$(32.3)(5.2)$$

$$\overline{R}^2 = 0.998;\ SE = 53.9;\ DW = 0.63. \tag{3.4}$$

The H indicates inflation-adjusted magnitudes, as distinguished from the same variables without the H, which are thus in current dollars. $M2$ is the money supply. The numbers in parentheses under the DIH and $M2H$ terms are the t-ratios. Since a t-ratio greater than 2 is generally considered significant, both variables appear to be extremely significant. Also, the R^2 appears to be extremely high.

To the first-time econometrician, this function, showing a near-perfect correlation between consumption and disposable income, might appear to be an excellent equation. In fact it is a very poor equation for predictive purposes, mainly because it is structurally deficient. An increase in income should raise consumption, but not by more than that increase in income; in this case the gain is 1.11 times as much. Second, the money supply may or may not be a very important determinant of consumer spending, but it certainly is not negative, as shown in this equation.

We can see the major changes that occur when the common trend is removed by using percentage changes. The R^2 drops sharply, but the coefficients make much more sense. The resulting equation is

$$\%\Delta CH = 0.86 + 0.58 * \%\Delta DIH + 0.24 * \%\Delta M2H$$
$$(8.8) \qquad\qquad (5.8)$$

$$\overline{R}^2 = 0.777; \; SE = 0.84; \; DW = 2.10. \qquad\qquad (3.5)$$

The $\overline{R}^2$ has decreased from 0.998 to 0.777, but the parameter estimates are much more reasonable. This equation says that every 1% increase in income will boost consumption by 0.58% the first year, while every 1% increase in the money supply will boost consumption by 0.24%. Again, both terms appear to be highly significant, and there is no autocorrelation of the residuals, so the goodness-of-fit statistics are not overstated.

The SE figures are not directly comparable because one is in levels and the other is in percentage changes. To compare these, we multiply the SE of 0.84 by the mean value of consumption over the sample period, which is 2579. For the levels equation, the standard error of estimate for consumption is 53.9, whereas for the percentage first-difference equation it is only 21.7 when converted to levels, or less than half as large. This finding can be verified by using EViews to print out the "forecast" values of consumption for both of these equations.

As an exercise, the student should estimate this equation using logs, first differences, first differences of logs, and the saving rate, which can be defined here as (income minus consumption)/income.[1] The summary statistics are given in table 3.2. In these examples, the constant terms have been omitted. The most important points to note are the following.

1   The goodness-of-fit statistics are about the same in logarithms as in levels, and the differences are very small. In this particular case, there has been no impact

---

[1]   In practice, saving equals disposable income minus personal outlays, which equals consumption plus interest paid by persons plus personal transfer payments to the rest of the world. These minor differences need not concern us at this juncture.

Table 3.2 Summary statistics of the example.

Form of equation	Income coefficient	t-ratio	Money supply coefficient	t-ratio	R^2	SE	SE converted to levels	DW
Levels	1.11	32.3	−0.27	−5.2	0.998	53.9	53.9	0.63
Logs	1.01	23.9	−0.01	−0.2	0.998	0.0213	55.4	0.33
First differences	0.71	8.3	0.24	3.9	0.754	27.6	27.6	1.39
Percentage changes	0.58	8.8	0.24	5.8	0.777	0.87	21.7	2.10
Log first differences	0.58	8.8	0.24	5.8	0.777	0.0084	21.7	2.10
Saving levels	−0.11	−3.2	0.27	5.2	0.752	53.9	53.9	0.63

on the importance of the trend by switching to logarithms because both consumption and income have risen at about the same rate throughout the sample period. In other cases, however, logarithms can make a bigger difference, such as an equation for stock prices, which rose much faster than profits during the 1990s.

2　The first-difference and percentage change equations have much lower R^2, but also much lower SE. Also, the DW is much better, which means the goodness-of-fit statistics are not overstated. From a theoretical point of view, the income coefficient is also much more reasonable. In this case, removing the trend generates a much better forecasting equation, even though the fit appears to be much lower.

3　There is very little difference between the first differences and the percentage first differences. In the latter case, SE is a little lower and DW is a little better. In general, the percentage form is to be preferred when forecasting variables with strong trends because the size of the dependent variable is trendless instead of increasing over time.

4　The results for the percentage first differences and the first differences of logarithms are virtually identical. That will always be true because of the way logarithms are defined; it is not just a fluke for this set of equations.

5　Note that the R^2 is much lower for the saving levels equation than for the consumption levels equation. However, also note that the SE is identical. There has been a major reduction in R^2 even though the equation is the same (with the signs reversed), because saving as defined here is identically equal to income minus consumption. That alone should convince you not to rely exclusively on R^2 as a measure of how well your equation will forecast.

As we progress through the next few chapters, it will become clear that:

- the apparently high correlation shown in the levels equation often represents a common trend rather than a true behavioral relationship
- several variables are missing in the levels equation, as shown by the low *DW*
- significant autocorrelation and heteroscedasticity are present in the levels equation
- because consumption accounts for about two-thirds of GDP and hence income, to a certain extent the same variable occurs on both sides of the equation.

Real-life econometric equations are obviously much more complicated than this simple example. However, even at this level we can see that simply judging an equation by its R^2 and the coefficients by their *t*-ratios will often lead to very disappointing forecasts.

3.3 MEASURING AND UNDERSTANDING PARTIAL CORRELATION

Quite often it is the case that two variables X and Y will appear to have a very high correlation, but when one calculates a regression equation that includes a third variable Z, the partial correlation between X and Y will disappear. That means the correlation between the Y and the residuals based on a regression between X and Z is zero. For example, the number of marriages might be quite highly correlated with the number of drunken drivers arrested, but when population is added to the equation, that correlation disappears, since it only reflects a common trend.

While not as frequent, it can also happen that X and Y are uncorrelated, but when variable Z is added to the equation, both Y and Z became significant because they are negatively correlated with each other. For example, we might find a very low simple correlation between capital spending and interest rates, but when the growth in output is added to the regression, that term is significantly positive, while interest rates become significantly negative. That is because, in a statistical sense, high interest rates are usually associated with low growth, and vice versa.

3.3.1 COVARIANCE AND THE CORRELATION MATRIX

It is a simple matter to calculate the covariance matrix for all the variables used in a given regression, but that doesn't impart much useful information because the variables are generally of different magnitudes (e.g., some are interest rates, some are in billions of dollars, some are percentage changes, and so on). However, this defect can be easily remedied by transforming the covariance matrix into the correlation coefficient matrix using the formula given in chapter 2, which is repeated here:

$$\rho(X, Y) = \frac{\mathrm{Cov}(X, Y)}{\sigma_X \cdot \sigma_Y}. \tag{3.6}$$

The correlation coefficient matrix can be easily observed in EViews by choosing a selected set of variables to be estimated in the equation, and then use the "Views" command to select this option.

3.3.2 PARTIAL CORRELATION COEFFICIENTS

The correlation matrix shows which variables have strong positive and negative correlations with each other. However, more information is needed to make useful choices in a multiple regression equation. For that purpose we use the concept of *partial correlation*, which is the correlation between the dependent variable and a given independent variable *once the impact of all the other independent variables in the equation have been taken into account.*

The formulas become somewhat tedious without matrix notation for the general linear model, so we restrict them here to the case of an equation with two independent variables, X_2 and X_3.[2] If the dependent variable is Y, then

$$r_{YX_2X_3} = \frac{r_{YX_2} - r_{YX_3} \cdot r_{X_2X_3}}{\left(1 - r^2{}_{X_2X_3}\right)^{1/2} \cdot \left(1 - r^2{}_{YX_3}\right)^{1/2}}. \tag{3.7}$$

Let us see what this formula means. The denominator is included just for scaling purposes; i.e., it converts a covariance matrix to a correlation matrix, so we focus on the terms in the numerator. Suppose that r_{YX_2} were 0. It might appear, from looking at the simple correlation matrix, that X_2 would not belong in the equation. However, suppose that X_2 and X_3 have a strong negative correlation, and r_{YX_3} was significantly positive. In that case, the partial correlation between Y and X_2 *given that X_3 is also in the equation* would be significantly positive.

The thrust of these comments is that it is not sufficient to look at a variance–covariance or correlation matrix and simply choose those variables that have a high correlation with the dependent variables. In a multiple regression equation, all of the interactions must also be considered.

No one can be expected to see all these partial correlations right off the bat. Some trial and error in estimating regressions is always to be anticipated. Most model builders run an initial regression, look at the residuals, and then try to

---

[2] For further discussion, see Pindyck, Robert S., and Daniel L. Rubinfeld, *Econometric Models and Economic Forecasts*, 4th edn (Irwin McGraw-Hill, Boston), 1998, pp. 100–1; and Johnston, Jack, and John DiNardo, *Econometric Methods*, 4th edn (McGraw-Hill, New York), 1997, pp. 76–83. The latter reference also presents the *k*-variable case.

find some other variable which fits the unexplained residuals. There is nothing wrong with this procedure if it is not carried to extremes.

3.3.3 PITFALLS OF STEPWISE REGRESSION

Given these comments, it might seem useful to have a regression program that chooses variables automatically. The model builder would select a fairly large set of all possible variables, the program would pick the one that initially had the highest correlation with the dependent variable and run that regression, then correlate the residuals with the variable that had the highest correlation with those residuals, run another regression, compare the residuals with the variable that had the highest correlation, and so on until no more significant variables were found. Such a program is known as *stepwise regression*, but in fact it doesn't work very well for several reasons. Indeed, the potential for misuse of partial correlation coefficients is probably greater than its potential usefulness.

The trouble with this approach, besides the obvious lack of any theory, is that it fails to take into consideration the possibility of negative covariance. It may be that neither variable X_2 nor X_3 has a significant correlation with Y, but when included in the same regression both of them are significant. As noted above, one key example might be capital spending as a function of output (or capacity utilization) and interest rates. The first-order correlations are not very strong, yet – as might be expected – there is a negative correlation between output and interest rates, especially when lags are taken into account. Mechanically using a stepwise regression package would miss this interaction. For reasons of this sort, the method is not recommended.

3.4 TESTING AND ADJUSTING FOR AUTOCORRELATION

Since autocorrelation is primarily a problem that occurs in time-series (as opposed to cross-section) data, only time-series data are considered here, with the notation adjusted accordingly.

The general linear time-series model with autocorrelation can be written as

$$Y_t = \beta_1 + \beta_2 X_{2t} + \beta_3 X_{3t} + \ldots + \beta_k X_{kt} + \varepsilon_t \text{ and } \varepsilon_t = \rho \varepsilon_{t-1} + v_t \qquad (3.8)$$

where ρ is calculated as

$$\rho = \frac{\text{Cov}(\varepsilon_t, \varepsilon_{t-1})}{\sigma_\varepsilon^2} = \frac{\text{Cov}(\varepsilon_t, \varepsilon_{t-1})}{[\text{Var}(\varepsilon_t)]^{1/2}[\text{Var}(\varepsilon_{t-1})]^{1/2}}. \qquad (3.9)$$

ρ is the correlation coefficient calculated for residuals in period t and $t - 1$.

3.4.1 WHY AUTOCORRELATION OCCURS AND WHAT IT MEANS

Autocorrelation is present in the vast majority of time series for the following reasons.

- *Errors of measurement.* Data reported by the government are based on incomplete information. Missing observations tend to be interpolated in such a way that the data are smoothed. Also, the same biases may occur systematically in the sampling program for different time periods.
- *Omitted variables.* This is probably the most serious problem. Positive correlation of residuals often signifies one or more significant variables are missing. In some cases, such as expectational variables, these missing variables cannot be measured precisely.
- *Misspecification of existing variables.* This often refers to a nonlinear equation. Sometimes the equation is piecewise linear, which means the underlying structural relationship has shifted during the sample period. The equation is linear in both periods but one or more of the coefficients has changed. In other cases, the coefficients vary with the phase of the business cycle. Sometimes one or one or more of the independent variables should be raised to some power other than unity. That could mean an exponential power such as squared, cubed, etc., or it could indicate an inverse correlation, where the form of the independent variable should be $1/X$ instead of X.
- *The effect of habit.* Even if the data are correct and the equation is correctly specified, economic decisions are often based on habit, so that the error term in this period after taking into account all the relevant variables really is correlated with the error term in the previous period. Sometimes this information can be used to help improve forecast accuracy, but using it runs the risk of generating poor forecasts whenever habits do change.

The presence of autocorrelation does not affect unbiasedness or consistency, but it does affect efficiency. That means the standard errors that are calculated using OLS are understated, and hence the significance levels of the individual terms (and often the entire equation) are overstated. Results that appear to be significant actually are not. I emphasize that the presence of autocorrelation in the residuals does not necessarily mean the parameter estimates are incorrect; it simply means that the sample period statistics will probably understate errors during the forecast period.

In working with time-series data, it is often the case that *quarterly* data will indicate significant autocorrelation, while the same equation estimated with *annual* data shows no autocorrelation. If this happens, and the coefficients in the annual equation are approximately the same, it is generally better *not* to include the autoregressive adjustment in the quarterly equation when using it for forecasting purposes. Such a result often means that the quarterly data are artificially smoothed, not that variables are missing. If on the other hand some of the coefficients in the corresponding annual equation become insignificant, the quarterly equation needs more work before it can be used for forecasting.

3.4.2 DURBIN–WATSON STATISTIC TO MEASURE AUTOCORRELATION

The Durbin–Watson (DW) statistic is used in statistics almost as widely as R-bar squared.[3] It is defined as

$$DW = \sum (\varepsilon_t - \varepsilon_{t-1})^2 \Big/ \sum \varepsilon_t^2. \tag{3.10}$$

This formula has a marked resemblance to the formula for ρ. We can expand the numerator and write

$$DW = \left(\sum \varepsilon_t^2 + \sum \varepsilon_{t-1}^2 - 2\sum \varepsilon_t \varepsilon_{t-1} \right) \Big/ \sum \varepsilon_t^2. \tag{3.11}$$

In large samples, $\Sigma \varepsilon_t^2$ is approximately equal to $\Sigma \varepsilon_{t-1}^2$, so

$$DW = 2 \left(\sum \varepsilon_t^2 - \sum \varepsilon_t \varepsilon_{t-1} \right) \Big/ \sum \varepsilon_t^2 = 2(1 - \rho). \tag{3.12}$$

Thus if $\rho = 0$, DW is 2; if $\rho = 1$, $DW = 0$; and if $\rho = -1$, $DW = 4$.

The significance level of DW for 95% confidence is generally around $DW = 1.4$, although it is lower for smaller samples and higher for larger samples. There is also an upper and lower bound; within this range, the results are indeterminate.

---

[3] For further discussion, see Pindyck and Rubinfeld, pp. 160–9; and Johnston and DiNardo, pp. 179–84. The original articles are Durbin, J. and G. S. Watson, "Testing for Serial Correlation in Least Squares Regression," *Biometrika*, 37 (1950), 409–28; and 38 (1951), 159–78. The tables for significant upper and lower bounds were extended in Savin, N. E., and K. J. White, "The Durbin–Watson Test for Serial Correlation with Extreme Sample Sizes or Many Regressors," *Econometrica*, 45 (1977), 1989–96. Modifications for the test when the equation contains no constant term are given in Farebrother, R. W., "The Durbin–Watson Test for Serial Correlation when there is no Intercept in the Regression," *Econometrica*, 48 (1980), 1553–63. Adjustments for this statistic when the lagged dependent variable is used in the equation are found in Durbin, J., "Testing for Serial Correlation in Least Squares Regression when some of the Regressors are Lagged Dependent Variables," *Econometrica*, 38 (1970), 410–21.

Since the significance level depends on the sample size and the number of independent variables, as well as containing this indeterminate range, another way to check the significance level is to run the regression with the AR(1) adjustment and see whether that coefficient is significant. If DW is above 1.6, that test is not necessary.

3.4.3 AUTOCORRELATION ADJUSTMENTS: COCHRANE–ORCUTT AND HILDRETH–LU

It is straightforward to calculate ρ by calculating the underlying regression and determining its value from the residuals, using the formulas given above. Such a value can then be inserted into the underlying equation, with the equation rewritten as

$$(Y - \rho Y_{-1}) = \beta_1(1 - \rho) + \beta_2(X_1 - \rho X_{1-1}) + \beta_3(X_2 - \rho X_{2-1}) + \ldots + (\varepsilon_t - \rho \varepsilon_{t-1}) \quad (3.13)$$

where the value of ρ is as calculated in (3.6). If we let $v_t = \varepsilon_t - \rho \varepsilon_{t-1}$, then v_t can be tested for autocorrelation, and a second iterative value of ρ can be obtained. This method can be repeated for as many iterations as desired until convergence is reached; generally it takes fewer than ten iterations.

This method is known as the *Cochrane–Orcutt* method,[4] and is by far the most popular method of adjusting for autocorrelation. In EViews this is listed as the AR(1) transformation, and is implemented by reestimating an equation with autocorrelation by adding the term AR(1) to the equation. It is not necessary to respecify each term individually.

Under unusual circumstances, though, it is possible that the initial ρ selected might not be the only one; there could be multiple values for ρ. For that reason, the Hildreth–Lu method[5] is sometimes used. This scans the values of ρ from -1 to $+1$ in a grid with units of, say, 0.1. This method then finds the global maximum and then zeros in on this value using a grid of, say, 0.01, until the answer is found to the desired degree of precision. However, this method isn't used very much because Cochrane–Orcutt usually gives the same answer and is easier to implement.

Sometimes ρ is very close to unity, in which case the equation reduces to a first-difference equation. *A useful rule of thumb is to use first differences or percentage changes if the value of the DW statistic is less than R^2.*

For example, if $\bar{R}^2$ were 0.99 for a levels equation (not unusual, as we have seen), and DW for that equation were 0.50 (also not unusual), the equation

[4] Cochrane, D., and G. H. Orcutt, "Applications of Least-Squares Regressions to Relationships Containing Autocorrelated Error Terms," *Journal of the American Statistical Association*, 44, (1949), 32–61.

[5] Hildreth, G., and J. Y. Lu, "Demand Relations with Autocorrelated Disturbances," *Michigan State University Agricultural Experiment Station Technical Bulletin* 276, November, 1960.

should probably be reestimated in percentage first differences. On the other hand, if *DW* were greater than 1.0, it would probably be better to stay with the levels equation and try to improve the equation by experimenting with lag structures or adding more variables. Other methods of trend removal are considered later in the book.

3.4.4 HIGHER-ORDER AUTOCORRELATION

So far we have considered only the possibility of first-order autocorrelation. The error term might also be correlated with own values lagged more than one time period, so that in the regression

$$\varepsilon_t = \rho_1\varepsilon_{t-1} + \rho_2\varepsilon_{t-2} + \ldots + \rho_k\varepsilon_{t-k} + v_t \tag{3.14}$$

the various ρ_i, $i > 1$, would also be significant.

It is unlikely, although not impossible, that a whole string of the ρ_i would be significant, but that is not usually what happens. Instead, we find that in time-series data there is some autocorrelation with residuals a year ago; so the term ρ_4 would be significant for quarterly data – but not the intervening ρ's. For monthly data, the term ρ_{12} would be significant – but not the intervening ρ's.

If this sort of situation does arise, there are four possible treatments. One is seasonally adjusting the data (which can be easily done in EViews) and see whether the problem disappears. If it does not, the three remaining options are as follows:

- Add the lagged variable with the 4(quarter) or 12(month) lag.
- Use the SAR term in EViews, which means calculating the fourth (or 12th order) autocorrelation factor but none of those in between, unless they are explicitly specified.
- Switch to a percentage first-difference equation, using the current period minus four quarters (or 12 months) ago.

If seasonal autocorrelation appears in the data, it is usually preferable to seasonally adjust the data or, if the data are robust enough, use percentage first-difference equations. Firms are generally interested in how well their orders or sales are doing compared with a year ago, rather than comparing them with periods that have different seasonal factors.

3.4.5 OVERSTATEMENT OF *t*-RATIOS WHEN AUTOCORRELATION IS PRESENT

Under reasonable values of ρ, the standard errors can be understated by more than 80%, thus providing grossly inaccurate measures for goodness-of-fit statistics. For the simple bivariate case $Y_t = \beta X_t + \varepsilon_t$, the variance of β in an equation with autocorrelated residuals can be as large as $(1 + r\rho)/(1 - r\rho)$, where ρ is the autocorrelation coefficient and r is the correlation coefficient of x_t and x_{t-1}. The proof is found in Maddala.[6]

In series with strong time trends, it would not be unusual to find that ρ is 0.8 or higher, and r is 0.9 or higher. Using these values, we would find that the ratio given above is 1.72/0.28, or 6.14. That means the stated t-ratios could be more than six times as high as the "actual" estimates. Hence a variable with a t-ratio of 10 under the above autocorrelation conditions might not even be significant at the standard 5% level. However, this is an upper limit. In most cases, positive autocorrelation of the residuals does not bias the standard errors down by the full amount. In relatively large samples (50 to 150 observations), the bias is usually between one-half and two-thirds of the amount given by this formula. Nonetheless, this formula should serve as a warning about the overstatement of t-ratios when significant positive autocorrelation is present.

In addition to overstating the t-ratios, it is likely that the existence of autocorrelation means the equation is misspecified, in which case trying to reduce autocorrelation by the use of the AR(1) adjustment will not improve forecasting accuracy. There is actually a fairly simple test for this. Consider the two equations

$$Y_t = \rho Y_{t-1} + \beta X_t - \beta \rho X_{t-1} + \varepsilon_t \tag{3.15}$$

$$Y_t = \alpha_1 Y_{t-1} + \alpha_2 X_t + \alpha_3 X_{t-1} + \varepsilon_t. \tag{3.16}$$

These are the same with the restriction that $\alpha_1 \alpha_2 + \alpha_3 = 0$. EViews contains a simple test to determine whether that relationship holds or not, known as the *Wald coefficient restriction*. If the relationship does not hold, then the AR(1) adjustment should not be used, and further experimentation with the form of the equation is warranted.

Autocorrelation does not bias the coefficients unless the lagged dependent variable is used. However, it does overstate their significance, which means the forecast error will probably be larger than indicated by the sample period statistics for the equation.

3.4.6 PITFALLS OF USING THE LAGGED DEPENDENT VARIABLE

A quick glance at the least-squares printouts will reveal that R^2 is much higher, and the standard error of estimate is much lower, when the lagged dependent variable is included, either explicitly or with an AR(1) adjustment.

[6] Maddala, G. S., *Introduction to Econometrics*, 2nd edn (Prentice Hall, Englewood Cliffs, NJ), 1992, pp. 241–4.

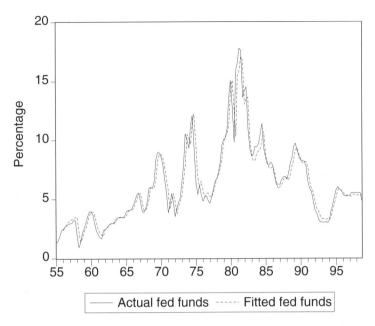

Figure 3.1 Fitted Federal funds rate as a function of inflation, and actual funds rate lagged one quarter.

For those who want to forecast only one period in advance, the use of all relevant information, including the lagged dependent variable, may improve forecast accuracy. This possibility is discussed in greater detail in Part III. However, a higher R^2 and DW statistic closer to 2 does not mean the multi-period forecasting accuracy of the equation has been improved by adding the lagged dependent variable. Indeed, beyond one period in the future, forecasting accuracy is often *diminished* by adding the lagged dependent variable as an additional independent variable.

To see the pitfalls involved, consider an equation in which the Federal funds rate is a function of the rate of inflation over the past year. This equation does not work very well because Fed policy was far different in the 1970s, under Arthur Burns and G. William Miller, than it was in the 1980s and 1990s, under Paul Volcker and Alan Greenspan. An equation in which the Fed funds rate is only a function of the inflation rate thus gives unsatisfactory results: it explains only about half the variance, the DW is an unsatisfactorily low 0.25, and the standard error is over two percentage points.

Now suppose the regression is recalculated by adding the funds rate lagged one quarter. On the surface, the results look much better: $\bar{R}^2$ has risen from 0.58 to 0.91, DW has improved from 0.21 to 1.51 (indicating no significant autocorrelation of the residuals), and the standard error has been cut in half.

However, upon closer examination, the equation misses all the turning points by one quarter (see figure 3.1). Maybe it seems as though the fitted values "catch up" after one quarter, but that is only because they depend on the actual lagged value. If the fitted lagged value were to be used, the simulated values would drift ever-further away from the actual value.

This is perhaps an extreme example, but it illustrates the point well. Using the lagged dependent variable on the right-hand side of the equation will often result in an equation with apparently superb sample period fits, but it will be useless for forecasting because the lagged dependent variable also has to be predicted. Even for single-period forecasting, the equation given above would miss virtually every turning point, and hence would be useless for actual forecasts.

Forecasting errors often arise when trying to predict Y if the most important independent variable is Y_{-1}, which means relying primarily on that variable for predicting Y. By definition, Y_{-1} never turns down ahead of time. Thus relying on the lagged dependent variable means missing almost all the turning points. Furthermore, Y_{-1} will not only rise during the first period that Y fell, but will continue to rise because the forecast will continue to contain erroneous feedback from the variable that failed to turn around. The more periods that are predicted with this equation, the worse the forecasts.

Thus it seldom if ever pays to put the lagged dependent variable on the right-hand side of an equation that will be used for multi-period forecasting. If that variable continues to be very significant in spite of all other changes that have been made, switch to percentage first differences, or other methods that eliminate the trend, many of which are discussed in detail in the next chapter.

3.5 TESTING AND ADJUSTING FOR HETEROSCEDASTICITY

The other major reason for non-normality of residuals is that, the larger the value of the dependent variable, the larger the value of the residual. In essence that means giving more weight to the larger sample points in the regression equation, which means that the goodness-of-fit statistics are overstated, just as is the case for autocorrelation.

Heteroscedasticity can arise from two major sources. The first is that as the size of the dependent variable increases, the absolute size of the error term increases, even though the percentage error does not rise. That happens primarily in cross-section data. The second cause stems from outliers, which can be handled either with dummy variables or by omitting those variables from the regression. Cross-section data are considered first.

3.5.1 CAUSES OF HETEROSCEDASTICITY IN CROSS-SECTION AND TIME-SERIES DATA

In cross-section data the causes and cures of heteroscedasticity are fairly straightforward, and can best be illustrated by an example. Suppose someone is estimating data from a panel survey of consumers, whose income ranges all the way from (say) $10,000 to $1,000,000. Let us assume for these purposes that the same factors govern consumption at all levels of income, so the various consumption functions are similar. In that case, the standard deviation for the $1 million consumers would be 100 times as large as the standard deviation for the $10,000 consumers. A few rich consumers would therefore dominate the sample in terms of the statistical tests.

The straightforward solution to this problem is to scale the results so that (say) a 5% error for the rich gets the same weight as a 5% error for the poor. That can be done using ratios or weighted least squares. However, as was pointed out earlier, most of the emphasis in forecasting is on time-series analysis. How does heteroscedasticity arise in those cases?

The simplest case stems from the fact that most time series increase over time (consumption, production, employment, prices, etc.). If the level of the dependent variable is, say, ten times as great at the end of the sample period as it was at the beginning, then the error term is also likely to be ten times as great. However, if this variable is correlated with an independent variable (income in the consumption function) with the same general trend, the residuals probably will not be heteroscedastic. Even if heteroscedasticity remains, this might have the net result of giving more recent observations greater weight, which in many cases is a good idea anyhow.

The other problem, which is not related to the trend, is one of extreme values. This can perhaps best be illustrated by looking at financial data. On Monday, October 19, 1987, the Dow Jones Industrial Average plunged 508 points, or 22% – a decline almost twice as much as the next largest percentage drop (including Black Tuesday in 1929). If all percentage changes are treated equally in a statistical sense, the results will be biased in the sense that the market will be shown to fall more on the 19th of each month, or each Monday, or each October.

In macroeconomic data, price equations might be dominated by energy shocks, thereby neglecting the importance of other key variables such as unit labor costs, capacity utilization, monetary policy, and so on.

These problems can be quite severe in the sense that not only are the goodness-of-fit statistics overstated, but the parameter estimates themselves will become biased, and forecasts based on these estimates will invariably generate the wrong answers. Case Study 3 illustrates how this can happen.

3.5.2 MEASURING AND TESTING FOR HETEROSCEDASTICITY

Researchers generally want to neutralize the distorting influence of extreme outliers without excluding them from the sample period entirely, assuming that they contain some relevant information. Using dummy variables essentially takes them out of the equation, although it overstates the goodness-of-fit statistics; omitting them entirely from the sample period will not distort these statistics. The usual procedure is to test the residuals to see whether heteroscedasticity is present.[7]

Unlike autocorrelation, there is no standard test such as the DW statistic. The two most common tests are the ARCH LM test (which stands for Autoregressive Conditional Heteroscedasticity – Lagrangian Multiplier) suggested by R. F. Engle,[8] and the White test, developed by Halbert White.[9]

The ARCH LM test is based on the comment made above that the most recent residuals are likely to be larger in typical time-series analysis. Engle thus suggests estimating the equation

$$\varepsilon_t^2 = \beta_1 + \beta_2 \varepsilon_{t-1}^2 + \beta_3 \varepsilon_{t-2}^2 + \ldots + \beta_k \varepsilon_{t-k-1}^2 \tag{3.17}$$

where the researcher picks the value of k (EViews asks you to supply this number). If the equation is significant, as measured by the F-ratio, then heteroscedasticity exists. The White test is a more general one and involves expanding the regression equation to include the value of the variables squared, and the cross-products among independent variables. Here too the F-ratio is used to determine whether the equation is significant.

Under the assumptions of the classical linear model, heteroscedasticity will affect the standard errors and goodness-of-fit statistics but not the parameter estimates. In other words, OLS (ordinary least squares) estimates are still unbiased even in the presence of heteroscedasticity. The most common adjustment to the variance/covariance matrix, and hence to the standard errors of an estimate, is known as White's correction. Another method, known as the Newey–West correction, gives consistent estimates even if both autocorrelation and heteroscedasticity are present (which is likely to be the case in standard time-series analysis). Generally the results do not vary much between the two methods.

While these two tests are theoretically sound, they still are not entirely satisfactory in the sense that, if a distortion or bias is introduced into the parameter estimate by an extreme outlier, these corrections will not fix the problem. These adjustments, like virtually all statistical tests, have been developed under the assumption of normal distributions, whereas in fact the existence of an extreme outlier indicates that the distribution is *not* normal.

While the t-ratios are a bit more realistic after applying these adjustments, one does not really get to the root of the problem of heteroscedasticity by apply-

[7] For further discussion, see Pindyck and Rubinfeld, pp. 146–57; and Johnston and DiNardo, pp. 162–7.

[8] Engle, Robert F., "Autoregressive Conditional Heteroscedasticity with Estimates of the Variance of United Kingdom Inflation," *Econometrica*, 50 (1982), 987–1008.

[9] White, H., "A Heteroscedasticity-Consistent Covariance Matrix Estimator and a Direct Test for Heteroscedasticity," *Econometrica*, 48 (1980), 817–38.

ing White's correction, or the Newey–West correction. There is nothing wrong in adjusting the standard errors and it should be done if heteroscedasticity is found to be present, but most of the time it does not make much difference. By experimenting, the reader can quickly determine that using these adjustments generally has much less effect on the parameter estimates than using the AR(1) adjustment, or changing from levels to changes.

Another method of diminishing heteroscedasticity is to use weighted least squares or put the dependent variable in ratio form. Weighted least squares (WLS)[10] is somewhat arbitrary in the sense the model builder must choose which weights to use; one common method is to use one of the independent variables that has the same trend or scale factor as the dependent variable. In the consumption function, for example, that would be income, whether time-series or cross-section data were being used. One could also take the ratio of consumption/income as the dependent variable; the impact of these changes is discussed in the following chapter. In most cases, using WLS does not change the parameter estimates very much either.

If one of the values of a time series has an extreme outlying value, thus leading to heteroscedasticity, it cannot be ignored; otherwise that one value will dominate the results, and the equation will eventually be reduced to fitting these one or two extreme points. One way to proceed is usually to treat this with a dummy variable, as discussed in chapter 4. Another is simply to disregard the errant observations completely. This process, often known as masking, consists of automatically excluding any observation where the error term is larger than a preassigned multiple of the standard error of the overall equation. One common rule of thumb is to exclude observations whose error term is more than three times the standard error.

In many cases, omitting outliers will generate parameter estimates that will produce forecasts with smaller errors than if the outliers were included. However, simply omitting all observations that cannot be explained can become a dangerous procedure. In particular, one should determine whether those outliers were caused by a specific exogenous development. For example, electric power usage would rise more during extremely cold winters or hot summers, insurance claims would rise dramatically after a hurricane, and entertainment expenditures for a given city – especially one of moderate size – would rise sharply after the local baseball team wins the World Series. At first glance it might appear these outliers should be discarded, but in fact they can usefully be correlated with the indicated exogenous development. Only in cases where outlying values do not appear to be related to any realistic independent variable should they be excluded from the equation.

---

[10] For further discussion see Pindyck and Rubinfeld, pp. 148–9; and Johnston and DiNardo, pp. 171–2.

3.6 GETTING STARTED: AN EXAMPLE IN EVIEWS

To provide a preview of many of the issues that occur in building forecasting models, a simple equation for annual constant-dollar department store sales is now presented. This series starts in 1967; thus for the percentage change equation, the first data point is 1968. The level of department store sales is a function of real disposable income less transfer payments, stock prices as measured by the S&P 500 index, and the availability of credit is measured by two variables: the amount of consumer credit outstanding, and the yield spread between long- and short-term rates, which measures the willingness of banks to make loans to consumers. The estimated values are

SALES

$$= 2.736 + 2.49 * YDHXTR + 8.78 * SP + 0.142 * YLDSPRD(-1) + 7.24 * CRED$$
$$\quad (2.3) \qquad\qquad (5.1) \qquad (2.2) \qquad\qquad\qquad (2.4)$$

$$RSQ = 0.992 \; DW = 0.42.$$

$$(3.18)$$

This is the standard form in which equations will be presented in this text. The numbers in parentheses under the coefficients are t-ratios. RSQ is R^2 adjusted for degrees of freedom. $SALES$ is the level of constant-dollar department store sales. $YDHXTR$ is real disposable income excluding transfer payments. SP is the S&P 500 stock price index. $YLDSPRD(-1)$ is the difference between the Aaa corporate bond yield and the Federal funds rate lagged one year. $CRED$ is the amount of consumer credit outstanding.

While this might appear to be an excellent equation, with an adjusted R^2 in excess of 0.99, most of the correlation is due to the upward trend; an equation in which the log of sales is a function only of a time trend would explain 98% of the variance. Also the residuals shown in figure 3.2 indicate this equation does a poor job of tracking changes in sales. The low DW of 0.42 indicates some structural defect. For this reason, as is so often the case in time-series variables with strong trends, we consider the percentage change equation

%SALES

$$= 1.19 + 0.592 * YDHXTR + 0.068 * \%SP + 0.673 * YLDSPRD(-1) \qquad (3.19)$$
$$\quad (3.6) \qquad\qquad (2.6) \qquad\qquad (3.2)$$

$$RSQ = 0.685; \; DW = 1.58.$$

This equation has a much lower adjusted R^2, but is a better structural equation. The graph of the residuals, as shown in figure 3.3, shows far less autocorrelation. Also, the consumer credit term has dropped out of the equation;

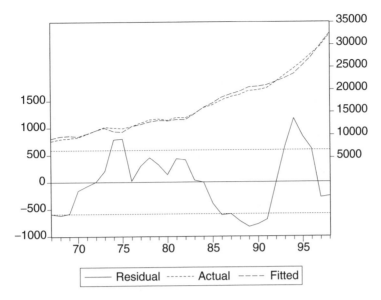

Figure 3.2 Example – see the text.

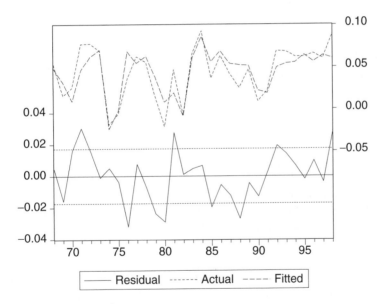

Figure 3.3 Example – see the text.

indicating it may have reflected reverse causality – consumer credit outstanding rose because department store sales rose, not the other way around. This is a fairly typical example of how an equation with a much lower R^2 is more likely to provide accurate forecasts.

Case Study 1: Predicting Retail Sales for Hardware Stores

One of the most important aspects of practical business forecasting is to provide actual examples and show how the equations were developed. In many cases, the problems that occur are as important as the successes, so the point of these case studies is to illustrate pitfalls as well as show impressive results. In general, each chapter from this point on will include three case studies. This chapter presents case studies where autocorrelation or heteroscedasticity play an important role in determining the equation that is actually chosen for forecasting.

The dependent variable in the first case study is retail sales at hardware and building materials stores in constant dollars. In general, hardware sales, like other types of consumer purchases, are related to real disposable income (YDH); this category of sales is also sensitive to the level of housing starts (HST). In addition, a reduction in interest rates, measured here by the corporate bond rate ($FAAA$), will boost home maintenance and additions, and a decline in the unemployment rate (UN) will also boost construction. In this example quarterly data are used; as is the case for department store data, they start in 1967.1. The equation with these four variables and their appropriate lags in quarters is

$$HDWSALES$$
$$= -2.375 + 2.78* \, YDH - 0.153* \, FAAA(-3) + 0.770* \, HST - 0.093* UN(-1)$$
$$(84.8) \qquad (7.2) \qquad\qquad (8.7) \qquad\qquad (3.1)$$
$$RSQ = 0.983; \, DW = 0.25.$$

All the variables appear to be significant, and RSQ seems quite high, but the DW statistic is far too low at 0.25. There are two standard ways to handle this: use the AR(1) adjustment or use a percentage first-difference equation.

With the AR(1) adjustment, the reader can verify that all the coefficients remain significant, RSQ reportedly rises to 0.996, and DW is slightly above 2. Nonetheless, an examination of the residuals shows that such an equation invariably misses the turning points.

Most hardware store owners (or manufacturers of hardware equipment) are interested in sales relative to year-earlier levels, which suggests taking the percentage change from year-earlier levels and treating the independent variables in the same fashion. When this is done, all four variables remain significant, but housing becomes relatively more important and income relatively less important, since the spurious correlation from the common trend is no longer present. In the equation below, the 4 at the end of each variable means a four-quarter change; % is percentage change; and Δ is first difference (used for variables without trends). Actual instead of percentage first differences are often used for variables without trends.

$$\%HDWSALES, 4$$
$$= 1.70 + 0.997 * \%YDH, 4 - 1.56 * \Delta FAAA(-3), 4$$
$$(6.3) \qquad\qquad (6.0)$$
$$+ 0.132 * \Delta HST, 4 - 1.84 * \Delta UN(-1), 4$$
$$(14.2) \qquad\qquad (5.9)$$
$$RSQ = 0.846; DW = 0.91.$$

All variables remain highly significant, and DW is slightly better at 0.91, although it still indicates significant positive autocorrelation. The histogram shows no significant heteroscedasticity. When the AR(1) term is used, all the coefficients remain significant and DW rises to 1.85.

Which equation is likely to give the better forecasts? The standard error of the percentage first-difference equation is 2.8% of the mean value, which is slightly more than $7 billion, which indicates a standard error of about $200 million. By comparison, the standard error of the levels equation is $325 million. On this basis the percentage change equation has a substantially smaller standard error.

Comparing this equation with one containing the AR(1) term (not shown here) shows very little difference in the value of the coefficients. That is not surprising in the sense that, according to standard statistical theory, the presence of autocorrelation biases the t-ratios but does not usually distort the estimates of the coefficients themselves, although as shown below that is not always the case.

The reader may also wish to calculate the same equation using annual data and verify that (i) the coefficients do not change very much, and (ii) there is no significant autocorrelation when annual data are used.

Since the coefficients are almost the same, either equation will generate almost the same forecasts. In this case, then, it does not matter which form of the equation is used. However, that is not always true, as seen in the next case study.

Case Study 2: German Short-term Interest Rates

We have already seen that the real Federal funds rate varies quite significantly depending on who is chairman of the Federal Reserve Board. It might be interesting to see how much real German short-term interest rates vary (the three-month bill rate is used, symbol TB3GER), depending on who is heading the Bundesbank.

To see this, regress the German short-term rate on the German rate of inflation and the growth in the German money supply (M2); the latter term reflects Bundesbank (BBK) policy that when money supply growth accelerates, the BBK tightens. The US Federal funds rate lagged one quarter is also included because US interest rates tend to dominate world financial markets. The US inflation rate is also included with a negative sign to show that the *real* Federal funds rate is more important: when US interest rates rise because of general worldwide inflation, the BBK is less likely to tighten than when the Fed raises real rates.

TB3GER

$$= -0.799 + 0.711 * GERINFL + 0.106 * \%GERM2,4 + 0.531 * FFED(-1)$$
$$\qquad\quad (9.2) \qquad\qquad\qquad (4.7) \qquad\qquad\qquad (12.0)$$
$$- 0.238 * INFL(-1) + 0.086 * \%GERM2(-4),4 + 0.602 * GERINFL * DUNIF$$
$$\quad (4.4) \qquad\qquad\qquad (3.1) \qquad\qquad\qquad\qquad (6.3)$$
$$RSQ = 0.847; \ DW = 0.79.$$

The prefix GER before inflation and M2 money supply indicate those variables are for Germany. *DUNIF* is a dummy variable for unification explained below. The term *%GERM2,4* means percentage change in the German money supply over the past four quarters.

This may seem like a reasonable equation, but once again *DW* is low. An examination of the residuals shows that German interest rates were well above their predicted values in the early 1990s. That occurred for a very specific reason: after unification, inflation rose because of questionable government policies that artificially equalized the value of the Dmark and the Ostmark, which should have been set no higher than half the value of the DM. The net effect was that unemployment rose dramatically in the former East Germany, leading to a massive increase in transfer payments and higher inflation. Since the inflation was due to political bungling, the BBK tightened more than previously when inflation rose.

That suggests using a dummy variable that is 0 before unification and 1 afterwards (*DUNIF*), and multiplying that variable by the rate of inflation. When that is tried, such a variable is highly significant and the fit improves substantially in later years. However, *DW* still indicates positive autocorrelation of the residuals, so the AR(1) adjustment is tried again.

This time, however, the value of the coefficients changes markedly. The dummy variable completely drops out of the equation, and so does the US inflation rate. Perhaps the latter variable is not appropriate after all, but the impact of inflation after unification would seem to be a theoretically justified variable. However, the result indicates otherwise once the AR(1) adjustment is included.

The histogram of the residuals shows that heteroscedasticity is present both with and without the AR(1) term. The White or Newey–West algorithms to adjust the variance–covariance matrix hardly changes the results; in this case, the presence or absence of heteroscedasticity is not very important. This leaves the main question: should the dummy variable term be used in the forecasting equation?

TB3GER

$$= 1.59 + 0.632 * GERINFL + 0.065 * \%GERM2,4 + 0.303 * FFED(-1) - 0.090 * INFL(-1)$$

$$(4.0) \qquad\qquad (1.9) \qquad\qquad\qquad (4.3) \qquad\qquad\qquad (0.9)$$

$$+ 0.037 * \%GERM2(-4),4 - 0.075 * GERINFL * DUNIF + 0.865 * AR(1)$$

$$(1.2) \qquad\qquad (0.2) \qquad\qquad\qquad (15.6)$$

$$RSQ = 0.917; DW = 1.74.$$

No one rule will always apply to this situation, but we can draw some specific conclusions in this case. First, in the equation with the dummy variable, the coefficients indicate that, after unification, a 1% rise in the inflation rate would boost short-term interest rates by 1.3%, whereas in the equation with AR(1) the coefficient is only 0.6%. On an a-priori basis, a coefficient of about 1% would seem reasonable. Second, the reaction of the BBK to the inept political decisions following unification is a one-time event that is unlikely to be repeated. It thus appears that neither version of the equation is totally satisfactory.

It is often the case that specific dummy variables designed to fit a few data points will disappear once the AR(1) adjustment is incorporated. In that sense, using the AR(1) term will often help the forecaster reduce the amount of "curve fitting" that is inherent in any econometric estimation procedure. Here, the AR(1) adjustment warns us off using a dummy variable that is highly significant but would probably reduce forecast accuracy. However, that does not necessarily mean the equation with AR(1) will forecast better; it probably means the equation needs to be respecified. More examples of this appear later in the text.

Case Study 3: Lumber Prices

The histogram for the percentage change in lumber prices is given in figure 3.4. Note that the changes are far from being normally distributed; severe heteroscedasticity exists because of a few outlying observations.

Classical statistical assumptions state only that the residuals of the equation should be normally distributed; that criterion does not have to apply to the original series itself. Nonetheless, the point of this example is to show what happens when we try to fit an equation that has severe outlying values. Sometimes the result is nonsensical.

To start, estimate an equation in which the percentage change in lumber prices is a function of housing starts, the change in the capacity utilization rate for manufacturing, lagged changes in the value of the dollar, changes in the price of oil, and a dummy variable for the imposition and termination of wage and price controls. That is not a very good equation in terms of the goodness-of-fit statistics, and explains only a little more than one-third of the total variance.

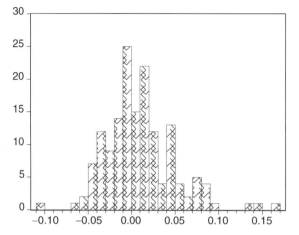

Figure 3.4 Case study 3 – see the text.

%*PPI LUMBER*

$$= -6.31 + 0.474^* HST(-2) + 0.000478^* \Delta CUMFG\char`\^2$$
$$\quad (5.5) \qquad\qquad (4.3)$$
$$- 0.083^* \Delta DOLLAR(-8), 4 + 0.058^* \%POIL(-1) + 5.55^* DUMWP$$
$$\quad (2.8) \qquad\qquad (3.0) \qquad\qquad (4.5)$$
$$RSQ = 0.356; DW = 1.50.$$

The residuals in figure 3.5 show that the price of lumber rose far more than is explained by the equation in 1980.1, and fell far more than is explained in 1980.2. Once again, there is a very specific reason. Paul Volcker became Fed chairman in late 1979; his predecessor, G. William Miller, appeared to be accommodating higher inflation, which led to runaway speculation in commodities. When Volcker tightened and imposed credit controls in early 1980, the speculative binge immediately collapsed. Since events of this sort had never occurred before, they are not drawn from the same sample. The Jarque–Bera test shows the residuals are not normally distributed.

Given this explanation, what should be done about the forecasting equation: add a dummy variable for this one period, eliminate those two observations, or add an economic variable that attempts to explain this abrupt shift in sentiment?

Adding a dummy variable improves *RSQ* but does not help the predictive accuracy of the model. Neither does eliminating these two points completely. Suppose the enterprising researcher scours the data for another series that would seem to measure the change in sentiment – which turns out to be the change in the price of gold. When that variable is added to the equation, the fit improves materially, and the residuals are now normally distributed, as shown

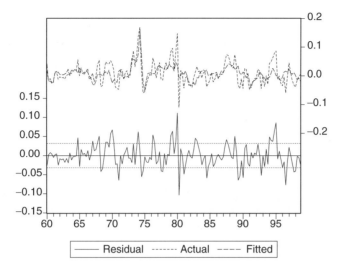

Figure 3.5 Case study 3 – see the text.

in figure 3.6. One could perhaps argue that the price of gold accurately reflects speculative fever.

%PPI LUMBER

$$= -4.92 + 0.378 * HST(-2) + 0.000511 * \Delta CUMFG^2 - 0.091 * \Delta DOLLAR(-8), 4$$

$$(4.7) \qquad\qquad (4.3) \qquad\qquad\qquad (3.4)$$

$$+ 0.038 * \%POIL(-1) + 5.40 * DUMWP + 0.049 * \Delta PGOLD$$

$$(2.2) \qquad\qquad (4.8) \qquad\qquad (5.6)$$

$$RSQ = 0.464; DW = 1.39.$$

However, the first half of 1980 was the only time that the change in the price of lumber was correlated with the change in the price of gold, which was really a proxy variable for runaway inflationary expectations. That can be tested by reestimating this equation starting in 1983.1, after inflation had returned to low levels; both that term and the change in oil prices drop out.

The price of gold actually has no economic relationship with the price of lumber. What happened, however, is that by estimating an equation with a few extreme outlying values – i.e., with severe heteroscedasticity – the least-squares formula gives a disproportionately high weight to these few values. Thus any other variable that has similar peaks and troughs, whether really related or not, will appear to be highly significant because it happens to fit those few periods. In recent years, the price of lumber and the price of gold have moved in opposite directions, and for good reason: when inflation is low, interest rates decline and housing starts rise, hence boosting the price of lumber. Yet low inflation also leads to a decline in gold prices. Hence using a positive correlation between

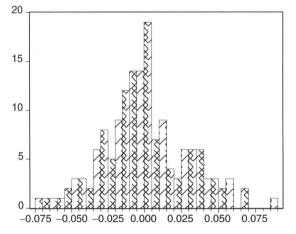

Figure 3.6 Case study 3 – see the text.

these two series to predict lumber prices in the 1990s would lead to a worse forecast than a naive model extrapolation stating that lumber prices would not change at all in the forecast period.

This case study illustrates the real problem with heteroscedasticity, and shows that adjusting the variance–covariance matrix will not really help in improving the forecasting accuracy of an equation that is dominated by a few outlying values. Later a variety of methods are discussed for treating this problem, but at this juncture it is suggested that such points should be handled with dummy variables or excluded from the sample period altogether. The diligent researcher who plows through thousands of series to find one that fits is likely to be rewarded with inferior forecasts.

Problems and Questions

1. You are in the paper manufacturing business and the company is trying to determine whether to build another plant.

(a) Your chief economist tells you that of all the manufacturing indus-tries, cyclical swings in the paper industry are most closely correlated with GDP. Annual data will suffice for this calculation. How strong is that correlation?

(b) By calculating the DW and testing for normality of residuals, how confident are you that this relationship will work well in the future? What changes, if any, would you make to the equation based on these statistics?

continued

(c) The CEO wants to build another plant only if paper production will rise an average of 5% or more per year over the next five years. Your forecast calls for GDP to rise an average of 4% per year. Based on this forecast, should the company build the plant or not?

(d) What other variables would you add to the equation to strengthen the correlation and provide better advice about building the paper plant?

2. Exports and imports in the US have both risen sharply as a share of total GDP over the post World War II period.

(a) Use regression analysis to calculate the average annual growth rate for constant dollar exports and imports. Use annual data.

(b) Imports are a function of the value of the dollar and industrial production. What happens when these two variables are both lagged? Explain your results. Which variables, if any, should be dropped?

(c) The DW for the import equation is extremely low, but improves somewhat when exports are added to the equation. Do you think that term improves the forecasting ability of this equation? Why or why not?

(d) Now estimate this equation in logarithms. What are the elasticities for the value of the dollar, industrial production, and exports? Do you think these make sense?

(e) Reestimate with an AR(1) adjustment. What happens to the coefficients? Do you think the forecasting properties equation have improved or not?

(f) Now estimate the function in percentage changes. What happens to R^2 and DW? What happens to the elasticities? Eliminate all non-significant terms and recalculate the equation. Explain which of these equations you would prefer to use for forecasting.

3. Corporate dividends are generally thought to be a function of three variables: corporate cash flow, interest rates, and capital spending. When cash flow rises, dividends rise; when interest rates rise, dividends also rise; and when capital spending rises, dividends decline because the firm decides to use more of its cash flow for investment. Use quarterly data.

(a) Using the data from the database, estimate a dividend function using these three variables. You should get an R^2 of about 0.98 and a DW of about 0.11. Comment on whether the parameter estimates seem to have the right signs. Based on these figures, what can you say about the robustness of the equation?

continued

(b)   Dividends change rather slowly over time, which means they reflect lagged as well as current values of these variables. Generate a better function by using both current and lagged values of these terms (since we have not yet covered distributed lags, a simple moving average will suffice). Explain how the equation has improved.

(c)   Look at the residuals, both on a time-series basis and with a histogram. What do you see about the residuals in recent periods? Correct this problem by using logarithms.

(d)   In all cases, *DW* remains very low. Correct this by using an AR(1) transformation. Explain whether or not the equations have improved.

(e)   Using the ratio of dividends to cash flow, see if you can find an equation that gives the correct sign for all three variables. What does this suggest about the problems of multicollinearity in this equation?

(f)   In late 2000 and 2001, corporate profits fell by the largest percentage in the post World War II period, but investment also fell by an unusually large percentage. What would you expect to happen to dividend payments in 2001 and 2002?

4.   The example for department store sales in the text used annual data in constant dollars. However, suppose management requested some forecasts for monthly data in current dollars without seasonal adjustment.

(a)   Plot this series. What pattern is immediately obvious?

(b)   To reduce this problem, run a regression in which monthly sales are a function of disposable income and a seasonal variable that is 1 in December and 0 elsewhere (in EViews, the symbol for that variable is @seas(12)). What problems remain? How would you reduce these errors?

(c)   What other seasonal variables should be added to this equation? Enter them and calculate the resulting regression.

(d)   What happens to most of the seasonal patterns from 1967 through 1998? How would you adjust for this problem?

5.   Copper prices are determined by many of the same factors as lumber prices, since they are both used in construction.

(a)   Estimate an equation for quarterly percentage changes in copper prices using the same variables that are included in the lumber equation given above. Which variables drop out of the equation? Why do you think that happens?

continued

(b) What other variables should be added to this equation? (Hint: what sectors use lots of copper but not much lumber?)

(c) Do you think the price of gold is a useful variable to help predict copper prices, assuming it could also be predicted? Plot the relationship between the change in gold prices and copper prices for the periods 1974 through 1982 and 1983 through 1999. Does this change your answer?

CHAPTER 4

ADDITIONAL TOPICS FOR SINGLE-EQUATION REGRESSION MODELS

INTRODUCTION

The previous chapter discussed the issues of autocorrelation and heteroscedasticity in the residuals, and illustrated the standard statistical adjustments that are used when these problems arise. It also pointed out the possible pitfalls of building forecasting models when those conditions are present.

Multicollinearity occurs when two or more of the independent variables in the regression equation are very highly correlated. Unlike autocorrelation and heteroscedasticity, there are no specific tests for multicollinearity, but it can be even more serious because it distorts the values of the coefficients themselves, rather than affecting only the goodness-of-fit statistics. The usual problem is that while the sum of the coefficients of highly collinear variables is close to the true underlying value, the individual coefficients contain significant errors. Thus unless the relationship between these values is exactly the same in both the sample and forecast periods, predictions from such a model are likely to contain serious mistakes.

The problems of multicollinearity stem from two major sources: *different* variables that are highly collinear, and *lagged values of the same variable*, which will be highly collinear if that series contains strong trends. The treatment of these causes is quite different. In the first case, variables should be combined, or the strong common trend should be removed by using first differences, percentage changes, ratios, or weighted least squares. In the second case, several lagged values of the same variable should be combined into only a few terms by the use of distributed lags. Both these methods are considered in detail.

4.1 PROBLEMS CAUSED BY MULTICOLLINEARITY

In equations where several variables have with strong time trends – consumption, investment, prices, sales, production, income, etc. – they are likely to be highly collinear. However, there is no explicit test that determines when this problem will distort the results. The equations must be examined on an individual basis. I will indicate how extreme multicollinearity can distort the parameter estimates, and the best way to reduce if not entirely eliminate this problem.

To see how multicollinearity can give ridiculous results, consider the admittedly far-fetched example in which consumption is regressed against:

- disposable income
- the major components of disposable income: wages, transfer payments, taxes, and all other components of personal income
- wages, transfer payments, and total income. (There is some double counting here, which is on purpose.)
- wages, transfer payments, taxes, other income, and total income. (This matrix ought to be singular, except we have introduced some rounding errors so it will convert. But since total income equals the sum of the first three variables, the results can reasonably be expected to be nonsensical.)
- wages, transfer payments, taxes, and other income, but all in percentage changes, so multicollinearity is no longer a problem.

The summary statistics for these regressions are as follows:

$$C = -21.4 + 0.923 * YD$$
$$(348.5)$$
$$R^2 = 0.999; \ SE = 32.8; \ DW = 0.23. \tag{4.1}$$

$$C = -20.5 + 0.556 * W + 1.212 * TR + 1.223 * YOTH - 0.364 * TX$$
$$(7.8) \qquad (9.8) \qquad (9.4) \qquad (1.8)$$
$$R^2 = 0.999; \ SE = 25.6; \ DW = 0.47. \tag{4.2}$$

$$C = -10.2 - 0.210 * W - 0.440 * TR + 0.975 * YD$$
$$(1.4) \qquad (9.8) \qquad (8.1)$$
$$R^2 = 0.999; \ SE = 28.4; \ DW = 0.38. \tag{4.3}$$

$$C = -18.3 - 40.95 * W - 41.57 * TR - 41.60 * YOTH - 40.36 * YD - 40.93 * TX$$
$$(1.0) \qquad (1.0) \qquad (1.0) \qquad (1.0) \qquad (1.0)$$
$$R^2 = 0.999; \ SE = 25.6; \ DW = 0.67. \tag{4.4}$$

$$\%C = 0.013 + 0.591 * \%W + 0.087 * \%TR - 0.066 * \%TX + 0.206 * \%YOTH$$
$$(5.3) \qquad (3.5) \qquad (2.1) \qquad (3.3)$$
$$R^2 = 0.784; \ SE = 0.0113; \ DW = 1.91. \tag{4.5}$$

All terms are in current dollars; all R^2 are adjusted for degrees of freedom. The numbers in parentheses are t-ratios. C is consumption, YD is disposable income, W is wages, TR is transfer payments, $YOTH$ is other personal income, and TX is personal income taxes.

Note that the overall goodness-of-fit statistics in the first four equations are all virtually the same when the components of income are disaggregated. That ought to be a tipoff something is wrong, for theory suggests that at least the short-term marginal propensity to consume from volatile components of income is smaller than from stable components. The fact that the estimated value of the coefficients for TR and $YOTH$ are greater than unity in equation (4.2) looks suspicious right away. In equation (4.3), the negative signs on W and TR are clearly inappropriate. In equation (4.4), with almost complete multicollinearity, the results are nonsensical – even though the R^2 stays the same.

When multicollinearity is eliminated by taking percentage changes, wages are the most important variable, and transfers are much less important because the major cyclical component of transfers is tied to the business cycle, and rises when other income declines. Later we will see that this consumption function is still seriously incomplete because no monetary variables are included. But you can't tell that from the statistics, since DW is 1.91.

Also note that the standard errors become enormous when extreme multicollinearity is present. That doesn't always happen; but when it does, that is an obvious hint this condition exists. In that case, the logical choice is to drop one or more of the variables.

There are a few tests that suggest multicollinearity is present, but they are not discussed here – nor are they included in EViews – because (i) they do not provide any additional information that cannot be gleaned from the correlation matrix and comparison of the sizes of the standard errors, and (ii) unlike with autocorrelation and heteroscedasticity, there is no simple way to fix the problem. There are some tests known as "complaint indicators," which tell you that multicollinearity is present, but not what to do about it.

If an equation with extreme multicollinearity is used for forecasting, the results will contain very large errors if there is even a tiny change in the relationship between the multicollinear independent variables, because the co-efficients have been blown up to unrealistically high values. Ordinarily, if the relationship between the independent variables changes a little bit, the forecast error will be quite small. Hence it is generally a poor idea to generate forecasts using an equation with extreme multicollinearity.

The following lessons can be drawn from the above example:

1 Extreme multicollinearity will often result in nonsensical parameter estimates, including the wrong signs, and unusually high standard errors.
2 Rearranging the *same data* in different linear combinations will often reduce the degree of multicollinearity.
3 If the levels form of the equation is retained, the degree of multicollinearity can be reduced by dropping one or more of the variables.
4 The best way to solve the problem is to remove the common trend, either through percentage first differences or other methods, which are discussed next.

Table 4.1 Empirical results for the example.

Form of equation	Current income	Lagged income	Current price	Lagged price	$\bar{R}^2$	SE	DW
Level	0.200 (2.9)[a]	0.025 (0.4)	7.0 (0.9)	12.2 (1.7)	0.985	21.7	0.52
Logarithm	1.77 (2.5)	0.41 (0.6)	−0.1 (−0.2)	0.4 (0.6)	0.993	0.15	0.37
Percentage change	1.40 (4.3)	1.12 (3.5)	−0.63 (−4.1)	−0.36 (−2.4)	0.675	0.041	1.73
Deviations from trend	1.85 (4.8)	0.86 (2.4)	−0.64 (−3.4)	−0.36 (−1.9)	0.941	0.039	0.60
Ratio	0.083[b] (1.4)	0.083 (1.4)	−0.0061 (−3.0)	−0.0011 (−0.6)	0.956	0.0060	0.27
Weighted least squares	0.207 (3.4)	0.032 (0.5)	9.8 (1.2)	11.8 (1.6)	0.995	21.2	0.67

[a] The numbers in parentheses are t-ratios.
[b] Constant term.

4.2 ELIMINATING OR REDUCING SPURIOUS TRENDS

There are several common methods for removing trends from the data in regression equations with time-series data. Each of these methods is discussed, followed by a list of the major advantages and disadvantages of each method. The results will be illustrated by empirical estimates of an equation for airline travel for each of these five cases. While the results from this example are fairly typical, varying results may be obtained for different functions. The point of the airline travel function is to illustrate how these various methods reduce multicollinearity and forecast error, not to define a set of rules that will work in all cases.

Case Study 4: Demand for Airline Travel

In this case study, an equation is estimated to explain the demand for airline travel using several different methods to reduce or eliminate the trend. In these equations, the dependent variable is revenue passenger miles traveled; the data are taken from the website of the Air Transport Association of America, www.air-transport.org. Income is real disposable personal income, and price is the price of airline fares measured in cents per mile divided by the CPI. This equation is first estimated in linear form, and then reestimated for the following five cases (the empirical results are shown in table 4.1):

- log-linear transformations
- percentage first differences
- deviations around trends
- ratios
- weighted least squares.

One would of course expect that airline travel is positively correlated with income, with an elasticity of greater than unity, and negatively related to the relative price of airline travel. However, the percentage change equation is the only one in which both current and lagged airline travel prices are significantly negative. In particular, in the levels equation, both price terms are positive, which makes no sense. The logarithm equation is only slightly better in this regard. However, note that when the trends are removed from the logarithm equation, it is much improved.

Also note that the results for weighted least squares are almost the same as those for the unweighted levels equation in spite of the strong upward trend in airline travel. The weights in this case are the values of disposable income, but approximately the same results would have been obtained with other similar weighting factors. That is a common finding; using this option seldom makes much difference.

The coefficients in the percentage change equation are elasticities, so they can be examined in terms of economic relevancy. The combined income terms show an elasticity of 2.52, suggesting that airline travel is a highly discretionary good that increases sharply during years of prosperity. The price elasticity is -1.00, an interesting finding for the following reason. The marginal costs of adding an additional passenger to the flight are close to zero; therefore economic theory would say that maximizing profit occurs at about the same price as maximizing revenue, which happens at a price elasticity of unity. The fact that the total result turns out to be exactly -1.00 is a coincidence, but it is nonetheless revealing to find this regression indicates airlines have priced their product at a point that maximizes profits.

4.2.1 LOG-LINEAR TRANSFORMATION

- *Main advantage:* removes some of the common trend, dampens outlying values
- *Secondary advantage:* coefficients easily interpreted as elasticities
- *Major disadvantage:* autocorrelation generally remains just as serious a problem
- *Secondary disadvantage:* implies underlying function has constant elasticities, which may not be the case
- *Related methods:* levels

Consider the form of the airline travel function

$$\log TR = \beta_1 + \beta_2 \log Y + \beta_3 \log Y_{-1} + \beta_4 \log P + \beta_5 \log P_{-1} \qquad (4.6)$$

where *TR* is airline travel and *P* is the relative price of airline travel, which has fallen an average of 3% per year over the sample period. There is nothing particularly wrong with this equation, except in levels form it would be

$$TR = e^{\beta 1} Y^{\beta 2} Y_{-1}^{\beta 3} P^{\beta 4} P_{-1}{}^{\beta 5}. \tag{4.7}$$

In fact, the underlying equation might or might not be multiplicative. There are no a-priori rules for determining when an equation is linear and when it is log-linear. In a log-linear equation, the elasticities remain the same over the entire sample period. That may or may not be an appropriate assumption.

A linear demand curve means that, at relatively low prices, the demand is inelastic, so an increase in price will boost total revenues; while at relatively high prices the demand is elastic, so a further increase in price will reduce total revenues. The log-linear demand curve assumes that the price elasticity is constant along the entire length of the curve. On an a-priori basis there is no way to determine which assumption is better. In the airline equation, both the levels and the logarithm equations give non-significant results for the price terms, so the issue cannot be decided with these equations.

Cost (or supply) curves are usually flat in the region of constant returns to scale, and then start rising at an increasing rate as diminishing returns set in. In that case, the function is neither linear nor log-linear, and must be estimated using nonlinear techniques, a method discussed later in this chapter. Production functions are generally thought to be log-linear, with constant elasticities of substitution. It is often assumed a certain percentage increase in costs results in the same percentage increase in prices whether the economy is in a boom or a recession. As a matter of fact, the change in the markup factor is probably due more to monetary policy and expectations than to the phase of the business cycle, leading to a complicated nonlinear relationship that usually is not estimated directly (i.e., a linear approximation is used by including monetary factors separately). But here again there is no conclusive empirical evidence that using logarithms is better or worse.

In many cases, the empirical evidence does not permit one to choose between linear and log-linear equations. If the theory provides strong reasons to expect constant elasticities, use the logarithmic formulation; otherwise use the linear form. For series with strong trends, the results generally do not differ very much. The logarithm form is often preferred because, as noted above, the coefficients are elasticities, making comparison easier if one is working with equations involving hundreds of commodities, countries, companies, or individuals.

As noted in chapter 2, using percentage changes is virtually the same as using first differences of logarithms, although there is one slight difference: in calculating percentage changes, there is some ambiguity about whether the denominator should be the current period, the previous period, or some average of the two periods. By taking differences of logarithms, this ambiguity is resolved.

However, except in unusual cases, the difference between the two choices of equations is minuscule.

4.2.2 PERCENTAGE FIRST DIFFERENCES

*   *Main advantage:* eliminates all traces of trend
*   *Secondary advantage:* eliminates "imbalances" between levels and rates
*   *Major disadvantage:* one or two outlying points, which might not make much difference in a levels equation, could distort the regression estimates
*   *Secondary disadvantage:* may obscure long-run relationships
*   *Related methods:* first differences (without the percentage) gives similar results, although over a long time period many first differences also contain a significant trend; also, since the percentage change coefficients are elasticities, they are easier to interpret; first differences of logarithms give essentially identical results

The equation for annual percentage changes for airline travel yields robust parameter estimates, as noted above. One point of interest is the much lower $\overline{R}^2$, which is just one more example of how that statistic can often be misleading. The standard error of the equation is 4.1%, and the mean value of the dependent variable is 270, which means in levels terms the error is 11.1. That is much lower than the standard error of 21.7 for the levels equation.

While this equation works well, percentage changes in quarterly or monthly data are often distorted by seasonal quirks and random factors. Hence the noise overwhelms the signal and the results are not robust. This problem is sometimes handled by taking percentage differences over the same quarter the previous year, which finesses the seasonal problem. The trouble with this method cannot be detected in a single-equation approach, but creates problems when these equations are combined in a simultaneous model with multi-period forecasts. Using annual percentage first differences sometimes creates a spurious two-year cycle in the forecasts, especially when reinforced by other equations of the same form. This problem can be reduced if not totally eliminated by using a four-quarter moving average, lagged one quarter, instead of the four-quarter lag itself. Thus we have

$$\Delta Y / Y_{-1} = \beta \Delta X / X_{-1} \text{ (often too much noise)} \tag{4.8}$$

$$(Y - Y_{-4}) / Y_{-4} = \beta (X - X_{-4}) / X_{-4} \text{ (could cause spurious cycles)} \tag{4.9}$$

$$(Y - \overline{Y}) / \overline{Y} = \beta (X - \overline{X}) / \overline{X} \tag{4.10}$$

where $\overline{X} = (X_{-1} + X_{-2} + X_{-3} + X_{-4})/4$ (preferred if equations are to be used in simultaneous-equation models).

4.2.3 RATIOS

- *Main advantage:* where applicable, eliminates trends
- *Secondary advantage:* series are "smooth" and not dominated by outliers; also, long-run parameters are better developed, and equation is "balanced" if untrended series are included
- *Major disadvantage:* must be sure the ratio of the dependent variable does not have a trend, or will not have a trend in the forecast period, otherwise the problem of spurious trends could remain.
- *Secondary disadvantage:* constant term may introduce nonlinearities
- *Related methods:* weighted least squares (see section (4.2.5))

We start with the levels function

$$TR = \beta_1 + \beta_2 Y + \beta_3 Y_{-1} + \beta_4 P + \beta_5 P_{-1} \tag{4.11}$$

where TR is airline travel, Y is disposable income, and P is relative price of airline travel.

In levels form this equation could have several drawbacks. In particular, Y and Y_{-1} could be collinear, and the effect of P might be swamped by the trends. One could take percentage first differences, but sometimes that understates the long-run change in the dependent variable due to a change in income or prices. This equation can be reformulated as

$$TR/Y = \beta_1 + \beta_2 Y_{-1}/Y + \beta_3 P + \beta_4 P_{-1}. \tag{4.12}$$

The relative price terms have not been divided by Y because that would introduce a spurious trend at least as serious as the one we are trying to eliminate.

Until now the constant term has not been discussed, since it is not very important. However, in this case, the β_1 term has some economic significance, since the actual forecasts will be calculated by multiplying the entire equation by Y, so β_1 becomes the coefficient of the income term. Thus in its linear form, this equation has no constant term at all.

To compare this equation to the levels and percentage change forms, it is useful to calculate the elasticities. The sum of the coefficients of the two income terms, which happen to be identical, is 0.166. Since the mean value of TR/Y is 0.071, and the mean value of Y_{-1}/Y is approximately unity, then the income elasticity is 0.166/0.071, or approximately 2.34 – quite similar to the 2.52 value contained in the percentage change equations.

The mean value of airline prices (cents/mile in constant dollars) is 12.8, so the price elasticity (combining terms) is $-0.0072 * 12.8/0.071$, or about -1.3. That is slightly higher than the -1.0 figure obtained from the percentage change equations. The standard error in levels form is obtained by multiplying the SE of the equation, which is 0.006, times the mean value of real disposable income, which is 3,355, yielding a comparable figure of 20.1. That is slightly lower than the levels equation SE of 21.7 but substantially higher than the comparable percentage change equation SE of 12; so on balance, the percentage change equation would appear to be a better choice.

4.2.4 DEVIATIONS AROUND TRENDS

*   *Main advantage:* by definition, trends are eliminated; don't have to worry about trends remaining, as in ratios
*   *Secondary advantage:* a backup if percentage changes or ratios do not work
*   *Major disadvantage:* in many cases, does not eliminate or reduce autocorrelation
*   *Secondary disadvantage:* changes in trend in the dependent but not the independent variables could result in poorly performing equation
*   *Related methods:* none

Once again consider the airline travel function in equation (4.11), but this time remove the trend from each variable. Representing the trend value for TR as TR_{TR} and using similar notation for the other variables, we can write

$$(TR - TR_{TR}) = \gamma_1 + \gamma_2(Y - Y_{TR}) + \gamma_3(Y_{-1} - Y_{TR}) + \gamma_4(P - P_{TR}) + \gamma_5(P_{-1} - P_{TR})$$

$$(4.13)$$

where in each case the trend variable is calculated by running a separate *regression equation* of the form $\log X = \alpha_1 + \alpha_2 t$ (where t is a time trend) for TR, Y, and P. In other words, these are logarithmic trends. This equation is equivalent to

$$\log TR$$
$$= \gamma_1 + \gamma_2 \log Y + \gamma_3 \log Y_{-1} + \gamma_4 \log P + \gamma_5 \log P_{-1} + (1 - \lambda_2 - \lambda_3 - \lambda_4 - \lambda_5)T_{TR}$$

$$(4.14)$$

where T_{TR} is the time trend for airline travel, and the λ are some linear combination of the γ and the trend rates of trend growth in Y and P. If the sum of the λ's is not approximately equal to zero, then the method of deviations around the trend can reintroduce a spurious trend back into the equation, hence offsetting some of the detrending that this method is designed to accomplish.

For this reason, the use of differences around trends will not always work. Yet in many occasions it is useful, especially when percentage changes in the data are erratic or look like a random series, or when the relevant ratios still contain strong trends.

To estimate this equation, first estimate a regression of the log of travel on a time trend, and then calculate the residuals. This process is repeated for income and for the relative price of airline travel. In EViews, then estimate *RESID1* (the difference between the log of travel and its trend value) as a function of current and lagged *RESID2* (the difference between the log of income and its trend value), and current and lagged *RESID3* (the difference between log of relative price and its trend)

The results are quite instructive. Unlike with the logarithm equation, where the combined price elasticity was only −0.13 and clearly not significantly different from zero, we find that the price elasticity in this equation (measured by the coefficients, since this is a logarithmic equation) is exactly −1.00, the same result obtained for the percentage change equation. The income elasticity is 2.71, slightly higher than the 2.52 figure in the percentage change equation.

The next issue is how to compare standard errors; this equation, which is in logarithms, has a standard error of 0.039, compared with 21.7 in the levels equation. The standard error must be converted from logarithms to levels to draw any meaningful comparison which is done as follows. The mean value of the airline travel variable is 270.5; the natural log of that number is 5.600. One standard deviation from that number is 5.639; the antilog of that is 281.2. Hence the standard error of this equation converted to levels if 10.7, only about half the *SE* of the levels equation. Hence in this regard, the deviations-from-trend equation is superior.

The other factor to note is that *DW* is only 0.60, which suggests the possible use of the AR(1) transformation. When that happens, the equation improves in the sense that the income elasticity falls to 2.43; the price elasticity remains at −1.00. While *DW* now shows no autocorrelation, that is not a valid test with AR(1). The major change is that the income elasticity is now lower.

In this case, virtually the same result is obtained as occurs in the percentage change equation; that does not always happen. Also, note that while the logarithm equation does not give reasonable results, the equation is substantially improved when the trends are removed. Hence this equation is yet another case where strong trends in time-series data obscure the underlying result.

4.2.5 WEIGHTED LEAST SQUARES

- *Main advantage:* best method for treating heteroscedasticity, although its use is more common for cross-section than time-series data
- *Major disadvantage:* essentially reduces equation to ratio form, which may still leave strong trends in key variables
- *Secondary disadvantage:* in most cases, arbitrary choices of weights
- *Related methods:* ratios

There are two cases: one where the variances are known, and the other where they are estimated. In the first case, the variables in the regression are simply divided by their respective variances. In practical terms, though, this information is hardly ever known.

In the more usual case, the changes in the variances are approximated by the changes in one of the trend variables (in the airline travel function, the obvious choice would be income). The equation is then divided through by that variable. In this case, weighted least squares has some similarity to ratios, but the results are usually closer to the OLS equations than the ratio equation.

There are few differences between the OLS and WLS equations because all of the independent variables have significant trends: income rises and relative price falls. When some of the independent variables do not have any trends, such as percentage changes or interest rates, WLS often improves the coefficients of these trendless terms, in which case the forecasting accuracy of the equation generally improves. Most of the time, however, there is not much difference between OLS and WLS estimates.

4.2.6 SUMMARY AND COMPARISON OF METHODS

Any time one is calculating regressions using time series with strong trends – whether they are components of aggregate demand and income, individual demand and supply functions, production functions, money supply, stock prices, or any other variable that grows over time – the original set of equations, based on the relevant theory, will usually show positive autocorrelation of the residuals, and will usually suffer from multicollinearity as well. These maladies could be due to a number of different factors, but most of the time the culprit is the strong common trend.

Both the sample period statistical results and the forecasting properties of the equation are likely to be unsatisfactory unless these problems are resolved. Using the lagged dependent variable on the right-hand side of the equation – or using an autocorrelation adjustment – will provide a "quick fix" in the sense that the sample period statistical tests will appear to be better, but often the multi-period forecasting record will become worse. It is better to use one of the methods mentioned here to eliminate the common trends.

Building econometric forecasting equations can never be reduced to a "cookbook" technique, and different problems call for different solutions, but the general checklist should be helpful in deciding which form of the equation to use.

1 It is usually easy to tell if strong trends are dominant simply by looking at the data. If not, check the correlation matrix. If a wide variety of different forms of the regression equation routinely yield $R^2 > 0.99$, it is reasonably clear all you are doing is measuring a common trend, and it is best to reduce or remove it.

2 Another hint will be a very low DW statistic; if DW is lower than R^2, that is usually a reliable signal that one should use percentage changes (or first differences of logarithms, which will give essentially the same result).

3 In equations with strong trends, high R^2, and low DW, percentage changes should be tried. The major drawback occurs if the resulting series is dominated

by random fluctuations, which usually means the absolute values of the parameter estimates are biased down. If monthly or quarterly data are being used, one logical choice is to try annual percentage changes (i.e., this month or quarter over the same month or quarter a year ago). For forecasting with multi-equation models, it is better for the lagged variable to be an average over the past year than simply a year ago, in order to avoid spurious cycles in forecasting more than one year out.

4 If the annual percentage change method does not work, consider either ratios or detrending each series. These methods often do not solve the problem of autocorrelation. Yet while an AR(1) adjustment will superficially solve that problem, it generally will not improve forecasting accuracy for multi-period predictions and often makes the errors larger.

5 For variables without trends – interest rates, inflation rates, foreign exchange rates of the dollar, etc. – levels equations are preferred. There may still be some autocorrelation, but that is best handled by improving the specification of the equation rather than by moving to percentage changes.

4.3 DISTRIBUTED LAGS

So far we have looked at the problem of multicollinearity as it applies to two or more independent variables with strong trends. For illustrative purposes we used annual data. However, an even more common cause of multicollinearity occurs when quarterly or monthly data are used and the theory suggests several lagged values of one or more of the independent variables. For example, consumption depends on lagged as well as current income. Because of multicollinearity, the estimated coefficients in regression equations will generally be nonsensical if an entire string of lagged variables is entered in a single equation. Yet theory does not tell us precisely how long the lag will be, nor what shape the distribution will take: whether 90% of the reaction will take place in the first time period, or whether it will be spread over several years.

In most key macroeconomic equations – consumption, investment, exports, interest rates, wages and prices, etc. – economic choices depend on lagged as well as current variables. The problem is obviously more important the shorter the time period considered: lagged values are more important for quarterly and monthly data than for annual data. At the industry level, changes in shipments, new orders, and inventories depend on what has happened in the past as well as the present. Only in cross-section data are lags generally considered unimportant.

4.3.1 GENERAL DISCUSSION OF DISTRIBUTED LAGS

Most of the time, the researcher must make some a-priori assumption about the shape and length of the lag distribution, otherwise the empirical testing can quickly get out of hand. As a general rule, the following four types of lag distributions are the most common in estimating regression equations.

The simplest kind of lag is the *arithmetic moving average with equal weights*. All terms have the same weight up to a certain point, beyond which all the weights are zero. For example, changes in wage rates this quarter might depend on changes in the inflation rate over the past four quarters with equal weights, followed by zero weights for longer lags. One could make a plausible case for such an assumption in the case where wages are changed only once a year, while price changes are continuous. In that case we might write

$$\%(wr) = \beta_0 + \beta_1[\%(cpi) + \%(cpi)_{-1} + \%(cpi)_{-2} + \%(cpi)_{-3}]/4 \tag{4.15}$$

where "%" is the percentage first difference operator; i.e., $\%(x) = (x - x_{-1})/x_{-1} * 100$.

This may not sound like a very realistic lag distribution, but could occur if, say, wage bargains incorporate all the inflation that has occurred since the previous contract was signed, but none of the inflation before that point. This is sometimes known as the "one-horse shay" assumption, based on the concept that a machine (originally a horse) would perform faithfully and at the same efficiency during its lifetime, and then, when it suddenly expired, wouldn't work at all. Most of the time, though, the weights on lag distribution do not suddenly become zero, so lag distributions are used that describe the actual situation more accurately.

The second type of lag distribution is a *declining weight moving average*, which can be either arithmetic or geometric. An example of an arithmetic distribution is:

$$(4Y_{-1} + 3Y_{-2} + 2Y_{-3} + Y_{-4})/10. \tag{4.16}$$

An example of a geometric distribution is

$$(0.8Y_{-1} + 0.64Y_{-2} + 0.512Y_{-3} + 0.4096Y_{-4})/\Sigma \tag{4.17}$$

where Σ is the summation of the weights used in the lag distribution.

The drawback to estimating the equation

$$C_t = \beta_1 + \beta_2\left(\sum_{i=1}^{k} \lambda^i Y_{-i}\right) \tag{4.18}$$

is that it requires a nonlinear estimation technique involving simultaneous estimation of both β_2 and λ (k is set by the researcher). As shown later, such results often fail to give satisfactory results; in addition, the significance levels of the parameter estimates can be tested only on a linear approximation. This equation can also be transformed into

$$C_t = \beta_2 Y + \lambda C_{t-1} \tag{4.19}$$

but estimating that equation means using the lagged dependent variable, which generally is not recommended.

The third type of lag distribution is an *inverted U* (or V). As the name implies, the weights start near zero, rise to a peak, and then tail off again. A common example would be the lag between orders and deliveries: immediately after the order is placed only a few goods are delivered, then the proportion rises, and eventually falls off to zero again. To a certain extent this lag structure is similar to the normal distribution. A typical example of an inverted U distribution is

$$Y_t = \beta_0 + \beta_1(X_t + 2X_{t-1} + 3X_{t-2} + 4X_{t-3} + 5X_{t-4}$$
$$+ 4X_{t-5} + 3X_{t-6} + 2X_{t-7} + X_{t-8})/25. \tag{4.20}$$

The fourth type of lag distribution is a *cubic distribution*. The initial weights are relatively large, then decline sharply, but then rise again before eventually declining to zero. This would occur in the case where an initial impact caused some variable to change; after that impact had worked its way through the economy, there would be a secondary impact, smaller but still significant. This lag distribution is often found in functions for capital spending: the initial plans are made based on variables with long lags, but then modified as more recent economic conditions change, especially when orders are canceled or construction is halted.

By now we are reaching the point of diminishing returns, since the researcher is basically specifying the overall lag structure without testing beforehand to see whether the assumption is a reasonable one. Hence a more general approach is needed. While one could certainly invent other, more complicated lag distributions, the exercise soon reduces to curve fitting and data mining rather than econometrics.

All the distributions described here have weights that eventually go to zero. There is no point in considering a lag distribution so long that the weights never go to zero. It doesn't really make any economic sense, and it couldn't be estimated anyhow. However, it is generally not known on an a-priori basis whether the weights are large or small at the beginning of the lag period, or whether they decline monotonically. A more generalized lag structure that can be estimated in the linear regression model is needed to fill this gap.

4.3.2 POLYNOMIAL DISTRIBUTED LAGS

This section discusses polynomial distributed lags; the geometric lag is a special case. The lag structure can indeed be specified as a geometrically declining lag. However, it could also turn out to be the shape of an inverted U or V, it could have two or more peaks, or the weights could first decline and then rise again. In the case of the lag between orders and contracts, and deliveries or completions of capital goods, the weights of the distribution would probably be relatively small at first, peak in the middle, and eventually decline to zero again. The concept of polynomial distributed lags, which was introduced into economics to estimate the lag structure between ordering and delivery of capital goods by Shirley Almon,[1] permits the user to choose the following values:

- whether or not the lag is constrained to zero at the near end
- whether or not the lag is constrained to zero at the far end
- the degree of the polynomial: linear, quadratic, cubic, etc.
- the total length of lag.

The PDL method is quite general: the user need only choose the parameters given above. On the other hand, the results are not always easy to interpret, since they often give very similar goodness-of-fit statistics for wide variations in length of lag and degree and shape of the polynomial. I will first explain the method, then give some standard examples. Since the general case involves a fair amount of tedious algebra, the example of a third-degree polynomial with a five-period lag and no endpoint restrictions is given next.[2] The lag specification is

$$Y_t = \beta_0 + \beta_1(w_0 X_t + w_1 X_{t-1} + w_2 X_{t-2} + w_3 X_{t-3} + w_4 X_{t-4}) + \varepsilon_t \qquad (4.21)$$

where

$$w_i = \gamma_0 + \gamma_1 i + \gamma_2 i^2 + \gamma_3 i^3, \; i = 0,1,2,3,4. \qquad (4.22)$$

If the equation were a higher order than cubic (say, quartic), then equation (4.22) would have an additional term for i^4.

The simplest case is a linear polynomial – i.e., a straight line. If the distribution were constrained at the far end, and the lag were (say) five quarters, the underlying lag distribution would be a declining straight line that intersected the x-axis after five quarters. For a geometric distribution, the specification would call for a quadratic polynomial constrained at the far end.

After a fair amount of arithmetic, which involves substituting the w_i of (4.22) into the original equation (4.21), it can be shown that

---

[1] Almon, Shirley, "The Distributed Lag Between Capital Appropriations and Expenditures," *Econometrica*, 33 (1965), 178–96.
[2] For further discussion, see Pindyck, Robert S., and Daniel L. Rubinfeld, *Econometric Models and Economic Forecasts*, 4th edn (Irwin McGraw-Hill, Boston), 1998, pp. 236–8. Also see Maddala, G. S., *Introduction to Econometrics*, 2nd edn (Prentice Hall, Englewood Cliffs, NJ), 1992, pp. 423–9).

$$Y_t = \beta_0 + \beta_1 c_0 (X_t + X_{t-1} + X_{t-2} + X_{t-3} + X_{t-4})$$
$$+ \beta_1 c_1 (X_{t-1} + 2X_{t-2} + 3X_{t-3} + 4X_{t-4})$$
$$+ \beta_1 c_2 (X_{t-1} + 4X_{t-2} + 9X_{t-3} + 16X_{t-4})$$
$$+ \beta_1 c_3 (X_{t-1} + 8X_{t-2} + 27X_{t-3} + 64X_{t-4}). \qquad (4.23)$$

Since the product of two parameters cannot be estimated with linear methods, it is generally assumed that β_1 is unity. That is essentially the same as dividing by β_1, which would not affect any of the coefficients except the constant term, whose value is generally unimportant.

If one wanted to impose the additional restriction that the weights were zero at the far end, that would simply entail adding an additional term in (4.21) that said $w_5 = 0$. A similar constraint $w_0 = 0$ would be used if the weights were constrained to zero at the near end.

It may not be intuitively obvious what is accomplished by this method of calculating new variables with different coefficients to various powers. A formal exposition involves Lagrangian multipliers and more algebra than is appropriate here. However, on a heuristic level, we can think of fitting a quadratic (or a cubic) as an approximation of a more complicated lag structure that exists in the real world. Such an exercise is little more than curve fitting; but as pointed out earlier, theory doesn't tell us the length or the shape of the actual lag structure, even if it does suggest the variables and the approximate magnitudes of the coefficients that should be expected.

The PDL method is useful because it sharply reduces the number of degrees of freedom that are used in the estimation of the equation, it reduces multi-collinearity, and it reduces the probability that one or two outliers will determine the shape of the estimated lag distribution. The major drawback to this method, as will be seen, is that for variables with strong trends, it is often difficult to determine empirically how long the lag should be, and what order the polynomial should be.

Two of the most common examples of the use of PDLs in macroeconomics are the consumption function, and the lag between capital appropriations and actual capital expenditures. In the case of the consumption function, Friedman estimated a 17-year lag on income to approximate permanent income, although his original work was done before the concept of PDLs were used in econometrics. The regressions of capital spending on appropriations by Almon was the seminal use of PDLs in econometrics.

While Friedman was correct in his belief that consumer spending depends on average or expected income, his lag of 17 years was far too long for two reasons. First, the average consumer does not have that long a memory. Second, consumers also look ahead to what they expect their income to be; the work on rational expectations had not yet been developed when Friedman published his pioneering *Theory of the Consumption Function*.[3] As a result, consumer spending generally does not depend on income with more than a three-year lag, and the use of PDLs is not usually utilized today to estimate consumption functions. The use of PDLs in the investment function is explored in case study 6.

4.3.3 GENERAL GUIDELINES FOR USING PDLS

The following guidelines should be useful when using PDLs.

1   Some textbooks suggest starting with a high-order polynomial and then dropping the insignificant terms; but in real life it does not make much sense to experiment with any polynomial higher than a cubic unless one has independent information that would suggest a more complicated lag structure.

2   Don't expect to be able to pinpoint the precise length of the lag structure. The R^2 will vary hardly at all for adjacent lags (e.g., 12 compared with 13).[4]

3   In long lags, the coefficients often have the wrong sign for a few months or quarters, which doesn't make any economic sense. However, it is often difficult to get rid of these erroneous signs without compromising the rest of the equation. My advice would be if the coefficients with the wrong sign are tiny, leave them in. "Tiny" in this context means a t-ratio with an absolute value of less than 0.5.

4   Often, the tendency is to keep adding lags as long as $\bar{R}^2$ keeps increasing. However, that generally tends to make the lag longer than is the case in the underlying population. As pointed out, the adjusted R^2 will keep increasing as long as the t-ratios of each additional term are greater than 1. However, in the case of PDL, this rule of thumb should be modified so that additional lag terms are not added unless the t-ratios of those additional terms exceed 2.

5   Since the average length of business cycles used to be 4–5 years, it is sometimes the case, when using time-series data before the 1980s, that long lags may simply be picking up a spurious correlation with the previous cycle; this is known as the echo effect. Since business cycles happen less frequently these days, splitting the sample period and reestimating the equations starting in 1982 should reduce if not eliminate any such effect. If the maximum length of lag is reduced in the more recent sample period, then the earlier correlation probably does represent an echo effect.

6   The use of PDLs is usually quite sensitive to the choice of variables in the equation. That makes testing the equation more complex. In general, you should include what are expected to be the relevant variables in the equation, rather

---

[3]   Friedman, Milton, *A Theory of the Consumption Function* (Princeton University Press for NBER, Princeton, NJ), 1957.

[4]   Further discussion on choosing the length of lag is found in Frost, P. A., "Some Properties of the Almon Lag Technique When One Searches for Degree of Polynomial and Lag," *Journal of the American Statistical Association*, 70 (1975), 606–12.

than trying to work out the precise form of the PDL on the key variable first and then watch it fall apart when other variables are added. Also, the equation is likely to be unstable if one uses several PDL variables with long lags.

Since several doubts have been raised about the efficacy of PDLs, what are some alternative suggestions?

(a) If weights of the distribution become insignificant after a short lag, estimate those terms directly and ignore the long tail. That is what we have done with the GDP term in the investment equation.
(b) Alternatively, if a function appears to have a peak with a fairly short lag but a long tail, try estimating the tail as a separate variable.
(c) If the mean lag seems to keep increasing indefinitely as more terms are added, set up another workfile with annual data and estimate the function with annual data and no PDL, and see if the result is about the same. If it is significantly different, the PDL method is picking up some spurious correlation.
(d) Finally, try calculating the equation in percentage change form, with each lagged variable entered separately. There will be a higher ratio of "noise" in the data points, but the parameter estimates will provide a clearer hint about whether the long lag structure is justified. Bear in mind, though, that the percentage change formulation usually *underestimates* the length of the underlying lag structure and the long-term elasticities.

4.4 TREATMENT OF OUTLIERS AND ISSUES OF DATA ADEQUACY

Before actually estimating a regression equation, it is always – without exception – best to plot the data and examine their characteristics. Besides spotting any possible errors of transposition or copying that might have crept into the data, all of the statistical formulas and goodness-of-fit statistics are based on the assumption that the residuals are normally distributed. Most of the time, that is a reasonable assumption under which to proceed. However, if some of the residuals are exceptionally large, the least squares algorithm will over-weight those observations, possibly distorting the parameter estimates, which would lead to inaccurate forecasts. This section discusses various methods for treating this problem.

4.4.1 OUTLIERS

Suppose that after estimating what appears be a satisfactory regression equation, some of the errors for individual observations are more than three standard deviations from the mean. Assuming normality, the probability that they are drawn from the same population is less than 1 in 1,000. Generally it should not be assumed that these points are drawn from the same data generation function. The major options facing the econometrician are the following:

- remove those observations from the sample period entirely
- try to find economic variables that explain these aberrant points
- add specific dummy variables for those periods.

It is possible that these outliers are "harmless," which means the parameter estimates of the dependent variables will be about the same whether the outliers receive special treatment or not. In that case, adding a dummy variable simply improves the sample period fit without improving forecast accuracy. In such cases, the treatment of these outliers is irrelevant, and they can be ignored. However, that is usually not the case. It is more likely that the disturbances causing these outlying values also affect the independent variables; several examples are provided next.

Before turning to economic relationships, we look at the statistical distortion that can occur from a purely random observation by choosing an artificial example where bad data are introduced into the sample observations. To illustrate how outliers and dummy variables can affect an equation, consider the equation in which the percentage change in consumption is a function of the percentage change in income and the yield spread with an average lag of half a year. The sample data are then altered by introducing one period of "bad" data for both consumption and income, and the regressions are recalculated with and without dummy variables to offset these outlying observations. The bad data used here are constructed by adding 100% to the actual change; e.g., if income rose 5% in that year, the bad data would show an increase of 105%. While such large errors are not likely to be encountered in actual forecasting, exaggerating the case emphasizes the distortions that can occur in the parameter estimates. The results are summarized in table 4.2.

It is clear that if the outlying data points are ignored, the equation is ruined. Not only is the R^2 close to zero and the coefficients insignificant, but their values are far different and, in one case, the value of the yield spread variable switches signs. If the error occurs in the *independent* variable and a dummy variable is added, the equation in this case is unchanged. If the error occurs in the *dependent* variable and a dummy variable is added, the resulting R^2 is far overstated, although the parameter estimates do not change. With an error of this magnitude, though, it is clear that some adjustment must be made: either a dummy variable must be added or the erroneous observations must be removed from the sample.

If dummy variables are used, it is usually a good idea to recalculate the regression without those data points as a cross-check to make sure the equation has not changed very much. That will also provide a better estimate of the underlying value of R^2 for this regression.

If the outlier occurs in the dependent variable, but that value is uncorrelated with any of the independent variables, regressions that are calculated (i)

Table 4.2   Illustration of statistical distortion

Equation	$\bar{R}^2$	SE	DW
%C = 0.35 + 0.765*%Y + 0.32*YLD	0.734	0.98	2.10
(8.7) (3.0)			
%C# = 1.69 + 1.688*%Y − 0.77*YLD	−0.022	1.71	2.09
(1.1) (0.4)			
%C# = 0.37 + 0.774*%Y + 0.31*YLD + 99.1*δ_C	0.997	0.98	1.95
(8.8) (2.9)			
%C = 0.26 + 0.008*%Y# + 0.48*YLD	0.105	1.79	0.97
(0.4) (2.4)			
%C = 0.35 + 0.765*%Y# + 0.33*YLD − 76.5*δ_y	0.725	0.99	2.10
(8.6) (2.9)			

%C = percentage change in consumption; %C# = same as %C with 100% added to one observation; %Y = percentage change in disposable income; %Y# = same as %Y with 100% added to one (different) observation; YLD = yield spread, lagged half a year. δ are dummy variables for C and Y respectively (1 in the outlying period, 0 otherwise). Numbers underneath the coefficients are *t*-ratios.

excluding the outlier, and (ii) including an outlier with a dummy variable for that period, will yield approximately the same coefficients, *t*-ratios, and standard error of estimate. The only difference is that R^2 will be much higher for the second equation.

Suppose the outlier is found in the independent variable. Then the coefficient of that variable is the same (i) without the bad data, and (ii) with the combination of the bad data and the dummy variable if in fact the cause of the outlying observation is uncorrelated with the independent variables. Had there been some correlation, the value of the Y coefficient would have differed from the equation with no outlier and no dummy variable.

Thus the appropriate test to be performed is to run the regression with and without the outliers (using a dummy variable when including the outlier) and see how much the coefficients change. If they are about the same, and the *t*-ratios are significant both with and without the outliers, the general rule of thumb is not to worry about these outliers; while they can be handled with a dummy variable, they will not affect forecasting accuracy.

The more serious issue occurs when the outlying observations are correlated with some of the independent variables. Consider, for example, a widespread reduction in production – due either to a natural disaster or a strike – that reduces sales and personal income because some workers are not being paid. Shortages would ordinarily be accompanied by higher prices; but if there is rationing, the price equation would not work properly and a dummy variable would be appropriate. Other cases are discussed in more detail in the next section. In a related example, suppose a major electric power plant fails and customers in that service area must purchase power from a nationwide grid at five times the usual price – a result that can occur under deregulation. That sample point is clearly drawn from a different underlying data generation function, yet there is a significant correlation between quantity and price. Simply treating that observation with a dummy variable may distort estimates of the actual price elasticity.

Before turning to the actual use of dummy variables in equations, however, it is useful to discuss briefly some of the problems that can occur with data series. These problems may or may not necessitate the use of dummy variables, but data errors will generally distort the parameter estimates just as much as actual outlying events. Hence the use of a dummy variable may be merited if the residual is well outside the sample period range, even if there does not appear to be any real-world event that would explain the outlying observation.

4.4.2 MISSING OBSERVATIONS

Suppose one is estimating a regression equation and some of the data are missing. What is the best way to proceed?

One possibility is simply to omit all those observations from the sample period. However, that is not always advisable. Suppose the independent variable in question is used in a 20-quarter distributed lag; then 20 observations would have to be omitted for each missing data point. Sometimes data are available in slightly different form and can be combined – spliced together. In other cases, quarterly data can be interpolated from annual series, or monthly data from quarterly series.

Naturally there is some risk in making up the data with a certain hypothesis already in mind, and then finding that the data support that hypothesis. All researchers would always prefer to have complete data sets. But when that is not possible, what are the "second best" alternatives?

The problem with omitting observations from the sample period is intensified when long lag structures are used. Suppose one of the independent variables enters the equation with a distributed lag of 20 quarters, and the entire sample period is only 80 quarters. The sample period has already been reduced from 80 to 60 observations to accommodate this lag. To lose another 20 observations just because of one single missing data point could reduce the sample size to the range where the results are inconclusive.

Another case arises with the equation for purchases of motor vehicles. Monthly and quarterly data are available for auto sales starting in 1959, domestic light truck sales starting in 1966, and foreign light truck sales starting in 1976. Before that, only annual data are available. One option is to start the equation in 1976; however, that reduces the sample period almost by half. Since light truck sales, and particularly foreign light truck sales, were not very important in the early years (presumably one of the reasons that monthly and quarterly data were not prepared), the results might be improved by extrapolating those data for the earlier period. The various ways of filling in missing data points include the following.

1   Simple interpolation is acceptable if the missing point appears in a series with a strong trend and a small variance around that trend.
2   If there is no trend and the observations appear to be serially uncorrelated, one could simply use the mean value of the variable. That might be the case for percentage changes, for example. If one is taking deviations around the trend, the missing value would then be 0.
3   Suppose one series (e.g., foreign truck sales) are available only on an annual basis for part of the sample period, while a closely related series (domestic truck sales) are available monthly or quarterly. Then one can interpolate monthly or quarterly series for foreign truck sales based on the annual data for that series and monthly and quarterly figures for domestic sales.
4   Calculate a regression relating the data series with the missing observation to other variables during the sub-sample period when all the data are available; then use the "predicted" value for missing observations. That is equivalent to estimating the equation by omitting sample points where data are missing if none of the variables is lagged; but where lagged values are used, the size of the sample period can be expanded.
5   In these examples it is assumed that monthly and quarterly data are seasonally adjusted. If they are not, the appropriate seasonal factor should be added to that month or quarter when estimating the missing data.

To a certain extent, it is not known how well these methods work, because by definition the missing data do not exist (although experiments can be constructed where one "pretends" not to have some of the observations). In general, though, (3) and (4) usually work fairly well where the relationships fit well during the periods when all the data are available. Conversely, assuming the value is equal to some sample period average generally does not work well and should be tried only as a last resort.

4.4.3 GENERAL COMMENTS ON DATA ADEQUACY

It is a truism, yet one that can be repeated often, that the estimated model is only as good as the underlying data. While examples of inaccurate data abound, it is useful to group them into the following general classifications:

- *Outright errors.* These are input errors, or changes in definitions that are not properly reflected in the published data.
- *Data revisions.* This is often a serious problem for macroeconomic data. The corrections are usually due either to (i) missing data in preliminary releases, or (ii) change in sample survey techniques. In some cases, such as the inclusion of

business purchases of software in capital spending, the entire concept of the term is changed.

- *Restatement of profits or other company information.* To a certain extent, some of this is due to mergers, acquisitions, or divestitures, but the main problem is retroactive writedowns.
- *Fraud.* In the international arena, intentional fraud may occur when the government wants to make the country's output appear better than was actually the case (primarily, but far from exclusively, the case in former communist regimes).
- *Defects in survey method or obsolete surveys.* For example, the CPI weights could be based on the market basket consumers bought almost a decade ago rather than what they buy today. If one is focusing primarily on the prices of apples and oranges, it probably doesn't matter. If the area of interest is CD-ROMs and Internet access, it probably does.
- *Lack of understanding of how to collect the underlying data.* This is probably more often the case for LDCs, although occasionally a new series even for the US will have to be completely revised when the underlying process is understood more thoroughly.
- *Changes in growth patterns due to rebasing.* In most cases, the growth rate will be reduced by moving to a more recent base year. However, in the case of computers, where the deflator declines, the opposite is true.
- *Seasonal data.* Seasonal patterns do change over time, but no method of adjusting for seasonal data is perfect, and sometimes these methods distort the underlying data. Also, when seasonal factors are revised, monthly or quarterly changes are often far different in the revised data.
- *Reclassifications.* Reclassification of companies from one industry to another often distorts industry data. This is particularly severe in the case of conglomerates, where small percentage change may shift the entire company from industry A to industry B.
- *Consumer misreporting.* For individual consumer data, individual income, assets, spending patterns, or saving might be misstated or misreported. In particular, people might understate their income because some of it was not reported to the Inland Revenue.

There are no "textbook" answers about how to determine whether the desired data series are reliable, and no exhaustive list that will include all possible data deficiencies. The above list, however, covers most of the areas where data problems occur.

4.5 USES AND MISUSES OF DUMMY VARIABLES

In general, a dummy variable takes a value of 1 during designated periods and 0 elsewhere. For a series with constant seasonal factors, the seasonal dummies for quarterly data are 1 in the ith month or quarter and 0 otherwise. Sometimes, however, dummy variables either take on a variety of values, or they are combined with other terms. Thus in addition to seasonal dummies, one can distinguish among the following principal types of dummy variables. Examples are provided for each of these cases.[5]

- single or isolated event changes: wars, energy crises, strikes, weather aberrations
- changes in institutional structure: floating of the dollar, deregulation of the banking sector
- changes in slope coefficients: variable becomes more or less important over time
- nonlinear effects: big changes are proportionately more important than small changes
- ceilings and floors: economic variables have a larger impact above or below a certain level.

As already noted, it is a simple matter to boost the sample-period goodness-of-fit statistics with dummy variables without improving forecasting accuracy. This section considers some of the economic issues.

Dummy variables are often properly introduced to reflect institutional changes: deregulation of a particular sector or industry. Compare, for example, the behavior of the airline, trucking, banking, or stock market sectors before and after deregulation.

Another type of far-reaching change could occur because of changed expectations. For example, when the Fed did not have a credible monetary policy, declines in the unemployment rate were widely thought to presage higher inflation. However, once credibility was reestablished, the tradeoff between unemployment and inflation disappeared.

Company data for sales, orders, profits, etc., would obviously change if the company acquired another entity, or divested some of its divisions. For accounting and investment purposes, earnings per share can be restated so they are comparable, but any time-series data for total sales would show major shifts.

In terms of econometric application, one of the primary issues is whether the dummy variable should be applied to the constant term of the equation, to some of the slope coefficients, or possibly to the entire equation. In the latter case, the same functional form can be reestimated for two or more subperiods.

It was already shown in the previous section that erroneous data can, under extreme circumstances, seriously distort the parameter estimates. That case was exaggerated to emphasize the point, which is that the significant criterion is whether the dummy variable is correlated with the other independent variables. If the outlier is due to a truly random event, then omitting a dummy variable will reduce the sample period fit but leave the parameter estimates unchanged. However, if the dummy variable is correlated with the other independent variables, then omitting it will bias the other coefficients.

---

[5]   For further discussion see Pindyck and Rubinfeld, pp. 122–5; and Johnston and DiNardo, pp. 133–9.

4.5.1 SINGLE-EVENT DUMMY VARIABLES

Consider the case of an auto strike. Consumers buy fewer cars because they realize there will be fewer choices in the showroom, so they may not be able to find their preferred make and model, and may also receive a smaller discount. If the strike is lengthy, that will not only affect the auto industry but the economy in general: disposable income will fall and, although striking workers are not counted as unemployed, the unemployment rate will rise as other workers are laid off. Without the use of a dummy variable for strikes, the coefficients for income and the unemployment rate would probably be overstated.

However, that is not the end of the story. The auto strike delayed sales, but it probably did not cancel them. The loss of sales during the strike period is generally made up in the following period. Thus the appropriate value of the dummy variable would be −1 during the strike and +1 in the next period. In other industries, such as the steel industry, if the strike were anticipated, the dummy variable might be +1 in the period before the strike and −1 during the strike. If the strike lasted longer than expected, the dummy variable might have the values +1, −2, and +1. Only if there were a permanent loss of sales would the values of the dummy variable sum to less than zero.

The same argument can be made for dock strikes: exports and imports both rise before the strike occurs, decline during that period, surge the next period, and then return to trend levels. In that case, the values of the dummy variable would also sum to zero over the period before, during, and after the strike.

In some cases, the sum of the values of the dummy variable might be greater than zero. Suppose a hurricane devastates coastal areas. In the period before the hurricane, construction is at normal levels. After the storm ends, construction expenditures rise sharply for a while. If the rebuilding phase lasts several periods but gradually tapers off, the dummy variable might take the values 4, 3, 2, and 1 in the four periods following the storm. On balance, though, construction activity over the entire period will be higher than if no storm had occurred.

Sometimes the interaction is more complicated. The Nixon Administration imposed a wage and price freeze on August 15, 1971, that lasted for 90 days. That was followed by Phase II of controls, lasting through the end of 1972, during which wages and prices could rise by only a certain percentage determined by the government. During Phase III, which started on January 1, 1973, prices could be raised only by the amount that costs increased. Controls were ended on May 1, 1974, at which point prices briefly rose by record amounts.

It might seem clear that a dummy variable that was negative during controls and then positive for a while would be appropriate. In some commodity price equations the dummy variable is important, as will be shown later. However, when the macroeconomic inflation rate is correlated as a function of labor costs, money supply, and oil prices, the residuals do not show any such pattern. A wide variety of dummy variables this author tried are not significant.

In this case the reason is not obvious. The inflation rate is, and should be, negatively correlated with productivity growth. During the period of controls, many firms had an incentive to understate the rise in prices and hence over-state the rise in output, since the current-dollar numbers could not be easily fudged. As a result, reported productivity growth soared to 3.5% during the period of controls and then declined to −1.6% when they were removed. It is quite unlikely that such a pattern actually occurred.

Yet both theory and empirical evidence suggest that productivity rises faster when inflation is lower, because capital goods are then purchased in order to earn their highest real rate of return, rather than being purchased as a hedge against inflation. Hence the strong negative correlation between productivity and inflation is theoretically as well as empirically robust. However, because of faulty data during that period, the correlation may be overstated. The use of a dummy variable should reduce that parameter estimate – if we had accurate data; but it is not available. In this particular example, a dummy variable is theoretically reasonable, but is not empirically significant.

This is perhaps an extreme example, but it illustrates how the use of dummy variables depends in large part on the correlation between the dummy variable and other independent variables. When they are correlated, it is good statisti-cal practice to include a dummy variable: in that case, when used within reason, it is not just merely curve fitting or ad hoc adjustment.

4.5.2 CHANGES IN DUMMY VARIABLES FOR INSTITUTIONAL STRUCTURE

Over the past 25 years or so the US economy has undergone many structural changes involving deregulation. One of the most important was the deregula-tion of the banking sector in the early 1980s. Before then, growth in the money supply (M2) closely followed changes in the monetary base – required reserves plus currency – which could be closely controlled by the Fed. Since then, there has been no correlation between percentage changes in the monetary base and M2. Thus in estimating an equation for the percentage changes in M2, it is best to multiply the percentage changes in the monetary base by DBR – a dummy variable for changes in banking regulations – which is 0 through 1980.3 and 0 afterward. A comparison of these two series shows that, starting in late 1980, money supply growth accelerated at the same time that the growth rate in the monetary base decreased.

After deregulation, changes in the money supply were more closely corre-lated to loan demand than to the monetary base, so the changes in business loans are multiplied by $(1 - DBR)$. Also, the spread between the Federal funds and the discount rate, while still a significant determinant of changes in the money supply, is much less important after 1980 than before, so that variable is also multiplied by *DBR*. After 1980 the term still has a negative sign but is only marginally significant. The dummy variable is also estimated as a separate term, otherwise there would be a discontinuity when the contribution of the monetary base dropped to zero.

The estimated equation is as follows. The first number after the symbol is the length of lag; most variables are four-quarter percentage changes. The number after the symbol in parentheses is the period when the lag starts.

$$\%M2, 4$$
$$= 2.86 + 0.991 * \%MBASE, 4 * DBR - 1.02 * (FFED(-1) - DISR(-1)) * DBR$$
$$\qquad (21.5) \qquad\qquad\qquad\qquad (7.0)$$
$$- 0.91 * DBR - 0.51 * \Delta INFL(-1), 4 - 0.16 * \Delta INFL(-5), 4$$
$$\quad (2.6) \qquad\quad (8.7) \qquad\qquad\qquad (3.2)$$
$$+ 0.152 * \%LOAN(-4), 12 * (1 - DBR)$$
$$\quad (17.3)$$

$$RSQ = 0.853; DW = 0.60.$$

$$(4.24)$$

In this equation *M2* is the money supply, *MBASE* is the monetary base, *FFED* and *DISR* are the Federal funds and discount rate, *INFL* is the rate of inflation, and *LOAN* is commercial and industrial loans.

4.5.3 CHANGES IN SLOPE COEFFICIENTS

Sometimes, variables become more or less important over the sample period because of changes in institutional structure. For example, before 1985, an increase in nominal income pushed many taxpayers into a higher tax bracket even if their real income did not rise. For that reason, Federal tax receipts were highly correlated with inflation. After 1985, however, the tax brackets were indexed, which means the upper end of each bracket increased by the percentage that the CPI rose the previous year. Nominal increases that were not accompanied by real increases no longer caused taxpayers to move into a higher bracket. Hence the equation for personal income tax receipts shows that inflation and wage rates are much more important before 1985 than afterwards. These terms are thus multiplied by a dummy variable that is 1 before 1985 and 0 afterward.

Another example might occur in situations where foreign trade has become an increasingly large proportion of total sales. In previous periods, changes in the value of the dollar would have relatively little impact on sales, but in recent years that variable has become increasingly important. In that case, the value of the dollar would be multiplied by a time trend.

4.6 NONLINEAR REGRESSIONS

So far we have avoided nonlinear regressions for a very simple reason. All the standard statistical tests discussed in this book are based on the assumption that the regressions are linear in the parameters. If they are not, these tests will not report the correct levels of significance. As a result, virtually all estimation procedures for econometric equations where nonlinear relationships may occur are based on linear approximations to nonlinear equations. This section discusses the most common methods of linearizing equations, which can be grouped into the following categories:

- log-linear
- quadratic and other powers, including inverse
- ceilings, floors, and Kronecker deltas
- piecewise linear.

4.6.1 LOG-LINEAR EQUATIONS

The most common case of an equation that is nonlinear in the variables is one that is linear in its logarithms. As already noted, logarithms would be appropriate if the elasticities were constant throughout the range of the independent variables. This assumption is often made in the case of demand and supply functions. Two standard cases are considered: the demand for gasoline by consumers, and the aggregate production function.

Consumer demand for gasoline is identically equal to the number of registered motor vehicles times the amount each vehicle is driven each year times the average fuel economy per vehicle (miles/gallon). This relationship can be written as:

$$CGAS \equiv \text{number of vehicles} * \text{miles}/\text{year} \div \text{fuel economy}. \qquad (4.25)$$

In the short run, an increase in the price of gasoline might result in fewer miles driven per year, whereas in the long run it might result in the purchase of more fuel-efficient motor vehicles. Also, a rise in the price of gasoline would reduce real disposable income, which might reduce the demand for new motor vehicles, although any such relationship would be captured by the income term.

Elsewhere in this text an equation is presented to explain the purchase of new motor vehicles. That is obviously not the same as the total number of vehicles on the road, which is a function of long-term trends in income and demographics and can be represented by those variables. The number of miles driven per year is a function of income and *short-term* changes in the relative price of gasoline, while average fuel economy depends on *long-term* changes in the relative price of gasoline.

First we show that real consumption of gasoline can be explained by the number of motor vehicles and average miles per gallon (MPG); the number of miles/year turns out not to be significant. *MPG* is then a function of a 12-year lag on the relative price of gasoline, reflecting the fact that most changes occur when consumers save by buying more fuel-efficient cars, not by reducing the number of miles traveled.

Consumption of gasoline in constant prices is thus a function of the number of motor vehicles registered and a 12-year average of the relative price of gasoline; the form used is PDL (12,3,2). Because of significant positive autocorrelation, the function is reestimated with an AR(1) term. The same equation is then estimated in logarithmic terms, both with and without an AR(1) term. Finally, these equations are compared with a percentage change equation using the same terms and lag structure.

All these functions look about the same in terms of goodness-of-fit statistics and patterns of residuals, but the elasticity estimates are significantly different. The price elasticities for gasoline in each form of the equation are:

Levels, no AR	−0.24
Levels with AR(1)	−0.42
Logs, no AR	−0.26
Logs with AR(1)	−0.39
Percentage change	−0.39

The equations in levels and logs yield about the same estimates of the elasticity without the AR term, but they are both much lower than with the AR term. The latter appears to be more accurate, since that is also the value obtained when percentage changes are used and autocorrelation is not present. The long-term price elasticity of gasoline for consumer use is thus estimated to be −0.4. Note that in this case, the choice of levels or logs makes little difference, but adjusting the equation for autocorrelation makes quite a bit of difference.

The next equation considered is a macroeconomic production function: constant-dollar GDP is a function of labor input, capital input, and the growth in technology, which is usually represented with a time trend. Such functions have been standard ever since the concept was introduced by C. W. Cobb and Paul Douglas in 1928.[6] The theoretical development assumes that a given percentage change in both labor and capital inputs causes in the same percentage change in output, which means the equation is linear in the logarithms. In this case all variables have strong trends, so the issue of mixing variables with and without trends does not arise.

---

[6] Cobb., C. W., and P. H. Douglas, "A Theory of Production," *American Economic Review*, 18 (1928), 139–65; and Douglas, P. H., "Are There Laws of Production?" *American Economic Review*, 38 (1948), 1–41.

According to the national income statistics, labor income accounts for about two-thirds of GDP and capital income for about one-third, so those ought to be the coefficients in the logarithmic equation. In fact the equation is

$$\log GDP = -0.60 + 0.626 * \log L + 0.411 * \log K(-1) + 0.0066 * t$$
$$(4.9) \qquad\qquad (4.6) \qquad\qquad (2.1)$$
$$RSQ = 0.998; \ DW = 0.48. \qquad\qquad\qquad (4.26)$$

The linear equation is far inferior; the results are

$$GDP = -1491 + 0.0384 * L + 66.37 * K(-1) - 50.65 * t$$
$$(3.0) \qquad (5.0) \qquad\qquad (4.8)$$
$$RSQ = 0.996; \ DW = 0.25. \qquad\qquad\qquad (4.27)$$

In both these equations, GDP is in constant dollars, L is non-farm payroll employment, and K is capital stock.

The results from the levels equation are considered far inferior because if the elasticities are calculated at the mean, the elasticity for labor is 0.70, which is quite reasonable, but the elasticity for the capital stock is 0.96. Also, the time trend has the wrong sign. In this case, the log equation is clearly superior.

However, the log estimates also leave something to be desired. The coefficient of the time trend is only 0.0066, implying an average annual advance in technology of 0.66%; the figure is usually estimated to be between 1% and 1½%. Also, the very low DW statistic can be worrisome; that led to an incorrect estimate of price elasticity in the consumption of gasoline equation.

Since the variable on the left-hand side is actual as opposed to potential GDP, the variables on the right-hand side of the equation ought to be utilized labor, which is employment times hours worked, and utilized capital stock, which is total capital stock times capacity utilization. If these variables are substituted, the results are

$$\log GDP = -4.27 + 0.667 * \log LH + 0.268 * \log KU + 0.0129 * t$$
$$(5.6) \qquad\qquad (5.4) \qquad\qquad (6.1)$$
$$RSQ = 0.998; \ DW = 1.10 \qquad\qquad\qquad (4.28)$$

and

$$GDP = -3336 + 0.00257 * LH + 0.1252 * KU - 12.61 * t$$
$$(8.0) \qquad\qquad (1.2) \qquad\qquad (1.3)$$
$$RSQ = 0.995; \ DW = 0.47 \qquad\qquad\qquad (4.29)$$

where LH is employment times hours worked per week and KU is capital stock times the rate of capacity utilization in the manufacturing sector.

The results are substantially improved in the log equation. The coefficient of the labor term is exactly 2/3, and the coefficient of the capital stock term is not significantly different from 1/3, although it is a little low. The coefficient of the time trend is equivalent to 1.3% per year, almost precisely in the middle of the 1% to 1½% range calculated by economists who measure productivity separately. The levels equation has not improved at all, and the time trend still has the wrong sign. In this case, using a logarithmic function clearly improves the results.

4.6.2 QUADRATIC AND OTHER POWERS, INCLUDING INVERSE

We referred briefly to the concept that including variables with strong trends and no trends in the same equation may lead to forecasting errors. By the same token, estimating an equation in which Y is a function of both X and X^2 is also likely to lead to additional forecasting errors. If Y and X are linearly related, the use of X^2, while it may improve the sample period fit, will almost always increase forecast error as that variable continues to grow more rapidly. Hence terms with powers different from unity should generally be used with trendless series. That usually means using actual or percentage first differences to powers other than unity, including the inverse of the variable. Here too one must utilize a certain degree of caution; squaring the first difference of series that contained both positive and negative numbers would result in all positive numbers, which presumably is not what is desired.

From an economic perspective, one likely use of nonlinear powers would occur in circumstances where big changes are proportionately more important than small changes. If the price of newsprint rises 5%, publishers may grumble about it but they are not likely to make any changes. However, if the price were to rise 50% they might invest in new technology that would make newspaper pages thinner. If an employee receives a 3% wage hike in real terms, he is not likely to change his lifestyle and buy a more expensive home, but if he receives a 100% increase because of a promotion or a new job, a move is much likelier.

An example can also be drawn from the agricultural sector. In most years, the price of soybeans is closely related to the price of corn and the price of livestock. However, in years when shortages are likely to occur, prices rise much more rapidly. Hence the price is related to the inverse of soybean stocks. This variable is also multiplied by @SEAS(6), a dummy variable that is 1 in June and 0 elsewhere, because that is the month when prices rise the most during years when shortages are likely. That variable is highly significant, whereas the reader may verify that the same term is insignificant in a linearized version of the same equation. In this equation, SOYSTOCK is the stock of soybeans, MOVAV stands for moving average, and all other variables are prices received by farmers:

SOYBEAN PRICES

$$= -0.017 + 1.901 * CORN\ PRICES + 0.852 * LIVESTOCK\ PRICES$$

$$(13.5) \qquad\qquad\qquad (3.4)$$

$$+ 37.1 * @\ SEAS(6)/@\ MOVAV(SOYSTOCK(-1),12) + 0.921 * AR(1)$$

$$(4.1) \qquad\qquad\qquad\qquad\qquad\qquad (42.0)$$

$$RSQ = 0.933;\ DW = 1.80 \qquad\qquad\qquad (4.30)$$

4.6.3 CEILING, FLOORS, AND KRONECKER DELTAS: LINEARIZING WITH DUMMY VARIABLES

In this type of formulation, a variable has little or no effect up to a certain level, then the relationship becomes increasingly important. For example, suppose a firm has excess capacity. If sales increase, initially there will be no need to expand. After a while, though, further increases in sales would result in more net capital spending. Suppose that a capacity utilization rate of 80% represents an average crossover point for the overall economy. Then we could write

$$I_{net} = b * \delta\ (CP - 80),$$
where CP is the rate of capacity utilization, and δ has a value of 1 when $CP >$ 80 and 0 otherwise. Such a term is known as a Kronecker delta.

This formulation works quite well when used to explain purchases of industrial equipment. The two independent variables are the Aaa corporate bond rate, lagged 1–5 years, and the rate of capacity utilization in the Kronecker delta form, lagged from 2 to 10 years. The reader can verify that using the overall rate of capacity utilization without the dummy variable provides substantially inferior results (*SE* of 0.00089 compared with 0.00069). The fit of the equation is shown in figure 4.1. The equation, estimated with annual data from 1959 through 1999, is

$$INDEQP/GDP$$

$$= 0.0174 - 0.000621 * RAAA(-1) + 0.000166 * DCU80$$

$$(7.6) \qquad\qquad\qquad (3.3)$$

$$+ 0.000483 * DCU80(-1) + 0.00067 * LAGDCU80$$

$$(9.5) \qquad\qquad\qquad (10.1)$$

$$RSQ = 0.931;\ DW = 1.02 \qquad\qquad (4.31)$$

Where *INDEQP* is purchases of industrial equipment in constant dollars, *RAAA* is the real Aaa corporate bond rate (nominal rate minus inflation rate) lagged 1 to 5 years, $DCU80 = \delta(CP - 80)$ as described above, and *LAGDCU80* is a PDL starting with lag 2, extending back for eight more years, set to 0 at each end.

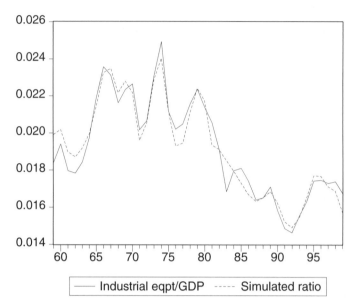

Figure 4.1 Ratio of purchases of industrial equipment to GDP, both in constant dollars, as a function of the Aaa bond rate and lagged rate of capacity utilization when over 80% (term is zero otherwise).

Microeconomics theory suggests that diminishing marginal returns results in rising costs and prices in the short run when the rate of capacity utilization rises above normal levels. That formulation would imply the use of a Kronecker delta in the equation for the producer price index. However, the term is not highly significant, suggesting that in most cases firms raise prices when costs increase but do not boost margins when capacity utilization rates are high. The equation is

$$\%PPI$$
$$= 0.30 + 0.110 * \%POIL + 4.36 * DWP - 0.100 * RFED(-2), 4$$
$$(17.6) \qquad\qquad (10.0) \qquad\qquad (4.3)$$
$$+ 0.166 * \%ULC, 4 + 0.086 * DCU80(-1), 2$$
$$(10.1) \qquad\qquad (2.8)$$
$$RSQ = 0.852; DW = 1.36$$

$$(4.32)$$

in which *PPI* is the producer price index for industrial commodities, *POIL* is the *PPI* for oil prices, *DWP* is a dummy variable for wage and price controls during the Nixon Administration, *RFED* is the real Federal funds rate, *ULC* is unit labor costs, and *DCU80* is the Kronecker dummy variable described above.

4.7 GENERAL STEPS FOR FORMULATING A MULTIVARIATE REGRESSION EQUATION

We have now covered some of the most common pitfalls found in estimating single-equation time-series structural forecasting models; chapter 5 presents the most common tests of structural stability, Part III examines time-series regressions – i.e., non-structural models – and Part IV covers a variety of fore-casting models. Hence this is an appropriate point to summarize the key rules to keep in mind when building single-equation structural forecasting models. The following general checklist indicates the usual steps that should be followed.

Step 1
Determine the underlying economic theory.

Step 2
Collect data and check for possible glitches in the data, sudden shifts in patterns, or outliers that need further explanation. Always plot the data series before actually calculating any regressions.

Step 3
Determine the lag structure. Often this will not be known in advance, but there should be some apriori structure to use as a starting point.

Step 4
Estimate the first pass at the regression. Most of the time, the results will be disappointing. Some variables will have the wrong sign and others will be insignificant. The residuals are likely to exhibit autocorrelation or het-eroscedasticity. For all these reasons, further refinements are necessary. But it is useful at this juncture to consider whether the insignificant variables and wrong signs occurred because:

(a)   the wrong theory was chosen
(b)   empirical choice of theoretical variable is wrong
(c)   lag structure is wrong.

It is always possible that (a) will turn out to be the answer, but before testing an alternative theory, (b) and (c) should be examined thoroughly. Search for other variables that will more closely represent the concept you are trying to measure. For example, someone might be trying to measure expected changes in, say, prices or interest rates. Since future events cannot be used in regression equations, try to figure out what past events best represent people's expectations of the future. It is not unreasonable to attempt several different formulations when trying to determine this.

Since theory does not indicate the precise form of the lag structure, it is appropriate to experiment with several different lag structures. However, it is generally inadvisable to use lags of 1, 2, 3 . . . , 10 in the same regression, because high multicollinearity will generally cause alternating signs. Some judgment is required. That is where PDLs can be useful.

Step 5
Virtually everyone who runs regressions compares their results by looking at R^2, including this author. Yet as noted previously, there is no point in improving the fit only to end up with the wrong signs or distorted coefficients, as well as all the other pitfalls listed above.

Step 6
If the variables seem to be measuring a common trend, consider other forms of the equation, such as percentage first differences, and see whether the results are consistent. That is particularly useful in time series with strong trends.

Step 7
Look at the residuals, and try to correlate them with some other variables or lag structures that haven't yet been tried; this can be done by graphing the residuals and the additional variable under consideration. Repeat the experiment until, at a minimum, all the variables are significant, the coefficients have the right sign, and the elasticities are reasonable.

Further steps
At this point, the researcher might think most of the work is done. Actually, for those building forecasting models, it is just starting. The estimated equation should now be put through a battery of tests designed to determine whether the goodness-of-fit statistics are really as high as the equation says, whether the coefficients are stable or unstable, whether they are biased or not, and whether this equation is likely to generate accurate forecasts. We will turn to these tests after looking at two case studies where distributed lags play an important role: the consumption function with quarterly data, and capital spending.

Case Study 5: The Consumption Function

Earlier in this chapter I discussed estimating the bivariate relationship between consumption and income in several different forms: levels, logs, first differences, and percentage changes. This case study shows what happens when the consumption/saving function is expanded to include monetary variables, expectational variables – inflation and unemployment – and other key economic variables, and examines how these variables change when the form of the equation varies.

According to the modern theory of the consumption function, consumption depends on some measure of average or expected income, not just current income. Expected income could be measured by some weighted average of past income, but variables representing consumer wealth – home prices and stock values – also measure expected income. Interest rates are an important determinant of consumption not so much because the cost of borrowing is important, but because lower interest rates also mean greater credit availability and the increased ability to refinance home mortgages at lower rates.

Attitudinal variables, such as the rate of inflation and the rate of unemployment, are also important; these are sometimes subsumed in an index of consumer attitudes, which is then entered as a separate variable. This approach is not used here because, as discussed later in this text, the fluctuations in consumer attitudes that are not related to inflation, unemployment, and stock prices do not appear to be correlated with consumer spending.

Hence the theoretical function says consumption is a function of current and lagged income, the Aaa corporate bond rate, the S&P 500 index of stock prices, the unemployment rate, the change in oil prices, and the relative price of homes. Given that function, we now consider the lag structure for each of these variables.

Since the changes in unemployment and inflation are expectational variables that affect the timing rather than the overall level of purchases, those lags should be relatively short. On the other hand, based on theoretical considerations, the lags for income, bond yield, stock prices, and home prices might be substantial. The first pass, then, is to use PDLs of 12 quarters, cubic polynomials, and constrained at the far end; 12,3,2 in the EViews formula.

However, these results are not useful. In particular, except for income, all the signs quickly reverse as the lags increase. Further experimentation, which the user may try, shows that even as the lag structure is shortened, the signs flip-flop. In the end, the optimal structure for the bond yield, stock price index, and relative price of homes has only a one-quarter lag. Even the coefficients of the income term drop off quickly, although they then recover with a longer lag. This indicates different lag structures for durable goods and services.

Having established a long lag on income and shorter lags on all other variables, we next consider whether these results are tainted by multicollinearity by using the battery of alternative formulations developed in this chapter: OLS, WLS, logs, percentage change, ratio, and deviations from logarithmic trends. Since this methodology has already been described in some detail earlier in this chapter, only the summary t-statistics are presented here (see table 4.3).

All equations except the one using percentage changes are adjusted with the AR(1) transformation. WLS is not listed since that is not applicable with the AR(1) transformation; without that adjustment, OLS and WLS were similar in all respects. In the ratio equation, the dependent variable is the ratio of consumption divided by disposable income; in that equation, the percentage change in income correctly has a negative sign, reflecting the fact that consumption adjusts to income with a lag.

These results are fairly instructive. Starting with the levels function, one could readily draw the conclusion that the stock market variable is much more important than the relative home price variable. That is also the case for the ratio function. In the logarithmic function, relative home prices are barely significant. In the percentage change equation, random changes overwhelm the

Table 4.3 Results for case study 5.

Form of equation	Income	t-ratios for:				
		Bond yield	Stock prices	Change in unemployment	Inflation	Relative home prices
Levels – OLS	68.6	−3.5	7.1	−2.5	−2.8	2.2
Logs	44.2	−8.4	3.4	−3.0	−2.4	1.8
Percentage change	4.5	−2.9	2.2	−3.7	−2.3	1.2
Ratio	−6.5[a]	−4.3	6.1	−1.2	−4.9	3.7
Deviation from trend	18.0	−2.3	2.5	−2.8	−2.3	3.1

[a] Percentage change in income over four quarters.

underlying function, and here too home prices are not significant. That might be expected because this is a longer-term effect. However, increasing the length of lag in the percentage change equation does not improve the fit, and the t-ratio for the change in stock prices turns negative.

In the deviations-from-trend equation, the results change significantly. While stock prices are still significant, the t-ratio drops sharply, and the importance of relative home prices improves sharply. An examination of the residuals from the levels and deviations-from-trend equations shows that, while both fail to track the negative impact of the first oil shock on consumption, the deviation-from-trend equation fits much better in the 1980s and 1990s. To the extent that future oil shocks are much less likely to disrupt consumer purchasing patterns, the deviations-from-trend equation appears to be the best forecasting equation.

This example shows that, while one could reasonably theorize that consumer spending patterns are based on long lags, that does not turn out to be the case empirically. That finding by itself does not invalidate the theory that long-run average or expected income is more important than current income as a determinant of consumption. Instead, it highlights several other results. First, the timing of many consumer purchases is dictated by the availability of credit. Second, expected income is more closely related to variables such as current stock prices and relative home prices than it is to lagged changes in real disposable income. As a result, long distributed lags do not work well in this equation. We will reexamine the forecasting efficacy of various consumption functions, with and without attitudinal variables, later in this text.

This case study also suggests that, while polynomial distributed lags are often useful, if they don't work, don't force them into the equation. In the case of functions for capital spending and the Federal funds rate (also bond yields), long lags are indeed important determinants. In the case of consumer spending, though, the lags are much shorter and, at least for discretionary purchases, the use of PDLs is inadvisable for building accurate forecasting equations.

Case Study 6: Capital Spending

Standard microeconomic theory states that, in equilibrium, the marginal product of labor is equal to the wage rate, and the marginal product of capital is equal to the cost of capital. However, whereas the wage rate is unambiguously defined in terms of dollars per hour, the cost of capital has a time dimension, since capital goods generally last for many years. In addition to the price of the capital good, one must also take into consideration the rate of interest, the cost of equity capital (stock prices), the rate of depreciation, and tax laws designed to affect capital spending – the accounting rate of depreciation and the rate of investment tax credit – as well as the corporate income tax rate. Also, the value of the marginal product of capital depends on the price of the product relative to the price of the capital good.

If the firm is operating on the constant part of its cost curve, the marginal product of capital is proportional to the average product of capital, which is output divided by capital stock. Under this assumption, then, optimal capital stock would be positively related to output and negatively related to the various components of the cost of capital.

This theory must be modified for several reasons. First, unlike labor, capital is "lumpy"; one cannot purchase half of a machine or a third of a building. Second, it takes time to fabricate a new machine or building. Third, firms may sometimes have excess capacity: thus even if output increases or the cost of capital declines, firms may not purchase new plant and equipment because the existing stock is adequate. Fourth, all the discussion so far has related to net investment; firms may replace existing plant and equipment as it wears out even if output has not increased.

These modifications make it difficult to estimate investment functions empirically. An additional complication, which is directly germane to the discussion in this chapter, is that the lag structures may differ for each of the variables. That is why PDLs are used to determine the lag structure. It is also possible that because of strong common trends, problems of multicollinearity will occur, which suggests using one of the methods of trend removal.

Differing lag structures may occur for each of the independent variables: GDP minus capital equipment, stock prices, the real Aaa bond rate, the effect of tax laws on investment, the price of capital equipment relative to the GDP deflator, and the relative price of oil. The latter term is included separately because the energy industry is more capital intensive than the rest of the economy, so when relative oil prices rise, the ratio of capital spending to GDP increases. That happened in both the late 1970s and the first half of the 1980s; when oil prices then fell, the ratio of capital spending to GDP dropped for several years.

At first one might expect the lag structure for all the terms to be about the same, since firms take both output and the cost of capital into consideration when determining their capital spending plans. However, that is not the case. The lags are much shorter for output than the cost of capital. There are several reasons for this that are beyond the scope of this discussion, but the overall argument can be summarized as follows. Consider two capital goods: one has a useful life of three years (personal computers, motor vehicles) and the other has a useful life of 20 years (electrical generating equipment, jet aircraft). The longer the economic life of the good, the more important the cost of capital becomes. A similar analogy can be drawn for consumers: the interest rate is much more important when buying a house than when buying a computer. Since a computer has a relatively short life, its purchase decision will be based primarily on the recent level of output. Thus the function for capital equipment can be viewed as a bifurcated model containing both the demand for both short-lived equipment, where output with a short lag is important, and long-lived equipment, where the cost of capital with a long lag is important.

That is indeed what we find, but one more adjustment must be made. During its lifetime, the investment tax credit was often used as a short-term policy variable to stimulate or reduce purchases of capital equipment: it was introduced in 1962, raised in 1964, suspended in 1966, reinstated in 1967, suspended in 1969, reinstated in 1971, raised in 1975, expanded in 1981, and modified in 1982 before being terminated in 1986. Depreciation allowances were also changed almost as frequently. That component of the user cost term has a shorter lag because it tended to affect the timing rather than the magnitude of capital spending.

Finally, note that the stock market variable serves a dual purpose. It is important with a short lag because it serves as a proxy for expected output. It is also important with a longer lag because it measures the equity cost of capital. As a result, the weights are quite high, then decline almost to zero, then rise again.

The levels function is given below. Including all of the individual terms for each of the PDLs would creates a listing of 63 separate terms, as given in the EViews program. That can be confusing for those not already familiar with equations containing PDLs. Hence the output is presented in summary form. The equation below presents the summary statistics for each of the independent variables; the sum of the coefficients and its standard error is given for each term estimated with PDLs. Figure 4.2 illustrates the lag structure for each of those variables.

PDE

$$= 505.6 - 291.0 * RPCG(-1) - 0.046 * KSTOCK(-4) + 0.128 * GDPXINV$$

$$(13.8) \qquad\qquad (10.6) \qquad\qquad (12.4)$$

$$+ 0.556 * SP500 - 102.8 * RCCE(-3) - 27.1 * RAAA(-3) + 69.4 * RPOIL(-8)$$

$$(29.2) \qquad\qquad (1.7) \qquad\qquad (19.8) \qquad\qquad (8.9)$$

$$RSQ = 0.9984; \ SE = 6.65; \ DW = 0.92.$$

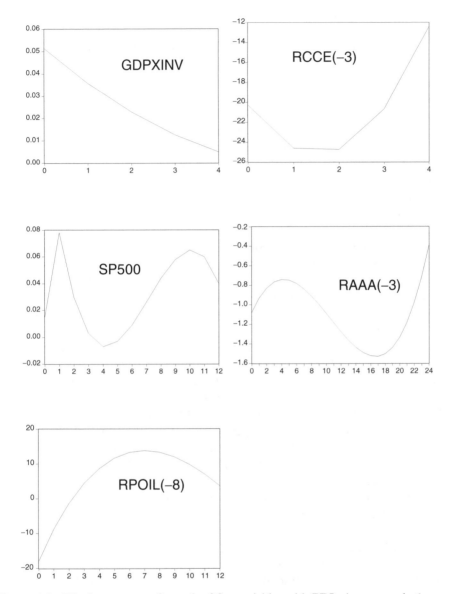

Figure 4.2   The lag structure for each of five variables with PDLs in case study 6.

In this equation, the dependent variable *PDE* is constant-dollar purchases of capital equipment. *RPCG* is the relative price of capital goods, *KSTOCK* is the capital stock of equipment, *GDPXINV* is real GDP excluding capital equipment, *SP500* is the S&P 500 index of stock prices, *RCCE* is the rental cost of capital for equipment, *RAAA* is the real Aaa corporate bond rate, and *RPOIL* is the relative price of oil.

This may appear to be a bewildering variety of lag structures. Some decrease monotonically; some start negative and turn positive; some decline and then recover; and some have two peaks. How does the researcher decide which lag structure is optimal?

The use of PDLs is more an art than a science. However, I offer the following general guidelines for determining the lag structure.

First, make an informed guess about the approximate length of the lag structure; if the guess turns out to be inaccurate, it probably won't affect the final result, but it will take more time. Since we know that capital spending decisions are based on information from several years, a reasonable starting point might be 3–4 years (12–16 quarters).

The default option for PDLs is usually a cubic polynomial constrained at the far end, which means that beyond the maximum length of lag specified, the coefficients are assumed to be zero. The value of the coefficients can also be constrained to zero at the near end of the lag structure, but that option is not generally used as an initial estimate. In EViews, the code for variable R (say) with this lag structure would be written as PDL(R, 12,3,2). R might be a level or percentage change, and it might also start with a lag. To estimate the percentage change of R starting with a three-quarter lag, the EViews code would be PDL(@PCH($R(-3)$),12,3,2).

Usually, the initial result will not be satisfactory. Some of the terms in the lag distribution will be insignificant, and some will have the wrong signs. In some cases, the cubic term may not be significant, so a quadratic equation would be sufficient (saving one degree of freedom).

In general, if the individual terms in the PDL equation have a t-ratio of less than 2, it is best to shorten the lag structure until all remaining terms satisfy this criterion. If the terms at the end of the lag distribution appear to be highly significant, it is reasonable to lengthen the lag structure as long as the terms remain significant.

Sometimes the terms will be close to zero at the beginning of the distribution. That suggests starting that variable with a longer lag. Occasionally it also suggests using the constraint of a zero value for the coefficients at the near end of the distribution.

Those are the "simple" cases. Sometimes, the variable will start out significant, then drop into insignificance or have the wrong sign, and then become significant again. In other cases, the variable will change sign, with significant values that are both positive and negative. Should these results be kept or discarded?

Sometimes results of this sort are statistical flukes and should be discarded. Other times, however, they make economic sense. I have included one example of each type in the investment function. The coefficients of the stock market variable are highly significant, then drop off, then rise again because of the dual function of this variable. When the coefficients do turn negative, the t-ratios of those negative terms are less than 1.0, meaning they are not at all significant, so the structure is kept intact.

The other unusual case is the value of the coefficients of the relative price of oil, which switch from negative to positive. Here the lag distribution can be justified by economic theory. When oil prices rise (say) the initial impact is to reduce real growth and profitability for most firms, hence cutting investment. Eventually, though, higher oil prices stimulate investment in the energy industry, so the positive impact outweighs the negative effect.

The use of PDLs is not recommended unless the lag structure is thought to be fairly long and complex; for example, if the weights were thought to decline monotonically, that assumption could be entered into the regression without using a PDL. In the case of the investment function, it is difficult to estimate an equation that generates accurate predictions without using PDLs.

A few other comments on this equation seem appropriate at this point. Specifically, in spite of the apparently high R^2, which is fairly typical for time series with strong trends, we note that the $RCCE(-3)$ term has a t-ratio of only 1.66; also, the DW is an uncomfortably low 0.92. Both these points are addressed below.

It would be tedious to repeat all this information for all six forms of the equation enumerated above; the interested reader may estimate these equations separately. The results are briefly summarized. In the logarithm equation, the $RCCE$ term is much more significant (t-ratio of 6.1) but the $SP500$ term drops out completely. The percentage change equation is dominated by random fluctuations and hence is of relatively little use; the capital stock, $RCCE$, $RAAA$, and $RPOIL$ terms all drop out. Using the ratio of capital spending to GDP as the dependent variable restores the significance of all the variables, but the $SP500$ term is now only significant with a short lag. All the terms are significant in the deviations-from-trend equation, and the $RPOIL$ term almost drops out. Finally, switching to weighted least squares hardly changes the results relative to the levels equation.

Except for the percentage change equation, where almost all the terms drop out, the Durbin–Watson statistic indicates substantial autocorrelation. When the AR(1) adjustment is used, most of the terms are little changed except for the relative price of oil, which becomes insignificant. This raises the question of whether it should be dropped from the final form of the equation.

It is not immediately obvious from these comments which one of the five forms of the equation will generate the best forecast (since WLS hardly makes any difference, it is not considered further). The percentage change form can be ruled out because such a large proportion of the variance appears to be random fluctuations. The logarithm equation has too large a coefficient for capital stock and too small a coefficient for stock prices relative to a-priori expectations. The user cost of capital term is not significant in the levels equation, which does not seem to be a reasonable result. Hence the choice is between the ratio and the deviations-from-trend. Further experimentation reveals that when the ratio equation is "tidied up" to remove PDL coefficients that are insignificant or have the wrong lag, several other terms become insignificant, so the final choice is the deviation-from-trend equation. Since DW is quite low at 0.52, the equation was reestimated with AR(1); all the terms remained significant, including the relative price of oil.

This lengthy example is designed to indicate how one chooses an optimal forecasting equation. The result that was chosen – the deviations from logarithmic trends – is not always the preferred choice. I do emphasize, however, that in cases where most of the variables have strong trends, it does seem better to choose some equation where the trend has been removed. Other methods of trend removal are discussed in Part III.

Problems and Questions

1. Estimate an equation to predict non-residential construction, following the outline given for the equation for purchases of producer durable equipment. The independent variables are real GDP, an index of stock prices, the Aaa corporate bond rate, the user cost of capital for structures, the relative price of oil, and capital stock. The one additional variable is the amount of consumer credit outstanding, since many of these smaller buildings are financed through the same changes as consumer credit.

(a) Estimate this equation in levels, using PDLs to determine the optimal lag structure. Use quarterly data (all series are on the website).
(b) You will notice that *DW* is very low. Try changing this by (i) using four-quarter percentage changes, and (b) logarithmic deviations from trends. Report your results. Explain why you think these equations are better or worse than the levels equation.
(c) How do the lag structures for the principal variables compare with the lags in the equation for *PDE*? What factors do you think explain the difference?
(d) The Durbin–Watson statistic remains low. Use AR(1) to remove autocorrelation and comment on the results. Now rerun the regressions taking into account the *t*-ratios with AR(1) and report those results.
(e) Why do you think the regression results are so poor? What factors cause changes in non-residential construction to be so difficult to explain? (Hint: how could economic conditions change between the time the structure is started and the time it is completed?)

2. Consumer purchases of medical care services should be a function of the proportion of the population over 65, real disposable income, health-care transfer payments (Medicare and Medicaid in the US), and the relative price of health care services.

continued

(a) Using quarterly data, calculate a regression that includes these variables. Use PDLs where appropriate.

(b) What can you say about the sign of relative prices? Does that agree with a-priori theoretical expectations? What factors do you think account for the difference?

(c) One would expect that medical care services would depend on the permanent rather than actual level of income (rich people get better medical care than poor people, etc.). How would you test this hypothesis? Report your results.

(d) Reestimate the equation using logs, and deviations from trend. Do these results seem more sensible or not?

(e) In all cases, the *DW* statistics are extremely low. Yet using the AR(1) adjustment shows a coefficient for the *AR* term very close to unity, which means this is essentially a first-difference equation. When AR(1) is used, all the other terms generally become insignificant. The standard statistical explanation is that the series is composed of random changes. That might be the case for the stock market, but does it make any sense for medical care? If not, how would one estimate a useful equation for consumer purchases of medical care services for budget planning in the future?

3. In the short run, consumer purchases of gasoline have a very low price elasticity, since in most cases the trip will be taken even if gasoline prices rise. In the long run, however, consumers can choose to buy cars with greater fuel efficiency.

(a) Taking this fact into account, how would you use distributed lags to estimate the short-term and long-term price elasticities of consumer purchases of gasoline?

(b) Estimate an equation in which consumption of gasoline is a function of income and the current and lagged relative price of gasoline.

(c) Based on this lag structure, how long do you think it might take before a major shift in oil prices is followed by a decline in oil prices?

4. Most corporations that pay a dividend on their common stock do not like to raise that dividend unless they are highly confident it will not have to be reduced in the foreseeable future. Hence dividend payments would probably depend on lagged as well as after-tax profits.

(a) Estimate a quarterly function for dividends as function of profits, using PDLs with maximum lags of 8, 12, 16, 20, and 24 quarters.

continued

Based on these results, what can you say about using PDLs to estimate the actual lag structure?

(b) What does the low DW statistic tell you about the structural robustness of the equation?

(c) Now try expanding the equation using (i) the corporate bond yield and (ii) capital spending as additional independent variables. How does that improve the equation? Should you use PDLs on these additional variables, or not?

(d) Because the DW is still so low and R^2 is high, try reestimating the function using the percentage change in dividends as the dependent variable, and percentage changes in all the independent variables. What happens to the coefficients and their significance levels? What happens to R^2? Is the result a useful forecasting equation?

(e) What happens to the equation when you use lagged dividends as an independent variable? Do you think that improves the forecasting accuracy of the equation?

(f) Taking all these factors into account, what form of the equation would you use to predict dividends? Would it contain PDLs, or not?

5. Most companies advertise in order to generate repeat business; the cost of advertising for the first-time sale generally exceeds the profit.

(a) Assuming that accurate company data were available for sales and advertising expenditures, how would you design a distributed lag model to determine the optimal level of advertising?

(b) What other data would you need to estimate this function?

(c) How would your model differ if you were estimating the effect of advertising for a new dot.com startup, as opposed to an old-line personal care company?

CHAPTER 5

FORECASTING WITH A SINGLE-EQUATION REGRESSION MODEL

INTRODUCTION

Checking the structural stability of individual equations is one of the key steps in model building. Unfortunately, it is sometimes ignored, because the results are not so easy to fix. Autocorrelation, heteroscedasticity, or multicollinearity can generally be reduced by straightforward and relatively simple adjustments. However, if tests show that the equation is unstable, that often means starting all over again with a different specification.

It is often difficult to find a reasonable equation that meets all the statistical tests, including the stability of coefficients. Of course, even accomplishing this goal provides no guarantee that the forecasts will be accurate. However, if the equation is unstable, misspecified, or omits relevant variables, that almost guarantees the forecasts will not be accurate. Thus satisfying the tests discussed in this chapter is a necessary condition for successful forecasting, even though it is not sufficient.

We first discuss further tests for the residuals of the equation, checking for normality, autocorrelation, and heteroscedasticity, then turn to some of the methods that allow the researcher to check for the stability of the equation. These tests are then applied to a quarterly equation for new motor vehicles. An equation for housing starts is used to illustrate various alternative methods for adjusting the constant term. Finally, an equation for the dollar/yen crossrate is used to illustrate some of the pitfalls of multi-period forecasting.

5.1 CHECKING FOR NORMALLY DISTRIBUTED RESIDUALS

As noted in previous topics, the various goodness-of-fit statistics are valid only if the error term is normally distributed. Thus unless tests indicate this condition holds, the R^2 and t-statistics are likely to overstate the actual goodness of fit.

One of the useful characteristics of the normal distribution is that it is completely described by the mean and variance. However, that is not true for other distributions. Hence if the residuals are not normally distributed, higher-order moments, particularly skewness and kurtosis, might be significantly different from the normal distribution. That is the basis of the Jarque–Bera test, previously mentioned when histograms were discussed. To review briefly, that test statistic is given as:

$$JB = \frac{(T-k)}{6}\left[S^2 + \frac{(K-3)^2}{4} \right] \tag{5.1}$$

where S is skewness, K is kurtosis, T is the number of observations, and k is the number of variables.[1]

The probability and significance levels of JB are included in EViews, but it is usually obvious whether or not the residuals are normally distributed by looking at the histogram. If more than one outlier are three or more standard deviations from the mean, those observations are presumably not drawn from the same population as the rest of the sample period data. You have to decide whether that unusual situation is a one-time event that will not recur, in which case it probably will not affect the forecast, or whether it should be treated by adding another variable, using dummy variables, omitting the outliers, or including some nonlinear transformation.

Even if the residuals are normally distributed, that is only a starting point. In particular, the residuals could still be serially correlated, as is often the case for economic time series. Since this is one of the most common results for regressions estimated with time-series data, further tests are often warranted.

5.1.1 HIGHER-ORDER TESTS FOR AUTOCORRELATION

The model builder has presumably already checked the Durbin–Watson statistic and determined whether or not significant first-order serial correlation exists. If it does, the equation may be altered by adding further variables, reducing or removing the trend, or including the first-order autoregressive adjustment AR(1). Using the lagged dependent variable on the right-hand side of the

---

[1] Most of the tests discussed in this chapter are also discussed in the EViews manual, ch. 7. The test was originally presented in Jarque, C. M., and A. K. Bera, "Efficient Tests for Normality, Homoscedasticity, and Serial Independence of Regression Residuals," *Economic Letters*, 6 (1980), 255–9.

equation is not recommended if the equation is to be used for multi-period forecasting.

Having made these adjustments, the residuals are now examined again. The procedure here follows the tests in EViews; while not all tests are included in this program, most others are duplicative or overlapping and are not discussed here.

It is sometimes useful to test for higher-order autocorrelation, especially if one is using quarterly or monthly data (it is unlikely to arise for annual data). While the DW test is obviously a useful starting point, it (i) tests only for first-order autocorrelation, (ii) does not work if the lagged dependent variable is included in the equation, and (iii) requires a constant term. For this reason, residuals are often tested with the Ljung–Box Q-statistic,[2] which is

$$Q_{LB} = T^*(T+2) \sum_{j=1}^{p} r_j^2 \bigg/ (T - j) \qquad (5.2)$$

where r_j is the jth order autocorrelation and T is the number of observations.

The Ljung–Box Q-statistic is often used with correlogram analysis, which is also available in EViews and other programs. That analysis shows two different correlations. The first is the correlation of ε_t with ε_{t-k}, where you pick the maximum value of k. The other is the partial autocorrelation, which shows the partial correlation of each coefficient when ε_t is regressed on $\varepsilon_{t-1}, \varepsilon_{t-2}, \varepsilon_{t-3}, \ldots,$ ε_{t-k}.

Ordinarily one would expect the value of the coefficients estimated in this equation to follow a geometrically declining lag. However, this test will also alert users to seasonality in the residuals.

Note that EViews includes two tests involving the Q-statistic. The first is for the levels of the residuals; the second is for the squared values of the residuals. Most of the time, both tests will generate the same results. However, sometimes the levels test will not show any autocorrelation while the squared test does, in which case it is likely that heteroscedasticity is also present. That does not happen every time, but it is a hint to look further.

The Breusch–Godfrey[3] test is an alternative test for autocorrelation. This test involves estimating a regression where ε_t is regressed on $\varepsilon_{t-1}, \varepsilon_{t-2}, \varepsilon_{t-3}, \ldots, \varepsilon_{t-k}$. The F-statistic is then calculated for this regression in order to see whether it is significantly different from zero. This is a large-sample test; the small-sample properties of the distribution are not known.

[2] Ljung, G., and G. E. P. Box, "On a Measure of Lack of Fit in Time Series Models," *Biometrika*, 66 (1979), 265–70.
[3] Breusch, T. S., "Testing for Autocorrelation in Dynamic Linear Models," *Australian Economic Papers*, 17 (1978), 334–55; and Godfrey, L. G., "Testing Against General Autoregressive and Moving Average Error Models when the Regressors Include Lagged Dependent Variables," *Econometrica*, 46 (1978), 1293–302.

Breusch–Godfrey does allow the user to test whether there is any autocorrelation up to the lag limit specified in the test. The results are generally thought to be more accurate in situations where one uses the lagged dependent variable on the right-hand side of the equation. Since that method often leads to error buildup in multi-period forecasting, the Breusch–Godfrey test does not provide much additional information about improving multi-period forecast accuracy. It does, however, indicate that researchers may be fooling themselves if they think putting the lagged dependent variable on the right-hand side of the equation really eliminates autocorrelation.

5.1.2 TESTS FOR HETEROSCEDASTICITY

Tests for heteroscedasticity are considered next. The ARCH test is based strictly on the values of the residuals, while the White test is based on the entire equation and hence is more general.

As noted previously, heteroscedasticity usually arises from one of two causes. The first is that the average size of the residuals increases as the size of the dependent variable increases. The second is that a few outliers dominate the regression estimates.

The simplest test is to correlate the residuals with each other. The only decision is how many lags to include. If the researcher chooses three lags, for example, estimate the equation

$$\varepsilon_t^2 = \beta_0 + \beta_1 \varepsilon_{t-1}^2 + \beta_2 \varepsilon_{t-2}^2 + \beta_3 \varepsilon_{t-3}^2 + V_t \tag{5.3}$$

and test whether the F-statistic from this regression is significant. One can also test whether the individual t-statistics are significant. This is known as the ARCH LM (Autoregressive Conditional Heteroscedasticity, Lagrangian Multiplier) procedure and is due to R. F. Engle.[4]

Halbert White[5] has developed a test to determine whether heteroscedasticity is present in the residuals; it can also be used to determine whether the equation is misspecified. First, estimate the basic regression

$$Y_t = \beta_1 + \beta_2 X_t + \beta_3 Z_t + \varepsilon_t \tag{5.4}$$

and then calculate an auxiliary regression

$$\varepsilon_t^2 = \beta_1 + \beta_2 X_t + \beta_3 Z_t + \beta_4 X_t^2 + \beta_5 Z_t^2 + \beta_6 X_t Z_t + V_t \tag{5.5}$$

---

[4]   Engle, R. F., "Autoregressive Conditional Heteroscedasticity with Estimates of the Variance of United Kingdom Inflation," *Econometrica*, 50 (1982), 987–1008.

[5]   White, Halbert, "A Heteroscedasticity-Consistent Covariance Matrix Estimator and a Direct Test for Heteroscedasticity," *Econometrica*, 48 (1980), 817–38.

If β_4, β_5, or β_6 is significant, heteroscedasticity is present, or the terms may not be linear. If the number of variables becomes large, the cross-terms (e.g., β_6) can be suppressed.

The White test is a more general test than merely determining whether heteroscedasticity of the residuals is present. If none of the coefficients is significant, it also suggests – although it does not verify – that the linear specification is correct.

5.2 TESTING FOR EQUATION STABILITY AND ROBUSTNESS

In some cases, the residuals of the estimated equations will be normally distributed, with no autocorrelation and no heteroscedasticity, yet the equations themselves will generate poor forecasts. In many cases, this occurs because there has been a shift in the parameters of the underlying structural equation. In the worst possible case, the structure remained constant during the entire sample period but then radically shifted just as the forecast period started. There is no cure for that disease, and when it does happen, the forecasts will be inaccurate. However, that is a fairly unusual circumstance (although see case study 21 on page 346). Usually, any shift in the structure can be detected during the sample period. Under those circumstances, a battery of standard tests can be used to uncover this shift, permitting the model builder to adjust the forecasts accordingly.

5.2.1 CHOW TEST FOR EQUATION STABILITY

The Chow test[6] was one of the first regression diagnostic tests to be developed, and is still one of the most important. The idea is quite straightforward. Divide the sample period into two (or more) sub-periods. Calculate the regression during all of these periods, and then calculate the regression separately for individual sub-periods. The Chow test then compares the sum of the squared residuals obtained by fitting a single equation over the entire sample period with the residuals obtained by estimating separate equations over each sub-sample period. If the residuals are significantly different, the coefficients have probably shifted, which increases the probability the equation is unstable and the co-efficients will shift again in the forecast period, generating poor forecasts.

The Chow test measures the *F*-statistic of the difference between the total and sub-period squared residuals divided by the sum of the sub-period squared

---

[6] Chow, Gregory C., "Tests of Equality Between Sets of Coefficients in Two Linear Regressions," *Econometrica*, 52 (1960), 211–22.

residuals, adjusted for the number of observations and parameters. For the simplest case with two sub-periods, the F-test is given as

$$F = \frac{(\varepsilon^2 - (\varepsilon_1^2 + \varepsilon_2^2))/k}{(\varepsilon_1^2 + \varepsilon_2^2)/(T - 2k)} \tag{5.6}$$

where ε^2 is the sum of the squared residuals over the entire sample period, ε_1^2 and ε_2^2 are the sums of the squared residuals over the first and second subperiods respectively, k is the number of parameters in the equation, and T is the total number of observations.

Sometimes when the Chow test shows unstable coefficients, the shift is caused by a readily identifiable economic or institutional factor, some of which have already been mentioned. For example, before the dollar was free to float, it was not possible to calculate a price elasticity for imports or exports because the dollar didn't change. Hence the coefficient would be different after 1971. Before the first energy crisis, the price of energy didn't change very much. Before banking deregulation, there were ceilings on interest rates; afterwards, the equations for both money supply and credit, as well as the importance of interest rates in the equations for aggregate demand, were far different. When wage and price controls were imposed, the impact of changes in demand on wages and prices was different than during normal periods. There are many such examples that must be treated explicitly, some of which can be handled with dummy variables. In other cases, the sample period can be truncated if it is likely that these circumstances will never reoccur, and hence are not relevant for current forecasting.

5.2.2 RAMSEY RESET TEST TO DETECT MISSPECIFICATION

No mechanical test will ever turn a bad equation into a good one, just as in the stock market no mechanical method will ever make anyone rich or successful. On the other hand, various mechanical methods in the stock market can keep traders out of a certain amount of trouble, such as not buying a stock when it has just turned down after a long runup, insider selling is intensifying, the Fed is tightening, and profits are declining. To a certain extent, these mechanical tests merely quantify some of the more obvious errors that should have shown up simply by eyeballing the results.

Nonetheless, the Ramsey RESET test[7] can sometimes uncover errors that are not obvious by visual inspection. Indeed, Ramsey and Alexander[8] showed that

[7]   Ramsey, J. B., "Tests for Specification Errors in Classical Linear Least Squares Regression Analysis," *Journal of the Royal Statistical Society, Series B*, 31 (1969), 350–71.
[8]   Ramsey, J. B., and A. Alexander, "The Econometric Approach to Business-Cycle Analysis Reconsidered," *Journal of Macroeconomics*, 6 (1984), 347–56.

the RESET test could detect specification error in an equation that was known a priori to be misspecified, but nonetheless gave satisfactory values for all of the more traditional test criteria – goodness of fit, high t-ratios, correct coefficient signs, and test for first-order autocorrelation.

The RESET test is designed to check for the following types of errors:

- omitted variables
- nonlinear functional forms (i.e., variables should be logs, powers, reciprocals, etc.)
- simultaneous-equation bias
- incorrect use of lagged dependent variables.

The Ramsey is developed as follows. In the standard linear model

$$Y_t = \beta_1 + \beta_2 X_{1t} + \beta_3 X_{2t} + \ldots + \beta_k X_{kt} + \varepsilon_t \tag{5.7}$$

consider the vector $\hat{\mathbf{Y}}_t$, which consists of the values fitted by the above equation. Ramsey now proposes the creation of a vector $\mathbf{Z}$, defined as

$$\left[\hat{\mathbf{Y}}_t^2 \ \hat{\mathbf{Y}}_t^3 \ \hat{\mathbf{Y}}_t^4 \ldots \hat{\mathbf{Y}}_t^k \right] \tag{5.8}$$

where the value of k is chosen by the researcher, and suggests that the powers of $\hat{\mathbf{Y}}$ be included in the equation in addition to all the other X_i terms that are already in the regression. The idea is that the various powers of the fitted values will reveal whether misspecification exists in the original equation by determining whether the powers of the fitted values are significantly different from zero.

The principal caveats can be grouped into three general categories.

(a)   The Ramsey test is most likely to warn you if some of the independent variables should be included to powers greater than unity. However, that sort of misspecification does not occur very often. More often, the misspecification is due to the type of nonlinearity that occurs when one of the independent variables is a reciprocal, or the dependent variable increases at a faster rate during certain phases of the business cycle or in response to changes in economic conditions (such as a cost curve). Often, the Ramsey test will not discover such errors.

(b)   Even if the Ramsey test signals that some variable(s) are omitted, it obviously doesn't tell you which ones.

(c)   Problems associated with the lagged dependent variable are better fixed simply by deciding not to include such variables in the first place. In that sense, the Ramsey test will tell you something that should have already been known. In the case of the motor vehicle equation, which is described below, the RESET test shows that something is missing. It turns out to be fourth-order autocorrelation, which should have been detected in the previous tests.

It is always a good idea to run the Ramsey RESET test as an elementary diagnostic, but you cannot realistically expect it to find the "missing" variables for you. That is the job of the economist and forecaster.

5.2.3 RECURSIVE LEAST SQUARES – TESTING OUTSIDE THE SAMPLE PERIOD

Econometricians realize that time-series regressions should be tested by omitting some of the data points. The Chow test provides just such a test. However, since the choice of break point chosen by the researcher is somewhat arbitrary, it would be better to examine the equation over time as sample points are added one by one. In the past, that used to represent a tremendous amount of regression time on the computer, and was seldom done. However, EViews provides the algorithms to combine these results and shows them on a single graph for each test, thus making the comparison and analysis much easier to absorb and analyze.

The EViews program performs six separate tests in this area; while some are more important than others, taken together they provide a comprehensive analysis of how the parameters change over time and whether the equation can reasonably be expected to remain stable over a reasonably long forecast period. All of these tests are illustrated in case study 7, the demand for motor vehicles.

RECURSIVE RESIDUALS

The program calculates values of the residuals in the period immediately after the end of the truncated sample period. For example, the equation would be estimated through 1975.4 and those coefficients would then be used to predict 1976.1. If that estimate falls outside two standard errors (as also calculated by the program), the test suggests the coefficients are unstable. This process is then repeated until the end of the full sample period.

CUSUM TEST

The acronym stands for CUmulative SUM of the residuals. In this test, the cumulative sum of the residuals are plotted; hence the 2σ bands widen over time. If the equation generates one-period errors that are random, CUSUM will show the cumulative residuals remaining within their error bands. On the other hand, if the errors are cumulative (as would likely be the case if one were to use the lagged dependent variable on the right-hand side of the equation), they would increasingly lie outside the 2σ bands as time progresses.

CUSUM OF SQUARES TEST

If w_t is the recursive residual, then this test examines the ratio

$$s_t = \frac{\sum_{\tau = k+1}^{t} w_t^2}{\sum_{\tau = k+1}^{T} w_t^2}.$$

(5.9)

The only difference between the numerator and the denominator is that the numerator is summed only to an intermediate point t, whereas the denominator is summed to the final point T. Thus at the end of the sample period, s_t must equal 1. The question is then how s_t performs throughout the sample period. It should rise linearly from 0 to 1; if it falls outside the bands, that provides further evidence that the coefficients are unstable.

ONE-STEP FORECAST TEST

This is similar to the one-period-ahead residuals, except the graph also supplies probabilities to indicate where the biggest errors occur.

N-STEP FORECAST TEST

This test provides a series of Chow tests without having to specify any particular break point. The program calculates all feasible cases, starting with the smallest sample size consistent with estimating the equation.

RECURSIVE COEFFICIENT ESTIMATES

This final test provides graphs of all the coefficients as the sample size increases from its minimum to the last observation. It enables one to determine whether the coefficients remain stable as more observations are added. In general, the coefficients tend to become more stable as the number of observations increases.

5.2.4 ADDITIONAL COMMENTS ON MULTICOLLINEARITY

As mentioned previously, there is no standard, mechanical test for multicollinearity. One has to rely on common sense when evaluating the parameter estimates.

It was previously noted that nonsensical parameter estimates and large standard errors were tipoffs that extreme multicollinearity is present. In addition, severe multicollinearity often is present if the coefficients change significantly as more data points are added. That is another reason why it is a good idea to estimate the equation over part of the sample period and then see whether the parameter estimates change significantly when additional observations are included.

Another test can be performed as follows. Suppose X and Y were highly collinear and also of the same size (as indicated by the correlation matrix), and suppose the coefficients were $0.4X$ and $0.75Y$. One possibility is to form a combination variable $Z_1 = 0.4X + 0.75Y$ and substitute that into the equation. Naturally that will generate the same result, except the goodness-of-fit statistics will be slightly better because one degree of freedom is added. Now vary the equation slightly by choosing $Z_2 = 0.3X + 0.85Y$. The other coefficients and the goodness-of-fit statistics should be just about the same. If they are not, the equation will probably be unstable in the forecast period and should be reformulated. Perhaps X or Y should be dropped, or the entire equation should be reformulated in percentage change instead of levels form.

If two of the independent variables are found to have an extremely high correlation with each other, ask yourself why. Are they really just two representations of the same economic phenomenon? If so, it is not necessary to include both terms in the equation. Or are they simply manifestations of the same common trend? I have dealt with that concern in previous chapters. Even if the equation remains in levels form, it is generally a good idea to check the stability of coefficients by calculating the corresponding percentage change function and see which variables remain significant.

Case Study 7: Demand for Motor Vehicles

We now turn to the regression for new motor vehicle (car and light truck) sales. The data are quarterly from 1959.1 through 1998.4. The key variables are real disposable income less transfer payments, the percentage change in real consumer credit, the relative price of gasoline, a dummy variable for auto strikes, stock prices, consumer credit, the unemployment rate, the yield spread between long and short-term rates, the ratio of two demographic variables – younger people between the ages of 16 and 24 buy more cars, and those between the ages of 45 and 64 buy fewer cars, ceteris paribus – and a dummy variable for the third quarter in 1985–7, described below. The complete equation is given in figure 5.1, and the actual and simulated fitted values are shown in figure 5.2.

All of the terms are highly significant. There is no autocorrelation in this equation, so no AR(1) adjustment is necessary. The reader should also rerun this regression without the DUMQ3 term to verify that all the terms remain significant and the equation is little changed except for a lower adjusted R^2 and higher standard error.

The first test is to whether the residuals are distributed normally. If the DUMQ3 variable is included, that is indeed the case. On the other hand, if that variable is omitted, the probability that the residuals are normally distributed is zero to six decimal places. Clearly those observations are drawn from a different population, which justifies the use of the dummy variable.

Dependent Variable: MOTVEH
Method: Least Squares

Sample(adjusted): 1959:1 1998:4
Included observations: 160 after adjusting endpoints

Variable	Coefficient	Std. Error	t-Statistic	Prob.
C	−3.03	0.56	−5.4	0.000
INCOME EXCL TRANSFERS	0.00172	0.00015	11.4	0.000
@PCH(REALCRED,4)	8.65	1.11	7.8	0.000
CPIGAS(-2)/CPI(-2)	−2.81	0.56	−5.0	0.000
DSTR	0.88	0.21	4.3	0.000
UNEMPL RATE	−0.397	0.048	−8.3	0.000
@MOVAV(YLDSPRD (-2),4)	0.347	0.045	7.7	0.000
POP RATIO	19.1	0.92	20.7	0.000
SP500(-1)	0.00260	0.00059	4.4	0.000
DUMQ3	2.78	0.39	7.2	0.000

R-squared	0.959	Mean dependent var	12.23
Adjusted R-squared	0.958	S.D. dependent var	2.71
S.E. of regression	0.56	Akaike info criterion	1.75
Sum squared resid	47.4	Schwarz criterion	1.94
Log likelihood	−130	F-statistic	392
Durbin-Watson stat	1.76	Prob(F-statistic)	0.000

Figure 5.1 Tabular EViews output for the equation for motor vehicles in case study 7.

These outliers occurred in 1985.3 and 1986.3, and to a lesser extent in 1987.3. Car manufacturers, finding they had excess vehicles left at the end of the model year, used unprecedented discounts, rebates, and inexpensive financing to clear showroom floors. In retrospect, the auto industry miscalculated the demand for domestic vehicles because the dollar was so strong that many buyers switched to foreign models. However, using the value of the dollar won't work because the residuals are negative during most of the year but strongly positive during the third quarter.

If the dummy variable for these three years is included, the residuals are normally distributed. The coefficients do not change very much when this dummy variable is added, so the incentive contests in those years are unrelated to the other variables in the equation. One could argue that these incentive programs were not known in advance, so the forecast would not be improved by including such a variable. Yet it could also be claimed that with production running

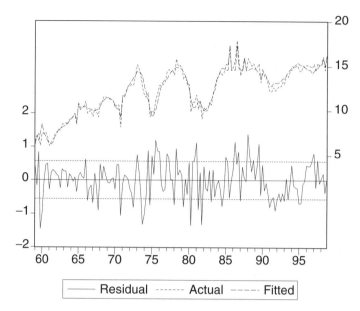

Figure 5.2 Graphical EViews output for the equation for motor vehicles.

ahead of sales for three years in a row, most ex ante forecasts would have adjusted for this discrepancy based on the grounds that the industry has never yet taken new cars back to the factory and melted them down.

The tests for autocorrelation and heteroscedasticity are inconclusive. The correlogram tests do not indicate positive autocorrelation. The Breusch–Godfrey test shows no significant autocorrelation with lags of 1 and 4, but some significant autocorrelation with lags of 2 and 3. The ARCH LM test shows no autocorrelation. The White test without cross-terms shows heteroscedasticity, but the test with cross-terms does not. That is fairly unusual; in most cases the two tests show the same results. Based on these results, autocorrelation and heteroscedasticity are probably not significant in this equation.

The Ramsey RESET test with lags of 2, 3, and 4 shows no misspecification. However, the reader should verify that if the population ratio variable is broken into two terms – those aged 16–24 and those aged 45–64 – the goodness-of-fit statistics of the equation are improved but the Ramsey equation indicates something is clearly amiss with the equation. While the test does not provide definitive answers, the most likely culprit is excessive multicollinearity when both population variables are entered separately.

The Chow breakpoint test shows a clear shift in the structural coefficients. The recursive coefficient tests show that most of the discontinuity occurs in the early 1970s, during the period of wage and price controls, the first energy crisis, and the first credit crunch. If the equation is reestimated starting in 1975, there are some minor changes in the coefficients, but the statistical problems autocorrela-

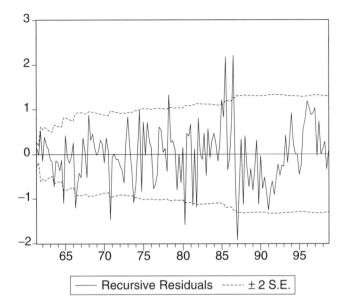

Figure 5.3   Recursive residuals test.

tion, heteroscedasticity, and shifting parameters disappear. Based on the 1975–98 sample period, the equation passes virtually all diagnostic tests.

Note that one cannot run the Chow test for most of the sample period because of the *DSTR* variable for auto strikes. Since there were no major strikes from 1970 through 1997, calculating the equation for during that period will result in the *DSTR* variable being entirely zeros, in which case the variance/covariance matrix won't invert. The way around this is to rerun the equation without the *DSTR* variable and then use the Chow test for various sample periods. However, the CUSUM tests provide a somewhat better way to handle this anomaly, so that method is used.

The first diagram of the recursive least squares testing shows what are called "recursive residuals," which are calculated as follows. The equation, which starts in 1959.1, is estimated through 1964.4. That equation is then used to predict 1965.1. The equation is then reestimated through 1965.1, and that version is used to predict the next quarter. The process continues through the end of the sample period. Note that in performing these tests, we must drop the *DUM3Q* variable because it is zero until 1985.3, If it were included, testing would be restricted to the period from 1986 to the present, and most of the information about shifting parameters would be lost.

The solid line in figure 5.3 shows the residuals calculated in this manner, and the dotted line shows the ranges defined by two standard errors. Points outside this range suggest the equation is unstable, particularly for the third quarters in the mid-1980s, although there is also some instability earlier. After 1987 there is no further instability.

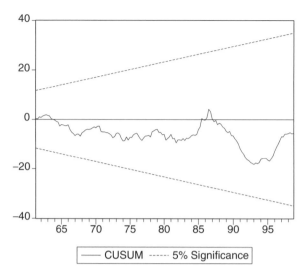

Figure 5.4   CUSUM of squares test.

Before drawing any firm conclusions, it is best to look at the next two tests, which are CUSUM and CUSUM of squares. CUSUM stands for cumulative sum of residuals, while CUSUM of squares is the cumulative sum of the square of the residuals. As the name implies, this is just the cumulation of the individual recursive residuals shown in the previous graph.

The recursive residuals test shows whether the forecasts are likely to be wide of the mark in any given quarter. But the CUSUM tests, illustrated in figures 5.4 and 5.5, show whether these one-time errors are just due to random factors or whether there is some systematic, long-lasting bias in the forecasts. For this equation, CUSUM shows that the errors do not accumulate over time, while CUSUM of squares shows structural instability before 1987.

The fourth test, known as the "one-step forecast test," is not shown separately, since it is more or less a repeat of the first graph. This test calculates the probability levels associated with each of these points. If the residual is well outside the two-standard deviation limit, the probability will be very close to 0 that the forecast point is drawn from the same population as the sample period. The fifth test known as the "N-step forecast test," also shows the same residuals as figure 5.3 and is not included separately. This test also shows that the probability of a stable sample is near zero until 1987. Before that date, the factors affecting car sales differed enough that the underlying equation changed almost every period. Some of these factors include the energy shocks, strikes, and deregulation of the banking sector, which led to alternative methods of credit allocation.

Finally, figure 5.6 shows the behavior of the individual coefficients except the constant term as sample points are added. Most of the coefficients are stable

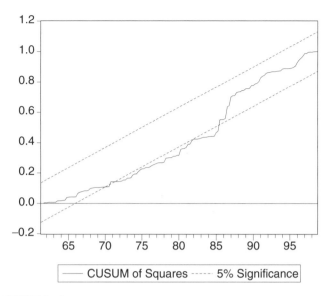

Figure 5.5   CUSUM of squares test.

after 1975; before then, some of them were buffeted by the first energy shock. Since then, the coefficients have remained generally stable except for the outliers in the third quarters of 1985, 1986, and 1987. The coefficients are shown in the order listed in figure 5.1.

This case study has illustrated the standard tests that should be used to determine whether the equation is statistically robust in the sample period and is likely to generate accurate forecasts. The main result we found was that the coefficients shifted during the early 1970s, and an equation estimated with post-1975 data provided much more robust statistics. However, that still does not answer the question of whether this equation would actually forecast well, since it requires accurate forecasts of the unemployment rate, stock prices, and consumer credit. Furthermore, in a complete macro model, it is also possible that the two-way causality in these variables would reduce forecasting accuracy.

5.3 EVALUATING FORECAST ACCURACY

So far the standard error of the equation has been used to measure the accuracy of any given equation. When we move beyond the sample period, the corresponding measure is known as the root mean square error, or RMS forecast error,[9] defined as follows:

---

[9] While this is the standard measure of forecast errors, it sometimes gives ambiguous results. For a discussion of this, see Clements, Michael P., and David F. Hendry, *Forecasting Economic Time Series* (Cambridge University Press, Cambridge, UK), 1998, ch. 3, esp. p. 68.

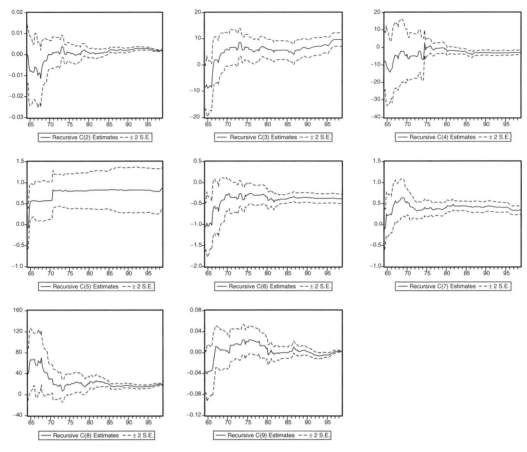

Figure 5.6 Recursive coefficient test.

$$RMSE = \sqrt{(1/T)\sum(Y_{ts} - Y_{ta})^2} \qquad (5.10)$$

where Y_{ts} are forecast values of Y, and Y_{ta} are actual values.

A somewhat similar measure, which generally gives comparable results, is the "absolute average error" (AAE), which is simply the actual error without regard to sign. The RMS error takes into account the greater penalty associated with very large forecasting errors, and is a more statistically robust term. However, both terms are often used to evaluate forecast accuracy, and both are used in this text.

An equation that generates forecasts with a continuing bias may still be very useful if one can adjust for that bias. Suppose, for example, that all recent residuals have been about 5% above the actual numbers; that 5% factor can be incorporated in the forecast. That raises the question of why the predicted values are too high; perhaps the parameters should be reestimated. However, there may have been a structural shift in recent periods that is noticeable in the residuals but has not occurred for a long enough time to warrant the inclusion of an additional variable.

This point is now illustrated with a quarterly equation for housing starts. It will be shown that (i) while the equation adequately tracks all the major cycles in housing starts, the residuals are highly autocorrelated; (ii) the residuals in recent years have all been positive; (iii) adjusting the forecasts by the average size of the recent residual materially improves the forecast: (iv) adding additional variables to try and explain the recent residuals worsens forecast accuracy, and (v) adjusting for autocorrelation using the AR(1) method also materially worsens forecast accuracy. While these results are based on only one equation, this author can state after many years of actual forecasting that results of this sort are the rule rather than the exception.

Using the RMS may not be appropriate in all circumstances. In particular, individuals or firms might face an asymmetric loss function: if the predicted values are below the actual values, the firms may lose some sales, whereas if the predicted values are higher than the actual values, the firm may go bankrupt. It is also possible that in certain applications, such as financial markets, predicting the direction in which the particular market will move is just as important as predicting the magnitude of that move.[10] In other cases, trend forecasts may be less important than accurate predictions of turning points.

The individual forecaster can, if desired, construct other asymmetrical loss functions. Yet even in these cases, smaller forecasting errors are much preferred to larger ones. Thus in a book on practical business forecasting, the emphasis should be placed on the source of these forecasting errors, which can be grouped into three main categories:

(a) errors that occur from the random nature of the forecasting process – in the case of normally distributed residuals, these are accurately measured by the standard error of the equation over the sample period
(b) errors that occur because the underlying data generation function has shifted – as a subset, this includes exogenous influences that have not previously occurred
(c) errors that occur because the actual values of the independent variables are not known at the time of forecast.

There is a massive literature discussing point (a), but very little on (b) and (c). Yet as a practical matter, those errors are likely to be larger than the errors indicated by the standard error of the equation during the sample period. One of the major tasks of forecasters is to reduce the errors from (b) and (c) by adjusting the equations outside the sample period, and taking extraneous information into account. Since this is often done on an individual basis and involves trial and error, the statistical results are not very robust and, in some cases,

---

[10] For a discussion of asymmetric loss functions, see Clements and Hendry, pp. 102–4.

cannot be precisely quantified. However, that does not make them any less important. The remainder of this chapter includes some examples of how these errors might be reduced; the subject is then discussed in greater detail in chapter 8, after the material on time-series models has been presented.

5.4 THE EFFECT OF FORECASTING ERRORS IN THE INDEPENDENT VARIABLES

There are many equations which, if correctly estimated and thoroughly tested, will generate forecasts that are well within the estimates indicated by the SE. In those cases, the econometricians have presumably done their work well, and no further comment is needed.

However, as this author can attest, there are often times when an equation that appears to be robust by all standard statistical tests generates very poor forecasts. The practical question is what to do in such situations. It is, of course, possible that the equation has been misspecified, so the only reasonable solution is to start all over again. In many cases, however, forecast accuracy can be improved by using some of the following tools. First, some econometricians suggest recalculating the equation with an AR(1) transformation. Second, it is often advantageous to adjust the constant terms based on recent residuals. Third, forecast error is often increased by faulty predictions of the independent variables; in some cases, using consensus forecasts may help. The advantages and disadvantages of these methods, together with several examples, comprise the remainder of this chapter.

It should also be noted that forecast error should be evaluated not only in comparison to the sample period error, but relative to errors generated from so-called naive models, which assume that the level or percentage change in a given variable is the same as last period, or – in a somewhat more sophisticated version – that the variable is a function only of its own lagged values and a time trend. Hence the forecasting record of naive models is also considered in these examples.

Case study 1 on page 90 presented an equation for the annual percentage changes in constant-dollar retail sales at hardware and building materials stores for the period from 1967 through 1998. The data series itself has a standard error of 6.6%, so if one assumed that hardware sales would rise at the average amount every year, the average forecast error would be 6.6%. A regression with current levels of the change in disposable income, housing starts, and the unemployment rate, and lagged changes in the Aaa corporate bond rate, explains 89% of the variance and reduces the standard error to 2.2%. It would appear this equation does indeed predict most of the change in the hardware sales.

Yet equations of this sort are always subject to multiple sources of possible forecast error. As noted above, the first is the random generation process that is reflected in the SE of the equation itself. The second test is the possibility that the structure will shift outside the sample period. The third is that the

Table 5.1   Errors generated by the following methods in the hardware store sales equation.

	Actual change (%)	Naive model	Errors		
			Within equation	Outside equation	With consensus values
1994	10.0	3.0	1.3	1.6	2.0
1995	1.4	8.6	1.8	1.9	3.4
1996	5.9	4.5	0.8	0.6	1.4
1997	5.5	0.4	0.2	0.1	0.7
1998	11.4	5.9	3.7	3.9	7.0
RMS		5.3	2.0	2.1	3.7

structure may remain unchanged, but forecasts for the unlagged values of the independent variables may be inaccurate.

Two major tests can be applied. The first one is to estimate the equation through a truncated sample period, ending in (say) 1993 and then forecast ahead, using the equation outside the sample period but inserting actual values of the independent variables. The second test is to use the consensus forecasts made each year for the percentage change in income, actual change in housing starts, and level of unemployment. Since the Aaa bond rate is lagged, it is known with certainty when the forecasts are made and hence does not contribute to any error for one-year forecasts.

SE for the 1994–8 period calculated with an equation estimated through 1993 is only 2.1%, virtually the same as the *SE* of the fitted residuals if the equation is estimated through 1998. This indicates stability of the equation. Of course this is never a perfect test, as it could be claimed the equation fits so well because we know what happened in the 1994–8 period and adjusted the sample period equation accordingly. In this particular case, however, the author actually used such an equation to predict hardware sales and can therefore warrant that the structural form of the equation did not change over that period.

The next test substitutes consensus forecasts for the actual values of income, housing starts, and the unemployment rate, and then recalculates *SE* for these five years. As shown in table 5.1, using predicted values for the unlagged independent variables boosted *SE* from 2.1% to 3.7%. These forecast errors are still smaller than the 5.2% error which would be generated by assuming the percentage change this year is the same as last year, but they are substantially higher than the ex post simulation errors. The error from the naive model is generated by assuming the change this year is the same as the change last year.

As shown in table 5.1, the difference in the RMS between the values when the sample period includes 1994–8 and excludes it is virtually nil. On the other hand, using the consensus instead of actual values almost doubles the error. This is not an atypical result, and illustrates one major reason why forecast errors are invariably larger than indicated by the sample-period standard error.

Because hardware sales are closely tied to housing starts and income, the structural stability is quite high, and most of the error stems from the inability to predict those variables. Examining errors from the equation for housing starts, on the other hand, shows that most of the error reflects a shift in the function rather than the inability to predict the independent variables; that case is considered next.

Case Study 8: Housing Starts

The equation for housing starts is estimated from 1959 through 1997. Data for housing starts are not comparable before 1959, and the sample period is truncated to allow several quarters to evaluate forecasting accuracy.

In the short run, housing starts are a function of both demand and supply variables, where supply in this case represents monetary factors: the cost and availability of credit. Short-run demand factors are represented by stock prices and the unemployment rate. Long-run demand factors are represented by demographic trends and the vacancy rate.

The availability of credit plays a key role; it is measured by the difference between the long-term and short-term interest rates, generally known as the yield spread. When the yield spread widens, credit becomes more easily available and financial institutions are more likely to lend money to both builders and homeowners. The change in the real money supply over the past two years is also an important variable. Because of changes in banking regulations, changes in the money supply were more important before 1973, while changes in the stock market were more important starting in 1980. Because housing starts are trendless, the ratio of stock prices to GDP and percentage changes of stock prices are used instead of levels. Similarly, the real money supply term is entered in percentage changes, and the number of people aged 20–24 is divided by total population. The dummy variable *DUM80* is included because of the discontinuity caused by starting the SP/GDP series in 1980.1. The equation is

$$HST$$
$$= 1.36 + 14.42 * POP20/POP - 0.148 * VACRAT(-5), 4 - 0.062 * UN(-2), 4$$
$$\qquad (9.3) \qquad\qquad\quad (10.3) \qquad\qquad\qquad (5.5)$$
$$+ 0.165 * \%RM2, 8 + 0.035 * \%RM2, 4 * DUM73 + 0.140 * YLDSPRD(-2), 8$$
$$\quad (8.5) \qquad\qquad (6.5) \qquad\qquad\qquad\quad (12.3)$$
$$+ 3.87 * [SP/GDP](-1) * DUM80 + 0.012 * \%SP, 4 - 0.271 * DUM80$$
$$\quad (2.0) \qquad\qquad\qquad\qquad (3.0) \qquad\quad (2.8)$$
$$RSQ = 0.884; \; SE = 0.110; \; DW = 1.01$$

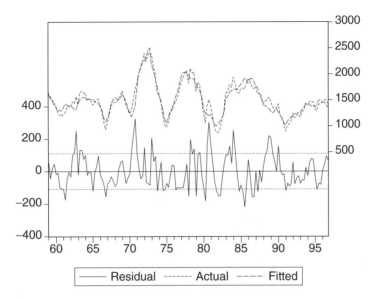

Figure 5.7 Residuals for the housing starts equation.

where *HST* is housing starts in millions, *POP20/POP* is the ratio of population aged 20–24 to total population, *VACRAT* is the vacancy rate for rental properties (the (−5),4 means it starts with a five-quarter lag and extends back an additional four quarters), *UN* is the unemployment rate, *RM2* is real money supply (M2 divided by CPI), *YLDSPRD* is the spread between the Aaa corporate bond rate and the Federal funds rate, *SP/GDP* is the ratio of S&P 500 stock price index to GDP, *DUM73* is a dummy variable (1 through 1972.4, 0 thereafter), and *DUM80* is a dummy variable (0 through 1979.4, 1 thereafter). The numbers after the commas indicate the length of lag. In levels terms, these lags represent the length of the moving average; in percentage terms, they indicate the length of lag for the percentage change.

The equation appears to track the data very well, as shown by the comparison of the actual and fitted values in figure 5.7. But how well does it forecast?

That all depends on what measuring stick is used. The first and easiest step is to calculate the difference between actual and estimated values for 1997.1 through 2000.4 generated by this equation. That period is outside the sample period, and appears to give very good results, as shown in table 5.2. However, that is not a true test for two reasons. First, this equation benefits from the hindsight of including the stock market variable. Second and more important, any such calculations assume that the values of all the independent variables – including the stock market – are known, which is obviously not the case. In particular, hardly anyone at the end of 1996 correctly predicted the actual increase in the stock market over the next three years.

For ease of exposition, the remaining forecasts are shown only for the annual totals. Table 5.3 shows the forecasts using the above equation when the actual

Table 5.2 Actual housing starts and forecast errors, with and without AR(1) transformation, using actual values for all independent variables.

Quarter	Actual	Error	Error with AR(1)
1997:1	1.459	0.098	0.062
1997:2	1.473	0.110	0.085
1997:3	1.457	0.075	0.046
1997:4	1.515	0.051	0.028
1998:1	1.585	0.079	0.034
1998:2	1.570	−0.003	−0.048
1998:3	1.637	0.012	−0.029
1998:4	1.701	0.077	0.009
1999:1	1.760	0.139	0.080
1999:2	1.591	−0.068	−0.097
1999:3	1.663	0.005	−0.016
1999:4	1.689	0.080	0.056
2000:1	1.732	0.137	0.117
2000:2	1.605	0.032	0.013
2000:3	1.527	−0.020	−0.034
2000:4	1.550	−0.004	−0.023

Table 5.3 Housing starts: comparison using actual values, consensus, and a naive model.

	Actual starts	Using eqn	AAE	With AR(1)	AAE	Consensus	AAE	Naive model	AAE
1997	1.48	1.39	0.09	1.42	0.06	1.40	0.08	1.35	0.13
1998	1.62	1.58	0.04	1.63	0.01	1.44	0.18	1.48	0.14
1999	1.67	1.64	0.03	1.67	0.00	1.53	0.14	1.62	0.05
2000	1.60	1.57	0.03	1.59	0.01	1.54	0.06	1.67	0.07
Average AAE			0.05		0.02		0.12		0.10

values of the independent variables are known, compared to the consensus forecast and a naive model. Table 5.4 shows the comparison when the consensus forecasts of the independent variables are used. The naive model assumes starts this year are the same as last year. In these tables AAE stands for absolute error.

The equation appears to do much better than the consensus forecast – but only if one knows the actual values of interest rates, the yield spread, growth in the money supply, and stock prices. Thus a more realistic comparison would use the consensus forecasts for these variables. Since consensus estimates for monetary variables are not available, it has been assumed that the yield spread

Table 5.4 Housing starts: comparison using consensus values in the equation.

	Actual	Using eqn	AAE	With AR(1)	AAE
1997	1.48	1.35	0.13	1.38	0.10
1998	1.62	1.40	0.22	1.43	0.19
1999	1.67	1.44	0.23	1.45	0.22
2000	1.60	1.45	0.15	1.46	0.14
Average AAE			0.18		0.16

Table 5.5 Housing starts: equation without stock market terms.

	No AR(1)	AAE	With AR(1)	AAE
1997	1.24	0.26	1.32	0.16
1998	1.36	0.26	1.43	0.19
1999	1.34	0.31	1.42	0.25
2000	1.27	0.33	1.32	0.28
Average AAE		0.29		0.22

remained at $1\frac{1}{2}\%$, real money supply rose 4% per year, and stock prices rose 12% per year. Entering these results in the above equation generates quite different results (tables 5.4 and 5.5).

Further analysis of these errors reveals that most of the mistake occurred because of the inability to predict the rapid rise in the stock market. In 1996, most economists did not include stock prices in the housing start equation; previously, the relationship had not been very robust, and indeed the significance levels of the two stock market terms are much smaller than the other terms; by 2000, these terms have become much more important.[11] Thus to generate a true ex ante forecast, it makes more sense to reestimate the equation through 1996 without the stock market terms and see how well it performs. The AAEs for these equations are so large as to render them useless for forecasting, since they are much bigger than the AAE for the naive model.

Note what has happened here. When actual values of the independent variables are used, the AAE is only 0.05 million starts. When the consensus values are used, that error rises to 0.18 million, and when the stock market term is omitted, it rises to 0.29 million. By comparison, the naive model AAE is only

---

[11] It remains to be seen whether this is a long-term stable relationship. When the stock market plunged in late 2000 and early 2001, housing starts improved because interest rates fell.

Table 5.6 Housing starts: using the equation without stock prices plus constant adjustment.

	Actual starts	Predicted	AAE
1997	1.48	1.38	0.10
1998	1.62	1.60	0.02
1999	1.68	1.61	0.07
2000	1.60	1.60	0.00
Average AAE			0.05

0.10 million. It might appear that the inability to predict the independent variables accurately vitiates the econometric approach. However, it is not yet time to give up.

It is possible to use the information in the residuals to adjust the forecasts each year. To do this, calculate the residuals – actual minus predicted values – each year for the previous four quarters; initially, the residual values are used for 1996. That average residual is then added to the 1997 forecasts generated using consensus estimates for the independent variables. The residuals for 1997 are then calculated, and added to the 1998 forecasts calculated from the estimates. The same procedure is used for 1999 and 2000. In other words, the forecasts for each year are adjusted by the errors of the previous year. When that relatively simple procedure is used, the results are much improved, as shown in table 5.6. The AAE is then seen to be much better than the consensus forecast – and as good as an equation using the stock price terms and the actual values for the independent variables.

The next two figures illustrate these various comparisons for quarterly values. In figure 5.8, actual housing starts are compared with the single-equation estimates including stock prices with and without AR(1) using the *actual* values of the independent variables, and using the consensus values of the independent variables. Clearly, most of the error stems from the inability to predict stock prices, money supply growth, and the yield spread.

Figure 5.9 shows the comparison of actual housing starts to forecasts made using an equation without the stock price terms and (i) no adjustment, (ii) the AR(1) adjustment, and (iii) the constant adjustment described above. There is no corresponding line for the equation with AR(1) and constant adjustments, because with AR(1) the residuals are random and hence any constant adjustment would be zero. It is clear that the improvement from using constant adjustments is much greater than the improvement from using the AR(1) transformation.

This case study is typical of the problems forecasters face when generating true ex ante predictions. In fact, the equation estimated in 1996 would have been misspecified by not using stock market terms – but that was not known

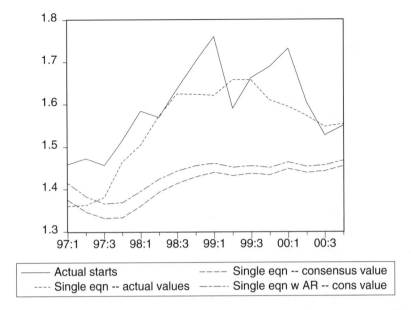

Figure 5.8   Actual and predicted levels of housing starts, comparing forecasts with actual and consensus estimates of the independent variables.

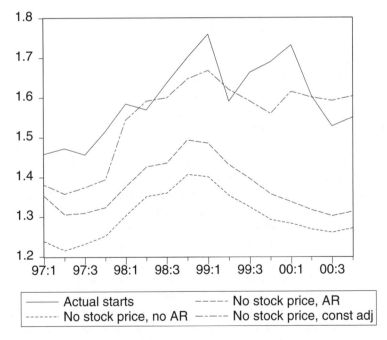

Figure 5.9   Actual and predicted levels of housing starts, using different assumptions about the independent variables and adjustment of the constant term.

at the time. The question is how to improve the forecasts in spite of not having perfect hindsight.

As these results show, using an AR(1) transformation helps very little; in other similar cases, it does not help at all. Using the consensus forecasts, while slightly better than a naive model, does not help very much either. The most successful method of improving forecast accuracy in this case, given a misspecified equation, is to adjust the constant term by the average of the previous year's residuals. That is a particularly helpful method when all the residuals have the same sign and approximately the same magnitude. Forecast accuracy can be significantly improved with this method, as will be shown further in Part IV.

5.5 COMPARISON WITH NAIVE MODELS

So far we have tested whether the residuals of the equations are normally distributed, whether autocorrelation or heteroscedasticity exists, and whether the coefficients are stable. However, even if all these conditions are met, the equation will not be very useful for forecasting if it does not produce smaller errors than a naive model that does not depend on any structural parameters. Two types of naive models are considered here. The first says the level – or change – this period is the same as last period. The second says that the variable is a function of its own lagged values.

5.5.1 SAME LEVEL OR PERCENTAGE CHANGE

If a variable has no trend – such as interest rates, capacity utilization, or the ratio of inventories to sales – the simplest naive model says the value of that variable this period is the same as last period. If the variable has a significant trend, that naive model says the percentage change this period is the same as the percentage change last period.

At first glance it might seem that any forecast at all could outperform a naive model; after all, that is the same as saying that R^2 in an equation is zero; none of the variance can be explained. Yet in some cases this is simply not the case. So far, no one has developed a model that will accurately predict the amount, or even the direction, that the stock market, interest rates, or foreign exchange rates will change the following day. A model that predicted as little as 10% of the variance would be extremely useful, but no such model has yet been found. Even if some formula were discovered that happened to work on some previous set of data, it would quickly become obsolete as traders and speculators rushed to take advantage of that information.

Nonetheless, it is easy enough to run so many regression equations that eventually some set of variables will turn up as highly significant. Such data mining exercises tell us nothing about the forecasting efficacy of such equations. Most

Table 5.7 Blue Chip Consensus forecasting record for percentage change in real GDP.

Forecast year	Consensus	Actual	Actual error	Naive error
1977	5.1	4.9	0.2	0.7
1978	4.3	5.0	−0.7	−0.1
1979	2.1	2.9	0.8	−2.1
1980	−2.0	−0.3	−1.7	−3.2
1981	0.7	2.5	−1.8	2.8
1982	0.3	−2.1	2.4	−4.6
1983	2.5	4.0	−1.5	6.1
1984	5.3	6.8	−1.5	2.8
1985	3.3	3.7	−0.4	−3.1
1986	3.0	3.0	0.0	−0.7
10-year absolute average error			1.1	2.6
1987	2.4	2.9	−0.5	−0.1
1988	2.2	3.8	−1.6	0.9
1989	2.7	3.4	−0.7	−0.4
1990	1.7	1.2	0.5	−2.2
1991	−0.1	−0.9	0.8	−2.1
1992	1.6	2.7	−1.1	3.6
1993	2.9	2.3	0.6	−0.4
1994	3.0	3.5	−0.5	1.2
1995	3.1	2.3	0.8	−1.2
1996	2.2	3.4	−1.2	1.1
1997	2.3	3.9	−1.6	0.5
1998	2.5	4.1	−1.6	0.2
12-year absolute average error			1.0	1.2
22-year absolute average error			1.0	1.8

of the time, however, it is difficult to perform actual ex post tests of forecasting accuracy.

Key macroeconomic variables represent one of the few cases where a documented track record of sufficient length exists, permitting the comparison of naive models with actual forecasts, as opposed to those generated from regression models when the results are already known.

The results for the Blue Chip Economic Indicators consensus forecasts are shown here (see tables 5.7 and 5.8), since they are the most widely used and

Table 5.8 Blue Chip Consensus forecasting record for change in CPI inflation rate.

Forecast year	Consensus	Actual	Error	Naive error
1980	11.0	13.5	−2.5	−2.2
1981	11.2	10.3	0.9	3.2
1982	7.8	6.2	1.6	4.1
1983	5.0	3.2	1.8	3.0
1984	5.0	4.3	0.7	−1.1
1985	4.2	3.6	0.6	0.7
1986	3.6	1.9	1.7	1.7
1987	3.2	3.6	−0.4	−1.7
8-year absolute average error			1.3	2.2
1988	4.2	4.1	0.1	−0.5
1989	4.7	4.8	−0.1	−0.7
1990	4.1	5.4	−1.3	−0.6
1991	4.8	4.2	0.6	1.2
1992	3.3	3.0	0.3	1.2
1993	3.1	3.0	0.1	0.0
1994	2.8	2.6	0.2	−0.4
1995	3.3	2.8	0.5	0.2
1996	2.8	3.0	−0.2	0.2
1997	2.9	2.3	−0.6	0.7
1998	2.2	1.6	−0.6	0.7
11-year absolute average error			0.4	0.6
19-year absolute average error			0.8	1.3

best documented of the consensus forecasts.[12] The actual forecasts, taken from tables prepared by Blue Chip, present estimates for both real growth and inflation, together with the naive models that say the rate of growth in real GDP and the CPI this year will be the same as last year. The consensus forecasts are those made at the beginning of January each year by 50 leading forecasters.

While these statistics are often calculated using the RMSE, they are shown here with the AAE, which is the statistic reported by Blue Chip; in any case,

---

[12] These are published and released on approximately the tenth day of each month by Panel Publishers, a division of Aspen Publishers, Inc., a Wolters Kluwer Company (Alexandria, VA).

the comparative results are not changed. The AAE for real growth is 1.0% for Blue Chip, compared with a naive model error of 1.8%. For inflation, the comparison also favors the Blue Chip consensus, with an AAE of 0.8% compared with a naive model estimate of 1.3%.

This test, however, is not conclusive. To understand the next point, it is necessary to understand the difference between quarterly average and annual average forecasts. This question has arisen in numerous presentations delivered by this author, and merits a brief explanation. The percentage change on an annual average basis, which are the numbers quoted in Blue Chip and many other sources, compares the average for the four quarters of this year with the four quarters last year. The percentage change on a quarterly average forecasts compares the fourth quarter of this year with the fourth quarter of last year.

The point can be expanded with an illustration. Suppose you are given data for the previous eight quarters and are asked to predict the following year based on the data in case A and the data in case B

Year/qtr	Case A	Case B
1.01	101	101
1.02	102	102
1.03	103	103
1.04	104	104
2.01	105	105
2.02	106	106
2.03	107	105
2.04	108	104

In case A, assume the forecaster knows nothing except that, over the long run, this variable grows at 4% per year. In that case, the forecast for the third year, using the first set of data, would probably be 110.5, showing (about) a 4% rate of growth; this simple example ignores the effects of compounding. In case B, the economy may be heading into a recession. Since recessions usually last 3–4 quarters, one reasonable forecast might be 103, 102, 103, 104, for an average of 103 for the year and a 2% decline from the previous year. However, suppose the forecaster is not astute enough to realize a recession has started and simply plugs in the 4% growth formula for the following year, giving figures of 105, 106, 107, and 108. That leads to an annual average of 106.5, which still shows only a $1\frac{1}{2}$% growth rate for the year. It appears the forecaster has accurately predicted at least part of the slowdown, when in fact he or she merely took into account those data that were already known. By comparison, on a quarterly average basis, those data would not be known in advance. In plain English, predicting annual average changes provides forecasters with a "head start."

Yet this test is not conclusive either. The consensus forecast, like any other forecast, is based on the most recent data published by the government, but often these series are substantially revised in the years ahead. BEA, which publishes these figures, has calculated that the AAE for real GDP caused by revisions from the first "advance" estimate to the final figure is 1.4%, which is in fact larger than the AAE generated by the consensus forecast. About half of that differential is due to more complete data for the previous quarter, and about half is due to changes in methodology (such as including business purchases of software in capital spending). Thus even if the consensus forecasts were perfect at the time they were made, they might contain substantial errors when those forecasts are compared with revised data.

For these reasons it is actually not possible to construct a "clean" test that determines how well the consensus forecast has performed relative to a naive model or any other similar standard. Based on experience in generating macro forecasts since 1963, it is this author's opinion that the consensus forecast for real growth is significantly better than a naive model, the consensus forecast for inflation is slightly better, and the consensus forecast for interest rates is no better at all. In what could be considered a market test, a service offered by Blue Chip to provide consensus interest rate forecasts was withdrawn after a few years, whereas the basic Blue Chip forecast service remains popular with subscribers.

5.5.2 NAIVE MODELS USING LAGGED VALUES OF THE DEPENDENT VARIABLES

The residuals in the housing starts equation discussed above have a high degree of autocorrelation. An alternative approach would be to estimate housing starts this quarter as a function of housing starts in previous quarters, eliminating any coefficients with t-ratios that are less than unity. Note this is a purely mechanical approach; no attempt is made here to estimate a structural equation.

While the most important variable is housing starts lagged one quarter, housing starts with lags of three and six quarters are also significant. The *SE* of 0.120 is slightly higher than the *SE* of 0.110 for the structural equation. The forecast errors are given in table 5.9; the AAE of 0.090 is higher than for either

Table 5.9 Absolute values of forecast errors from naive housing starts model.

1997.1	0.081	1998.1	0.007	1999.1	0.214	2000.1	0.060
1997.2	0.058	1998.2	0.017	1999.2	0.090	2000.2	0.069
1997.3	0.079	1998.3	0.078	1999.3	0.017	2000.3	0.140
1997.4	0.021	1998.4	0.173	1999.4	0.043	2000.4	0.090
1997	0.060						
1998	0.069						
1999	0.140						
2000	0.090						

4-yr average forecast error = 0.090

the equation with stock prices or the adjustment of the previous yearly residuals. At least for housing starts, the naive model does not work.

5.6 BUILDUP OF FORECAST ERROR OUTSIDE THE SAMPLE PERIOD

We have seen that it is important to distinguish between unconditional forecasts, where all of the dependent variables are known with certainty – because they are non-stochastic or are lagged – and conditional forecasts, where the independent variables must also be predicted. Most practical business forecasts are of the latter variety, whereas the standard statistical tests are developed for the former case. This section provides further commentary on the additional error that is likely to occur in the forecast period even if the underlying structure of the equation remains unchanged. Three cases are discussed: error as the dependent variable moves further away from the mean; error because the values of the independent variables are not known; and error buildup in multi-period forecasting.

5.6.1 INCREASED DISTANCE FROM THE MEAN VALUE

The algebra is fairly cumbersome without matrix notation for the multivariate case, so to illustrate this principal, consider the bivariate case, first for unconditional and then for conditional forecasts. Starting with the standard bivariate model[13]:

$$Y_t = a + bX_t + \varepsilon_t \qquad (5.11)$$

one can generate a forecast

$$\hat{Y}_t = \hat{a} + \hat{b}X_{t+1}. \qquad (5.12)$$

Remember that a and b are not known, but are estimated, so there are some errors attached to these estimates. Then

$$e_{t+1} = \hat{Y}_{t+1} - Y_{t+1} = (\hat{a} - a) + (\hat{b} - b)X_{t+1} - \varepsilon_{t+1}. \qquad (5.13)$$

Note the two sources of error: one because of the random nature of the parameters that are being estimated, and the other because of the error term ε_{t+1}. After doing the arithmetic we have

[13] For further discussion of this point, see Pindyck, Robert S., and Daniel L. Rubinfeld, *Econometric Models and Economic Forecasts*, 4th edn (Irwin McGraw-Hill, Boston), 1998, pp. 204–9 and 221–3.

$$s_f^2 = s^2 \left[1 + 1/T + (X_{T+1} - \overline{X})^2 \Big/ \sum (X_t - \overline{X})^2 \right] \qquad (5.14)$$

where s_f^2 is the standard error in the forecast period and s^2 is the standard error in the sample period.

The second term in the square brackets, $1/T$, is a small-sample adjustment that disappears as the sample size increases. The third term is of more interest. In general, it means that the more the forecast value moves away from the sample period mean, the larger the forecast error. Hence the error is more likely to increase for a series with a strong trend, such as consumption or stock prices, than for a series with no trend, such as housing starts or interest rates.

To see how large that error might be, consider the consumption function. Over the 50-year period from 1949 through 1998, consumption had a standard deviation of $1200 billion, which means the denominator of the above term is $[50*(1200)^2]$, or $72,000,000 billion. In 1999, the difference between the actual and mean value of consumption was about $2600 billion, so its square would be $6,760,000 billion, or about 9%. When $1/T = 2\%$ is added, the variance in the forecast period would be about 11% more than indicated by the sample period statistics – provided that the value of income is known with certainty (remember, this is just the bivariate case).

This source of error can be compared with a trendless series. The series for housing starts has a standard error of 0.3 million, so it has a variance of 0.09 million times 40 annual observations, or 3.6 million. As shown above, the error in forecasting housing starts is about 0.15 million, so the numerator is 0.02, or about $\frac{1}{4}\%$ of the denominator. Thus in the case of a variable without any trend, the increase in error during the forecast period from this source is minuscule.

5.6.2 UNKNOWN VALUES OF INDEPENDENT VARIABLES

We next consider the more realistic case of conditional forecasting. The same bivariate forecasting model is used, except that the value of X_t is not known at the time of forecast, so one also has to consider the error made in forecasting this variable. This time, add the assumption that $\hat{X}_{t+1} = X_{t+1} + u_{t+1}$, where u_{t+1} is the error in predicting X_{t+1}. Again skipping the algebra, the formula is

$$s_f^2 = s^2 \left[1 + 1/T + \left\{ (X_{T+1} - \overline{X})^2 + s_u^2 \right\} \Big/ \sum (X_t - \overline{X})^2 \right] + \beta^2 s_u^2. \qquad (5.15)$$

In the case of the consumption function, the error in predicting income would generally be about the same as the error in predicting consumption when income was known. Also, β would be fairly close to unity. As a result, the term $\beta^2 s_u^2$ could turn out to be almost as large as s^2, in which case the forecast error would be almost doubled because the value of the independent variable was not known. Furthermore, if the number of variables in the equation is expanded, the error accumulation can become quite substantial. The result is not generally additive because there are usually some negative covariances – some offsetting errors – but nonetheless can be quite large relative to the SE.

We have already seen how the forecast error almost doubled in the equation for hardware store sales when the consensus values were substituted for the actual values of the unlagged independent variables. This formula explains how such an error buildup could occur. The practical lesson is that when building a forecasting model, if there isn't much difference in the goodness-of-fit statistics between the lagged and unlagged values of the independent variable, single-period forecast accuracy will almost always be improved by choosing lagged values of the independent variables.

5.6.3 ERROR BUILDUP IN MULTI-PERIOD FORECASTING

A major source of error buildup in multi-period forecasting, in addition to the sources already mentioned, stems from using the lagged dependent variable on the right-hand side of the equation. Even if this term is not entered explicitly, the same general effect is generated any time an AR(1) transformation is used. Also, error buildup may occur from the predicted values of lagged independent variables. Even if all the independent variables in the equation are lagged, which means this source of error is absent for single-period forecasting, eventually these variables will become endogenous – and hence contain forecasting errors – if the forecast period is extended far enough in the future.

Foreign exchange rates are notoriously difficult to predict in any case, but illustrate the point well. The following case study utilizes an equation for the cross-rate between the Japanese yen and the US dollar. When the yen strengthens, it takes fewer yen to purchase one dollar, so $ ratio declines. From 1971, when the US went off the international gold standard, to early 1995, the yen rose from 360/$ to 80/$. It subsequently fell back to 140/$.

Explanations for the stronger yen during those years are plentiful: relative to the US, Japan had a lower rate of inflation, faster growth, and a big net export surplus. An equation estimated for 1971.1 through 1994.4 is examined next.

Case Study 9: The Yen/Dollar Cross-rate

The summary statistics for the yen/dollar equation estimated through 1994.4 are given in table 5.10. The key variables are the relative inflation rates, the Japanese growth rate, the US Federal funds rate, the change in the US rate of inflation, and the Japanese net export ratio. The residuals are shown in figure 5.10.

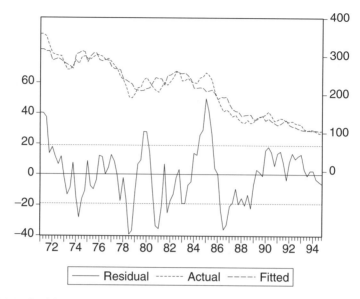

Figure 5.10 Residuals for the yen/dollar equation.

$$YEN$$
$$= 478.7 - 2.82 * (USINFL - JPNINFL) - 73.3 * JPNGDP$$
$$\quad\quad (5.4) \quad\quad\quad\quad\quad\quad\quad\quad (19.7)$$
$$- 677 * JPNNEX - 3.17 * \Delta USINFL + 3.04 * RFF(-4)$$
$$\quad (3.0) \quad\quad\quad\quad (3.9) \quad\quad\quad\quad\quad (3.8)$$
$$RSQ = 0.928; DW = 0.44$$

where *YEN* is the yen/dollar cross-rate, *USINFL* is the US inflation rate, *JPNINFL* is the Japanese inflation rate, *JPNGDP* is Japanese real GDP, *JPNNEX* is Japanese ratio of net exports to GDP, and *RFF* is the Federal funds rate minus annual rate of inflation.

This equation fails to capture the spike in the dollar in 1985, but economists generally agree that was a speculative bubble unrelated to underlying economic forces; an offsetting opposite reaction occurred in 1986 after the G-7 took concerted action to reduce the value of the dollar. In recent years, the equation appears to be tracking the continued increase in the yen. At the end of 1994, one might have been pardoned for predicting that the yen would continue to appreciate indefinitely.

The other problem with this equation is the very high degree of auto-correlation, so the equation is rerun with AR(1). Ex post forecasts for the 1995.1–1998.4 period with (i) the original equation, (ii) the equation with AR(1), and (iii) in-sample estimates where the equation is reestimated through 1998.4 are presented in table 5.10.

Table 5.10 Residuals from alternative formulations of the yen/dollar equation.

Year/qtr	Actual yen/$	Equation 1		Equation 2		Equation 3	
		Predicted	Error	Predicted	Error	Predicted	Error
1995:1	96.2	99.6	−3.5	98.9	−2.8	101.4	−5.2
1995:2	84.5	101.1	−16.6	100.7	−16.2	103.1	−18.6
1995:3	94.2	105.9	−11.7	103.8	−9.5	108.1	−13.8
1995:4	101.5	108.5	−7.0	105.6	−4.1	111.0	−9.4
1996:1	105.8	98.9	6.9	103.5	2.3	102.1	3.8
1996:2	107.5	100.0	7.5	106.3	1.2	103.4	4.1
1996:3	109.0	100.1	8.9	108.6	0.4	103.7	5.3
1996:4	112.9	99.6	13.3	110.9	2.0	103.4	9.5
1997:1	121.2	106.4	14.9	113.8	7.4	110.2	11.0
1997:2	119.7	109.8	9.9	115.8	3.9	113.8	6.0
1997:3	118.1	110.7	7.4	116.9	1.1	114.7	3.4
1997:4	125.4	112.8	12.5	118.5	6.9	116.8	8.6
1998:1	128.2	120.4	7.8	121.0	7.2	123.7	4.4
1998:2	135.7	118.8	16.8	119.1	16.6	122.1	13.5
1998:3	140.0	118.0	22.0	117.9	22.1	121.1	18.9
1998:4	119.5	116.8	2.7	116.4	3.1	119.8	−0.3

None of the equations generate adequate forecasts. The equation with the AR(1) transform shows a gradually increasing trend in the yen/dollar ratio, while the original equation fails to track the turnaround in the yen until early 1997, whereas it actually turned up in mid-1995. An equation estimated through 1998 captures part of this turnaround but fails to predict the weakness in the yen in mid-1998 – a pattern that was again reversed in 1999. However, most of the forecasts in the AR(1) equation show a steadily increasing trend that fails to capture any of the turning points. Furthermore, this problem becomes more severe as the distance from the last sample point increases. Thus even though the equation appears to be robust from a theoretical viewpoint, the forecasts are not satisfactory. Adding the consensus forecast would not reduce forecast error either, since consensus forecasts of foreign exchange rates are almost random.

I stated at the outset of this book that it would occasionally be useful to show the failures as well as the successes of forecasting models. Perhaps this case study may seem to be carrying that principal to extremes, yet the following lessons can be gleaned.

1 Reestimating the equation with the AR(1) does not improve forecast accuracy. This point has already been emphasized several times.
2 This equation can be used to indicate the underlying value of the yen, and show when the actual rate diverges from equilibrium. Hence, for example, if the

rate is well above equilibrium, it would be more likely to decline in the future. However, the equation provides few hints about the timing.

3 Expanding somewhat on that previous point, note that the yen tends to overshoot equilibrium – in both directions – for several quarters before turning around. That is also true for most other foreign exchange rates. One cannot generalize, but in this case it appears to take about two quarters between the time the underlying economic factors suggest a turnaround in the yen and the currency actually reversing course. That could be a useful finding for a company that wants to hedge its position in yen over an extended period.

4 Finally, this equation suggests that predicting foreign exchange rates by using econometric models will seldom if ever pinpoint the timing of turning points. Even if someone were to discover a "magic formula," changes in market dynamics would soon render that formula obsolete. The best one can reasonably expect from an equation of this sort is to identify the periods when the yen or other currencies are far overvalued or undervalued.

Problems and Questions

1. Look again at the equation for purchases of motor vehicles (case study 7).

(a) What happens when you rerun the equation with the two population terms entered separately? What do you think causes this result?

(b) Given the results from the Chow test, do you think the equation would generate more accurate forecasts if the sample period were truncated? Test this hypothesis by starting to estimate the equation in (i) 1975 and (ii) 1982 through 1998, and then compare the forecasts for 1999 and 2000. What conclusions can you draw from these comparisons?

(c) How much would the forecasts vary if the *DUMQ3* term were omitted?

2. Estimate the Federal funds rate equation starting in 1987.2, when Greenspan became Fed Chairman, using a "Taylor" rule, in which the independent variables are the unlagged rate of unemployment and the percentage change in the core rate of inflation over the past year.

(a) What is the standard error of that equation? Do you think that forecasts using this equation for the following year will have a root mean square error equal to or less than the sample-period standard error? (Hint: who will be the Fed chairman "next" year?)

(b) Identify the largest residuals in the above equation. What exogenous world events caused these large residuals? Design an experiment to

continued

determine whether forecast error would be reduced by including dummy variables for these quarters.

(c) Suppose the core inflation rate remained at $2\frac{1}{2}$% but a recession caused the unemployment rate to rise to 6%. Based on this equation, how much would you expect the Fed to reduce the funds rate? How does this compare with the funds rate during the previous recession?

(d) In the first four months of 2001, the Fed reduced the funds rate from $6\frac{1}{2}$% to $4\frac{1}{2}$% even though the unemployment rate rose only 0.3% and the inflation rate did not change significantly (it actually rose slightly). What happened to the Taylor rule? How would you adjust your forecasts of the Federal funds rate in the future based on this development?

3. An electric utility company faces the following forecasting problem. Because of restrictions set by state regulatory agencies, it is not profitable to build another greenfield plant. Averaged over the year, it has adequate excess capacity but faces a peak-load problem. On average, peak demand is about the same during cold winter days and hot summer days, but peaks in individual years depend on the weather, which cannot be predicted in advance. If capacity is not adequate, the company must buy power on the deregulated free market at five times the normal cost. You are asked to design a forecasting model to determine whether it is better to do routine maintenance during the winter or summer months.

(a) How would you use past historical data to determine whether excess demands are more likely to occur in the winter or summer, given that weather forecasts are random?

(b) How would you determine whether the price elasticity for electric power is higher in the winter or in the summer? How would that affect the model?

(c) How would these results be modified if "global warming" were significant? Assuming that the utility had historical data on degree-days for the region it serves, what type of tests would you use to determine whether or not the trend was significant?

4. You are asked to estimate an equation for net exports of consumer durable goods excluding motor vehicles as a proportion of GDP (the data series begin in 1967.1).

(a) Use a PDL to determine the optimal structure for the trade-weighted average of the dollar.

(b) Add a nonlinear trend of the form $1/(10+@\text{trend})$ to the equation to reflect the increasing dependence of consumers on exported goods,

continued

but at a decreasing rate. How does that affect the estimate of the trade-weighted average of the dollar?

(c) Now add a series for consumption of consumer durables excluding motor vehicles to the equation. The sign is negative and highly significant. Why is that appropriate?

(d) Now add the same variable lagged one period. This time, the sign is positive. What does that mean?

(e) In some cases, changes in exports and imports may reflect changes in inventories rather than final sales. Add current and lagged inventory investment to the equation. In view of the difficulty in predicting changes in inventory investment, do you think this variable should be included in the forecasting equation even if it is highly significant?

(f) Use the recursive residual tests to determine whether the forecasting accuracy of the equation is likely to be improved by truncating the sample period.

(g) What terms drop out of the equation when the AR(1) term is added? Do you think they ought to be included in the final equation or not?

(h) Taking all these factors into comparison, present the optimal equation to be used for forecasting.

5. You are asked to develop a model to predict the volume of new orders for steel. The first step is to correlate constant-dollar new orders with the key components of aggregate demand that use steel: motor vehicles, household appliances, producers durable equipment, housing, non-residential construction, inventories, exports, and imports (with a negative sign).

(a) Estimate this equation. Explain why it is not useful for forecasting.

(b) One of the most surprising results in this equation is that the motor vehicle term is not significant. Try adding industrial production in the motor vehicle industry to this equation. What happens to the sign of the term for consumption of motor vehicles? Does that make sense or not? What about changes in the other signs – are they sensible or not?

(c) Even with this additional term, the equation tends to underpredict early in the sample period and overpredict later in the sample period. What additional variable(s) could be added to eliminate this problem? (Hint: try total capacity of the steel industry.)

(d) Rerun the equation by omitting variables that appear to have the wrong sign. Now reestimate the equation by truncating the sample period in 1997.4. Reestimate the equation by omitting any terms that have become insignificant or have the wrong sign. Compare the ex post forecasts for 1998.1 through 2000.4 with the sample period

continued

residuals when the equation is estimated through 2000.4. What conclusions can be drawn about the stability of the equation in recent years?

(e) Reestimate the equation starting in 1982.1, omitting terms that are now insignificant or have the wrong sign.

(f) Now calculate forecast errors for (i) the original equation estimated over the entire sample period, (ii) the truncated sample period starting in 1982.1, (iii) the original equation with the AR(1) adjustment, and (iv) the truncated equation with the AR(1) adjustment. Based on these results, which version of the equation will you present to top management for forecasting purposes?

PART III

CHAPTER 6

ELEMENTS OF UNIVARIATE TIME-SERIES METHODS

INTRODUCTION

Econometric modeling started in the 1920s and 1930s. Early attempts to build forecasting models centered on the estimation of equations to predict agricultural prices and quantities and stock market prices. The discipline then spread to building models for macroeconomic forecasting purposes. While early models included only 20 to 30 equations, the size rapidly increased, and by the 1970s some macro models contained thousands of individual equations.

While initial expectations for these macroeconomic models were quite optimistic, the quality of forecasts they delivered was disappointing. The nadir was reached in the 1970s and early 1980s, when models were unable to predict the simultaneous occurrence of double-digit inflation and unemployment. In particular, these models were also unable to predict any of the four recessions occurring between 1970 and 1982.

These well-publicized failures, coupled with the inability of econometric models to predict financial markets accurately, led to a reexamination of the sources of error in structural models and a movement away from this approach toward non-structural models. As already noted, error from structural models occurred not only because of random elements but because the underlying data generation function often shifted, and it was difficult to predict the independent variables accurately.

For these reasons, econometric analysis and development of forecasting models has shifted in the past 30 years toward placing a greater emphasis on non-structural models. This part of the book analyzes single-equation models; multi-equation models are considered in chapters 11 and 12. In these non-structural models, a given variable is a function only of its own lagged variables, lagged error terms, and truly exogenous variables such as time trends.

This author has been using econometric models to generate macroeconomic and industry forecasts since 1963. Even initially, it was obvious that forecast accuracy was improved by adjusting the constant terms of the regression equations. There was always a certain amount of independent judgment used in that procedure, but the changes often tended to be based on ad hoc rather than systematic methods. Sometimes, judgment played a greater role in determining the forecast than the underlying structure of the equations. Thus it became logical to raise the issue that forecast accuracy might be improved by systematizing the adjustment procedure or, in some cases, jettisoning the structural approach completely.

The position taken in this text is that the choice of model is an empirical rather than a theoretical question. It is quite likely that some combination of methods – structural models, time series models, and exogenous information in the form of field surveys or indexes of sentiment – can provide more accurate forecasts than any single method, and this possibility is examined later in the text. That approach is not a new development; the original Wharton econometric forecasting model, developed in the early 1960s, contained equations with terms for consumer and business sentiment as well as econometrically determined variables.

Even large sophisticated structural models can be reduced to the form where each variable is a function only of its own lagged values and truly exogenous variables. Admittedly, such models contain no estimates of elasticities or multipliers, and cannot be used for policy prescriptions. Nonetheless, if the two approaches can be shown to be logically equivalent, it is worth testing these alternative statistical methods to see whether in fact they can reduce forecast error.

Sometimes forecasting models are developed to track a large number of individual product lines, inventories, or production schedules. It may not be feasible to generate structural models for each individual item, so time-series regression equations represent a more realistic approach for forecasting and tracking these individual items.

Hence there are several reasons why time-series models are considered part of practical business forecasting. In most cases, these models perform better when the trend and seasonal factors have been removed from the original data. Hence we first turn to a discussion of those issues before focusing on the estimation of autoregressive and moving average models in chapter 7. Chapter 8 then discusses the possible benefits of combining different forecasting methods to reduce error.

6.1 THE BASIC TIME-SERIES DECOMPOSITION MODEL

Earlier it was indicated that removing the seasonal and trend factors from the data will generally improve forecast accuracy. That statement remains valid. However, practical business forecasters may also be interested in explicitly identifying and predicting these factors.

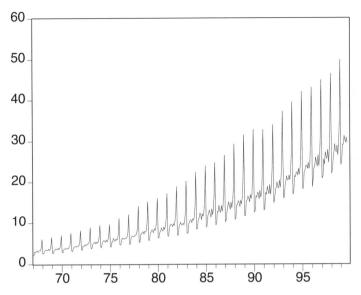

Figure 6.1   General merchandise sales before seasonal adjustment (monthly data, billions of current dollars).

Theoretically, any time series can be decomposed into trend, seasonal, cyclical, and irregular factors. Under certain conditions, the irregular factor will be randomly distributed. However, this decomposition is often not straightforward because these factors interact. Also, the cyclical factor does not follow some preassigned function such as a sine curve, but contains random elements of timing and magnitude. Thus most of the discussion in this chapter will focus on removing the trend and seasonal factors. In some cases, the Hodrick–Prescott filter can be used to remove cyclical factors.

Case Study 10: General Merchandise Sales

We first consider monthly data for general merchandise sales and discuss various methods for extracting the trend and seasonal factors. General merchandise sales, which comprise SIC 53, are similar to department store sales, but include discount stores, variety stores, and other establishments that sell a wide variety of goods. Sales in stores that sell a specific class of items – hardware, apparel, furniture, home appliances, jewelry, etc. – are reported in other two-digit SIC codes in the retail sales sector. Later in this chapter the data for apparel sales (SIC 56) are used to illustrate the concept of shifting seasonal factors because of moving holiday dates. The seasonally unadjusted data for general merchandise sales are shown in figure 6.1.

Several important features of this graph can be noted:

- Sales rise every December and decline every January.
- The seasonal swings are much greater in more recent years, although one cannot tell from this graph whether the *percentage* changes are greater.
- The December peaks were smaller in 1990 and 1991, when there was a recession. As shown below, this is also true for earlier recessions, although it is not as obvious from the graph.

These points reveal substantial interaction between the trend, seasonal, and cyclical component. Furthermore, if one were to correlate retail sales with the usual economic variables – income, cost and availability of credit, expectations, etc. – the residuals would be serially correlated, so the "irregular" component would not be random.

6.1.1 IDENTIFYING THE TREND

General merchandise sales exhibit a strong upward trend. However, it is not obvious whether that trend is linear. Indeed, regressing sales against a linear time trend quickly reveals that the residuals are large and positive near the end of the sample period. This is not surprising; it is more likely that the rate of growth of sales, rather than the actual change, would be constant. This equation can thus be refitted using the logarithm of sales as a function of a linear time trend.

However, that doesn't work so well either, because the residuals in the middle of the sample period are larger, suggesting the growth rate of sales is smaller now than was the case earlier. Since these data are in current dollars, that is presumably due to lower inflation. The trend is not removed from the residuals until a quadratic function is used, in which the logarithm of sales is a function of time and time-squared. These three cases are illustrated in figures 6.2–6.4. Another possibility, considered later, is to reestimate the function using constant-dollar sales, which may be useful for econometric analysis but would not answer the question of how much actual sales are likely to change in the near future without also predicting the change in prices.

6.1.2 MEASURING THE SEASONAL FACTOR

The appearance of the seasonal factors in the residuals is clearly seen in these graphs. The most obvious pattern is that sales rise in December and fall in January, but other seasonal patterns that cannot be seen as easily in these graphs also occur.

The seasonal factors have shifted over time; e.g., the holiday shopping season has extended further into November – and January – in recent years. This is an

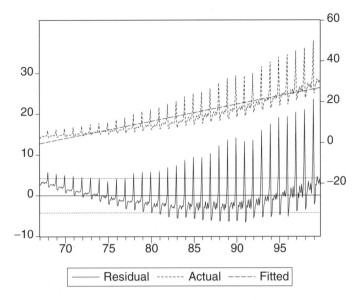

Figure 6.2 General merchandise sales regressed against a linear trend.

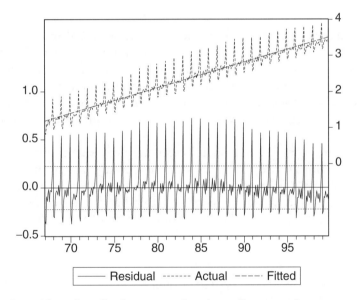

Figure 6.3 Logarithm of retail sales regressed against a linear trend.

important point and one that is discussed in detail in section 6.4. For the moment, however, we assume the seasonal factors are fixed, with their magnitude measured by estimating a regression using the residuals shown in figure 6.4 as the dependent variable. The independent variables are seasonal factors

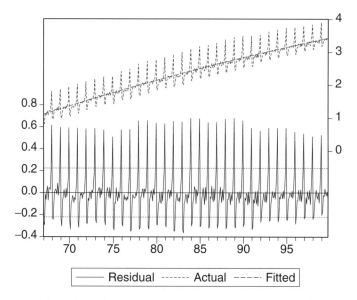

Figure 6.4 Logarithm of retail sales regressed against a quadratic trend.

that are 1 in the designated month and 0 elsewhere; in EViews these are entered as @seas(1), . . . , @seas(12). One word of caution: when running this regression, the constant term must be excluded, or the matrix will be singular. Alternatively, one could include the constant term and omit one of the seasonals, but since we are concentrating on the seasonal factors here, that alternative is not chosen. The reader can verify that the results are identical for both methods.

In this regression, the seasonal factors are very significant for November, December, January, and February, and moderately significant for the other months. The residuals obtained from regressing the residuals on the seasonal factors are shown in figure 6.5. Since the trend and seasonal factors have now been removed, what remains is some combination of the cyclical and irregular factors.

6.1.3 SEPARATING THE CYCLICAL AND IRREGULAR COMPONENTS

The residuals shown in figure 6.5 contain a significant cyclical component that is associated with business cycle fluctuations. Recessions occurred in 1970, 1974–5, 1980, 1981–2, and 1990–1. The dips in the residual series for each of these recessions are apparent in the graph. In most cycles, general merchandise sales remained sluggish for several months after the upturn had started. That

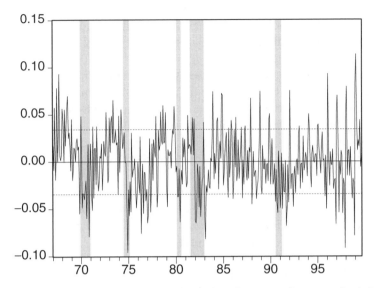

Figure 6.5 Residuals for general merchandise sales after extracting a quadratic log trend. Shaded areas represent business cycle recessions.

is because upturns generally begin with a recovery in housing and the end of inventory disinvestment, while the pickup in consumer spending usually begins a few months later.

In an attempt to identify the cyclical component further, one could then run a regression equation using income, the cost and availability of credit, and consumer expectations as the principal independent variables. However, the remaining component, which is the irregular factor, would not be random, but would exhibit significant autocorrelation. It has already been demonstrated how this problem is likely to remain even after a wide variety of alternative formulations and specifications of structural equations have been tried. Indeed, that is one of the reasons why non-structural equations have become widely used for forecasting purposes. Since this chapter focuses on non-structural methods, we now turn to several alternative methods for measuring and removing the trend from this series.

6.2 LINEAR AND NONLINEAR TRENDS

Nonlinear trends can be grouped into the following major categories.

- *Constant rate of growth* (log-linear trends). Most macroeconomic series with significant time trends – consumption, income, capital spending, exports and imports, stock prices and volume, price indexes, etc. – follow this pattern. This category could also include a constant rate of decline, such as the famed Moore's law, which states that the cost of integrated circuitry will fall by half every 18 months.

• *Growing, but at a slower rate.* The ratio of consumer credit outstanding to income rose quite rapidly after World War II, but after consumers caught up on their backlog of durables, this series advanced at a much slower rate.

• *Declining, but at a slower rate.* The big rise in oil prices in the 1973–80 period initially caused a big decline in the so-called energy coefficient – the amount of energy used per unit of real GDP – but that coefficient now declines much more slowly.

• *Saturation curve.* The percentage of market penetration starts at zero, rises slowly for a while, then accelerates, and later levels off near the saturation level. That is particularly useful for life cycle analysis of individual products. These curves are examined in more detail in chapter 10.

It is possible to consider other types of trends, such as explosive trends in which the rate of increase rises at an accelerating rate. That might be the case for situations such as hyperinflation. However, those episodes are generally short-lived and are better handled by data smoothing methods discussed in the next section rather than fitting a long-term trend.

While a large variety of methods has been developed to fit trends under these various circumstances, the power of these methods is somewhat limited, and it is often difficult if not impossible to distinguish which method will provide better trend forecasts in the longer run. With some oversimplification, it can be said that trend analysis usually consists of fitting the logarithm of the variable to some combination of a linear, quadratic, or inverse time trend. Several practical examples are presented next; more complicated methods often dissolve into exercises in curve-fitting. More advanced methods of treating nonlinear trends are also discussed in chapter 10.

The following example illustrates the volume on the New York Stock Exchange from 1947 through 1998; the data are shown in figure 6.6. It initially appears that volume has followed a pattern of explosive growth because of the termination of fixed commission rates, the roaring bull market of the 1990s, and trading over the Internet.

However, that is actually not the case at all. The logarithm of that series reveals an entirely different picture; as shown in figure 6.7, a simple trend explains 98% of the variance. While the actual change in volume in recent years is much greater, the percentage change in volume in the late 1990s is about the same as in earlier years, as shown in figure 6.8. Would-be model builders are cautioned that before reaching the conclusion that any series is rising at an increasing rate, it is always useful to examine the log-linear transformation.

Figure 6.7 also shows that the residuals are generally positive at the beginning, negative in the 1970s and early 1980s, and then positive starting in 1983,

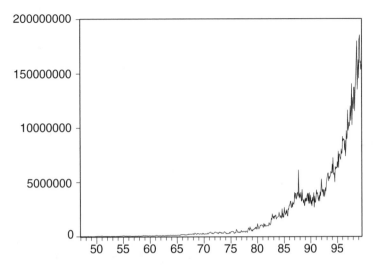

Figure 6.6 Volume on the New York stock exchange, which appears to have exhibited explosive growth in recent years.

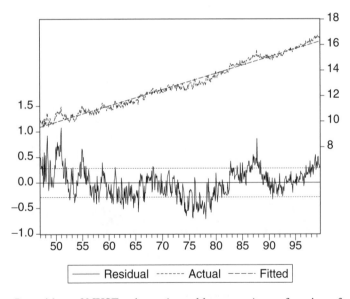

Figure 6.7 Logarithm of NYSE volume (monthly average) as a function of a time trend.

especially in 1987. That pattern might suggest an equation in which the trend is entered with a quadratic as well as a linear term.

The resulting graph is shown in figure 6.9. The residuals no longer follow the pattern of sagging in the middle, but volume in the years leading up to the 1987 crash is still above trend. The R^2 rises only from 0.98 to 0.985, and it is not

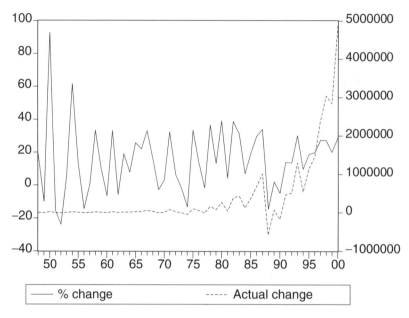

Figure 6.8 Actual and percentage changes in NYSE volume. While the actual changes are much larger in recent years, the percentage change is about the same.

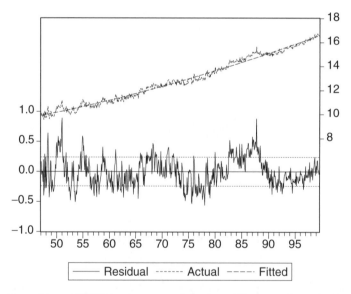

Figure 6.9 Logarithm of NYSE volume as a function of linear and quadratic time trends.

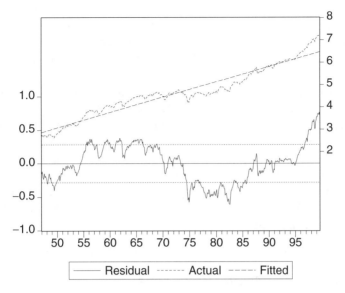

Figure 6.10   Logarithm of the S&P 500 stock price index as a function of a time trend.

clear if adding a quadratic term – which implies an accelerating rate of growth in the future – is appropriate.

What about the surge in stock prices themselves in the late 1990s? At first glance, the levels appear to follow the same explosive curve as stock exchange volume, so perhaps a logarithmic function would fit the long-term trend quite closely. However, when the log of the S&P500 price index is correlated with a time trend, as shown in figure 6.10, the values are still substantially above trend in recent years; even after the extended slump in 2001, stock prices remained above their long-term trend. In this case, trend analysis is not appropriate, as many would-be investors have found as they retired to the sidelines when the Dow was "overvalued" at 6000. This particular example emphasizes that trend analysis is most useful in situations where marketing or technology factors, rather than economic factors, dominate the growth pattern.

6.3 METHODS OF SMOOTHING DATA

The previous section focused on removing the trends from long time series. However, many applications with univariate time-series analysis utilize monthly data, where it is often useful to smooth the data. The methodology differs depending on whether the principal goal is to smooth random elements or repetitive patterns. The latter are discussed in the next section under the rubric of seasonal adjustment; here various processes are discussed for smoothing random elements in data series to discern the underlying trend. Most practical business applications are concerned with monthly and quarterly data, so we concentrate on those examples. In financial markets, daily data are often subject to smoothing (e.g., the familiar 20-, 40-, or 50-day moving averages for stock prices).

The most common methods of smoothing data involve either arithmetic or exponential moving averages. The Holt–Winters method adjusts for both random elements and the trend factor; it can also be expanded to include a seasonal adjustment variable. The Hodrick–Prescott filter was designed to measure long cyclical swings, and provides a smooth estimate of those patterns, hence removing both trend and cyclical factors. In these cases, smoothing methods are used to remove random fluctuations from the data and identify the underlying patterns, which can then be correlated with economic variables or used for further univariate time-series analysis.

6.3.1 ARITHMETIC MOVING AVERAGES

The simplest moving average is calculated by weighting each variable equally for a specified number of periods. This can be expressed as

$$\tilde{Y}_t = 1/(m+1)\sum_{i=0}^{m} Y_{t-i}. \tag{6.1}$$

Except for the current period, all the values are in the past, so this is often known as a one-sided moving average.

If the series has a time trend, it is often more useful to center the data on the current observation; this will become clearer when seasonal adjustment methods are discussed. The corresponding two-sided moving average is given by

$$\tilde{Y}_t = 1/(2m+1)\sum_{i=-m}^{m} Y_{t-i}. \tag{6.2}$$

A weighted moving average gives larger weights to more recent observations. A typical example is

$$\tilde{Y}_t = (1/21)\sum (6 * Y_t + 5 * Y_{t-1} + 4 * Y_{t-2} + 3 * Y_{t-3} + 2 * Y_{t-4} + Y_{t-5}). \tag{6.3}$$

To illustrate these examples, it is easier to inspect the differences in these weighted averages visually for series without any trend; the case of series with trends, which is more common, is covered in sections 6.3.3 and 6.3.4. The following two graphs show different types of moving averages for percentage changes in the stock market over the past three years. Figure 6.11 shows arithmetic moving averages; figure 6.12 shows weighted moving averages.

These graphs do not answer the question of how to choose the optimal lag, which is often a difficult decision. Some answers are provided in the next

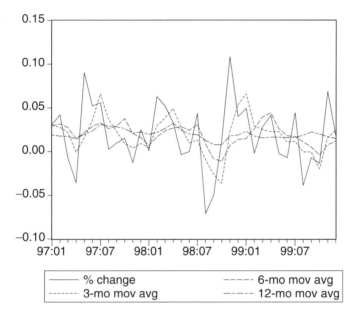

Figure 6.11 Moving averages of the percentage change in S&P 500 stock prices with different weight. As the length of the moving average increases, random monthly fluctuations become less important.

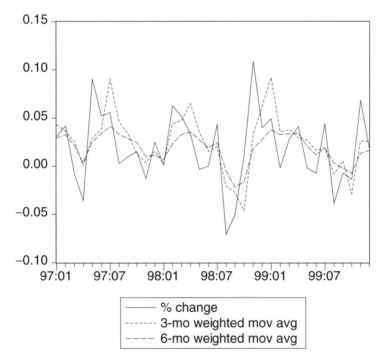

Figure 6.12 Weighted moving averages of the percentage change in S&P 500 stock prices, using arithmetically declining weights.

chapter; at this point we note that a six-month average seems to iron out most of the random fluctuations without obscuring the underlying pattern of changes in the stock market.

6.3.2 EXPONENTIAL MOVING AVERAGES

The concept of a weighted moving average can be generalized – and simplified – by moving to a method where the weights decline exponentially. Consider a series of fairly long length that can be represented as

$$\tilde{y}_t = \alpha \left[y_t + (1-\alpha) y_{t-1} + (1-\alpha)^2 y_{t-2} + \ldots + (1-\alpha)^n y_{t-n} \right] = \alpha \sum_{i=0}^{n} (1-\alpha)^i y_{t-i}. \quad (6.4)$$

Now consider the same equation lagged one period multiplied through by $(1 - \alpha)$. That yields

$$(1-\alpha)\tilde{y}_{t-1} = \alpha \left[(1-\alpha) y_{t-1} + (1-\alpha)^2 y_{t-2} + (1-\alpha)^3 y_{t-3} + \ldots + (1-\alpha)^{n+1} y_{t-(n+1)} \right]. \quad (6.5)$$

If (6.5) is subtracted from (6.4), all the intermediate terms drop out, leaving

$$\tilde{y}_t = \alpha y_t + (1-\alpha)\tilde{y}_{t-1} \quad (6.6)$$

except for the last term, which is very small and hence can be dropped without affecting the accuracy. The exponentially weighted moving average of y thus depends only on the current value of y, the moving average lagged one period, and α, which is known as the smoothing factor. The lower the value of α, the more heavily smoothed the series. Examples of different levels of α are given for the monthly percentage change in stock prices in figure 6.13. This formula makes estimating exponential weighted moving averages much simpler than compiling lengthy lists of arithmetic weights, a factor that becomes increasingly important when utilizing the concept of parsimony for non-structural models considered in the following chapter.

So far it has been assumed that the series being smoothed contain no trend, but that is seldom the case for time series. Two principal methods have been introduced to adjust for random elements when a time trend is present. The simpler of the two is known as double exponential smoothing, and involves the estimation of only a single parameter. The second, known as the Holt–Winters method,[1] involves estimating two or three separate parameters. That reduces parsimony but in most cases increases accuracy.

---

[1]   Holt, C. C., "Forecasting Seasonals and Trends by Exponentially Weighted Moving Averages," ONR Research Memorandum 52, Carnegie Institute of Technology, Pittsburgh, 1957; and Winters, P. R., "Forecasting Sales by Exponentially Weighted Moving Averages," *Management Science*, 6 (1960), 324–42.

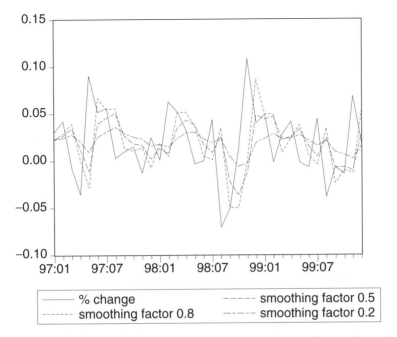

Figure 6.13 Exponential moving averages of monthly percentage changes in stock prices for $\alpha = 0.8$, 0.5, and 0.2.

The double-smoothing method starts out the same way as the exponential weighted moving averages considered earlier in this section. Repeating equation (6.6), the series can now be smoothed a second time using the same formula, which gives

$$\tilde{\tilde{y}}_t = \alpha \tilde{y} + (1-\alpha)\tilde{\tilde{y}}_{t-1}. \tag{6.7}$$

The forecast for $\tilde{y}$ in period k is given as:

$$\tilde{y}_{t+k} = (2\tilde{y}_t - \tilde{\tilde{y}}_t)^t \frac{\alpha}{1\alpha}[\tilde{y}_t - \tilde{\tilde{y}}_t]k \tag{6.8}$$

The major problem with this approach is that sometimes it may be advisable to apply a heavy smoothing factor to the trend but not give very large weights to previous values. That combination cannot be accomplished with a single parameter, which is why the two-parameter method is more common and usually gives better results. That case is considered next.

6.3.3 HOLT–WINTERS METHOD FOR EXPONENTIAL SMOOTHING

The two-parameter method for exponential smoothing was developed by C. C. Holt in 1957, and expanded to include a seasonal adjustment parameter

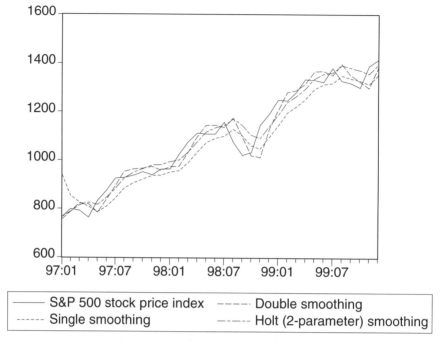

Figure 6.14 S&P 500 stock prices smoothed with different methods of exponential weighting, for $\alpha = 0.5$ in all cases.

by P. W. Winters in 1960. This considers only the contributions of Holt; the incorporation of seasonal factors is deferred until the next section.

Once again, $\tilde{y}_t$ is the smoothed series; the Holt method determines $\tilde{y}_t = a + bk$, where

$$a_t = \alpha y_t + (1-\alpha)(a_{t-1} + b_{t-1}) \tag{6.9}$$

$$b_t = \beta(a_t - a_{t-1}) + (1-\beta)b_{t-1} \tag{6.10}$$

and α and β are the two smoothing parameters. In these formulas, note the slope and intercept terms of the equation that determines $\tilde{y}$ change over time, which is the meaning of the time subscripts attached to the coefficients. The smoothing parameters α and β do not change, but the intercept and slope terms do. Essentially the Holt method adjusts the smoothed value of the intercept and trend of the previous period based on the addition of the next sample point. The smoothed values thus incorporate the new data and decrease the weights of the older data.

Monthly data for the S&P 500 stock price index for 1997 through 1999 are shown in figure 6.14. These data have been exponentially smoothed, using $\alpha = 0.5$ in all cases, for the methods of single smoothing, double smoothing, and the Holt (two-parameter) method. While again cautioning that no general conclusions can be drawn from one example, it is seen that the double-smoothing method simply lags behind the stock price series and does not do a very good job of smoothing.

In general, the Holt method with two parameters works better than the double-smoothing method that relies only on one parameter. Most of the time, a single parameter is asked to do "too much" and cannot adequately track both the random component and the trend, so a second parameter is generally advisable. Also, the Holt method permits an adjustment of the intercept and trend term based on more recent data.

In the next example, monthly data are smoothed for the manufacturing inventory/sales ratio (TRMH) starting in 1991, a period during which this ratio has exhibited a strong downward trend because of continued prosperity and the growing application of just-in-time and zero-inventory methods of production. The series is smoothed by three different methods, as shown in figure 6.15. In this case the algorithm chooses the value of α instead of arbitrarily assigning a value of 0.5. The single-smoothing method yields $\alpha = 0.84$, double-smoothing $\alpha = 0.28$, and the Holt method $\alpha = 0.63$.

While no unequivocal conclusions can be drawn from these graphs, the value of α for the double-smoothing method seems far too low, indicating that once again the attempt to make one parameter measure two different effects is not usually successful. The Holt method has the advantage of smoothing the series while retaining the underlying trend movements.

6.3.4 HODRICK–PRESCOTT FILTER

The methods in the previous section have been applied to relatively short data series. While there is nothing inherent in these methods that requires the use of only a few years of data, data smoothing methods for inventory and production control usually focus only on recent data. When extracting the underlying trend of an economic time series over the entire postwar period, a more common procedure is to use the Hodrick–Prescott filter. Indeed, this filter was expressly designed to analyze postwar US business cycles, as opposed to the smoothing methods used for inventory and production data.

Once again let $\tilde{y}$ be the smoothed series. Then the Hodrick–Prescott (HP) filter[2] minimizes the *variance* of y around its moving average, subject to a penalty that constrains the second difference of $\tilde{y}$. If the so-called penalty parameter is denoted by λ, then the HP filter chooses $\tilde{y}$ to minimize

$$\sum_{t=1}^{T}(y_t - \tilde{y}_t)^2 + \lambda \sum_{t=2}^{T-1}[(\tilde{y}_{t+1} - \tilde{y}_t) - (\tilde{y}_t - \tilde{y}_{t-1})]^2. \tag{6.11}$$

[2] Hodrick, R. J., and E. C. Prescott, "Postwar U.S. Business Cycles: An Empirical Investigation," *Journal of Money, Credit, and Banking*, 29 (1997), 1–16. While not published until 1997, this paper was circulated in the early 1980s.

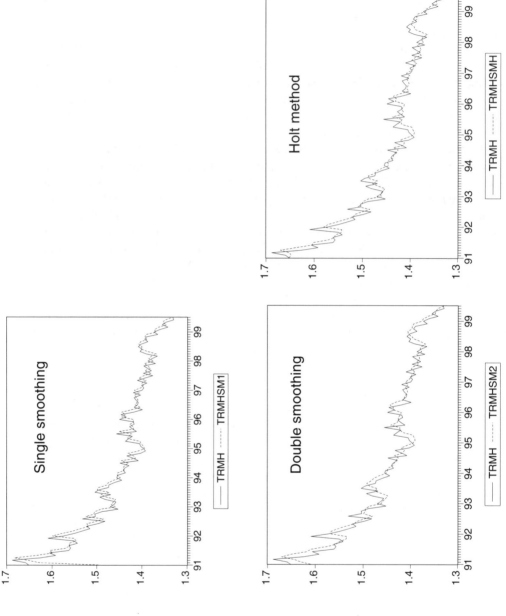

Figure 6.15 Smoothing the manufacturing inventory/sales ratio by different methods.

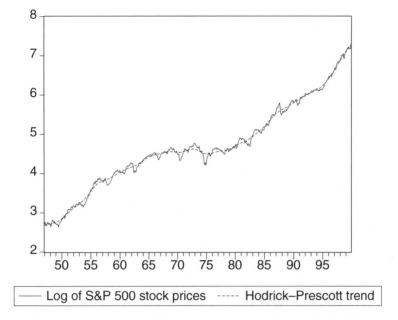

Figure 6.16 Logarithm of monthly S&P 500 stock prices with the Hodrick–Prescott filter. The trend of stock prices has shifted several times in the post World War II period, as reflected in the HP filter.

The larger the value of λ, the smoother the series. As $\lambda \to \infty$, $\tilde{y}$ approaches a linear trend. In EViews, the defult parameters for λ are 100 for annual data, 1,600 for quarterly data, and 14,400 for monthly data.

In figure 6.16, the HP filter is used on the logarithms of the monthly data for the S&P 500 stock price index from 1947 through 1999. Unlike simple linear or quadratic trends, it can be seen that this trend value changes its slope several times throughout the period. Stock prices rose rapidly through 1966, then almost leveled off through 1981, regained their earlier growth rate from 1982 through 1994, and then accelerated through 1999. While the economic reasons for these shifts may also be of interest, the HP filter allows one to analyze short-term cyclical and random fluctuations around a shifting trend.

6.4 METHODS OF SEASONAL ADJUSTMENT

At the beginning of this chapter we presented the classical dichotomy of a time series into trend, seasonal, cyclical, and irregular components. It is now time to examine methods of adjusting for seasonal variation.

In some cases the researcher or model builder will want to identify and estimate the seasonal factors. This would be the case, for example, if someone wanted to know how much additional stock to order before the holiday shopping season, or how much to cut back on inventories before summer plant closings.

In other cases, model builders want to use seasonally adjusted data to avoid spurious correlations. As already shown, retail sales rise sharply each December. Because people earn and spend more money, income and credit outstanding also rise sharply each December. Thus a simple correlation between these two series without seasonal adjustment would overstate the correlation between consumption and income, and consumption and credit.

The methods for seasonal adjustment discussed in this section can be used for either of two purposes. In some cases, the desired objective is to prepare seasonally adjusted data. In other cases, the seasonal adjustment factors themselves are desired for forecasting purposes.

The underlying principal behind seasonal adjustment is quite simple *if the seasonal factors remain constant*. The problem is that, in most economic time series, they do not. The causes of changing seasonal factors can be divided into three categories: random changes, such as those associated with the weather; shifting patterns associated with variations in the calendar (such as the movable date of Easter, or different number of weekends per month); and shifts in factors related to economic decisions. The latter case is represented by such phenomena as the lengthening of the Christmas holiday shopping season, or fewer plant shutdowns during the summer.

One well-known example of the first type of change in seasonal factors is the pattern of housing starts in the Northeast and Midwest regions of the US, which decline sharply every January and February because of the cold weather. While a similar pattern occurs every year, the severity of winter varies considerably from one year to the next. The seasonal factor for housing starts in January and February for these regions is about 2, which means actual housing starts are multiplied by 2 to obtain the seasonally adjusted figure.

Suppose actual housing starts in these two regions of the country usually average about 20,000 per month in January and February, or about 480,000 on a seasonally adjusted annual rate basis. Because of unusually mild winter weather one year, that figure rises to 27,000 per month. The seasonally adjusted annual rate figures would increase to 648,000. Assuming no offsetting weather effects in the South and West, seasonally adjusted housing starts at annual rates would increase 168,000, which might lead some economists to conclude that housing activity was accelerating.

Other, wiser hands would point out that the surge was due to mild weather, but even that is not the end of the story. If in fact the underlying demand for housing has not changed, then housing starts in the Northeast and Midwest will actually total 480,000 by year-end. However, the seasonally adjusted data will tell another story. Suppose houses were started ahead of schedule in January and February, resulting in fewer starts during the peak months of June and July, when the seasonal factor is about 0.8. The switch of 7,000 starts from Jun/Jul to Jan/Feb will add 168,000 at seasonally adjusted annual rates in the first two months of the year, but subtract only 67,000 from the Jun/Jul figures. Hence the seasonally adjusted total for the year will be 101,000 more than the actual number.

Obviously this discrepancy cannot remain on the books. The Bureau of the Census, which prepares these figures, goes back and adjusts the numbers so that the seasonally adjusted and actual totals are identical. Yet in the meantime, the figures reported on a monthly basis are misleading. Furthermore, the equilibration of the two series means the seasonal factors for January and February will be adjusted because of the mild winter, so if there is a severe winter the following year, the seasonally adjusted housing start data will understate the true level of starts. No method will entirely compensate for this anomaly, and as a result, "seasonally adjusted" data from the government often contains unintended inaccuracies. This is an unavoidable error, not a criticism of the highly sophisticated methods used at Census, yet it does lead to forecasting errors. In recent years, the seasonal adjustment programs have been refined to isolate or reduce the importance of outliers due to weather or other exogenous causes.

In other cases, changes in seasonal adjustment factors are due to predictable patterns. Since these changes are not random, the problems are usually less severe. In the case of changes in the calendar, the adjustments are straightforward. Some months may have more trading days than others, or more weekends; the seasonal adjustment algorithms can easily be adjusted to take this into account. The other major source of seasonal variation in this category revolves around changing dates for holidays, notably Easter. We show below how changes in the date of Easter Sunday affects the seasonal factor for apparel sales in March and April.

The more complicated issue arises when the seasonals shift due to economic factors. For example, the Christmas shopping season now extends further in both directions. Another example is that many manufacturing plants do not shut down as much in summer as they used to. Demand for power used to peak on cold days in the winter; now it peaks on hot days in the summer. More people vacation in Florida in August than used to be the case.

Many firms, such as hospitals and educational institutions, raise their prices only once a year. During years of rapid inflation, hospital costs rose an average of 10% per year. Since these changes usually occurred in January, the seasonal adjustment factors gradually incorporated this change. During the 1990s, the annual increase in hospital costs fell to about 3% per year. Thus for a while, the seasonally adjusted figures for hospital costs in January would show a 7% decline. Eventually this problem was fixed, but when the rate of inflation slowed down in the US in the 1980s and 1990s, the seasonally adjusted data for the CPI initially showed an actual decline in January (the current revised data have fixed this error, so you won't find it now).

Seasonal factors can also be affected by outlying values. Suppose some exogenous event – an oil shock for the PPI – caused a change in one given month that was 10 times as large as an ordinary seasonal factor. If that one point is treated the same as all other observations, it will dominate the seasonals in other years. One possibility is to omit it entirely; another way is to dampen it. However, it cannot be ignored entirely without distorting the seasonal factors in subsequent years.

Census Bureau programs have been designed to treat all these and other factors, and the methods they use will be briefly outlined. First, however, it is useful to understand how seasonal adjustment factors are calculated when the weights do not change and random fluctuations are relatively small.

6.4.1 ARITHMETIC AND MULTIPLICATIVE FIXED WEIGHTS

To illustrate these points, consider a typical monthly series before seasonal adjustment. The first step is to calculate a centered moving average, which for monthly data is

$$\tilde{y} = (y_{t+6} + 2y_{t+5} + \ldots + 2y_{t-5} + y_{t-6})/24. \tag{6.12}$$

The seasonal factors for each month can then be calculated as $y - \tilde{y}$. All the seasonals are collected for the first, second, . . . , twelfth month and averaged for each month.

Sometimes the sum of the seasonally adjusted data for any given year will not be equal to the actual data, as already discussed for housing starts. When that occurs, the seasonal factors must be re-scaled to eradicate that anomaly. One simple way would be to adjust each year separately: if the sum of the seasonally adjusted data were 102% of the actual data, all observations would simply be divided by 1.02. There is a problem with this method. Suppose in the following year the seasonally adjusted data were 98% of the actual data; then the seasonally adjusted series would have an unwarranted 4% rise from December to January. Hence the seasonal factors themselves must be smoothed by a moving-average method to eliminate the jumps that would occur when the seasonally adjusted data for any given year do not sum to the actual data.

If one wants to obtain the seasonal factors themselves, rather than the seasonally adjusted data, and if it is assumed the factors remain constant, a regression can be calculated in which the actual data are a function of seasonal dummy variables that are 1 in the appropriate month and zero elsewhere. Recall the earlier warning that you cannot include all 12 monthly seasonal factors plus the constant term, or the matrix will not invert. It is necessary to omit one of the seasonals, or the constant term itself.

The major problem with this method is that it usually does not work if the time series has a strong trend; as we have often seen, most of them do. In these cases, the methodology is similar except that the seasonal factors are calculated as $y/\tilde{y}$ instead of $y - \tilde{y}$. That way, the percentage difference of the ith month

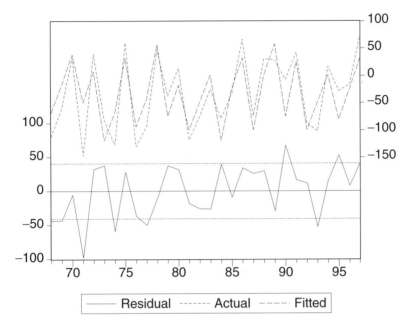

Figure 6.17   The difference between March and April seasonal factors for apparel sales, depending on which date Easter falls.

relative to its moving average is assumed to remain constant, rather than the actual amount.

Multiplicative factors can be used as a quick and easy method of obtaining seasonal factors for series with strong time trends when the evidence suggests calendar variations are unimportant, outlying values are within 2.5σ, and the seasonal patterns do not shift over time. Since these conditions seldom occur, we next discuss how each of these issues should be treated.

6.4.2 VARIABLE WEIGHTS

At the beginning of this chapter the seasonal factors for general merchandise sales were presented. The data for apparel sales will now be used to illustrate the issue that arises because of changing seasonals due to a variable holiday, which in this case is Easter. First, take the seasonally unadjusted data for apparel sales and remove the trend calculated by using a log-linear equation. Second, take the actual residuals from this equation and divide by a two-sided 12-month moving average to obtain the seasonal factors for March and April. The difference between these two seasonal factors is then correlated with a series that has the values equal to the day of April on which Easter falls; if it occurs in March, a negative figure is estimated (e.g., March 30 = −2). The resulting regression, for which the residuals are shown in figure 6.17, indicates that

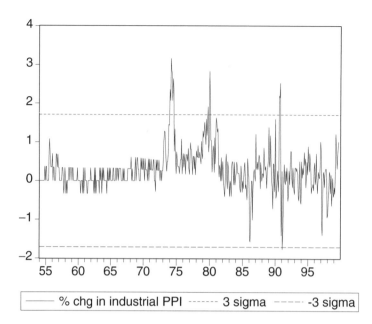

Figure 6.18 Monthly percentage changes in unadjusted industrial producer price index (PPI). During energy shocks the percentage change was more than three standard deviations from the mean.

70% of the shift in the seasonal factors between these two months can be explained by the timing of Easter. The remaining factors are random, as indicated by a *DW* of 2.00.

This simple regression does not take into account a possible nonlinear relationship (e.g., the difference between Easter on April 12 and April 19 may not be as great as the difference between Easter on March 31 and April 7), nor does it smooth for outlying observations, as occurred in 1971 when sales were postponed because the economy was just recovering from a recession. Nonetheless, the pattern is clearly significant; the *t*-ratio for the coefficient of the Easter variable is −7.1. Building a calendar into the seasonal adjustment algorithms is a relatively simple way to adjust for holiday variations.

6.4.3 TREATMENT OF OUTLYING OBSERVATIONS

The next topic to be considered is what happens when an economic time series is dominated by a few outlying observations. To illustrate this point, look at the seasonally unadjusted PPI for industrial commodities. Figure 6.18 shows monthly percentage changes for seasonally unadjusted data.

The standard error is 0.57%. Yet there are several periods when the actual percentage change is more than 3σ. Apparently these are drawn from a different population. These periods correspond to the removal of price controls in 1974, the energy shock in January 1980, the plunge in oil prices in February and March 1986, the Iraqi invasion of Kuwait in August through October 1990, and the return to normalcy after the US and UN victory in the Persian Gulf War in February and March 1991.

Note in particular that the two biggest declines both occurred in February and March. Thus if no further adjustments were made, the seasonal adjustment program would assume that prices always fell sharply in those two months. Hence in normal years, the seasonally adjusted data would show big increases. The Census programs allow the user to specify a certain σ beyond which the observations are discarded and replaced with some weighted moving average of nearby values. In most cases, σ is set at a range between 1.5 and 2.5, with the weights given to the outlying values gradually declining to zero as σ increases over this range.

In the Census X-11 program,[3] the raw data are generally adjusted for (i) trading day variations where appropriate, (ii) movable holidays where appropriate, and (iii) outliers, following the methodology sketched above. This program then recalculates the moving average taking the adjusted data into account, and generates another set of seasonal factors. The seasonal factors are scaled so they sum to 12.000 for monthly data and 4.000 for quarterly data. The process is then refined several more times until the differences between iterations are insignificant. In some versions of these programs, the duration of the moving average is adjusted by the amount of randomness in the series, and can range (for monthly data) from 9 to 23 months.

Hence a sophisticated seasonal adjustment program modifies the data based on the different number of trading days or the existence of moving holidays, reduces or eliminates the undue influence of outliers, and adjusts the length of the moving average based on randomness, continuing to refine this process until a convergence process is reached. These methods are all straightforward if somewhat lengthy and do not raise any statistical questions.

The method described above, which calculates the seasonal factors based on modified data divided by a smoothed trend, permits these factors to change over time. That is entirely appropriate; failure to do this would often generate subpar results. Nonetheless, that procedure raises additional questions in terms of both statistical procedure and economic inference.

---

[3] A refinement of this program, the X-12-ARIMA program, is discussed in Findley, D. F. et al., "New Capabilities and Methods of the X-12-ARIMA Seasonal-Adjustment Program," *Journal of Business & Economic Statistics*, 16 (1998), 127–52.

6.4.4 SEASONAL ADJUSTMENT FACTORS WITH THE CENSUS BUREAU X-11 PROGRAM

One of the standard methods for seasonally adjusting data is the Census Bureau X-11 program, which is important for forecasters because it is used to calculate all the seasonally adjusted government data: national income accounts, employment and unemployment, prices and productivity, and so on. The principal steps utilized by this program are:

1 Adjust data for trading day or holiday differences.
2 Take the resulting data and calculate a 12-month (or four-quarter) moving average.
3 Smooth this series with another moving average, usually over three or five periods.
4 Calculate preliminary seasonal factors as the actual data divided by this twice-smoothed average.
5 Identify the outlying values. The default option is to scale their weights from 100% to 0% when σ is between 1.5 and 2.5. Replace these outliers with trend values.
6 Calculate the seasonal factors based on actual data adjusted for outliers divided by smoothed trends.
7 Smooth the existing trend cycle again and recalculate the seasonal factors. In some versions, the length of the moving average chosen is longer if the underlying series has more randomness.

We now return to the data for general merchandise sales. Table 6.1 shows the seasonal factors from the Census Bureau X-11 program. Note that over the period 1988 through 1998 the December seasonal declined from 184.7 to 167.2, while the January seasonal rose from 70.3 to 76.7. Also note that the February and July seasonals rose substantially, while the November seasonal also declined. In preparing estimates of seasonally adjusted data for the current year, the Census Bureau uses these formulas to project future seasonal factors based on recent trends in the past. The program prints out these estimates; the November and December seasonals are expected to decline further, while the January and February seasonals are expected to rise further.

Yet eventually these trends must come to an end, otherwise shopping in December would be no higher than in any other month. If this declining seasonal pattern ends gradually, the program may be able to track it accurately. However, sometimes the seasonal pattern changes suddenly. For example, the seasonal pattern showed virtually no change through 1987, and then started declining about 1.5 points per year. That may not seem like a very big change, but data reported by Census that retail sales rose only 4% instead of 5% in

Table 6.1 X-11 seasonal adjustment factors for general merchandise sales.

	Jan	Feb	Mar	Apr	May	Jun	Jul	Aug	Sep	Oct	Nov	Dec
1979	71.366	69.967	87.697	93.337	98.439	93.569	89.135	97.851	92.141	101.610	119.746	185.034
1980	71.253	69.929	87.944	93.368	98.484	93.709	89.110	97.632	92.138	101.327	119.688	185.485
1981	71.040	70.015	88.140	93.295	98.698	93.784	89.000	97.373	92.087	100.909	119.665	186.310
1982	70.732	70.100	88.363	93.214	98.843	93.958	88.679	97.141	91.944	100.235	119.805	186.690
1983	70.427	70.403	88.858	93.080	99.413	93.866	88.318	97.219	91.661	99.525	120.054	186.772
1984	70.180	70.711	89.542	92.865	99.854	93.792	87.925	97.511	91.286	98.967	120.288	186.556
1985	70.002	71.144	90.216	92.519	100.288	93.591	87.671	97.910	90.867	98.706	120.388	186.079
1986	70.021	71.483	90.823	92.434	100.198	93.624	87.564	98.104	90.517	98.616	120.450	185.701
1987	70.065	71.763	91.393	92.294	99.798	93.853	87.644	98.184	90.296	98.388	120.559	185.239
1988	70.292	71.991	91.956	92.074	99.238	94.249	87.883	98.208	90.089	98.007	120.596	184.653
1989	70.808	72.393	92.314	91.791	98.717	94.541	88.250	98.301	89.989	97.716	120.631	183.294
1990	71.625	72.932	92.484	91.706	98.403	94.512	88.870	98.380	89.974	97.653	120.473	181.380
1991	72.539	73.662	92.620	91.616	98.194	94.359	89.633	98.504	90.088	97.934	120.036	179.039
1992	73.437	74.438	92.576	91.669	98.128	94.252	90.525	98.505	90.313	98.319	119.318	176.821
1993	74.246	75.250	92.354	91.750	98.081	94.409	91.184	98.565	90.630	98.739	118.616	174.560
1994	74.990	76.017	91.985	91.826	98.156	94.734	91.795	98.715	90.862	98.928	118.084	172.334
1995	75.583	76.884	91.591	91.840	98.442	95.161	92.106	99.032	90.859	98.936	117.738	170.323
1996	76.100	77.602	91.281	91.893	98.881	95.502	92.404	99.404	90.689	98.889	117.663	168.847
1997	76.422	78.107	90.949	91.923	99.351	95.593	92.494	99.739	90.447	98.873	117.543	167.831
1998	76.677	78.414	90.825	91.978	99.699	95.570	92.520	99.943	90.258	98.857	117.402	167.203
Seasonal factors, one year ahead												
1999	76.804	78.568	90.762	92.005	99.873	95.558	92.534	100.045	90.164	98.849	117.331	166.889

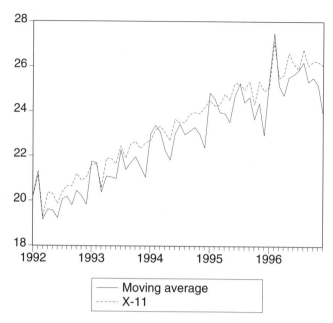

Figure 6.19 Department store sales adjusted by fixed and moving-average seasonals. The series adjusted by the X-11 method contains far fewer seasonal aberrations than that adjusted by a simple multiplicative model.

December might signal a substantially slower growth rate in the economy – or it might represent only a changing seasonal factor. To the extent that financial market and economic policy decisions are based on the growth rate, changes of this magnitude can be quite important.

The seasonally adjusted department store sales using X-11 are shown relative to the seasonal factors using a simple multiplicative model in figure 6.19. In this case, it is clear that the X-11 adjusted series is much smoother than the constant-weight seasonal factors.

This chapter has contained examples where several economic time series have been decomposed into their components: trend, cyclical, seasonal, and irregular. When a significant long-term shift in seasonal factors can be identified, the X-11 program will generally provide better results than fixed-weight seasonals. Yet at least so far, the term "better" applies to sample period tracking, rather than actual forecasting. Forecasting has not been covered in this chapter because the results from decomposition need to be combined with other methods to produce useful forecasts. The next chapter shows how autoregressive and moving-average models can be combined with time-series decomposition to build non-structural forecasting models.

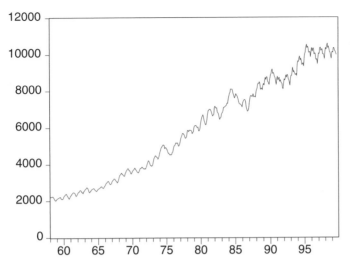

Figure 6.20   Case study 11: Manufacturing inventory stocks for textile mill products (SIC-22) (millions of current dollars, not seasonally adjusted).

Case Study 11: Manufacturing Inventory Stocks for Textile Mill Products

Step 1
Inspect the graph visually, as shown in figure 6.20 (this is always a good idea in any case). There is a clear upward trend, but it is not monotonic: in particular, the trend dips in the 1983–5 period, suggesting there are some longer-term cyclical effects as well. Also, there is a definite seasonal pattern, although visual inspection from this graph does not reveal whether the seasonals shift over time.

Step 2
Try extracting the trend using a log-linear transformation, as shown in figure 6.21. As it turns out, the trend does not fit very well, especially near the end, when the errors are likely to be most important for forecasting. Thus a different approach is suggested.

Step 3
Fit a Hodrick–Prescott filter through the residuals, then examine the new residuals (see figure 6.22).

Step 4
Examine the residuals from figure 6.22 for seasonal patterns, observe whether the seasonals are stable or not, and whether they increase over time. The residuals are shown in figure 6.23.

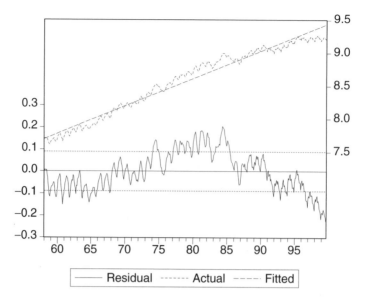

Figure 6.21 Log-linear trend of textile mill inventories.

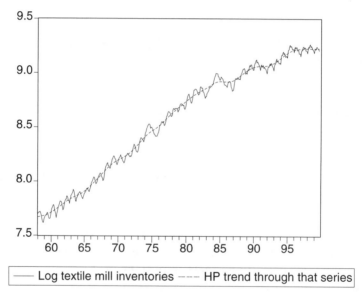

Figure 6.22 Textile mill inventory trend determined by HP filter. The trend fits the series much better than a straightforward log-linear trend.

Step 5
Calculate a linear regression of these residuals on the monthly seasonal factor and a time trend (figure 6.24). That term turns out to be insignificant, which means the seasonals are stable over time. This regression will also supply the monthly seasonal factors for forecasting purposes.

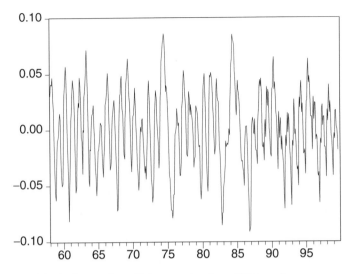

Figure 6.23 Residuals for textile mill inventories from HP trend.

Since the process has already identified the trend, cyclical, and seasonal factors, the residuals left in figure 6.24 represent the irregular component. The major outliers are associated with the energy crisis in 1974, which sent raw material prices soaring and created temporary shortages; those factors were reversed the following year. The other major disturbance occurred in 1983–4. Because of the unprecedented high level of real interest rates, the previous year, firms reduced their inventory stocks below equilibrium levels; the sharp increase in demand during the first year of recovery in 1983 caught manufacturers by surprise, and they did not rebuild inventories to equilibrium levels until the following year. Since neither of these events are likely to occur again, the irregular component can reasonably be assumed to be random in the near future. Also, since the seasonals are stable, there is no need to use the X-11 seasonal adjustment program.

Hence the trend, cyclical, and seasonal patterns identified in the various stages of decomposition can serve as a useful guide for forecasting textile mill inventories in the near future. In the case where a firm has many such product lines, similar results could be used to track inventories and help the plant managers determine when inventory levels are diverging from their expected values so they can make the appropriate operating decisions.

Case Study 12: Seasonally Adjusted Gasoline Prices

The data for gasoline prices at the consumer level before seasonal adjustment are shown in figure 6.25. Note this is different from the other examples

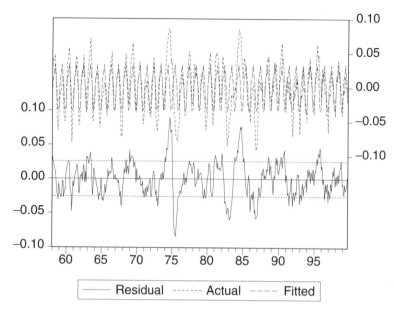

Figure 6.24 HP residuals for textile mill inventories as a function of seasonal dummy variables.

given in this chapter, because there is no discernible long-run trend or cyclical pattern. While gasoline prices are much higher now than they were in the 1950s, they are no higher in *relative* terms. Furthermore, there has been no upward trend since 1980 even in nominal terms. Hence neither a log-linear transformation nor a Hodrick–Prescott filter will identify major trends or cycles in this series.

This series represents a major challenge for analysis and forecasting because the irregular component – dominated by energy shocks – overwhelms the trend, cycle, and seasonal factors. What is the proper procedure for analyzing and predicting gasoline prices?

From the perspective of identifying any trend, it is more useful to look at the price of gasoline relative to the overall CPI. While there were substantial increases from 1973 through 1980, the long-term tendency is for the relative price of gasoline to remain unchanged. That is probably the most reasonable working assumption for trend analysis. In particular, there is no reason to expect rising relative prices to reemerge, in spite of frequent stories about the "shortage" of petroleum. Other methods of forecasting long-range trends, some of them non-econometric, are discussed in chapter 10.

There is no identifiable cyclical pattern for gasoline prices, since they do not rise in booms and fall in recessions. If anything, a sharp increase in gasoline

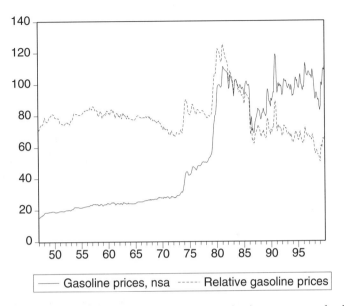

Figure 6.25 Seasonally unadjusted gasoline prices in absolute terms, and relative to the overall CPI.

prices leads to a recession the following year. In the future, the most reasonable assumption is one of no cyclical pattern.

Turning to the seasonal pattern, regressing the percentage change in gasoline prices as a function of seasonal dummy variables reveals significant positive seasonals in April, May, and June: the percentage change data are given in figure 6.26. This regression reveals that the price of gasoline rises an average of 1.2%, 1.2%, and 0.9% in those three months, while on balance it does not change for the rest of the year. However, with all the shifts in energy markets over the past 50 years, one might reasonably want to test for variable seasonal weights by using X-11. The comparison of the unadjusted and X-11 seasonally adjusted data is shown in figure 6.27. As shown there, the seasonals are overwhelmed by the irregular component.

Readers may wish to run the X-11 program and examine the actual and seasonally adjusted data. The program shows that, after the big drop in gasoline prices in February and March 1986, seasonally adjusted data for the next few years showed bigger increases in those months than actually occurred. Also, note that the single biggest monthly percentage increase in gasoline prices occurred not during any of the energy crises, but in April 1999, when prices rose 15%. Eventually these anomalies will be removed; but in previous years, the revised seasonally adjusted data showed a big decline in

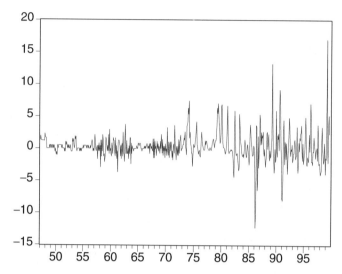

Figure 6.26 Monthly percentage change in CPI-gasoline prices before seasonal adjustment. The biggest percentage change in the CPI for gasoline prices did not occur during or immediately after any of the energy crises, but in April 1999.

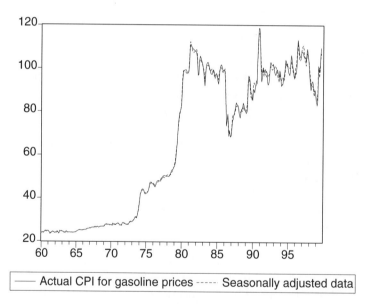

| —— Actual CPI for gasoline prices ----- Seasonally adjusted data |

Figure 6.27 CPI-gasoline prices unadjusted and with X-11 seasonal adjustment. The seasonal pattern is overwhelmed by the irregular component.

April gasoline prices – whereas in fact they rose by the usual amount. Unless specific adjustments are included, the X-11 seasonal adjustment program tends to distort the actual data in the years before and after a big move in prices.

Admittedly, the CPI for gasoline prices is an unusual series in that the irregular component dominates the decomposition: usually the trend, cycle, and seasonal are all more important. However, this example does show how to proceed when these circumstances do arise.

Problems and Questions

1. Plot the monthly data for the index of industrial production before seasonal adjustment.

(a) Calculate a linear and log-linear trend. Which is more appropriate? Do you think these data should be fitted using a quadratic trend?

(b) Calculate the seasonal factors using a linear regression. Compare these with the seasonal factors calculated with the X-11 program. Do you think the seasonals are stable?

(c) Calculate the seasonals using percentage first differences of industrial production. How do the results differ? What is the economic interpretation of that difference?

(d) Repeat the same exercise for seasonally unadjusted industrial production for the steel industry. Are the seasonal factors stable for that industry? To what do you attribute the differences?

2. Taxes received by the Federal government are much higher in the second quarter of each year than during other quarters. Plot the seasonally unadjusted quarterly series from 1959 to the present.

(a) Run a regression using a time trend and seasonal dummy variables for linear and log-linear forms of the equation. Based on those figures, what has been the average growth rate of tax receipts over this period?

(b) Which seasonal factors, if any, are significant in addition to the second quarter? Which are not? What accounts for that finding?

(c) The X-11 program shows that the weights have shifted substantially over the past 30 years. In particular, the weights have increased for the second quarter and declined for the other three quarters. What factor caused that to happen?

(d) Run the X-11 program using the logarithm of seasonally unadjusted Federal income tax receipts. Do the weights still show the same pattern? What accounts for the difference? How would you modify your answer to (c) in view of this result?

(e) Many years ago, Federal income taxes used to be due on March 15 instead of April 15. When that occurred, the bulk of tax payments

Continued

were made during the first quarter. Examine the data going back to 1947 and determine in what year the change was made. As a government statistician, you are asked to develop seasonal factors for tax receipts as part of the preparation of National Income and Product Accounts (NIPA) figures on a seasonally adjusted basis. Explain how you would calculate the change in seasonals, taking the change in regulations into account. (Hint: did the quarterly pattern change all at once, or did it take taxpayers several years to adjust to this change?)

(f) Following the 1973–4 recession, Congress passed an income tax rebate that was distributed during 1975.2. Thus for that year only, seasonally unadjusted tax receipts fell during the second quarter instead of rising sharply. In designing a seasonal adjustment program, how would you treat that one quarter? Check the results using X-11 and determine whether or not 1975.2 is used in calculating the final seasonal factors that the government actually used. (Hint: compare these data with the published seasonally adjusted data.)

3. New orders for capital goods are often considered one of the most reliable leading indicators of where the economy is heading, but the monthly data are very erratic. The major issue is to try to determine when significant changes represent trends and when they represent only temporary factors. Aircraft orders tend to be "lumpy" and show huge monthly changes, so data are presented separately for aircraft and all other private sector capital goods.

(a) Plot the series for non-defense capital goods new orders excluding aircraft and parts (NORXA) from the beginning of the series in 1968 through to the end of 1999. Calculate the smoothing factors for single exponential smoothing, double exponential smoothing, and Holt–Winters. How do these compare? Which estimate do you think is most reliable for ascertaining the underlying trend?

(b) Calculate a smoothed series using the Hodrick–Prescott filter. Compare the results over the sample period. Use the HP filter to estimate how much NORXA would be likely to increase in 2000 if the smoothing factor remained unchanged. Compare this with the actual data for 2000. Based on that comparison, do you think capital spending slowed down in 2000?

(c) Now use the seasonally unadjusted series for NORXA. Calculate the multiplicative seasonal factors using Holt–Winters. How have the other parameters, α and β changed? What is the economic interpretation of that shift?

(d) Calculate the smoothing factors for aircraft orders using single exponential smoothing, double exponential smoothing, and

Continued

Holt–Winters. You will find that α is very close to zero. What is the economic interpretation of that result?

(e) Calculate the smoothed series for aircraft orders using the Hodrick–Prescott filter for the sample period ending in 1999. Now go back and recalculate the same smoothed series through 2000 (EViews will automatically give that series another name). Plot the two smoothed series. What conclusion can be drawn from this comparison about using the HP filter as a forecasting tool?

4. It is usually claimed that stock prices (and other financial market indicators) contain no stable seasonal factors, for if they did, leveraged instruments such as options and futures could be used to make tremendous profits.

(a) Calculate the monthly seasonal factors for the Nasdaq index to determine whether there are any significant seasonal factors. In determining whether this is the case, calculate the seasonals for (i) levels, (ii) logs, and (iii) percentage changes.

(b) You will find significant seasonal factors for percentage changes for January and February. This result, which has been the subject of many articles in financial journals, is related to what is generally called the "January effect" and has been well known for several years. Given that is the case, how would you expect seasonals for those months to shift in recent years? Has that happened or not?

(c) It is often claimed that short-term changes in stock prices reflect changes in interest rates. Calculate the seasonal factors for changes in the Federal funds rate and the Aaa corporate bond yield. Are there any significant seasonal factors for those variables? Why do you think the seasonal pattern persists for equities but not for debt instruments?

(d) It is often claimed that the stock market is a leading indicator; the problem is that wide monthly swings may disguise underlying trends. Using the tools developed in this chapter, calculate the optimal smoothing parameters for the S&P 500 index that would enhance its value as a leading indicator (for purposes of comparison, the index of coincident indicators tells the current state of the economy). Perform the same exercise for the Nasdaq composite. Which one – if either – of these two series would serve as a useful leading indicator? In this answer, consider what happened in both 1987 and 1998: the stock market suffered a severe correction, but real GDP growth accelerated the following year.

Continued

5. One of the major responsibilities of production managers is to keep track of inventories and determine when they are diverging relative to sales. If stocks are too low, production activity should be increased, and if they are too high, it should be diminished. In many capital-intensive industries, however, there are substantial costs to changing production schedules if the changes are only temporary. Hence one major challenge is to determine when deviations of the inventory/sales ratio from its trend indicate a change in production schedules, and when they are due to short-term factors that will soon be reversed.

(a) Plot the inventory/sales (I/S) ratio for the paper industry (SIC 26). Test to see whether there are any significant seasonal factors (although both inventory stocks and sales are seasonally adjusted, the ratio itself might have some seasonality).

(b) Since 1983, this I/S ratio – like most manufacturing industries – has exhibited a significant downward trend. Do you see any sign that the trend is leveling off, or would you include it in predictions for future years? How would you design a test to determine whether the downward trend is continuing?

(c) Calculate three-month and six-month unweighted moving averages, and three-month and six-month geometrically weighted moving averages. Which of these do you think would be most useful in indicating recent trends in the I/S ratio that exclude short-term temporary factors?

(d) Now consider the I/S ratio for the chemical industry (SIC 28). A comparative plot of these two series will show that the I/S ratio for both declined sharply in the mid-1980s, but after that, the I/S ratio for the paper industry had much more cyclical volatility. Keeping that in mind, explain how the optimal smoothing series you designed for the paper industry would change for the chemical industry.

(e) Over an extended period of time, the I/S ratio for any industry obviously cannot continue to decline the same amount indefinitely; yet it is not clear whether the inflection point has yet been reached. For the chemical industry, determine whether a nonlinear trend that decreases at a diminishing rate would provide a better method of tracking the I/S ratio than a linearly declining trend.

CHAPTER 7

UNIVARIATE TIME-SERIES MODELING AND FORECASTING

INTRODUCTION

The previous chapter covered the decomposition of economic time series into their components: trend, cyclical, seasonal, and irregular. Methods were explained for extracting the trend, long-term cyclical swings, and seasonal patterns, but virtually nothing was said about the irregular component. That is because in the classical linear model it is assumed to be random.

Yet as has already been seen, that assumption is unlikely to be met. This chapter focuses on methods that can be used to improve forecasting accuracy based on the information found in the irregular component. Two principal methods are considered: autoregressive models, which are important if the residuals are serially correlated, and moving-average models, where forecasts are adjusted by previous values of the residuals. Note that in this context, a moving-average model refers to a regression in which the dependent variable is a function of previous residuals – as opposed to the meaning in the previous chapter, when a moving average was some weighted combination of current and lagged values of the variable itself.

The models considered in this chapter are known as ARIMA models, which stands for AutoRegressive Integrated Moving Average models.[1] Integrated means the trend has been removed; if the series has no significant trend, the models are known as ARMA models. These models are, of course, non-structural; they contain no economic variables. The only independent variables are lagged values of the dependent variable and previous residuals; in all cases where it is relevant, the time trend has been removed.

---

[1] For additional treatment of this material, see Pindyck, Robert S., and Daniel L. Rubinfeld, *Econometric Models and Economic Forecasts*, 4th edn (Irwin McGraw-Hill, Boston), 1998, chs 16–17; and Johnson, Jack, and John DiNardo, *Econometric Methods*, 4th edn (McGraw-Hill, New York), 1997, ch. 7. A more statistically intensive treatment is found in Granger, C. W. J., and Paul Newbold, *Forecasting Economic Time Series* (Academic Press, San Diego, CA), 1986, ch. 1.5–1.7.

The approach taken earlier in this text was to build structural models, on the grounds that the best attempt to estimate the underlying population parameters would probably generate the best forecasts. However, we have attempted to show, both by examples that worked and examples that did not, the possible pitfalls to that approach. Some of these examples also indicated how forecasting accuracy can be improved by using constant adjustments, but so far this has involved somewhat of an ad hoc approach. It is likely that forecasting accuracy can be improved by using the best features from both structural and nonstructural forecasts; this topic is explored in chapter 8.

There are several possible reasons why the structural approach could be suboptimal. First, the underlying structure may shift over time. One notable example of this is the Federal funds rate; the underlying parameters change every time a new Fed Chairman is appointed. Second, a non-structural approach may be more feasible for thousands of individual product lines. Suppose someone is dealing with 10,000 parts or SKUs; it would take a tremendous amount of time and effort to build a structural econometric model for each separate item and keep all those models updated. In such cases, a nonstructural approach would be much more efficient.

Non-structural models can also serve as a yardstick: if a structural equation cannot explain a higher proportion of the variance than a model that uses only the lagged dependent variable and previous residuals, its forecasting efficacy should be severely questioned. It was also shown earlier that, while a single-equation model may generate accurate forecasts if the values of all the independent variables are known, errors in predicting those variables may significantly reduce forecasting accuracy. For all these reasons, the non-structural approach deserves serious consideration.

7.1 THE BOX–JENKINS APPROACH TO NON-STRUCTURAL MODELS

The use of autoregressive (AR) and moving-average (MA) models dates to the early days of econometrics. The seminal papers on moving-average and autoregressive models were published by G. Udny Yule in 1926 and 1927; his article, "Why Do We Sometimes Get Nonsense Correlations Between Time Series," was the first to point out that the usual tests of statistical significance were invalidated when the residuals were serially correlated.[2] So-called "mixed models" – i.e., combining AR and MA models – were first studied by Herman Wold in 1938 and M. S. Bartlett in 1946.[3] However, these papers were primarily focused

[2] Yule, G. U., *Journal of the Royal Statistical Society*, 89 (1926), 1–64.

[3] Wold, H. O., *A Study in the Analysis of Stationary Time Series* (Almqvist & Wicksell, Stockholm), 1938. Also Bartlett, M. S., "On the Theoretical Specification of Sampling Properties of Autocorrelated Time Series", *Journal of the Royal Statistical Society, Series B*, 8 (1946), 27–41.

on examining the statistical properties of AR and MA models, as opposed to using them for forecasting. At the time, it was still generally assumed structural models would provide superior forecasts.

The first major attempt to show how AR and MA models could be used for forecasting is generally credited to George E. P. Box and Gwilym Jenkins.[4] The principal contribution of Box and Jenkins was not in developing new statistical techniques, but in showing how AR and MA models could be combined, as Granger and Newbold have said, into "an integrated and well-defined approach to time series forecasting via model building stimulating a good deal of practical application over a wide range of actual time series."[5]

Box and Jenkins developed an iterative three-step approach: identification, estimation, and diagnostic checking. Identification is discussed in section 7.4; at this point we can summarize by saying it involves checking the residuals for serial correlation and choosing the length of lag for the AR and MA models, using the principle of parsimony – the fewer terms, the more likely the model is to generate accurate forecasts, ceteris paribus. Estimation includes various methods of removing the trend as well as applying standard least squares methods. In many cases, seasonal adjustment of the data is also appropriate. Since several different models are likely to provide apparently similar results, diagnostic checking includes calculating how well the equation forecasts outside the sample period, and then modifying the model appropriately.

The statistical formulas and tests originally developed for AR and MA models were based on the concept of *stationarity* – the assumption that the series contain no trends. Since most economic time series do indeed contain trends, those trends must first be removed. Several tests have been developed to determine whether the trend in any given series is significant, but those tests often give ambiguous results and should be used with caution.

When in doubt, take it out; removing the trend is generally the best way to proceed in estimating these models. The approach used here first assumes the series do not have any trend; the standard methods for estimating ARMA models are developed in section 7.2 under that assumption. Section 7.3 then discusses various ways to remove the trend where it does exist and test for stationarity. The remaining sections of this chapter cover the three steps of the Box–Jenkins procedure: identification, estimation, and diagnostic checking.

7.2 ESTIMATING ARMA MODELS

ARMA models combine an autoregressive model and a moving-average model; at this stage of the analysis, the series is assumed to have no trend. These models

---

[4] Box, G. E. P., and G. M. Jenkins, *Time Series Analysis, Forecasting, and Control* (Holden-Day, San Francisco), 1970, rev. edn 1976.
[5] Granger and Newbold, p. 153.

used to be known as Box–Jenkins models, although that term is not used so frequently now.

An autoregressive model is one in which the dependent variable is a function of its lagged values. A moving-average model is one in which the dependent variable is a function of current and lagged exogenous shocks, as represented by the residual term. The concept of integration is somewhat more complicated and is discussed in detail in the next section. Technically, the order of integration equals the number of autoregressive unit roots. In practice, most economic time series are either integrated of order zero – no adjustment is needed – or order one – first differencing is required. In everyday terms, an integrated model is one with the trend removed.

Compared to the detailed discussion in Part II on choosing the right set of economic variables and the optimal lag structure, it might seem that calculating regressions where the detrended dependent variable is a function of its own lagged values and exogenous shocks would be much simpler. Indeed, one of the advantages of these models is that they can quickly be estimated for thousands of different series without having to develop separate theories for each function. Nonetheless, the model building procedure is not quite as simple as it might initially appear, since the forecasting results will generally be enhanced if relatively few parameters are estimated. This concept of *parsimony* is discussed separately in section 7.4 as part of the larger issue of identification.

7.2.1 First-order Autoregressive Models – AR(1)

First consider the simple first-order autoregressive model of the form

$$y_t = \alpha y_{t-1} + \varepsilon_t. \tag{7.1}$$

The constant term can be omitted without loss of generality, since the results are the same if this equation contained a separate constant term. This is known as an AR(1) model.

The ε_t term has a mean of zero, a constant variance, and is serially uncorrelated. It is known as a *white noise* process, a term taken from engineering that is analogous to white light, which is composed of all colors of the spectrum in equal amounts. The ε_t term need not be normally distributed; if it is, the process is known as Gaussian white noise. This term consists of random, exogenous shocks.

If the expected value of y_t is denoted by μ, indicating its mean value, then

$$\mu_t = \alpha \mu_{t-1}. \tag{7.2}$$

As has already been shown when discussing exponential moving averages, the solution to this equation is

$$\mu_t = \alpha^{t+N}\mu_{t-N}. \tag{7.3}$$

if the autoregressive process starts at time $-N$.

Since this discussion is confined to stationary series – i.e., those without trends – which means that $|\alpha| < 1$. If the process began in the infinite past, then $\mu_t = 0$ for all t. That means y_t will not diverge from its mean value no matter how large t becomes. By comparison, for a series with an increasing trend, the mean value of y would diverge from zero.

Squaring both sides of (7.1) and taking expected values yields the equation

$$E(y_t^2) = \alpha^2 E(y_{t-1}^2) + E(\varepsilon_t^2) + 2\alpha E(y_{t-1}\varepsilon_t)$$
$$\text{or } \sigma_y^2 = \alpha^2\sigma_{y_{t-1}}^2 + \sigma_\varepsilon^2, \text{where } \sigma_y^2 \equiv \text{var}(y_t) \text{ and } \sigma_\varepsilon^2 \equiv \text{var}(\varepsilon_t). \tag{7.4}$$

The cross-product term vanishes because, by definition, ε_t is uncorrelated with all lagged values of y_t, although it may be – and often is – correlated with y_t itself. If the series is stationary, then

$$\sigma_y^2 = \sigma_\varepsilon^2 / (1 - \alpha^2). \tag{7.5}$$

Multiplying through by the denominator, this becomes

$$\sigma_y^2 = \alpha^2\sigma_y^2 + \sigma_\varepsilon^2. \tag{7.6}$$

To obtain the autocovariance coefficients, go back and multiply (7.1) by y_{t-1} instead of y_t. That yields

$$E(y_t y_{t-1}) = \alpha E(y_{t-1}^2) + E(y_{t-1}\varepsilon_t). \tag{7.7}$$

In AR models, the usual convention is to denote σ_y^2 as λ_0 and the autocovariance coefficients as $\lambda_1, \lambda_2, \ldots, \lambda_n$. Using this notation, (7.7) can be rewritten as $\lambda_1 = \alpha\lambda_0$, and in general

$$\lambda_N = \alpha^N\lambda_0, \, N \geq 0. \tag{7.8}$$

The larger the value of α, assuming it is between 0 and 1, the smoother y_t will be. If $\alpha < 0$, the series will exhibit a jagged-edge pattern; technically, it will be less smooth than a pure white noise series. It is very unusual in practice for first-order autocorrelation to be negative, but as will be shown later, higher-order autocorrelations are often negative.

The autocorrelation coefficients for a stationary series are defined as

$$\rho_k = \frac{E(y_t y_{t-k})}{\sqrt{\text{var}(y_t)} \cdot \sqrt{\text{var}(y_{t-k})}} = \frac{\lambda_k}{\lambda_0}. \tag{7.9}$$

Since these coefficients are symmetrical around lag zero, it is only necessary to consider positive lags. The autocorrelation coefficients for the AR(1) process can thus be written as

$$\rho_k = \alpha \rho_{k-1} = \alpha^k, \ k = 1, 2, \ldots, N. \tag{7.10}$$

This formula is known as the autocorrelation function of the series, abbreviated as ACF. Its graphical representation is known as the *correlogram* (figure 7.1 is an example).

7.2.2 AR(2) MODELS

We next proceed to the AR(2) case, when second-order autocorrelation occurs, and examine some of the specific properties of this equation before advancing to the general case. Once again the variable is taken around its mean, so that

$$y_t = \alpha_1 y_{t-1} + \alpha_2 y_{t-2} + \varepsilon_t. \tag{7.11}$$

If both sides of the equation are multiplied by y_t and expected values are taken, then the analogous equation to (7.8) is

$$\lambda_0 = \alpha_1 \lambda_1 + \alpha_2 \lambda_2 + \sigma_\varepsilon^2. \tag{7.12}$$

Multiplying (7.11) by y_{t-1} and y_{t-2} and taking expected values yields

$$\lambda_1 = \alpha_1 \lambda_0 + \alpha_2 \lambda_1 \tag{7.13}$$
$$\lambda_2 = \alpha_1 \lambda_1 + \alpha_2 \lambda_0$$

as the two autocovariance coefficients.

We state without proof[6] that (7.13) can be restated in terms of the autocorrelation coefficients ρ_1 and ρ_2 as

$$\rho_1 = \alpha_1 + \alpha_2 \rho_1 \tag{7.14}$$
$$\rho_2 = \alpha_1 \rho_1 + \alpha_2.$$

These are known as the Yule–Walker equations for the AR(2) process. If both α_1 and α_2 are greater than zero, the autocorrelation function will be monotonically dampened toward zero. However, it is quite possible, as shown in the example below, that while the sum of $\alpha_1 + \alpha_2 < 1$, thus satisfying the stationarity

---

[6] For the proof, see Johnson and DiNardo, p. 210.

condition, $\alpha_1 > 1$ and $\alpha_2 < 0$. Since calculating these values involves solving a quadratic equation, it can be shown that if $\alpha_1^2 + 4\alpha_2 < 0$, the resulting equation will have complex roots, and hence the function will oscillate, following a general sinusoidal pattern, before dampening to zero.

Before presenting actual cases of exponential and sinusoidal dampening, the concept of the partial autocorrelation function (PACF) will be discussed. As seen in the correlograms presented later, it is often difficult to distinguish the optimal number of periods of autocorrelation, since a large number of lags are significant. For this reason, it is useful to use the PACF, which shows the net additional correlation due to adding one more lag.

Recall that the partial correlation coefficient in a three-variable case can be written as

$$r_{13.2} = \frac{r_{13} - r_{12}r_{23}}{\sqrt{(1 - r_{12}^2)} \cdot \sqrt{(1 - r_{23}^2)}} \tag{7.15}$$

For a stationary series, this definition can be simplified. Let 1, 2, and 3 denote y_t and its first and second lags. Because this is a stationary series, $r_{12} = r_{23} = \rho_1$ and $r_{13} = \rho_2$. Then

$$r_{13.2} = \frac{\rho_2 - \rho_1^2}{1 - \rho_1^2}. \tag{7.16}$$

If (7.14) is solved for α_2, it turns out that α_2 is equal to $r_{13.2}$. Thus the autocorrelation coefficient is also the partial correlation coefficient.

7.2.3 AR(N) MODELS

The correlograms shown later include AR terms with many lags; the default option in EViews, for example, is 36. To show the possible significance of these longer lagged terms, we now consider the AR(N) case, and then examine how significance levels for each term in ACF and PACF are determined.

In order to expand the case of two independent variables (7.15) to the general case, it is first convenient to introduce the generalized formula for the partial correlation coefficient. The symbol ϕ is used here as a partial autocorrelation coefficient to distinguish from ρ, the overall autocorrelation coefficient, while r_k is the simple correlation coefficient between the unlagged variable and its lag k periods ago. The general formula is given as

$$\phi_k = \frac{r_k - \sum_{j=1}^{k-1} \phi_{k-1,j} r_{k-j}}{1 - \sum_{j=1}^{k-1} \phi_{k-1,j} r_{k-j}} \tag{7.17}$$

where $\phi_{k,j} = \phi_{k-1,j} - \phi_k \phi_{k-1,k-j}$.

The Yule–Walker equations (7.15) can be expanded to the N-variate case as follows:[7]

$$\rho_1 = \phi_1 + \phi_2\rho_1 + \ldots + \phi_p\rho_{p-1} \qquad (7.18)$$

$$\vdots$$

$$\rho_p = \phi_1\rho_{p-1} + \phi_2\rho_{-2} + \ldots + \phi_p.$$

If $\rho_1, \rho_2, \ldots, \rho_p$ are known, the equations can be solved for $\phi_1, \phi_2, \ldots, \phi_p$.

However, solution of the equations in (7.18) requires knowledge of the value of p, which is in fact one of the parameters the researcher is trying to determine. As a result, the equations are solved sequentially. First, the hypothesis that $p = 1$ is tested to see whether ϕ_1 is significant. If it is, then solve the first two equations and determine whether ϕ_2 is significant. This process can be repeated until a value of ϕ_k is obtained that is not significant.

Recall that the ϕ_k are *partial* autocorrelation coefficients. Hence some way is needed to measure their level of significance – in addition to determining whether the overall autocorrelation function is significant.

The standard procedure is to test whether the overall autoregressive equation is significant or not; that is analogous to testing the F-ratio for a structural equation. Box and his colleagues devised what is known as a Q-statistic to measure whether there is a significant degree of autocorrelation up to and including degree k. The original Box–Pierce $Q = T\Sigma r_k^2$ has been replaced by the Ljung–Box statistic,[8] often denoted as Q_{LB}, which has better small-sample properties. It is given as

$$Q_{LB} = T(T+2) \sum_{k=1}^{P} r_k^2/(T-k). \qquad (7.19)$$

Q_{LB} is distributed as χ^2 with $P - p - q$ degrees of freedom, where P is the total number of autocorrelation coefficients tested and p and q are the degrees of the AR and MA modeling process. Because this covers the whole range of possible autocorrelation coefficients, Q_{LB} is sometimes known as a "portmanteau" statistic. The validity of the test rests in large part on the number of observations being fairly large. The test is not very powerful for moderate size samples, probably less than 50. The higher the number, the higher the probability that autocorrelation is present.

In most cases, Q_{LB} will be highly significant, but the real question will be whether the partial autocorrelation coefficients are significant. The small-sample properties of the significance levels are not known; for large samples, the standard error of the PACF coefficients is approximately equal to $1/\sqrt{T}$, so

[7]   For further discussion, see Pindyck and Rubinfeld, p. 533.

[8]   Ljung, G. M., and G. E. P. Box, "The Likelihood Function of Stationary Autoregressive–Moving Average Models," *Biometrika*, 66 (1979), 265–70.

the bounds of significance are $2/\sqrt{T}$. The dotted lines in the plots of the auto-correlations in EViews are the approximate two-standard-error bounds computed as $2/\sqrt{T}$. This is only an approximation but serves as a useful guide indicating the degree of autocorrelation.

What is the significance of all these formulas for practical business forecasting? In the real world, we have seen time and again that economic time series are likely to contain a high degree of serial correlation. AR models permit the researcher to capture this correlation in a systematic matter and use it to reduce forecasting error. The problem arises because, just as in structural modeling, spurious correlations may arise that provide robust sample period statistics but do not improve forecasting accuracy.

At this point it is useful to examine some typical correlograms, the Q-statistic, and PACF coefficients. Since stationarity is assumed at this state of the analysis, these graphs are presented for data series with no trends. Figure 7.1 presents the correlogram for single-family housing starts, Note there is a very high autocorrelation, and the first-order autocorrelation statistic is almost unity (0.908). Second- and third-order coefficients also appear to be highly significant; after that, the others become insignificant. Note that the ACF fades away very slowly. That is a typical pattern for highly autocorrelated series. It also appears that the PACF for lags 1, 2, and 3 are significant. The practical implications for estimating AR models will be discussed later.

Figure 7.2 shows the correlogram for the monthly rate of inflation; the pattern is substantially different. As is often the case with percentage changes, the first-order autocorrelation coefficient is much smaller. Also, the ACF has a slight sinusoidal wave, which suggests that random shocks are also important in addition to autocorrelation. Also note that the coefficients appear to be significant up to a lag of 12. That is far too many to include in a regression, and as shown in the next subsection, that number can be pared down by combining an AR model with an MA model.

7.2.4 MOVING-AVERAGE (MA) MODELS

The previous chapter discussed arithmetic, weighted, and exponential moving averages. In all cases, these were combinations of the current and lagged values of a given variable that were used to smooth the data. However, that is not what is meant by MA models in this context.

Suppose ε_t is a zero-mean white noise. Then the series $y_t = \varepsilon_t + \varepsilon_{t-1}$ will be smoother than white noise. The general formula for an MA(1) model is given as

$$y_t = \varepsilon_t - \beta_1 \varepsilon_{t-1}. \tag{7.20}$$

In fact, any stationary AR(1) process can be *inverted* to give an MA process of infinite order, which is

Sample: 1947:01 1999:12
Included observations: 489

Autocorrelation	Partial Correlation		AC	PAC	Q-Stat	Prob
.|*******|	.|*******|	1	0.908	0.908	405.58	0.000
.|*******|	.|** |	2	0.863	0.219	772.54	0.000
.|****** |	.|* |	3	0.837	0.161	1119.0	0.000
.|****** |	.|. |	4	0.801	0.004	1437.0	0.000
.|****** |	.|. |	5	0.762	−0.031	1725.0	0.000
.|****** |	.|. |	6	0.720	−0.056	1982.8	0.000
.|***** |	*|. |	7	0.675	−0.066	2209.7	0.000
.|***** |	*|. |	8	0.629	−0.058	2406.9	0.000
.|**** |	*|. |	9	0.580	−0.059	2575.2	0.000
.|**** |	.|. |	10	0.534	−0.028	2718.3	0.000
.|**** |	.|. |	11	0.488	−0.029	2838.0	0.000
.|*** |	.|. |	12	0.447	0.006	2938.6	0.000
.|*** |	.|* |	13	0.422	0.094	3028.2	0.000
.|*** |	*|. |	14	0.375	−0.078	3099.3	0.000
.|*** |	.|. |	15	0.331	−0.040	3154.8	0.000
.|** |	*|. |	16	0.280	−0.116	3194.4	0.000
.|** |	.|. |	17	0.244	0.016	3224.7	0.000
.|** |	.|. |	18	0.208	−0.009	3246.8	0.000
.|* |	.|. |	19	0.170	−0.017	3261.5	0.000
.|* |	.|. |	20	0.135	−0.001	3270.9	0.000
.|* |	.|. |	21	0.104	0.006	3276.5	0.000
.|* |	.|. |	22	0.071	−0.016	3279.0	0.000
.|. |	*|. |	23	0.031	−0.070	3279.5	0.000
.|. |	.|. |	24	−0.004	−0.032	3279.5	0.000
.|. |	.|* |	25	−0.019	0.081	3279.7	0.000
.|. |	.|. |	26	−0.046	−0.049	3280.8	0.000
*|. |	.|. |	27	−0.074	−0.018	3283.6	0.000
*|. |	.|. |	28	−0.096	−0.022	3288.4	0.000
*|. |	.|. |	29	−0.126	−0.045	3296.7	0.000
*|. |	.|. |	30	−0.154	−0.051	3309.2	0.000
*|. |	.|. |	31	−0.177	−0.016	3325.5	0.000
**|. |	.|. |	32	−0.197	−0.009	3345.9	0.000
**|. |	.|. |	33	−0.218	−0.015	3370.8	0.000
**|. |	.|* |	34	−0.223	0.072	3397.1	0.000
**|. |	.|. |	35	−0.241	−0.046	3427.8	0.000
**|. |	.|. |	36	−0.249	0.047	3460.8	0.000

Figure 7.1 Correlogram for single-family housing starts (monthly data).

$$y_t = \varepsilon_t - \beta\varepsilon_{t-1} - \beta^2\varepsilon_{t-2} - \ldots - \beta^k\varepsilon_{t-k} + \ldots \tag{7.21}$$

In MA models, then, the dependent variable is expressed solely in terms of unobservable shocks. Of course, it is not possible to estimate a model with unobservable data. However, one can use previous errors – i.e., observable

Sample: 1947:01 1999:12
Included observations: 629

Autocorrelation	Partial Correlation		AC	PAC	Q-Stat	Prob
.|****	.|****	1	0.561	0.561	199.05	0.000
.|****	.|**	2	0.490	0.256	351.28	0.000
.|***	.|*	3	0.447	0.153	477.79	0.000
.|***	.|*	4	0.410	0.097	584.60	0.000
.|***	.|*	5	0.418	0.128	695.51	0.000
.|***	.|*	6	0.406	0.091	800.59	0.000
.|***	.|*	7	0.405	0.088	905.04	0.000
.|***	.|*	8	0.421	0.110	1018.6	0.000
.|***	.|*	9	0.428	0.099	1135.7	0.000
.|***	.|*	10	0.441	0.103	1260.3	0.000
.|***	*|.	11	0.340	−0.090	1334.6	0.000
.|**	*|.	12	0.239	−0.167	1371.4	0.000
.|**	*|.	13	0.229	−0.060	1405.3	0.000
.|**	.|.	14	0.217	−0.034	1435.6	0.000
.|**	.|*	15	0.265	0.069	1480.8	0.000
.|**	.|.	16	0.261	0.026	1524.8	0.000
.|**	.|.	17	0.233	−0.019	1560.0	0.000
.|**	.|.	18	0.216	−0.027	1590.2	0.000
.|*	.|.	19	0.197	−0.016	1615.4	0.000
.|**	.|.	20	0.202	0.043	1642.0	0.000
.|*	.|.	21	0.191	0.065	1665.9	0.000
.|*	.|.	22	0.162	0.037	1683.1	0.000
.|*	*|.	23	0.116	−0.067	1691.9	0.000
.|*	*|.	24	0.102	−0.073	1698.8	0.000
.|*	.|.	25	0.128	−0.012	1709.6	0.000
.|*	.|.	26	0.122	−0.010	1719.4	0.000
.|*	.|*	27	0.159	0.108	1736.0	0.000
.|*	.|*	28	0.168	0.094	1754.6	0.000
.|**	.|*	29	0.208	0.129	1783.1	0.000
.|**	.|.	30	0.198	0.025	1809.2	0.000
.|**	.|.	31	0.210	0.038	1838.4	0.000
.|**	.|*	32	0.232	0.099	1874.1	0.000
.|*	.|.	33	0.170	−0.011	1893.4	0.000
.|*	.|.	34	0.149	−0.026	1908.2	0.000
.|*	*|.	35	0.144	−0.069	1922.2	0.000
.|*	.|.	36	0.175	−0.027	1942.7	0.000

Figure 7.2   Correlogram for the monthly rate of inflation, CPI.

residuals – which are actually used when estimating an MA model. An MA model of order 1 means the most recent forecast error is used, order 2 means the errors from the two most recent periods are used, and so on.

In most cases, the residuals are taken from an equation that contains several independent variables, but the concept of correlating the dependent variable with previous errors is still the same. In fact, it has a certain resemblance to adjusting the equation for forecast errors, as discussed in chapter 5. In particular, the MA process is often used in conjunction with AR models. However, before providing specific examples of ARMA models, we briefly examine some of the other properties of MA models themselves.

AR models can be sinusoidal, but MA models cannot. In an MA(1) model, the autocorrelation coefficient for the model given in (7.20) is

$$\rho_1 = \beta_1 / (1 + \beta_1^2). \tag{7.22}$$

That term can never be bigger than 1/2 because β cannot be bigger than 1 in a first-order stationary MA model.

In everyday terms, one can think of an AR model as one that is heavily weighted by past values, while an MA model is one that is influenced by exogenous shocks. Thus a very smooth series would have very high coefficients for the AR model and low ones for the MA, while a series that was primarily buffeted by shocks would have low AR values but high MA values.

A model might have an MA order greater than one if an exogenous shock affected the dependent variable for several periods. For example, an oil shock might affect the inflation rate that month and for the next several months. Furthermore, an increase in the price of gasoline might affect consumer spending for the next several quarters. In cases of this sort, MA models may be appropriate. The number of terms in the MA process would presumably increase as the time interval decreased; so it would be greater for daily data than for weekly, greater for weekly than monthly, and so on.

7.2.5 ARMA PROCEDURES

At this point the two processes, AR and MA, can be combined into what is known as an ARMA(p,q) process, where p is the number of terms in the AR function and q is the number of terms in the MA function. Most of the time, p and q will not be greater than 3. The generalized model can be written as

$$y_t = \sum_{j=1}^{p} \alpha_j y_{t-j} - \sum_{j=1}^{q} \beta_j \varepsilon_{t-j}. \tag{7.23}$$

First consider the simplest case, namely ARMA(1,1), which can be written as

$$y_t = \alpha y_{t-1} + \varepsilon_t - \beta \varepsilon_{t-1}. \tag{7.24}$$

The variance of y_t, which has previously been denoted as λ_0, equals

$$\lambda_0 = \frac{(1 - 2\alpha\beta + \beta^2)}{(1 - \alpha^2)} * \sigma_\varepsilon^2 \tag{7.25}$$

The first-order covariance is given as

$$\lambda_1 = \alpha\lambda_0 + \beta\sigma_\varepsilon^2 = \frac{(\alpha - \beta)(1 - \alpha\beta)}{(1 - \alpha^2)} * \sigma_\varepsilon^2 \tag{7.26}$$

with higher-order covariances equal to

$$\lambda_k = \alpha\lambda_{k-1}, \; k = 2, 3, \ldots, n. \tag{7.27}$$

The autocorrelation function of the ARMA(1,1) process is

$$\rho_1 = \frac{(\alpha - \beta)(1 - \alpha\beta)}{1 + 2\alpha\beta + \beta^2} \tag{7.28}$$

$$\rho_k = \alpha\rho_{k-1}, \; k = 2, 3, \ldots, n.$$

We now indicate what these various terms imply for the ARMA(1,1) process. The first coefficient of the autocorrelation function (ACF) depends on both α and β; i.e., on both the AR and MA part of the process. After that, however, the terms of ACF decline exponentially and depend only on the AR process.

Earlier it was shown that the terms of the *partial* autocorrelation function (PACF) fell to zero in the population after lag p; the sample period estimates may not be exactly zero, but they will usually be insignificant. However, in the ARMA procedure, the PACF terms dampen out indefinitely and do not automatically drop to zero after lag p. The comparison of these processes can be summarized as follows for a stationary series:

Process	ACF	PACF
Pure AR	Infinite	Zero after lag p
Pure MA	Zero after lag q	Infinite
Mixed ARMA	Infinite	Infinite

An examination of the correlogram should thus indicate whether the process is primarily AR or MA. That will help in determining the degree of p and q in the mixed model.

Assuming the process is stationary, there is always an AR or an MA process of infinite length that is equivalent to the mixed ARMA model.[9] Also, the coefficients in the mixed model will, after the setting of q starting values determined by the MA process, take the same shape as the pure AR process.

In that case, why bother with the mixed model? On statistical grounds, the answer is parsimony: there are fewer parameters to be estimated. On economic grounds, one can argue that most economic time series tend to follow past patterns except when there is a shock, in which case the pattern diverges for a while.

---

[9] See, for example, Granger and Newbold, p. 26.

So far we have indicated that any mixed ARMA process can be represented by either an infinite AR or MA process, but the mixed model is generally better on the grounds of parsimony. At this juncture several major issues must still be decided. First, the best ways to extract a significant trend must be examined; that is the case for most economic time series. Second, more information is needed on how to apply the principle of parsimony to reduce the number of terms in the equation to its optimal level. Third, introduction of seasonal factors introduces additional complications.

First, however, two examples are given, one of which is dominated by an AR process and the other by an MA process. For this purpose, refer back to the correlograms for single-family housing starts and the monthly inflation rate given in figures 7.1 and 7.2.

The series for single-family housing starts is chosen because it contains no trend. Note that the ACF coefficients dampen out very slowly, whereas the first-order PACF coefficient is quite large, but the others are much lower; the second- and third-order coefficients might be significant, but after that they are clearly insignificant. That suggests an AR process of order 2 or 3, and an MA process of order 0 or 1. As it turns out, the optimal equation is ARMA(1,1), although AR(1) would be almost as good; the reasons for this are explored in section 7.4. For the moment, the reader can note that, although additional terms appear to be quite significant, the adjusted R^2 hardly improves at all and the efficiency decreases.

The correlogram for the monthly rate of inflation as measured by the CPI has a much different pattern. First, the PACF coefficients appear to be significant up to a lag of 12. Second, the ACF coefficients first decline but then increase for a while before eventually dampening to zero. This pattern suggests that a mixed model is necessary; if a low-order MA model were appropriate, the ACF coefficients would fall to zero beyond lag q, whereas if a low-order AR model were appropriate, the PACF coefficients would fall to zero beyond lag p.

7.3 STATIONARY AND INTEGRATED SERIES

A series is said to be integrated of order d (an integer) if differencing that series d times will produce a stationary process. In most cases, d is 0 or 1. If $d = 0$, the process is already stationary – it does not have a significant trend. If $d = 1$, then the process becomes stationary after taking the first difference. In many cases, the process will yield more accurate forecasts if first differences are applied to logarithms rather than levels, since that implies a constant rate of growth. Technically it is possible that $d = 2$ or more, but the practical applications of such examples are extremely limited, so none is presented in this text. The issue discussed in this section is the conditions under which differencing is optimal, and when it should not be used.

So far we have assumed that the autocorrelation coefficients ρ_k are all less than unity; if that is not true, the variance will be infinite and the usual tests and measures for goodness of fit will be biased. Chapter 4 contained a detailed discussion of the methods for removing a time trend from the data. That is known as a deterministic trend. However, it is also possible that the trend is stochastic.[10] These two cases can be illustrated as follows:

$$y_t = \alpha_1 + \beta T + \varepsilon_t \text{ (deterministic trend, } T \text{ is a time trend)} \tag{7.29}$$

$$y_t = \alpha_2 + \rho y_{t-1} + \varepsilon_t \text{ (stochastic trend if } \rho = 1). \tag{7.30}$$

Suppose $\rho = 1$. In that case, the series is known as a random-walk model, which means the series does not revert to some previous point if randomly shocked, but wanders around aimlessly. The practical significance of this means any random shock would send the variable off on a different track. If, for example, GDP had a stochastic trend – i.e., an autocorrelation coefficient of unity – then a shock, such as an oil shock, would send GDP off on a different course, and it would not return to its previous path.[11]

Also, because the variance is not finite, correlation of a dependent variable with one or more series that exhibit random walks would generally result in spurious correlations. Many economic series that appear to be significantly correlated with a time trend are in fact random walks, in which case the estimated equations will generate forecasts with much larger errors than would be expected from the sample period statistics.

Suppose that some economic time series y increases over time. We can combine the two equations given above as

$$y_t = \alpha + \beta T + \rho y_{t-1} + \varepsilon_t. \tag{7.31}$$

One possibility is that the growth in y occurs because $\beta > 0$, but if the trend were removed, the resulting series would be stationary, which means $\rho < 1$. That is essentially the case discussed in chapter 4. The other possibility is that the growth in Y occurs because $\rho = 1$ and $\alpha > 0$, which means the series follows a random walk with a positive drift. If that is the case, taking deviations around the trend would *not* make the series stationary, and spurious correlations would still result; only first differencing would yield a stationary series.

[10]   This treatment follows Pindyck and Rubinfeld, pp. 507–10. Also see Maddala, G. S., *Introduction to Econometrics*, 2nd edn (Prentice Hall, Englewood Cliffs, NJ), 1992, pp. 258–62; and Diebold, F. X., *Elements of Forecasting* (South-Western, Cincinnati), 1998, ch. 10.2.

[11]   This may at first seem far-fetched, but precisely that conclusion was reached in a widely quoted study by Nelson, C. R., and C. I. Plosser, "Trends and Random Walks in Macroeconomic Time Series: Some Evidence and Implications," *Journal of Monetary Economics*, 10 (1982), 139–62. However, most economists do not share this opinion; see, for example, Choi, I., "Most U.S. Economic Time Series do not Have Unit Roots: Nelson and Plosser's (1982) Results Reconsidered," manuscript, Ohio State University, 1990. A later paper that reaches similar conclusions is Rudebusch, G. D., "Trends and Random Walks in Macroeconomic Time Series: A Re-examination," Federal Reserve Paper 1139, Washington, DC, 1990. For further references see Maddala, pp. 584–8.

To determine whether or not the series describes a random walk – or contains significant components of a random walk – it is useful to test (7.31) to see whether ρ is significantly different from unity. If it is not, actual or percentage first differencing of the series is indicated.

It might seem to be a relatively straightforward matter to determine whether a variable has a significant trend; simply run a regression of that variable, or its logarithm, against a time trend and see whether the resulting coefficient is significant. The trouble with that approach is that the DW statistics are usually extremely small, so the significance tests are biased. Furthermore, that problem cannot be solved by estimating the logically equivalent equation of $\Delta y = a + bt + cy_{-1}$, even though those residuals generally would not be serially correlated. The problem is that the ratio of c to its standard error does not follow the t-distribution and is *not* normally distributed, because the assumption of stationarity was required in the derivation of the distribution, and it is precisely the hypothesis of non-stationarity that is being tested. Also, recall that if ρ is in fact equal to unity, the variance is not finite and hence the standard OLS tests of significance are invalid. In particular, the OLS estimate of ρ is biased toward zero.

This problem has led to the development of a series of alternative tests to determine whether ρ = 1; these are generally known as *unit-root tests*. The original methodology and calculations were prepared by D. A. Dickey and W. A. Fuller, so this test is generally known as the Dickey–Fuller test.[12] Later this test was extended to take into account the common case where the residuals are serially correlated; these results are known as the augmented Dickey–Fuller (ADF) test. These results have been extended by using a much larger set of replications by MacKinnon,[13] which are given in EViews and similar programs. These tests were necessary because the experiments by Dickey and Fuller, while pathbreaking, were based on a fairly small number of examples. They obtained limiting distributions for several important cases and then approximated the distributions empirically; the results were expanded by MacKinnon.

Researchers can thus use several sophisticated tests to determine whether the economic time series in question does or does not have a unit root. If it does, first differencing is indicated. Nonetheless, econometricians are not always convinced of the wisdom and merit of this approach. Diebold claims, "[A]t least asymptotically we are probably better off estimating forecasting models *in levels*

---

[12] The original sources are Dickey, D. A., *Estimation and Hypothesis Testing in Nonstationary Time Series*, unpublished PhD dissertation, Iowa State University, 1976; and Fuller, W. A., *Introduction to Statistical Time Series* (John Wiley, New York), 1976. Further discussion is found in Dickey, D. A., and Fuller, W. A., "Likelihood Ratio Statistics for Autoregressive Time Series with a Unit Root," *Econometrica*, 49 (1981), 1057–72, with tables on p. 1063.

[13] MacKinnon, J. G., "Critical Values for Cointegration Tests," ch. 13 in R. F. Engle and C. W. J. Granger, eds, *Long-Run Economic Relationships* (Oxford University Press, Oxford), 1991.

with trends included, because then we will get an accurate approximation to the dynamics in the data . . . differencing is appropriate only in the unit-root case, and inappropriate differencing can be harmful, even asymptotically." [14] (emphasis added). On the other side of the issue, Plosser and Schwert claim it is always best to work with differenced data rather than data in levels,[15] and Maddala claims "it is better to use differencing and regressions in first differences, rather than regressions in levels with time as an extra explanatory variable."[16] Many other references both pro and con could be quoted here.

More recently, other unit-root tests have been proposed to deal with the problems of serial correlation in the residuals,[17] the best known being the Phillips–Perron (PP) test. However, in most cases the results are similar to those found by using the ADF test. A comparison of these and other tests can be found in several references.[18] However, when it comes to practical business forecasting, these tests do not really tell us very much. The entire concept of ARMA models was based on the concept of stationarity, and if that condition is violated the results are likely to provide inferior forecasts. Also, these tests often provide inconsistent or erroneous answers.

Given this somewhat bewildering method of alternative tests, what method should the practical business forecaster employ?

Before answering this question, note that the results from ADF and associated tests are often not very robust. In many cases there is not much difference between $\rho = 1$, which indicates a unit root and calls for differencing and (say) $\rho = 0.95$, which indicates a stationary process and no need for differencing. Often, the available tests will give conflicting answers about whether the trend in a given series is due to a correlation with time, or a unit root with positive drift. In a widely quoted result, Rudebusch tested real GNP[19] (as it was then) for a unit root and found that it failed to reject the unit-root hypothesis, but also failed to reject a stationary hypothesis. That is typical of the results for many macroeconomic time series.

Even Maddala, who generally favors differencing, concedes that one of the major drawbacks to this procedure is that it results in the loss of valuable long-run information in the data; it is indeed this loss that leads Diebold to conclude

---

[14]   Diebold, p. 261.
[15]   Plosser, C. I., and G. W. Schwert, "Money, Income, and Sunspots: Measuring Economic Relationships and the Effects of Differencing," *Journal of Monetary Economics*, 4 (1978) 637–60.
[16]   Maddala, p. 262.
[17]   See Phillips, P. C. B., and P. Perron, "Testing for a Unit Root in Time Series Regression," *Biometrika*, 75 (1988), 335–46.
[18]   See, in particular, Pantula, S. G., G. Gonzalez-Farias, and W. A. Fuller, "A Comparison of Unit Root Test Criteria," *Journal of Business and Economic Statistics*, 12 (1994), 449–59.
[19]   Rudebusch, G. D., "The Uncertain Unit Root in Real GNP," *American Economic Review*, 83 (1993), 264–72. See also Diebold, F. X. and G. D. Rudebusch, "Deterministic vs. Stochastic Trend in U.S. GNP Yet Again," *American Economic Review*, 86 (1996), 1291–8.

that levels should ordinarily be preferred for estimating equations. Hence the answer to the question posed above depends in large part on what type of result the researcher is seeking. If one is primarily interested in determining and predicting the long-run trend for a given variable, the levels approach is generally preferable even at the risk of some spurious correlation with time trends; earlier it was suggested this problem could be at least partially alleviated by using ratios. On the other hand, many ARIMA models are designed to capture short-term fluctuations, either for predictive purposes or as tracking models to determine when inventories, shipments, production, or other individual firm or industry are going off track. In such examples, this author has found that the weight of the evidence points strongly to the use of differencing if a trend might be present. That is generally true whether or not the ADF or PP tests indicate the presence of a unit root.

Retail sales, the consumer price index, and the S&P 500 stock price index all have significant trends, whereas first differences of these series do not. Admittedly, sometimes it is not clear whether series such as interest rates or inventory/sales ratios contain significant trends. Theoretically, the real rate of interest does not contain any long-term trend. Yet it is entirely possible that over the past 50 years the series is significantly correlated with a time trend, which could represent a random walk with a positive drift.

When removing the trend, most textbooks indicate that the standard method is to take first differences. However, in many cases it is better to take percentage changes, which are equivalent to first differences of logarithms. To see this, consider the graphs of monthly changes for stock prices in first differences and percentage changes, as shown in figure 7.3.

Both the ADF and PP tests clearly reject the existence of a unit root in the first difference of stock prices. Nonetheless, the graph shows that the fluctuations are much larger near the end of the sample period, so that the assumption of a constant variance is violated. Of course the test applies to the residuals rather than to the original series, but if we calculate an ARMA(1,1) equation for d(sp500) and examine the residuals, which are shown in figure 7.4, virtually the identical pattern occurs. Hence the ADF and PP tests, which are based on the assumption of a constant variance, are inappropriate; the problem of heteroscedasticity can easily be eliminated here by taking percentage changes.

We next review the time series for unadjusted and seasonally adjusted apparel sales, which were analyzed in the previous chapter. Figure 7.5 shows that both series have the same upward trend, although the variance is much larger for the unadjusted data. Yet the unit-root tests give contradictory results. According to the calculations of McKinnon contained in the EViews program, the critical values for rejecting a unit root for this series are −4.0 at the 1% level, −3.4 at the 5% level, and −3.1 at the 10% level. The values for the seasonally adjusted series are −1.9 for the ADF test and −2.2 for the PP test. The hypothesis of no unit root is clearly rejected, as it should be, since apparel sales clearly have a strong trend.

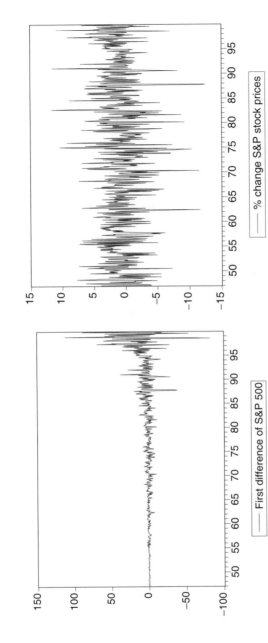

Figure 7.3 Absolute and percentage changes in S&P 500 stock prices. The first differences increase greatly as the market rises, while there is no trend increase in percentage changes.

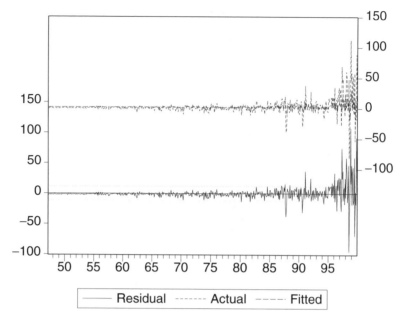

Figure 7.4 Residuals of changes in monthly stock prices from an ARMA(1,1) equation.

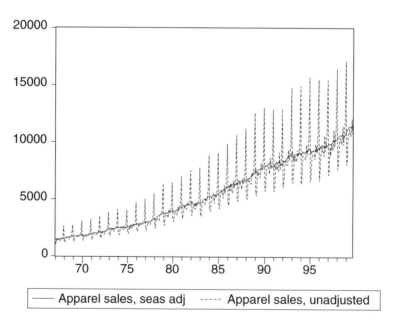

Figure 7.5 Seasonally adjusted and unadjusted apparel sales.

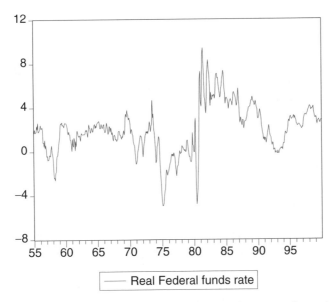

Figure 7.6 The real Federal funds rate. There appears to be no trend, yet the first order auto correlation coefficient is almost unity.

However, the tests for a unit root with the *unadjusted* data give the opposite results; the statistics are −7.7 for the ADF test and −18.4 for the PP test. The test statistics show that the monthly fluctuations are so large that the trend is obscured, although that is not really the case. The lesson is that the tests for stationarity are not always reliable. If the series appears to have a trend, and the principal purpose of the forecast is to examine short-term fluctuations rather than long-term trend values, that trend should be extracted by using either first differencing or taking percentage changes before proceeding to ARMA models.

Figure 7.6 shows monthly data for the real Federal funds rate, defined as the nominal rate minus the percentage change in the CPI over the past 12 months. Visual inspection suggests there is no trend. The ADF and PP tests indicate no unit root at the 5% level of significance. Also, a regression where the real funds rate is a function of a time trend and an AR(1) transformation also shows an insignificant *t*-statistic for the time trend.

Even in this case, forecasting accuracy is likely to be improved by taking first differences. There is no "proof" to this statement, but the evidence that does exist can be found in the correlogram diagram, which shows a first-order auto-correlation coefficient of 0.958. When this coefficient is not significantly differ-ent from unity, it is often better to take first differences in any case. The forecasting record of different forms of this equation will be examined in section 7.7. This example suggests that the trend should be removed for a high first-order ACF even if the traditional tests do not indicate any significant unit root or time trend.

7.4 IDENTIFICATION

The process of choosing the optimal (p,d,q) structure in an ARIMA model is known as *identification*.[20] This process involves some guesswork, since theory does not indicate the optimal length of lag or degree of differencing. In virtually all cases, d is either 0 or 1, so the following comments about identification are confined to determining the optimal values of p and q.

In general, a tradeoff exists. The adjusted R^2 will rise as more terms are included, but the use of additional terms increases the probability that curve-fitting will reduce forecast accuracy. Essentially, a measure is needed that will balance the rise in adjusted R^2 against the spurious increase in correlation that occurs when additional terms are added. Some sort of "penalty" term is needed to account for the extra terms.

Hannan and Rissanen (HR)[21] have suggested the following three-step procedure. First, determine the maximum length of lag for an AR model. Second, use the Akaike Information Criterion (AIC) – which contains a "penalty" term – to determine the maximum length of lag in an AR model. Third, use the Schwarz criterion (SC), which imprises a larger penalty for additional coefficients, to determine the maximum lags for a mixed ARMA model. AIC and SC are discussed below.

Step 1
Determine the maximum length of lag. The original HR procedure suggested running a pure autoregressive equation – on a stationary series – until the adjusted $\bar{R}^2$ was maximized. However, in the author's experience, a more efficient procedure is to look at the correlogram and determine the maximum length of lag as the point where the partial autocorrelation coefficients (PAC) stop being significant. In a case where, say, lags 1 through 4 were significant, 5 through 9 were not, but 10 was significant again, the usual procedure is to treat that long lag as being due to one-time exogenous factors and ignore that result. The only exception is where monthly data show a significant PAC at lag 12; this is discussed in section 7.6 under seasonal adjustment procedures in ARIMA models.

Step 2
In general, the lag determined from the correlogram (or regression equation) will be too long. Here is where the "penalty" term comes into play. For a pure autoregressive model, the general idea is to balance the decreasing standard error as the number of AR terms increases with some penalty for adding

---

[20] For a brief discussion, see Johnston and DiNardo. pp. 228–9. A more complete analysis is given in Granger and Newbold, sect. 3.2, pp. 77–87.
[21] Hannan, E. J., and J. Rissanen, "Recursive Estimation of Mixed Autoregressive–Moving Average Order," *Biometrika*, 69 (1982), 81–94. A correction appears in 70 (1983), 303.

additional variables. The usual test is known as AIC,[22] which is included in EViews and most other regression packages. k is chosen to minimize

$$AIC = \log \frac{(\Sigma_{\varepsilon_i^2})}{N} + 2k/n \qquad (7.32)$$

where $\Sigma_{\varepsilon_i^2}$ is the sum of the squared residuals, k is the maximum degree of auto-correlation and n is the number of observations.

Shibata[23] has shown that this estimate is inconsistent, and overstates the optimal degree of the model. This is not a trivial difference; the AIC criterion often overstates the optimal degree by a factor of 2 or 3. That is why we suggest looking at the correlogram rather than a pure autoregressive equation. However, this point is not too serious because at this stage of the analysis the aim is to identify the maximum probable lag, not the optimal lag. Hence over-stating that lag will result in a few additional computations but should not affect the final choice of model.

Step 3
Using the maximum lag as determined by the AIC criterion, now estimate a mixed ARMA model and reduce the lag according to SC,[24] k is chosen to minimize:

$$SC = \log \frac{(\Sigma_{\varepsilon_i^2})}{N} + \frac{k}{n} \log n \qquad (7.33)$$

As is the case for all the formulas in this section, these steps are guidelines rather than absolute rules and must be applied with some discretion. In this case, one possible flaw with SC is that it will often give different results based on the length of the time series. To see how this can occur, consider the comparison with a short and a long time series; the short one has, say, 60 monthly observations, while the long one has 600 monthly observations. The term (log n)/n is 0.068 for $n = 60$ but only 0.011 for $n = 600$. Thus adding another lag term will raise the Schwarz criterion by 0.068 for the short series but only 0.011 for the long series. It is possible that the change in σ^2 from adding another lag term would also be different for a short and long series, but it is usually about the same. *Hence the Schwarz criterion would tend to indicate a longer lag distribution for a longer series than a shorter one.* For this reason, the Schwarz criterion should not be used exclusively. In general, it is best to choose two or three different ARMA models and then check their forecasting accuracy outside the sample period.

[22] Akaike, H., "Fitting Autoregressive Models for Prediction," *Annals of the Institute of Statistics and Mathematics*, 21 (1969), 243–7.
[23] Shibata, R., "Selection of the Order of an Autoregressive Model by Akaike's Information Criterion," *Biometrika*, 63 (1976), 117–26.
[24] Schwarz, G., "Estimating the Dimension of a Model," *Annals of Statistics*, 6 (1978) 461–4.

Table 7.1 Schwarz criterion values for ARMA models (monthly rate of inflation).

ARMA	Schwarz (SC) criterion	
	630 observations	60 observations
(5,5)	−8.987	−10.013
(5,4)	−8.985	−10.072
(4,4)	−8.962	−10.107
(4,3)	−8.953	−10.175
(3,3)	−8.964	−10.286
(3,2)	−8.936	−10.355
(2,2)	−8.923	−10.420
(2,1)	−8.933	−10.411
(1,1)	−8.910	−10.477

These concepts can be usefully illustrated with the series for monthly inflation data, which was also analyzed in section 7.2. The correlogram was given in figure 7.1. To review briefly, visual inspection indicates a maximum AR lag of 5. However, if we calculate a pure autoregressive equation, the AIC criterion indicates an optimal lag of 15, which is far too long.

This aberration did not occur just because the monthly inflation data series was used. The reader may verify that the correlogram for the first difference of apparel sales, which were also discussed in section 7.2, shows a maximum lag of 4, whereas the AIC criterion indicates an optimal lag of 13.

We now estimate an ARMA model starting with a maximum lag of (5,5) and gradually dropping the terms one at a time, using the Schwarz criterion. The results are given in table 7.1. Results are also presented for a short series of only 60 observations.

First, note that while the (5,5) model has the lowest SC value for the long series, the (1,1) model has the lowest value for the short series. This reinforces the point made earlier. Second, the SC values for the long series do not follow a monotonic trend; there is a reversal of (3,3). In conjunction with the short series results, this strongly suggests (3,3) is probably the longest model that should be considered. Third, the gradient for the short series declines after (2,2), suggesting that is probably the shortest model that should be considered. On this basis, we should experiment with the forecasts from the (3,3), (3,2), and (2,2) models.

It should be apparent by this point that AIC and SC, while they may serve as an aid to identification, do not provide definitive answers. However, before turning to some useful rules for checking forecasting accuracy, a short detour is taken to examine the estimation procedure, including seasonal adjustment, and description of the terms contained in EViews.

7.5 SEASONAL FACTORS IN ARMA MODELING

So far we have ignored the issue of whether the data used in the ARMA process are seasonally adjusted or not, implicitly assuming they have already been adjusted by X-11 or similar processes. In the examples given above, seasonally adjusted data are used for inflation, and interest rates do not contain any significant seasonal factors. However, in many cases, it is useful to identify and measure the seasonal factors themselves; also, forecasting accuracy may be improved using data before seasonal adjustment in cases where the seasonal factors are not random but are related to the economic environment – such as retail sales and housing starts.

The discussion here centers on the use of monthly data; the same general analysis would apply for quarterly data, with the critical lag being four periods instead of 12. It is assumed throughout this discussion that the seasonal factors are multiplicative, as opposed to additive. Additive seasonal factors would be used only in the case where some of the observations were zero or negative; e.g., when the series is already a first difference or percentage change.

We first consider the AR and MA processes separately. Suppose a seasonally unadjusted series has significant PACF for 1 and 2, then a long string of insignificant coefficients, then a significant coefficient again for a lag of 12. Omitting the constant term, the underlying equation would thus be

$$y_t = \alpha_1 y_{t-1} + \alpha_2 y_{t-2} + \eta_1 (y_{t-12} - \alpha_1 y_{t-13} - \alpha_2 y_{t-14}) + u_t. \tag{7.34}$$

For MA processes, the equation with two lagged terms and a seasonal factor can be written as

$$y_t = \varepsilon_t + \beta_1 \varepsilon_{t-1} + \beta_2 \varepsilon_{t-2} + \eta_2 (\varepsilon_{t-12} - \beta_1 \varepsilon_{t-13} - \beta_2 \varepsilon_{t-14}). \tag{7.35}$$

Hence the generalized model can be written as

$$y_t = \sum_{i=1}^{p} \alpha_i y_{t-i} + \eta_1 \left[y_{t-12} - \sum_{i=1}^{p} \alpha_i y_{t-i-12} \right] + \varepsilon_t$$

$$+ \sum_{i=1}^{q} \beta_i \varepsilon_{t-i} + \eta_2 \left[\varepsilon_{t-12} - \sum_{i=1}^{q} \beta_i e_{t-i-12} \right] + u_t. \tag{7.36}$$

To understand the practical significance of these terms, assume for the moment that α_1 is fairly close to unity and α_2 is fairly small in the AR equation, so (7.34) can be reasonably approximated as

$$\Delta y_t = \eta_1 \Delta y_{t-12}. \tag{7.37}$$

If in addition η_1 is also fairly close to unity – which we will see is often the case for seasonally unadjusted data – this equation simply says the change in

Table 7.2 Coefficients for the ARMA housing starts model with one- and 12-month lags.

Variable	Coefficient	SE	t-statistic
C	48.18	542.60	0.1
AR(1)	0.94	0.02	61.6
SAR(12)	1.00	0.00	283.4
MA(1)	−0.21	0.05	−4.4
SMA(12)	−0.89	0.00	−6327.2

y this month is equal to the change in y in the same month last year. This is a stationary series; if the first differences are increasing over time, the problem can be resolved by taking percentage changes.

The pure MA case is somewhat more difficult to interpret intuitively, because there are no guidelines for the usual sizes of β_1, β_2, and η_2. A fairly typical case for a series that is actually composed primarily of random elements would have β_1 and β_2 fairly close to 0 and η_2 fairly close to unity. The economic interpretation is that the value of y in the current period is highly correlated with the error term a year ago. However, if the series has not been seasonally adjusted, that error term would probably reflect the seasonal factor, and hence could also be measured by SAR(12).

This strongly suggests that, in a seasonal ARMA model, the SMA(12) term should not be included without at least trying the SAR(12) term as well; otherwise, the SMA(12) term itself serves as a suboptimal proxy variable for the seasonal factor. However, when both of these terms are tried together in the same equation, the results often look quite unusual.

To see this, consider an equation in which the monthly data for unadjusted single-family housing starts are a function of AR(1), MA(1), SAR(12), and SMA(12). As shown in table 7.2, the results show an absurdly large t-ratio of 6,327 for the SMA(12) term. The adjusted R^2 for this equation is 0.91. If the equation is estimated without the SMA(12) term, the other variables remain significant and the adjusted R^2 drops only slightly, to 0.87.

How could the t-ratios for SAR(12) and SMA(12) be so large when the equation itself does not fit that well? To answer this question, consider a simpler equation where SAR(12) and SMA(12) are the only two independent variables. In such a case, the variance of the second parameter estimate is given by

$$\text{Var}(b_2) = \sigma^2 / \sum_i y_i^2 * (1 - r_{23}^2). \tag{7.38}$$

In this case it should be clear what happened. The absolute value of the simple correlation coefficient r_{23} is almost unity; SAR(12) and SMA(12) are almost the same variable with opposite signs. The adjusted R^2, on the other hand, has

Dependent Variable: @PCH(SP500)
Method: Least Squares

Sample: 1959:01 1997:12
Included observations: 468
Convergence achieved after 15 iterations
Backcast: 1957:12 1958:12

Variable	Coefficient	Std. Error	t-Statistic	Prob.
C	0.007	0.002	4.5	0.000
AR(1)	0.116	0.159	0.7	0.465
SAR(12)	0.829	0.025	33.2	0.000
MA(1)	0.163	0.159	1.0	0.306
SMA(12)	−0.886	0.000187	−4743.2	0.000

R-squared	0.102	Mean dependent var		0.00676
Adjusted R-squared	0.094	S.D. dependent var		0.03355
S.E. of regression	0.032	Akaike info criterion		−4.04
Sum squared resid	0.472	Schwarz criterion		−4.00
Log likelihood	950	F-statistic		13.2
Durbin-Watson stat	1.99	Prob(F-statistic)		0.000

Inverted AR Roots	.98	.85+.49i	.85 −.49i	.49+.85i
	.49 −.85i	.12	−.00 −.98i	−.00+.98i
	−.49 −.85i	−.49+.85i	−.85 +.49i	−.85 −.49i
	−.98			
Inverted MA Roots	.99	.86+.49i	.86 −.49i	.49 -.86i
	.49+.86i	.00 −.99i	−.00+.99i	−.16
	−.49 −.86i	−.49+.86i	−.86+.49i	−.86 −.49i
	−.99			

Figure 7.7   ARIMA model for monthly percentage changes in the S&P 500 stock price index.

not improved very much when SMA(12) is added. Hence this extremely high t-ratio – which is actually fairly typical – does not improve the sample period fit very much, and in general does not improve the forecasting accuracy at all.

To illustrate the possible pitfalls, consider an ARMA model for monthly percentage changes in the S&P 500 stock price index. This variable does not have any seasonal pattern, yet the t-ratios for SAR(12) and SMA(12) are 33 and −4,743 respectively (see figure 7.7).

Common sense says you can't make money in the market assuming that what happened last month – or in the same month a year ago – will happen this month. With the possible exception of the "January effect" (see problem 6.4) there are no seasonal patterns to stock prices in spite of folklore about the "summer rally," "September swoon," and other fictitious characters. On the other hand, changes in stocks are often influenced by exogenous events, which argues for an MA process. If the monthly percentage change in stocks is estimated using an ARMA model, the results show that MA(1) is significant, AR(1) is not, and SMA(12) is not either. This equation explains only about 7% of the variance. So far there are no surprises.

However, the above equation shows what happens when the SAR(12) term is added. The adjusted R^2 of the equation hardly improves at all, rising from 0.07 to 0.09. However, the SAR(12) term becomes quite significant while the SMA(12) term becomes bizarrely significant, with a t-ratio of 4,743. That makes no sense when we consider that the overall adjusted R^2 is only 0.09. Also recall that in an equation with a single independent variable, $t^2 = F$, so even if the net contribution of the other variables were zero, the F-ratio for the equation would be about 22.5 million, whereas in fact it is 13.

These results are further evidence of a spurious negative correlation between SAR(12) and SMA(12). On the one hand, the equation says the change in stock prices is positively correlated with the change a year ago, while the SMA term says the change in stock prices is negatively correlated with the error term a year ago. Essentially these two factors cancel each other, but simply glancing at the regression one might get the opinion they are both highly significant contributors to forecasts of the stock market.

To a certain extent this example is somewhat of a "ringer" because stock prices have no seasonal factor. It is included as a lesson to the unwary of what happens for those who blunder into an equation with no idea of the underlying structure. To avoid such nonsensical results, the following procedure is recommended. First, don't use either SAR or SMA terms unless the underlying series has a strong seasonal component. Usually this is apparent by eye, but if not, calculate a regression with seasonal dummy variables. If the seasonal pattern is strong, test for the significance of SAR(12). If that term is significant, add SMA(12), which is usually important if the values of the seasonal factors are changing. However, this procedure is best attempted one step at a time rather than adding all the variables at once and finding they are all significant.

The use of SAR(12) and SMA(12) terms often introduces spurious correlations. On the other hand, where seasonal patterns are strong, they cannot be ignored. Using seasonally adjusted data solves some but not all of the problems, because changing seasonal patterns are based on recent trends, which means that the forecaster must predict the seasonal factors as well as the underlying data.

One alternative to these problems is to take first differences, or percentage changes, for the data over the past 12 months; i.e., the value of y in any given month this year minus the value of y in the same month last year. If the underlying variable has a significant trend, percentage changes are usually better, in which case the dependent variable would have the form $(y_t - y_{t-12})/y_{t-12}$. If this formulation is used, the seasonal factors do not have to be estimated independently. Also, any shift that does occur can be estimated in the regression using either economic variables, truncated time trends, or dummy variables.

In summary to this point, the following options can be chosen to minimize forecasting error using an ARIMA model with data that are not seasonally adjusted.

1   Seasonally adjust the data using the X-11 program or a similar method. Assuming the variable has a significant trend, calculate first differences or percentage changes with the seasonally adjusted data, and then calculate the ARMA model.
2   Do not seasonally adjust the data; take first differences or percentage changes, and then calculate the ARMA model with the original data using SAR(12) and possibly SMA(12)
3   Use seasonal differencing – take first differences or percentage changes over the past year instead of the past month, and then calculate an ARMA model using those differences as the dependent variable.

To illustrate some results, reconsider three examples that have been used previously. The series for apparel sales has a strong trend and a strong seasonal pattern. The series for housing starts has no trend and a strong seasonal pattern. The monthly rate of inflation, this time as measured by the PPI for industrial commodities, has no trend and a weaker seasonal pattern; it is more influenced by random elements. For each series the following regressions are calculated:

(a)   seasonally adjusted data, ARMA
(b)   unadjusted data, ARMA, SAR(12)
(c)   unadjusted data, ARMA, SAR(12) and SMA (12)
(d)   12-month differencing, ARMA
(e)   12-month differencing, ARMA, SAR(12) and SMA(12).

All these results are based on equations estimated from 1959.1 through 1997.12, with the period from 1998.1 through 1999.12 used for forecasting. In each case, the ARMA model includes the optimal lag structure based on the t-ratios of the individual terms, the overall adjusted R^2, and the Schwarz and Akaike criteria, although in general those did not have much influence on the optimal choice.

The results in table 7.3 show no consistent pattern, which may seem discouraging to the researcher. However, they do illustrate there is no one method that works best all the time. There are no cut and dried rules for choosing the ARMA model that will minimize forecast error. Also, of course, testing forecasting accuracy over a two-year period is hardly a comprehensive sample.

Nonetheless, the results are illustrative. In particular, note that the seasonally adjusted data are best for apparel sales and worst for housing starts, for which seasonal differencing gives the best results. The results for the monthly inflation rate for industrial commodities are about the same for seasonally adjusted data and seasonally differenced data when SAR(12) and SMA(12) are used. The big changes in the PPI are due primarily to the oil shocks, which

Table 7.3 Results.

	Single-family housing starts			Apparel sales			Inflation rate – PPI industrial commodities		
	ARMA lag	RMS	AAE	ARMA lag	RMS	AAE	ARMA lag	RMS	AAE
(a)	(2,2)	19.7	18.8	(2,2)	315	262	(3,3)	1.60	1.24
(b)	(1,1)	18.0	15.8	(2,1)	475	352	(3,3)	1.75	1.40
(c)	(2,1)	15.7	14.6	(2,1)	364	294	(1,1)	2.10	1.63
(d)	(3,3)	12.6	11.0	(2,2)	480	358	(3,3)	5.95	4.67
(e)	(1,1)	12.8	11.8	(1,1)	471	361	(1,1)	1.71	1.37

have no seasonal component, so the method of adjustment does not matter very much.

The main conclusion to be drawn from these experiments is that the optimal type of seasonal adjustment method depends critically on the nature of the seasonal factors. If they are always the same each year, the method does not matter at all. However, that is rarely the case for economic time series. The following rule of thumb can be used. If the seasonal process is predictable – e.g., the day on which Easter falls is obviously known in advance – the X-11 program will work better. If the fluctuations are due to random events, such as weather, oil crises, strikes, or other unforecastable interruptions, X-11 is likely to introduce spurious changes that will not reoccur. As a result, it is probably better to use seasonally differenced data in those cases.

7.6 ESTIMATION OF ARMA MODELS

The discussion of autocorrelation in chapter 3 noted that whenever an AR(1) or higher power process is used, a nonlinear estimation procedure is generally utilized. The same comment applies to ARMA models. The reason for reintroducing the topic at this juncture is that, fairly often, ARMA models do not converge or generate results that are clearly ridiculous, such as the t-ratios of 4,000 or higher illustrated above.

In using the common nonlinear algorithms, the answer that is obtained may differ depending on the starting point that is chosen. To understand this, think of a hilly terrain, with several peaks and valleys. One peak is the highest, so if you were doing aerial scanning, there would be no difficulty in identifying that peak. However, suppose you are in one of the valleys – all directions are up. It may be that the slope up to peak A is steeper than the slope to peak B – but peak B is higher. Because of the steeper slope, you start up A. When you get to the top, you are unable to see from your vantage point that B is higher than A, so you think you have climbed the right hill when it was the wrong one. Alternatively, the valley may be so flat for a while that you have no idea which way to turn, so you remain stuck in the valley indefinitely.

Mathematically, then, any nonlinear algorithm could produce an incorrect answer for two reasons. First, it could reach a local rather than a global maximum. Second, it could fail to converge at all.

Are these common enough to be of concern, or are they merely statistical lacunae of no practical significance? As it turns out, they happen quite often. In estimating ARMA models, it is not unusual for EViews or other programs to print out a message that convergence was not achieved after 100 iterations. Also, you will sometimes receive a message that the equation "failed to improve" after a certain number of iterations. In other cases, the results are obviously nonsensical; in that case, it is usually a good idea to simplify the model somewhat by dropping a term and see whether the problem persists. If it does, the most likely answer is that the algorithm is starting from the wrong spot, in which case the researcher should specify estimated values to help get the estimation procedure pointing in the right direction.

Of course, the values of the coefficients are not known in advance; if they were, it would not be necessary to estimate the equation in the first place. However, when working with ARMA models that have been properly integrated, we are always dealing with stationary processes. That means $\Sigma \alpha_j < 1$ and $\Sigma \beta_j < 1$. Thus reasonable starting points might be 0.5; other possibilities are 0.75 and 0.25. This will usually give you a better chance of reaching the right value, but if not, the remaining possibility is to simplify the model until convergence is achieved.

EViews printouts for ARMA models contain two additional terms: backcasts, and AR and MA roots. Backcasting simply means the program fills in the residuals, so the sample period is not truncated by the number of periods equal to the longest lag. In practice that makes very little difference.

The bottom part of the EViews printout for ARMA models contains information about the values of the inverted AR roots and inverted MA roots. They may be either real or imaginary; that doesn't matter. The key danger point occurs if the value of either of these roots is greater than unity, in which case the AR or MA process is explosive. If you have already taken first differences or percentage changes, that is unlikely to happen. If you are working with levels and one or more of the roots is greater than unity, then the trend should be removed.

7.7 DIAGNOSTIC CHECKING AND FORECASTING

We now turn to testing different types of models. At this point it is assumed the trend has been removed, and either the data have been seasonally adjusted, or seasonal factors have been incorporated in the estimation procedures (by using SAR(4) for quarterly data and SAR(12) for monthly data). Those steps are generally straightforward.

It is usually more difficult to choose the optimal length of the AR and MA processes, denoted as p and q. In general, the overall goodness-of-fit statistics will look about the same for a large variety of different lag structures; however, the forecast accuracy of these equations may vary significantly. In general, the more parameters that are estimated, the more likely that the equation simply represents an exercise in curve fitting that will not generate accurate predictions. The rule of parsimony is used here: use fewer rather than more parameters. However, this rule by itself explains very little. Does that mean ARMA(1,1) models are preferable to ARMA(2,2) models? Clearly more information is needed to make an informed choice.

The ultimate choice of model depends on forecasting accuracy, which generally is not known in advance. In the estimation phase, the suggested steps are as follows.

Step 1
Plot the data (presumably in first difference or percentage change form) to make sure there are no severe outliers. The parameters of ARMA processes, like other statistical models, are based on the assumption of a constant variance. If that is not the case, the equation may not generate accurate forecasts although the parameter estimates appear to be quite robust.

Step 2
When there appears to be any trend, it is usually better to remove the trend before proceeding further. If the trend is weak, the forecasts will be about the same whether the trend is removed or not, and no harm will be done by removing it.

Step 3
Start by estimating ARMA models of low order, such as (1,1). Then expand the model as long as the terms remain significant. Occasionally the terms in a (2,2) or (3,3) model will not be significant, but the coefficients will then become significant again as the model is expanded further. That simply represents very high correlations among the terms and does not improve the model. That is often a warning sign that curve fitting is invading the equation. In general, the concept of parsimony should be observed.

Step 4
Theoretically, the residuals should be randomly distributed (determined by looking at the correlogram). However, in practice that will not happen very often, and generally cannot be used as a criterion for determining the order of the ARMA model. Except for seasonal factors, the maximum structure will occur at the first PACF that becomes insignificant, but that sets the maximum rather than the optimal length of lag.

In order to indicate the practical difficulties associated with ARMA models, we look at several alternative equations for the Federal funds rate; the data series begins in 1955. First, we estimate a simple ARMA(1,1) model. Although the R^2 is high, that means nothing in this sort of model; the test comes when we

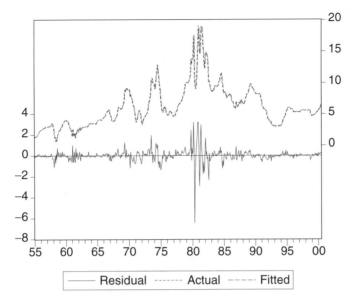

Figure 7.8 Residuals from an ARMA(1,1) equation of the Federal funds rate.

examine the correlogram to see whether the residuals are randomly distributed. Quite clearly they are not: PACF are significant for several lags, including lags of 7, 8, 9, 11, 12, and 13 months. This is not a very encouraging start, since one would hope to find that the significance of the residuals decreases as the length of lag increases. Also, there are no seasonal factors in the Federal funds rate, so significant coefficients a year ago are puzzling.

Expanding the equation to ARMA(2,2) and then (3,3) does not help matters at all; the same PACF are still significant.

It is possible to add terms AR(7), AR(8), AR(9), MA(7), MA(8), and MA(9) but that does not help matters either. In that case, those PACF are no longer significant but we now find that PACF for lags 11 through 14 are all significant. If even more terms are added, the equation no longer converges, and it becomes clear this expansion process cannot continue indefinitely.

What is causing the problem? In this case – and in many similar examples – it is best to go back and look at the economics. Figure 7.8 shows the residuals from a simple AR(1) model; it is clear that something very unusual happened in early 1980. More specifically, the standard error of the equation is 0.58, but the error for May 1980 is 6.44 – more than 10 times the standard error. Clearly that observation is drawn from a different population. That error is so large that it affects the estimated parameters for the entire sample period.

In March 1980, the Volcker Fed imposed credit controls, whereupon the economy declined at a record pace. By May the damage was becoming clear, so the Fed slashed the funds rate from 17.6% to 11.0%. Of course this decline would not have been predicted by any econometric model either, so it does not necessarily follow this is a failure of ARMA modeling. However, it illustrates what can happen when there are severe outliers – and serves as yet another reminder that it is always a useful idea to plot the data before calculating any regressions.

By 1983, monetary policy had returned to normal, so an ARMA model is estimated starting in that year. Once again the process starts with a (1,1) model; the correlogram shows a very high PACF with lag 2, which strongly suggests trying a (2,2) model. For that model, the residuals are randomly distributed, but neither the MA(1) nor MA(2) terms are significant, raising the question of whether they are needed. First MA(2) is eliminated, and then MA(1); the resulting ARMA(2,0) model still has random residuals, so that is the one that is chosen. The economic interpretation of this equation says the Federal funds rate is highly influenced by its values one and two months ago, but is not as subject to exogenous shocks.

Three case studies are now presented that offer a richer variety of possibilities for ARMA models, including detrending and seasonal factors. While some ex post forecasts are offered in these examples, the forecasting properties of similar equations are assessed in greater detail in the next chapter.

Case Study 13: New Orders for Machine Tools

This study analyzes both seasonally adjusted and unadjusted data, since in some cases the seasonal factors themselves may be of interest. The procedure is as follows. First, several different methods for removing the trend are examined. Second, an ARMA model is estimated with seasonally adjusted data, choosing the optimum p and q. Third, the model is estimated with seasonally unadjusted data, including AR(12) and MA(12) terms. In all cases, the sample period is truncated at the end of 1997, and the forecasting accuracy is assessed for the 1998–2000 period. The series used is in constant dollars; i.e., the dollar figures are deflated by the PPI for machine tools. The series for the volume of machine tool orders is shown in figure 7.9; the series has a significant trend, although it only explains about 5% of the variance. Both the ADF and PP tests indicate a unit root for this series, so the trend is removed.

While this series has a significant trend, the first differences are not materially larger at the end of the sample period, so they are used instead of percentage changes. The initial step, after plotting the data, is to estimate an ARMA(1,1) equation. The correlogram shows significant PACF at lag 6 and again at lag 12 – even though the data are seasonally adjusted. The next step is to try an ARMA(2,2) equation; the additional terms are highly significant, but the same PACF correlations remain.

When an ARMA(3,3) equation is tried, ridiculous t-ratios start showing up for some of the terms, and the equation almost does not converge. Another

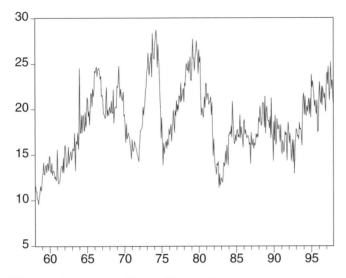

Figure 7.9   Volume of new orders for machine tools.

possibility is to try ARMA(2,2) plus AR(6), MA(6), AR(12), and MA(12), since that is where the significant correlations occurred. All these terms were significant but the correlogram revealed that the residuals remained serially correlated.

None of the ARMA models gives very useful predictions. There was a big increase in machine tool orders in January 1998, which this sort of model is not designed to capture. Note that when longer lags are added, the forecast error *increases*. This suggests that the correlations with longer lags are spurious or due to outliers rather than an integral part of the process. The forecasts for the period 1998.01 to 2000.12 are shown in figure 7.10.

The seasonally unadjusted data series is considered next. In this case the ARMA(1,1) model with AR(12) and SA(12) gives results that are just about the same as when further terms are included; so using the principle of parsimony, the simpler form of the model is used. It can be seen that ARMA(1,1), (2,2), and (3,3) all give almost identical results when AR(12) and MA(12) terms are included. Figure 7.11 also shows that using these latter two terms without any additional terms gives significantly inferior results.

However, just as was the case for the seasonally adjusted data, the correlogram shows that the residuals are serially correlated no matter how many lags are added (within reason). At least in this case, it is apparently no easier to obtain random residuals in time-series models than it was in structural econometric models.

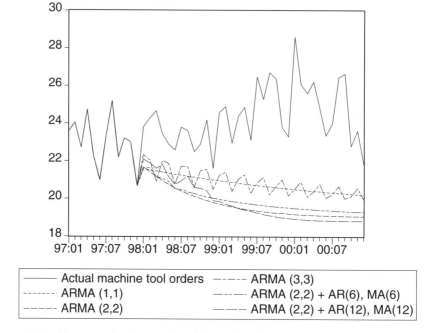

Figure 7.10 Forecast of volume of machine tool orders (seasonally adjusted).

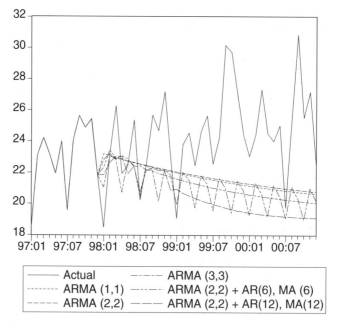

Figure 7.11 Forecast of volume of machine tool orders (not seasonally adjusted).

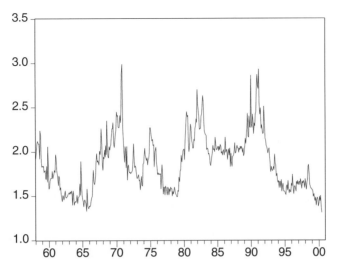

Figure 7.12   Inventory/sales ratio for transportation equipment (SIC 37).

It might appear that the forecasts for the seasonally unadjusted data are more accurate than the adjusted data, but that is just an illusion. The seasonal factors can be predicted by the seasonal adjustment procedure without any further modeling. The RMS error for the unadjusted data are actually slightly higher than for the adjusted data.

Case Study 14: Inventory/Sales (I/S) Ratio for SIC 37 (Transportation Equipment)

Figure 7.12 shows the values of the I/S ratio for transportation equipment, using seasonally adjusted data for inventories and sales. It is one of the few I/S ratios in the manufacturing sector that does not have a long-term downward trend.

Since there is no trend to be removed – and both the ADF and PP tests verify this finding – it is possible to proceed directly to estimating ARMA models. First, the ARMA(1,1) model is tried; the correlogram shows significant PACF for several lags. The ARMA(2,2) model is tried, but there is no improvement; similarly for the ARMA(3,3) model. Even an attempt to estimate an ARMA(6,6) model, which violates the principle of parsimony and generally gives inferior forecasts, still results in serially correlated residuals, so no useful purpose would be served by adding all those additional terms to the model.

The forecasts for these three models are shown in figure 7.13. None of them works very well; the big increase in the I/S ratio in 1998 and the decline in 1999 and 2000 are not tracked by any of the ARMA models. In this graph, the actual data for 1997 are shown in comparison with the actual and forecast values from 1998 through 2000.

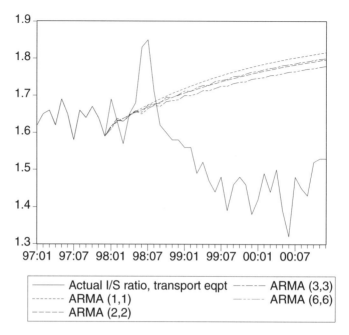

Figure 7.13 I/S ratio forecasts with different ARMA models for the SIC 37.

Case Study 15: Non-farm Payroll Employment

The previous two case studies have contained examples where the trend explains only a very small proportion of the sample period variance. We now turn to a case where a simple trend explains over 99% of that variance, and determine whether ARMA models can improve forecasting accuracy in this case. It is not initially clear whether trend removal using levels or logarithms will produce better results, so both methods are tried.

Once again, there is little difference on which to choose simply by looking at sample period statistics. ARMA(1,1), (1,2), (2,1), and (2,2) appear to give very similar results in terms of the correlogram analysis, levels of significance, and the Akaike and Schwarz criteria. Also, there seems to be little information that would enable one to choose between the detrended series using levels and logs. The (1,1) and (2,2) equations are shown in figure 7.14; the (1,2) and (2,1) results are virtually identical.

However, in this case the forecast results are instructive. While the ARMA models are all about the same, the forecasts using the detrended series for the logs are substantially better than those using the levels. That is not just a random result; the rate of growth in employment has been fairly steady over the sample period, and since the series has a strong time trend, that implies the actual changes in recent years will be greater than the sample period average, whereas that is not the case for the logarithmic approach. In this example, then, a clear difference emerges.

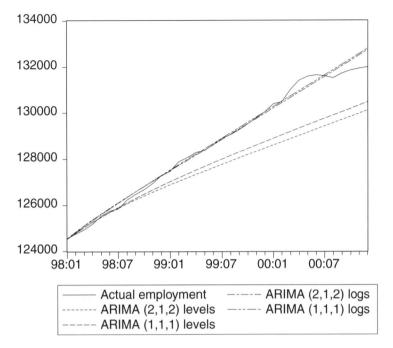

Figure 7.14   Forecasts of non-farm payroll employment.

The superiority of the logarithmic equation still leaves the question unanswered of whether a simple equation log(employment) = α + β (time trend) would give essentially the same results; these results can also be compared with a naive model which says the percentage increase is equal to the average increase over the entire sample period 1947.01 to 1997.12. Figure 7.15 shows how those forecasts compare with the ARIMA models. An equation in which log(employment) is a function of a time trend and an AR(1) adjustment provides forecasts that are very similar to the ARIMA(2,1,2) model; the AR(1) term provides virtually all the forecasting information, even though the other terms are also significant. That is often the case for government data with strong time trends where the data collection process often causes some artificial smoothness. The naive model falls below the actual level in 1998 and 1999 but, when slower growth ensues, is almost exactly equal to the level of employment by the end of 2000. Hence the naive model does just as well as ARIMA or trend models.

SUMMARY

The results of the case studies in this chapter might appear to be quite unimpressive, since they consist primarily of inaccurate forecasts. However, a few

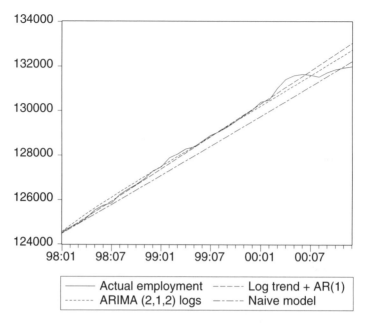

Figure 7.15 Alternative forecasts of non-farm payroll employment, comparing ARIMA with trend and naive models.

instructive comments can be found in these results. In general it is the case that when series have weak trends or no trends, ARMA models will give poor forecasts if an upward or downward trend develops in the forecast period. Of course, the same criticism could be levied against structural models as well.

Where series do have strong trends, use of an autoregressive adjustment can reduce forecasting error, as was the case for payroll employment. In the past, these constant adjustments were often attempted on an ad hoc basis. ARMA processes often provide a more systematic method of handling this problem.

In building ARMA models, results are seldom improved by extending the model beyond ARMA(2,2), plus seasonal factors where appropriate. The individual coefficients may appear to be highly significant but the forecasts are no better and, in many cases, are worse because of the increased proclivity toward curve fitting with an extended model.

The statistical tests devised to determine the optimal ARMA model are not very useful because they are based on the assumption that the residuals are independent, whereas observation of the correlograms shows that is seldom the case. For this reason, the Akaike and Schwarz criterion do not provide much useful information. In general, a parsimonious approach is preferable.

In most cases, ARMA models do not provide very accurate forecasts. However, it is also true that in most cases, adjustment of the forecast to take into account past forecasting errors can improve accuracy. Thus the combination of structural models plus ARMA adjustments may very well lead to superior forecasts – and forecasts may be further enhanced by combining these types of models with other result. This topic is discussed in detail in the next chapter.

Problems and Questions

1. Figure 7.16 shows monthly data for employment in the steel industry before seasonal adjustment. It is clear that the data are dominated by strikes in 1949, 1952, 1956, and 1959.

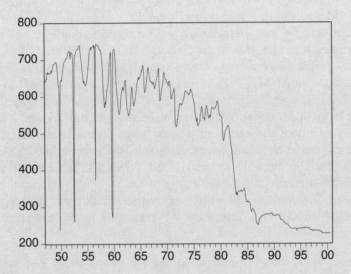

Figure 7.16 Problem 1.

(a) Discuss how you would modify the data for these strikes before proceeding further.
(b) Over the entire sample period, the data clearly exhibit a downward trend. Verify this by running a regression, and also calculating the ADF and PP tests.
(c) If you wanted to develop a forecasting model for steel employment in the future, explain whether you would use the downward trend.

Continued

(d) These data are not seasonally adjusted. Check to see whether seasonal factors are significant. How does your answer differ whether 1948–67 or 1980–99 is used as the sample period? What seasonal factors, if any, would you use in your forecasts?

(e) After taking the strike periods, trends, and any seasonal factors into account, estimate an optimal ARMA model up to 1999 and then use it to predict monthly employment in 2000. Show whether the forecasts are better or worse by using (i) seasonal factors, (ii) a trend adjustment, and (iii) choice of sample period.

2. Plot the data for seasonally unadjusted new home sales. A significant seasonal pattern is apparent.

(a) Calculate the seasonal factors (i) using a regression equation, (ii) using X-11 for the sample period 1963–81, and (iii) using X-11 for the sample period 1982–2000. Which set of seasonal factors would you use in a forecasting model?

(b) Calculating a linear regression with a trend variable shows a highly significant t-ratio of 9.8. Yet both the ADF and PP tests indicate no unit root. In forecasting, would you include a trend term or not?

(c) Estimate an ARMA(1,1) model up to 1999.12 with SAR(12) but not SMA(12), then with both SAR(12) and SMA(12). Calculate the RMS error for 2000. Which equation gives better results?

(d) Now estimate the same equations using d(new home sales) as the dependent variable, and calculate the RMS error for 2000. Would you use the trended or detrended series for forecasting with an ARMA model?

(e) Based on your decision in (d), experiment with additional lags in the ARMA model and determine whether they improve forecast accuracy for 2000.

3. Figure 7.17 shows monthly prices for citrus fruit, not seasonally adjusted. The sharp peaks represent freezes.

(a) How should these outliers be handled? Do you think the trend should be removed before using the data to build an ARMA model? Does your answer change if the sample period starts in 1980?

(b) Estimate an optimal ARMA model, including SAR(12) and SMA(12) terms if applicable.

(c) Seasonally adjust the data from 1980 through 1999. Construct seasonally adjusted data for 2000 by using the forecast seasonal factors contained in X-11 applied to the actual data. Now estimate an optimal ARMA model.

Continued

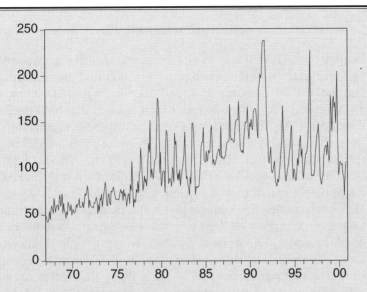

Figure 7.17 Problem 3.

(d) Take that ARMA model and add SAR(12) and SMA(12) terms. Are they significant? Why do you think that result occurred on seasonally adjusted data? (Hint: is it just a data fluke or is there something inherent in citrus prices that high prices caused by a freeze one year would be followed by lower prices the next year?).

(e) Test ARMA models built with seasonally adjusted and unadjusted data on the actual data for 2000. Based on these results, which series would you prefer to use to predict citrus prices in the future using an ARMA model?

4. By definition, the number of unemployed workers is equal to the labor force minus total employment as measured by the household survey. However, the monthly figures for both these series are quite erratic, so most economists look at the *payroll* figures for employment and the *household* figures for unemployment. Indeed, Fed Chairman Alan Greenspan has said he ignores short-run changes in the household employment data. Yet an attempt to predict short-term changes in the unemployment rate using payroll data for employment does not give very robust results. Indeed, short-term changes in the unemployment rate appear to be due to random factors and statistical data flukes, which means forecasting accuracy might be improved by an ARMA model. Here we use quarterly data, since that is the time span that provides more information about the strength of the economy, and also the likelihood of changes in monetary

Continued

policy. All data in this example are seasonally adjusted.

(a) Estimate an ARMA(1,1) model using changes in the unemployment rate and examine the correlogram. You will find significant negative correlations for quarters 4, 8, and 12. Given that these are seasonally adjusted data, what factors might explain this behavior?

(b) Expand the ARMA modeling process until these significant correlations disappear. Show your results. Now use this model to predict the four quarters of 2000, compared with the ARMA(1,1) model. Now try other ARMA models with fewer lags, even if the PACF correlations return. Which equation has the smallest RMS error for 2000? What does this suggest about the principle of parsimony?

(c) Calculate a regression between the percentage changes in payroll employment and household employment (theoretically these are the same variable). The adjusted R^2 is only 0.59 and the correlogram shows several significant PACFs. It is likely that differences in data collection could account for these divergences, so an ARMA model might help predict the difference. Reestimate the equation with AR(1) and MA(1). Which terms are significant? Check the correlogram to see if the significance of the PACFs has diminished.

(d) Now expand the ARMA process to (2,2). What happens to the t-ratios of the AR and MA terms? Compare this change with the change in the adjusted R^2 and the PACFs in the correlogram. Do you think these additional terms would improve forecast accuracy?

5. Daily closing prices for Microsoft stock (MSFT) for one year are shown in figure 7.18. During this period, the stock price has a strong downward trend, and both ADF and PP tests indicate a unit root.

(a) Explain why (or why not) you would take this trend into consideration in forecasting future changes in MSFT prices.

(b) Calculate the first difference of this series, and then plot a histogram. You will find the distribution is not normal because there are too many outliers. This result, which is the rule rather than exception in financial market variables, is often known as "fat tails." Given the lack of normality, what conclusions can be drawn about any forecasting model using these data?

(c) Calculate an ARMA(1,1) model on the first differences. You will find that adjusted R^2 is less than zero. Is that result surprising? The correlogram shows a significant PACF at a five-day lag. How would you interpret that result?

(d) Expand the model to ARMA(5,5). The F-statistic now shows that the overall relationship is significant at the 1% level, even though the

Continued

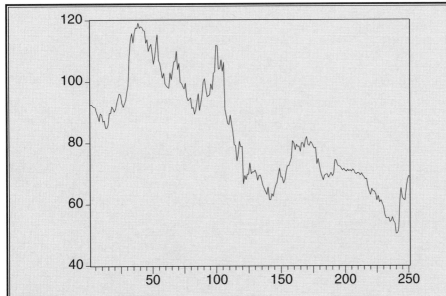

Figure 7.18 Problem 5.

adjusted R^2 is a modest 0.075. Note that the AR(5) and MA(5) terms are highly significant but the value of the parameters is almost identical with different signs. What is the economic interpretation of that?

(e) How does the equation change as more terms are added? Do you think additional terms would help improve forecasting accuracy?

(f) It seems logical to argue that one cannot really make any money by trading MSFT stock based on any simple ARMA model, or else someone would have already discovered the road to success. However, certain lag structures appear to be significant. How can you explain that apparent discrepancy?

PART IV

CHAPTER 8

COMBINING FORECASTS

INTRODUCTION

The previous seven chapters presented a variety of different methods of forecasting for both structural econometric forecasts and non-structural time-series processes. In both cases, failures as well as successes were presented to emphasize that there are no perfect forecasts.

Over three decades ago, econometricians found that forecast errors could often be reduced by *combining* different methods of forecasting; since then, many studies have been undertaken to verify this point. Yet this view is not universally accepted. If one forecast appears to be better than the others, why not just use that forecast? Or to look at it from another perspective, should forecasts based on carefully developed and estimated models be modified by random views of some itinerant off the streets?

Combining forecasts does not always reduce forecast error. In particular, as pointed out by Clements and Hendry, "when forecasts are based on econometric models, each of which has access to the same information set, then combining the resulting forecasts will rarely be a good idea . . . when models do not draw on a common information pool, and are essentially of a different nature or type, or when models are differentially susceptible to structural breaks, then the case for combination is more persuasive."[1]

As is the case with most areas of forecasting, the advantages from combining forecasts remain a contentious issue. Clements and Hendry also point out that "The combination of forecasts may be superior . . . to each of the constituents. However, forecast combination runs counter to the concept . . . of a progressive research strategy. The latter would suggest that a better approach is

---

[1]   Clements, Michael P., and David F. Hendry, *Forecasting Economic Time Series* (Cambridge University Press, Cambridge), 1998, p. 227.

to refine a model when it is found to be wanting in some dimensions. The goal is a model which . . . forecast[s] the process better than its rivals."

It was shown many years ago that if the predictions from two or more different sources are unbiased, if the error variance remains constant, and if the underlying function has not shifted, then combining forecasts with weights inversely proportional to the errors will reduce forecast error.[2] An extensive literature has developed to show the advantages of combining forecasts; many of these studies have been reviewed by Clemen.[3]

Nonetheless, these conditions – under which combining forecasts will reduce forecast error – are seldom met in practice. If in fact the underlying function and the error variances did not shift over time, standard regression analysis alone could be used to generate optimal forecasts. However, most of the problems of practical business forecasting arise precisely when these conditions are not met.

In this chapter the following methods of combining forecasts are considered:

- non-structural methods: ARIMA, Box–Jenkins, and Holt–Winters
- combining structural and non-structural methods
- the role of judgment, as measured by indexes of sentiment and consensus forecasts
- adjusting constant and slope terms in structural equations
- combining all of the above methods.

The results for these categories can be summarized as follows. *First*, combining non-structural methods occasionally reduces forecast error, but not as often as might be expected from the standard statistical measures. *Second*, the evidence is mixed on combining structural equations and the ARIMA process, with the answer depending on the underlying nature of the particular time series and the amount of serial correlation. *Third*, the role of judgment can often improve forecast accuracy even if the forecasts from the consensus or sentiment index alone are no better than from a naive model. *Fourth*, intelligent adjustment of the constant and slope terms in a structural equation will invariably improve forecast accuracy. *Fifth*, optimal forecasts generally use several of these methods for adjusting the original structural equations.

Before turning to these specific cases, however, it is useful to discuss briefly some of the theories used to support the combination of forecasting methods.

---

[2] See, for example, the discussion in Granger, C. W. J., and P. Newbold, *Forecasting Economic Time Series* (Academic Press, San Diego, CA), 1986, section 9.2, pp. 266–76.

[3] Clemen, R. T., "Combining Forecasts: A Review and Annotated Bibliography," *International Journal of Forecasting*, 5 (1989), 559–81.

8.1 OUTLINE OF THE THEORY OF FORECAST COMBINATION

To start, consider two forecasts, and consider a regression equation where the actual values are estimated as a function of forecast values generated from model (a) and forecast values generated from model (b). If the estimate of the regression coefficient for the first forecast is 1, and the estimate of the second forecast is 0, then all the relevant information is contained in the first forecast, and nothing is gained by combining forecasts. In such a case, model (a) is said to forecast-encompass model (b), and forecast accuracy will not be improved by combining forecasts. This is a simple test to undertake, provided of course that one has a reasonably long period of true ex ante forecasts; it cannot be used to test a new model with no forecasting record.

The original work in this area dates back to the seminal article by Bates and Granger,[4] and is known as the variance–covariance forecast combination method. However, this was later shown by Diebold[5] to be a special case of the regression-based forecast combination method, so our comments are restricted to the latter treatment.

Diebold starts with the regression equation.[6]

$$y_{t+k} = \beta_0 + \beta_1 \, y^a_{t+k} + \beta_2 \, y^b_{t+k} + \varepsilon_t, \tag{8.1}$$

where y^a and y^b are forecasts from models (a) and (b). As already noted, that is a very simple calculation if an adequate history of forecasts are available *and* the conditions noted at the beginning of this section – unbiased, constant variables, and unchanged data generation function – are observed. Most of the time they are not. Hence Diebold proposes four types of adjustments to take shifting conditions into account. These can be classified as (i) time-varying combination weights, (ii) adjustments for serial correlation, (iii) shrinking of combining weights toward equality, and (iv) nonlinear regressions.

The first case might apply under circumstances in which one forecasting method becomes increasingly important over time; for example, stock market forecasts might depend more on changes in monetary policy now that they are more transparent. Statistically, this method involves adding a time trend (T) to each of the coefficients in equation (8.1) above, or

$$y_{t+k} = (\beta_0 + \gamma_0 T) + (\beta_1 + \gamma_1 T) y^a_{t+k} + (\beta_2 + \gamma_2 T) y^b_{t+k} + \varepsilon_t. \tag{8.2}$$

---

[4] Bates, J. M., and C. W. J. Granger, "The Combination of Forecasts," *Operations Research Quarterly*, 20 (1969), 451–68.

[5] Diebold, F. X., "Forecasting Combination and Encompassing: Reconciling Two Divergent Literatures," *International Journal of Forecasting*, 5 (1989), 589–92.

[6] For further discussion, see Diebold, *Elements of Forecasting* (South-Western College Publishing, Cincinnati, 1998). pp. 349–52.

The second case is often important because residuals from structural equations based on economic time series often exhibit autocorrelation. Hence this method essentially amounts to combining structural or judgmental forecasts with some adjustment of the constant term to take into account the recent residuals from the structural equation. As will be shown later in this chapter, this method often reduces forecast error. Statistically, one estimates the same equation as in (8.1), but the residuals follow an AR(1) scheme. It is also possible to extend this method to include an ARMA(p,q) process, but that is less likely to improve forecast accuracy.

The third case has some similarities to the first case in that the β coefficients shift over time. In this case, however, the user assumes that the farther the time horizon extends, the more likely it is that weights will both approach $\frac{1}{2}$. Thus while one may be able to assign a much larger weight to model (a) in the near term, as the length of the forecast horizon increases, the accuracy of that method fades relative to model (b). In practice, this method is not used often.

The fourth case can apply in cases where one method appears to generate the best forecasts during periods of normal growth, but a different method is more useful during periods of unusually large changes. In this case, the optimal forecast might consist of, say, a regression on the actual value of the forecast from model (a) and the square of the forecast from model (b). Thus, for example, when the likelihood of business cycle recessions, or energy shocks, or stock market crashes is higher, this alternative method would provide a better warning signal without predicting "doom and gloom" almost every year.

In general, combining forecasts depends in large part on the forecaster's estimate of the relative accuracy of these two methods. While the common-sense conclusion might be to use the model that has previously generated the smaller error, the above discussion indicates where that might not be appropriate. First, the weights may shift over time. Second, forecast error can often be reduced by taking serial correlation of the residuals into account. Third, as the time horizon lengthens, the relative advantage of one method may diminish. Fourth, one method may be better for forecasting trends; another for forecasting turning points. Before turning to some practical examples of combining forecasts, though, it is worthwhile discussing the major sources of error, if only to emphasize that when a heretofore unknown situation arises, combining forecasting methods may not improve accuracy at all.

8.2 MAJOR SOURCES OF FORECAST ERROR

If the residuals are normally distributed, the best forecast is the one that minimizes the root mean square error (RMSE), which is the square root of the variance in the forecast period. If all the assumptions of the classical linear model were satisfied, this would be a very short section. However, that is seldom the case.

Sometimes the residuals are not even normally distributed over the sample period. However, the adjustments previously discussed for autocorrelation and heteroscedasticity in structural equations, plus the use of ARIMA methods for time-series analysis, can be used to minimize that problem. Yet forecast errors are invariably larger than would be indicated by sample period statistics. The main sources of error – in addition to the random variation associated with the sampling technique – can be summarized as follows.

1   The equation is misspecified: some of the variables are missing, or they are entered improperly (e.g., the underlying relationship is really nonlinear).
2   In the forecast period, incorrect values are assumed for exogenous variables, or predictions of endogenous variables are incorrect.
3   Data series are revised, so the equations are estimated on what later turn out to have been inaccurate data. Also, what appears to have been an excellent forecast at the time has a much larger error based on revised data.
4   In multi-period forecasts, error buildup accumulates when the lagged dependent variable appears on the right-hand side of the equation, as is always the case for AR processes. That result argues against using equations with AR terms for multi-period forecasting. In many cases, it is better to take autocorrelation into account by adjusting the constant term.
5   The structure of the equation has shifted, either within the sample period or after it has ended. As a result, none of the standard statistical tests apply, and the forecast is invariably improved by judgmental factors.

Most of the time, some combination of structural equations, time-series processes, and informed judgment will significantly reduce forecast error. In particular, reason (5) often accounts for the bulk of forecasting error, so combining forecasts will be examined with that possibility in mind. We emphasize in advance that different combinations will produce the best forecasts, depending on the characteristics of the underlying data series.

It is general practice when examining the issue of optimal forecasts to use RMSE as a measure of forecast accuracy; a related measure, known as the absolute average forecast error (AAFE), is sometimes used, but RMSE is usually preferred on the grounds that if the residuals are normally distributed, RMSE is an optimal measure of forecast accuracy. Even if the assumption about normality does not hold, it is seldom if ever the case that an alternative distribution is known with sufficient accuracy to substitute an alternative measure.

In the case of macroeconomic forecasts – which have been the most thoroughly documented and are important because they serve as the starting point for so many industry and company forecasts – data revisions that occur long after the fact sometimes cloud the issue of how accurate a forecast was at the time it was made. One example out of many can be used to illustrate this point. In the January 10, 1980, issue of the Blue Chip Economic Indicators, Robert J. Eggert calculated that the consensus error for predicting the real growth rate over the previous three years had been only 0.2%, 0.1%, and 0.1%. The data were subsequently revised several times; the National Income and Product Accounts (NIPA) revisions issued in late 1999 showed these errors to be substantially larger: 0.6%, 1.4%, and 1.3%. In determining forecasting accuracy, there is a huge difference between an average error of 0.1% and 1.1%, since a naive model error for real GDP generates an error of about 1%. Thus data revisions made long after the forecasts have been released can often reduce predictive accuracy through no fault of the individual forecasters.

This situation can be even more severe for individual company earnings. Who is right – the analyst who predicted a big gain in earnings, which is what the company initially reported the next quarter, or the analyst who predicted a big decline in earnings, which turns out to be the case when the SEC uncovers accounting irregularities?

Having made this point, we will concede that data revisions are not the principal source of inaccurate macroeconomic model predictions; in most cases, revisions account for only a small proportion of forecast error. Nonetheless, in the cases where it does make some difference, one needs to determine which is more important: the data that will be released soon, or the final revised data? This question can never be answered with the usual statistical techniques, since it is a judgment call; however, most practical business forecasters would prefer to predict the next year accurately based on data that will be released during the following year, rather than data that will be revised 5, 10, or even 20 years later.

Macroeconomic forecasters in the US were generally unable to predict the shifting patterns of the 1970s and 1980s: four recessions in 12 years after no recessions in almost a decade, two bouts of double-digit inflation, and unprecedented increases in interest rates, including a rise in the prime rate to $21\frac{1}{2}$%. Afterwards, many reasons were advanced for this failure. Those who viewed econometric models more kindly proclaimed that "nobody" could have predicted the two energy shocks. Many members of the "Chicago School" attacked the models on the grounds they were Keynesian instead of monetary, while Bob Lucas added that the older models failed to incorporate rational expectations. Other researchers, notably Christopher Sims, thought that structural models were inferior, and suggested replacing them by the use of autoregressive models known as VARs.[7]

All these alternative methods of macroeconomic forecasting were thoroughly discussed during the 1980s, with the belief that the combination of these various methods might lead to more accurate macroeconomic forecasts in the future. However, the 1990–91 recession was not predicted by any of these methods; a detailed discussion of these failures can be found in a NBER study,

[7]   See in particular, Sims, Christopher A., "A Nine-Variable Probabilistic Macroeconomic Forecasting Model," in *Business Cycles, Indicators, and Forecasting*, James H. Stock and Mark W. Watson, eds (University of Chicago Press for NBER), 1993.

Business Cycles, Indicators, and Forecasting, published in 1993. Forecasts generated by Keynesian econometric model builders were wrong. Forecasts generated by monetarist econometric model builders, and by rational-expectations theorists, were wrong. Forecasts from models built with VARs were wrong. Forecasts based on the index of leading indicators, and the various indexes of consumer and business sentiment, were wrong. Of the 52 contributors to the Blue Chip Economic Indicators survey, the July 1990 report showed not a single one predicted a recession – yet that was the month, according to the National Bureau, that actual recession began. Thus no one predicted the downturn in spite of the advances in forecasting methodology during the previous decade.

What is the point of presenting this litany of mistakes – or to ask the question somewhat differently, what lessons can be learned from this forecasting failure?

Before providing some tentative answers, we might usefully try to determine, with the benefit of hindsight, what *did* cause the downturn. One factor was undoubtedly the decision by Saddam Hussein to invade Kuwait, which was soon followed by a doubling of oil prices. However, after the UN forces recaptured Kuwait and defeated Hussein, oil prices returned to previous levels, yet the US economy remained unusually sluggish for the next $2\frac{1}{2}$ years. Obviously some other factors were at work.

In retrospect, primary cause of the recession turned out to be the restriction of credit following the aftermath of the collapse of the savings and loans industry. Following the liberalization of banking laws as part of deregulation in 1982, many lending institutions made loans that, at least in retrospect, had a very small probability of being repaid. Whether this was mistaken judgment or outright fraud is not germane here; when the laws were changed in 1989, many financial lending officers were terrified of being thrown in jail for making unsound loans, and drastically tightened credit conditions. As a result, during 1990, 1991, and 1992, constant-dollar consumer credit outstanding fell by an average of 3.9% per year, while constant-dollar business loans fell by an even greater 6.2% per year; over the previous three decades, both of these measures of credit availability had risen an average of about 4% per year in real terms, roughly in step with overall real growth.

This cutback in credit availability was unprecedented in the post-Korean War period, and in spite of the headlines given to the change in legislation, forecasters were unable to gauge the actual drop accurately or determine its impact on consumer spending, capital spending, and housing. In this case, then, combining various forecasting methods would not have reduced forecast error.

This example serves as a good illustration of our underlying point that the major source of forecast error is a shift in the structure of the underlying data generation function. When the underlying structural relationships shift, any forecasting method based on what has happened in the past – which means virtually all methods – will generate errors that are much larger than would be expected from previous experience.

We can reasonably assume that no one foresaw the full impact of the credit squeeze, the Iraq–Kuwait war, or the brief doubling of oil prices. However, suppose you were asked to predict the economic outlook in early 1991, when all of these factors were known. What would be the best way to proceed?

Historical business cycle experience would have indicated that, in the past, real growth always rebounded to above average rates during the first full year of recovery. This time, however, real growth remained below average for the next two years. How could that development have been foreseen?

For one thing, as this author can attest, historically estimated functions overstated the gains in consumption and investment. For that reason, the use of *constant adjustments* based on recent experience would have been warranted. Adjustment of the *slope terms* in the equations for consumer credit and business loans would also have been appropriate. The use of *judgment* about how long the credit restrictions would remain in effect would also have improved forecast accuracy. These can be considered three of the most important methods for reducing forecast error using structural models. After a brief review of the comparison of several non-structural methods, the remainder of this chapter focuses on these elements in the context of structural equations.

8.3 COMBINING METHODS OF NON-STRUCTURAL ESTIMATION

Several studies have combined different non-structural methods of forecasting and found that the resulting forecasting errors have been reduced. One of the best-known studies is by Makradakis and eight other authors. They studied forecasts of 1,001 series predicted for a time horizon of 18 periods.[8] The methods for comparison they used include naive models, various types of exponential smoothing including Holt–Winters, and regression models. Without reporting on all these details, this study finds that the average forecasting error by combining some of these methods is about 8% smaller than the single best method, which is Holt–Winters. Newbold and Granger report a 6% improvement for a similar test.[9]

In this author's experience, some of which is summarized below, these figures are probably near the maximum that can be expected from combining methods of non-structural estimation. Indeed, after discussing their results, Granger and Newbold comment that "the examples of combination given so far are not really designed to show the procedure in its best possible light. After all, it would be

---

[8] Makridakis, S., et al., "The Accuracy of Extrapolation (Time Series) Methods: Results of a Forecasting Competition," *Journal of Forecasting*, 1 (1982), 111–53. These results are also discussed in Makridakis, S., S. C. Wheelwright, and R. J. Hyndman, *Forecasting Methods and Applications*, 3rd edn (John Wiley, New York), 1998, pp. 525–37.
[9] Granger and Newbold, p. 272.

reasonable to expect combination to be most profitable when the individual forecasts are very dissimilar in nature."[10] That is precisely the point mentioned earlier. As will be shown when dealing with actual economic time-series data, the combination of several non-structural methods seldom improves forecast accuracy, particularly for multi-period forecasts.

To illustrate this point, we consider six economic time series used previously in this text. All these are monthly data. Three of these are not seasonally adjusted: apparel sales, single-family housing starts, and the PPI for industrial commodities. The other three series are either seasonally adjusted or have no seasonal factors: the real Federal funds rate, the S&P 500 index of stock prices, and the monthly rate of inflation as measured by the CPI. In all cases we compare (i) the optimal ARIMA model, (ii) Holt–Winters (HW) exponential smoothing, using seasonal factors where appropriate, and (iii) a naive model that says the percentage change this period is the same as the previous period; for seasonally unadjusted data, the percentage change over the past 12 months is used. The naive model may not seem to be a very serious competitor, but is often included in combinatorial forecasts. In the vast majority of cases the HW method is superior to other exponential smoothing methods – as also shown by Makradakis et al. – so there is little to be added to our analysis by including additional smoothing methods.

In all cases, the equations were estimated either from 1947.01 or the first month when consistent data became available, through 1997.12, with 1998.01 through 1999.12 reserved for the forecast period. In all cases, trends were removed by using first-differencing or percentage changes even if the ADF and PP tests did not indicate a unit root (when levels were used, the forecast errors were larger in all cases).

Initially, the results appear promising. For seasonally unadjusted apparel sales, the RMS error of the average of these three methods during the forecast period is significantly smaller than any of the individual methods. The reason, as shown in figure 8.1, is that the ARIMA model consistently overestimates actual sales, while the naive model consistently underestimates them. The combination forecast, on the other hand, averages these errors, so the average forecast error is much smaller.

However, *that is not true for the other five variables that are predicted.* In the case of housing starts, the HW method generates the smallest forecast errors; for the industrial PPI, it is the ARIMA model. For the series without seasonal factors, the best forecast for the real Federal funds rate is actually generated by the naive (no change) model. The best forecast for the stock market is HW, and the best forecast for the CPI is ARIMA – a complete split. The summary RMSE statistics are shown in table 8.1.

These six series were not chosen in order to generate these diverse results; before performing the calculations, it was not clear which method would be

---

[10] Granger and Newbold, p. 272.

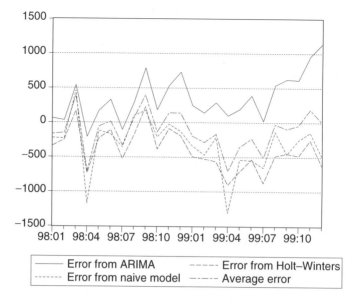

Figure 8.1 Errors for three alternative methods of predicting apparel sales. Combining non-structural methods reduces forecasting error for seasonally unadjusted data.

Table 8.1 RMSE for different methods of predicting economic time series, 1998.01–1999.12.

	Apparel sales	Housing starts	PPI industrial	Real Fed funds rate	Stock prices	Monthly inflation
ARIMA	487	12.3	1.7[a]	0.55	168	0.15[a]
Holt–Winters	495	9.8[a]	8.8	0.65	92[a]	0.16
Naive Model	484	15.4	6.5	0.35[a]	114	0.28
Combined	326[a]	11.6	2.4	0.45	123	0.17

[a] Indicates smallest error for the 1998.01–1999.12 time period.

superior. However, tests with many other economic time-series models provides a similar result. Combination of non-structural forecasting methods seldom reduces forecast error significantly.

It is straightforward to duplicate these calculations and show that, in most cases, the mean value of the forecast error is significantly different from zero. That in turn leads to the conclusion that the underlying structure must have shifted. In all cases except apparel sales, that is probably true. During the 1998–9 period, inflation was much lower than would have been expected from previous experience, given that the US economy was at full employment. The real Federal funds rate was virtually unchanged, whereas it had previously fluctuated significantly. Both the stock market and housing starts rose more than would have been indicated from historical evidence.

Other studies were apparently constructed in an atmosphere where the underlying structure did not change. Practical business forecasters know that, in the real world, that is seldom the case.

Also, except for apparel sales, the errors are closely correlated. All methods tend to miss the high and low values. As the correlation coefficient of the forecast series approaches unity, the advantage of combining forecasts diminishes.

We conclude at this point that combining forecasting methods will usually reduce forecasting error significantly only if (i) the correlation between the errors is small, and (ii) the underlying structure – the data generating function – remains unchanged. In practice these conditions are seldom the case. Hence combining ARIMA, exponential smoothing, and naive models in practice will not generally improve forecasting accuracy very much.

This does not necessarily mean that combining forecasts does not improve forecasting accuracy. It does mean that the combination of various non-structural, mechanical methods does not yield optimal results. Instead, better results are more likely to be obtained by combining structural, non-structural, and judgmental methods that use different processes, have uncorrelated errors, and take structural shifts into account. The rest of this chapter explores some of these combinations.

8.4 COMBINING STRUCTURAL AND NON-STRUCTURAL METHODS

It is certainly possible to combine structural and non-structural methods of forecasting. However, many structural equations are estimated in levels rather than actual or percentage differences even if the key series contain strong time trends. That is not just because levels equations invariably provide higher goodness-of-fit statistics. The model builder may be interested in obtaining long-term forecasts under equilibrium conditions, or predicting the trend itself. Also, the value of long-term elasticities may be important. An auto manufacturer might want to estimate the short-term and long-term impact of a change in energy prices on sales of various types of new cars, or a steel producer might want to estimate both the short-term and long-term price elasticity of substitution for aluminum. Computer manufacturers might well be interested in estimating how much their long-term sales growth rate would increase for different percentage reductions in prices.

For these and similar reasons, many structural equations are estimated in levels form. However, most economic time series contain significant time trends, whereas ARMA processes are derived under the specific assumption that the variables do not contain a significant trend, so the processes are stationary.

This presents a dilemma, and not only one that appears in ARMA models. Suppose the independent variables are mixed: some have strong time trends, such as sales and income, and some do not have any time trend, such as interest rates, relative prices, or percentage changes. Over an extended period, the value of the sales or income variables might rise 10-fold, while the value of interest rates and relative prices would stay about the same.

Consider a typical equation, $Y = c + 1.5X - 50r$, where Y and X are trend variables and r is trendless (such as the real rate of interest). Suppose at the beginning of the sample period, $Y = 200$, $X = 200$, and $r = 5$. A 1% change in X would change Y by 1.5%. A 1% change in r (i.e., from 5.00 to 5.05) would change Y by 1.25%. At the end of the sample period, assume Y is 2,000, X is 2,000, and r is still 5. A 1% change in X will still change Y by 1.5%, but a 1% change in r will change Y by only 0.125%. The larger X and Y get, the less important r is. This problem could be eliminated by taking the percentage change of Y and X and leaving r in levels, but then the fluctuations might outweigh the trend to the point where the parameter estimates would be distorted. An intermediate choice, which has often been used in estimating macro models, is to take four-quarter percentage moving averages. Yet even that would not provide long-term estimates; where those are desired, equations in levels form may be preferred. However, if levels are combined with ARMA processes the equation will contain both stationary and non-stationary variables, and the usual statistical tests will be invalid. Also, the forecasts are likely to contain relatively large errors.

Several different methods can be employed to minimize this problem, some of which involve combinations of forecasts. On a structural basis, the equation can be changed to ratio form, so that the ratio of Y/X is estimated as a function of r. In that case, both variables are likely to be trendless. Another possibility is to generate two sets of forecasts: one that predicts the trends in both X and Y, and the other that correlates changes in Y with changes in r. These forecasts can then be combined using the weights estimated by methods described in section 8.1. A third possibility is to relate cyclical changes in the real rate of interest to some type of sentiment variable; when the Fed tightens, consumer and business sentiment may weaken. Examples of this are found when the stock market reacts vigorously to unexpected changes in the Federal funds rate; these changes might also affect purchases of consumer and capital goods. The main choice, then, is between a structural equation that reduces or eliminates the common trend in Y and X, or, alternatively, uses some sort of combined forecast to give greater weight to cyclical variables.

For example, suppose purchases of constant-dollar consumer durables (hereafter, durables) are a function of current and lagged disposable income, lagged housing starts, the yield spread, and several attitude variables that include stock prices, unemployment, inflation, relative oil prices, and the index of consumer sentiment. The yield spread has no trend at all, and most of the attitudinal variables generally have no significant trends. On the other hand, durables, income, and stock prices all do have significant trends. The issue of how to

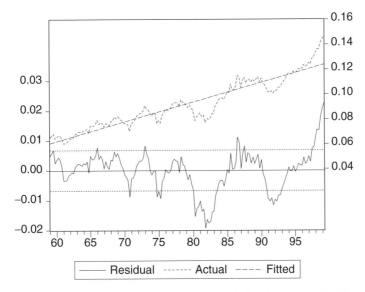

Figure 8.2 Ratio of durables to income (in constant dollars) compared with a linear time trend.

combine the importance of these variables to generate optimal forecasts is explored in the next case study.

Case Study 16: Purchases of Consumer Durables

This case study presents an equation used to predict durables on a quarterly basis, with emphasis on the issues of detrending and simultaneous causality as well as improving forecasting accuracy by combining methods, in this case with an index of consumer sentiment.

The ratio of durables to disposable personal income in constant dollars is shown in figure 8.2. Two facts are obvious from this graph. First, over the past 40 years or so, durables have risen much faster than income; while both two series have strong trends, it is not the same trend. Second, this ratio rose quite rapidly from 1996 through 2000. We want to determine whether that surge can be explained by some combination of forecasting methods.

The key variables in an equation for durables are disposable income, the cost and availability of consumer credit, housing starts (since homeowners purchase furniture and appliances when they move into a new home), and various attitudinal variables such as stock prices, the unemployment rate, the inflation rate, relative oil prices, and an index of consumer sentiment. All these terms were tried in an equation that is estimated in both levels and four-quarter percentage changes. For purposes of assessing forecast accuracy, the sample period for this equation is truncated in 1995.4. Also, the sample period does not starts

Table 8.2 Percentage change and levels equations.

Constant term	Income distribution lag	Housing starts	Yield spread	Unemployment rate	Inflation rate	Relative oil prices	Consumer sentiment	R^2 [DW]
Percentage change								
−0.92	2.60	0.081	0.90	−1.24	−1.05	−	−	0.716
	(3.8)	(4.0)	(3.4)	(2.4)	(5.0)			1.47
−2.26	1.70	0.071	0.077	−	−0.74		0.111	0.791
	(4.4)	(4.1)	(3.6)		(4.2)		(6.3)	1.79
Levels								
−116.7	0.125	16.6	−	−11.7	−1.96	−59.8		0.988
	(85.2)	(3.0)		(7.6)	(2.0)	(10.6)		0.59
−231.5	0.130	24.5	3.78	−	−	−30.0	0.685	0.993
	(97.5)	(6.8)	(5.3)			(5.8)	(11.8)	0.98

until 1967.1 because we want to test the importance of the index consumer sentiment, and consistent quarterly data are not available until that date.

The primary focus of this chapter is improving forecasting accuracy by combining methods of forecasts. However, one should not lose sight of the point that forecasting accuracy will be impaired if the underlying equation is not structurally sound. In particular, that means not mixing trends and trendless series unless the importance of the latter will be adequately represented in the forecast period, and not using independent variables that could suffer from simultaneity bias. If such variables are included, the forecast errors will generally be much larger than indicated by the sample period statistics.

The equations for durables were estimated from 1967.1 through 1995.4, except that the percentage change equations started in 1968.1 (see table 8.2). All of the variables mentioned above were tried, insignificant coefficients are not reported. Equations were estimated with and without the index of consumer confidence, which worked best with no lag on a quarterly basis. Note that the variables included in the equations differ substantially depending on which option is chosen.

Over the sample period, the inclusion of the index of consumer sentiment improves the percentage of explained variance and reduces serial correlation of the residuals. It is not surprising that the unemployment rate drops out of the equation with consumer sentiment, since the two are highly correlated. However, there are also some anomalies. It is not clear why relative oil prices are so significant in the levels but not the percentage change equation; one suspects spurious correlation. Also, it is somewhat surprising that the yield spread term disappears when consumer sentiment is added. Finally, the equation is notable by the absence of the stock market term; this point is addressed shortly.

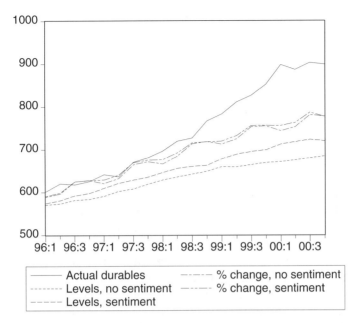

Figure 8.3 Forecast of purchases of real consumer durables, using alternative equations, 1996.1 through 2000.4.

The next step is to compare the forecasts for 1996.1 through 2000.4 generated by these four equations; the results are shown in figure 8.3. The errors are much larger than would be expected from the sample period statistics – even though the actual values of all the independent variables are used, which means the results are better than would have been obtained on a true ex ante basis. The errors are somewhat smaller for the percentage change equations, since the levels equations probably suffer from spurious trend correlation. However, the sentiment variable does not help very much for the levels equation, and does not help at all for the percentage change equation. The RMSE for the best equation is 68.3, compared to the SEE of 13.4. It would appear that the underlying structural relationship shifted after 1997.

The consensus forecasts are no help in this regard. Blue Chip Consensus forecasts are not available for consumer durables per se, but figures do exist for total consumption and sales of light motor vehicles (new cars and light trucks). The corresponding data for 1998–2000, when the function severely underestimated the growth in durables, are shown in table 8.3.

Consumer sentiment also failed to improve these forecasts because, over this five-year period, that index hardly rose at all even though durables boomed. As shown in chapter 12, the index of consumer sentiment did not improve forecast accuracy during the 1990s; the highly significant terms in the above regressions reflect its greater importance in previous decades.

Table 8.3 Blue Chip Consensus data predictions.

	1998		1999		2000	
	Predicted	Actual	Predicted	Actual	Predicted	Actual
Change in new car sales	−0.1	0.4	0.1	1.8	−0.4	0.7
Percentage change in total consumption	2.8	4.9	3.2	4.9	3.8	5.3

Even using constant adjustments would not improve the forecasting record, since the residuals for 1996 and 1997 were close to zero before the actual gains far outpaced those predicted by the equation or consensus forecasts.

There is almost always an answer on an ex post basis; if the regressions are rerun up to 2000.4, the stock market term emerges as one of the most important variables; also, the forecasting errors are randomly distributed. However, the reader can verify that if the stock market term is added to the regressions given above, or any similar equations for the sample period ending n 1995, that term is insignificant and in many cases has the wrong sign. In fact, rerunning the levels equation without the index of consumer sentiment for an additional five years changes the t-ratio on the stock price term from −1.1 to +22.0 – clear evidence of a structural shift.

Yet even combining forecasts by giving a higher weight to a stock market does not really solve the issue. Early in 2001, stock prices plunged dramatically – yet purchases of light motor vehicles rebounded sharply from a seasonally adjusted annual rate of 15.8 million in 2000.4 to 17.2 million in 2001.1. Furthermore, it is not a question of depending on lagged stock market values, as motor vehicle sales continued to improve later in the year and when they dipped following the terrorist attacks of 11 September, they rebounded sharply in October because of zero interest rate financing.

There is an important lesson to be learned here, which we will illustrate shortly. However, let us quickly review the evidence to this point. An estimated structural equation, which appeared to track consumer durable sales closely to the end of 1995, also gave reasonable results for 1996 and 1997, although they were also somewhat below actual levels. However, the forecasts for 1998–2000 were far too low even when several different forecasting methods were combined: use of constant adjustments to reflect serial correlation of the residuals, introduction of a sentiment term, and giving greater weight to trendless cyclical variables such as the unemployment rate, the inflation rate, and the yield spread. What went wrong?

Figure 8.4 shows the ratios of (i) purchases of motor vehicles and parts to disposable income, and (ii) other consumer durables to disposable income; all figures are in billions of 1996 (chained) dollars. There is virtually no trend to the motor vehicle ratio, and indeed the levels in the late 1990s are well below

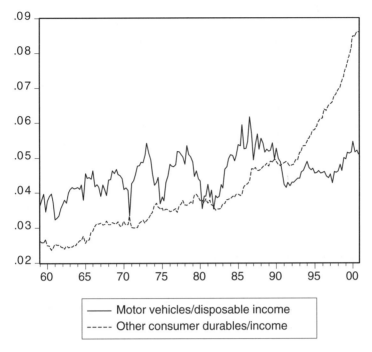

Figure 8.4 The ratio of other consumer durables to disposal income (both in constant dollars) is dominated by the rise in purchases of personal computers.

peak levels reached in the 1970s and 1980s. By comparison, the ratio of other durables – dominated by personal computers – has risen sharply since 1990, especially in the latter half of the decade. Purchases of personal computers have very little correlation with housing starts, the inflation rate, relative oil prices, or the yield spread; yet it was that category of durables that dominated sales in the latter half of the 1990s.

Thus we find that, although the structural equation looked sound based on standard techniques, it was built on a shifting foundation. The forecasts would have been much more accurate if motor vehicles, personal computers, and household durables had been estimated separately. In that case we would have found that purchases of motor vehicles remained tied to traditional cyclical variables, and rose in early 2001 because interest rates had declined in previous quarters.[11] On the other hand, sales of personal computers soared because of the roaring stock market; when it collapsed in 2001.1, sales of personal computers also fell 3.5% that quarter.

---

[11] This is not a new finding. In 1982, when the auto industry was in the middle of a severe slump, Lee Iacocca said the three problems with car sales were "interest rates, interest rates, and interest rates." As soon as they fell, car sales recovered.

The issue once again turns out to be structural instability. Bad equations do not generate good forecasts no matter how many other forecasts they are combined with. The main problem with the equation presented in case study 16 is that it mixes, so to speak, apples and bicycles. Consumer durables are not a homogenous commodity. In particular, that category contains two major components with diverging trends: "traditional" durables, such as motor vehicles and household appliances, that grow at about the same rate as income, and "high tech" durables, mainly personal computers, that grow much faster than income. These two categories should be treated separately, as is indeed done in the macro model presented in chapter 12.

The same dilemma often occurs when a forecaster is asked to predict "sales" for a given company or industry. If the product is not homogeneous – and especially if it consists of some components where sales are growing rapidly and some that are declining – the forecasts are likely to be inferior even when combined with other methods. A sound structural approach is invariably the best starting point for accurate forecasts.

8.5 THE ROLE OF JUDGMENT IN FORECASTING

Economists have long observed that consumer spending patterns are partially based on past habits, so purchases in the current time period are based on previous behavior as well as current values of income and monetary factors. To the extent that the index of consumer sentiment reflects these factors, many consider it a significant determinant of purchases. In addition, expected future changes in economic and financial well-being are important. Indeed, the index of consumer sentiment continues to be one of the key variables that is closely followed by economic forecasters and financial analysts. In that sense, it has passed a "market test," and one could reasonably argue that it must contain useful information or it would not remain popular.

8.5.1 SURVEYS OF SENTIMENT AND BUYING PLANS

The first surveys developed for macroeconomic forecasting were not indexes of sentiment; instead, they were indexes of consumer purchasing plans, business forecasts of what firms expected their sales and capital expenditures would be. It was initially thought that "hard" indexes of actual purchase plans would be more valuable than "soft" indexes of consumer or business sentiment. However, the reverse turned out to be true: indexes of consumer and business buying plans have been consigned to the dustbin, while indexes of sentiment continue to flourish and are eagerly awaited by forecasters and market analysts.

It was also thought initially that the sector of the economy most amenable to the use of business indexes of planning or sentiment would be capital spending. Unlike consumer spending, much of which is "impulse buying," most purchases of capital goods are made by large companies, which carefully prepare capital budgets well in advance of the actual decision to purchase. Furthermore, most goods and structures are delivered or completed with a substantial lag, so data on orders and appropriations should provide additional valuable information about where capital spending in particular and the economy in general were heading.

Based on this logic, shortly after the end of World War II, both government and private agencies started to issue reports of investment anticipations on an annual basis; the Commerce–SEC data were also available on a quarterly basis. However, these reports are no longer issued for the simple reason they were not very useful. Here again the "market test" issue arises: since the anticipations data did not improve forecast accuracy, they were eventually phased out. In a similar manner, data on capital appropriations by large corporations are no longer published by the Conference Board. Data for new orders for capital goods are issued every month, but they turn out to have a very low correlation with future capital spending; only the current quarter correlation is significant. As a result, this report seldom influences financial markets.

There are several reasons why investment anticipations, appropriations, and orders are not useful in predicting actual capital spending. Some are related to the variable time lag for deliveries and construction. More fundamentally, though, this lack of correlation reflects the fact that businesses change their plans based on emerging economic events. Hence the anticipations indexes represented factors that have already happened, rather than what was likely to happen in the future. In that sense, they contain little or no new information.

8.5.2 SENTIMENT INDEX FOR PROSPECTIVE HOME BUYERS

We now consider a sentiment index of prospective home buyers, which is collected and provided by the National Association of Home Builders (NAHB). This index starts only in 1985, so the sample period is more limited, but the results are fairly clear-cut. The equation for housing starts was estimated in chapter 5, where it was found that the key independent variables were demographic factors, the percentage change in income, the vacancy rate, the unemployment rate, the percentage change in the real money supply, and the yield spread. That equation turned out to generate very inaccurate predictions unless they were adjusted by the constant term, and I said this issue would be revisited later.

As it turns out, the forecast error is dramatically reduced by using the NAHB index of homebuyer sentiment. The reader may verify that the index of consumer sentiment does not improve the forecast of single-family housing starts. The RMS errors for the 1998.1–1999.4 period are given in table 8.4; the estimated equation is also shown. The demographic and vacancy rate variables dropped out of the housing start equation presented earlier because of the shorter sample period and the use of the homebuyer sentiment variable.

Table 8.4 RMS errors for housing start equation, 1998.1–1999.4.

	Neither	AR	AR and MA
Without sentiment	117.2	176.8	177.6
Sentiment alone	33.6	–	–
Combined	29.9	31.8	31.1

HST1

$$= 0.628 + 0.127 * \%SP,4 + 1.75 * \%YXTR,4 - 0.022 * RAAA(-3)$$
$$(2.5) \qquad (3.8) \qquad (3.5)$$
$$+ 0.0066 * HSENT + 0.0031 * HSENT(-1)$$
$$(5.4) \qquad (2.4)$$
$$RSQ = 0.892; DW = 1.51$$

HST1 = single-family housing starts; *SP* = S&P 500 stock price index; *YXTR* = real personal disposable income excluding transfer payments; *RAAA* = real AAA corporate bond rate; *HSENT* = NAHB index of homebuyer sentiment.

The relationship of the NAHB index and housing starts is graphed in figure 8.5.

Why does the NAHB index of sentiment for home buyers reduce forecast error so much more than the better known indexes of consumer sentiment? The short answer is that the homebuilding index reflects factors that are not included in the housing start equation, whereas the various indexes of consumer sentiment can be adequately explained by changes in inflation, unemployment and the stock market – and the small fraction of the variance that cannot be explained is not correlated with consumer spending patterns.

The NAHB index plunged in December 2000 and did not recover for several months, probably because of the weak stock market; yet housing starts rose substantially in the first half of 2001, mainly because of lower mortgage rates. On the other hand, the NAHB index turned down later in the year before the terrorist attacks, and housing starts followed. In this case, the combination of financial and confidence variable materially improves the forecast of housing starts precisely because they represent different factors.

8.6 THE ROLE OF CONSENSUS FORECASTS

While economists have had some success in predicting real growth, inflation, and unemployment, they have been notably unsuccessful at predicting interest rates. As noted previously, consensus surveys published in the *Wall Street Journal* for interest rates for the next six months get the direction wrong more often than they get it right.

Several different sources of consensus forecasts can be used. In addition to the *Wall Street Journal* surveys, consensus forecasts for key macroeconomic vari-

Figure 8.5 Housing starts and the NAHB index of homebuyer sentiment. Since its inception, the NAHB index has tracked housing starts much more closely than any other indicator.

ables have been collected and tabulated in a joint effort by NBER and ASA; financial writer Joe Livingston has compiled consensus forecasts for several decades, and several of the regional Federal Reserve Banks also publish consensus forecasts.[12]

In the author's opinion, the most complete and best documented consensus forecasts are those compiled by Blue Chip Economic Indicators. These forecasts have been available every month since January 1977 and contain the forecasts of 50 or more contributors. The series are internally consistent and many of the same panelists have participated in the survey since its inception. The panelists are also identified by name and institution, so it also would be possible to determine whether, for example, large New York City financial institutions are more accurate in predicting interest rates than economists elsewhere in the country – or whether consulting economists have a better track record than those economists who work for large corporations.

Since the record of economists in predicting interest rates has been unusually poor – and since interest rates are of great importance in determining both where the economy is heading and how financial markets will perform – we next examine whether the consensus forecasts for interest rates can improve forecasting accuracy.

---

[12]   For a discussion of other macroeconomic surveys, see Zarnowitz, Victor, and Phillip Braun, "Twenty-two Years of the NBER–ASA Quarterly Economic Outlook Surveys: Aspects and Comparisons of Forecasting Performance," in Stock and Watson, op. cit. (footnote 7).

Case Study 17: Predicting Interest Rates by Combining Structural and Consensus Forecasts

This case study uses the Blue Chip Consensus forecasts for short-term interest rates, measured by the three-month Treasury bill rate on a discount basis, and long-term rates, measured by the ten-year Treasury note yield. For some years in the past, the Blue Chip consensus used the 4–6 month commercial paper rate to measure short-term rates, and the Aaa corporate bond yield and Aa utility bond yield to measure long-term rates. All of the calculations here have been adjusted to reflect these shifts.

Since the Blue Chip forecasts are issued monthly, it would be possible to calculate the impact of the consensus forecasts of a monthly basis. However, there is usually very little change in the consensus outlook from one month to the next; fluctuations that do occur in that narrow a time frame are largely due to speculative trading patterns and short-term disturbances. Hence for the purposes of identifying the possible contribution of the consensus predictions to forecasting accuracy, we examine the forecasts on an annual basis. The consensus forecasts used are those provided to Blue Chip on the first working day of each January. These forecasts can be compared to (i) a naive model that says the level of interest rates this year will be the same as last year, and (ii) a structural model that relates interest rates to the inflation rate, the Federal budget surplus or deficit ratio, loan demand, and the unemployment rate. In addition, the bond rate forecast is also correlated with the Treasury bill rate lagged one year as well as these other variables.

The only unlagged variable that is significant is the change in the unemployment rate. However, using an unlagged variable with an assumed error of zero could bias the results. Thus instead we have used the difference between the consensus forecast of unemployment this year and the actual unemployment rate last year. This term is almost as significant as the actual change in unemployment, and removes any simultaneous-equation bias.

The equations, with and without the consensus forecasting terms, are summarized in table 8.5. The coefficients and t-ratios are given for each variable used in the equation.

The equations for the three-month Treasury bill rate and the Aaa corporate bond rate are estimated for the period from 1977 through 1999, using annual data. The independent variables are the difference between the consensus estimate of the unemployment rate this year and its actual value last year, and lagged values of the inflation rate, the percentage change in business loans, and the ratio of the Federal government surplus or deficit to GDP. Also, the lagged Treasury bill rate is used in the Aaa corporate bond equation.

The quarterly and monthly functions for interest rates discussed elsewhere in this text are more complex, but these annual functions capture the essence of those factors that have determined interest rates in the past. Also, as mentioned above, note that only lagged or consensus variables are used. The RMS

Table 8.5 Alternative formulations of annual interest rate functions.

Dependent variable	$\Delta(UN)$	Infl(-1)	$\Delta(infl(-1))$	$\%\Delta$ loans (-1)	Def ratio	Lagged T-bill rate	Consensus forecast
T-bill rate	−1.56	0.66	0.24	0.26	−0.67		
	(3.4)	(6.0)	(1.7)	(6.0)	(2.5)		
T-bill rate	−0.86	0.32	0.15	0.11	−0.30		0.67
	(2.3)	(2.8)	(1.4)	(2.3)	(1.3)		(3.8)
Aaa bond rate	−0.92	0.22	–	–	−0.18	0.65	
	(3.0)	(3.2)			(1.8)	(8.2)	
Aaa bond rate	−0.71	0.17	–	–	–	0.46	0.33
	(2.3)	(2.4)				(4.0)	(2.5)

UN = consensus forecast of unemployment rate this year minus actual rate last year; Infl = percentage change in the CPI; Loans = business loans; Def ratio = ratio of Federal budget surplus or deficit to GDP.

Table 8.6 RMS errors for interest rates using consensus forecasts.

	Naive Model[a]	Structural	One-step ahead	Consensus	Combined
Short-term rates	1.63	0.82	0.98	1.10	0.59
Long-term rates	1.19	0.58	0.65	1.23	0.54
				0.64[b]	

[a] Interest rates this year are the same as last year.
[b] Also using the lagged value of the Treasury bill rate.

errors with and without the Blue Chip Consensus figures are summarized in table 8.6.

Since the RMS errors for the structural equations might be understated because the data were fitted over the sample period, these errors are also shown for the one-period ahead forecasts, in which the equation is truncated and then the next year is predicted. EViews calculates these results automatically. As expected, the RMS errors are somewhat higher with this procedure, since they are actual ex post forecasts. However, the differences are not very large.

For short-term interest rates, both the structural and consensus forecasts have substantially smaller errors than the no-change naive model. The structural equation has a somewhat lower error than the consensus forecast, but the difference shrinks considerably when the one-step-ahead estimate is considered; i.e., when out-of-sample forecasts are used. *More important, the error from a combined equation that contains both structural terms and the consensus forecast is only slightly more than half that of the average of these two methods taken separately. That is a firm endorsement for combining these methods of forecasting.*

Turning to long-term interest rates, there is no significant difference between the RMS for the naive error and the consensus forecast, which might suggest the assembled panel of experts can do no better than merely assuming long-term rates will be unchanged. However, that is not actually the case. For while the structural equation does much better, that is due in large part to the use of the lagged Treasury bill rate. Hence a more reasonable comparison might be to calculate the RMS error for an equation that uses the consensus forecast of the Aaa bond rate together with the *lagged actual* value of the bill rate, since that is always known at the time of forecast. The RMS error for that equation is cut almost in half, to 0.64%, virtually the same as the error from the one-step-ahead structural equation.

Thus when the consensus forecast is combined with the information contained in the actual value of the bill rate the previous year, the forecasts are almost as good as those generated from a structural model alone. Furthermore, when the structural and consensus forecasts are combined with the lagged value of the bill rate, the RMS error is reduced to 0.54%, slightly less than either the structural or consensus forecast; combining forecasting methods also reduces the forecast error in this case. Note, however, that the biggest reduction occurs when the lagged T-bill rate is added.

In this respect, we note that when the lagged T-bill rate is added to the equation to predict the current T-bill rate, it is not at all significant (the t-ratio is a minuscule 0.05). This means lagged short-term rates are a good predictor of *long-term* rates when combined with the consensus forecast and lagged structural variables, but provide no information about what the level of *short-term* rates will be this year. That reflects the fact that long-term interest rates are a weighted average of short-term rates, whereas the reverse is not true.

There seems to be little doubt, especially for short-term interest rates, that forecast errors are significantly reduced when the structural variables are combined with the consensus forecast. Later we will see that is also the case for inflation, although these findings cannot be extended to all macroeconomic variables. For example, the consensus forecast of capital spending does not improve the forecast accuracy at all. The usefulness of the consensus forecast invariably depends on whether that forecast contains information that is not included in the structural variables.

In the case of short-term interest rates, the additional information included in the consensus forecast reflects hints provided by the Federal Reserve about its near-term policy goals; this information is related to expected future changes and hence is not incorporated in lagged variables. Furthermore, this information changes substantially depending on the choice of Fed Chairman. Arthur Burns was more interested in boosting real growth, while Paul Volcker was more interested in subduing inflation even at the cost of recession and sluggish growth. Alan Greenspan has followed a more balanced approach, in which the level of the Federal funds rate is determined largely by recent and expected levels of the unemployment and inflation rates. It is both logical and empirically valid to assume that these changes in Fed policy, which cannot be measured quantitatively, are incorporated in the consensus forecast.

8.7 ADJUSTING CONSTANT TERMS AND SLOPE COEFFICIENTS

So far we have seen how judgment can improve forecast accuracy by using survey results and consensus forecasts. The third major method of incorporating judgment on a statistically consistent basis – as opposed to using qualitative expert opinion from the field – is to adjust the constant term and slopes that have been estimated by least squares.

The methodology for these two types of adjustment is quite different. In the case of the constant term, the appropriate procedure is to examine the residuals of recent periods and adjust the constant term in the forecast period based on those residuals; the other parameter estimates themselves are not changed. By comparison, changing the slope terms assumes the estimates of the slope terms vary over the sample period.

Most forecasters adjust their predictions by including some information from the residuals of the equation over the past few periods. If the actual values start to drift off from those predicted by the equation, it would be foolish to ignore that evidence. Nonetheless, such adjustments invariably raise the question: what factors are causing this drift?

We have already examined the reasons why this might happen, but to review briefly, this type of forecast error usually occurs either because some unobservable variable is missing, or the underlying structure has changed.

By definition, unobservable variables such as expectations cannot be measured precisely. In the equation for single-family housing starts, adding the index of homebuyer sentiment materially reduced forecasting error for the 1998–9 period. However, it is not always possible to find useful indexes of sentiment or confidence. Besides, the shift might be due to other factors: the introduction of a new product, or a new process for manufacturing or distributing that product. Sales of personal computers jumped when Internet usage became popular, and the rate of inflation declined when the use of the Internet permitted people to purchase goods at lower prices. Changes of this sort would presumably be captured by the recent patterns of residuals of equations used to explain computer sales, or prices of goods that can be purchased "on the computer."

8.7.1 ADVANTAGES AND PITFALLS OF ADJUSTING THE CONSTANT TERM

There are no hard and fast rules for estimating what proportion of the recent residuals should be incorporated into the forecast. Basically the forecaster is exercising judgment: either the shift is permanent, in which case the full value of recent residuals should be included, or the shift is temporary, in which case the adjustment should gradually return to zero over the next few quarters.

If the residuals of the estimated equation have a high degree of serial correlation, and all the recent residuals have approximately the same value, it is reasonable to apply that adjustment to the forecast. However, that raises the question of why the autocorrelation coefficient is so high: perhaps the equation is misspecified, and not all of the variables are actually linear. Perhaps one or more variables is missing. Other times, a shift has occurred outside the sample period, as was the case for the consumer durables equation after 1997. Usually the reason for a series of positive or negative residuals is not immediately obvious.

If the residuals are not highly autocorrelated, the usual procedure is to assume that any adjustment in the constant term will return to zero. Yet the drawback of quickly moving back to zero is as follows. Suppose the error over the past year is an amount equal to 4% of the mean value, and the series usually changes by an average of 6% per year. If the last period is used as the starting point, the slope estimates indicate that the change the following year should be equal to the average change of 6%. But if the constant term returns to zero, the predicted change would be only 2%. In that case, the forecast would be based almost entirely on judgment, with the values predicted by the equation almost ignored.

This dilemma emphasizes there is no mechanical way to adjust the constant term in the forecast period unless the source of the error is known, in which case the obvious remedy is to improve the equation over the sample period.

Forecasting, like politics, is the art of the possible. Often, the best equation that can be estimated over the sample period will have significant autocorrelation and residuals that bunch near the end of the sample period. Such cases suggest that combined methods of forecasting be used, perhaps by including expert judgment, surveys, or consensus forecasts. But suppose the item to be predicted is sales of an individual firm, for which none of these alternative methods exist.

If the forecaster thinks the recent residuals can be explained as a result of some development that has affected the dependent variable but cannot yet be quantified, the average value of the recent residuals should probably be continued into the forecast period. If, on the other hand, there does not seem to be any available reason for the bunching of these residuals, and hence the effect appears to be random, the forecast should be generated without incorporating the values of the recent residuals.

This "hand-crafted" approach will work for someone who is forecasting just a few variables, but is not efficient when thousands of variables are being predicted, such as a system designed to keep track of sales and inventories. That is one of the reasons why ARMA procedures are used to keep these equations on track. The examples in this text are primarily designed to show how forecasts can usefully be improved when the model builder has the time and resources to examine each equation individually.

There are no definitive answers about how to treat constant adjustments. In general, though, we suggest the following. If there are strong reasons for estimating an equation in levels form even though the residuals exhibit significant autocorrelation, future forecasts should probably be adjusted by recent levels of the residuals. Otherwise, it is better to remove the trend from the equation, respecify it so the residuals are not autocorrelated, and then use constant adjustments only when clearly identifiable changes have occurred in the underlying relationship.

8.7.2 ESTIMATING SHIFTING PARAMETERS

We next consider the possibility of estimating an equation in which the values of the parameters change over the forecast period. Perhaps the importance of a particular variable has increased over time, is more important in downturns than in upturns, or exhibits other forms of nonlinearity.

The sample period fit can almost always be improved by shifting the slope estimates, but the question is whether that will really improve the forecast accuracy, or just boost the goodness-of-fit statistics in the sample period – so-called "curve fitting." The tendency, especially for those without considerable experience in actual forecasting, is to over-engineer the equation during the sample period.

Keeping that caveat in mind, the three most common methods of changing the slope coefficients over the sample period are (i) dummy variables for truncated periods and nonlinearities that make the equation piecewise linear, (ii) slope coefficients that are a function of a time trend, and (iii) changes that occur continuously over the sample period but are not tied to specific economic developments. The latter category involves the use of Kalman filters, which are not covered in this book. The use of dummy variables has already been discussed. Hence the discussion now focuses on slopes that are a function of a time trend.

One key example of parameter shifts can be seen in the equation to predict net exports of the US economy. Since this series itself has a strong trend, some method should be used to reduce if not eliminate the trend, since trendless variables such as the value of the dollar are important independent variables. In this case, the best method is to take the ratio of net exports to total GDP, both in constant dollars; the graph is shown in figure 8.6. The data start in 1969 because all major foreign exchange rates were fixed before that date, so the underlying data generation function was clearly different.

Net exports are defined as exports minus imports, and are negatively correlated with the trade-weighted average of the dollar. Imports are positively related to changes in US GDP, whereas exports are positively related to foreign GDP. Hence net exports would be positively correlated with various measures of GDP in other countries and negatively related with changes in GDP in the US.

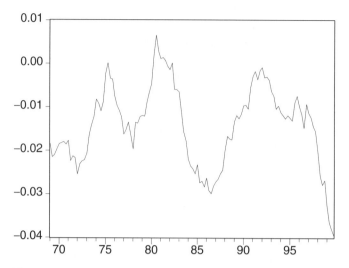

Figure 8.6 The ratio of constant-dollar net exports to constant-dollar GDP shows no trend, but declined sharply in the second half of the 1990s.

As the US has become more integrated into the world economy, foreign trade represents an increasing proportion of total GDP. Thus it would be reasonable to assume that in more recent years, a given change in US GDP or the value of the dollar would cause a greater change in the net export balance. Also, the weights have changed: trade with Europe, Japan, and OPEC has become relatively less important, whereas trade with Canada, Mexico, and the emerging nations in Asia has become relatively more important. The coefficients might also reflect these changes.

The forecasting challenge here is formidable because of the unprecedented decline in the net export ratio from 1996 through 1999. On an ex post basis, it was caused by the collapse of the Asian economy and the increased strength of the US economy. The question is whether that decline can be accurately predicted using an equation estimated only to the end of 1995. Using standard variables – changes in real GDP in the US and its major trading partners, plus the value of the dollar – an equation with constant parameters will do a very poor job of predicting this downturn, whereas an equation with changing parameter estimates related to a time trend generates much more accurate forecasts.

Table 8.7 provides the approximate weights of US exports to major regions of the world in 1974 and 1999. While the source of imports has also changed, that does not affect the equation because import growth is tied to changes in US GDP.

GDP for Canada is not included in the equation because it mirrors the US economy so closely. Thus one would expect that the importance of GDP for

Table 8.7 US export shares by major region.

Region	1974	1999
Canada	0.21	0.24
Mexico	0.05	0.12
Western Europe	0.30	0.24
Japan	0.11	0.08
Other Pacific Rim[a]	0.10	0.17
OPEC	0.10	0.03
South America[a]	0.08	0.08
All other	0.05	0.04

[a] Excluding OPEC nations.

western Europe and Japan would diminish over time, and for Latin America and the Pacific Rim would increase over time. Changes in GDP for OPEC nations can be reasonably approximated by changes in the price of oil, which is the term used in the equation.

Imports generally react to changes in real GDP with a short lag, while changes in exports have a longer lag. As a result, GDP for other countries and the value of the dollar all enter the equation with a lag of 2–4 quarters. To avoid problems that arise from mixing variables with and without trends, percentage changes are used for all measures of GDP. Since the value of the dollar does not have any long-term trend, the level of that variable is used. The estimated equation is.

$$XNETRAT$$
$$= 0.043 - 0.193 * \%GDP, 4 * TR - 0.054 * DOLLAR, 4$$
$$\quad\quad\quad (9.1) \quad\quad\quad\quad\quad\quad (21.0)$$
$$- 0.156 * \%GDP(-4), 4 * TR + 2.52 * \%IPJPN(-2), 4 + 1.61 * \%POIL(-4) * TR$$
$$\quad (8.1) \quad\quad\quad\quad\quad\quad (4.0) \quad\quad\quad\quad\quad\quad (4.0)$$
$$- 0.0015 * \%POIL(-4), 4 * TR + 0.096 * \%GDPASIA(-4), 4 * TR$$
$$\quad (3.0) \quad\quad\quad\quad\quad\quad\quad (5.7)$$
$$- 0.036 * \%IPOECD(-2), 4 * TR$$
$$RSQ = 0.914; \ DW = 1.02$$

where *XNETRAT* is the ratio of US net exports to GDP in constant dollars, *GDP* is US GDP in constant dollars, *DOLLAR* is the trade-weighted average of the dollar, *IPJPN* is the index of industrial production for Japan, *POIL* is the PPI for petroleum products, *GDPASIA* is the real GDP for the emerging nations in Asia, *IPOECD* is industrial production for OECD Europe, and *TR* is a time trend.

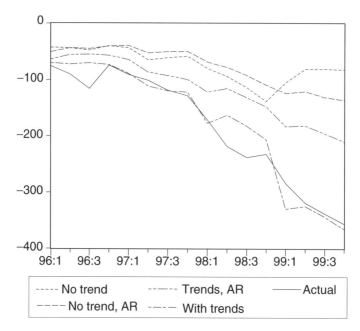

Figure 8.7   Forecasts of the ratio of constant-dollar net exports to GDP, with and without slope terms adjusted by trend factors, for 1996.1 through 1999.4.

The equation is not optimal, in the sense that not all of the terms mentioned above are significant. *IPOECD* without the trend, *IPJPN* with the trend, *GDPH* without the trend, *GDPASIA* without the trend, and *DOLLAR* with the trend were not significant and hence were dropped. Also, *GDP* for Latin America was not significant. Nonetheless, as shown in figure 8.7, this equation predicts the 1996.1–1999.4 period much better than an equation without trend-adjusted parameter estimates.

One could perhaps argue that the use of trends, even though the sample period is truncated in 1995.4, reflects the wisdom of hindsight. Yet it is sensible to claim that these parameter estimates have indeed changed over time as international trade has become a more important part of the US economy, and regional patterns have shifted. It remains to be seen which version of the equation will provide better forecasting in future years, but this example would seem to offer impressive testimony to the benefits of using shifting parameter estimates where underlying economic conditions have changed.

8.8 COMBINING FORECASTS: SUMMARY

This chapter has considered combining the following methods of forecasting:

• structural models
• ARMA processes, especially the use of the AR(1) transformation

- judgmental information incorporated in surveys
- consensus forecasts
- adjusting the constant term based on recent residuals
- modifying the slope coefficients by adding time trends.

No hard and fast rules can be drawn because most of the conditions found in practical business forecasting do not match the classical statistical assumptions. Nonetheless, the examples given in this chapter, combined with many other equations and models estimated by this author, point to several general conclusions:

1   Combination of forecasting methods works best if the methods that are combined are dissimilar.
2   Combining methods of forecasting will invariably improve forecasts from structural equations that are misspecified, but generally the improvement is not any greater than would be obtained by respecifying the equation more accurately.
3   Adjusting the parameters of structural models to take account of shifts in institutional structure, exogenous linkages, or changes in data methodology should not be considered *ad hoc* adjustments but can provide significant improvements in forecast accuracy.
4   For equations that are properly specified, a combination of (i) structural modeling, (ii) adjustment of the parameters of the equation as indicated by recent values of the residuals or shift in the underlying structure, and (iii) an appropriate measure of consumer or business sentiment is likely to produce forecasts with the smallest error.

We next consider an annual equation for predicting inflation to show how combining some of these methods can be used to reduce forecasting error, although the error does not necessarily continue to decline as additional methods are added. This indicates that combining forecasts per se is not a panacea for reducing forecast error.

Case Study 18: Improving the Forecasting Record for Inflation

The independent variable here is the annual percentage change in the CPI. We show examine the forecasting record of the following possibilities:

- ARMA model
- structural equation with fixed coefficients
- structural equation with variable coefficients
- structural equation with consensus CPI forecast
- structural equation with consensus and ARMA terms
- structural equation with consensus, ARMA, and a survey of inflation as calculated by the National Association of Purchasing Managers (NAPM).

Since the dependent variable is in percentage change form, no further differencing is required, so an ARMA(2,2) model is estimated. It gives relatively large forecasting errors, so we quickly move on to the next phase.

The standard price markup equation indicates that the inflation rate is a function of the percentage change in unit labor costs adjusted for supply shocks, primarily food, and energy. A dummy variable for wage and price controls is not significant. The claim that prices rise more rapidly when the unemployment rate is low, or the capacity utilization rate is high, cannot be verified statistically; these terms invariably have the wrong sign and are excluded.

Unit labor costs equal wage rates divided by productivity. However, since wage rates depend critically on the rate of inflation, using unlagged wage rates would bias the results in favor of the structural equation. Hence the estimated equation essentially involves a two-step procedure, in which the principal factors that affect wage rates – other than the inflation rate itself – are used as independent variables in the inflation equation. These variables are lagged percentage changes in the money supply and percentage changes in the minimum wage. Since productivity is determined more by long-run conditions, both lagged and unlagged changes for that variable are included. The estimated equation, shown with the Blue Chip Consensus estimates, is as follows. There are 50 annual observations from 1950 through 1999.

$$INFL$$
$$= 1.13 - 0.318 * \%PEOD - 0.197 * \%PROD(-1) + 2.86 * \%POIL * ENCOEF$$
$$\quad (5.4) \qquad\qquad (3.0) \qquad\qquad\qquad (7.6)$$
$$+ 0.025 * \%MINW + 0.052 * \%MINW(-1) + 0.077 * \%M2(-1),2$$
$$\quad (3.4) \qquad\qquad (5.9) \qquad\qquad\qquad (4.1)$$
$$+ 1.65 * \%PFOOD * (FOODCO - 0.15) + 0.496 * CONSCPI$$
$$\quad (6.4) \qquad\qquad\qquad\qquad\qquad (11.0)$$
$$RSQ = 0.961; \; DW = 2.20$$

where INFL is the inflation rate as measured by CPI-U, PROD is the productivity of the non-farm business sector, POIL is the producer price index of refined petroleum products, ENCOEF is the energy coefficient (the amount of energy used per unit of real GDP), MINW is the minimum wage, M2 is the M2 measure of the money supply, PFOOD is the producer price index of farm products, FOODCO is the ratio of consumer spending on food to total consumption, and CONSCPI is the Blue Chip Consensus forecast of inflation.

Note that we have introduced a more sophisticated measure of changing weights in this equation. Rather than use a simple time trend, the price of energy is multiplied by the energy coefficient, and the price of food is multiplied by the food coefficient minus 0.15 (representing an estimate of the proportion of consumer food prices not directly related to farm prices, mostly value added at restaurants). While the standard error is about the same with and without these structural changes, the forecast error is smaller with these terms included.

Table 8.8 Standard error and RMS error statistics for different methods of predicting inflation.

Method of calculation	SE of estimate	RMS error 1990–9
Separate measures		
Structural (fixed weights)	1.18	1.00
Structural (variable weights)	1.18	0.94
ARMA(2,2)	1.98	1.62
Naive model	2.01	0.70
Blue Chip Consensus	1.83	0.55
NAPM survey	2.28	2.35
Combined measures		
Structural + Consensus	0.60	0.47
Structural + ARMA	0.97	1.53
Structural, Consensus and ARMA	0.58	0.41
Structural, Consensus, ARMA, and NAPM	0.58	0.41

The Blue Chip data begin only in 1977, which would have drastically short-ened the sample period; so for data before then we used the actual rate of infla-tion the *previous* year for the consensus estimate. That would tend to understate the importance of the consensus forecast but, as is seen above, it is still highly significant.

The RMS errors have been calculated two ways. First, the equation was esti-mated over the entire sample period, from 1950 through 1999, and the stan-dard error of the equation was used as an estimate of the RMS error. Obviously that understates the actual forecasting error; the question is by how much. To determine that, the equation was estimated for the 1950–89 sample period, with the RMS error calculated for the out-of-sample 1990–9 time span. The com-parative statistics are given in table 8.8.

On the basis of the full sample period, it would appear that when separate measures are compared, the structural equation generated the lowest forecast error. However, that is a misleading statistic: in the forecast period, both the naive and the Blue Chip Consensus estimates are lower, because inflation did not change very much in the 1990s.

The combined measures indicate the advantage of combining the structural and consensus forecast; adding ARMA helps slightly if the consensus is not included. Adding the estimate of price changes provided by the National Association of Purchasing Managers does not improve forecast accuracy at all. This is not an attempt to denigrate the NAPM survey; only to point out that combining different types of forecasts does not necessarily improve forecast accuracy. The additional method must bring new information to the fore-casting exercise.

SUMMARY

The results presented in this chapter have been variegated. Nonetheless, some general conclusions can be drawn from these results.

1   The equation should be structurally sound, in the sense that variables with strong trends should not be correlated with trendless series unless further adjustments have been made. If this is not the case, various combinations of forecasting methods are likely to reduce forecast error, but the error is still likely to be larger than would be the case for a properly specified equation.
2   If the recent residuals share a common pattern – all positive, or all negative – forecast error will be diminished by using the average of recent residuals in the forecast period. However, that method will not always provide optimal forecasts. If the degree of serial correlation is high, the equation may be misspecified.
3   While using the AR(1) adjustment will eliminate serial correlation, it generally will not improve forecast accuracy relative to a properly specified equation, and will lead to larger errors in multi-period forecasts. Also, using the MA(1) term seldom improves forecast accuracy in a properly specified equation.
4   Permitting the slope coefficients to change over time can reduce forecast error when the underlying weights of the variables have changed. The likelihood of this occurring can be determined by checking the recursive residuals graph in EViews, or similar tests in other software programs.
5   Using surveys measuring consumer and business sentiment is more likely to improve forecast accuracy if they contain independent information not reflected in the variables in the structural equation.
6   Consensus surveys can improve forecast accuracy even if the consensus forecasts by themselves are no better than a naive model. However, as is also the case for surveys, the consensus forecasts must contain information not included in the structural variables.

Problems and Questions

1. You are asked to predict the demand for cigarettes.

(a)   Estimate an equation in which the volume of cigarettes purchased is a function of the relative price and income. What happens to the income term? Is that a sensible result? How would you test to see whether there any difference between the short-term and long-term price elasticity for cigarettes?

continued

(b) Now estimate the same equation in log form. What is the price elasticity estimated in logs, and how does it compare with the elasticity in the levels equation?

(c) Reestimate both the level and log functions by truncating the sample period in 1995 and then predict cigarette consumption in 1996 through 1999. Which equation gives more accurate predictions?

(d) Does adjusting the equation by adding an AR(1) term improve forecast accuracy?

(e) Based on these results and an examination of the residuals, what other factors should be incorporated into your forecasts of cigarette consumption?

2. Chapter 7 showed that using an ARMA model alone to predict machine tool orders did not work very well. However, it is possible that some combination of a structural equation, ARMA process, and the NAPM consensus forecast of new orders would provide better forecasts.

(a) First, using monthly data, estimate a structural equation for the volume of machine tool orders using the rate of capacity utilization, industrial production in manufacturing, the rate of investment tax credit, and the real Aaa corporate bond rate as independent variables. Use PDLs where appropriate. Truncate the sample period at the end of 1997.

(b) Reestimate the equation with an AR(1) term, and with both AR(1) and MA(1) terms. Now calculate ex post forecasts for 1998–2000 using these three equations.

(c) Add the NAPM series for new orders to the equation that provides the most accurate forecasts. Use lags if appropriate. Now use that equation to forecast 1998–2000. Has the accuracy improved?

(d) Examine the residuals for the 1996–7 period. Is there any information there that could be used to improve the forecast accuracy? If so, how would you incorporate it?

3. This problem examines various methods of predicting housing starts. While housing start data are available from 1959, consensus forecasts begin only in 1977 and the NAHB index of housing sentiment starts only in 1985. All regressions in this example are to be calculated using annual data.

(a) Calculate regressions from 1959 through 1990 for housing starts based on (i) a naive model, in which housing starts this year are a function of starts during the previous two years, (ii) the optimal

continued

Table 8.9 Extra data for problem 3.

Year	Blue Chip Consensus	NAHB index
1977	1.82	
1978	1.89	
1979	1.65	
1980	1.42	
1981	1.40	
1982	1.26	
1983	1.45	
1984	1.74	
1985	1.72	55.1
1986	1.77	60.1
1987	1.71	56.0
1988	1.54	53.2
1989	1.44	47.5
1990	1.43	34.3
1991	1.16	35.8
1992	1.21	48.3
1993	1.33	58.5
1994	1.39	56.0
1995	1.36	46.6
1996	1.36	56.6
1997	1.40	56.5
1998	1.44	70.3
1999	1.53	73.3
2000	1.54	62.0

ARMA model (choose the lag structure), and (iii) a structural equation *using only lagged values*. (Hint: try lagged percentage changes in real disposable income, real money supply, and the level of the yield spread.) Compare the sample period standard errors. Now choose the equation that combines these methods and generates the lowest standard error.

(b) Repeat this process for 1977–2000 but add (iv) an equation that relates housing starts to the consensus forecast, and (v) housing starts to the consensus forecast and lagged structural variables. Calculate the standard errors, and choose the best combined forecasting equation.

continued

(c) Repeat this process for 1985–2000 but add (vi) an equation that relates housing starts to the NAHB index of housing sentiment, (vii) an equation that relates housing starts to the consensus forecast and the NAHB index, and (viii) an equation with these two variables plus relevant structural variables. Now calculate the best combined forecasting equation.

(d) Based on the comments about when combining forecasts work best, explain why the equation with the consensus forecast and the NAHB index works so much better than any other combination.

4. Estimate a function using monthly data, where constant-dollar retail sales are a function of real personal disposable income and the ratio of the S&P 500 stock price index to real disposable income. Use PDLs where appropriate.

(a) Show the optimal equation.

(b) Now add the index of consumer sentiment to this equation. Should it be included in levels or percentage change form? Explain why you chose that form, based on economics as well as the statistical estimates.

(c) Now try adding ARMA processes to this equation. Start with ARMA(1,1). It will immediately become obvious that the AR(1) coefficient is very close to unity. Under those circumstances, the use of ARMA processes is inapplicable. Reestimate the equation using (i) one-month percentage differences and (ii) 12-month percentage differences. What happens to the structural variables? Should AR and MA terms be included in the forecasting equation? (Hint: check the RMS errors.) Should AR(12) and MA(12) terms be included in the forecasting equation?

(d) The results are quite different depending on what form the dependent variable takes. Derive the optimal forecasting equations, including consumer sentiment and ARMA processes if appropriate, for a client who wants you to predict (i) the level of sales, month by month, over the next 12 months, (ii) the percentage change next month, (iii) the percentage change over the next 12 months. Use out-of-sample ex post forecasts for recent years to defend your choices.

5. This example uses quarterly data for producer price indexes. Two dependent variables are used: total industrial prices, and industrial prices excluding energy. Estimate quarterly percentage changes in each of these variables as a function of the percentage change in unit labor costs over the past four quarters, and the NAPM diffusion index of prices paid.

continued

(a) Report your results.

(b) It is immediately obvious that there is a huge positive residual in 1974.2, which is the quarter in which the price controls were removed. That is true for the core rate as well as the total rate, so higher oil prices are not the major factor. In terms of designing a forecast equation, should that data point be treated with a dummy variable, or would it be better to start the sample period after the impact of the wage and price controls had ended?

(c) Now introduce ARMA processes into the equation containing unit labor costs and the NAPM index. Do any of those terms help improve forecast accuracy? Use RMS error data to support your conclusion.

(d) How do the results differ for a sample period starting in (i) 1948, (ii) 1976, and (iii) 1983? The sample period error is smaller for the latter period because prices did not fluctuate as much – no major oil shocks or price controls. However, that does not necessarily mean the equation with the shorter sample period would provide better ex ante forecasts. What other criteria would you use to determine which of these equations to use as a forecasting model? Explain why your answer depends on whether the variable to be predicted is total industrial prices or the core rate.

CHAPTER 9

BUILDING AND PRESENTING SHORT-TERM SALES FORECASTING MODELS

INTRODUCTION

The first eight chapters of the text focused on developing the statistical theory and empirical implementation for estimating and testing business forecasting models. This material also showed how to improve forecast accuracy as well as test for the robustness of parameters over the sample period. The remaining four chapters will present actual examples of forecasting models. Chapter 9 discusses short-term sales forecasting models, while chapter 10 focuses on long-term models that can be used for projecting both trends and changes. Chapter 11 examines the additional problems that occur when using multi-equation models for forecasting. In some cases, each of the individual equations may perform adequately, but forecast accuracy diminishes when they are combined. Chapter 12 discusses a small macroeconomic forecasting model, emphasizing the actual methodology that is used to choose exogenous variables and adjust constant terms in the model; it also evaluates how much macroeconomic forecasts can be improved by combining structural methods, constant adjustments, and various exogenous inputs such as indexes of sentiment or consensus forecasts.

This chapter presents methods to prepare and present short-term sales forecasts to management. This material is developed with the client in mind – how to provide information about the underlying theory and assumptions behind the model, the outlook, and alternative forecasts.[1] For this reason, only structural models are considered here; while the forecasts may be enhanced by

---

[1] Previously referenced textbooks do not contain much information on sales forecasting and the role of judgment. For this purpose, useful background reading can be found in four leading texts. See especially Makridakis, S., S. C. Wheelwright, and R. J. Hyndman, *Forecasting Methods and Applications*, 3rd edn (John Wiley, New York), 1998, chs 10–12. Also see Hanke, J. E., and A. G. Reitsch, *Business Forecasting*, 6th edn (Prentice-Hall, Upper Saddle River, NJ), 1998, ch. 11; and Wilson, J. H., and B. Keating,

using various ARMA processes or constant adjustments, these details are not typically presented to management or consulting clients.

9.1 ORGANIZING THE SALES FORECASTING PROCEDURE

Before starting to estimate multiple regression equations, it is best to determine precisely what the forecasting model is expected to accomplish. In particular, the forecaster should determine the following.[2]

Step 1: Variables that are to be predicted
In some cases, management wants a forecast of total sales, or sales by product line or region. Sometimes they are interested in projected market share for a variety of products. In other cases, the model will be used more as a tracking mechanism to determine whether sales, production, and inventories remain in line with expectations.

Step 2: Principal use of the forecasts
Management might request forecasts to predict actual or percentage changes, determine the probability that sales or cash flow will fall below a certain level, indicate the growth rate above which expansion is desirable, or monitor product lines to see whether they remain on track.

Step 3: Time frame – monthly, quarterly, annually, etc.
In some cases, annual forecasts may be desired, but forecasts will be tracked on a monthly basis to see whether goals and targets are being met. In the short run, airlines want to know how best to deploy existing aircraft to maximize the percentage of seats that are filled; in the long run, they want to know how many new airplanes to buy. Utilities need to allocate existing resources to meet the peak-load problem in the short run; in the long run, they need to determine how much to expand capacity.

Step 4: Data adequacy
The modeling effort is unlikely to be robust unless the data series are long enough, and variable enough, to permit meaningful correlations with the independent variables. In an extreme example, suppose a firm had data showing that sales rose 10% per year for each of the past 10 years; there is not enough variation to provide reliable parameter estimates. The data should cover at

---

Business Forecasting, 3rd edn (Irwin/McGraw-Hill, Burr Ridge, IL), 1998, ch. 9. DeLurgio, S. A., *Forecasting Principles and Applications* (Irwin/McGraw-Hill, Burr Ridge, IL), 1998 contains an interesting discussion of business forecasting methods in ch. 15, but most of those comments apply to long-term forecasting.

[2] For a somewhat shorter alternative list, see Wilson and Keating, pp. 409–14. Also see Lawless, M. J., "Ten Prescriptions for Forecasting Success," *Journal of Business Forecasting*, 16 (1997), 3–5; and "Effective Sales Forecasting: A Management Tool," *Journal of Business Forecasting*, 10 (1990), 2–11.

least one period of significant cyclical variation. Robust models should be based on 40–50 observations, which is rarely the case for individual product line data unless monthly and quarterly data are used. Sometimes, however, these observations are not really independent, so the true degrees of freedom are far less than indicated by the number of observations minus the number of variables.

Step 5: Acceptable error range

Don't overpromise. In general, it would be unrealistic to expect that forecast period errors would be smaller than indicated by sample period statistics. Those who claim that can be accomplished run the risk of losing credibility even if the forecasting procedure is robust. It is often useful to provide a forecast range as well as a point estimate.

Step 6: Symmetric or asymmetric loss function

In some cases, failing to meet targets is much more serious than having sales grow faster than anticipated. In other cases, failure to estimate growth rates accurately could force the company to put customers on allocation and lose business to competitors. Know the risks on both sides before presenting the forecasts.

Step 7: Conditional or unconditional forecasts

Sometimes management wants the best estimate regardless of what could happen. For example, financial analysts are paid to pick stocks that outperform the overall market, not stocks that will outperform the market if the Fed eases, oil prices decline, or there is a revolution in Russia. In other cases, management wants to know how much sales would be affected if real growth declines by 2% next year, or the value of the dollar appreciates. In these cases, alternative scenarios are desired. These alternatives are not always based on macro factors. Managers may want to know how their business will be affected if a new competitive threat emerges, and the best way to react.

Step 8: Top-down or bottom-up forecast

In some cases, overall growth may be determined by economic activity, but one brand may gain at the expense of the other. For example, total auto sales are largely determined by macroeconomic factors, but the market share of SUVs may rise at the expense of "traditional" cars for a while – and then, after the market has been saturated, start to decline again. Management may want to know when that turning point is most likely to occur. Total airline miles may be determined within a fairly narrow range, but consumers may take more business trips and fewer vacations – or vice versa.

Step 9: Structural or time-series models

To a certain extent this depends on whether the forecast involves a few relatively aggregate items or thousands of individual product lines. It also depends on whether management is more comfortable with a forecast that is linked to key economic factors, or one that is mechanically generated and relies less heavily on judgment. In this author's experience, most clients expect an explanation of the underlying reasons for your predictions. A forecast that says "Sales will rise 6% next year" based strictly on lagged values and error terms without any other supporting logic generally will not be well received even if it turns out to be accurate.

Step 10: Identifying the main drivers

In a structural model, the key independent variables must "make sense" to those who will be using the forecasts. There is little point in presenting an apparently statistically robust model if the terms used in the model have little or no apparent relation to the variables being predicted. Clients will suspect that spurious correlations are being applied.

Step 11: Use of judgment

In some cases, management wants you to incorporate judgment, sales forecasts, consensus estimates, management goals, and other internal company information into the forecasting procedure; in other cases, they have hired an econometrician to move away from this method of forecasting. Where data are available, one should try to determine the degree to which judgmental information has previously improved forecasts generated from structural models.

Step 12: Determining the sample period error

In general, the forecast period error will be larger, but to establish credibility you need to show that the model has tracked accurately in the past. Find out whether the sample period error is acceptable to management, or if they were expecting a smaller error. Most executives realize that, in the vast majority of cases, the forecast period error will be larger than the sample period error, so if the latter is larger than desired, an alternative method may have to be tried.

Step 13: Alternative methods of forecasting

Determine the extent to which the sample period error is reduced by combining different methods of forecasts. However, note that these methods also need to sound plausible; simply throwing in another forecasting method because combining methods sometimes reduces forecast error will not satisfy management.

Step 14: Scenario buildup and intervention analysis

In many cases, it is useful to present alternative scenarios: optimistic, consensus, and pessimistic. However, in some cases more specific alternatives are desirable. In the case of the oil industry, alternatives might be based on a scenario buildup where another armed conflagration breaks out in the Middle East. Intervention analysis could be used to model a change in government regulations, such as a decision to phase out the internal combustion engine and substitute more energy-efficient methods of transportation. In these cases, changes in the specific variables would generally override the importance of changes in the macroeconomic climate.

Step 15: Accuracy of independent variables
How accurate are your predictions of the drivers? If only lagged values are used for the period being predicted, this is not an issue. However, if you find a strong correlation with an unlagged variable that provides an extremely low sample period error but that variable cannot be predicted very well, the results may not be useful. In the same vein, double-check to make sure that a disguised form of the dependent variable has not ended up on the right-hand side of the equation.

Step 16: Selling to top management or other clients
If you can't convince the end user to buy the forecasts, the exercise has been a wasted effort even if the results are superb. Presentation must be offered in easy-to-understand, credible terms.

Many of these hints focus on presentation as well as statistical robustness. While that factor should not be overlooked, providing accurate forecasts is generally a necessary but not sufficient condition for success. This author is aware of many circumstances where economists were fired in spite of accurate forecasts. In some cases, the process was viewed as obscure; the economists were not able to defend their positions with well-reasoned methodology. In other cases, it was a question of "shooting the messenger"; when the economy went into recession and sales declined, the economics staff was fired in spite of having predicted the downturn accurately. If management stresses "think positive" but the economy is weakening, it may often be advisable to show the conditions under which sales will continue to grow as well as the conditions that will cause them to decline. An unconditional statement that "sales are going to decline next year and there is nothing you or anyone else can do about it" is not likely to win kudos in performance reviews or lead to retention as a consultant.

9.2 ENDOGENOUS AND EXOGENOUS VARIABLES IN SALES FORECASTING

The independent variables used in the models discussed in this chapter can be grouped into the following three categories:

- macroeconomic variables that are external to the firm, such as interest rates, the value of the dollar, growth rate in GDP, consumer attitudes, or total capital spending;
- variables that the firm can control, such as investment or advertising and sales expenditures;
- variables affecting the specific product that are the result of competitive situations; reactions of firms already in the industry, domestic firms that might enter the industry, or international penetration of domestic markets.

9.2.1 MACROECONOMIC VARIABLES

In most cases, individual firms are not large enough for changes in their sales to affect the overall economy; the major exception is the auto industry. Hence using variables such as interest and inflation rates, industrial production and capacity utilization, and credit availability should not generate any simultaneity bias in the parameter estimates. However, unless lagged values are used, these variables do not satisfy the condition of being known at time t. Using unlagged values of macroeconomic variables is likely to increase forecast error relative to what would be expected from sample period statistics.

The following hints are often useful in generating predicted values for the key independent variables (drivers).

1   If the period to be predicted is just a few months or quarters, use lagged values of the independent variables wherever possible. Sometimes it is advisable to use a distributed lag that incorporates both lagged and unlagged values.

2   Consensus forecasts can be used for key drivers. That choice provides a reasonable estimate of what can be expected if there are no major surprises in the economy. Also, the use of consensus forecasts can serve as a platform for alternative scenarios. If the consensus expects interest rates to decline but you think they will rise, the implications of this difference should be communicated to management.

3   If the drivers are not the type of variables usually predicted by consensus forecasts, the model should probably be expanded to predict these variables as well.

4   In general, don't use variables that cannot be predicted accurately unless they are critical to the model, in which case scenario analysis can be used. For example, stock prices are notoriously difficult to predict; but if they have a material influence on the variable that is being predicted, the logical approach would be to present alternative estimates based on realistic guesses about the stock market. In general, it does not do much good to find an extremely high correlation with a variable that cannot be predicted accurately.

9.2.2 VARIABLES CONTROLLED BY THE FIRM

Next consider some of the major issues that arise when forecasting the type of variables that the firm can control. Firms sometimes confuse actual growth in sales with targeted goals. Suppose a bank wants to increase its loan portfolio by 15% every year. For a time, it can meet that goal by making riskier loans – but in the long run, it may be forced to merge or even shut its doors if enough of these loans default. On the other hand, improved risk management models may permit the bank to enhance the chances of success, thus boosting lending activity without significantly raising the risk.

In using growth targets, the first step is to determine how much sales are likely to increase based on national, regional, and demographic trends. The firm can then decide to try and enhance this growth rate by expansion, merger, or moving into new products and services. The firm can expand sales of its existing product lines faster than total sales only by purchasing competitors or taking market share away from other firms, whether domestic or international. That latter result might be accomplished by reducing costs through new capital spending, enhancement of product quality, more advertising, or starting operations in regions that had previously been neglected. All of these can be useful methods for expanding market share; but since all of them are costly, management must consider whether the rate of return is justified. They must also be aware that other firms may counterattack with similar strategies. Mindless expansion is usually a recipe for disaster, as many high-tech firms belatedly found out in 2000.

Perhaps all this sounds obvious when stated so baldly, but the author is aware of many circumstances where firms operate under the illusion that their sales can grow faster than the rate indicated by economic conditions simply by exhorting the sales staff to "do better" without spending the additional funds necessary to accomplish this goal. In this case, econometric models serve as a useful guideline for what can be expected in terms of overall national or international growth for a given product or service.

Most manufacturing or trade firms utilize a system that closely monitors inventory stocks. Many programs that exist are designed to compare inventory/sales ratios with previous levels and longer-term trends. These programs generally work well if recent trends continue; but when sales change unexpectedly, econometric modeling often provides an additional dimension that will help optimize stocks and increase profit levels.

A typical problem encountered is the following. Sales have been rising at an average of 6% per year. One month they increase by 10% over year-earlier levels. That could mean (i) the economy is improving, (ii) the demand for the product has risen in spite of no change in macroeconomic conditions, (iii) the firm has gained market share relative to its competitors, (iv) the gain is a one-time fluke caused by exogenous conditions (batteries and flashlights were purchased ahead of a hurricane warning), or (v) random fluctuations have produced an increase that is not related to either economic conditions or exogenous variables. The challenge of the econometric model-builder is to help determine what really happened.

Alternatively, profits have been rising at a steady 15% per year, but in one quarter they do not increase at all. When reporting to stockholders, top management is likely to blame a variety of exogenous sources: bad weather, rising (or falling) commodity prices, the election, the World Series, insurrection in Afghanistan, and so on. Some of these events may have actually affected sales, but it is more likely that underlying demand slowed down or costs rose faster than anticipated. If top management cannot sort out these reasons quickly, their jobs are likely to be in jeopardy.

To answer questions of this sort, many firms belong to associations that publish industry data collected and processed by a third party (in order to avoid antitrust implications). That will indicate whether your gain has been shared by competitors or is at their expense. At the retail level, monthly figures published by the Census Bureau can provide guidance about how rapidly broad retail lines are growing; that data can also be used for comparative purposes.

In many cases, inventory decisions will be made at the micro level. Apparel stores will quickly find out what are "hot" items and which fashions are no longer being purchased this year. Supermarkets will stock their shelves with items that will move quickly – especially for perishable goods. Steel service centers will soon realize whether the demand is rising or falling for rods, beams, wire, and other items. When tens of thousands of items must be tracked, inventory management systems will invariably rely on ARIMA models, since it is difficult to keep track of the economic factors affecting thousands of different types of products or SKU items. Nonetheless, macro factors play an important role in determining overall demand. In many cases, optimal modeling efforts will blend these two types of variables.

Econometric models can help firms determine the level of capital spending, degree of expansion, amount spent on advertising, and method of managing and controlling inventories. Where past values are known, these data can be used as independent variables and elasticities can be calculated. Even if that information is not available, decisions can be made in the context of what growth rate can be expected from economic conditions, and how much that growth rate can be enhanced by variables that are determined internally.

9.2.3 VARIABLE REFLECTING COMPETITIVE RESPONSE

The third type of variable to be considered is the possible response by competitors. These variables are obviously not under the control of the firm – at least if it is acting legally – but in many cases can be anticipated. A price reduction will invariably be matched by the competition; if there are shortages, a price increase would be the more appropriate response. The news that a competitor plans to open a store across the street may initially come as a surprise, but during the construction period the existing firm will have time to react. The real issue is whether these competitive moves can be modeled econometrically.

We consider how these different types of variables might be incorporated into a model determining how fast loans are likely to grow for an individual bank. Federal privacy laws do not permit the dissemination of individual credit information on a public basis. However, based on work done by this author and his colleagues, the general approach can be sketched here.

First, determine the aggregate growth in the particular category of loans – consumer credit cards, auto loans, equipment leasing, home mortgages, commercial real estate, etc. – that can be expected based on macroeconomic conditions. Then estimate a regression equation relating the growth in loans to these variables plus interest rates, and generate forecasts using a specific macro model or consensus estimates. Suppose that, based on this regression, the projected growth in a particular category of loans was 8% per year for the next two years.

Second, the bank has to determine whether it wants to specialize in loans in its geographical area, where loan officers can meet potential borrowers personally and assess their character, or whether it wants to expand to other regions of the country. If the latter option is utilized, it can determine how much loan demand is likely to grow in rapidly expanding areas.

Third, it determines the amount that should be spent on (i) advertising, (ii) additional loan officers, and (iii) computerized credit scoring models in order to boost demand. In some cases, data will be available to estimate these parameters empirically; in other cases, the figures will be based on judgment by senior management.

Fourth, the bank needs to assess the competitive response by other banks. If, for example, a large bank in a major city mounts a vigorous advertising campaign stating that "for a limited time only, you can borrow money from us BELOW PRIME," they must take into consideration how competitors will react in order to preserve their market share. To a certain extent, reducing interest rates will increase loan demand; but since it will also cut into margins, it may be unprofitable. At a minimum, the bank would like to have estimates of how much a ½% cut in interest rates would boost its loan demand.

For the most part, forecast values for macroeconomic variables are estimated outside the firm. However, for variables under control of the firm, or those representing competitor response, top management may believe that judgment from the field can enhance forecasting accuracy. This raises the more general issue of how judgment should be incorporated in sales forecasting models.

9.3 THE ROLE OF JUDGMENT

Most executives assume they understand their business better than some outside consultant hired to build a model, or a staff economist who generally does not have the depth of experience. As a result, they sometimes claim that statistical modeling is no substitute for informed judgment. However, forecasts by management could be inaccurate for a variety of reasons. First, executives may prefer an optimistic forecast for reasons of morale. Second, they may be poorly informed about factors affecting the overall domestic or world economy, even though they understand the dynamics of their own business very well. Third, they may have a vested interest in seeing their own product lines perform well; that is particularly the case for new product development, which is discussed in the next chapter.

9.3.1 DEFLECTING EXCESS OPTIMISM

One of the hurdles many corporate economists face is that management prefers an optimistic forecast.[3] It may be seen as a morale booster, or an incentive to the sales force to sell more product. Many firms believe it is worthwhile to set sales targets "too high" in order to discourage slack performance by sales personnel. Top management might "tweak" credit scoring models in order to accept a larger proportion of loans. Production schedules may be set above realistic levels in order to encourage the sales force to increase their effort.

It is always possible that sales personnel will *underestimate* the likely sales growth, thus permitting them to exceed their quotas and earn additional bonuses. However, such attempts are generally seen as self-serving and are not likely to influence company forecasts. In this author's experience, it is much more common to hear that *this* company doesn't want any recession forecasts demoralizing their staff. Negative economic conditions ahead are seen as "opportunities" and "challenges" rather than nightmares, and many corporations like to infuse their staff with a "can do" mentality.

The problem is particularly severe for new product development, where the manager in charge of the new product or service naturally tends to have an optimistic outlook for its future. Yet even with existing products, the usual puffery that "our" product is better than anyone else's sometimes gets translated into overly optimistic forecasts. When these are not reached, excess inventory accumulates, too many people are hired, too many plants are built, and in extreme cases the company is forced to close. Mindless expansion of retail outlets is one key example of this sort of thinking, as is spending hundreds of millions of dollars on dot.com advertising without giving more than a passing thought to how much sales will rise.

Admittedly, the headline cases in the financial press generally tend to be the failures; when a company performs well because sales or product managers accurately predicted demand, that is deemed far less newsworthy. And turning a novice loose with an econometric model who has little understanding of the industry will invariably generate poorer forecasts than the expert judgment of an experienced product manager. Nonetheless, having said all this, there tends to be a "cheerleader" effect in which pessimistic forecasts are viewed as unwelcome.[4]

---

[3] For examples of this, see Walker, K. B., and L. A. McClelland, "Management Forecasts and Statistical Prediction Model Forecasts in Corporate Budgeting," *Journal of Accounting Research*, 29 (1991), 373–82. Also see Winklhofer, H., A. Diamantopoulous, and S. F. Witt, "Forecasting Practice: A Review of the Empirical Literature and an Agenda for Future Research," *International Journal of Forecasting.* 12 (1996), 193–221.

[4] The severe drawbacks to judgmental forecasts have long been noted. In an early work, P. E. Meehl found that judgmental forecasts were inferior to decision rules because people applied different factors at different times. See his book, *Clinical Versus Statistical Predictions: A Theoretical Analysis and Review of the Literature* (University of Minneapolis Press, Minneapolis), 1954. More recently, R. Hogarth and

Seasoned business judgment certainly should not be ignored. If sales of a particular product have been rising at 15% per year over the past 10 years, exogenous factors that could cause growth to decline to 5% next year must be carefully considered. Senior management may be aware of changes in the product, or in its method of delivery, that will have a material impact on its sales growth in the future. Econometricians ignore such factors at their own peril.

One of the oldest but nonetheless useful clichés in the financial sector is "never confuse genius with a bull market." This aphorism also applies to situations where sales of a particular good, after stagnating or growing at modest rates for several quarters, suddenly surge. Often the tendency is to assume that there has been a change for the better, whereas in many cases this improvement represents a temporary one-time shift. In these situations, management forecasts will often become too optimistic.

As these comments should make clear, no blanket statement can be issued about when judgment will or will not improve forecasting accuracy. However, in this author's experience, a number of useful rules of thumb have emerged, which can be summarized as follows.

1   In the *long run*, forecasts based primarily on technology invariably understate the actual growth that will occur; but in the *short run*, management tends to overstate the benefits from emerging technology. See: dot.com companies in 2000.
2   Judgmental forecasts are generally weighted too heavily by events of the recent past. If sales have been above average, that superior performance is expected to continue indefinitely. If sales have been sluggish, it is often the case that subpar performance is expected to continue.
3   Most judgmental forecasts miss turning points. Of course that is also true for many econometric forecasts. However, if signs of a recession are brewing, management too often assumes their sales will not be negatively affected.

9.3.2 THE IMPORTANCE OF ACCURATE MACROECONOMIC FORECASTS

Regardless of their expertise at running individual businesses, most top managers possess no special knowledge about the general state of the economy. Hence forecasts of company sales that override macroeconomic concerns are apt to be inaccurate. On the other hand, sales forecasts based on detailed knowledge of products or markets – precisely the sort of information that generally

---

S. Makridakis reached a similar conclusion in "Forecasting and Planning: An Evaluation," *Management Science*, 27 (1981), 115–38. For further discussion, see Makradakis et al., pp. 496–502.

cannot be used in an econometric model – will often help produce more accurate forecasts.

In this author's experience, forecasting errors that senior management generally make are not generally tied to individual product performance but reflect an inaccurate assessment of macroeconomic conditions. That is one of the reasons why the importance of macro forecasts is highlighted throughout this text. However, as also noted, macro forecasts have not had an outstanding track record in the past, which leads to the following suggestion.

In terms of communicating with top management, one of the best ways to overcome this problem is to prepare alternative scenarios for the macroeconomic drivers: optimistic, consensus, and pessimistic. In the past, it has been observed (say) that sales of a particular product line increase an average of 2% per year faster than the underlying economic drivers. Thus if the economy is expected to continue to advance at average rates, that relationship would continue to hold. If, however, the economy stumbles, sales would probably grow at a much slower rate. The same analysis could be applied to international developments – especially in view of the collapse of various economies around the world throughout the 1990s.

There may also be another reason for top management to phrase forecasts in conditional terms. Public companies are invariably requested to provide "guidance" to investment analysts, although in mid-2000 the requirement of "greater" public disclosure paradoxically led to less guidance to selected analysts. Sometimes, when earnings fall far short of expected targets, class action suits follow. If management were to state their expectations in terms of conditional forecasts, such lawsuits could usually be avoided. This will not solve all these problems all the time, but will often provide an additional safety net. Even if lawsuits are not the issue, management performance may appear to be more satisfactory in the eyes of the Board of Directors if the shortfall in sales reflects an unexpected decline in economic activity rather than poor business planning.

9.3.3 ASSESSING JUDGMENTAL INPUTS

These generalizations do not take us very far in determining the weight that should be given to judgment, field input, surveys, and consensus forecasts in generating sales forecasts. We need to be more specific.

As a first pass, one should judge the usefulness of such input on what has happened previously. If a given method – whether econometric or judgmental – has been used previously, one can determine whether these inputs have improved forecast accuracy. Even this method is not foolproof; if a bad forecast is made, it can be pointed out that Sales Manager X is no longer on the job, having been fired for his poor estimates, but Manager Y is much more adept at prediction. Conversely, Manager X did such a great job of forecasting that he moved on to a better job, and his replacement Y isn't as good. Nonetheless, in spite of the cliché that past performance is no guarantee of future accuracy, the track record of how well these methods have worked in the past should provide valuable guidance about whether they will be helpful in the future.

However, this doesn't cover all cases. Indeed, suppose that because of inferior forecasting performance in the past, a new team is assembled to try a new approach to forecasting. As part of this new approach, field surveys are commissioned, and input from the sales force, which had not previously been utilized, is also solicited.

In some cases, these judgmental factors should be included. Suppose that the quality of a particular product had been subpar, but the manufacturer remedied this defect, and various consumer surveys now show that quality has improved and consumers are beginning to recognize this. Sales would then be expected to rise much faster than levels predicted from a regression equation based on past experience. Sales and orders may also be influenced by new product lines, major trade shows, or a new advertising campaign. In such cases, judgment factors can reinforce the trends and cycles that would otherwise be predicted by regression analysis.

Sometimes independent judgment reinforces factors that would be captured by the underlying economic relationships. For example, a rise in housing starts will boost sales of home furnishings over the next several months, a relationship that presumably would be reflected by the regression equation and also indicated by input from the sales force.

What happens when the input from the field is markedly different from what the modeling process is showing? In most cases, the input is more optimistic; it is unusual for informed opinion to be unduly pessimistic. It is important to examine the reasons for this optimism. Claims that the sales force is better motivated, a new management team is in place, the company lost market share last year but will gain it back this year, etc., are generally worthless pieces of information. The customers will not buy more product just because the management team has improved. On the other hand, significant changes in product quality or service, different market positioning, increased advertising, etc., may have a significant impact on sales that would not be captured in the modeling process.

The importance of judgmental input can also depend on the degree to which product identification is important. A company selling steel finds its demand will not magically increase if the underlying demand for autos, construction, and machinery remains unchanged. Possibly one firm can take market share away from another, but except for price-cutting – which will invariably be matched by the competition – this is often wishful thinking. Conversely, a no. 1 rating by J. D. Power & Associates for an automobile brand that had not previously been ranked near the top would presumably boost sales over the following year. However, no econometric model would have adequately predicted the sales of Firestone tires in late 2000.

In this author's experience, the attempt to impose a greater degree of optimism on the forecasts based on outside experience, sales force input, and judgment of top management is usually unwarranted. Surveys are a different matter: surveys of consumer and homebuilder sentiment can improve forecast accuracy. General guidelines in these matters are as follows.

1   One should be cautious about using input from the field if there is no prior track record. Determine whether informed judgment or surveys improves forecast accuracy before incorporating it into the methodology.
2   Judgmental forecasts that are more optimistic than the econometric model approach should be supported by actual changes that have occurred, not just wishful thinking that this year will be better than last year.
3   Negative surprises, such as a competitor building a new plant or opening up across the street, a new international competitor, or the discovery of a product defect, should be taken into account even if they are not part of the previous modeling experience. If there has been a major change in government regulations, intervention analysis – the use of dummy variables to capture a shift in the underlying data generation function – may be warranted.

To the extent that judgment from the sales force and senior management reflects a change in product quality, advertising strategy, or expansion, the forecast should also be adjusted by those explicit factors. Conversely, claims that sales really ought to be better this year because they were disappointing last year are unlikely to have any correlation with sales performance. The vaguer the reasoning, the less likely the input will affect the actual change in sales.

To summarize this section, if judgmental factors are based on changes in product design or quality or marketing strategies, they should usually be included in the forecast equation. If they are based on vague assurances that "we really ought to do better this year," they can safely be ignored.

9.4 PRESENTING SALES FORECASTS

This section offers abbreviated versions of the type of presentations this author has made to top management. However, before presenting these examples, we offer several comments about presenting the forecast to top management. These comments are based on factors found to be useful in presentations over the past 30 years.

In making a presentation, management invariably wants to know what is going to happen to sales and profits of their company, usually by major product line or division. A general discussion of where the overall economy is heading is only of limited interest. Having said that, however, a simple declarative statement that sales are going to rise 6.3% next year – *even if accurate* – will not impress very many managers. The thought process is at least as important as the ultimate result, although both are expected to be clearly presented and accurate.

Any presentation of the overall economic environment should be tailored to the type of product or service being forecast. If the product is a cyclical consumer or capital good, variables that determine overall consumer and capital spending are generally most important, including consumer and business sentiment. Indeed, where consumer goods are being predicted, a brief discussion of consumer confidence is usually appropriate. There is no comparable variable of business confidence for capital spending; the NAPM (National Association of Purchasing Managers) index is generally viewed as an accurate snapshot of the current state of manufacturing, but has little predictive value.

Interest rates are almost always important; even if the industry is not cyclically sensitive, the cost of financing inventories, new capital expenditures, expansions, or mergers and acquisitions is also important. In many cases, the fluctuations in the stock market are an important determinant of sales, but since most people think "you can't predict the market," alternative scenarios are generally considered useful.

If the foreign arena is of interest and importance, the forecasts of key foreign currencies – the yen, pound sterling, euro, Canadian dollar, and possibly the Mexican peso and the Australian dollar – should be presented. A general scenario of growth in major regions of the world will usually suffice, although if the company or industry in question has a major investment in some volatile part of the world, that deserves further mention.

Early in the presentation, the consultant should present a list of the key drivers that affect their markets. The forecasts for these variables should be summarized, followed by a discussion of how variables affect the company or industry markets being predicted. After these have been presented, it is often useful to show the actual and simulated values for the underlying equations. In some cases it may be worthwhile to show what would happen if estimated instead of actual values were used for the independent variables (dynamic simulations)

Managers and clients generally will often want to see how well the equation fits over the sample period, on the logical ground that it certainly will not do any better when true ex ante forecasts are generated. The actual statistics should always be held available in case anyone questions the results, but most managers are not interested in t-ratios, Durbin–Watson statistics, or the Schwarz criterion. Instead, a simple graph showing actual and forecast values should be sufficient.

The drivers should usually be represented in elasticities: for example, a 1% change in variable X causes an 0.4% change in the dependent variable. If lags are used for the independent variables, the lag structure should be briefly summarized, although few are interested in the intricacies of polynomial distributed lags.

Finally, managers generally expect to hear a discussion of the forecast risks, usually by including alternative scenarios with estimated percentage for each case. Especially after a recovery has been ongoing for several years, a discussion of when the next recession is likely to occur is usually relevant. If the company or industry has an international presence, a discussion of the economic trouble spots around the world is appropriate at this juncture. If the business of the client is directly related to commodity prices – agriculture, energy, metals, or lumber – a synopsis covering the alternative possibilities of major changes in prices in either direction is warranted.

The remainder of this chapter consists of abbreviated versions of actual presentations made by this author to various clients. The confidential company or industry data used cannot be reproduced here, so published industry data are substituted, but the systematic approach is the same. Two examples are presented: one for capital goods, where management is primarily interested in annual changes, and the other for consumer goods, where the key factor of interest to management is the level of sales this month relative to a year ago. Both presentations are designed for short-term forecasting one to two years in advance; long-term trend projections are covered in the following chapter. In both cases, the general approach follows the same structure:

- graphical explanation of the key drivers affecting the variable to be predicted
- presentation of the actual equation used for forecasting
- discussion of the macroeconomic outlook
- discussion of other key factors in the equation (if relevant)
- presentation of standard forecast for the next two years
- discussion of other variables that could be relevant, including judgmental factors
- alternative scenarios and associated probabilities
- presentation of alternative forecasts for next two years

In general, these graphs and charts are extracted from PowerPoint presentations; in the interests of space, some of the intermediate text has been omitted. The message is to indicate what is relevant for presentations to clients or top management, and what should generally be omitted. While the researcher will presumably have undertaken a wide variety of structural tests to verify stability, they are not included in these presentations because the client is seldom interested in a barrage of statistical details.

9.4.1 PURCHASES OF CONSTRUCTION EQUIPMENT

Predicting changes in various components of capital spending is one of the areas in which econometric modeling is often thought to be useful because the wide cyclical swings are tied to clearly defined and measurable economic forces. In the presentation given below, NIPA[5] data are used; in practice, this author used confidential industry data collected by an association of firms in this industry.

---

[5] National Income and Product Accounts.

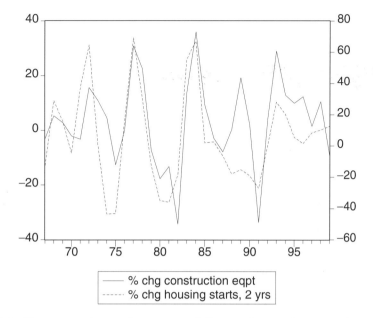

Figure 9.1   Percentage changes in constant-dollar purchases of construction equipment and housing starts over two years.

PRINCIPAL DRIVERS

- Change in housing starts over the past two years
- Credit availability, as measured by the yield spread between the Aaa corporate bond rate and the Federal funds rate, also over the past two years
- Change in oil prices, lagged one year

Correlations of the dependent variable with key drivers are shown in figures 9.1 and 9.2. The dependent variable is the annual percentage change in purchases of construction equipment in constant dollars. (Note: the change in oil prices is not shown here, for while it has a high partial correlation, the simple correlation is low.)

PRESENTATION AND DISCUSSION OF EQUATION

The equation used for forecasting is as follows. The actual and simulated percentage changes are shown in figure 9.3. The figures in parentheses are *t*-ratios.

%chg(*construction equipment*)
$$= 9.00 + 0.363 * \%chg(\textit{housing starts}) + 0.146 * \%chg(\textit{oil prices}) + 5.46 * \%\textit{yldsprd}$$
$$(5.9) \qquad\qquad\qquad (2.7) \qquad\qquad\qquad (5.0)$$
$$RSQ = 0.70; DW 2.02.$$

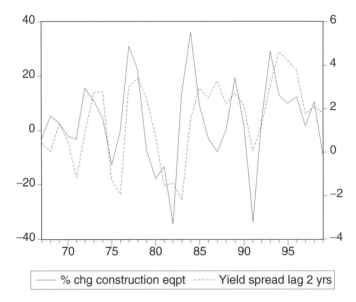

Figure 9.2 Percentage change in constant-dollar purchases of construction equipment, and the yield spread between the Aaa corporate bond rate and the Federal funds rate lagged two years.

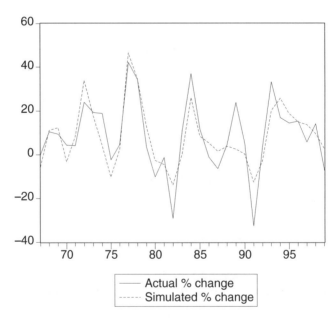

Figure 9.3 Percentage change in investment in construction equipment (constant dollars) as a function of the change in housing starts, the yield spread, and change in oil prices.

The percentage changes in housing starts and oil prices are calculated over the a two-year period. The *yldsprd* term is the difference between the Aaa corporate bond rate and the Federal funds rate; it also has a two-year distributed lag, with weights of 0.4 for the first year and 0.6 for the second year.

Except for the yield spread term, the coefficients are elasticities. Purchases of construction equipment will change 0.36% for each 1% change in housing starts, and 0.15% for each 1% change in oil prices. A one percentage point change in the yield spread – e.g., from 1% to 2% – will change purchases by 5.5%.

THE MACROECONOMIC OUTLOOK

The macroeconomic outlook is discussed next. At the end of 2000, the main points of interest were the following. First, the economy is slowing down, and the Fed is expected to ease in early 2001. Because of the lags involved, though, that would not boost purchases of construction equipment very much until 2002. Second, housing starts are expected to improve substantially in 2001, although to a certain extent the decline in interest rates would be partially offset by weaker consumer confidence and a sluggish stock market. Third, it was assumed oil prices would return to about $25/bbl, but an alternative scenario analysis was prepared since no one really knows what will happen to oil prices. Several slides were prepared (not included here) showing the most likely forecasts of these three variables.

At this point some questions from management or the client can be anticipated. First, the availability of credit has been discussed, but what about the cost? Second, what about the F. W. Dodge index of construction contracts, since only residential construction appears to be included in this equation? Third, what about attitude variables as represented by the index of consumer sentiment and stock prices?

In fact all of these variables and many others were tried in the regression equation and were found to be insignificant, but that is not usually the answer management wants to hear. Another approach is warranted. You should explain that while the cost of credit is also important, it is highly correlated with the availability of credit, and is also included indirectly through the importance of mortgage rates in the housing start equation. You can also note that since bond rates already declined in the second half of 2000 in anticipation of Fed easing, they are unlikely to decline much more over the next year or two.

The second issue needs to be finessed somewhat differently, since one would ordinarily expect that changes in non-residential construction would be a major variable in this equation. Initially we had also expected to find that. The actual result is shown in figure 9.4, which illustrates the lack of correlation between the percentage change in construction contracts as measured by F. W. Dodge and the residuals from the equation on which the forecasts are based. However, that is not the best answer to management. It is better to base your answer on

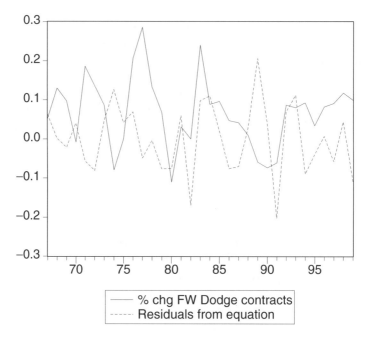

Figure 9.4 There is no correlation between the percentage change in construction contracts reported by F. W. Dodge and residuals from the equation for construction equipment.

the relationship shown in figure 9.5, which indicates that the correlation between Dodge contracts and actual purchases of construction equipment has weakened in recent years. Explain that contracts for non-residential construction increasingly lag behind changes in economic activity because of the increased delays in obtaining permits and other legal documents, so they now serve as a lagging rather than a leading indicator.

Finally, consumer confidence and the stock market can be discussed. In this case it is useful to point out that the surge in both these variables in 1999 was actually accompanied by a decline in purchases of construction equipment, largely because of the decline in oil prices and the aforementioned difficultly in obtaining permits. One can also concede that, although these variables are still important over the longer run, they have not recently been correlated with annual changes.

DISCUSSION OF STANDARD AND ALTERNATIVE SCENARIOS

At this point, forecasts should be presented for (i) the most likely, or "standard" economic forecast, (ii) an optimistic forecast in which the Fed eases soon and housing starts rebound rapidly, (iii) an alternative in which oil prices remain at $35/bbl but interest rates are little changed, and (iv) another alternative in

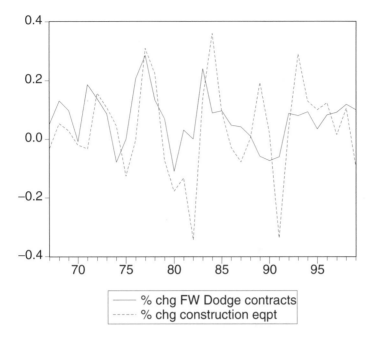

Figure 9.5 In recent years, changes in construction contracts as reported by F. W. Dodge have not closely tracked changes in purchases of construction company equipment.

which high oil prices causes the Fed to tighten, hence reducing the availability of credit and housing starts. Ordinarily these would be termed "pessimistic," but in the case of construction equipment, higher oil prices helps their business. In terms of the model, these assumptions can be summarized as in table 9.1.

The outlook for the percentage change in purchases of construction equipment in constant dollars based on these four alternatives is given in the bar graph in figure 9.6.

Note that the gain in construction equipment purchases in 2001 is likely to be robust in spite of slower growth in the economy because of the lagged impact of higher oil prices and previous increases in housing starts. In 2002, by comparison, the lagged effects of the tightening of credit conditions and slowdown in housing starts should result in much more modest gains in purchases of construction equipment. Also, oil prices probably will not rise above peak 2000 levels.

That concludes this presentation. However, the reader may legitimately raise the issue of whether this example is "too simple," in the sense that it does not seem to use many of the sophisticated statistical and econometric tools discussed elsewhere in this text. Also, annual data have been used instead of quarterly data, which greatly simplifies the lag structure. These points are addressed in the next example.

Table 9.1 Forecasts.

	2000	2001	2002
Level of housing starts			
Standard	1.60	1.60	1.65
Optimistic	1.60	1.70	1.80
High oil prices	1.60	1.55	1.55
Fed tightens	1.60	1.40	1.50
Yield spread			
Standard	1.4	1.0	1.5
Optimistic	1.4	2.0	2.0
High oil prices	1.0	1.0	1.0
Fed tightens	1.0	−1.0	0.0
Level of oil prices ($/bbl)			
Standard	27	25	25
Optimistic	27	20	20
High oil prices	27	35	35
Fed tightens	27	35	35

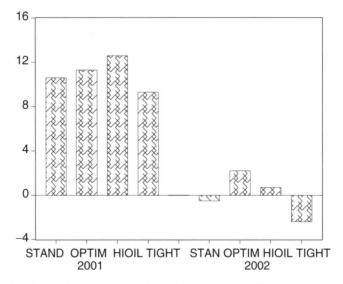

Figure 9.6 Forecasts for percentage change in purchases of construction equipment (in constant dollars), 2001 and 2002.

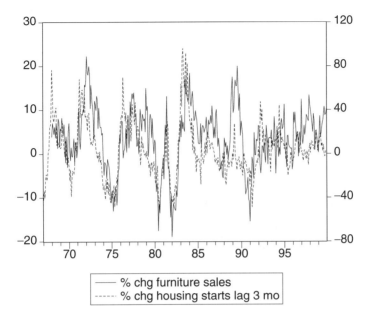

Figure 9.7 Percentage change over year-earlier levels for constant-dollar furniture sales and housing starts lagged three months.

9.4.2 RETAIL FURNITURE SALES

This example focuses on percentage changes from year-earlier levels at retail furniture stores. In this case the list of drivers is substantially larger and the lag structure is more complicated, although the specific details are not communicated to the client. The dependent variable is the percentage change in retail furniture store sales from year-earlier levels in constant dollars. All independent variables are also 12-month percentage changes except the yield spread, which is in levels.

PRINCIPAL DRIVERS

- Disposable income
- Housing starts
- Sales of new homes
- Yield spread between corporate bonds and the Federal funds rate
- Stock prices
- Consumer confidence
- Price of furniture

Figures 9.7–9.10 show the correlation of the change in furniture sales with housing starts, consumer confidence, stock prices, and the yield spread.

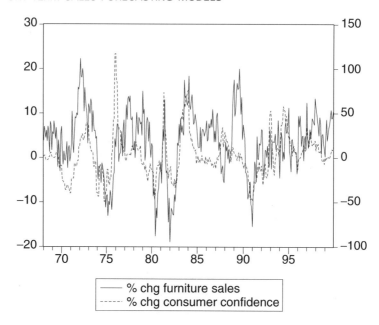

Figure 9.8 Percentage change over year-earlier levels for constant-dollar furniture sales and the Conference Board index of consumer confidence.

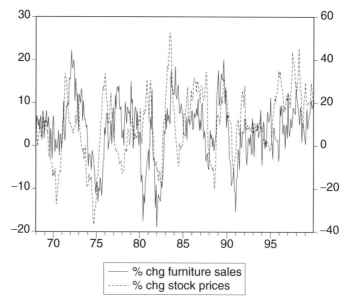

Figure 9.9 Percentage change over year-earlier levels for constant-dollar furniture sales and the S&P 500 index of stock prices.

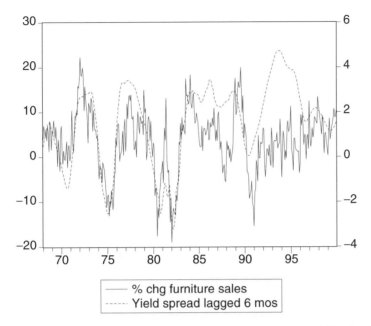

Figure 9.10 Percentage change over year-earlier levels for constant-dollar furniture sales and a 12-month moving average of the yield spread lagged six months.

PRESENTATION AND DISCUSSION OF EQUATION

The actual equation is given below. A 24-month cubic PDL constrained at the far end is used for real disposable income, but that detail is not included in the presentation. Instead, we say that a weighted average of disposable income over the past two years is used. The percentage changes of all other variables are over one year, with the starting points of the lag indicated in the regression equation. In this and all other equations presented in the chapter, a number in parentheses following the variable indicates the beginning period of the lag, while the number after the comma is the length of lag.

$\%\,furniture\ sales,12$

$$= -5.14 + 0.61 * yldsprd(-8),12 + 0.066 * \%consumer\ confidence,12$$

$$(3.5) \qquad\qquad\qquad (5.0)$$

$$+ 0.053 * \%stock\ prices,12 - 0.41 * \%\,furniture\ prices,12$$

$$(2.8) \qquad\qquad\qquad (3.5)$$

$$+ 0.035 * \%new\ home\ sales(-2),12 + 0.051 * \%housing\ starts(-3),12$$

$$(2.2) \qquad\qquad\qquad (3.6)$$

$$+ 2.49 * \%disposable\ income,24$$

$$(11.9)$$

$$RSQ = 0.61;\ DW = 0.80.$$

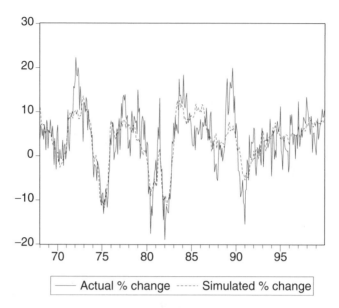

Figure 9.11 Percentage change over year-earlier levels for constant-dollar furniture sales compared with simulated values.

The discussion of the equation follows next. Note the high income elasticity, which is almost $2\frac{1}{2}$; a 1% change in real personal disposable income will change furniture sales by $2\frac{1}{2}$%. Also note the longer lag on the yield spread, which is a true leading indicator: it changes well before any components of aggregate demand. The actual and simulated percentage changes are given in figure 9.11.

DISCUSSION OF STANDARD AND ALTERNATIVE SCENARIOS

At this point, the macroeconomic outlook is discussed. However, since those comments were already provided in the previous example, they are not repeated here. Instead, we move directly to the table showing alternative assumptions for the next two years. In this case the "wild card" – the variable that is most unpredictable – is the stock market. Hence the following four scenarios are considered: (i) the standard forecast, (ii) a pessimistic "hard landing" forecast for 2001, (iii) an optimistic forecast with a major stock market rally, and (iv) an optimistic forecast with only a modest stock market rally. The assumptions are given in table 9.2.

The price of furniture is not listed explicitly. If these forecasts are designed for an industry or trade association, offering predictions of explicit prices could be construed as a violation of antitrust law. Instead, the assumption is made

Table 9.2 Assumptions.

	2000	2001	2002
Level of housing starts			
Standard	1.60	1.60	1.65
Pessimistic	1.60	1.40	1.50
Optimistic, large gain in stock prices	1.60	1.70	1.80
Optimistic, moderate gain in stock prices	1.60	1.68	1.75
Level of new home sales			
Standard	900	850	900
Pessimistic	900	800	850
Optimistic, large gain in stock prices	900	925	950
Optimistic, moderate gain in stock prices	900	925	950
Yield spread			
Standard	1.4	1.0	1.5
Pessimistic	1.0	−1.0	1.0
Optimistic, large gain in stock prices	1.4	2.0	2.0
Optimistic, moderate gain in stock prices	1.4	2.0	2.0
Change in personal disposable income			
Standard	3.1	2.5	3.5
Pessimistic	3.1	2.0	2.5
Optimistic, large gain in stock prices	3.1	4.0	4.0
Optimistic, moderate gain in stock prices	3.1	4.0	4.0
Index of consumer confidence			
Standard	138	142	144
Pessimistic	138	120	130
Optimistic, large gain in stock prices	138	148	152
Optimistic, moderate gain in stock prices	138	144	146
S&P 500 index of stock prices, % change			
Standard	−2.0	5.0	8.0
Pessimistic	−5.0	−15.0	20.0
Optimistic, large gain in stock prices	−2.0	20.0	15.0
Optimistic, moderate gain in stock prices	−2.0	5.0	8.0

that furniture prices will continue their pattern of recent years, which is no change – the level of furniture prices, according to BEA, was the same in late 2000 as it was in late 1994. For those who wish to pursue the issue further by inserting their own price forecasts, the estimated price elasticity is approximately −0.4.

Figure 9.12 shows the forecasts for 2001 and 2002 based on these four alternative assumptions.

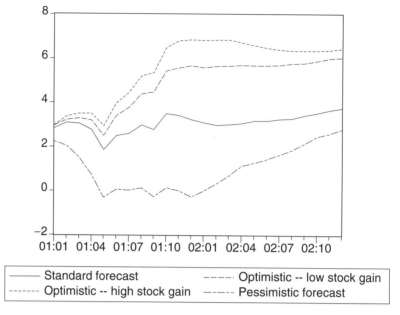

Figure 9.12 Percentage change over year-earlier levels for constant-dollar furniture sales based on alternative macroeconomic assumptions.

Unlike the forecast for construction equipment, which depends largely on lagged variables, this graph shows a wide variety of options for furniture sales, ranging from 7% for the very optimistic forecast to an actual decline for the pessimistic forecast. Under the standard forecast, sales would rise only about 3% per year over the next two years, compared with about 9% in 2000. That reflects the decline in housing starts and stock prices that have already occurred. Sometimes it is appropriate to assign weights to these various forecasts; for example, 50% to the standard forecast, 20% to the moderately optimistic outlook, 20% for the very optimistic outlook, and 10% for the pessimistic forecast. That would give a weighted average gain of about 4% for furniture sales in 2001 and about 5% in 2002. If management is pessimistic about the overall economy, however, they should be made aware of the fact that, at least based on historical evidence, that would point to virtually no gain in furniture sales next year.

Case Study 19: The Demand for Bicycles

We now turn to the development of a sales forecasting model for bicycles. The data are based on monthly figures for total bicycle sales calculated by the US Commerce Department, and start in 1959. Rather than simply presenting the final results, we will show how this model is derived step by step.

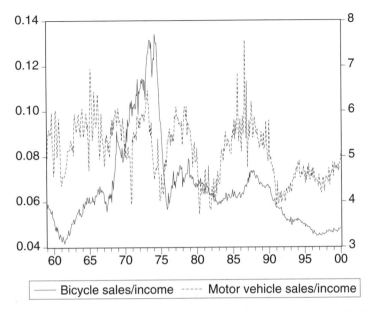

Figure 9.13 Bicycle and motor vehicle sales as a percentage of disposable income (all figures in constant dollars).

The first step is to graph the ratio of bicycle sales to total disposable income, and compare this with the ratio of car sales to income to see whether there is any correlation. Car sales are chosen because (i) both are methods of transportation, and (ii) car sales is a macro variable for which consensus forecasts are already available. The results are shown in figure 9.13.

Several factors are apparent from this graph. First, bicycle sales lag motor vehicle sales by an average of 1–2 years; the precise lag structure can be determined empirically. Second, a huge surge in bicycle sales occurred in the early 1970s that has never been repeated. Third, the overall correlation between these two variables is not very high; other variables will obviously be needed.

The surge in bicycle sales from 1968 to 1973, and its disappearance thereafter, deserves further comment, and indeed points out the limitations of econometric analysis. It would be possible, by judicious juggling of independent variables for population, income, credit, and other terms, to explain this bulge, but that would be a useless exercise for forecasting purposes. What really happened is that the social unrest associated with the Vietnam War generated a desire in some younger members of society to move away from "gas guzzlers" and other material goods and move back to a simpler age when bicycles were more important. The end of the Vietnam war, the resignation of Nixon, and the ensuing recession after the first energy shock brought that era to a quick end.

Is this just ex post rationalization, or was this known at the time? In fact, this example is based on an actual model the author and colleagues built many years ago for a leading bicycle manufacturer. In the late 1960s, there was a sharp upsurge in the number of bicycles purchased by "trendy New Yorkers," so it was assumed that trend would spread to the rest of the country, which did indeed occur later. When those same New Yorkers stopped buying bicycles, the national sales curve dipped about a year later. The fact that income dropped, unemployment rose, interest rates increased, credit was tightened, and oil prices rose may all have been contributing factors, but could not explain most of the cyclical effect that actually occurred. In this case, exogenous judgment was required to generate accurate forecasts.

Now fast forward to 2000, and assume you are given the assignment of building – or updating – a model to predict bicycle sales. For practical purposes, the era of the late 1960s and early 1970s is irrelevant for predicting sales in the future; on a statistical basis, one can quickly verify that assumption by estimating the function for pre-1977 and post-1977 periods and noting that the parameter estimates are significantly different.

Consider the data from 1977 through 1999. The correlation with motor vehicle sales lagged one to two years still exists, but what other variables should be added? One likely choice is population: younger people are more likely to buy bicycles than older people. After experimenting with the ratio of population for various age groups divided by total population, the most significant ratios were for people aged 16–19, 20–24, and 25–29.

However, that equation does not work very well. The population ratio for those aged 20–24 is not significant, even though that should be one of the prime age groups. Second, the DW is very low. Third, that equation misses the declines in 1980, 1985, and 1991, and the surge in 1987.

Perhaps some index of consumer sentiment, such as the one published by the Conference Board, should be added. Also, while oil prices should not affect bicycle sales negatively, high oil prices may be associated with negative sentiment that is not measured in the usual indexes, whereas a drop in oil prices boosts sentiment and also increases discretionary income. The unemployment rate and stock market might also serve as useful measures of consumer sentiment.

The equation is reestimated with those variables, but they are barely significant, and the DW remains very low. The next step is to try adding an AR(1) adjustment. However, that merely reveals that the series is essentially a random walk; the AR coefficient is 0.997, and none of the other variables is significant with the correct sign except for the unemployment rate. So far it might seem that nothing has been accomplished.

The trend has already been removed from the series for bicycle sales through dividing by disposable income; yet the residuals still exhibit a very high degree of serial correlation. That suggests using some differencing method. Taking percentage changes of the monthly data yields essentially a random series with an adjusted R^2 of only 0.03. However, taking annual percentage changes – i.e., this

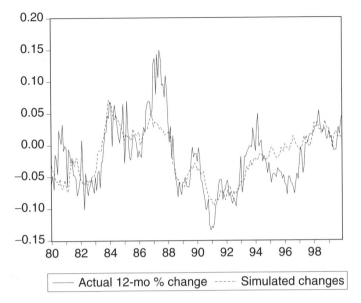

Figure 9.14 Actual and simulated 12-month percentage changes in the ratio of bicycle sales to personal income (both in constant dollars).

month relative to the same month a year ago – provides more usable figures. The regression estimated in annual percentage change form is as follows; the actual and simulated values are shown in figure 9.14.

$$\%BIRAT,12$$
$$= -0.009 + 0.367 * \%POPRAT16,12 + 0.626 * \%POPRAT20,12$$
$$\quad\quad (2.9) \quad\quad\quad\quad\quad\quad\quad\quad (3.2)$$
$$+ 0.766 * \%POPRAT25,12 - 0.084 * \%RPGAS,24 + 0.102 * \%SPRAT(-6),12$$
$$\quad (5.2) \quad\quad\quad\quad\quad\quad (5.6) \quad\quad\quad\quad\quad\quad (4.8)$$
$$- 0.012 * \Delta UN,12 + 0.0062 * CARRAT(-12),12$$
$$\quad (3.5) \quad\quad\quad\quad (4.7)$$
$$RSQ = 0.530; DW = 0.49$$
$$\text{Sample period } 1980.01 - 1999.12$$

where *BIRAT* is the ratio of bicycle sales to disposable income, *POPRAT16* is the ratio of population aged 16–19 to total population, *POPRAT20* is the ratio of population aged 20–24 to total population, *POPRAT25* is the ratio of population aged 25–29 to total population, *RPGAS* is the relative price of gasoline, *SPRAT* is the ratio of S&P 500 stock price index to disposable income, *UN* is the unemployment rate, and *CARRAT* is the ratio of motor vehicle sales to disposable income.

At this point, we should quickly review the steps that have been taken. *First*, the dependent variable was divided by income and compared with the ratio of car sales to income. *Second*, various population variables were added. *Third*, various attitudinal variables were added. *Fourth*, the equation was tried with an AR(1) transformation, but without success. *Fifth*, monthly percentage first differences were used, but also without success. *Sixth*, the variables were transformed into annual percentage changes, with much more satisfactory results. This is typical of the amount of experimentation that is necessary in building a forecast model.

This equation is still far from perfect – note the low DW statistic – but at least all of the variables make sense. Both population terms are significant with the correct sign, gasoline prices are significant with a negative sign, motor vehicle sales are significant with an average lag of 18 months, and stock prices and the unemployment rate are also significant. Since the residuals are still highly correlated, the equation is once again reestimated using the AR(1) transformation. Here again, the results are not very robust, and most of the variables are only marginally significant; in particular, the stock market variable drops out.

The final equation – without the AR(1) adjustment – shows that the annual percentage change in the ratio of bicycle sales to disposable income is a function of the ratio of motor vehicle sales to disposable income, lagged $1\frac{1}{2}$ years; changes in population for groups aged 16–19, 20–24, and 25–29; the change in the relative price of gasoline over the past two years; and consumer attitudes as represented by changes in the stock market and the unemployment rate. When these variables are included, the Conference Board index of consumer sentiment is not significant.

There is still the bothersome detail of the low DW statistic. One standard test is to reestimate the equation to the end of 1997 with and without the AR(1) term and then use those parameters to predict 1998 and 1999 sales. The results are revealing: the RMS error with the AR(1) term is 72.4 (million dollars), while it is only 53.2 without the AR(1) term. For comparative purposes, the average value of bicycle sales during that period was $3.04 billion. That result is fully comparable with results obtained for other equations in this text.

One final note on the low DW statistic. Recall that the data used here are on Commerce Department statistics and hence are smoothed; the regressions that we calculated with actual company data did not exhibit the same autocorrelation problem. In many cases, where data have been artificially smoothed by methods of data collection, a low DW does not necessarily indicate that the equation is misspecified, or that variables have been omitted. It often means the Commerce Department has smoothed the data.

Only a small proportion of the steps actually taken to estimate this model have been shown; the rest represented empirical experimentation with the lag structure. The variables included in this equation are what one would ordinarily expect in an equation for a discretionary purchase: income (as reflected by using the ratio form), population trends, and attitudinal variables. While it would have been possible to improve the sample period fit by "squeezing" some of the larger outlying residuals, our experience suggests this would not improve the forecast accuracy.

What about using an ARMA model? The optimal structure is (2,2) for levels, but the process is non-stationary, so an ARIMA model is indicated. The optimal structure is (2,1,2). However, the RMSE error for the 1998.01–1999.12 period is 157 when converted back to levels form, compared with 53.2 for the structural equation, so that approach is not useful here.

The lessons that can be learned from this example that are generally applicable to building short-term sales forecasting models and using them for forecasting and are summarized next:

1   If the series in question shows growth rates that are inconsistent with historical perspective, check to see whether one-time exogenous factors are at work. If they are, the econometric approach should be combined with judgment.
2   Determine the relationship between sales of this product and relevant consumer or capital spending variables, with particular attention to the lag structure, since short-term forecasting accuracy will be improved if lagged values of the independent variables can be used.
3   It may be necessary to experiment with alternative forms of the dependent variable: in this case, neither levels nor monthly percentage changes generated reasonable results, but annual percentage changes worked much better.
4   Adjusting for autocorrelation is likely to result in larger forecasting errors, even though the sample period statistics appear to be more robust. Hence one should always generate ex post forecasts with and without the AR(1) term to check this possibility.

Case Study 20: New Orders for Machine Tools

New orders for machine tools, besides being an important variable in its own right, are often considered a key leading indicator for the entire economy, since "machines that build machines" are at the heart of industrial investment. Admittedly this series does not carry as much clout in the high-tech era, but the equation is still indicative of many similar equations that could be estimated for capital goods new orders.

The data for constant-dollar new orders for machine tools are graphed, and appear to have no significant trend. Hence the initial choice of independent variables would also be trendless. The usual variables in an equation for capital goods would include both variables that measure output or capacity utilization, and variables that reflect the cost and availability of credit, such as the real bond rate and the percentage change in real commercial loans. Both of these variables are lagged, although since the dependent variable is a series for orders rather than shipments, the lags are shorter than would be the case for an equation predicting shipments or purchases of capital goods.

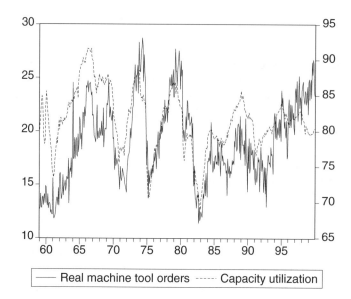

Figure 9.15 While both these series are trendless, machine tool orders have tended to rise over time relative to capacity utilization.

Figure 9.15 shows the data for machine tools and the rate of capacity utilization for the manufacturing sector. Note that while neither series has a strong time trend, machine tool orders have tended to rise over time relative to the rate of capacity utilization. That suggests the introduction of an additional variable that does include a time trend, one logical choice being the level of industrial production.

The cost of credit is measured as the Aaa corporate bond yield minus the five-year average rate of inflation, and the availability of credit is measured by the percentage change in real commercial and industrial loans. The unemployment rate represents the fact that when unemployment is low, firms are more likely to increase their capital spending, ceteris paribus. Most of the estimation work undertaken is used to determine the lag structure that appears to provide the best sample-period statistics and the best ex post forecasts. The final equation is

$$MCHTOOL$$
$$= -18.43 + 0.081 * CUMFG, 3 + 0.080 * IP(-8) - 0.694 * UN, 12$$
$$(16.1) \qquad\qquad (19.8) \qquad\qquad (7.6)$$
$$+ 0.046 * \%LOANS(-12), 12 - 1.324 * RAAA(-3), 12$$
$$(4.3) \qquad\qquad\qquad (22.3)$$
$$RSQ = 0.781; DW = 0.88; SE = 1.67;$$
$$\text{Sample period } 1980.01 - 1999.12$$

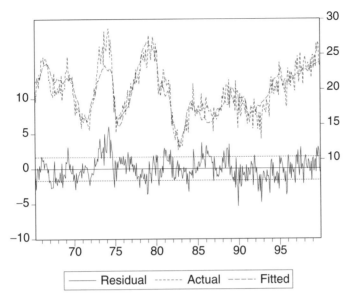

Figure 9.16 Actual and predicted values of machine tool orders.

where *MCHTOOL* is new orders for machine tools in constant dollars, *CUMFG* is the capacity utilization rate for manufacturing (lag weights are 3:2:1), *IP* is industrial production for manufacturing, *UN* is the unemployment rate, *LOANS* is commercial and industrial loans in constant dollars, and *RAAA* is the real Aaa corporate bond rate.

The graph of the actual versus simulated values is given in figure 9.16. Most of the cyclical swings are adequately tracked, as is the increase during the 1990s. The DW statistic is still too low by standard tests; however, if the sample period starts in 1977, it rises substantially; furthermore, all the variables remain significant and the coefficients do not change very much.

One again the issue arises about whether this equation would predict better with an AR(1) adjustment. The sample period is truncated in 1997 and then used to predict 1998 and 1999 values with and without the AR(1) term. The RMS error is 2.01 without the AR(1) term and 2.18 with it. Here again, the autocorrelation adjustment increases the forecast error. The standard error for the 1997–9 period for the ARIMA(2,1,2) model is 4.30, so that formulation is not considered further.

Nonetheless, this equation does not predict very well. The equation can be reestimated through 1996 and then used to predict monthly values for 1997 through 1999, with the results shown in figure 9.17. Almost all of the actual values are above the simulated estimates. This suggests adjusting the constant term. The average absolute error of the residuals shown in figure 9.16 for 1997 is $1.22 billion; almost all the residuals are positive. That average error can be

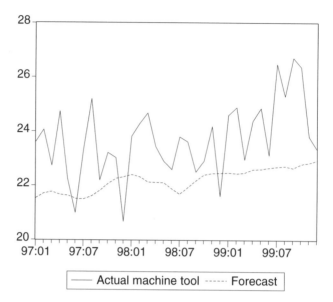

Figure 9.17   From 1997 through 1999, actual values of machine tool orders were above predicted values.

added to the 1998 forecasts, raising each monthly prediction by 1.22. Since the average error is 1.19, that means the adjusted 1998 error would be almost zero. For 1999 the error is a somewhat larger 2.08; but even so, using the 1.22 adjustment would reduce the forecast error by more than half, lowering it to 0.86. If the equation is reestimated to 1999, the average absolute error for the 1999 residuals is 1.12, still higher than 0.86.

While the demand for machine tools was above the simulated value for the 1997–9 period, the error was within the range indicated by the standard error of the estimate, so there is no evidence of a shifting function. Since almost all of the residuals were positive, using this information means that a constant adjustment based on the 1997 residuals can help improve the forecasts for the next two years. When the residuals follow a consistent pattern, forecasting error can generally be reduced significantly by using this additional information.

Case Study 21: Purchases of Farm Equipment

The final case study in this chapter presents the estimation of a quarterly function for constant-dollar purchases of farm machinery. Since both machine tools and farm equipment are components of capital spending, this may appear to be a similar exercise, but there is an important difference. Purchases of machine

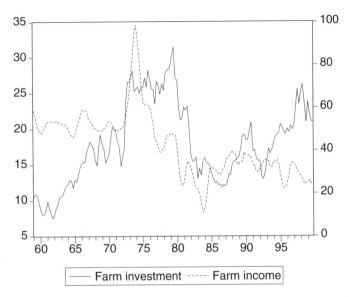

Figure 9.18 There is no simple correlation between farm investment and farm income (both in constant dollars).

tools are tied primarily to macroeconomic variables. Purchases of farm equipment, on the other hand, are primarily related to agricultural variables: prices, production, income, and exports. Credit conditions are important but other macroeconomic variables are not.

It is often said that economists – like most other researchers – would much rather present their successes rather than their failures. The farm equipment equation provides an example of an equation that appeared to work well for years, but went off the track recently. Nonetheless some important lessons can be learned.

The first step is to graph the pattern of constant-dollar purchases of farm equipment and farm income, as shown in figure 9.18. However, that is not a very promising start, since there appears to be no correlation between these two variables; even with a substantial lag.

As shown below, farm income is an important determinant of farm investment, as would be expected, but only when other variables are included in the equation. In this case, a snap judgment cannot be made just by looking at simple correlations.

The estimated equation is as follows. An earlier version of this equation was prepared for several leading farm equipment manufacturers in the mid-1960s and updated periodically. In general, it worked well for several decades.

INVFARM

$$= 37.5 + 0.132 * \%ACREAGE, 4 + 0.463 * INFL, 8 + 0.658 * \%CRED$$

$$(4.5) \qquad\qquad (9.1) \qquad\qquad (5.1)$$

$$-1.04 * FAAA + 0.077 * \%YFH, 4 + 39.5 * DITC, 4 - 30.1 * D67$$

$$(9.6) \qquad\quad (5.8) \qquad\qquad\quad (8.2) \qquad\qquad (20.9)$$

$$-0.196 * DOLLAR, 4 * D67 + 0.062 * \%LOAN + 5.25 * DFARM$$

$$(15.0) \qquad\qquad\qquad (2.6) \qquad\qquad (7.3)$$

$$RSQ = 0.939; DW = 1.03; SE = 1.52;$$

sample period 1959.1–1996.4

where *INVFARM* is the constant-dollar investment in farm equipment, *ACREAGE* is total planted acreage, *INFL* is the rate of inflation, *CRED* is constant-dollar consumer credit outstanding, *FAAA* is the Aaa corporate bond yield, *YFH* is constant-dollar net farm income, *DITC* is the rate of investment tax credit, *DOLLAR* is the trade-weighted average of the dollar, and *LOAN* is constant-dollar business loans. *D67* is a dummy variable, 0 before 1967.1 and 1 thereafter, because the value of the dollar was fixed before 1967. *DFARM* equals 1 in the fourth quarter of years when the investment tax credit was in force and farm income rose; otherwise 0 (see below).

Purchases of farm equipment are closely related to the cost and availability of credit as well as farm sector conditions. The relevant farm variables are net farm income in constant prices, the value of the dollar, and farm acreage. The value of the dollar is included because it impacts farm profitability: when the dollar is overvalued, the volume of farm exports may not drop very much if farmers have excess supplies, but profitability is sharply curtailed. Because the trade-weighted average value of the dollar did not change very much before 1967 – the international gold standard remained in place to 1971, but in the intervening four years the British pound devalued, the DM appreciated, and the US devalued the dollar by 15% – the value of the dollar is multiplied by a dummy variable that is zero before 1967. Because this would introduce a discontinuity, a dummy variable that starts in 1967 is also entered separately.

Credit conditions are also important. The real Aaa corporate bond rate – divided into the nominal rate and the inflation rate over the past two years – consumer credit, business loans, and the rate of investment tax credit are all significant. These terms have the signs that would be expected for an investment function in a commodity-based industry, and the elasticities appear reasonable.

The equation also includes a nonlinear variable, which was found in empirical work in the 1960s. When farm income rose during the year, farmers boosted their capital expenditures of farm equipment late in the year (generally the fourth quarter) in years when the investment tax credit was operative, thus reducing their tax burden. In years when income declined, so the tax burden was lower, the ITC (investment tax credit) was not used. After the ITC ended, this pattern disappeared.

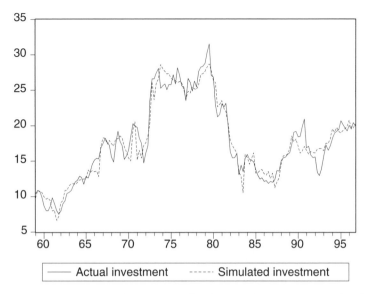

Figure 9.19 Actual purchases of constant-dollar farm equipment compared with simulated values generated from the text equation.

The fitted values for this equation for the period 1959.1 through 1996.4 are shown in figure 9.19. While there are a few misses, the equation appears to capture all the major swings fairly closely. However, the forecasts from this equation are very poor when used to predict 1997.1–1999.4, as shown in figure 9.20.

Furthermore, estimating this equation to 1999.4 shows a similar pattern of missed forecasts, even though all the parameter estimates remain significant. In this case, the root mean square error for the last three years is 6.71, compared with a standard error of the estimate of 1.52. Clearly a structural shift occurred.

As usual, it is much easier to explain what happened in retrospect. In 1996, Congress voted to end most crop supports, permitting farmers to grow as much as they wanted and sell it all on the free market. Many farmers thought their net income would improve, so they purchased additional equipment. Most economists could have predicted what would happen: output rose, prices fell and net farm income actually declined. The situation was exacerbated by the rise of the dollar and the unexpected collapse of markets in Japan and Southeast Asia because of recessions there. Hence many of the "reasonable" variables used in the farm equipment equation suddenly became inappropriate.

In the past, investment in farm equipment was always positively correlated with farm income, farm exports, and farm acreage. Yet after 1996, when farm supports were withdrawn, the relationship changed. Given that development, how should one have predicted purchases of farm equipment for the 1997–9 period – and what methods should be used for future years?

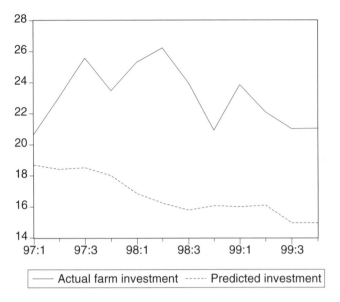

Figure 9.20 Actual and predicted constant-dollar purchases of farm equipment, using the text equation estimated up to 1999.4.

This example represents a classic case of a shift in the underlying data generation function. Before 1996, the government limited the amount of acreage that could be planted for corn and wheat, but farmers were guaranteed a minimum price. Then those restrictions – and benefits – were terminated. Net farm income declined even though production and acreage increased. Yet farmers did not cut back on their purchases of farm equipment; indeed, the spur of the free market caused many of them to purchase more new equipment to boost productivity and offset the impact of falling prices.

What can be salvaged from this equation? To answer this question, the equation was reestimated from 1990 through 1999. Some of the variables, such as the dummy variable for the period of fixed exchange rates and the investment tax credit, are irrelevant. The change in business loan demand, which was not as significant as the change in consumer credit, disappears. The lags are somewhat longer, probably reflecting a longer-term perspective now that free-market conditions are in play. The value of the dollar is no longer significant, since farm exports have increased in spite of the stronger dollar from 1995 through 2000. Not surprisingly, the acreage variable has become more important. The modified equation, given below, tracks the 1997–9 period quite well, as shown in figure 9.21, although the obvious question remains of how well it will work in the future.

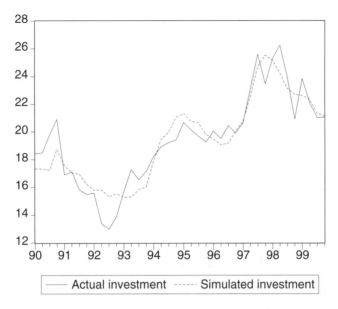

Figure 9.21 Actual and simulated purchases of constant-dollar farm equipment, based on the text equation estimated for the 1990.1–1999.4 sample period.

$INVFARM$
$$= -107.1 + 0.347 * \%YFH(-4), 4 + 0.393 * ACREAGE, 4 + 0.265 * \%CRED, 4$$
$$\qquad (5.6) \qquad\qquad\qquad (10.5) \qquad\qquad\qquad (6.0)$$
$$-1.46 * FAAA, 4$$
$$\;\;(4.5)$$

$$RSQ = 0.841; DW = 1.20; SE = 1.25;$$
$$\text{sample period } 1990.1 - 1999.4$$

The following lessons can be drawn from this example.

1 No matter how well an equation seems to fit – and how accurate the forecasts have been – all models should be updated systematically as new data become available. With today's PCs, this has become a very simple task.

2 Ordinarily, it is useful to have more rather than fewer observations; but in this case, the relationship should have been reexamined when foreign trade became more important, the investment tax credit was canceled, and farm support prices were removed. Whenever some of the key underlying terms are no longer operative because of changes in institutional structure, the model should be reestimated.

3 Once farm sector restraints were removed, it was reasonable to assume that acreage would increase and farmers would need to purchase additional farm

equipment. That is one area where judgmental factors can be usefully incorporated into the forecast.

4   Some of the terms in the older equation remains relevant. In particular, net farm
income and the cost and availability of credit are still important. However, it
does not make any sense to use an econometric equation to predict when the
underlying structure has shifted radically.

Problems and Questions

1. Figure 9.22 shows the data for the ratio of soft drinks (including
juices and bottled waters) to disposable income from 1959 through 1999
(data are on the disk).

(a)   What variables would you use to explain this declining trend? Estimate an appropriate regression on the annual data, including the
relevant population groups.

(b)   Predict this ratio five years into the future based on what is currently
known about population ratios. For purposes of this model, assume
that all other variables grow at the same rate as occurred in the
1995–9 period; or if the variables are trendless, they remain at their
average value over the past five years.

(c)   Suppose you are advising the soft drink industry about plans for the
future. Explain how you would determine whether to (i) move away
from cola-based beverages into non-carbonated drinks, (ii) expand
abroad, (iii) change marketing strategy aimed at teenagers,
(iv) change pricing policy, or (v) target major fast-food chains to sell
more drinks.

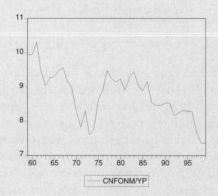

Figure 9.22   Problem 1.

continued

2. This chapter includes an equation for the demand for household furniture. Monthly data are also available for purchases of business furniture on the website.

(a) Graph this series, both in levels form and relative to total GDP.

(b) Estimate the equation with the same drivers as were given for the retail furniture equation. Which terms remain significant? Which are dropped? Based on other capital goods equations given in this text, which terms should be added?

(c) Should the equation be presented to management in levels, ratios, or percentage change form?

(d) Briefly describe the importance of each of the key drivers in terms of their elasticities.

(e) Prepare alternative forecasts based on optimistic, standard, and pessimistic scenarios.

3. The market for automobile and truck tires can be divided into four separate segments: tires for new cars, replacement tires for cars, tires for new trucks, and replacement tires for trucks; net exports are a very small percentage of total sales and can be ignored in this example. Assume, however, the only data you have are production data for tires (from the Federal Reserve Board).

(a) Describe how you would select the key drivers for each of these four markets.

(b) Estimate an equation using the Fed industrial production data. Based on your results, which of these four markets appears to be the most important?

(c) The actual percentages are about 40% for new car tires, and about 20% each for replacement car tires, new truck tires, and for replacement truck tires (these are dollar amounts rather than the number of tires, since truck and bus tires are much bigger and more expensive). How do these agree with your estimates in (b)?

(d) What factors explain why some sectors appear to have greater weights than the actual percentages, and some have smaller weights. How would you explain this discrepancy to management?

4. A financial services firm notices that delinquency rates on a wide variety of loans has declined during the 1990s. That is not surprising in view of the increase in real growth, the booming stock market, and the decline in the unemployment rate. However, that firm would also like to be prepared for periods of slower growth and rising unemployment, and asks you to build a model to answer these questions. Annual data are

continued

available from the Fed for residential real estate loans, commercial real estate loans, consumer credit cards, other consumer loans, and commercial and industrial loans; historical data on the website can be updated at www.bog.frb.fed.us/releases/CharteOff/delallsa.txt.

(a) Estimate annual equations for delinquency rates through 1999 based on real growth, unemployment, and stock prices. What other variables should be included?

(b) How do you handle the issue that, during the 1990–9 period, the economy improved steadily, whereas management wants to know what will happen during leaner times?

(c) Prepare an optimistic, standard, and "worst case" scenario for delinquency rates for each of the above categories for 2000, 2001, and 2002.

(d) Now go back and test your forecasts against the actual data for 2000. Indicate what adjustments should be made to the equations before presenting the results to management the next time.

CHAPTER 10

METHODS OF LONG-TERM FORECASTING

INTRODUCTION

The previous chapter focused on short-term forecasting models that are designed to predict the next one to two years. While exceptions such as an energy crisis or a change in government policy sometimes arise – such as the 1996 farm bill discussed in the previous chapter – these functions are usually estimated under the assumption that the underlying data generation function remains unchanged. Long-run forecasting, on the other hand, is generally based on the assumption that the researcher does not know how the data generating function will change in the long run, which means classical statistical methods will not apply.

Sometimes the problems arise *de novo*. For example, in May 2000, the Commerce Department released its estimate that E-commerce sales were $5.3 billion for 1999.4, or 0.68% of total retail sales. Various consulting groups have prepared estimates of how fast E-commerce sales will grow over the next 5–10 years. Some of these estimates may be correct; others may be wildly off the mark. But in any case it is clear that structural equations cannot be estimated based on one – or even three or four – data points. Later in this chapter, we present some alternative estimates of how fast these sales might rise.

In other cases, adequate data exist, but long-run trends may not follow previous patterns. Data for oil prices exist for over 150 years, yet that long time series has provided no hint about how prices will change in the future. No one predicted a fourfold increase in oil prices in 1973, but after it happened it was widely considered a one-time phenomenon that would not be repeated. Oil prices then rose from $13 to $35/bbl in 1980, revising expectations to the point where many economists expected that prices would soon rise to $100/bbl, yet five years later they were back to $13/bbl. After that, the consensus energy forecast showed a modest long-term increase in the real price of oil, but that prediction was temporarily derailed in 1998 when prices fell to $10/bbl.

That in turn brought forth a whole new round of forecasts explaining why oil prices would remain low indefinitely, which quickly lost credibility when prices zoomed to $35/bbl in the summer of 2000.

To date, no one has been able to use these data to generate accurate forecasts of oil prices. Indeed, in 2000 "expert" opinion was sharply divided between those who think the world will soon run out of oil, pushing prices sharply higher, and those who think emerging alternative sources of energy will push prices so much lower that eventually oil will be left in the ground, just as is now the case for coal. Later in this chapter we also examine these alternative hypotheses.

A third major case occurs when a strong trend suddenly disappears. One notable example of that occurred in Southeast Asia, when the so-called Growth Tigers – South Korea, Taiwan, Indonesia, and Malaysia – suffered declines of 5% to 15% in real GDP in 1998 following several decades of near double-digit growth. In retrospect the reasons were readily identified: an overvalued currency, excessive borrowing abroad, and a decline in exports that caused massive devaluations, which in turn triggered retrenchment. However, hardly anyone foresaw this disruption ahead of time. It is worthwhile examining the factors that can cause long-term trends to change so quickly.

Three main themes are discussed and analyzed in this chapter: (a) *de novo* forecasting with little or no data; (b) the effect of exogenous changes when plentiful data are available; and (c) shocks that disrupt previous dominant trends. Section 10.1 covers a generalized discussion of non-parametric methods of long-term forecasting: surveys, scenario analysis, consensus forecasts, and Delphi methods. Since these methods have generally turned out to be ineffective, we return to the available statistical methods. Section 10.2 presents some examples of estimating trend growth based on purely statistical models – i.e., without any judgmental input and without taking into account any of the economic factors that might affect these variables. The tools can be valuable when used in conjunction with other information, but can provide inaccurate long-run projections when trend factors change.

This chapter also covers a variety of examples and cases where determining the long-term trend is an important part of the projection, but structural forces are also important. These are treated in three separate sections. Section 10.3 examines cases where significant cyclical patterns are imposed on continuing strong trend growth, as is the case for computers and semiconductors. Section 10.4 examines changes in long-term growth rates of GDP for various countries; these may reflect either an increasing or a decreasing rate of growth. The rapid buildup of the Japanese economy after World War II, followed by a slowdown, is compared with a similar pattern in the Korean economy approximately 20 years later. The underlying logic of the Solow growth model is used in these cases. Finally, section 10.5 focuses on very long-range trends for population and natural resource pricing, taking supply and demand factors into consideration as well as log-linear or nonlinear trends.

10.1 NON-PARAMETRIC METHODS OF LONG-TERM FORECASTING

Corporate planners are often faced with situations where no prior data exist. Perhaps a new product or service is being introduced, or new technology is being unveiled. Alternatively, a firm may plan to expand; it notices how other firms have fared, but has no data of its own. In still other cases, an unprecedented event occurs, which may be expected or unexpected. The first energy shock and the fall of the Berlin Wall were unexpected. Government regulations for fuel economy, requiring seat belts, deregulation of airline travel, etc., changed the way in which firms do business but were announced well before the laws were actually enacted. Even so, guesswork plays a major role in those forecasts. The challenge is to identify the superior guesses.

A large variety of non-parametric forecasting methods exist, which can be grouped into four major categories. The *first* comes under the general rubric of market research, and includes consumer survey methods and focus groups. The *second* incorporates analogy and precursor analysis, in which an upcoming situation is related to a similar set of circumstances that has already occurred. The *third* is scenario analysis by corporate planners or executives: logical outcomes are examined under alternative assumptions. The *fourth* is known as the Delphi method, in which various opinions are collected in the first round and are then adjusted in subsequent rounds based on the consensus estimates and the alleged expertise of the survey participants. Each of these is considered briefly.

10.1.1 SURVEY METHODS

Entire curricula are devoted to methods of market research and testing new products; here we offer only a few suggestions that apply to forecasting models. The major drawback of these methods is mistakes in survey methods and focus groups that stem from biased results. In market research studies, consumers are often provided with some "hint" of what they are expected to like. In focus groups, one relatively strong opinion in that group may bias the overall findings, causing others in the group who disagree to suppress their opinions. Survey methods can be a helpful tool but should not be used by themselves.[1]

We can distinguish among surveys taken for products or services that are already being offered, new products and services that are being introduced but

---

[1] For a more detailed discussion of forecasting with survey methods, see Dalrymple, D. J., "Sales Forecasting Practices," *International Journal of Forecasting*, 3 (1987), 379–91; and Mentzer, J. T., and J. E. Cox, Jr., "Familiarity, Application and Performance of Sales Forecasting Techniques," *Journal of Forecasting*, 3 (1984), 27–36.

are closely related to existing products – a new type of processed food, or a new style of motor vehicle – and products and services that represent a distinct break from the past, such as Internet access in 1995. In the first case, standard statistical analysis can be used to determine what consumers like and do not like; those procedures are straightforward. In the third case, market research and focus groups will not accomplish very much; until consumers have actually tried a new product or service, they will not be able to provide informed opinions about the likelihood of purchase in the future. In general, new product development is not as amenable to survey methods or focus groups. Hence these brief comments are concentrated on the intermediate category.

In the mid-1980s, Chrysler successfully introduced the concept of the minivan, which spawned what might be called the SUV Revolution. That company was several years ahead not only of the faltering Detroit giants but also of leading-edge foreign manufacturers. By comparison, IBM stumbled badly when it failed to appreciate the importance of the personal computer; Digital Equipment also fared poorly. Employees of Xerox at the famed Palo Alto Research Center (PARC) essentially invented Windows at least a decade ahead of the competition, but senior management didn't know what to do with the idea.

It seems highly unlikely that Chrysler succeeded where IBM, Digital Equipment, and Xerox failed just because the market researchers and statisticians at Chrysler were more intelligent. Part of the reason may have been the adaptation of an existing product as opposed to the introduction of a new concept – although IBM did quite well when rolling out the mainframe computer. Instead, these are examples where large, successful companies were hindered by the burden of previous successes, whereas Chrysler was forced to become innovative or go out of business completely.

This need not always be the case. The first "light" beer was introduced not by Anheuser–Busch or Miller Brewing, but by a company known as Gablinger. It was, of course, an ignominious failure. In this case the advertising was misdirected, aimed at weight watchers rather than "macho" men, so the company missed what should have been its principal target. In a similar vein, almost everyone remembers the failure of New Coke, but not so many recall Coke's original foray into diet soft drinks, known as Tab. The product was also an abject failure until it was repositioned and reformulated as Diet Coke.

Sometimes new products simply do not fill any desired niche. Pringles never took off in the US, and reduced-fat potato chips with Olestra were also poorly received. Proctor & Gamble is one of the most respected and successful consumer marketing companies in the world, but they could not create demand for a product that few wanted to buy, regardless of what survey results or focus groups told them.

The small sample of examples cited above is clearly biased because it includes many of the highly publicized major failures. There are presumably many more examples of products that were tried and found wanting by market research surveys and focus groups, and for precisely that reason never saw the light of day. Nonetheless, the above examples can be used to identify several useful rules for using survey methods in forecasting, which can be summarized as follows.

1   Forecasting the demand for new products – or even minor changes to existing products – is far different from asking people how much they like existing products. In the latter case, appropriately designed and tabulated surveys will generally produce highly accurate results. However, most individuals do not know what they will like in advance, and as a result, some people try to guess what they think the interviewer wants to hear. It is human nature to want to give a positive rather than a negative answer. For this reason, such results must be examined with more than the usual degree of skepticism.
2   It is also human nature for business executives who have spent a great deal of effort and resources into developing a new product or service to assume there must be a market for it. As a result, results from market research tests and focus groups are likely to be skewed in that direction.
3   Tests should be designed to ask the customers whether they prefer product A or product B, as opposed to product A or not product A. Even this will not always work, such as the case when consumers said they liked the sweeter taste of New Coke in tests, but did not embrace that view when it was actually offered for sale. Nonetheless, the survey or focus group leader should try to disguise the answer that the company "wants" to hear.
4   Multiple tests should be used with different wording. Groucho Marx once found that the line "Is this man dead or has my watch stopped?" elicited only assorted guffaws, whereas "Either this man is dead or my watch has stopped" brought down the house. Similarly, different focus groups with a wide variety of individuals should be used, since the opinions of any one focus group can be swayed by a dominant individual.

Perhaps the most important point to remember in survey groups is that forecasting is an inexact science – and in many cases, consumers do not know what they like in advance. In statistical methods, one generally assumes the existence of an underlying data generation function, even if the properties of that function are not very well known. In the case of surveys, there is no good reason to assume that the function for any one group is the same as for the next group. Thus market research tests generally do not provide useful information for long-term projections; alternative methods must be considered.

10.1.2 ANALOGY AND PRECURSOR METHODS

Anyone who has traveled extensively by car in the US quickly observes that some Interstate interchanges feature large clusters of motels, fast-food restaurants, and gas stations, while at other interchanges there are no such facilities. In some cases the reasons are obvious: the crossroad is an important highway, or the local population density is relatively high. In other cases, however, the reasons are not as obvious. Many times, one of the biggest firms – McDonald's or Holiday Inn – will have done extensive research to determine the optimal locations, and smaller firms will then piggyback on those results. That is one crude example of what might be called analogy or precursor methods of forecasting: see what has worked well in the past, and replicate that effort.

That immediately raises the question of how McDonald's or Holiday Inn decided on those locations in the first place. In general, they went back and examined which of the existing locations had done the best, and then built new locations where situations seemed to be similar: they too used analogy and precursor methods. Only the very first locations were selected without prior information or experience; Howard Johnson built restaurants along busy cross-country highways in the 1930s; the company almost went out of business when road traffic was curtailed during World War II before its original vision was finally justified.

Perhaps this example seems too simple: find a location with lots of long-distance automobile travel and build a restaurant, gas station, or motel. However, the same general methodology can be applied to more sophisticated problems as well.

One of the most successful marketing gimmicks of recent years has been the concept of frequent flyer miles: many travelers will choose one airline or another because of its frequent flyer mileage program and the benefits it offers. How did such an idea arise?

It was not possible to offer benefits of this sort until the barrier of regulated airline fares was lifted in the late 1970s. Airlines often ask their passengers what they like and dislike about the flights, and tabulate this information. In spite of universal griping about airline food, the quality of meals turned out not to be a reason why passengers switched from one airline to another. The same was true for baggage handling, on-time performance, and the relatively friendliness of airline personnel. Conversely, fares were very important, and upgrades were also very important; almost everyone would like to sit in first class if it doesn't cost extra. Hence the concept of frequent flyer miles was born, since it specifically permitted people to fly "free" or receive "free" upgrades. Such a discovery is presented as an example of precursor analysis because it was based on how people had reacted in the past.

In a similar vein, Harrah's used precursor analysis to determine what factors would attract more gamblers to their casinos. In the past, one of the preferred tools was "comping": free meals, hotel rooms, and similar accoutrements. However, Harrah's found that one of the most valuable tools was "free money"; giving people chips or tokens to use at the slot machines or gaming tables. That was not only popular with the patrons, but also cost-effective because it turned out that customers who received those chips or tokens stayed at the machines or tables longer and actually ended up spending more than those who were not given "free" money. In this case, a careful analysis of what customers had done in the past proved to be a useful and effective forecasting tool.

10.1.3 SCENARIO ANALYSIS

It is often useful to evaluate future options under different assumptions about key underlying variables. Such an approach is known as scenario analysis. Some examples of short-term scenario analysis were presented in the previous chapter, but the focus here is on long-term projections. In these cases, alternative scenarios would encompass such factors as geopolitical shifts, new developments in technology, trends in health and aging, and the long-term outlook for natural resource prices.

The first example chosen here is the long-term outlook for the stock market. For some traders, the long run is after lunch: each trade represents a new opportunity, and their portfolio adjustments are based only on the latest news. The existence of such traders tends to make the stock market very efficient. However, most individuals and institutions, such as those managing pension funds, do not follow this modus operandi. Instead, they base their decisions on perceived long-run changes in the market.

That is not necessarily an inferior way to invest. A decision to move 100 percent into stocks in the summer of 1982, based on the logic that inflation had finally been conquered and interest rates were headed for an extended decline, would have generated results far superior to those generated by most money managers and investment firms. Specifically, purchasing a market basket consisting of the S&P 500 stocks in August 1982 would have generated an annual rate of return of 20% per year for the next 18 years, including reinvested dividends. Only a handful of geniuses managed to top that return.

That may be of some interest to history buffs, but the would-be long-term investor in early 2000 faced an entirely different set of parameters; the price/earnings ratio rose to what had previously been considered twice its equilibrium value based on current levels of inflation and interest rates. The last time that happened was in 1929. By now we know that over the following year, the S&P 500 fell 25%, the Nasdaq composite fell 70%, and various assorted indexes of Internet stocks fell 80–95%. Any savvy money manager could have beaten the averages by moving into cash; aggressive managers could have doubled their money by going short. However, since the market correction apparently surprised most investors, this situation is a useful one for applying scenario analysis.

We start with the fundamental discount model for expected future earnings, which says

$$P/E = (1+g)/(\rho + g - r) \tag{10.1}$$

where P/E is the price earnings ratio of a standard market basket (such as the S&P 500), g is the expected future growth rate of corporate earnings, ρ is the risk premium of stocks relative to bonds, and r is the high-quality bond rate (usually the Aaa corporate bond rate).

Before the bull market of the late 1990s, it was generally assumed that in equilibrium situations – i.e., stable monetary policy, normal growth, and low, stable inflation – $g = r$ and $\rho = 0.06$. Hence the equilibrium P/E ratio was estimated to be about 17. Since the long-run stable rate of inflation was widely thought to be about 3%, this led to the well known "rule of 20," which said the inflation rate plus the P/E ratio summed to 20. Until the late 1990s it worked quite well.

Why should one expect g to be equal to r? Over the long run, the ratio of corporate profits to GDP has remained constant, which means g is the same as the growth rate in nominal GDP. In equilibrium, the bond rate is approximately equal to the inflation rate plus the underlying growth rate of the economy, which is also the growth rate in nominal GDP.

In early 2000, the P/E of the S&P 500 more than doubled, rising from 17 to a peak of 36. In designing alternative scenarios, we first need to determine why it rose so much. The combination of an acceleration in productivity growth, the Federal budget surplus, and low inflation and full employment boosted long-run expected profit growth to 8%. Also, many of these same factors had led to the assumption that the long-term corporate bond rate would decline to 7%. Plugging these numbers into equation (10.1) yields 1.08/0.03 = 36, the peak P/E ratio that was in fact observed in early 2000.

Several alternative scenarios can now be derived using this basic formula.

- Expectations were correct and the P/E returns to 36.
- Because of the superior rate of return on stocks over the long run, the risk premium declines and the P/E ratio rises to 100. That may sound ridiculous given what happened, but that forecast was made by James Glassman in late 1999[2] and was apparently taken seriously by some "investors."
- Profits cannot continue to rise faster than GDP indefinitely, so eventually the market will return to its previous P/E of 17, and stock prices will fall 50%.
- Some intermediate correction is necessary, because the economy cannot continue to grow faster than its long-term equilibrium rate indefinitely. However, because of the emerging budget surplus, productivity growth will exceed its long-term average, so profits might keep rising 8% per year compared to a 7% bond yield. In that case, the P/E ratio would decline to 24, implying a severe market correction, but not the crash indicated in the previous scenario.

If one assumes that inflation remains low and stable and interest rates do not change very much, the real issue boils down to whether profits can continue to rise faster than GDP, as was the case from 1982 through 1999, or whether that gap will eventually disappear. The arguments in favor of an increase in the ratio of S&P 500 profits to GDP include (i) faster growth in productivity, (ii) cost

---

[2] Glassman, J. K., and K. Hackett, *Dow 36,000: The New Strategy of Profiting from the Coming Rise in the Stock Market* (Times Books, New York), 1999.

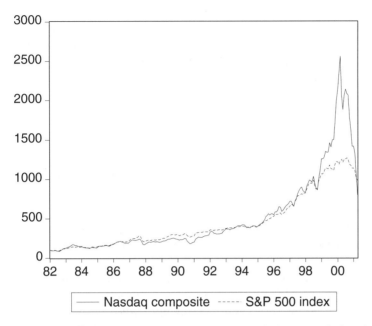

Figure 10.1 Both the S&P 5000 and Nasdaq composite indexes are indexed at 100 in January 1982.

savings from mergers and acquisitions, (iii) a decline in the ratio of interest payments to GDP as firms use more equity financing, and (iv) faster growth in overseas markets.

No one knows how fast profits will rise over the long run, but an intelligent use of scenario analysis would assign probabilities to each of the factors listed in (i) through (iv) above and then decide whether, at the end of 2000, the stock market was still overvalued, fairly valued, or undervalued.

I have chosen this particular example because no regression equation fitted for the period to 1997 would have predicting a doubling of the S&P 500 index from late 1997 to early 2000. Nor would it have predicted the increase in the Nasdaq composite from 1500 in October 1998 to over 5000 in March 2000 – or, for that matter, the subsequent decline to 1600 in April 2001. In statistical parlance, the underlying data generation function changed. We have identified those factors that shifted, but do not know the degree to which they will shift back. That question can usefully be explored using scenario analysis.

One further brief comment about the performance of the stock market in 1999 and 2000. Figure 10.1 shows the behavior of the S&P 500 and Nasdaq composite indexes; both indexed to 100 in January 1982. Until the end of 1998, the indexes moved almost in tandem. Starting in 1999, the unprecedented climb in the Nasdaq index was unsupported by any economic scenario – higher profits, lower interest rates, or more rapid long-term growth – and took on the nature of a Tulip Bulb mania. Of course it is easy enough to point all this out in retrospect. The important point to be made here is that the rise in Nasdaq could not have been supported by *any* reasonable scenario analysis, so that by early 2000, a sell signal was indicated regardless of one's particular estimates of economic variables. When all plausible scenarios point in the same direction, one can usually generate a very powerful forecast.

10.1.4 DELPHI ANALYSIS

In the previous section, probabilities were assigned to various scenarios based on arbitrary guesses about the likelihood of various scenarios. However, suppose you had picked scenario A, and the results were shown to a panel of ten other people, many of whom were supposed to be experts, and two picked B, five picked C and three picked D; no one else picked A. Would you still stick with your choice?

Maybe you would, but many others would not. There would seem to be some merit in a method of forecasting where expert opinion receives a higher weight than average opinion, and where forecasters could modify their predictions in subsequent rounds based on the projections provided by experts. The Delphi method incorporates just such a method.

The Delphi method originated at the Rand Corporation, which was originally founded after World War II in order to keep the Whiz Kids of the Army Air Force together to think of ingenious new solutions in peacetime. The acronym originally stood for *Research And Development*; the corporation currently explores a wide variety of research projects, not just those submitted by the military. Currently, the Delphi method is widely used to generate forecasts in technology, education, medicine, and other socioeconomic issues.[3]

In organizing a Delphi forecast, a questionnaire is sent to a variety of participants from various disciplines; the point is to select a group of people who are likely to provide different answers. The participants not only answer each question but rank their expertise in answering, using a scale that often ranks from 1 to 5. The results are then weighted by the degree of expertise and the results – weighted median and range – are resubmitted to the participants, who are encouraged to change their answers if the results are not in line with their own thinking and they do not consider themselves experts. This process usually continues for three or four rounds. But does it work?

---

[3] For general sources on the Delphi method, see Gordon, T. J., "The Delphi Method: An Illustration," in *Technological Forecasting for Industry and Government*." J. Bright, ed. (Prentice Hall: Englewood Cliffs, NJ), 1986; Martino, J., *Technological Forecasting and Decision Making*, 3rd edn (North Holland, Amsterdam), 1993; and Levary R., and D. Han, "Choosing a Technological Forecasting Model," *Industrial Management*, 37 (1995). For a more recent reference on the use of Delphi methods for socioeconomic issues, see Adler M., and E. Ziglio, eds., *Gazing Into the Oracle: The Delphi Method and Its Application to Social Policy and Public Health* (Kingsley Publishers, London).

Table 10.1   A selection of results from Granger's Delphi methods.

In what year will there be . . .	Median	Interquartile range
Economically useful desalination of seawater	1970	1970–1983
Automated language translators	1972	1968–1976
New organs through transplanting or prosthesis	1972	1968–1982
Reliable weather forecasts	1975	1972–1988
Controlled thermonuclear power	1985	1980–2000
Feasibility of limited weather control	1990	1987–2000
Economically useful farming of ocean to produce at least 20% of world's food	2000	2000–2017
Use of drugs to raise level of intelligence	2012	1984–2023

Questions were asked in 1965.

Once again, the answer is empirically determined. Granger[4] has reported on several experiments; some of those results are reproduced in table 10.1.

In a related test, experts were asked in 1967 to pick the year by which at least 50% of all cars would be electrically powered. The original answer was 1990; after the fourth iterative round, the data advanced to 1995.

Other experiments have shown that even in a Delphi-type process, the forecast will invariably move toward the consensus even if someone who is generally acknowledged as an expert holds a strong contrary opinion. We have already seen that short-term consensus forecasts for a variety of macroeconomic variables can improve forecasting accuracy when combined with other methods. However, when a change in technology is under discussion, sometimes the Delphi method does not produce results that are better than a random sample. Having participated in several such experiments, the general rule this author and colleagues have found – which is borne out by the studies quoted by Granger – is that the use of experts and the iterative process will reduce the error slightly, but the question still remains whether these results are usable.

Opinion is thus sharply divided about whether the Delphi method is effective. Of course there are some errors; the relevant question is whether these errors are smaller than would be obtained by other methods. A related relevant question is whether there is any inherent bias in the Delphi method.

The major criticisms of the Delphi method have been adequately categorized by Makridakis and Wheelwright and by Martino[5]; these are summarized here as follows.

---

[4]   Granger, C. W. J., *Forecasting in Business and Economics*, 2nd edn (Academic Press, San Diego, CA), 1989, p. 229.
[5]   Martino, J., "The Precision of Delphi Estimates," *Technological Forecasting and Social Change*, 1 (1970), 292–9.

- The results appear to be heavily dependent on the particular judges selected.
- The results are sensitive to the ambiguity in the questionnaire.
- It is difficult to assess accurately the degree of expertise of each panelist (i.e., almost everyone thinks they are "experts").
- Current events receive too large a weight relative to future events.
- Experts tend to judge the future of a given event in isolation from other developments.
- Even if the panelists have expert knowledge about the current state of a given project, they may have no experience or expertise in forecasting.
- The responses are sometimes altered in an attempt to move the next round of responses in a desired direction.

I am not aware of any Delphi study that was undertaken to determine the future direction of the stock market in March 2000; but while a few respected analysts recognized that the market was overvalued and called for a correction, no one predicted that a little more than a year later, the Nasdaq composite would have declined almost 70%. No survey technique would have uncovered that result.

Yet not all the reviews are negative. DeLurgio[6] provides an example of one of the original uses of the Delphi method, namely general aviation aircraft, where engineers were asked what kind of engines, materials, fuselages, control surfaces, and avionics were expected in the future. The study was successful in identifying 32 technological adoptions, implementations, or breakthroughs to improve the industry. In a more recent paper, Rowe and Wright[7] reviewed several empirical studies and found that Delphi groups outperformed statistical groups by 12 to two with two ties, and outperformed standard interacting groups by five to one with two ties.

Evaluation of any forecasting method is always difficult because of the large element of subjectivity. In the case of macroeconomic, industry, or financial forecasts, however, the actual results are known soon after the fact – although, except for the financial sector, these data can be revised. In the case of the Delphi method, however, the facts often remain unknown for many years; in the interim, unforeseen events often interact with the original premise. Also, there are no measures of error such as are found in statistical models, so the exercise invariably reduces to comparing one group's forecast with another group. Yet most of the time the forecasts are made under different circumstances, with different underlying assumptions, and with different questions asked.

Having said all this, it cannot be denied that the Delphi method has passed a "market test" in the sense that the method remains widely used by corpora-

---

[6] DeLurgio, S. A., *Forecasting Principles and Applications* (Irwin McGraw-Hill, Burr Ridge, IL), 1998, p. 637.

[7] Rowe, G., and G. Wright, "The Delphi Technique as a Forecasting Tool: Issues and Analysis," *International Journal of Forecasting*, 15 (1999), 353–75.

tions and institutions; if it did not have substantive value, it probably would have been discontinued by now. As someone whose professional experience is directly related to "what works," this author views such market tests as significant. What, then, are the appropriate circumstances under which the Delphi method is likely to give useful results?

- The forecasting exercise makes more sense in situations where the likelihood of human interaction will not be directly affected by recent events. For example, the consensus forecast for inflation taken in the early 1980s called for an average rate of 6%; that was widely decried as unacceptable, but "experts" wrung their hands and proclaimed nothing could be done. In fact, widespread unhappiness with that rate led to a major shift in monetary policy and a reduction in underlying inflation to half that rate. Widespread agreement with this point has led to the use of cross-impact analysis, which tries to define interrelationships between possible future events.[8]
- In general, the bulk of the evidence suggests that weighting the results by the degree of expertise will give somewhat better results than an unweighted average. Of course, that statement by itself does not imply the results will be very good. We are back to the question posed at the beginning of this text "compared to what?"
- Delphi methods can be usefully employed relative to statistical methods when there is strong evidence to suggest that the underlying data generating function has changed. For example, a forecast made in 1978 about the future of airline travel would presumably have been more accurate by taking into consideration forthcoming changes caused by deregulation than by assuming the older model would remain intact. I presented another example of this in the previous chapter when explaining farm investment; farmers increased their purchases of capital equipment when given the opportunity to grow more crops. These changes could have been foreseen by experts, whereas statistical methods probably would have completely missed these shifts.
- Delphi methods generally work better in situations where there has not been a major change recently. Experience with forecasting oil prices, for example, shows that the forecast generated by expert opinion is generally far different after a major increase or decrease in prices than it was just a few months earlier.[9]

In situations where the above criteria are observed, the Delphi method is likely to provide more accurate long-term forecasts than projections generated by an unweighted sample, or methods using statistical analysis. However, such

---

[8] For further information, see Helmer, O., "Problems in Future Research – Delphi and Causal Cross-Input Analysis," *Futures*, 9 (1977); and Martino J., *Technological Forecasting and Decision Making*, 3rd edn (North Holland, Amsterdam), 1993.
[9] Even if the results are accurate, they may not be accepted. This author participated in a modified Delphi experiment in the early 1980s, when the group agreed crude oil prices would decline from $35 to $20/bbl later in the decade. The result was rejected out of hand by management.

situations do not arise very often. Thus for the remainder of this chapter we return to the use of statistical methods to generate long-term projections.

10.2 STATISTICAL METHODS OF DETERMINING NONLINEAR TRENDS: NONLINEAR GROWTH AND DECLINE, LOGISTICS, AND SATURATION CURVES

Often some data series will grow very rapidly at first, but after a while the growth rate declines to a long-term sustainable level. That might be the case for a new product or service; eventually growth declines to its long-term trend rate. At the macroeconomic level, the economy of a country might grow very rapidly until it catches up with the existing technology frontier, then grow much more slowly. After a new cure for a disease is found, the death rate might drop very quickly for a while, but then level off after virtually all patients have been successfully treated. In these and other examples, a nonlinear trend can be fitted to existing data that can then be used to project a different rate of trend growth in the future.[10]

The quadratic curve, where the series in question is a function of a linear and quadratic time trend, has already been discussed. Three additional cases are presented in this section. In the first, the rate of growth – or decline – is rapid at first, but then diminishes to a trend rate. The second case is often known as an S-curve: growth starts off slowly, then accelerates, then slows down again. The third case is a subset of the second: the same general pattern is observed, but eventually the saturation level is reached, at which point the series does not grow at all. All three cases have some similarities and involve the use of exponential and asymmetrical functions; examples are provided to indicate when one method should be preferred over the others.

10.2.1 NONLINEAR GROWTH AND DECLINE CURVES

We first consider the case where a series increases at a decreasing rate, but the growth rate remains positive; the methodology is the same for a series that might decline at a decreasing rate, but its growth rate remains negative. Curves that follow these patterns can be estimated as:

$$y = a + b/(c+t) \tag{10.2a}$$

where t is a time trend that starts in the first year of the sample. Sometimes this equation is estimated in its logarithmic form, namely

$$\log y = a + b/(c+t). \tag{10.2b}$$

---

[10] For further discussion, see DeLurgio, pp. 643–53.

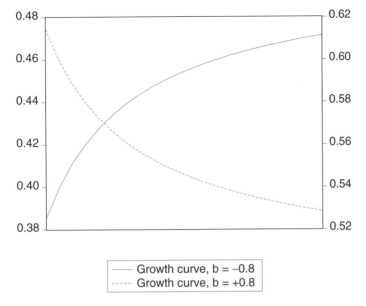

Figure 10.2 Rising and falling nonlinear growth curves.

If b is positive, the curve will be declining at a decreasing rate; if it is negative, the curve will be rising at a decreasing rate. Typical examples are shown in figure 10.2.

An example of a rising nonlinear growth curve is presented below for the ratio of consumer credit to income. An example of a declining curve might be the proportion of steelworkers to total employment; steel has become a decreasingly important part of the total US economy, but in recent years that ratio has declined much more slowly than it did during the 1970s and 1980s.

10.2.2 LOGISTICS CURVES (S-CURVES)

The general form of the logistics curve is given as

$$y = 1/(a + b * c^t), \quad b > 0. \tag{10.3}$$

Sometimes this curve is written in exponential form as

$$y = 1/(a + be^{-ct}) \tag{10.4}$$

where e is the base of natural logarithms. This form will be useful when developing saturation curves.[11] Because of the difficulty of estimating this nonlinear function, it is usually estimated in the form

---

[11] For further discussion of this point, see DeLurgio, p. 649

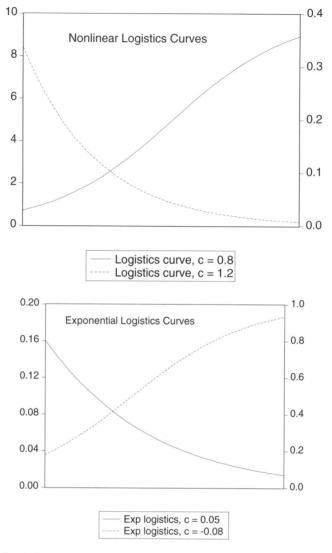

Figure 10.3 Logistics curves.

$$1/y = a + be^{-ct}. \tag{10.5}$$

A graphical comparison of typical logistics curves is shown in figure 10.3. These diagrams may look almost the same as figure 10.2, and indeed there are certain similarities. However, note that the positive growth curve has a larger slope in the middle of the sample period, giving rise to the S-shaped phenomenon.

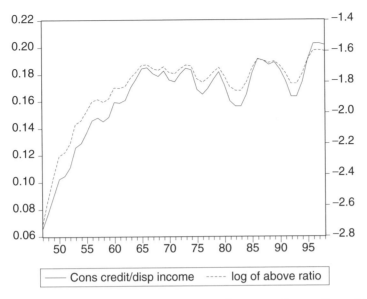

Figure 10.4 Level and log of ratio of consumer credit outstanding to disposable personal income.

A similar curve to the exponential version of the logistics curve is known as the Gompertz curve, and is

$$Y = Se^{-ae^{-bt}} \tag{10.6}$$

where S is the saturation level. This concept will be developed in the next subsection.

We now examine the ratio of consumer credit outstanding to personal income, which rose very rapidly from the end of World War II until the early 1960s, but since then has increased much more slowly. The levels and logs of this ratio are shown in figure 10.4. Since this is a ratio, the level and log forms have very similar shapes, so it does not make much difference which form of the dependent variable is used.

A nonlinear trend is fitted to the consumer credit ratio using (i) a nonlinear growth curve with levels, (ii) nonlinear growth curve with logs, (iii) a nonlinear logistics curve, and (iv) an exponential logistics curve, shown here in inverted fashion. As shown in figure 10.5, the results are fairly similar. Thus further tests are often needed to choose among these various nonlinear equations, as discussed later in this chapter.

The next example calculates the trend for real GDP for Japan from 1947 through 1998. Since this series is a level rather than ratio, the appropriate choice

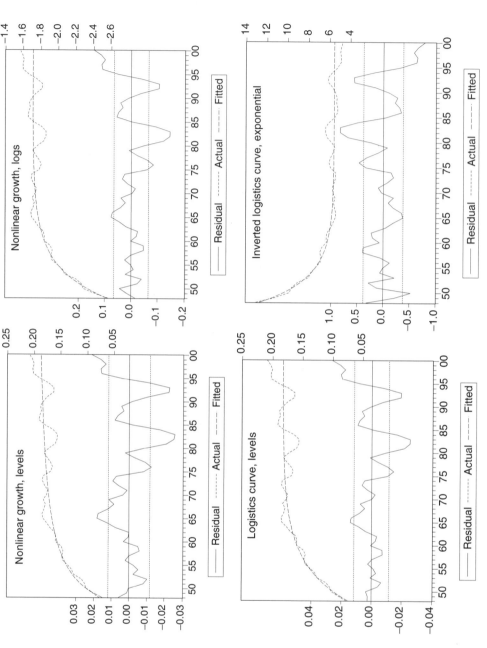

Figure 10.5 Nonlinear methods of estimating the consumer credit ratio.

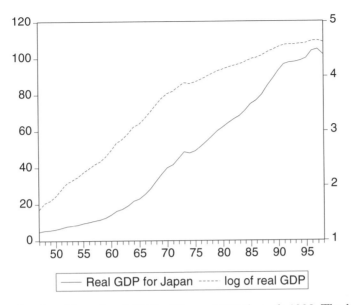

Figure 10.6   Level and log of real GDP of Japan, 1947 through 1998. The logarithm of GDP shows a much steadier path than the level of GDP.

is to use logarithms; otherwise, small percentage growth rates in recent years will be much larger in absolute value than large percentage changes shortly after World War II. Plotting the data shows that the growth rate has slowed down substantially since 1973, and again since 1991. The data are shown in figure 10.6. The logistics curve fits very poorly, and the S-curve estimate does not converge (the R^2 keeps increasing as the value of b keeps rising). The R^2 is 0.990 for the quadratic and 0.992 for the Gompertz curve.

No one knows how fast the Japanese economy will grow in the future, but we can explore the characteristics of the alternative trends. The quadratic time trend assumes an average growth rate of only 0.3% per year over the next decade, with real GDP actually declining in later years as the negative weight of the quadratic term increases. The S-curve fails to catch slower growth in recent years; it assumes the decade-long recession is an aberration and growth will return to its early period, so the catch-up will cause real growth to rise 4.4% over the next decade. That forecast consists of an unusually large gain in 1999 followed by 3% growth thereafter. The forecasts from the Gompertz curve are in the middle; they show an average gain of 3.5% per year from 1998, or 2.3% from 1999 after almost a 20% jump in the first year. All forecasts are far off the trend initially because of the 2.8% decline in real GDP in 1998.

The quadratic curve probably provides the worst forecasts even though it has the best sample period fit. The longer the extrapolation period, the more real

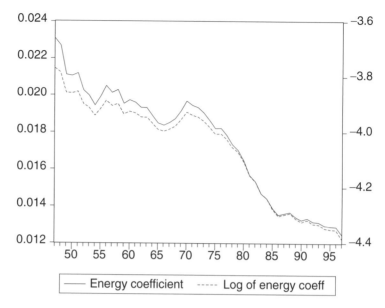

Figure 10.7 Level and log of energy usage per dollar of real GDP. Both series declined sharply during the period of high energy prices from 1973 through 1985, and fell more slowly during other periods.

GDP declines. The Gompertz curve probably generates the most realistic esti-mates in this case; an educated guess is that once Japan pulls out of its decade-long recession, real growth will average about 3% per year. However, trend extrapolation does not really seem to work very well here, so we return to the question of the Japanese growth rate in section 10.6, where trend factors are combined with economic variables.

In the next two examples, the indicated series is declining, but at a slower rate. The first is the energy coefficient; the second is the motor vehicle traffic fatality rate per 100 million miles traveled. The energy coefficient is the amount of energy used (measured in Quadrillion British Thermal Units) divided by real GDP. The data are shown in figure 10.7.

All the regression results yield R^2 in the range of 0.88 to 0.94, but there are substantial differences. In the quadratic time trend function, the rate of decline is projected to accelerate, whereas it is actually leveling off. The Gompertz curve does not work well, since it is designed more for stable rates of growth or decline. The S-curve is thrown off the track by the *rise* in the energy coefficient from 1965 through 1972; generally, this type of curve works better when the change in the series is small at first, then increases, and then slows down again. The graph of the logistics curve, which probably gives the best results, is shown in figure 10.8.

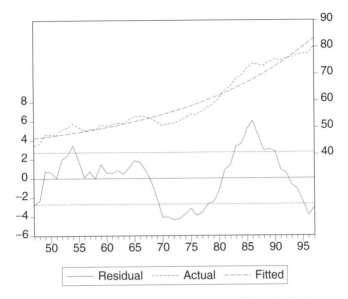

Figure 10.8 Reciprocal of the energy coefficient estimated as a logistics curve (actual and fitted values).

The last example in this section looks at the motor vehicle traffic fatality rate measured as deaths per 100 million vehicle miles traveled. The first data are available in 1925. In spite of regularly scheduled "scare stories" about how highways are becoming ever more dangerous, the death rate has fallen by 90% since 1925 and continues to decline. The data, in level and log form, are shown in figure 10.9.

In this case, the strong negative trend in the logarithmic form of the data means the Gompertz curve works best, as shown in figure 10.10. The quadratic function also fits well, and in this case shows the trend leveling off, which appears to be a reasonable assumption. The S-curve projects too rapid a decline in the future, while the logistics curve does not fit the data very well. That is because the log curve keeps falling fairly steadily and does not exhibit an S shape.

It is, of course, not possible to draw any firm conclusions about which method of trend measurement generally should be chosen from only four cases. However, the Gompertz curve generally yields the best results when the trend is fairly stable, while the logistics and S-curves work better when the series changes slowly, then more rapidly, then slows down again – provided the rate of change does not reverse course in the middle, as happened with the energy coefficient. The quadratic time trend works well only in specialized cases, since the quadratic term dominates outlying observations. If the coefficient is

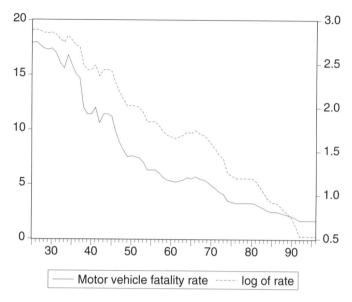

Figure 10.9 Traffic fatality rate per 100 million vehicle miles traveled, in levels and logs.

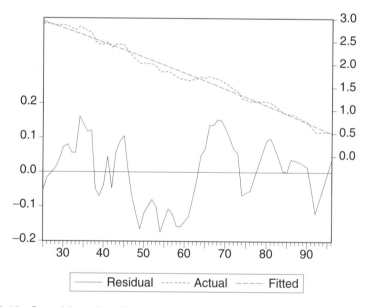

Figure 10.10 Logarithm of traffic fatality rate with trend fitted as a Gompertz curve.

positive, the equation may generate an explosive trend in later years; if it is negative, it may generate a reversal of the trend and an actual decline in later years.
Only if these developments are expected to occur would a quadratic trend equation be used.

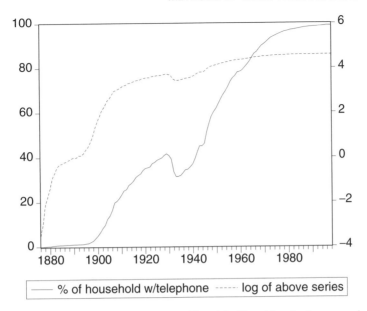

Figure 10.11 Level and log of percentage of households with telephone service. The log series rises much more rapidly in earlier years, but both series level off in recent years.

10.2.3 SATURATION CURVES

This section examines a specialized case of nonlinear trend fitting known as saturation curves. These curves are often thought to be useful for product life-cycle analysis, when firms would like to know the most likely path of the growth rate over an extended period based on a relatively few observations.

The saturation rate can be applied in two different cases. The first occurs when the upper limit is 100%, such as the percentage of households that have telephones. The second occurs when the upper level of saturation is not known, such as the number of microcomputers per person. With the proliferation of laptops, separate machines for office, primary residence, vacation home, and computers in motor vehicles, the number could rise well above 1 in the future. Examples of saturation curves are offered (i) when saturation has already been achieved, and (ii) when the product is still in the early stages of acceptance. It might seem that case (i) is only an academic exercise if the answer is already known, but this example permits us to estimate the function over a short period of time and see how well it would have performed.

The percentage of households with telephone service is a useful series to examine because data exist all the way back to 1876, the year the telephone was invented, thus providing a much longer and complete series than is available for most product life cycles. The data in levels and log form are shown in figure 10.11; note the dip in the Great Depression of the 1930s.

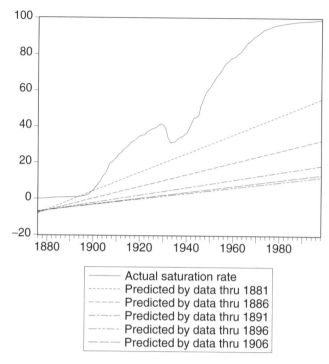

Figure 10.12 Percentage of households with a telephone service, compared with predictions from saturation curves generated using various sample periods.

Saturation curves are a special case of logistics curves. Consider a modified logistic equation written as $\log y = S + b*c^t$, where S is the saturation level. If $c < 1$, then as $t \to \infty$, $c^t \to 0$, so the function becomes $\log y = S$. Rearranging some terms and taking logarithms a second time, this equation can be rewritten as

$$\log(y/(S - y)) = b + c*t. \tag{10.7}$$

Similar manipulation with the Gompertz function yields the linear regression

$$\log(\log(S/y)) = b + c*t. \tag{10.8}$$

In this example, the first step is to determine which function fits the telephone data better over the 1876–1998 period. The reader may wish to estimate both these functions; an inspection of the residuals clearly shows the logistics curve fits better.

Next, consider how well this curve would have predicted telephone service saturation levels if it has been used with data after 5, 10, 15, 20, and 30 years. The results, which are shown in figure 10.12, are quite disappointing in the sense that they all severely underestimate the rate at which households added telephone service starting after 1906.

In spite of the apparent failure of this method, there is a valuable lesson to be learned from this case, one that could have had practical significance in recent decades. It doesn't make much sense to own a telephone if you are the only one with such an instrument; the parties with whom you plan to speak must also own telephones. Until switching networks had been generally established, relatively few households purchased telephone service. It was only after 1906, when networks became much more broadly based, that the percentage of households with phone service accelerated.

Maybe this sounds like an outmoded example, yet the same type of misguided saturation analysis was applied by AT&T statisticians in the 1970s when they tried to project how many area codes would be needed. As is well known by now, they failed to predict how the proliferation of lines for fax machines, computers, cell phones and the Internet would cause an explosion in the demand for individual phone numbers. While those statisticians were among the best in the country, they had no idea of what the future would bring. The lesson here is that saturation analysis generally does not work well in situations where the direction of future technology is unknown. It is more useful in marketing studies where technology remains constant. For this reason, these methods are generally most useful when combined with economic factors, which will be examined in the remainder of this chapter.

Case Study 22: Growth in E-commerce

The growth pattern for E-commerce, or on-line retail sales, has been hotly debated, since no one knows the ultimate potential of on-line shopping. Also, very little data are yet available. The first figures prepared by the Bureau of the Census indicated that E-commerce sales were 0.63% of total retail sales in 1999.4, 0.70% in 2000.1, 0.68% in 2000.2, and 0.78% in 2000.3. Census defines E-commerce sales as "sales of goods and services over the Internet, an extranet, Electronic Data Interchange, or other online system. Payment may or may not be made online." These figures are then compared with total retail sales, a useful approximation but one that is not directly comparable because it does not include services such as airline travel.

Combining our own estimates with those of the Census Bureau, we can estimate that E-commerce sales as a percentage of total retail sales were 0.1% in 1997, 0.25% in 1998, 0.5% in 1999, and 0.8% in 2000. These data are then combined with a saturation curve to estimate the growth in E-commerce sales over the next 10 years.

The eventual saturation level is unknown, of course, so several plausible estimates are presented in table 10.2. Those can be used to provide a range of growth rates and rule out some of the more extreme predictions.

Table 10.2   Retail sales by category and E-commerce saturation rates.

	Percentage of sales	Saturation rates	
		Min–Max	Most likely
Total retail sales	100.0	10–27	17.7
Building materials and hardware stores	5.6	0–20	10
Motor vehicles and parts	24.6	5–30	10
Furniture and appliances	5.3	20–50	30
Other durables (books, jewelry, etc.)	5.5	40–70	50
General merchandise (department) stores	12.6	20–40	30
Grocery stores	14.8	0–20	5
Gas stations	6.9	0–10	0
Clothing stores	4.4	20–40	30
Restaurants	9.5	0–15	5
Drug stores	4.2	30–60	45
Other nondurables (variety stores, etc.)	6.6	20–60	40

A saturation curve is fitted based on the four data points given above using the assumptions of saturation rates of (a) 10%, (b) 17.7%, and (c) 27% of total retail sales. Figure 10.13 shows the projected saturation rates under these three assumptions for each year from 2001 through 2010. Table 10.3 shows the level, in millions of dollars, and the percentage growth rate for E-commerce sales, based on the assumption that total retail sales rise 5% per year.

How realistic are these numbers? E-commerce sales in 2000, according to Census Bureau estimates, were slightly in excess of $26 billion. That number may seem high, but it represents gross revenues for sales, not net revenues or profit margins. Retail sales profits were approximately $90 billion in 2000, or about 3% of total gross sales. Applying the same percentage to E-commerce sales would yield a profit of about $750 million. Of course that figure is grossly overestimated for 2000 because of the amount spent on advertising and start-up costs, but it provides some estimate of what steady-state profits might be once the industry stabilizes. Then again, cut-throat competition on the Internet could drive profit margins to zero: we are not making any prediction here about profits, merely putting the sales figures in perspective.

Maybe the problems of late deliveries, chargebacks, consumer credit fraud, warehousing and inventory bottlenecks, on-line misrepresentations, and legal roadblocks from car dealers and others, will all be resolved, and the figures for E-commerce sales given in table 10.2 will turn out to be far too low. Yet this author vigorously disagrees with that conclusion, and thinks the sparse data nonetheless provide a reasonable upper bound for the growth rates in

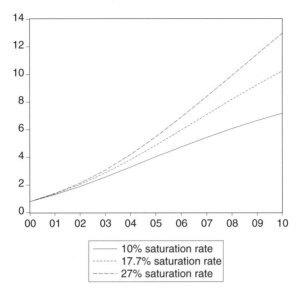

Figure 10.13 E-commerce sales as a proportion of total retail sales based on alternative assumptions about saturation rates.

Table 10.3 E-commerce sales and growth rates for alternative saturation assumptions.

Year	10% saturation	Growth (%)	17.7% saturation	Growth (%)	27% saturation	Growth (%)
2000	25,992	73.6	25,992	73.6	25,992	73.6
2001	44,487	71.2	46,187	77.7	47,236	81.7
2002	67,689	52.2	72,779	57.6	76,039	61.0
2003	96,266	42.2	107,560	47.8	115,109	51.4
2004	129,549	34.6	150,610	40.0	165,319	43.6
2005	166,636	28.6	201,517	33.8	226,970	37.3
2006	206,563	24.0	259,507	28.8	299,821	32.1
2007	248,434	20.3	323,583	24.7	383,189	27.8
2008	291,494	17.3	392,677	21.4	476,084	24.2
2009	335,171	15.0	465,756	18.6	577,353	21.3
2010	379,070	13.1	541,903	16.3	685,802	18.8

E-commerce sales that are far below some of the blue-sky estimates currently circulating. Implicit in this forecast is the assumption that E-commerce does not really represent a new technology but merely a simpler, more efficient way of ordering existing merchandise.

10.3 PREDICTING TRENDS WHERE CYCLICAL INFLUENCES ARE IMPORTANT

Many people think the use of personal computers is still in its infancy. That may very well turn out to be the case. Yet applying logistics curves or other similar nonlinear trends may not give very useful results because computer sales also contain a significant cyclical pattern that may disguise underlying trends. The following case study evaluates different measures for projecting sales of personal computers.

Case Study 23: Sales of Personal Computers

The dependent variable is the number of personal computers (PCs) sold each year. The series is actually an amalgam of estimates of annual sales by Dataquest and the figures published by BEA for the amount spent on personal computers by individuals (personal computers bought by businesses are not reported separately). For the years when the data series overlap, the ratios appear to be consistent, so the BEA series on expenditures is probably a reasonable approximation of the number of PCs purchased. It also has the advantage of extending back to 1977.

The reader can easily verify that the logistics and Gompertz curves do not fit the data very well, so the discussion is confined to an S-curve, a saturation curve, and a log-linear regression with and without economic variables. The most important economic variables are the change in real disposable income, consumer confidence, and the Federal funds rate. The major conclusions can be summarized as follows.

- A linear regression in which the log of computer sales is correlated with a trend and the percentage change in relevant economic variables provides very poor estimates. It is clear that a nonlinear formulation improves the forecasting accuracy of the equation.
- The S-curve formulation fits the existing data much better than a saturation curve that assumes everyone will eventually purchase a new PC each year, or even that everyone will eventually own one PC (these are discussed below). If this analysis is correct, the heyday of rapid growth in PCs had passed by 2000.
- The use of cyclical variables does not change the parameters of the trend terms very much, but these terms are highly significant. This result suggests that an acceleration or deceleration in computer sales in any given year should be analyzed in terms of the current economic conditions as well as the underlying long-term trends.

The simulation over the 1977–99 period for an S-curve with and without the economic variables listed above is shown in figure 10.14. There is not a great

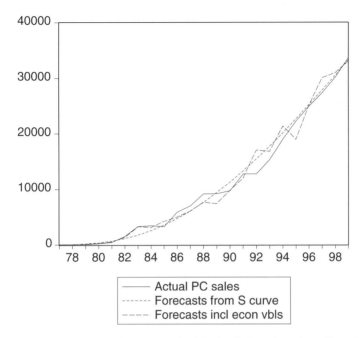

Figure 10.14 Actual sales of PCs compared with simulations based on (i) an S-curve with no economic variables, and (ii) an S-curve with changes in the Federal funds rate, real disposal income, and consumer confidence.

deal of difference between the two simulations; the equation with economic variables overstates the drop in PC sales in 1995 resulting from higher interest rates, but it captures other cyclical swings more closely. Readers can verify that the slowdown in income and decline in consumer confidence in late 2000 and early 2001 actually did reduce the growth in PC sales, as would be indicated by the S-curve equation with economic variables.

Using the S-curve equation to predict the number of PC sales out for 10 years shows the growth rate in sales slowing from 8.4% in 2000 to 4.6% in 2010, barely higher than the growth rate for the overall economy. For those who see the use of PCs still in its infancy, those growth rates may appear far too low. Thus it is worth examining the results that would be obtained from modifying the S-curve so it is a saturation curve.

No one knows how many personal computers will be purchased each year in the future, but alternative estimates can be prepared as follows. One assumption might be that, at saturation, every person in the US has an average of three computers: at work, at home, and a portable computer. Also, assume computers are replaced an average of every three years. Then the ratio of personal computers purchased each year to the population would rise to 1.0. More conservative assumptions can be prepared under the assumption that everyone

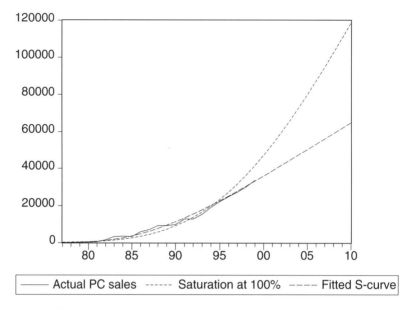

Figure 10.15 Simulation of PC sales using an S-curve and a saturation curve assuming 100%.

has an average of two computers, or that everyone has an average of one computer at saturation levels. Those assumptions would correspond to saturation ratios of 0.50 and 0.33 of the population, assuming a new computer is purchased once every three years.

Some experts would say even those optimistic estimates are far too low. In the future, they would claim, a computer in one's motor vehicle will be as common as a radio is today. Most households will have a computer in every room: one in the kitchen to organize the appliances, one in the den to complement TV viewing, one in the garage to monitor lawn care and sprinkling, one in the bedroom to set the alarm clock and tell the kitchen computer to start the coffee, and so on.

The statistical analysis shows just the opposite. If one fits the existing figures to an S-curve and compares it with more optimistic projections of saturation curves along the lines expounded above, saturation curve estimates are already far too high, overestimating actual PC sales in 2000 by almost 30%, as shown in figure 10.15. Even using more modest saturation rates overstates recent sales growth, as shown in figure 10.16. Of course, fitting a logarithmic curve through existing data without incorporating any variables representing economic progress or technological change may provide long-term estimates that are way off the mark. That is always the risk attendant in generating long-term forecasts.

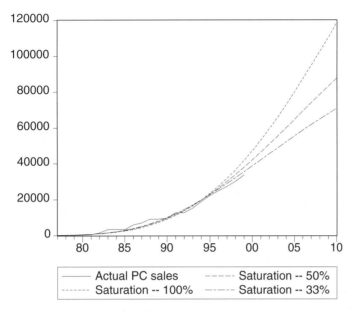

Figure 10.16 Actual and forecast values of PC sales assuming saturation rats of 100%, 50%, and 33%.

Nonetheless, the statistics have a compelling story to tell, namely that growth in sales of PCs – at least in their present configuration – will be quite limited in the future. Electronic computing devices that perform the types of tasks listed above will probably not look like PCs and will be called something else. Based on the typical PC configuration used for word processing, Internet access, modest computing tasks, and electronic games in 2000, the curves fitted above strongly suggest only moderate growth in future years.[12]

Maybe we are making the same mistake as those AT&T statisticians did 30 years ago by failing to grasp that the information revolution is still in its infancy. That may well be the case. Yet the point here is far different, namely that the PC *as presently configured* is already an anachronism: able to perform a large variety of tasks, but none of them as efficiently as devices designed for specific purposes. In the future, then, the growth rate of PCs as they are currently known should diminish sharply, while explosive growth will occur in products and services still in their infancy or not yet even invented.

---

[12] This point may seem obvious to the reader, but when this example was actually prepared in the spring of 2000, many analysts thought PC sales would continue to rise at double-digit rates indefinitely.

10.4 PROJECTING LONG-RUN TRENDS IN REAL GROWTH

Productivity is technically defined as output per employee-hour, but over very long periods of time, and for cross-country comparisons, this can be closely approximated by real GDP per capita. During the 20th century, this measure of productivity growth averaged just under 2% per year for the US economy. Major deviations from this trend occurred only twice: during the Great Depression of the 1930s, when productivity hardly advanced at all, and during World War II, when capacity was stretched to its limits.

However, fairly steady growth has not been the case for most other countries of the world. Europe and Japan were devastated during World War II; after 1945, growth proceeded very rapidly for two decades, after which it slowed down again. South Korea was a very poor country for several years after the Korean War ended, but its growth rate then started to spurt in the mid-1960s.

Rapid growth halted for both Japan and Korea in the 1990s. From 1992 through 1999, real GDP in Japan advanced an average of less than 1% per year. The Korean economy grew very rapidly to 1995, but growth slipped in 1996 and 1997, followed by a 6% decline in real GDP in 1998. Both of these slowdowns were generally unanticipated; in fact, during the early 1990s it became fashionable to present the "Asian growth model" as superior to the engines of growth that drove the US economy.

The Solow growth model, first introduced in 1956, shows that as countries become more mature, their growth rate will decline even if the ratio of capital spending to GDP remains steady, because more investment will be used for replacement purposes and less for expansion. In a similar vein, it can be argued that when countries are poor, they can make great strides by quickly adopting new methods of technology and shifting workers from agriculture to manufacturing; but as they approach the leading edge of technology, growth will diminish.

A comprehensive model that predicts the growth rate in any given country would also include variables measuring the amount of education, degree of freedom and acceptance of capitalism, development of financial institutions and transportation infrastructure, and other policy variables. In some cases a switch from a totalitarian state to one with some measure of democracy does not improve real growth, as witnessed by the collapse of the Russian economy during the 1990s.

Nonetheless, except for major political upheavals and reversals, the growth rate of a country is usually closely related to (i) the ratio of investment to GDP, and (ii) the gap between its level of productivity and productivity in the US. The latter variable can be fitted using the various nonlinear methods explained in this chapter, including a saturation curve where the maximum level of per capita GDP is given by the US level. Fluctuations in this trend can then be related to capital spending ratios. The next case study utilizes this approach to project long-term growth rates in Japan and Korea.

Case Study 24: Projecting Long-term Growth Rates in Japan and Korea

This case study uses long-term trend methods of projection to predict real GDP in Japan and Korea. We seek to determine which method gives better forecasts: log-linear, S-curve, or saturation curve analysis – and whether the answer differs by country. It is also of interest to determine whether the addition of economic variables improves the forecasts generated from saturation curves. In terms of actual forecasting, this raises the issue of being able to predict the economic variables, but the question remains whether they improve the fit during the sample period. If that is not the case, it is extremely unlikely that they would generate accurate forecasts when the values of the independent variables are unknown.

The Solow growth model states that the ratio of investment to GDP is an important long-run determinant of the growth rate. Another key variable might be the foreign exchange rate; that is important for Japan, but less so for Korea. When the yen is undervalued, growth is stimulated; when it is overvalued, exports and growth are reduced. That is not the case for the US because the world is on a de facto dollar standard, so a stronger dollar boosts investment by attracting foreign capital and consumption by reducing the price of imports. However, in a semi-closed society such as Japan, foreign investment is not as welcome, and consumers are not permitted to reap the benefits of a stronger currency through lower import prices.

The following equations are estimated:

$$\log GDP = a_1 + a_2 * trend$$
$$+ a_3 * investment\ ratio + a_4 * foreign\ exchange\ rate \qquad (10.9)$$

$$\log GDP = b_1 - b_2 (b_3 + trend)$$
$$+ b_4 * investment\ ratio + b_5 * foreign\ exchange\ rate \qquad (10.10)$$

$$\log(\log(prodUS / prodX)) = c_1 + c_2 * trend$$
$$+ c_3 * investment\ ratio + c_4 * foreign\ exchange\ rate. \qquad (10.11)$$

These equations are estimated for Korea and Japan; *prodUS* is the per capita real GDP in the US, and *prodX* is the per capita real GDP in Japan or Korea, converted to dollars at 1997 purchasing parities.

Equation (10.11) utilizes a saturation curve where real growth slows down as per capita GDP (productivity) in those countries approaches US levels. A four-year moving average of the investment ratio is used for Japan; the unlagged

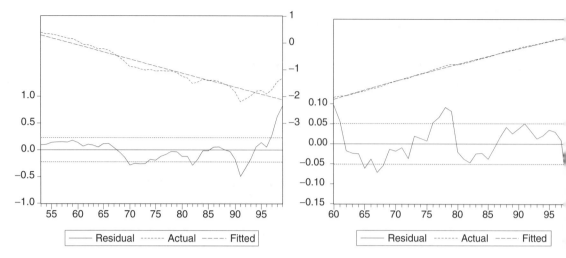

Figure 10.17 The left chart shows Japanese real GDP fitted to a saturation curve. The right chart shows Korean GDP fitted to an S-curve.

ratio is used for Korea. Also, the Korean equation is estimated starting in 1960; before then, the economy was still recovering from the ravaging effects of the Korean War.

We first examine how well these equations work without the economic variables. The saturation curve approach does not work very well in the 1990s, as shown in figure 10.17. The results are similar for log-linear and S-curves. Hence we proceed directly to the next step, which includes economic variables as indicated above.

Figure 10.18 shows the residuals for Japanese real GDP using these three regression equations. As it turns out, none of them fit very well. The linear regression is by far the worst, since it implies the growth rate before 1990 would continue indefinitely. Of the other two regressions, the S-curve provides somewhat better forecasts than the saturation curve. For the Korean economy, as shown in figure 10.19, the behavior of the regressions for the 1998 recession depend on the relative importance of the investment ratio; since that term is significant in the saturation curve equation, the simulated value of GDP does not turn down at all. The S-curve regression gives the best results, with the linear regression in an intermediate position.

This case study illustrates that using nonlinear methods of trend projections will give substantially better long-term forecasts than even fairly complex log-linear equations. Furthermore, these projections can be helped by including economic variables. In the case of Japan, the investment ratio had been declining throughout the 1970s and 1980s, so a forecast that real growth was about to diminish would not have been unrealistic. In the case of Korea, the 1998 recession was an exogenous event brought about by excessive borrowing

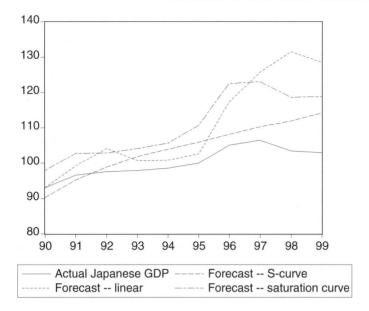

Figure 10.18 Forecasts of Japanese real GDP using a log-linear regression, S-curve, and saturation curve. All equations contain the Japanese investment/GDP ratio and foreign exchange rate.

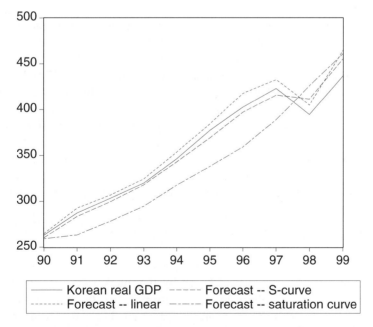

Figure 10.19 Predictions of Korean GDP using a log-linear regression, an S-curve, and a saturation curve. All regressions include the ratio of investment to GDP.

overseas in dollars, the collapse of semiconductor prices in 1996, and the 1997 recession in Japan. Yet even without taking these factors into account, the S-curve analysis would have shown a slowdown in Korean growth from 10% to 7% in the 1990s – and indicated that investment decisions and forecasts based on continued 10% growth would lead to a disequilibrium situation and a severe adjustment later in the decade.

10.5 FORECASTING VERY LONG-RANGE TRENDS: POPULATION AND NATURAL RESOURCE TRENDS

This section contains some general guidelines on generating forecasts for very long-run trends. Starting in the early 1970s, the "Limits to Growth" movement became popular because, it was claimed, if the world economy kept growing at recent rates, we would soon "run out of everything" and the standard of living would start to decline. This theory became increasingly popular as the price of crude oil rose from $3 to $35/bbl, although it recently sold at a discount when oil prices fell back to $10/bbl in early 1999.

The main error made by most long-term forecasters is they confuse recent changes with long-term trends. That error may occur for two reasons. First, developments of recent years may be temporary. Second, and probably generally more important, if these trends were to continue, economic forces would work to reverse them. If prices rise sharply, for example, demand would decrease and supply would increase.

Often, the factors that cause trends to reverse are based on political decisions. The US budget remained in deficit continuously throughout the 1970s and 1980s, rising to a peak deficit of $290 billion in fiscal year 1992. At that point, most economists and financial analysts assumed the deficit would continue to rise indefinitely. Eight years later, the surplus was $237 billion, so most economists switched and predicted a steady rise in the surplus for the next several years. That turned out to be wrong too. In 1993, Congress and the President decided to reduce the rate of growth in government spending; tax rates were also raised slightly, although that increase accounted for less than 10% of the total swing in the budget position. In 2002, the pace of government spending accelerated, and tax rates were reduced. Problem 3 in this chapter explores some of the ramifications for budget projections in the future.

10.5.1 PREDICTING LONG-TERM TRENDS IN POPULATION GROWTH

One of the most common issues faced by demographers is how fast the US (and world) population will grow in the future. Since the end of World War II, population has risen at an average annual rate of 1.34%. According to the 2000 decennial census, US population was 281 million, up from 76 million in 1900. If this rate of growth were to continue indefinitely, US population would rise

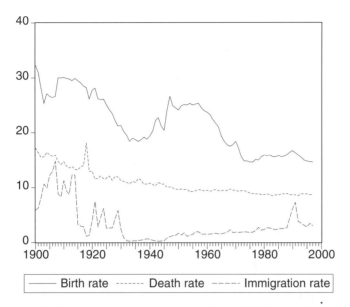

Figure 10.20 Birth, death, and immigration rates for the US during the twentieth century (per 1,000).

to over 1 billion by 2100, and for that matter over 134 *trillion* by 3000. Population density would exceed 5 million people per square mile, compared with just under 10 people per square mile now.

Obviously these are ludicrous projections; they are provided to show what happens when one assumes that long-run trends continue without change. However, they do raise the valid issue of how fast US population is likely to grow in the coming decades and centuries.

Figure 10.20 illustrates the data for birth, death, and immigration rates for the US during the 20th century. The birth rate has been cut in half from approximately 30 to 15 births per 1,000 people, and has stabilized near that level since the early 1970s. The 1918 spike in the death rate was due to casualties in World War I and the influenza epidemic of that year. In recent years the death rate has shown virtually no change at 8.6 deaths per 1,000 people. The immigration rate hit rock bottom during the decade of the Great Depression, but has increased almost steadily since then; the spike in 1990 represents a change in the counting of undocumented aliens. If recent trends were to continue, the annual growth in the population would be 1.5% from new births minus 0.8% from deaths plus 0.3% from net immigration, or a growth rate of 1.0%. That is the current rate, which is slightly less than the 1.3% average annual growth rate during the 20th century. The key question, of course, is how long these rates will remain in effect.

As of 1998, the Census Bureau reported that the average number of children per female was 2.00 for whites, 2.43 for blacks, 2.15 for American Indian and

Eskimo, 1.95 for Asian, and 2.98 for Hispanics. Because of infant deaths, demographers calculate that the birth rate needed to hold the population constant in the absence of any immigration is 2.11. If current birth rates do not change very much, the number of people classified as white and Asian in the US will decline over time, while the number of people classified as black and Hispanic will continue to rise.

These are the raw materials from which one can construct a long-range projection of population trends in the US. It is logical to assume that the birth rates for white and Asian women will remain below 2.11 indefinitely; the question is what happens to the birth rates for black and Hispanic women, and what happens to the immigration rate. As black and Hispanic families become more affluent, their birth rate would probably follow the same type of declining curve as occurred for white women throughout the century. Hence the key factor becomes the rate of immigration. If that rate remains near current levels, not only will that serve as a source of population growth because of new immigrants, but women in that category can reasonably be expected to have a birth rate near the current level of 3 children per women for at least the first generation after arriving in the US.

One logical economic argument would claim that immigration of Hispanics will be negatively correlated with the growth rate of the Latin American economy. The more economic conditions improve, the fewer workers will be tempted to uproot their families and move to the US. That requires increased investment in Latin America, more free trade flows, and the establishment of a rule of law and democratic government throughout that region. No one pretends these are easy variables to predict.

The other argument that could affect population growth would be a sharp decline in the death rate, as "miracle drugs" and replacement parts enable people to live much longer. If that were the case, population could grow at abnormally rapid rates for several decades.

In order to offer long-term projections of immigration rates into the US, it would be necessary to assess future developments in medical care, growth in Latin American and Asian nations, and the political climate regarding immigration. This author has no strong views on these issues; this discussion is presented to show the methodology for analyzing this problem, as opposed to simply trying to extrapolate existing trends of the previous century. If population growth were to average 1.0% in the 21st century, 0.5% in the 22nd century, and 0.0% thereafter, US population would level off at about 1.2 billion around 2200.

10.5.2 PREDICTING LONG-TERM TRENDS IN NATURAL RESOURCE PRICES

This section discusses methods of forecasting long-term trends in prices for two key natural resources: farm prices and oil prices. "Conventional wisdom" states

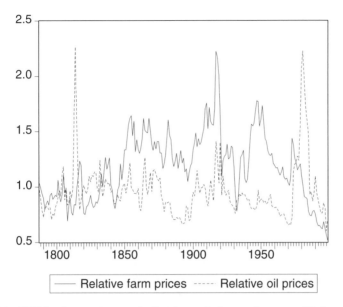

Figure 10.21 PPI for farm prices and oil prices relative to the cost of living.

that farm prices are under continuing downward pressure because productivity in the agricultural sector is rising much faster than population, and as income rises, people spend a smaller proportion of their budget on food, especially food consumed at home (omitting the value added of restaurants). In contrast, it is often claimed that some day the world will "run out" of oil, both because, unlike food, it is not a renewable resource, and as income rises people spend a larger proportion of their budget on energy needs for motor vehicles, larger residences, air conditioning, and so on.

While that possibility cannot be ruled out, it has been completely false over the past 200 years. Figure 10.21 shows that the wholesale price of *both farm products and energy products* has declined at about the same rate relative to the cost of living since 1787. Of course there have been some notable fluctuations, including the recent surges in energy prices that started in 1973; but as of 1999, the price of energy relative to the cost of living was only about 70% of its level during the founding years of the Republic.

Of course, this historical evidence does not guarantee that these downward trends will continue. Some natural resource economists not employed by the oil industry argue that eventually the world will run out of oil reserves, at which point the relative price will rise sharply. This "shortage" argument is based on both demand and supply considerations. On the demand side, it is claimed that the rising standard of living in the Third World will eventually result in a substantial demand for petroleum products, even if – as has been the case since 1973 – the demand for petroleum in the industrialized world has actually declined. On the supply side, even at present levels, the huge reserves in the Arabian peninsula will eventually be exhausted, and whatever oil is pumped in the rest of the world will be available only at sharply higher prices.

The demand argument is more straightforward. It has already been shown in section 10.2 that the energy coefficient in the US has declined sharply since 1973; a very similar curve could be observed for Western Europe and Japan. While two cars in every garage and a central air conditioning unit in every house in India and China may eventually occur, we estimate that development would be at least several hundred years in the future. From 1973 through 1999, the demand for petroleum products excluding North America, Western Europe, and Japan rose only about 2% per year, even though those years coincided with extraordinarily rapid growth in Southeast Asia.

The key questions are thus on the supply side, which is indeed where the argument is centered. Since 1985, crude oil production has risen almost 2% per year. If that rate were to continue, it would outpace the rise in demand. However, projecting that trend is of dubious accuracy, since petroleum is indeed a non-renewable resource. The main argument actually hinges on alternative sources of fuel. There are several possibilities: nuclear, alternative non-renewable sources (oil shale and tar sands), crops such as corn and sugar, reprocessed waste material and other biomass, wind, geothermal, and solar. According to the Energy Information Administration, in 2020 nuclear power will account for about 5% of total US energy requirements, renewable sources – mainly ethanol and waste recycling – will account for about 10%, and "other" exotic types will account for less than 1%. For comparison, the 1999 figures were about 9% for nuclear, 9% for renewable, and less than 1% for other.

Alternative energy sources were prominently discussed in the first half of the 1980s, when benchmark crude oil prices averaged $35/bbl, but attention quickly faded when oil prices plunged. The technology still exists, but these methods are not cost-effective at recent levels of oil prices.

To take one much-discussed example, consider the costs of ethanol. One bushel of corn yields approximately 2½ gallons of ethanol. If corn sells for $2.50/bushel, that is equivalent to $1.00/gallon of ethanol. If the price of crude oil is $25/bbl, or about 60c/gallon, ethanol is not competitive unless it is subsidized.

Because of continuing advances in technology, including but not limited to biotechnology, the price of corn is likely to stay at or below $2.50/bushel over the next 20 years. If the current equilibrium price of oil is $25/bbl and it remains constant in *real* terms, meaning it rises about 3% per year in nominal terms, the nominal price would be $45/bbl by 2020, so the price of crude oil price would rise slightly above $1/gallon. At that point, ethanol would be fully competitive.

No one suggests that ethanol will completely replace petroleum. Currently, world petroleum use is about 68 million barrels per day, or 25 billion barrels per year, which is equivalent to about 1 trillion gallons. The total current world

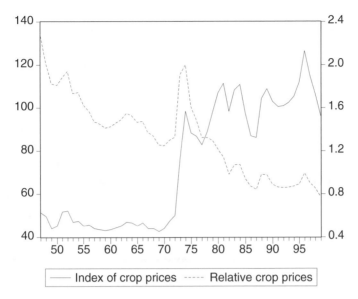

Figure 10.22 Index of crop prices received by farmers – actual level and relative to the PPI.

corn crop is about 25 billion bushels, or 62.5 billion gallons of ethanol – and most corn is used to feed animals.

However, no one is suggesting the world will completely run out of petroleum by 2020. Instead, a realistic scenario suggests that the gap between demand and supply of petroleum will be about 2% per year by then, or 20 billion gallons per year. The continuing advance in technology means the world corn crop will double by 2020 to 50 billion bushels. If the demand for meat animals rises 2% per year, then half of the increase in production, or about 12.5 billion bushels, would be available for ethanol production. That is equivalent to more than 30 billion gallons of gasoline per year.

Focusing on ethanol does not even take into consideration energy that could be obtained from industrial waste, crops such as sugar, and other forms of biomass, plus the increase in energy supply from wind, geothermal, and solar power that would become cost effective if energy prices rose far enough. The supply of solar energy is almost infinite; it is expensive to harness and new methods of technology would have to be invented to transform it into power for motor vehicles (perhaps through batteries) and heating buildings. If oil prices rose enough, though, it would be fatuous to claim that no one could develop this technology.

For much of the 21st century, though, the clear alternative to oil and natural gas will be renewable sources. For that purpose, the long-term projection of prices received by farmers for crops is of interest. The data for actual and relative price indexes since the end of World War II are shown in figure 10.22.

A simple log-linear regression shows that the average price of crops received by farmers has declined 1.7% per year relative to the non-farm PPI. In approximate terms that reflects a $3\frac{1}{2}$% average annual gain in productivity in the farm sector, compared with a $1\frac{3}{4}$% gain in the non-farm sector. It is likely that trend will continue in the future. Since 1982, the non-farm PPI has risen an average of 1.7% per year, which is the basis for the assumption that corn prices will remain constant in nominal terms.

This brief sketch certainly will not settle the question of where oil prices are heading in the long term. However, the relevant facts are as follows. As soon as the nominal price of oil rises to the $45–50/bbl level, alternative sources of energy become cost-efficient, at which point the demand for petroleum products declines. Hence this analysis would indicate that price range represents an upper limit on oil prices for at least the next several decades even if supply does start to diminish.

Problems and Questions

1. This problem is based on annual data for the semiconductor industry. While they share some similarities with the computer data, there are also some important differences, as will be seen in this example. The annual data are compiled by the semiconductor industry association (SIA), available at www.semichips.org. This website also contains data, free of charge, for monthly billings and shipments, plus data by region. More detailed data can also be purchased from this organization.

The data compiled by SIA are actually available back to 1954, but before 1961 the industry was in its infancy, with growth rates exceeding 100%, and the data are necessarily somewhat sparse and incomplete. In 1961, however, the industry posted only a 7.6% annual growth rate, and since then annual sales have been subject to cyclical fluctuations. Starting with that date, the log of shipments, together with a simple trend that rises at 15% per year, explains more than 99% of the variance, as shown in figure 10.23.

However, an entirely different picture emerges when percentage changes are considered, as shown in figure 10.24. The annual change in semiconductor shipments has ranged from a high of 72% in 1973 to a low of −16% in 1985. If monthly or quarterly data were to be considered, the swings are so erratic that one would use some sort of smoothing model to predict short-term movements in shipments.

Much of the annual fluctuation in shipments is due to changes in price, which in turn are due to changes in capacity. A model to explain these adequately would have to include variables and equations for total capacity in each major country for each major type of semiconductor,

continued

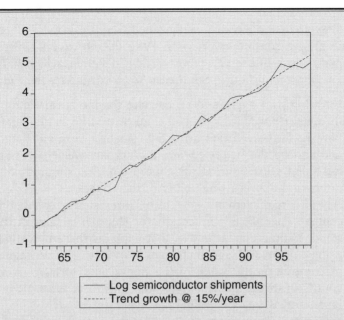

Figure 10.23 Logarithm of semiconductor shipments. A simple trend explains over 99% of the log of shipments.

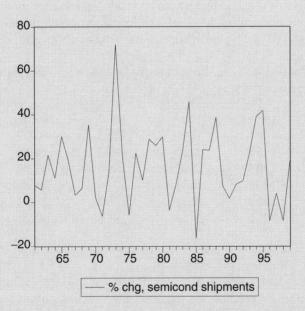

Figure 10.24 Annual percentage changes in semiconductor shipments. In spite of a strong upward trend, shipments have grown at highly variable annual rates.

including Japan and Korea as well as the US and Europe. Indeed, the sharp decline in semiconductor prices in 1996 due to excess capacity was the proximate cause of the net export deficit in Korea, which led to the collapse of the won and other Southeast Asian currencies the following year.

(a) Fit a logistics curve and an S-curve for the annual data from 1955 through 1999. Which do you think would be better for forecasting? Now re-fit these curves using data starting from 1961 through 1999, and choose the better equation. Compare these curves to a simple log-linear regression. Do the more complex methods of estimation improve the forecasting ability of the equation?

(b) Suppose management were more interested in predicting the percentage changes in semiconductor shipments than in the long-run trend. Estimate an equation that explains these percentage changes using current and lagged changes in industrial production, purchases of computers, the value of the dollar, and foreign growth rates of countries in the Far East (for this purpose, testing with GDP for Japan and Korea will suffice). Show your results.

(c) Using the results from the percentage change equation, determine whether a better forecasting equation for semiconductor shipments can be developed that includes both a nonlinear trend and some combination of these variables.

(d) Would fitting a saturation curve help improve the forecast accuracy? In order to test this hypothesis, consider alternative assumptions that current per capita level of semiconductor shipments is equal to (i) 50%, (ii) 25%, and (iii) 10% of saturation levels.

2. The following data show cellular telephone subscribership in millions, starting in 1985:

1985	0.34	1992	11.03
1986	0.68	1993	16.07
1987	1.23	1994	24.13
1988	2.07	1995	33.79
1989	3.51	1996	44.04
1990	5.28	1997	55.31
1991	7.56	1998	69.21

(a) Fit these data to a log-linear regression. Comment on the advisability of using that equation for forecasting.

(b) Fit the data using an S-curve. Based on the fit, would you use this equation to predict the demand for cellular phone subscribers in 2010, 2020, and 2030? Now calculate the forecasts for those years.

continued

Do you think the numbers are realistic? (For comparative purposes, assume US population in 2000 is 281 million and it rises by 1% per year.)

(c) Reestimate the equation using a saturation curve in which every person in the US is a cellular telephone subscriber by 2030. Compare the forecasts generated by this equation with those from the S-curve.

(d) Based on these findings, identify the equation you would use for cell phone subscribers for the period from 2000 to 2030.

3. In this example, you are asked to supply long-range forecasts for the Federal budget surplus or deficit and the social security fund surplus or deficit to the year 2050. In some cases, you will be required to use government assumptions; in other cases, the results will depend on alternative estimates about the economy and fiscal policy. The fixed assumptions are as follows:

- Total population will rise 1% per year.
- Population aged 65 and over will rise 2% per year.
- Social security benefits will rise at a rate of 2% plus the rate of inflation to 2010, and 3% plus the rate of inflation after that.
- Federal tax receipts will rise 1.2 times as fast as the growth in nominal GDP (e.g., if nominal GDP grows 5% per year, Federal tax receipts will rise 6%).
- Interest rates will average 6% per year (actually they would vary depending on the inflation rate and the budget position, but this is a simplifying assumption).
- Government expenditures will rise by a rate equal to 2% plus the rate of inflation plus an adjustment for real growth. To simplify matters, assume this adjustment is equal to 3% minus the actual growth rate (e.g., if growth is 4%, spending would rise 1% less than inflation plus 2%; if it fell to 2%, spending would rise 1% more than inflation plus 2%).
- Currently, there is a $2 trillion surplus in the social security "trust fund"; this number will rise to $4 trillion by 2010. After that, social security receipts will rise by the same rate as nominal GDP increases, while benefits will rise by inflation plus 2%. The annual change in the total balance in the trust fund will equal receipts plus interest earned on the balance minus benefits. In 2000, social security benefits paid were $410 billion and social security receipts were $550 billion.
- For the first three parts of the problem, assume the inflation rate averages 3%. This assumption is then relaxed in part (d).

(a) Project the Federal budget surplus or deficit position annually from 2000 to 2050 based on assumptions that real GDP will rise (i) 2%, (ii) 3%, and (iii) 4%.

continued

(b) The total national debt held by the public at the end of fiscal year 2000 was approximately $3.4 trillion. Using the working assumption that the debt will be reduced by the amount of the surplus each year, calculate the year in which the national debt will be reduced to zero under the three growth rate assumptions given above. Once that date is reached, indicate how you would alter your projections of the surplus in the future.

(c) Now calculate the position of the social security trust fund from 2000 to 2050 under the three alternative assumptions about real growth. Calculate the year in which the trust fund runs out of money. If you have done the calculations correctly, the fund remains in the black under 4% growth indefinitely. Given this finding, why do you think there has been so much concern about the "bankruptcy" of the social security system?

(d) Recalculate the Federal budget and social security trust fund positions under the assumption that nominal GDP rises 6% per year but (i) real growth is 4% and inflation is 2%, and (ii) real growth is 2% and inflation is 4%. This should provide as good an answer as any about why it is in the long-term interests of US policymakers to keep the inflation rate low and stable.

4. At the end of World War II, Germany was devastated by the war effort and Allied bombing, whereas the UK emerged relatively unscathed. According to available data, per capita GNP in 1948 was $530 for Germany, compared with $1769 for the US and $1126 for the UK. However, the German economy then grew almost 10% per year, compared with about 3% per year for the UK economy. After 1973, the growth rate in Germany slowed down much more than in Japan.

(a) Using S-curve and saturation analysis, determine how much of the growth pattern for Germany can be explained by catch-up with the US and the investment ratio (data are on the website) and how much can be ascribed to other causes.

(b) Using this analysis, explain why the slowdown in growth in Germany occurred before it happened in Japan.

(c) Even though per capita GDP in the UK was only about two-thirds of that in the US, it grew more slowly than in the US after World War II even though its investment ratio was higher. That was largely attributed to a larger government sector and, for many years, an overvalued currency. Using these factors, determine the best method for projecting the growth in the UK economy in the future.

PART V

CHAPTER 11

SIMULTANEOUS-EQUATION MODELS

INTRODUCTION

To this point, the examples in this book have consisted entirely of single-equation forecasting models, or models that are solved sequentially. For most practical business forecasts, that will be sufficient. However, sometimes two or more equations must be solved interactively. That is clearly the case at the macroeconomic level, where consumption, income, interest rates, stock prices, prices, and wages are all determined simultaneously. At the company and industry level, this problem would also arise if some simultaneous causality exists. That might be the case, for example, in a commodity model: the quantity demanded depends on the price, which depends on the quantity supplied, which is equal to the quantity demanded plus the change in stocks. Sales of an individual product line depend on its price, which might depend on how much the firm or industry decides to produce. A firm could obtain economies of scale and produce goods less expensively if sales rise enough; but sales will not be stimulated unless the price declines sufficiently. In the international arena, a decision by OPEC to produce more oil in order to boost revenue could have the unintended effect of lowering prices enough that revenue would actually decline. In a few industries, such as motor vehicles, the product may be important enough to impact the overall economy.

In addition to the issues raised by simultaneity bias, a one-equation model might produce accurate forecasts if the values of all of the independent variables are known, but would generate very poor forecasts if these variables could not be predicted accurately. For example, stock prices are an important determinant of both consumer and capital spending, but are difficult to forecast accurately. An equation to forecast the consumption of gasoline might work well for known values of oil prices, but energy prices are often influenced by factors that are unpredictable. A model to predict electricity generation where demand is closely tied to weather variables might be useful in identifying likely peak-load levels, but will not provide accurate forecasts unless one can also predict the weather accurately. Interest rates depend on inflationary expectations, which are not measurable and may be only imperfectly tied to the previous inflation rate, labor costs, and the gap between demand and supply. Net exports depend on the value of the dollar and growth in foreign countries; predicting them accurately might require a full-scale world model.

One of the key assumptions of the classical linear model is that all the independent variables are known at time t. As shown throughout this text, that is seldom the case. One suggested solution has been to use only lagged values of the independent variables wherever possible. However, that is not always feasible for two main reasons. First, unlagged relationships may be important in certain cases, such as the impact of current or expected future inflation on interest rates. Second, for multi-period forecasting, the independent variables will become unknown whenever the number of periods in the forecasting horizon exceeds the minimum lag chosen for those variables.

Several additional problems arise in using multi-equation forecasting models that do not occur for single-equation models. First, the model may be structured so that $a = f(b)$, while $b = f(a)$. Mistakes are seldom this obvious, but sometimes the two-way causality is disguised. In such cases, each equation may contain very robust goodness-of-fit statistics, but the forecasts will be no better than from a naive model. Second, this circular logic may be further disguised by lags, which will become apparent in multi-period forecasting; in this case, one might have $a = f(b)$ and $b = f(a_{-j})$. In this case, the faulty logic would not affect the forecasts until j periods had been predicted.

A detailed discussion of the possible pitfalls found in using a full-scale macroeconomic model for forecasting is deferred to the next chapter. To a certain extent, this chapter is an introduction, providing examples of these issues using individual equations and subsets of the macro model. Section 11.1 discusses some of the methods used to adjust for simultaneity bias in a single equation, including two-stage least squares. Section 11.2 examines how well these methods work for a submodel of the interaction between prices and wages. Section 11.3 provides some examples of the problems that arise from two-way causality among equations with both unlagged and lagged variables, including a submodel with equations for inflation, interest rates and stock prices, and examines methods to reduce this error. These case studies also examine the impact on AR(1) transformations and constant adjustments on multi-period forecasting accuracy. Section 11.4 provides a brief summary of the principal forecasting lessons illustrated in this chapter.

11.1 SIMULTANEITY BIAS IN A SINGLE EQUATION

At the macroeconomic level, one of the most prominent examples of simultaneous causality arises in the consumption function. An increase in disposable income boosts consumption, which in turn raises production, employment, wages and salaries – and disposable income. Similarly, a decline in the unemployment rate raises consumption, which in turn reduces unemployment further. More stringent credit conditions will reduce growth in consumer spending; but if consumer spending slows down, the amount of consumer credit outstanding will decline as well, ceteris paribus. If stock prices rise, consumption will increase, but if an increase in consumer spending boosts profits, stock prices would rise for that reason. This simultaneous link between consumption and income was one of the earliest to be studied in the econometric literature, and many proposed solutions have been offered.

Suppose that instead of using the *actual* unlagged values of income, unemployment, consumer credit, and stock prices, the regression were calculated based on *estimated* values of the unlagged endogenous variables. These estimates would in turn be calculated from regression equations that used only lagged and exogenous variables. Then that assumption of the classical linear model would be satisfied, since variables would be known at time *t*. As a result, no simultaneous-equation bias would exist.

Such a process is known as two-stage least squares (TSLS). In the first stage, the unlagged independent variables – unlagged income and credit conditions in the consumption function – are estimated exclusively as a function of exogenous and lagged variables. This is known as a reduced-form equation. The second stage then consists of estimating the original structural equation with estimated rather than actual values of the unlagged endogenous variables.[1]

One obvious drawback to this method is that the exogenous and lagged variables used in these regressions must be arbitrarily selected. The other possibility is to use *all* of the variables in the model and compute maximum likelihood estimates. That is theoretically superior only in the case of large samples that contain far more observations than the typical forecasting model. In small samples, empirical evidence indicates that, since the entire model is no stronger than its weakest equation, the simulated values usually do not track actual values very closely. Hence we do not consider maximum likelihood methods in practical business forecasting applications.

There are no set rules for choosing the optimal set of exogenous and lagged variables to be used in these regressions. In general, using endogenous variables lagged one quarter for series with high autocorrelation means the results will be virtually indistinguishable from ordinary least squares (OLS) estimates. On the other hand, if one uses only truly exogenous variables such as trends in these first-stage regressions, much of the valuable information will be lost and the forecasts are likely to contain large errors.

The consumption function presented here is similar to the function estimated earlier in this text. First, real disposable income is included with a 16-quarter lag; a cubic PDL is constrained at the far end. Second, unlagged stock prices are used; lagged values were not significant. Third, the unlagged unemployment

---

Table 11.1 Summary statistics for alternative consumption equations.

	YPDH	CRED	UNEMPL	SP500	YLD SPRD	AR(1)	R^2	SEE	DW
OLS	0.881	3.92	-13.6	0.366	7.99		0.9994	27.1	0.42
	(139.3)	(5.6)	(-5.8)	(11.8)	(4.0)				
OLS/AR	0.878	3.98	-13.8	0.397	6.87	0.799	0.9998	16.6	2
	(79.3)	(3.8)	(-3.3)	(7.4)	(2.2)	(14.4)			
TSLS EXOG	0.758	-14.55	5.2	0.923	6.3		0.993	95	0.25
	(2.6)	(-0.4)	(0.1)	(0.7)	(0.3)				
TSLS/AR EXOG	0.794	-10.22	-2.1	0.757	4.2	0.083	0.996	73.6	0.28
	(4.4)	(-0.4)	(-0.1)	(0.9)	(0.3)	(0.6)			
TSLS LAG	0.881	4.75	-12.4	0.371	7.83		0.9994	27.4	0.41
	(58.2)	(1.5)	(-4.1)	(6.9)	(1.7)				
TSLS/AR LAG	0.859	-1.44	-9.3	0.44	15.89	0.827	0.9997	18.3	1.89
	(49.7)	(-2.1)	(-1.2)	(5.3)	(3.9)	(14.8)			
OLS LAG	0.874	4.11	-9.2	0.417	13.38		0.9992	32.9	0.48
	(109.7)	(5)	(-3.1)	(9.9)	(6.1)				
OLS/AR LAG	0.872	3.97	-3.7	0.421	15.55	0.832	0.9997	20.7	2.14
	(58.1)	(3.1)	(-0.7)	(5.8)	(4.0)	(13.8)			

In all cases, the dependent variable is consumption in constant dollars. Figures in parentheses are t-ratios. $YPDH$ = real disposable personal income, cubic PDL with 16-quarter lag; $CRED$ = four-quarter percentage change in real consumer credit outstanding; $UNEMPL$ = unemployment rate; $SP500$ = S&P 500 index of stock prices; $YLDSPRD$ = Aaa corporate bond rate minus Federal funds rate, four-quarter moving average lagged two quarters; $AR(1)$ = autoregressive adjustment.

Table 11.2 RMSE for alternative estimates of consumption functions.

	Without AR(1)	With AR(1)
OLS	67.2	60.1
TSLS EXOG	545.1	402.3
TSLS LAG	66.6	52.4
OLS LAG	47.9	72.1

rate is used; lagged values were not significant. Fourth, the percentage change in real consumer credit is used over the past four quarters. Fifth, a four-quarter moving average of the yield spread between the Aaa corporate bond rate and the Federal funds rate is used, starting with a two-quarter lag. Notice that both monetary terms measure the availability rather than the cost of credit.

The efficacy of TSLS is now tested as follows. First, the consumption function is estimated using OLS. Second, the equation is estimated with TSLS, using trend factors, policy variables (such as changes in tax rates or monetary policy), and the lagged value of the yield spread as the independent variables in the first-stage regressions. Third, the TSLS equation is reestimated using the lagged values of all the independent variables; e.g., the instruments now include the lagged values of real disposable income, stock prices, consumer credit, and the unemployment rate. These two regressions are labeled TSLS EXOG and TSLS LAG. Fourth, the OLS equation is reestimated using only lagged values of the same variables; those results are labeled OLS LAG.

All equations are estimated from 1959.1 through 1997.4, with the 1998–2000 period reserved for ex post forecasts. In estimating TSLS equations, EViews and other programs automatically calculate both stages of the estimation procedure, so it is not necessary to extract the forecast values from the first stage and re-enter them. Also, the number of lagged and exogenous variables used as instruments must equal or exceed the number of parameter estimates in the equation; otherwise the matrix will not invert and no solution will be obtained. Finally, because the residuals are serially correlated, all these regressions are also rerun with an AR(1) adjustment, but as will be seen, the relative importance of using TSLS is not affected.

The summary statistics for each equation are given in table 11.1. The residuals and RMS errors are given in table 11.2, and the graphs of actual versus predicted values for the equations without the AR(1) adjustment is shown in figure 11.1.

It is immediately clear that the TSLS EXOG equation does not work. In this equation, the instruments are all truly exogenous variables such as changes in tax rates, credit conditions, banking regulations, and the price of oil. None of the variables is significant even though the adjusted R^2 remains above 0.99. This example indicates that when using TSLS, reasonable results will generally be

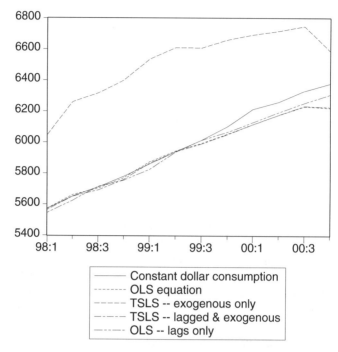

Figure 11.1 Predictions of constant-dollar consumption using a variety of equations estimated with OLS and TSLS.

obtained only by using lagged values of the independent variables. In the TSLS LAG equation, lagged values of income, credit, stock prices, and unemployment are included in the list of instruments.

The reasons for poor results using TSLS have been explored using simulation methods by Nelson and Startz.[2] Essentially these results show that the main problem arises when the correlation of the exogenous variables and the independent endogenous variables in the equation is low. However, when the correlation is very high, the results of OLS and TSLS are quite similar. Thus where, possible, simultaneous-equation bias should be minimized by using lagged values of the independent variables wherever appropriate.

Except for the TSLS EXOG equation, the terms for income, stock prices, and the yield spread remain robust. However, these alternative methods do cast some doubt about whether the unemployment rate and the percentage change in consumer credit should be included in the final equations; these terms may be distorted by simultaneity bias. The unemployment term is also suspect

---

[2] Nelson, C., and R. Startz, "Some Further Results on the Exact Small Sample Properties of the Instrumental Variables Estimator," *Econometrica*, 58 (1990), 967–76. The results are summarized in Johnston, Jack, and John DiNardo, *Econometric Methods*, 4th edn (McGraw-Hill, New York), 1997, pp. 357–8.

because it becomes insignificant with an AR(1) adjustment even for the OLS equations.

Before deciding which terms should be included and excluded, it is useful to look at the ex post forecasting errors for the period 1998.1 through 2000.4, which are summarized in table 11.2 and figure 11.1. As would be expected, the TSLS EXOG equation has much higher forecasting errors, which is no surprise since only one of the coefficients is significant. Comparing the other three equations, the lowest RMS error occurs with the OLS LAG equation. In fact, in the other equations, actual values of the independent variables would not be known; so if the RMS error were the same for two or more equations, the OLS LAG equation would be preferred for that reason alone.

Also note that while the AR(1) term reduces the RMS error for the OLS and TSLS equations, it actually increases it for the OLS LAG equation. That often happens; it is not an unusual result. If the AR(1) term reduces forecasting error in the OLS and TSLS equation, that is because lagged values have greater weights. However, since that is already accomplished by using only lagged values, adding the AR(1) term does not improve forecast accuracy.

It is not appropriate to draw any general conclusions from one example, especially because this equation has not yet been included in a simultaneous-equation model. Nonetheless, some preliminary results can be suggested. First, the earlier statement that it is often preferable to use only lagged values of endogenous variables wherever possible has been strengthened. Second, using TSLS does not reduce forecast error very much if the instruments chosen are lagged values of the independent variables. Further conclusions will become apparent after reviewing several simultaneous submodels.

11.2 ESTIMATING SIMULTANEOUS-EQUATION MODELS

We now turn to a submodel with two simultaneous equations: prices and wages. Annual percentage changes are used in both equations for several reasons. First, in the context of an actual macro model, the Federal Reserve uses the change in the rate of inflation over the past year for determining monetary policy. Second, changes in wage rates are invariably based on changes in inflation over the past year. Thus even though quarterly data are used, it is appropriate to estimate these equations using four-quarter percentage changes. Third, quarterly percentage changes contain too much "noise," so the parameter estimates are biased downward and the equations generate inaccurate forecasts.

Case Study 25: Submodel for Prices and Wages

The procedure used for this case study is as follows. First, equations are estimated for the four-quarter percentage change in the consumer price index, ("inflation"), and hourly earnings, ("wages"). Because inflation depends on unlagged changes in wages, simultaneous-equation bias may be present. Wages depend on lagged values of inflation, but in multi-period forecasting, those values may also be unknown. Hence the price and wage equations are re-estimated using a two-step procedure. First, the estimated values of wages and prices are determined from the OLS regressions; second, those estimated values are used to recalculate the equations. These equations are estimated up to 1997.4; the sample period is truncated to permit experimentation with ex post forecasts. Because of the different sample period, the coefficients are not exactly the same as in the inflation and wage equations used in the macro model pre-sented in the following chapter. Also, the inflation equation presented there includes a dummy variable for the change in BLS methodology, a point dis-cussed below.

This two-equation model is simulated for the three-year period 1998.1 through 2000.4, using both the OLS and two-stage estimates, and the RMS errors are compared. After that, two other forecasting adjustments are explored. First, the DW statistics indicate significant positive serial correlation of the residuals in spite of using percentage changes, so the forecasting properties of the submodel are reassessed using the AR(1) adjustment. Second, as an alter-native method of forecasting, the equations are adjusted by the average value of the residuals in recent quarters. While the effect of these methods on fore-casting accuracy has already been examined for a variety of single-equation models, additional problems can arise in multi-equation models.

Before presenting these results, I hasten to point out that all of the forecasts are better than would be obtained in true ex ante situations, since the values of many of the independent variables, notably the price of oil, are assumed to be known. Nonetheless, this is an important first step in diagnosing the sources of forecasting error in multi-equation models.

The price equation is a markup function over unit labor costs, with addi-tional terms for changes in oil prices, food prices, and the minimum wage. Non-linear terms are used for oil and food prices because of their decreasing importance as consumers spend a smaller proportion of their total budget on energy and food purchases as real income increases. In the wage equation, the change in wages is related to lagged inflation, with additional terms for changes in the minimum wage, food, and oil prices. A dummy variable is included for wage/price guidelines during the Kennedy–Johnson years. Initially, these guide-lines kept wage gains smaller than would otherwise be the case; but when the economy returned to full employment, wages then rose faster than would be expected, so the net effect of these guidelines turns out to be zero; wage and price controls "work" only when they are not needed. In contrast, a dummy variable for wage and price controls during the Nixon Administration was not significant, mainly because reported productivity growth was overstated during those years.

The wage equation also contains terms for changes in the money supply and, until Paul Volcker became Fed Chairman and started fighting inflation more vigorously, the inverse of the unemployment rate. That term is 0 after 1980.4 and, as the reader can verify, has the opposite sign after that date if included separately.

Note that in these equations, demand factors – money supply and the unemployment rate – are included directly in the wage equation, but only indirectly (through wages) in the price equation. The reader can verify that these variables are not significant in the price equation; also, the rate of capacity utilization has the wrong sign, although it is insignificant. The practical meaning of this asymmetry is that, when pressures of demand increase, wages rise more rapidly in the absence of stringent monetary policy. While prices also rise more rapidly, the *margin* between prices and unit labor costs does not widen. When the monetary authorities take the appropriate stance, the core inflation rate does not increase at all when the economy grows more rapidly or approaches full employment, as was seen in the late 1990s.

Summary statistics are given for both wages and prices in table 11.3. The equations marked "TSLS" are based on the modified two-step procedure outlined above, where the estimated values of wages and prices are actually substituted as independent variables. When the traditional TSLS methods are used, some very unusual results are likely to occur, so this method is not followed here. The sample period for all equations is truncated in 1997.4 so that the 1998–2000 period can be used for ex post forecasting.

The modified TSLS results may be surprising because the coefficient for the estimated wage rate term in the price equation is larger and more significant than the coefficient for the actual wage rate. Also, the equation fits slightly better, although the difference is small. How could the regression yield better results using estimated instead of actual values?

As it turns out, the wage rate data sometimes contain erratic short-term fluctuations that are not reflected in pricing decisions. These might include payment of one-time bonuses, such as those associated with the signing of a new labor contract, or year-end bonuses. Also, changes in these figures could reflect changes in overtime hours or interindustry mix (auto workers are paid more than textile workers).

The same argument is *not* true for the wage equation. Since wage rates reflect actual changes in prices, whether temporary or permanent, the actual and estimated changes of the price term in the wage equation have virtually the same coefficient; the other terms in both versions of that equation are also virtually identical. Also cost-of-living increases are based on the actual rise in the CPI, not the "normal" or core rate increase.

The next step is to create a model in EViews, which is done by clicking on "objects," "new object," and "model." One of the most useful features in EViews is that it is not necessary to copy or otherwise transfer the equation into the model; simply enter the name of the equation preceded by a colon. Thus, for example, if the name of the equations are eqcpi and eqwage, simply type in :eqcpi and :eqwage and then solve the model for the indicated periods. This two-equation submodel is solved for the period 1998.1 through 2000.4, using

Table 11.3 Coefficients of wage and price equations.

Inflation equation

	WAGE	FOOD PRICES	OIL PRICES	MINIMUM WAGE	FRINGE BEN RAT	PRODUCTIVITY	$\bar{R}^2$	DW
OLS	0.757	0.994	0.198	0.394	0.152	-1.496	0.952	0.73
	(25.3)	(9.3)	(14.7)	(3.7)	(14.6)	(-5.7)		
TSLS	0.814	0.879	0.186	0.478	0.153	-1.499	0.958	0.80
	(27.6)	(7.7)	(14.5)	(4.7)	(15.7)	(-6.0)		

Wage rate equation

	CPI	FOOD PRICES	OIL PRICES	MINIMUM WAGE	MIN WAGE LAGGED	MONEY SUPPLY	UNEMPL RATE	DUMMY GUIDELINES	$\bar{R}^2$	DW
OLS	0.418	0.265	2.24	0.035	0.045	0.908	0.069	-0.703	0.908	0.94
	(21.1)	(6.4)	(5.4)	(5.5)	(8.2)	(10.2)	(13.5)	(-5.3)		
TSLS	0.426	0.192	2.41	0.051	0.026	1.01	0.068	-0.658	0.908	0.89
	(20.3)	(4.4)	(5.8)	(5.5)	(2.9)	(10.9)	(13.0)	(-5.0)		

Variables are four-quarter percentage changes except where indicated. Figures in parentheses are *t*-ratios.

WAGE = moving average of wage rates over most recent three quarters with weights of 3:2:1; *FOOD PRICES* = percentage change in prices received by farmers times the "food coefficient," which is the ratio of food consumption to total consumption minus 0.15; *OIL PRICES* = four-quarter differences in PPI for petroleum products times the "energy coefficient," which is ratio of energy expenditures to total GDP in constant dollars minus 0.01; *FRINGE BEN RAT* = ratio of fringe benefits (mainly employer contributions for social security and private pension plans) divided by total wages and salaries; *MINIMUM WAGE* = minimum wage rate, included unlagged and with a lag of two quarters; *UNEMPL RATE* = inverse of four-quarter moving average of the unemployment rate, lagged one quarter, times a dummy variable that is 1 before 1980.4 and 0 thereafter; *DUMMY GUIDELINES* = dummy variable for guidelines during the Kennedy–Johnson administration: 1 for 1961–4, and –1 for 1966–9.

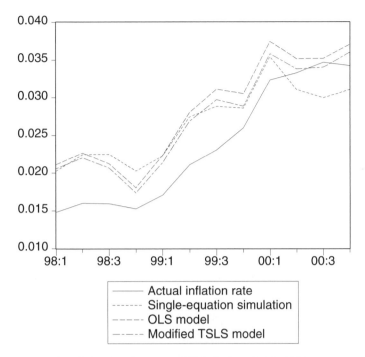

Figure 11.2 Actual and simulated rates of US inflation, 1998–2000.

actual values for all variables expect inflation and wages, which are calculated simultaneously. Figures 11.2 and 11.3 show the comparison of (i) actual changes, (ii) single-equation predictions, (iii) model predictions using the OLS equations, and (iv) model predictions using the modified TSLS equations.

Several points are worth mentioning. First, the simulated values for inflation in 1998 and 1999 are all well above the actual rate of inflation; this point is addressed below. Second, the forecasts from the submodel are generally *more* accurate than those from the single equation. Third, while there is not very much difference, the errors from the OLS model are slightly smaller than those from the TSLS model. That may seem surprising because TSLS estimates are supposed to reduce simultaneity bias, plus the single-equation results for inflation were slightly better when estimated with TSLS; however, when all the interactions are considered, the results are reversed. Since TSLS introduces an additional complexity but does not improve the model results, it is not used to estimate the equations in the macro model.

Figure 11.3 shows that the simulated values of the change in wage rates are below the actual changes in 1998, slightly higher in 1999, and substantially higher in 2000. Furthermore, the errors in 1999 and 2000 are substantially larger for the model simulations than for the single-equation estimate. That is because the model, without adjustment, overestimates the rate of inflation, which then enters the wage equation with a four-quarter lag.

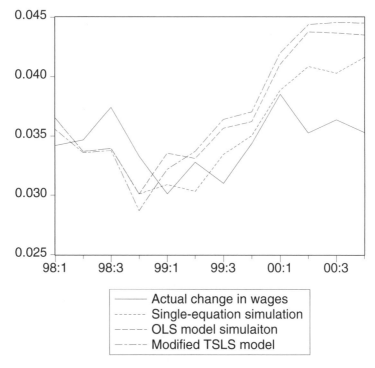

Figure 11.3 Actual and simulated changes in US wage rates, 1998–2000.

We now look for the reason why the forecasts of the inflation rate for 1998 and 1999 are above the actual values, which in turn causes wage gains to be overestimated in 1999 and 2000. One possibility is to adjust the equation by AR(1), which might be justified because of the low value of the DW statistics; a similar adjustment could also be considered for the wage equation, since that DW statistic is also less than unity. However, as shown in figures 11.4 and 11.5, using the AR(1) transformations actually increases forecast error.

The other possibility is to check the residuals during the recent quarters of the sample period. If a consistent pattern were apparent in the sample period, the next step would be to determine whether one or more variables were missing, or if some exogenous change had occurred. For the CPI equation, the average residual from 1994.1 through 1997.4 was −0.45%. Furthermore, all the residuals were negative. At first this might seem like a misspecification of the inflation equation, but in this case there is a very specific and valid reason for the negative residuals. Starting in 1994, the BLS revised its methodology, with the net result that – according to the BLS – the reported rate of inflation was approximately 0.6% per year lower than if all prices had changed the same amount using the old basis. This change followed the finding of the Boskin Commission that the CPI overstated the actual increase in the cost of living by

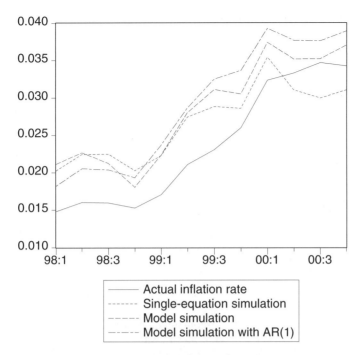

Figure 11.4 Alternative forecasts of inflation rate with AR(1) transformation in both price and wage equations.

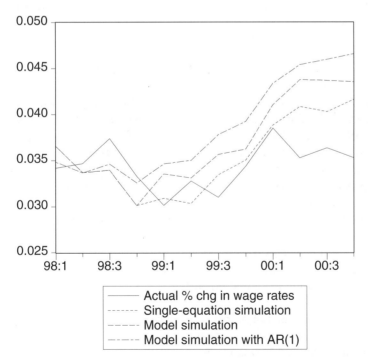

Figure 11.5 Alternative forecasts of the percentage change in wage rates with AR(1) transformation in both equations.

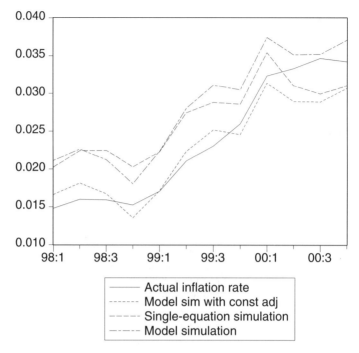

Figure 11.6   Alternative forecasts for inflation rate with the inflation equation adjusted by values of recent residuals.

an average of 1.1% per year, so the BLS move was widely viewed as a major step in the right direction.

Hence the equation based on the old methodology would overstate the reported rate of inflation after 1994 by approximately 0.6% per year, ceteris paribus. Since the average negative residual for the four-year period was −0.45%, the constant term for the price equation was adjusted by that amount and the submodel was re-simulated. Figures 11.6 and 11.7 show that the forecasts improve substantially when the constant term of the price equation is adjusted.

The results of this case study can be summarized as follows:

1   In properly specified equations, simultaneity bias is generally not very important, especially if lagged values of the independent variables are used. In particular, reestimating the equations using TSLS usually does not reduce forecast error.
2   The AR(1) transformation results in larger forecast errors for multi-period forecasting. That is almost always the case.
3   At least in small multi-equation models, most of the error usually stems from the single-equation residuals rather than from the use of predicted values for the independent variables.

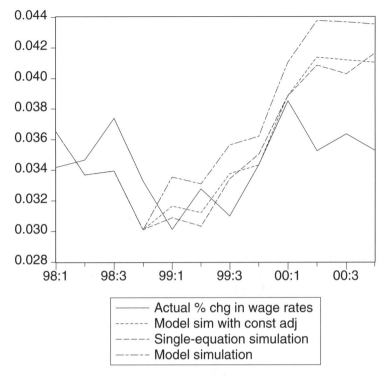

Figure 11.7 Alternative forecasts of percentage change in wage rates with a constant adjustment term in the price equation.

4 Forecast accuracy can be substantially improved by using constant adjustments, especially when the residuals all have the same sign for an extended period of time, and an underlying economic reason for this shift can be determined.

11.3 FURTHER ISSUES IN SIMULTANEOUS-EQUATION MODEL FORECASTING

The major issues that remain to be discussed can best be handled within the confines of small simultaneous-equation models. These issue include (i) simultaneous causality when unlagged endogenous variables are used, (ii) further examples of dual causality, where $a = f(b)$ and $b = f(a)$, and (iii) disguised use of the lagged dependent variable on the right-hand side of the equation. Two additional case studies are used to illustrate these points. The first is the simultaneous prediction of inflation, interest rates, and stock prices. Unlagged endogenous variables are important here because interest rates depend on inflation, long-term rates depend on short-term rates, and stock prices depend on both interest rates and inflation. The second involves the simultaneous prediction of purchases of producers durable equipment (PDE), inventory investment, imports, and industrial production. All three of these aggregate demand components are a function of industrial production; yet production depends primarily on these three variables. This case study not only examines how that simultaneous interaction affects the joint forecasts of all these variables, but provides an example of how simultaneous model determination can help uncover poorly specified equations.

Case Study 26: Simultaneous Determination of Inflation, Short-term and Long-term Interest Rates, and Stock Prices

The same equations given above for prices and wages are used here. However, since the Fed bases its monetary policy decisions on the "core" rate of inflation – inflation excluding changes in food and energy prices – an additional equation is added to explain the core rate of inflation, using the same terms and lag structure except for the omission of the terms for food and energy prices. Equations are also included for the Federal funds rate, the Aaa corporate bond rate, and the S&P 500 index of stock prices. In some forms of the stock price equation, one of the independent variables is the dividend ratio, in which case a separate equation is added for S&P 500 dividends.

This submodel is designed to analyze several specific features. First, both short and long-term rates depend on unlagged values of inflation, and in addition, the Aaa corporate bond rate depends on the Federal funds rate. Hence additional elements of simultaneity are introduced. Second, while the dividend ratio turns out to be an important variable in the stock price equation, that term is defined as the ratio of dividends to prices, so to a certain extent this is akin to estimating $SP = f(SP(-1))$, something cautioned against earlier in this text. We examine whether this relationship causes additional problems in multi-period forecasting, and for that purpose calculate long-term simulations of the submodel for the entire decade of the 1990s.

Economists disagree about the best way to predict the Federal funds rate, partly because, unlike forecasts for real growth and inflation, actual consensus forecasts of interest rates have been no better than a no-change naive model. This is not through lack of trying; as is true for all financial market prices, tremendous riches await anyone who can consistently predict them accurately. Yet failure to offer any guidance about where these variables are heading almost defeats the purpose of business forecasting generally, since there are very few businesses – whether cyclical, defensive, or high-tech – whose operations and financial decisions are not affected by changes in interest rates or stock prices.

There are several reasons why predicting the Federal funds rate has proven to be difficult. First, interest rates are based on expectations about the future as well as what has happened in the past. Second, the Federal funds rate is determined by a vote of the FOMC (Federal Open Market Committee) members, who may have specific reasons (such as an unexpected financial collapse or panic) for changing the funds rate in a manner that would not be consistent with previous changes in key economic variables. Third, the reaction of the Federal funds rate to a given change in the rate of inflation or unemployment has been significantly different under different Fed chairmen. The partial correlation coefficients of unemployment and inflation in the Federal funds rate equation are quite different under William McChesney Martin, Arthur Burns, Paul Volcker, and Alan Greenspan – and could quite possibly change again under the next Fed Chairman.

Economists disagree about the best way to solve these knotty problems. This author and others include those variables that the Fed probably considers when trying to divine future trends in inflation. It is probably not possible to predict how the Fed will react to unforeseen financial crises; forecasters will always make errors when these occur. Thus the major remaining question is whether it is best to estimate the Federal funds equation over a longer period, or restrict it to the time that Alan Greenspan has been in charge at the Fed.

Many economists favor the latter approach. It has often been observed that during the tenure of Alan Greenspan as Chairman of the Federal Reserve Board, the Federal funds rate can be explained as a function of the unemployment rate and the core inflation rate over the past year. This formula is known as a Taylor rule, after John Taylor, professor of economics at Stanford University and one-time member of the President's Council of Economic Advisors. The actual and simulated values appear to fit quite well to the end of 1997, as in figure 11.8.

However, the use of this function to predict the Federal funds rate for 1998 through 2000 generates some remarkably bad forecasts, shown in figure 11.9. We can label them "remarkably bad" by comparing them to the Blue Chip consensus forecasts made at the beginning of the year, which are well within the forecasting range that would be indicated from the sample period statistics for the Taylor Rule equation ($SEE = 0.5$). Yet if the Taylor rule equation is reestimated to 2000.4, the equation continues to fit well and the SEE of the equation rises only slightly to 0.6. However, the coefficients change dramatically. The coefficient for the unemployment rate drops from -1.8 to -1.5; the coefficient for inflation rises from 1.5 to 1.7; and in the biggest change of all the constant term drops from 11.2 to 8.7, which means in the 1998–2000 period the Fed set the funds rate $2\frac{1}{2}\%$ lower than would have been indicated by the earlier function.

Thus while the Taylor rule may be a useful shorthand description of Fed policy under Greenspan, it is a very ineffective forecasting tool. In hindsight, the Fed raised the funds rate less than usual at full employment because inflation did not rise. In addition, inflationary expectations remained stable, as the surge in real growth was generated by unprecedented gains in productivity instead of excessive use of credit. Another popular hypothesis, namely that the funds rate remained lower than usual because of the budget surplus, could not

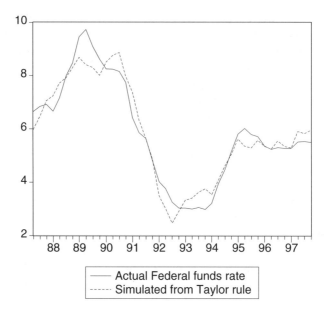

Figure 11.8 Estimating the Federal funds rate with a Taylor rule: actual and simulated rates for 1987.2 through 1997.4.

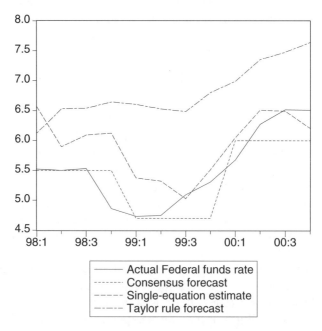

Figure 11.9 Alternative forecasts of the Federal funds rate, 1998 through 2000.

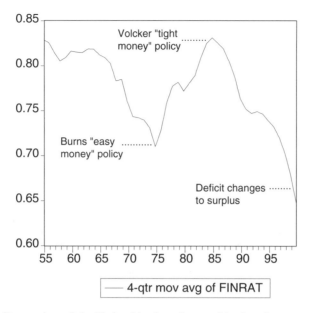

Figure 11.10 Proportion of the Federal budget financed by bonds.

be verified empirically. Taking these factors into account, the Federal funds rate equation used here includes the following additional variables.

- When consumer credit and business loans are expanding faster than GDP, the Fed is more likely to tighten; when they are growing less rapidly or actually declining, the Fed is more likely to ease. Thus if rapid growth is being driven by faster productivity, the Fed is less likely to tighten than if it is driven by excessive use of credit. Empirically, changes in business loans are more important than changes in consumer credit. During the years when Paul Volcker was chairman, changes in the money supply (M2) were also important.
- The proportion of the Federal budget financed by selling bonds is an important determinant of the Federal funds rate; this series has been constructed by the author and is shown in figure 11.10. During the period when Arthur Burns was Chairman, interest rates were held artificially low because the Fed "printed money" instead of selling bonds; during the term of Paul Volcker, the opposite strategy was followed. This term also reflects the fact that, during years of surplus, there are far fewer bonds to be sold, so the ratio drops. This term explains the Federal funds rate better than simply including the Federal budget surplus or deficit ratio.
- The unemployment rate should be considered in relative rather than absolute terms, by comparing it to the full-employment rate of unemployment. This series is not published by the government, but has been estimated by the author and is shown relative to the actual unemployment rate in figure 11.11.

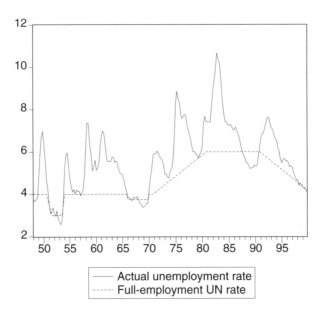

Figure 11.11 The full-employment rate of employment declined from 6% to 4% during the decade of the 1990s.

- An index of sensitive materials prices can provide advance warning about whether inflationary pressures are likely to build. If these prices are rising rapidly, the Fed is more likely to tighten whether or not the actual inflation rate has risen; if they are not, it might leave rates unchanged even when the economy is at full employment. That variable was one of the main reasons the Fed tightened in 1994 even though the inflation rate as measured by the CPI did not rise.

One lesson to be learned here is not directly related to simultaneity; instead, it is the questionable value of making the equation too simple. So often forecasters are told, KISS – Keep it Simple, Stupid. However, that can be overdone. Estimating the more complicated equation definitely improves its forecasting accuracy in the 1998–2000 period.

This result also raises the issue of how well this more complicated equation would work if it were estimated only during the quarters when Greenspan headed the Fed. The change in constant-dollar business loans and the financing ratio terms remain significant, but the change in the money supply, the change in sensitive materials prices, and the full-employment level of unemployment drop out. The forecasting accuracy over the 1998–2000 period is about the same.

The forecaster is thus faced with the decision whether to use an equation fitted only during the Greenspan years, or including data all the way back to

1955. In this author's opinion, it is probably better to forecast with an equation that includes these terms in order to be able to predict what would happen if inflationary expectations did flare up again in the future. I suspect the Fed would keep tightening even as the unemployment rate rose, as was indeed the case under Volcker. While that is a guess, it is typical of the kind of decisions forecasters must make regularly. More often than not, the author has found that an equation fitted over a longer sample period usually provides more accurate forecasts.

In the first four months of 2001, the FOMC voted to reduce the Federal funds rate by two full percentage points, from $6\frac{1}{2}\%$ to $4\frac{1}{2}\%$, following a substantial slowdown in the economy; when an actual recession developed, the funds rate was reduced to 20% by late 2001. Over the same period, the core rate of inflation actually rose slightly, although not by very much. The financing ratio was virtually unchanged. Early in the year, the FOMC members apparently reacted to what they feared would be a full-scale recession if easing were not applied promptly. Also, they were probably influenced by the massive decline in stock prices, although their public statements denied this. Leaving aside the terrorist attacks, which could not have been foreseen, the rapid decline in the funds rate stemmed from yet another shift in the underlying function, not simultaneous equation bias or the inability to predict the independent variables accurately. In this case, judgmental forecasts taking into account the increased importance of the stock market would have improved forecast accuracy.

The Aaa corporate bond rate equation is considered next. The key terms in that equation are a 20-quarter PDL on the rate of inflation, a four-quarter PDL on the Federal funds rate, both starting with zero lag, and an eight-quarter PDL on the real Federal funds rate, starting with a two-quarter lag. The last term reflects the fact that if Fed policy has been relatively tight in the past, bond rates will decline, ceteris paribus, as investors expect some easing, and vice versa. The index of sensitive materials prices is also important; and the deficit ratio is important for the full sample period but not the Greenspan period. Both the Federal funds rate and Aaa corporate bond equation include a dummy variable that is 1 starting in 1980.4, when the change in banking regulations caused a change in monetary policy. For those who would prefer not to use equations with dummy variables, the equation starting in 1987.2 would be chosen. The equations estimated for the full period for which Federal funds rate data are available, and for the subperiod when Greenspan was Fed Chairman, are shown in table 11.4.

The model simulations are considered next, with particular emphasis on how the simultaneity affects forecasting accuracy as opposed to errors caused by structural shifts in the underlying equations. Figure 11.12 compares the simulation values of the Federal funds rate generated by solving the model with those from a single-equation estimate where inflation is known, while figure 11.13 shows the simulation values of the Aaa corporate bond rate using the model

Table 11.4 Estimated equations.

Federal funds rate estimated 1955.1–1997.4:

FFED
$$= -7.68 + 0.383 \star INFL + 0.564 \star INFL(-4) + 0.080 \star \%LOAN + 0.058 \star \%PWSENS$$
$$\qquad (6.5) \qquad\qquad (8.4) \qquad\qquad\qquad (5.6) \qquad\qquad\qquad (7.4)$$
$$+ 11.72 \star FINRAT,4 + 0.203 \star \%M2,8 \star DBR - 0.717 \star (UN - FULLN)$$
$$\quad (4.6) \qquad\qquad\qquad (17.2) \qquad\qquad\qquad (8.2)$$
$RSQ = 0.921; DW = 0.72.$

Federal funds rate estimated 1987.2–1997.4:

$$FFED = -8.24 + 0.807 \star INFL + 0.559 \star INFL(-4) + 0.114 \star \%LOAN$$
$$\qquad\qquad (9.0) \qquad\qquad (4.5) \qquad\qquad\qquad (7.7)$$
$$+ 23.15 \star FINRAT,4 - 1.057 \star UN$$
$$\quad (7.0) \qquad\qquad\qquad (7.1)$$
$RSQ = 0.960; DW = 0.81.$

Aaa corporate bond rate estimated 1957.2–1997.4:

$$FAAA = 2.38 - 16.41 \star DEFRAT(-4),4 + 0.031 \star \%PWSENS \star DBR + 0.889 \star DBR$$
$$\qquad\qquad (4.2) \qquad\qquad\qquad (5.2) \qquad\qquad\qquad\qquad (7.7)$$
$$+ 0.590 \star FFED,6 + 0.248 \star INFL(-8),12 - 1.104 \star \Delta RFED(-2),8$$
$$\quad (34.5) \qquad\qquad (10.3) \qquad\qquad\qquad (8.2)$$
$RSQ = 0.980; DW = 0.74.$

Aaa corporate bold rate estimated 1987.2–1999.4:

$$FAAA = 2.98 + 0.058 \star \%PWSENS \star DBR + 0.586 \star FFED,6 + 0.446 \star INFL(-8),12$$
$$\qquad\qquad (5.0) \qquad\qquad\qquad\qquad (10.9) \qquad\qquad\quad (3.1)$$
$$- 1.758 \star \Delta RFED(-2),8$$
$$\quad (5.1)$$
$RSQ = 0.906; DW = 1.46.$

FFED = Federal funds rate; *INFL* = inflation rate (CPI); *LOAN* = business loans; *PWSENS* = index of sensitive materials prices; *FINRAT* = proportion of Federal budget financed by selling bonds; *M2* = money supply; *DBR* = dummy variable for change in banking regulations; 0 before 1980.4, 1 thereafter; *UN* = unemployment rate; *FULLN* = full-employment rate of unemployment; *FAAA* = Aaa corporate bond yield; *DEFRAT* = ratio of Federal budget surplus or deficit to GDP; *RFED* = Federal funds rate minus annual inflation rate.

---

compared to a single-equation estimate where inflation and the Federal funds rate are both known.

The actual Federal funds rate is well below both the single-equation and model simulation values in 1998 and the first half of 1999. To a certain extent that represents the financial market collapse in the fall of 1998 that could not have been foreseen, although even before then the funds rate was below simulated values; later on we discuss how adjusting the constant term would reduce that error. Starting in the middle of 1999, both methods of prediction capture

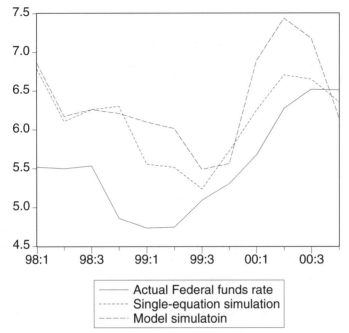

Figure 11.12   Actual and predicted values of the Federal funds rate.

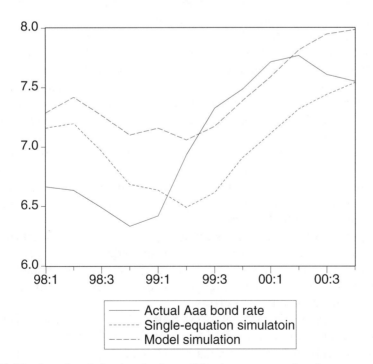

Figure 11.13   Actual and simulated values of the Aaa corporate bond rate.

the rise in the funds rate, although the simulated values remain above actual level until mid-2000. Note that the simulations from the model, where the calculated instead of the actual inflation rate is used, are actually somewhat more accurate than the single-equation estimate. Simultaneity bias is not an issue here.

The forecasts of the Aaa corporate bond rate for 1998 are too high because the predictions of the Federal funds rate are too high. Note, however, that the single-equation estimates are also too high. The relatively low actual value of the bond rate reflects other factors; investors may have expected the Fed to ease later in the year. In the same vein, the rise in the actual bond rate in 1999 occurs before the increase in the simulated values. In recent years, bond market investors have anticipated changes in the Federal funds rate before they occur, owing to a change in Fed philosophy that now sends clearer signals about future activity. Similarly, the decline in the bond yield in the second half of 2000 reflects the expectation that the Fed would ease in early 2001, which was indeed the case. Because of the importance of expected future changes in the funds rate, both the single-equation and model simulation values lag behind actual changes. In this case, the bond market equation is mis-specified because we cannot accurately measure unobservable changes in expectations.

Figures 11.14 and 11.15 show the simulation values of these two interest rates when (i) an AR(1) transformation is used for both equations, and (ii) a constant adjustment is used for the Federal funds rate equation. Since it may be difficult to interpret all these crossing lines, table 11.5 also contains the absolute average errors for each forecast during this 12-quarter period.

The results are quite different for the two equations. The Federal funds equation exhibits the more typical result: the AR(1) transformation makes the forecast much worse, while the constant adjustment makes them much better. However, there is virtually no difference in the various predictions for the Aaa bond yield. There is no constant adjustment because the residuals average to zero over the past 16 quarters, and no pattern is apparent. The AR(1) transformation does not worsen the bond market forecasts only because there is very little autocorrelation, so the value of that term is close to zero. The fact that the model simulation error is lower than the single-equation estimate suggests that bond markets react more to what they think the Fed will do in the near future than to what it has actually done.

Here again, most of the errors stem from the residuals that occurred in the single-equation estimate. Even though unlagged values are used, simultaneous equation bias is not very large. The errors from the model simulation values, which are based on predicted rather than actual values of inflation, are about the same as the single-equation errors.

Before drawing any final conclusions from this submodel, we shall discuss the stock market equation and show how actual and predicted values of interest rates affect those forecasts. As already indicated on page 361, the price/earnings ratio of the stock market at any given time is equal to the discounted future

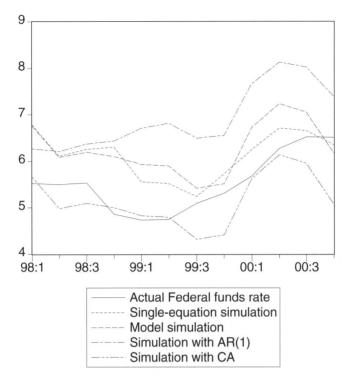

Figure 11.14   Alternative forecasts of the Federal funds rate, 1998 through 2000.

value of expected earnings, where the discount factor is usually taken to be the Aaa corporate bond rate, and is adjusted by tax rates, particularly changes in the capital gain tax rate. Empirically, however, that statement is an empty vessel unless one can identify those factors that determine expectations about earnings. Several variables have been found to be empirically valid, including the growth rate of the economy, level and recent changes in profits, the budget surplus or deficit position, and (with a negative sign) the rate of inflation. Also, to the extent that firms plow back earnings into expansion instead of paying them out in dividends, expected future growth in profits is higher. That is true for individual stocks as well as for the overall market.

Taking all these factors into consideration, the following equation (table 11.6) is estimated for the S&P 500 index of stock prices. Because the market rose so rapidly throughout the 1990s, table 11.6 shows estimates of this equation both for 1947 through 1990 as well as 1947 through 1999. Note that most of the parameter estimates do not change very much when the additional decade of data is added. In both cases, the dependent variable is the ratio of stock prices to current-dollar GDP.

In the first simulation, the sample period is truncated in 1997 and the model is simulated from 1998.1 through 2000.4 to determine the values of (i) the

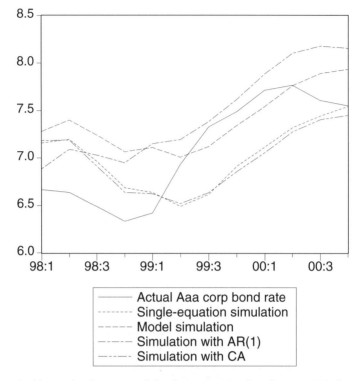

Figure 11.15   Alternative forecasts of the Aaa corporate bond rate, 1998 through 2000.

Table 11.5   Absolute average errors for different forecasting methods.

	Federal funds	Aaa bond yield
Single-equation estimates	0.63	0.42
Model simulation	0.78	0.38
Model simulation with AR(1)	1.40	0.39
Model simulation with CA	0.43	0.43

single-equation forecast, (ii) forecasts assuming only the dividend ratio is endogenous (i.e., simulated instead of actual values are used for lagged stock prices), and (iii) forecasts assuming the dividend ratio, interest rates, and inflation are all endogenous. The results are shown in figure 11.16.

It is probably no surprise that the model failed to capture the 20% gain in stock prices in early 1999 following the Fed easing after the collapse of the Russian rouble and the rescue of Long-Term Capital Management. What may be more surprising is that the forecasts are virtually the same whether the actual or predicted values of dividends, interest rates, and inflation are used, and

Table 11.6 Parameters of stock market equation estimated to 1990 and to 1999.

Equation estimated to	1990	1999
Profit ratio	0.428	0.365
	(5.7)	(5.1)
Change in profits	1.39	1.57
	(2.6)	(3.1)
Aaa corporate bond rate	−0.182	−0.153
	(4.2)	(4.0)
Capital gains tax rate	−0.050	−0.049
	(6.1)	(5.9)
Change in inflation rate	−0.010	−0.011
	(3.6)	(4.2)
Surplus/deficit ratio	0.464	0.599
	(7.2)	(11.5)
Dividend ratio	−1.50	−1.43
	(25.7)	(30.2)
Adjusted R^2	0.904	0.909
DW	0.53	0.47

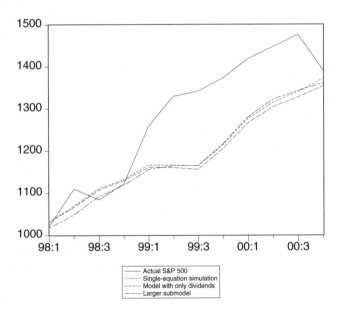

Figure 11.16 Alternative forecasts of stock prices. In the large submodel, inflation and interest rates are endogenous.

Table 11.7 RMSE for stock market simulations, 1990.1 through 1999.4.

Single equation, dividend ratio exogenous	77.4
Single equation, dividend ratio endogenous	108.7
Submodel, dividend ratio exogenous	74.7
Submodel, dividend ratio endogenous	139.6
Submodel, no dividend at all, just time trend	94.4
Single equation, truncate sample period in 1990	131.1
Submodel, AR(1)	187.7

almost all the error occurs in the single-equation estimate. However, this result may occur because of the unusually large error in forecasting the stock market in 1999. Before drawing any overall conclusions, it is useful to simulate this submodel using a wider variety of choices and over a longer time period.

To assess the long-term viability of using the dividend ratio in the equation, several tests are performed. First, the model is simulated over a longer period, from 1990 through 1999. Second, the sample period for the equations is truncated in 1990, so all the simulated values are outside the sample period. Third, the stock market equation is modified by eliminating the dividend ratio completely. Fourth, the stock market equation is modified by adding an AR(1) transformation. The RMSE for these and other combinations, all based on simulations from 1990.1 through 1999.4, are summarized in table 11.7.

In this table, the submodel includes endogenous equations for the Federal funds rate, Aaa corporate bond rate, overall inflation rate, core inflation rate, wage rate, and (where indicated) the dividend ratio.

First note that the RMSE from solving the submodel with an exogenous dividend ratio is 74.7, or slightly *lower* than the single equation RMSE of 77.4. The use of unlagged endogenous interest and inflation rates in the model does not increase forecast error. As previously noted, that is because, to a certain extent, stock market investors act on what they expect the Fed to do, not what it has already done. Changes in Fed policy that are not congruent with the underlying economic indicators apparently do not move stock prices as much as changes that are supported by the economic data. In any case, the simultaneous determination of inflation, interest rates, and stock prices does not increase forecast error even over a ten-year simulation period.

On the other hand, the use of the dividend ratio in the equation – which is a disguised use of lagged stock prices – causes the RMSE almost to double over the simulation period, as shown in figure 11.17. Hence the use of that term would be a serious error. An even worse error would be the use of an AR(1) transformation, which further balloons the RMSE from 139.6 to 187.7, compared to 74.7 for the model simulation with dividend ratio exogenous. Hence

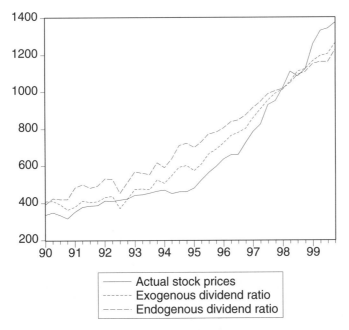

Figure 11.17 Using simulated values of lagged stock market prices almost doubles the RSME.

both of these errors should be avoided. The alternative, which is to include a nonlinear time trend in place of the dividend ratio, increases the RMSE to 94.4.

Figure 11.18 shows the simulated values of the single equation for stock prices when that equation is reestimated with an AR(1) transformation. As can be seen, the values drift off more and more as the time horizon increases. This provides yet another example how the use of an AR(1) transformation increases forecast error for multi-period forecasting.

A simulation was also calculated using an equation where the sample period for the stock market equation was truncated in 1990. It is not surprising that the RMSE was somewhat larger, rising to 131.1. However, figure 11.18 shows that the simulations from that equation err in being further *above* the actual values. On this basis, the stock market was undervalued during the early 1990s, and it was only in 1998 and 1999 that it rose above equilibrium values. Based on these simulations, it seems clear that the general upward trend in the predicted values of the stock market in the 1990s stems from underlying economic conditions that were also influential from the 1950s through the 1980s. In particular we find that the P/E ratio rose in the 1990s because of lower inflation, higher productivity growth, and the return to a budget surplus. Indeed, even after the severe market contraction of 2001, the P/E ratio remained well above previous levels, indicating the importance of these variables and validating this approach.

The methods used in this case study can be expanded into a larger context for practical business forecasting and summarized as follows.

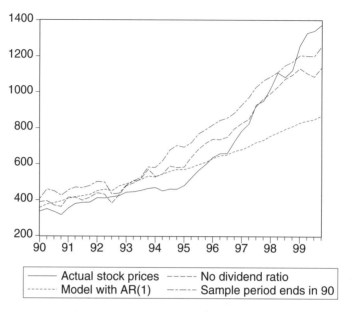

Figure 11.18 Alternative stock price simulations with an AR(1) transformation, no dividend ratio, and truncating the sample period in 1990.

1 For properly specified equations with reasonable lag structures, most of the forecast errors stem from errors in the single equations. Simultaneity bias is not a major issue in these circumstances.

2 Although the statistical properties of the model (particularly the DW statistic) may appear to be superior for a shorter time span, it is often better to include a longer sample period where possible to include more variety in the independent variables. For example, an equation based on a sample period that contained only an upward trend would probably not predict turning points.

3 Both habit formation, as represented by previous patterns, and expectations about the future, can be important in forecasting equations. This is not an either/or dichotomy; both sets of variables can improve forecasting accuracy. While expectations cannot be measured directly, changes in current conditions sometimes serve as useful proxy variables. Changes in the stock market, for example, depend on both expected future changes and previous changes in financial market conditions.

4 Long lags for some of the independent variables – even when estimating financial prices that change instantly upon the receipt of new information – can enhance forecasting accuracy when properly specified. In particular, long-term bond yields have depended on the average rate of inflation over the past five years for over a century. More recently, even though monetary policy under Paul Volcker conquered inflation, it took investors many years to believe that the Fed had successfully accomplished this goal.

Case Study 27: Simultaneous Determination of Industrial Production, Producers Durable Equipment, Inventory Investment, and Imports

The two case studies presented above focused on variables where expectations are quite important: inflation and financial market prices. This case study turns to a set of macro variables where production decisions are the key driving force. This submodel contains equations for purchases of producers durable equipment (PDE), inventory investment, imports, and industrial production. In the first three equations, the principal independent variable is industrial production. Yet industrial production itself is primarily a function of these three variables. Thus even if each individual equation provides accurate forecasts using the actual values of the independent variables, solving these equations simultaneously could cause the forecasts to go off the track.

The summary statistics for the equations are shown in table 11.8.

The industrial production equation differs from the others in that it is estimated in levels rather than percentage change or ratio form. That increases the possibility of spurious trends; however, when it was estimated in percentage form, the coefficients were too low in the sense that they did not accurately reflect the weights of the various sectors in industrial production. The simulation and forecasting properties of the levels equation also turned out to be more accurate than the percentage change form.

All equations were estimated from 1959.1 through 1997.4, with the submodel simulated from 1998.1 through 2000. In general the results remain on track except for PDE, where both the single-equation and model simulation results are far below the actual values until 2000.4, when purchases of transportation equipment fell sharply. The results are graphed in figures 11.19–22.

To perform a more stringent test, the model was also simulated over the period from 1989.1 through 1991.4, the last time the US economy actually was in recession. The results are fairly similar; in particular, the PDE equation continues to have the largest errors, especially for the model simulation results, so they are not shown separately.

Since the PDE equation has the biggest errors, in this case, the next logical step would be to see if this equation could be improved with an AR(1) transformation or a constant adjustment (CA) term. The CA term based on recent residuals improves the forecast accuracy but the simulated values are still too low. When an AR(1) transformation is added to all the equations except inventory investment, the PDE results improve – but the results for imports and industrial production are far worse. In this case, neither method seems to improve the forecast results very much.

Examining these results leads to the conclusion that the PDE equation is flawed in a way that is only peripherally related to the issue of simultaneity. The problem is that, empirically, the PDE data series consists of two entire separate components: one is information processing equipment and software, which

Table 11.8 Summary statistics for case study 27.

$\%chg(PDEH,4) = 17.4 + 0.920\star \ \%chg \ (IPMFG(-1),4) + 0.041\star \ \%chg \ (SP(-2),14)$
        (12.5)   (2.8)
    $+ 1.02\star \ YLDSPRD(-3),4 - 0.460\star \ RCCE \ (-4) + 6.26\star \ DITC - 4.92\star \ RELPR \ (-1)$
     (4.8)   (4.1)   (7.2)   (3.5)
$RSQ = 0.833; \ DW = 1.04$

$\%chg(MH,4)$
    $= 2.75 + 0.954\star \ \%chg \ (IP,4) + 0.321\star \ \%chg \ (CDH \ (-1),4) + 1.41\star \ DOL(-2),10$
          (8.8)   (3.8)   (4.0)
    $+ 5.25\star \ DDSTR - 7.36\star \ DUMWP$
     (2.1)   (5.5)
$RSQ = 0.808; \ DW = 1.13$

$IIH/GDPH = - \ 0.028 + 0.037\star \ \%chg(IPMFG(-1)) + 0.036\star \ CP(-1) + 0.071\star \ \%YPDH,4$
                    (2.0)   (5.1)   (4.5)
    $+ 0.0063\star \ DSTR - 0.031\star \ \%chg(CDH) + 0.023\star \ \%chg(CDH(-1),4)$
     (3.9)   (3.2)   (2.9)
    $+ 0.024\star \ \%chg \ (MH,2)$
     (3.4)
$RSQ = 0.561; \ DW = 1.67$

$IPMFG = -13.60 + 0.062\star \ PDEH + 0.036\star \ IIH + 0.029\star \ XH - 0.043\star \ MH$
                    (4.7)   (6.1)   (4.7)   (4.6)
    $+ 0.049\star \ CNH + 0.011\star \ GFDH + 0.026\star \ IPSH + 0.028\star \ IRH + 0.798\star \ MOTVEH$
     (11.5)   (3.0)   (2.4)   (3.4)   (4.9)
$RSQ = 0.997; \ DW = 0.54$

The number after the symbol but before the comma represents the quarter in which the lag starts, and the number after the comma represents the length of lag. Thus, for example, $\%chg(IP(-1),4)$ means a four-quarter percentage change in IP starting with a lag of one quarter. In all cases, H after a symbol means constant dollars.

$PDEH$ = purchases of producer durable equipment; $IPMFG$ = index of industrial production for manufacturing; SP = S&P 500 index of stock prices; $YLDSPRD$ = difference between Aaa corporate bond yield and Federal funds rate; $RCCE$ = rental cost of capital for equipment (see pages 137–8); $DITC$ = dummy variable for change in rate of investment tax credit; $RELPR$ = relative price of capital goods.

MH = imports; CDH = purchases of consumer durables; DOL = index of the trade-weighted average of dollar; $DDSTR$ = dummy variable for dock strikes; $DUMWP$ = dummy variable for wage/price controls – during these controls, in some cases firms could not pass along the higher price of imports, so they declined.

IIH = inventory investment; CP = index of capacity utilization for manufacturing; $DSTR$ = dummy variable for major auto and steel strikes.

XH = exports; CNH = purchases of consumer non-durable goods; $GFDH$ = defense purchases; $IPSH$ = non-residential construction; IRH = residential construction; $MOTVEH$ = consumer purchases of motor vehicles (number).

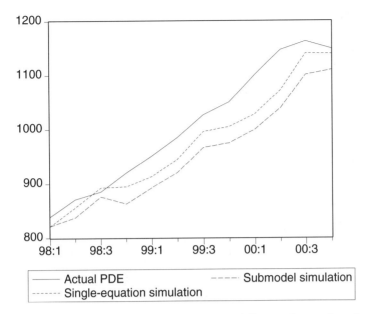

Figure 11.19   Actual and predicted values of constant-dollar purchases of producer durable equipment.

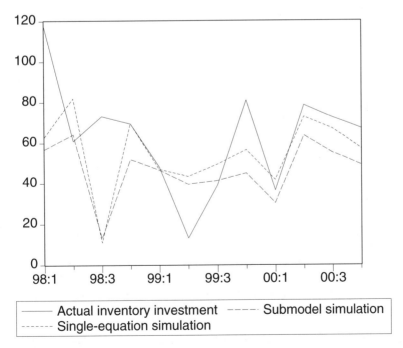

Figure 11.20   Actual and simulated values of constant-dollar inventory investment.

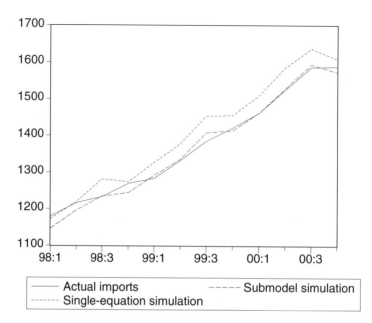

Figure 11.21 Actual and simulated values of constant-dollar imports.

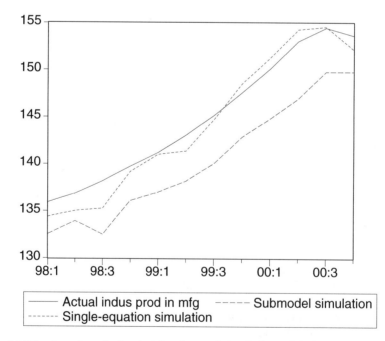

Figure 11.22 Actual and simulated values of the index of industrial production for manufacturing.

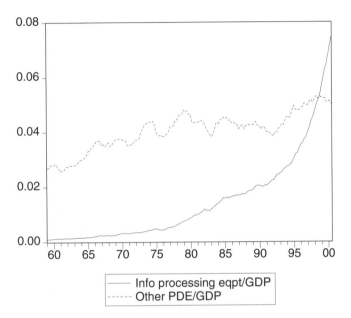

Figure 11.23 Ratios of purchases of information processing equipment and software to GDP, and all other PDE to GDP (all in constant dollars).

has grown very rapidly relative to GDP over the past few decades, and the other is industrial and related equipment, which has shown only a very slight upward trend relative to GDP. This is the same problem we saw earlier in the equation for consumer durables. The behavior of the two series is shown in figure 11.23.

As a result of this dichotomy, the upward trend in information processing equipment and software dominates the total PDE figures in recent years, distorting the coefficients in the equation and overstating the importance of industrial production, which has also grown rapidly in recent years because of other factors. For this reason, more accurate forecasts can be generated by estimating two separate functions for PDE. That is done in the macro model presented in the next chapter. Also, it turns out the results are somewhat more accurate if the industrial production equation is reestimated in logarithms. The point of presenting the suboptimal form of the equation is to show how it can lead to forecasting errors, and indicate the best way to correct these errors.

The principal lesson to be learned here is the following. When an equation appears to be drifting off, even if the simulated forecast values can be improved by adding an AR(1) term, it is likely that defects in the structure of the equation will lead to larger forecasting errors under true ex ante conditions. In that case, the equation should be respecified. To reiterate, if the simulated results improve when the AR(1) term is used, that often means the equation is misspecified, which is the main reason for significant autocorrelation of the residuals when it is not caused by data smoothing or habit formation. *If the ex post simulation forecasts appear to be materially improved by using an AR(1) transformation, that should be construed as a warning sign that true ex ante forecasts are likely to contain large errors.*

11.4 SUMMARY

Most of this chapter has consisted of three case studies designed to show how forecasts are likely to be affected when simultaneous-equation models are used to generate values of the independent variables. Only a small sample of the submodels contained in the overall macro model have been illustrated here, but the choices shown are representative of the issues that most often arise. This summary is also based on other submodels not shown here that reinforce the conclusions based on these examples.

In the early days of building econometric models, it was generally thought that simultaneous-equation bias was severe, so methods that reduced or eliminated that bias would produce more accurate forecasts. However, that hypothesis has not been validated. The use of TSLS or similar methods generally does not improve forecasting accuracy, and carries with it the risk that some of the parameters will become distorted. Using strictly exogenous variables – trends and policy variables – in the first stage of TSLS often wipes out cyclical behavior. Using lagged values of the independent variables restores these patterns, but often produces results that are virtually indistinguishable from OLS estimates.

Simultaneity bias can be reduced by using lagged values or, where that is not appropriate, PDLs that start with the unlagged value. Using lagged values has the additional benefit that these values are known when the forecasts are generated.

Using the AR(1) transformation generally increases forecasting error as the time horizon expands. This transformation works best if the forecast range is only one period in the future. Furthermore, if the AR(1) transformation improves ex post forecast accuracy, that is often a warning sign that the underlying equation is misspecified and will provide inferior ex ante forecasts.

Forecast errors from a properly specified equation generally will not increase very much because of simultaneity, whereas a poorly specified equation will usually generate poor forecast results even if no simultaneity bias exists. In simulating the submodel that contained PDE, it was seen that the simultaneity bias was much worse because the equation was misspecified.

Constant adjustments based on recent values of the residuals will often help to improve forecast accuracy, especially if the recent positive or negative residuals can be related to some shift in exogenous forces, policy decisions, or data methodology.

The last chapter analyzes the simulation, forecasting, and dynamic properties of a prototype macro model similar to the one used by this author for forecasting the US economy for many years. Some of the key interactions have already been explored in submodels; additional problems that arise within the context of a complete model will be considered next. In addition, we examine the degree to which constant adjustments, consensus forecasts, surveys, and other information can improve macro forecasting.

Problems and Questions

1. Construct a model in which the endogenous variables are purchases of motor vehicles, the rate of unemployment, and the percentage change in real consumer credit over the past year. The exogenous variables are real disposable income, the relative price of gasoline, the stock market, and the yield spread.

(a) Estimate an equation for motor vehicles using these terms, some of which may be lagged. Also estimate an equation in which the change in the unemployment rate is a function of the change in real GDP, which is exogenous, and the change in purchases of motor vehicles, which is endogenous; lagged values may also be used. Also estimate an equation where the percentage change in real consumer credit is a function of the change in real disposable income, the yield spread, and the change in purchases of motor vehicles; here again, some of the terms may be lagged.

(b) Truncate the sample period in 1997.4 and solve this three-equation submodel for 1998.1–2000.4. Compare each of the three endogenous variables with their actual values. Comment on the usefulness of this submodel for forecasting purposes.

(c) Adjust the constant terms in each of these three equations by the average value of the residuals for 1997. Show the improvement, if any, in the forecasts.

(d) Now reestimate the motor vehicle equation using lagged unemployment and consumer credit. These terms will definitely become less significant. Resimulate the model for the 1998.1–2000.4 period and compare the forecasting errors with those obtained in (b). Based on this result, what can you say about the possibility of simultaneous-equation bias among these variables?

2. The submodel in this example contains equations for stock prices, corporate profits (*YCP*), and the value of the dollar. It can logically be argued that an increase in stock prices boosts corporate profits, especially in the financial sector, while a rise in profits will definitely boost stock

continued

prices, ceteris paribus. In addition, a rise in the value of the dollar is likely to boost stock prices because it will attract more foreign capital, while a rise in stock prices will generally boost the value of the dollar. It may not be immediately obvious which way the causality flows. Finally, a rise in the value of the dollar may reduce profits from overseas in dollar terms; in addition, some firms may be priced out of foreign markets. Taking all these linkages into account, we have

$$SP = f(\$, YCP)$$
$$YCP = f(SP, -\$)$$
$$\$ = f(SP).$$

All three of these terms are simultaneously determined, but an additional complication ensues when we note the theoretical negative correlation between YCP and the $\$$.

(a) Reestimate the stock price equation given above in the chapter and add the $\$$ term.

(b) The equation for the value of the dollar is complicated and includes several terms for foreign variables. However, for purposes of this exercise use the following variables: the ratio of SP/GDP, the Aaa corporate bond rate unlagged and lagged four quarters; the inflation rate lagged and unlagged four quarters; and a time trend (you may, of course, add further variables if desired).

(c) Estimate an equation for the ratio YCP/GDP using the following independent variables: the ratio of personal income to GDP, productivity, SP/GDP, and a four-quarter moving average of the value of the dollar.

(d) Simulate the model for the 1998.1–2000.4 period and compare the actual and predicted results. By changing the constant term on the dollar, determine whether an increase in the dollar raises or lowers profits.

(e) To reduce simultaneity, try lagging the $\$$ in the SP and YCP equations, and SP in the $\$$ equation. Report your results, and indicate how these changes improve forecast accuracy.

(f) Even with these changes, the forecasts are far off the mark. Indicate which of the simultaneous links should be omitted in order to improve forecast accuracy even though that reduces the sample period fit.

3. In the profit equation given above, we sidestepped another issue of simultaneity by stating that the ratio of corporate income to GDP was negatively correlated with personal income to GDP. That is indeed the case,

continued

but in many respects it is almost an identity: except for depreciation, transfer payments, and a few residual terms, personal income plus corporate income equals GDP. Hence a full-scale model would have to be address that issue as well.

(a) The most important components of personal income are wage rates, employee-hours, productivity, fringe benefits, transfer payments, and interest payments, which are closely related to the bond rate. Estimate a profit function that includes these separate terms. Which are significant and which are not?

(b) Indicate how forecast accuracy might be improved if some or all of these terms are lagged. Which ones appear to be most important without any lag? In which cases do lagged terms improve the sample period fit as well as the forecast?

(c) One would expect profits to increase, ceteris paribus, if the spread between the increase in prices and the increase in wage costs widened. Test this hypothesis to determine whether it is empirically valid. How do you explain this result?

(d) In a complete macro model, it is also possible to treat profits as a residual after predicting GDP and all the other components of national income. Discuss the pros and cons of proceeding in this fashion instead of estimating profits directly and facing the issues of simultaneity.

4. In recent years, the corporate bond rate has changed before the Federal funds rate moves, reversing a long-standing pattern. That is because the Fed is now more open about announcing its forthcoming moves. However, these moves are not made in a vacuum, and there is no reason to expect that either FOMC members or bond traders can predict the economy better than anyone else.

(a) By truncating the sample period from the back end (i.e., using 2000.4 as the ending point but moving up the starting point), determine the time when lagged values of changes in the Aaa bond rate first became a significant determinant of the funds rate. Incorporate the variables in the funds rate equation that remain significant.

(b) The more difficult issue is to determine what factors now move the bond rate. Likely candidates would be the change in sensitive materials prices, changes in measures of economic activity such as real GDP or industrial production, and possibly the unemployment rate, although that is generally a lagging indicator. Using the same sample period as was identified in (a), use regression analysis to determine which of these terms is significant in addition to the other determinants of the bond yield.

continued

(c) Now solve for the funds rate and bond rate simultaneously; because of the paucity of observations, use data up to 2000.4 in the sample period. Does this help improve the forecasts of interest rates, given that the actual economic data are known? To what extent does solving these two equations simultaneously increase forecast error?

(d) Based on your observations, which equations and models would you use to predict the funds rate and the bond rate in 2001?

5. The sharp decline in the Federal funds rate in 2001 was probably due to the severe decline in stock prices.

(a) Reestimate the Federal funds rate equation given in this chapter by including current and lagged percentage changes in the S&P 500 stock price index, and the Nasdaq composite index. How do your results differ depending on whether the starting point is 1955.1 or 1987.1?

(b) Using the stock market equation, solve a small simultaneous model with the Federal funds rate, the Aaa corporate bond rate, stock prices, and the inflation rate. How well does this model capture the decline in the Federal funds rate in 2001? How much does your result vary depending on the lag of the stock market term in the Federal funds rate equation?

(c) Based on these results, would you want to make future forecasts of the Fed funds rate using an equation with or without the stock market term? (Hint: what is your forecasting time horizon?)

CHAPTER 12

ALTERNATIVE METHODS OF MACROECONOMIC FORECASTING

INTRODUCTION

This chapter reviews and discusses the major methods used to predict the overall economy. These include structural models, the index of leading indicators, consensus forecasts, and survey methods for consumer, business, and homebuilder sentiment.

Most users of this book, whether students or actual practitioners of forecasting, will probably never build a macroeconometric model. They will either use someone else's forecast – such as the consensus outlook – or develop their own forecast by simulating one of the commercially available macroeconomic models and entering their own assumptions. Most of the actual forecasting work will be done at the individual firm or industry level. In that case, why an entire chapter on macroeconomic forecasting?

In our view, this material is warranted for two reasons. First, virtually all forecasts of economic variables, even at the detailed micro level, depend on what is happening in the overall economy. That is also the case for technologically driven product demand: for example, those who thought the demand for personal computers would continue to rise exponentially for an indefinite period were rudely surprised when they fell 3.5% during 2001.1, the direct result of the accompanying slowdown in the economy. The cost and availability of debt and equity credit will always depend on macroeconomic conditions even for those companies whose sales are not determined by cyclical factors.

Nonetheless, one could simply suggest a variety of sources for macroeconomic forecasts, ranging from the "free" updates in the *Wall Street Journal* twice a year, to the monthly subscriptions to the Blue Chip Economic Indicators forecasts, available in 2001 for $597 per year, to the macroeconomic forecasting services offered by several competing firms for several thousand dollars per year.

However, examining the macroeconomic forecasting record provides a much greater wealth of detail than is available for individual industry or company forecasts. A detailed track record of consensus forecasts is available for 30 years, with some consensus forecasts extending back 50 years. Actual ex ante forecasts have been available for most of this period, allowing anyone to examine the actual track record, as opposed to results generated with model simulations. Several surveys of sentiment exist for key components of the economy – consumer spending and housing in particular – as opposed to the lack of any sentiment index for, say, sales of International Paper or Abbott Laboratories. Furthermore, the existence of an actual track record permits us to examine how that record might be improved by adjusting the constant terms and slope coefficients. In many cases, industry and company data are confidential and forecasting projects undertaken by this author and others cannot be published or examined for this reason. Hence macroeconomic models provide by far the best opportunity of examining methods that can be used to improve a wide variety of forecasts in the future.

12.1 STRUCTURAL VERSUS VAR MODELS

So far we have concentrated almost exclusively on structural macroeconomic models. However, over the past two decades, many academic papers have been written about forecasting the economy using vector autoregressive (VAR and BVAR) models, with those authors claiming that forecasts generated by this approach are superior to those produced by the structural econometric approach. Before proceeding with the present approach, that hypothesis should be investigated.

Starting in 1980, the failure of large-scale econometric models during the previous decade led several economists, notably Robert Litterman[1] and Christopher Sims[2] to develop alternative macro models in which the independent variables in all of the equations are lagged values of the dependent variables. The original model estimated by Litterman contained six equations: the M1 measure of the money supply, constant-dollar GDP, the GDP deflator, constant-dollar capital spending, the three-month Treasury bill rate, and the unemployment rate. Sims later extended this model to include the trade-weighted average of the dollar, the S&P 500 stock price index, and the PPI for sensitive materials prices.

We already noted in chapter 8 that the Sims model, like all other forecasts, failed to predict the 1990–1 recession. However, since no one correctly anticipated that downturn, this may not be a valid test. As always, the question is whether this method can produce more accurate forecasts than other methods

---

[1] Litterman, Robert B., "Forecasting with Bayesian Vector Autoregressions – Five Years of Experience," *Journal of Business and Economic Statistics* (1986), 25–30.

[2] For a detailed discussion of his methodology, see Sims, Christopher A., "Macroeconomics and Reality," *Econometrica*, 48 (1980), 1–48.

– or whether this method, in combination with other methods, can produce the most accurate forecasts.

It is quite clear that Litterman and Sims developed these models with the expectations that they would generate superior forecasts. In 1986, Litterman declared that "a statistical time series model has been developed that, for the first time, appears to generate forecasts that compare favorably in terms of accuracy with those generated by the best judgment of economic forecasters." Later, Sims was less ebullient, stating that "The model has done 'well' by historical standards, but such performance in a period when naive models are also doing 'well' is weak support at best for this model." As far as the inability of the model to predict any downturn in the 1990–1 recession, Sims concedes: "The model did not perform brilliantly in tracking the 1990–1 recession . . . the two quarters of negative growth were almost completely unanticipated by the model."

Yet in spite of this mixed performance, many econometricians and forecasters continued to trumpet the virtues of these models relative to econometric and judgmental performance. Thus as late as 1998, Diebold[3] felt motivated to claim that "the reports of the death of large-scale macroeconomic forecasting models are not exaggerated," adding that in his opinion, the future of modeling would be found in more complex nonlinear VAR models.

It remained for Charles Bischoff, with Nalefom Belay and In-Bong Kang, to show that this particular emperor has no clothes. Appearing in *Business Economics*, their article was entitled "Bayesian VAR Forecasts Fail to Live Up to Their Promise,"[4] with the subhead that "For the period 1981–1996, judgementally adjusted large structural macroeconomic models forecast more accurately than Bayesian VAR models." Most of the comparisons presented in this study are with the DRI model[5]; Bischoff also asked this author for back forecasts of Chase Econometrics and Evans Economics, but complete records were not available. Thus forecasts from these models were not included in their study.

Bischoff and colleagues find that "The BVAR forecasts of GNP (or GDP) deflator were worse than those of DRI and the combinations by wide margins, for all horizons, and for all sub-periods." When the three additional Sims variables were added, "forecasts of inflation improved, but those for real variables deteriorated," and "BVAR was never 'best' for any variable, horizon, or measure of accuracy." They conclude: "The evidence presented here suggests that big

[3]   Diebold, F. X., "The Past, Present, and Future of Macroeconomic Forecasting," *Journal of Economic Perspectives* (1998), 175–92.
[4]   Bischoff, C. W., N. Belay, and I. Kang, "Bayesian VAR Forecasts Fail to Live up to Their Promise," *Business Economics* (July 2000), 19–29.
[5]   Data Resources, Inc., was sold by founder Otto Eckstein and Chairman Donald Marron to McGraw-Hill in 1980 for a reported $103 million. Later DRI was combined with other financial service divisions at McGraw-Hill and became known as Standard & Poor's DRI. In 2001, the former DRI was sold to a company that also owned Wharton Econometric Forecasting Associates, known as WEFA.

macroeconometric models are more accurate forecasting tools than BVAR models."

The VAR models have never passed a market test. No one offers a forecast service based on these models, nor are they used by any of the leading in-house economists for major corporations, institutions, or associations. There is no evidence that the use of this approach improves forecasting accuracy, and for that reason we do not consider it further.

Bischoff et al. are somewhat more cautious in their conclusions, conceding that "perhaps future nonlinear methods, may be the future of macroeconomic forecasting." However, they also state that "our own hypothesis is that nothing is really stable; all structures are changing slowly."

In this author's view, that is an important and correct assessment of the state of econometric modeling. With today's PCs and widely available data bases, there is no excuse for not reestimating models frequently to take into account shifts in the underlying structure. Nor is there any reason not to include parameter estimates with changing weights, or make full use of adjusting the constant terms to reflect recent changes in economic, political, or sociological conditions. Hence the view taken throughout this book, and reemphasized in this chapter, is that structural econometric modeling should serve as the basis of accurate economic forecasting, aided and abetted by frequent updates and shifts in parameter estimates, including additional information from surveys, judgment, and consensus forecasts where appropriate.

To a large extent, assessing the value of the leading indicators, consensus forecasts, and surveys is quite straightforward: either they work or they don't. There are no "tricks" about how to estimate equations, the optimal lag structures, and decisions about which information should be included or discarded. Hence the main focus of alternative methods of forecasting in this chapter will be to determine whether they can improve forecast accuracy when used in conjunction with a structural macroeconomic model.

12.2 SOLVING STRUCTURAL MACROECONOMIC MODELS

Before describing and illustrating some of the features of an actual macroeconomic model, we first briefly discuss the method of solving simultaneous equation models in order to maximize the probability of obtaining the correct solution, since there is not always a unique solution. Even if all of the equations are linear, the model itself is generally nonlinear; for example, current-dollar GDP is defined as real GDP times the deflator, both of which are estimated separately. As a result various algorithms must be used that do not always converge to a unique solution. Occasionally the model converges to a secondary root; in some cases, it does not converge at all.

After estimating the individual equations, the complete model should be simulated over several years to insure that it remains on track. Multiplier analysis can then be used to determine that small changes in the exogenous variables do indeed produce reasonable results. Once the stability of the model has been certified, the forecaster must consider various adjustments to improve forecast accuracy. This chapter discusses the use of mechanical constant adjustments through the use of the AR(1) transformation, judgmental adjustments of the constant terms, and the inclusion of outside information to improve forecast accuracy.

The simulations based on the chosen specification are far from perfect, as will become obvious when the graphs are presented. It would not only be presumptuous but inaccurate to suggest that these are the best results that can be obtained; forecasters always try to improve their accuracy in the future. Nonetheless, these results indicate what can reasonably be expected from macroeconomic forecasts under alternative scenarios, and what diagnostics can be used to aid forecasters in specifying equations and entering constant adjustments in forecasting models.

12.2.1 OUTLINING THE EQUILIBRIUM STRUCTURE

In building a multi-equation forecasting model, the first thing to do, after estimating the individual equations, is check that the number of equations is identical to the number of endogenous variables. This will usually involve adding several identities in the model. While this is an obvious step, it is sometimes overlooked. For example, the equations for consumer or capital spending might contain a term for the real rate of interest. However, interest rates will usually be estimated in nominal terms, so an identity defining the real rate of interest is required. Also, each endogenous variable can appear on the left-hand side of an equation only once. Any variable that is not determined by a stochastic equation or an identity must be exogenous, which means the user must supply estimated values for the forecast period. All constant terms used to adjust the equations are considered to be exogenous variables in the solution algorithm.

EViews is well designed for solving multi-equation models. Instead of copying or pasting the equations into the model solution algorithm, the name of the equation can simply be entered, preceded by a colon. If that equation turns out to have some defect that becomes apparent during testing, the equation can be reestimated and the model can then be re-solved without making any other changes. In most cases, the model converges quickly; even for models with several hundred equations, it takes only one or two seconds to solve each period. Occasionally, though, the model will not converge, or will converge to the wrong values.

It is assumed that by this point, the estimated equations do not contain the lagged values of the independent variable on the right-hand side of the equation; the checklist has been vetted for circular functionality among equations, e.g., $a = f(b)$ and $b = f(a)$; and lagged rather than current values of the endogenous variables have been used wherever appropriate.

12.2.2 NEWTON–RAPHSON METHOD AND THE GAUSS–SEIDEL ALGORITHM

Consider a very simple model that is linear in the individual equations but nonlinear in solution. Suppose the components of aggregate demand are linear functions of various measures of income (Y) and monetary variables (M), and prices are also linear functions of income and monetary terms. However, the national income identity holds only in current prices. To simplify matters, assume there is only one consumption and investment function, which can be written as

$$CH = a_0 + a_1 Y/pc + a_2 M$$
$$IH = b_0 + b_1 Y/pk + b_2 M$$
$$pc = c_0 + c_1 Y + c_2 M$$
$$pk = d_0 + d_1 Y + d_2 M$$
$$Y = pc * CH + pk * IH.$$

A nonlinear model of this sort cannot be solved by simple matrix inversion, so some method of approximation must be used. Originally, the solution was to divide the model into block-recursive systems, and then iterate among these blocks. In this example, prices would be held constant in the aggregate demand block, and the system solved for output; in the price block, demand would be held constant, and the system solved for prices, using the values obtained in the previous iteration. This method would continue until some desired level of error between successive iterations was obtained for each variable. In the early days (circa 1950s and early 1960s), econometric forecasting models were solved by this method, known as the Newton–Raphson method.

Even a fairly small model would contain several blocks with nonlinearities; the case shown above is far simpler than even the prototype model discussed later in this chapter. Thus for large-scale models, that method quickly became very cumbersome. However, that need not concern us, since it has been replaced by a much simpler and more efficient method.

Today, most multi-equation models are solved using the Gauss–Seidel algorithm. The idea is a natural extension of the block-recursive method, except that each individual equation is treated as a separate block and solved sequentially. All the equations are estimated in their preferred structural form; it does not matter whether or not they are linear: percentage changes, logarithms, ratios, functions with Kronecker deltas, etc. are all acceptable. However, each endogenous variable must appear on the left-hand side of an equation once and only once, which may necessitate restating a few of the equations.

The equations are solved sequentially, using preassigned values for each of the independent variables on the right-hand side of the equation. In practice, the first iteration for each time period is last period's actual values. After the equations are solved, the solution values from the first iteration are inserted as values of the independent variables and the model is solved a second time. The values of all unlagged endogenous variables from the first and second iterations are compared, and if the differences are larger than some preassigned tolerance level, the program automatically moves to a third iteration, using the second iterated set of values for all unlagged endogenous independent variables. This process continues until the differences for all variables becomes less than the preassigned level. When that occurs, the model has converged, and those values are used to start the iterative process for the next time period.

The Gauss–Seidel method is simple, direct, and efficient, and is used in EViews and other similar programs. However, it does not always converge to the correct value. Two possible problems can arise. One is that the preassigned tolerance level ε is usually set as a percentage (e.g., 0.01%) of each variable: an absolute magnitude is not used because some variables such as prices are denominated in very small units compared to GDP or money supply. However, occasionally one of the variables is very close to zero (inventory investment, net exports, or the budget surplus/deficit) so convergence is not reached. That problem can be remedied by a dual assignation in which ε is set either to 0.01% or an absolute difference of, say, 0.1, whichever is smaller. Most programs contain that option.

The second problem is more serious; sometimes the model does not converge to the right value, or does not converge at all. It turns out that the order in which the variables are solved sometimes makes a difference, and ordering the variables in the "right" order will give convergence whereas listing them in the "wrong" order will not.

12.2.3 THE TRIANGULAR STRUCTURE

How can the user tell if the model converges to the wrong solution? Most of the time, the answers will look "wrong" in the sense that the system solution will not be similar to the answer one would have obtained by putting the solved values of the independent variables into the individual equations. The test for this is to change one of the exogenous variables by a small amount and see whether the solution values are almost the same. If they are not, the model is unstable and the solution point reached is probably incorrect.

However, that happens rarely. A much more common problem occurs when the model does not converge at all. To see how this could happen, suppose the demand for capital goods (the capital spending function) is negatively related to the relative price of capital goods. Also, suppose the model contains more than one equation for capital goods. The implicit deflator for computers has been falling for many years. Suppose capital spending rises (because of lower interest rates), which boosts capital spending, causing the implicit deflator for capital goods to diminish. That boosts the demand for capital goods, which reduces the implicit deflator further, hence boosting the demand for capital goods even more, and so on. Under certain circumstances the model might not converge at all.

If the implicit deflator for capital goods were lagged or exogenous, so that it was fixed at time t, convergence would always occur in that time period. Most of the time, one should use lagged values of endogenous variables on the right-hand side of the equation whenever appropriate. However, sometimes the actual linkages in the economy dictate the use of unlagged variables. When that occurs, convergence is more likely to be reached if the equations are ordered so that the ones containing primarily or exclusively lagged and exogenous variables are solved first, with the fully simultaneous equations at the end of the list. Placing the equations in this form is known as triangular ordering. Even if the model will converge regardless of how the equations are ordered, using a triangular structure will reduce the time of iteration – although that is admittedly a moot point with today's powerful personal computers.

The first equations listed in the model should thus be those where all the independent variables are either lagged or exogenous. That way, when later equations are solved, known values for those independent variables will be used in all iterations. Those would be followed by equations where the right-hand endogenous variables are relatively unimportant. Variables that depend primarily on unlagged endogenous variables, such as interest rates, would be solved last.

12.3 A Prototype Macroeconomic Model

The prototype macro model presented here is very similar to models used by this author for predicting the US economy, but the number of equations has been reduced for pedagogical purposes. First, disposable income is estimated with one equation instead of by individual components. Second, the Federal budget surplus or deficit is estimated with a single equation instead of by individual components – personal income taxes, corporate income taxes, social security taxes, excise taxes, transfer payments, interest payments, and so on. Third, separate equations for the various deflators of the components of GDP are not estimated. Instead, the GDP identity holds in constant prices, with a separate equation for the GDP deflator so that the model can also predict current-dollar GDP; the implicit consumption deflator is also estimated separately because that is a key link in relating current and constant-dollar disposable income. Fourth, the equations for consumption and investment are presented at a higher level of aggregation than in most actual forecasting models.

12.3.1 SUMMARY OF MACROECONOMIC MODEL EQUATIONS

For ease of exposition, the equations in the prototype model are discussed in the order more attuned to economic structure rather than the order in which the equations are actually solved. The prototype model contains 34 stochastic equations, which can be subdivided into five "blocks": consumption; other components of aggregate demand; production and employment; prices, wages, and income; and financial sector variables. There are also 12 identities, for a total of 46 endogenous variables:

- Block I: consumer spending – five stochastic equations
- Block II: other components of aggregate demand – eight equations
- Block III: production and employment – five equations
- Block IV: prices, wages, and income – eight equations
- Block V: financial sector (interest rates, money supply, government deficit, loans and credit, stock prices, and value of dollar) – eight equations.

Consumer spending depends primarily on lagged and unlagged income and monetary variables: the cost and availability of credit, and stock prices. The relative prices of food and energy are important, and the equations for durables contain variables reflecting demographic trends. As noted in case study 16 (page 285), forecasting accuracy is improved by treating motor vehicles and other consumer durable goods separately.

In Block II, equations are estimated for the components of capital spending, housing, inventory investment, and exports and imports. Purchases of computers are treated separately for the same reason as is the case for consumption, as noted in case study 27 (page 433). Except for the inventory investment equation, almost all of the independent variables are lagged; these include measures of income and output (mainly industrial production) and the cost and availability of credit. Inventory investment is related to recent changes in other components of aggregate demand and production.

In Block III, production depends on the unlagged components of aggregate demand, and payroll employment and employee-hours depend on unlagged production. The unemployment rate is defined as total labor force minus total household employment divided by the labor force. The labor force is entirely a function of lagged and exogenous variables. Household and payroll employment move together in the long run, but in the short run differ because of cyclical conditions; e.g., during good times, more people are likely to have two jobs.

Block IV starts with the wage and price equations, then moves to the major components of income. Wages and prices depend on exogenous and lagged variables: the money supply, food and energy prices, in productivity trends and the minimum wage. Personal income is closely related to wage rates and employment. Separate equations are included for transfer payments, personal income taxes, and corporate income.

Financial sector equations are estimated in Block V, which contains a high degree of simultaneity. Interest rates are a function of inflation, unemployment, loan demand, and the Federal budget surplus or deficit ratio. The money supply depends on lagged loan demand; before 1982, it was controlled closely by the monetary authorities. Business loan demand and consumer credit outstanding depend on interest rates, inflation, components of aggregate demand, and monetary policy variables. The S&P 500 index of stock prices is a function of corporate profits, bond yields, the rate of capital gains taxation, the rate of inflation, and the Federal budget surplus or deficit ratio. Finally, the trade-weighted average of the dollar is a function of domestic stock prices, domestic interest rates, and growth rates in Europe and Asia.

The reduced form of the model indicates that the most important exogenous variables are (i) changes in monetary policy that affect the availability of credit, (ii) exogenous food and energy prices, (iii) the level of Federal government spending, and (iv) income tax rates. Demographic variables affect longer-term movements in the economy, but not short-term fluctuations. According to this model, the major causes of recessions are exogenous shocks. The model does not contain any mechanism for generating endogenous business cycles. In particular, there is no linkage whereby an increase in wages and prices at full employment causes monetary tightening and a decline in real GDP; the model contains no "Phillips curve." The simulation record of this prototype model will be examined shortly.

Most actual macroeconometric models contain more variables than this prototype for two reasons: it strengthens the empirical estimates of some of the linkages, and users often desire more detail. In most forecasting models the individual components of personal income are estimated separately, whereas in this model a single equation suffices. Similarly, a single equation is estimated here for the Federal surplus or deficit ratio, instead of including separate tax and transfer equations.

The actual equations included in this model, and an explanation of the particular variables chosen, can be found in the website associated with this textbook. Besides the fact that space limitations preclude a detailed discussion in these pages, the model itself changes frequently and is regularly updated. It is reestimated with new data every quarter, and respecified with new variables and new lag structures every year. Some might see this as an admission that the model did not generate perfect forecasts over the previous year, but of course we already know that. Frequent updating of all econometric models is indeed an integral part of the entire modeling process.

Many users require more detailed estimates of consumer and capital spending that permit the user to link these variables to individual company or industry models, but this additional detail would not enhance the understanding of how a model is built, nor improve the explanation of the interaction between equations. Also, there is no evidence that bigger models predict the overall economy more accurately; the increased size is useful primarily because it provides greater industry detail. Even when that is desired, though, forecasting efficacy and accuracy are generally improved by estimating a fairly small core model of 50–75 stochastic equations, and then building satellite models to generate detailed predictions for prices, employment, production, and other industry variables rather than creating one large interactive model with thousands of equations.

12.3.2 TREATMENT OF TRENDS AND AUTOCORRELATION

In most cases where the dependent variable exhibits a strong upward trend, the variable is estimated in ratio or percentage change form. When percentage changes are used, the dependent variable is usually estimated in the form $(x - \bar{x})/\bar{x}$, where $\bar{x} = (x_{-1} + x_{-2} + x_{-3} + x_{-4})/4$; otherwise spurious four-quarter cycles are introduced into the forecast after the first year or two.

There are some exceptions to the treatment of trend removal. Where the equation is a quasi-identity (such as productivity as a function of output and employee-hours), the levels form is generally used, with the variables transformed to logarithms. Occasionally, a percentage equation drifts off the track whereas the levels equation does not; so levels equations are used even though the DW statistic is very low. In the equation for purchases of computers, a logarithmic formulation is used to capture the strong upward trend of the technological revolution.

Just as a low DW does not necessarily reduce forecast accuracy, a high DW does not necessarily improve forecasting accuracy. Suppose, for example, that the residuals of a given equation estimated in percentage change form are negative for a few quarters, and then are randomly distributed after that, so the sample period DW statistic is not significantly different from 2. Even in that case, prediction of the *levels* of that variable may be too low for many years into the future. In this example, once the forecasts move off the track, they stay off the track. In that case, a relatively high DW disguises the fact that the model generates inaccurate forecasts.

Even after the trends have been removed, virtually all of the residuals exhibit significant positive autocorrelation. Statistically, that issue can be resolved by adding the AR(1) transformation. However, that will usually increase forecast error, as has been shown in several examples. Hence the AR(1) adjustment is not used in any forecasting equations even when the DW statistic is low. It is used only for diagnostic purposes; if a variable becomes insignificant when AR(1) is added, it is often excluded from the final equation.

Theoretically, a low DW means one or more variables are missing, or the underlying equation is not linear. It is, of course, quite possible we have missed some variables or incorrectly specified the equations. However, there are many reasons why the existence of positive autocorrelation of the residuals might not reduce forecasting accuracy, which can be summarized as follows.

- Suppose the inclusion of a missing variable would sharply reduce autocorrelation – but it is not possible to predict that variable accurately. In that case, while the sample period statistics would be improved by the inclusion of that variable, forecasts would not.
- Sometimes strings of positive or negative residuals reflect a change in expectations, which cannot be measured statistically. Taking that information into account through constant adjustments will improve forecast accuracy.
- In most cases when the dependent variable is transformed into percentage changes, a four-quarter change is used. Transforming that variable into a one-quarter percentage change generally eliminates serial correlation of the residuals – but the resulting series consists mainly of random noise, so those changes are uncorrelated with many of the relevant economic variables. As a result, forecasting accuracy is decreased.
- Often the degree of autocorrelation can be sharply reduced by shortening the sample period; however, that usually results in worse forecasts if underlying economic conditions change. For example, an equation estimated only during a period of uninterrupted growth would probably do very poorly in predicting the next recession. As a result, our equations generally incorporate the maximum amount of data available on a consistent basis.
- In this author's experience, excessive use of nonlinear terms in equations, while they improve the fit and raise the DW, usually reduce to an exercise in curve fitting that does not improve forecast accuracy.
- Except for financial market variables, the data prepared by government agencies are based on sampling techniques. Highly sophisticated methods are used, and the US government economic data are generally of high quality. Nonetheless, these techniques are likely to introduce some spurious smoothness into the data, especially for monthly or quarterly series. Hence it often happens that, while the residuals from a quarterly function contain significant autocorrelation, residuals from the same function estimated with annual data do not. If that is indeed the case, positive autocorrelation probably does not indicate an incorrect specification of the equation.
- Economic agents base their decisions in part on habit and past performance. In that sense, the residuals actually are correlated – and through judicious use of constant adjustments, that information can be used to improve forecast accuracy.

The DW statistic has been used as follows. All the equations have been rerun with the AR(1) term and, in most cases, variables that were not significant were omitted or modified. Hence most of the variables included in these equations are significant at the 5% level even after taking into account the serial

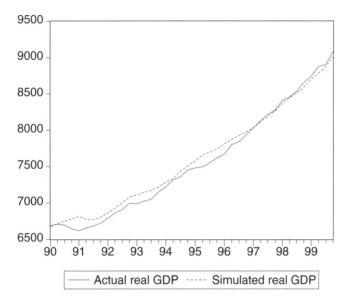

Figure 12.1   Actual and simulated values in real GDP.

correlation of residuals. However, using the equations with an AR(1) term does not improve forecasting accuracy, so it is not included in any of the model equations.

12.4 SIMULATING THE MODEL

Before using any model to generate actual forecasts, it is important to simulate it over historical periods to determine whether it remains on track. It is quite possible that, although each of the individual equations fits the sample period well, simultaneous causality could cause the overall model solution to diverge from actual values. Results are shown for 40-quarter simulations from 1990.1 through 1999.4 for a few of the key variables; similar comparisons were actually calculated for all endogenous variables in the model. Also, these calculations were performed for an 80-quarter period starting in 1980.1; since the results were similar, they are not illustrated here. Figures 12.1–12.8 show actual and simulated values for real GDP, growth rate, unemployment rate, inflation rate, Aaa corporate bond rate, Federal funds rate, stock prices, and the M2 money supply.

The next step in testing a structural model is to calculate multipliers in order to determine how the model reacts to changes in key policy variables such as changes in fiscal or monetary policies, or exogenous shocks. While this is an important step for models used for policy purposes, it is abbreviated here for two reasons. First, the emphasis of this book is on forecasting. Second and more

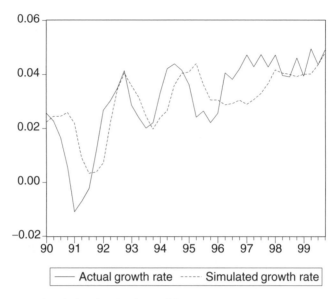

Figure 12.2 Actual and simulated values of four-quarter percentage changes in GDP.

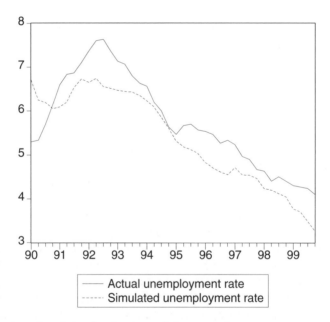

Figure 12.3 Actual and simulated values of the unemployment rate.

important, policy changes invariably depend on "what else" happens. If the Federal budget deficit is increased, the impact will be entirely different depending on whether the additional deficit is financed by "printing money" or selling bonds. Hence multiplier analysis is used here mainly to check that small changes

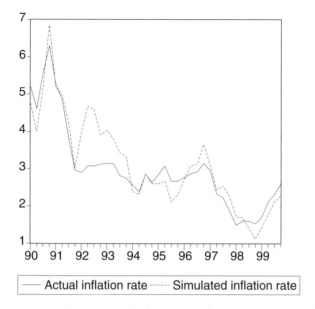

Figure 12.4   Actual and simulated values of four-quarter changes in the CPI.

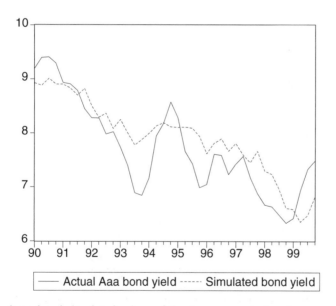

Figure 12.5   Actual and simulated values of the Aaa corporate bond rate.

in exogenous variables do not cause unrealistic changes in the simulated values. The multiplier analysis here confirms that the model generates realistic values and does not go off the track when exogenous variables are changed by small amounts.

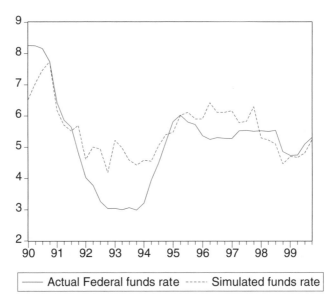

Figure 12.6 Actual and simulated values of the Federal funds rate.

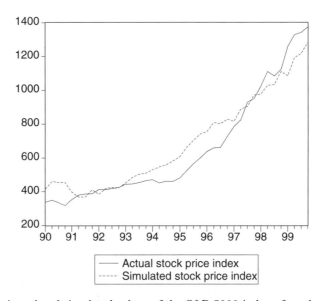

Figure 12.7 Actual and simulated values of the S&P 5000 index of stock prices.

Three multiplier simulations are described here: a reduction in the Federal funds rate by 1%, a reduction in personal income taxes by $50 billion, and an exogenous increase in purchases of motor vehicles by 1 million units. Since the results are basically similar, in the interests of space the simulation results are shown only for the first case.

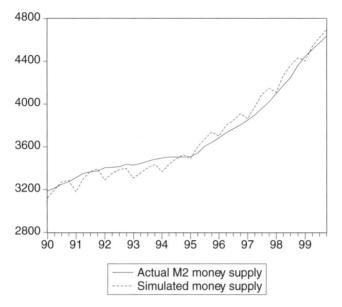

Figure 12.8 Actual and simulated values of the M2 measure of money supply.

A reduction in the Federal funds rate boosts real growth and raises stock prices. There is no measurable impact on inflation because there is no Phillips curve tradeoff in this model. Summary statistics are shown for the unemployment rate, real growth rate, Federal funds rate, and stock prices in figure 12.9.

When personal income taxes are cut by $50 billion, real growth initially rises, but the increase in the deficit boosts the bond yield, and the combination of a bigger deficit and higher interest rates offsets the increase in real growth and profits, so stock prices decline. As a result, the long-term tax cut multiplier is approximately zero.

The third multiplier simulates the impact of an exogenous 1 million increase in purchases of motor vehicles. The initial multiplier is about $2\frac{1}{2}$, but this eventually declines to about 1, as the increased demand for credit results in somewhat higher interest rates. Motor vehicle sales remain more than 1 million above the baseline value, so there is some "crowding out" as investment declines. That result happens whether the increase in consumption stems from a tax cut or an exogenous boost in consumer spending, although that effect is somewhat smaller if the shift occurs in the private sector.

Many other multipliers were calculated, but the results are basically the same. If aggregate demand rises and the Fed does not accommodate by reducing interest rates or expanding credit availability, the initial multiplier impacts are substantially reduced. In the case of public sector multipliers, long-term fiscal policy multipliers are close to zero under a wide variety of assumptions.

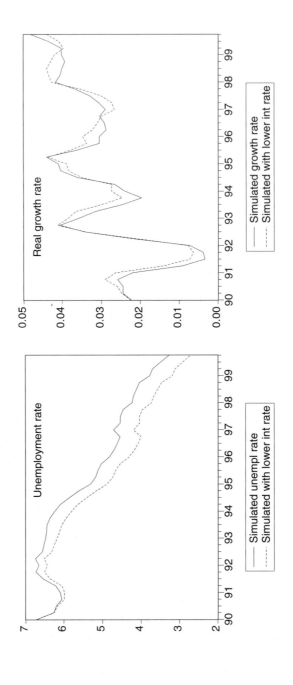

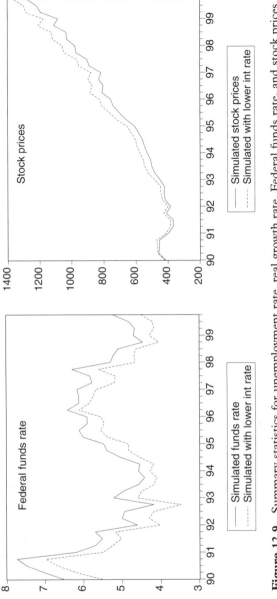

Figure 12.9 Summary statistics for unemployment rate, real growth rate, Federal funds rate, and stock prices.

12.5 PREPARING THE MODEL FOR FORECASTING

At this point we assume the testing of the model is complete, and now proceed to adjust it in order to minimize forecasting errors. The three principal methods considered here are adjusting the equations automatically with AR(1) transformations, changing the constant adjustments by recent values of the residuals, and using information from the consensus forecasts or surveys to reduce forecast error.

12.5.1 FORECASTING WITH AR(1) ADJUSTMENTS

Throughout this text it has been emphasized that using the AR(1) transformation does not improve forecast accuracy. This hypothesis is now tested on a full-scale model. To perform this test, all of the stochastic equations in the model are reestimated with an AR(1) transformation, and the model is then resimulated for the 1990–9 period. It is not necessary to show all the results; in virtually all cases, the forecast errors are larger. Figure 12.10 presents graphs for actual values, simulated values without AR, and simulations with AR(1) for real growth, stock prices, inflation, and the Federal funds rate.

In chapter 8 it was noted that virtually all forecasters failed to predict the 1990–1 recession. This model does not track the 1991 recession very well either, although the errors are even larger with AR(1) transformations. The actual four-quarter growth rate drops to −1%, while the model simulation shows a decline only to +0.5%; the AR version assumes it does not fall much below 2%. As a result, it does not capture the ensuing recovery very well either. Finally, the AR version of the model substantially underpredicts the rise in the growth rate in the late 1990s, whereas the actual model tracks that improvement fairly closely.

The results are even poorer for the Federal funds rate simulation with AR. Admittedly, the model fails to capture the Fed easing in 1993, which brought the nominal funds rate down to 3% and the real funds rate down to 0%, its lowest value ever in a non-recession period. The model simulation shows a decline in the nominal rate only to about $4\frac{1}{2}$%. However, the funds rate remains above 6% when the model equations are used with AR transformations. This presents one of the clearest examples of how the use of the lagged dependent variable – including using the AR transformation – causes errors to increase in multi-period forecasting. Indeed, in the AR(1) simulation, the Federal funds rate remains above its actual value for the entire 10-year period.

Similar results can be seen in the graphs for stock prices and the unemployment rate. In the case of stock prices, the AR simulation shows a much smaller increase in stock prices in the late 1990s. Furthermore, even though the simulated values of real growth and stock prices are lower and interest rates are higher than in the actual model simulation, the forecasts of the unemployment rate which should be higher because of the lower growth rate are further below the actual level than in the unadjusted model simulation. These results clearly indicate that multi-period forecasting is seldom if ever enhanced by reestimating structural equations with the AR(1) transformation even if the DW statistic appears to show less serial correlation of the residuals.

12.5.2 FORECASTING WITH CONSTANT ADJUSTMENTS

Table 12.1 lists the actual residuals for each of the stochastic equations for the four quarters of 1999, followed by the actual constant adjustment term used to forecast in 2000. The asterisk indicates that, in actual forecasting, the apparent trend in the constant term would be continued through the four quarters of 2000.

If the residuals changed sign during the four quarters of 1999, a value of 0 was generally assigned to the constant adjustment for 2000. If the value of the constant adjustment increased over time, generally the highest value, or an extrapolated value, was used for 2000. In practice this author often continues the trend of the constant adjustment, but since part of 2000 was already known, it seemed that the conditions of an actual ex ante forecast would be more closely followed if the constant adjustments were the same for all four quarters. Finally, if the residuals were all positive or negative and did not change very much, the average 1999 value was used for the constant adjustment in 2000.

The only major dilemma arose on the adjustment for the stock price term. It was clear that, by historical measures, the market was overvalued at the end of 1999; however, it was not known how much more it would rise, or when it would decline. Thus an alternative simulation was simulated in which the value of the constant term of the stock price index linearly declined to zero throughout 2000, closely approximating what did happen. However, because of the lags involved, the forecast of real GDP changed by less than $\frac{1}{2}\%$, and other key variables were similarly unaffected. Hence failure to predict the turnaround in the stock market was not the major reason why the model did not predict the sharp reduction in growth in the second half of the year.

12.5.3 COMPARISON OF ALTERNATIVE FORECASTS

One of the most contentious issues among forecasters remains the validity of judgmental adjusting of the constant terms of the equations; these are often referred to as ad hoc adjustments, with the implication that such adjustments cover up the inability of the forecaster to generate accurate equations.

From a philosophical viewpoint, there probably will never be an answer to this dispute. From a practical business forecasting viewpoint, however, the questions is much simpler and more direct: how much is forecast error reduced by using constant adjustments?

As shown here, the forecasts for 2000 were more accurate when the constant terms of the equations are adjusted by hand than when constant terms are adjusted automatically with AR(1) transformations. This author has also

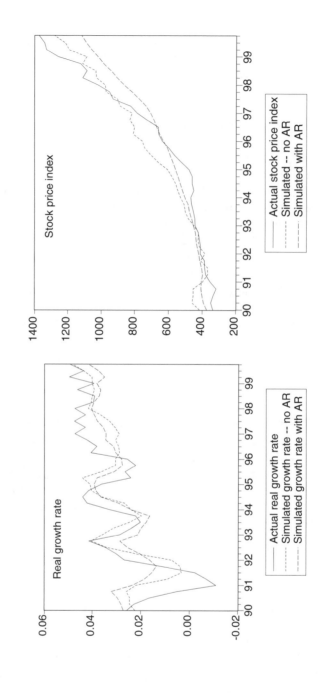

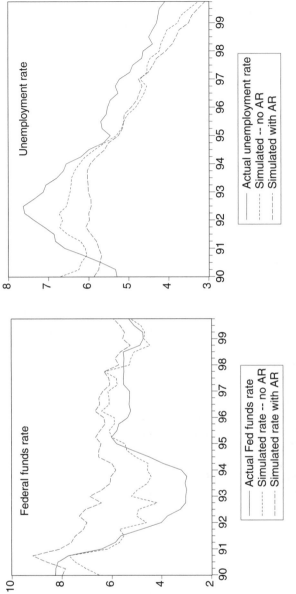

Figure 12.10 Forecasts with AR(1) adjustment.

Table 12.1 Single-equation residuals for 1999.

Equation	Actual residuals in 1999				Year 2000 constant adjustment
	99.1	99.2	99.3	99.4	
Motor vehicles	−0.1	−0.4	−0.2	0.2	0.0
Consumption autos/parts	15	23	12	16	17
Consumption other durables	−6	−4	9	21	30
Consumption non-durables	20	20	23	38	38
Consumption services	−13	−10	−4	−10	−10
PDE – computers & software	12	31	51	60	70*
PDE – other	−3	−12	−9	−15	−10
Non-residential construction	−3	−10	−9	−12	−8
Housing starts	0.07	−0.13	−0.02	0.05	0
Residential construction	13	17	15	14	15
Inventory Investment	−3	−32	−4	−12	0
Exports	−6	−16	0	0	0
Imports	−6	4	16	2	0
Industrial production	−2	0	−2	−2	−1
Employee-hours	−0.5	−1.1	−1.0	−0.9	−0.9
Productivity	−0.3	−1.6	0	0.6	0
Household employment	0.2	−0.1	−0.2	−0.6	−0.6
Labor force	0.7	0.3	0.2	0.2	0.4
Inflation – CPI	0	−0.2	−0.2	0.2	0
Wage rates	0	0.2	−0.2	−0.4	0
Implicit consumption deflator	0.8	0.5	0.8	0.9	1.0
Implicit GDP deflator	0.0	0.0	0.0	0.0	0.0
Personal income	35	22	33	67	40
Personal income taxes	−15	−13	4	18	0
Transfer payments	8	5	5	4	5
Federal budget surplus/deficit	0.2	0.4	0.5	0.3	0.4
Corporate income	29	9	−23	−31	−40*
Federal funds rate	0	0	0	0	0
Aaa corporate bond rate	0.0	0.7	0.9	0.8	0.6
Money supply	35	50	47	−15	0
Commercial loans	8	0	−16	−24	−32*
Consumer credit	−35	−43	−47	−50	−63*
Stock prices	115	199	205	191	180
Value of dollar	0	1	3	4	5

prepared one-year forecasts starting in 1990 where the sample period is trun-cated in the previous year, constant terms are adjusted by methods described below, and these results are then compared with those generated by the same model with AR(1) transformations and no constant adjustments. The results are just what would be expected from the comparison shown in figure 12.10; the AR(1) results are inferior for virtually all variables in all years.

However, that still leaves unanswered the larger question of whether forecasts generated by a model plus constant adjustments are better than forecasts generated by other methods. There are substantial difficulties in constructing such a test because macroeconomic forecasts made by different methods are not really independent. Suppose someone was able to build a macro model which, when used with constant adjustments, consistently generated very accurate forecasts. It would not be long before other forecasters would duplicate those methods, or at least issue forecasts that were very similar to the ones generated by this expert model builder. Under such circumstances, the consensus forecast would also turn out to be very accurate. However, a comparison of the consensus and model forecasts would show virtually no difference, and it would not be long before some economists would point out that the consensus forecast was just as accurate as predictions from macro models.

The problem with going back and calculating ex post simulations with actual consensus forecasts is that researchers have the benefit of hindsight. They use the actual values of exogenous variables, and even if the sample period is truncated, they will know what happened beyond the sample period, which will shape their judgment about which variables and which lag structures to use. Many years ago, this author attempted to analyze the true ex ante forecasting record of several models, then go back and insert the actual exogenous variables and determine what proportion of the error was caused by incorrect assumptions, and what proportion by errors in the equations. In many cases, using actual data made the forecasts worse because economists had already adjusted for what appeared to be questionable data at the time. Later, Stephen McNees and others have shown that no single method of forecasting – econometric model, leading indicators, consensus, back of the envelope, etc. – has compiled a superior forecasting record over the years.

Our experiment is thus a modest one. In preparing the book, this author estimated the model shown above in early 2000, made constant adjustments based on the 1999 residuals, and generated a forecast. These values were then compared to actual values at the end of the year. In that sense the results can be considered a true ex ante forecast, and can usefully be compared to forecasts generated with the same model using AR(1) transformations and no constant adjustments, and the Blue Chip consensus forecasts issues in January 2000. The 4.2% growth in real GDP for 2000 shown here is identical to the forecast of this author included in the January 2000 Blue Chip Economic Indicators newsletter. The results for key variables are shown in table 12.2. The variables chosen are the ones for which quarterly consensus estimates are available from Blue Chip except for the PPI, which is not estimated in the prototype model. That is because short-term fluctuations in the PPI are almost entirely dependent on exogenous food and energy prices.

Please keep in mind that the "actual" values are based on government data published in early 2001. These data are always revised later in the year,

Table 12.2 Comparison of forecast errors for 2000.

	2000.1	2000.2	2000.3	2000.4	*AAE*
Growth rate – actual	4.8	5.6	2.2	1.1	
Growth rate – const adj	4.1	4.9	3.6	4.2	1.5
Growth rate – AR adj	2.1	3.6	2.8	4.0	2.1
Growth rate – consensus	3.0	3.2	3.4	3.2	1.9
Unemployment rate – actual	4.1	4.0	4.0	4.0	
Unemployment rate – const adj	4.0	3.8	3.6	3.5	0.3
Unemployment rate – AR adj	3.9	3.8	3.6	3.5	0.3
Unemployment rate – consensus	4.1	4.1	4.1	4.1	0.1
CPI inflation rate – actual	4.2	3.6	3.0	3.0	
CPI inflation rate – const adj	2.5	3.1	2.5	3.4	0.8
CPI inflation rate – AR adj	1.4	2.5	1.8	2.5	1.4
CPI inflation rate – consensus	2.5	2.4	2.5	2.5	1.0
Implicit GDP inflation rate – actual	3.3	2.4	1.6	1.9	
Implicit GDP inflation rate – const adj	4.5	1.3	1.9	2.2	0.7
Implicit GDP inflation rate – AR adj	3.9	1.5	1.4	2.1	0.5
Implicit GDP inflation rate – consensus	1.8	1.7	1.8	1.8	0.6
Federal funds rate – actual	5.7	6.3	6.5	6.5	
Federal funds rate – const adj	5.6	5.9	6.0	6.1	0.3
Federal funds rate – AR adj	5.6	5.8	5.9	6.0	0.4
Federal funds rate – consensus	5.7	5.9	6.0	6.0	0.4
Aaa corporate bond rate – actual	7.7	7.8	7.6	7.4	
Aaa corporate bond rate – const adj	7.5	7.6	7.6	7.6	0.2
Aaa corporate bond rate – AR adj	7.4	7.3	7.2	7.1	0.4
Aaa corporate bond rate – consensus	7.7	7.7	7.7	7.7	0.1
% chg industrial production – actual	6.9	7.7	3.6	−0.8	
% chg industrial production – const adj	1.7	5.0	1.7	1.9	3.1
% chg industrial production – AR adj	1.9	2.6	2.7	3.1	3.7
% chg industrial production – consensus	3.0	3.3	3.4	3.3	3.2
% chg disposable income – actual	1.9	3.7	2.6	0.6	
% chg disposable income – constant adj	3.3	5.6	4.2	4.9	2.3
% chg disposable income – AR adj	2.4	4.1	3.2	3.4	1.1
% chg disposable income – consensus	3.4	3.3	3.4	3.1	1.3
% chg real consumer spending – actual	7.3	3.1	4.5	2.8	
% chg real consumer spending – constant adj	6.6	5.0	4.6	4.7	1.1
% chg real consumer spending – AR adj	3.9	3.9	4.0	4.0	1.5
% chg real consumer spending – consensus	3.4	3.3	3.2	3.0	1.4
Inventory investment, const $ – actual	37	79	73	56	
Inventory investment, const $ – constant adj	42	46	57	45	16
Inventory investment, const $ – AR adj	55	50	52	49	19
Inventory investment, const $ – consensus	38	38	38	38	24
Net exports, const $ – actual	−377	−403	−425	−442	
Net exports, const $ – constant adj	−373	−384	−392	−390	27
Net exports, const $ – AR adj	−373	−377	−377	−373	37
Net exports, const $ – consensus	−355	−361	−356	−362	56

Const adj, with constant adjustments; AR adj, with AR adjustments.

so by the time you are reading this, the "actual" figures will have changed somewhat.

Assigning a ranking of 1 to the smallest forecast error, 2 to the median, and 3 to the largest, the rankings for these 11 variables are 1.4 for the model with constant adjustments, and an identical 2.3 for both the consensus forecast and the model with AR adjustments. Thus in most cases, the forecast error of the econometric model without AR adjustments was smaller than the consensus forecast or the econometric model with AR adjustments.

Nonetheless, the forecasting experience must once again be judged unsatisfactory in the sense that no method predicted the sharp decline in the fourth-quarter growth rate to only 1.1%. Later we examine whether forecasts generated with other methods caught this downturn at the beginning of the year; several forecasters, including this author, saw it developing by midyear. So far, however, the results must be considered discouraging.

One cannot, of course, offer sweeping conclusions from one year of forecasts. However, the following observations appear pertinent not only for 2000 but, based on additional testing by this author, for macroeconomic forecasting generally.

- In virtually all cases, a model forecast based on AR(1) adjustments but no judgmental constant adjustments has larger errors than a forecast generated with constant adjustments based on residuals of the past one or two years.
- In most cases, where the model forecasts were inaccurate, the consensus forecast was also inaccurate; they generally made the same mistakes. That is hardly surprising, considering that most consensus forecasts are based directly or indirectly on model forecasts issued by the major econometric consulting firms. Also, all economists are looking at the same data.
- The model failed to capture the major exogenous shifts that occurred during 2000: further tightening by the Fed, sharply higher oil and natural gas prices, and the plunge in the stock market. So did the consensus forecast. According to the model, real growth was expected to decline from $4\frac{1}{2}$% in the first half of the year to 4% in the second half, compared with an actual decline from 5.2% to 1.6%. An alternative simulation (not shown here) using the actual values of the Federal funds rate and stock market prices shows predicted real growth of slightly over 3% in the second half. That is a small step in the right direction but clearly did not capture the full effect of the slowdown. Hence the model failed to capture the decline in consumer and business spending not directly related to higher interest rates or lower stock market prices.

This simple prototype model, with its forecasting record analyzed for only one year, cannot be expected to generate conclusive evidence. Also, it is possible that other forecasters have records that are dissimilar from this author's. However, several studies have indicated that is probably not the case. In a series of articles, Steven McNees finds that no one forecaster has a consistently superior record, either over time or with respect to individual variables.[6] Zarnowitz and Braun[7] compared the results from the macroeconometric model with the longest historical record – the Michigan model – with consensus forecasts and VAR models. They found little difference between the performance of the Michigan model and the NBER–ASA consensus forecast, although both were superior to BVAR and ARIMA model projections. Also, they found that the consensus forecast was generally more accurate than most individual forecasts. Hence we can reasonably claim that the results here are representative of these larger studies.

What conclusions can be drawn with respect to using macroeconomic models for forecasting purposes, leaving aside the issue of whether one model is better than another?

1 In the past, no econometric model has been able to provide accurate forecasts of unexpected exogenous developments, and it would be unrealistic to expect them to be successful in the future.
2 Models that incorporate adjustments in the constant and slope terms, and are frequently reestimated, generally provide more accurate forecasts than "pure" models that are not adjusted.
3 Along the same lines, pure modeling efforts such ARIMA and VAR models give far poorer macroeconomic forecasts than either econometric models or the consensus.
4 It usually takes two to three quarters for exogenous factors to affect the major economic indicators: real growth, inflation, and unemployment. Hence well-informed and intelligent modelers can predict accurately two to three quarters in advance by utilizing current information. Beyond that time horizon, model forecasts are always based on patterns of past relationships. So far, no one modeler has a distinguished record in this area.

12.6 USING THE LEADING INDICATORS FOR MACROECONOMIC FORECASTING

We now examine whether non-econometric methods are useful in predicting turning points in economic activity in general and the slowdown in the second half of 2000 in particular. The index of leading indicators is considered first,

---

[6] See, for example, McNees, Stephen K., "How Accurate are Macroeconomic Forecasts," *New England Economic Review* (July/August 1988), 15–36; and "Which Forecast Should You Use?" *New England Economic Review* (July/August 1985), 36–42.

[7] Zarnowitz, Victor, and Phillip Braun, "Twenty-two Years of the NBER–ASA Quarterly Economic Outlook Surveys: Aspects and Comparisons of Forecasting Performance," in James H. Stock and Mark W. Watson (eds), *Business Cycles, Indicators, and Forecasting* (University of Chicago Press), 1993.

since they have been used to predict business cycles for over 50 years and are still widely followed.

The concept behind the leading indicators is quite simple: given the linkages in the economy, some variables must turn down before others. Thus, for example, housing starts turn down before residential construction, new orders for capital goods turn down before capital spending, and the length of the work-week turns down before employment. Also, it could logically be argued that the stock market moves ahead of turning points in economic activity, since it immediately discounts all future information. There is no "theory" behind the leading indicators, nor is any intended: the idea is simply to identify those series that consistently change well in advance of changes in the major measures of economic activity: GDP, production, income, and employment.

For many years, the index of leading indicators was compiled by the Commerce Department; in 1996, that job was turned over to the Conference Board, but the overall methodology stayed remained similar. It should be noted, however, that the list of economic indicators included in the Leading Index has changed almost completely over the years, and the variables included now are not the ones used earlier. Presumably the list will change again in the future.

A comprehensive study of the predictive performance of the index of leading indicators was undertaken by Stock and Watson in 1991, and published in 1993.[8] Their results were quite disappointing, especially the inability of any such index to predict the 1990–1 downturn. According to this study, "An analysis of a broad set of 45 coincident and leading indicators, including the seven in the experimental index, demonstrates that almost all performed quite poorly during this episode. Only a few, such as housing building permits, consumer expectations, a measure of business sentiment, oil prices, help wanted advertising, and stock prices, signaled that the economy would suffer a sharp contraction . . . the challenge is how they could have been identified ex ante."

At this point the reader may wonder whether we are adding yet another straw man to the long list of methods that cannot predict very well. The answer is a little more complicated than that. First, using the "market test" criterion, this index may very well contain some useful information, since it is still closely followed. Second, perhaps we can pick up the gauntlet thrown down by Stock and Watson and in fact identify the correct subset of leading indicators on an ex ante basis.

Although this method is not supposed to involve any theory, a brief discussion of how the economy works at turning points is not amiss. Why do housing starts turn down? Because the cost of credit has risen and the availability has

---

[8]   Stock, J. H., and M. W. Watson, "A Procedure for Predicting Recessions with Leading Indicators: Econometric Issues and Recent Experience," *Business Cycles, Indicators, and Forecasting* (University of Chicago Press for NBER), 1993.

decreased. Why do new orders turn down? Basically because of the same reasons. Why do firms reduce their demand for labor? Because the demand for their products has declined, due in large part to the same factors. When the individual components of the index are examined, it can be seen that, in recent years, the monetary indicators are much more important than the non-monetary factors.

Thus in examining the individual leading indicators, it turns out that, in recent years, changes in stock prices, changes in the real money supply, and the yield spread have been the three most important components of the index of leading indicators. The other seven indicators detract rather than add to its predictive accuracy. When percentage changes in GDP are regressed against lagged values of the monetary and non-monetary components of the leading indicators, the latter term has a non-significant negative sign.

Currently, the other components of the index of leading indicators are the length of the manufacturing work week, initial unemployment claims, new orders for capital goods, new orders for consumer goods and materials, building permits, vendor performance (percentage of firms reporting slower deliveries), and consumer expectations. Consumer expectations might seem to be a better leading indicator than consumer sentiment, but repeated testing has shown just the opposite; in regressions used to test the importance of these variables, consumer expectations has a negative sign. New orders and vendor performance should theoretically serve as leading indicators, but in fact they turn out to be coincident. In the housing sector, building permits are sometimes countercyclical. The length of the manufacturing workweek is too erratic to be a useful leading indicator, and the series for initial unemployment claims is also a coincident indicator.

This suggests that some combination of changes in stock prices, changes in the real money supply, and the value of the yield spread might be useful in predicting turning points two to three quarters in advance.

Table 12.3 shows the performance of the monetary components of the index of leading indicators for the period from 1988.1 through 1991.4. The real money supply (M2) did indeed decline throughout 1990, and the yield spread had already turned negative in 1989. The stock market was more erratic, but on balance it did decline during 1990, although most of the drop occurred from July to October. Thus it seems likely that greater emphasis on these variables would have generated better predictions of the performance of the economy than any other methods considered in this chapter.

How well have these indicators done since then? Figure 12.11 shows their behavior from 1988 through the end of 2000; the percentage changes are shown in quarterly rates to make the graph easier to read. Unfortunately, however, the results are not very robust. The real money supply declined in 1991, 1992, 1993, and 1994, yet the economy steadily improved. The yield spread, defined as the difference between the Aaa corporate bond rate and the Federal funds rate, remained positive before and during the sharp drop in real growth in late 2000.

Table 12.3 Behavior of monetary components of the index of leading indicators, 1998 through 1991.

	Percentage change in M2	Yield spread	Percentage change in S&P 500
1988:1	4.1	2.9	4.3
1988:2	3.1	2.7	7.8
1988:3	−1.1	2.0	5.7
1988:4	−0.9	1.0	12.1
1989:1	−2.4	0.2	22.6
1989:2	−3.6	−0.2	31.6
1989:3	4.4	−0.1	36.5
1989:4	3.9	0.3	4.1
1990:1	−1.3	0.9	−10.6
1990:2	−0.6	1.1	15.7
1990:3	−2.6	1.2	−16.3
1990:4	−3.7	1.6	−21.8
1991:1	1.9	2.5	46.1
1991:2	2.1	3.0	28.4
1991:3	−1.6	3.1	7.3
1991:4	−1.9	3.6	1.5

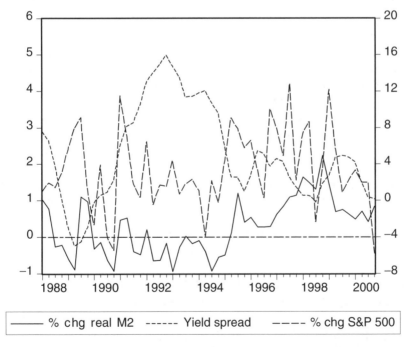

Figure 12.11 Monetary components of the index of leading indicators, 1988 through 2000. Percentage changes are shown at quarterly rates.

Table 12.4 Percentage changes in Real GDP.

	Actual	Predicted by Blue Chip	Predicted by monetary components lead indicators
2000.1	2.3	3.0	3.6
2000.2	5.6	3.2	3.7
2000.3	1.3	3.4	3.3
2000.4	1.9	3.2	2.4
2000.1	1.3	1.9	1.9
2000.2	0.3	2.5	1.6
2000.3	−0.4	3.1	1.3
2000.4	−2.0	3.5	1.0
AAFE	–	2.3	1.5

Nonetheless, the monetary components of the leading indicators did a better job of predicting slower growth in 2000–2001 than the consensus forecasts, although they missed the depth of the decline following the terrorist attacks of 11 September, 2001. Table 12.4 shows an AAFE of 1.5% for these components, compared to 2.3% for the consensus forecast. Furthermore, in 2001 the difference was even greater: 1.7% compared to 3.1%.

This author has closely followed the various manifestations of the index of leading indicators for the past 40 years, and has found that they did not miss actual recessions but they did give too many false signals. The sharp decline in the stock market in February through September 2001 was the single best leading indicator of the forthcoming recession. The problem, however, is that an even bigger decline in the fall of 1987 was followed by an *increase* in the growth rate the following year. Hence this indicator is too erratic to be used consistently.

While the leading indicators will presumably continue to be reported in the business and financial press, this author has not found any credible evidence to suggest that they improve forecast accuracy in non-recession years. After more than 50 years of failed results, it is time to move on to other methods.

12.7 USING INDEXES OF CONSUMER AND BUSINESS SENTIMENT FOR FORECASTING

This section considers the forecasting efficacy of the indexes of consumer sentiment, the national association of purchasing managers index of manufacturing activity (NAPM), and the NAHB index of homebuilders' sentiment. The

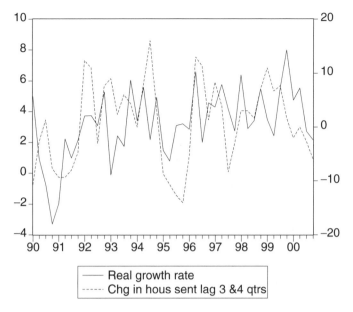

Figure 12.12   Real growth rate compared with the change in the NAHB index of housing sentiment, lagged three and four quarters.

performance of these indexes is evaluated over the past 10 years, with particu-lar emphasis on those periods before (i) the 1990–1 recession, (ii) the slow-down in the first half of 1995, and (iii) the slowdown in the second half of 2000. The comparisons of these indicators and percentage changes in real GDP are shown in figures 12.12–12.14.

As already shown, the NAHB index can be used to improve forecasts for housing starts; but housing often tends to be a countercyclical indicator – it often weakens during the latter stages of business cycles because of higher inter-est rates even though consumer and capital spending continue to rise – so its usefulness for predicting turning points in GDP is limited. In particular, the index turned up in early 1990 as interest rates fell, just before the economy plunged into recession. In 1995 it overstated the degree of decline, although it did fairly well in 2000.

The Conference Board index of consumer sentiment has not performed well at turning points. It completely missed the 1990–1 recession, then rose sharply after the conclusion of the Persian Gulf War, leading to the prediction that growth would rebound strongly, which did not occur. It failed to gauge the severity of the slowdown in 1995. Even worse, it remained near record-high levels through September 2000 and did not turn down until several months after the slowdown in consumer spending had already begun.

The NAPM index failed to predict the 1990–1 recession, and like the con-sumer sentiment index, indicated a much stronger rebound in 1991 and 1992

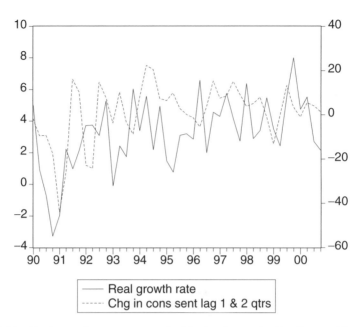

Figure 12.13 Real growth rate compared with the change in Conference Board index of consumer sentiment, lagged one and two quarters.

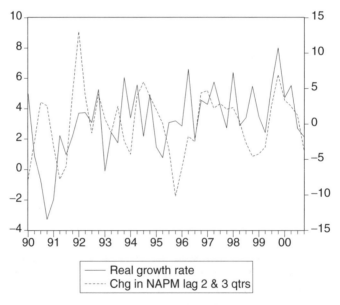

Figure 12.14 Real growth rate compared with the change in the NAPM index of manufacturing activity, lagged two and three quarters.

than actually occurred. It fell coincidentally with the slowdown in early 1995 but did not give a warning signal. Conversely, the slowdown in 2000 was correctly anticipated. However, note that the NAPM index fell sharply in 1998, yet real growth accelerated in 1999.

We now turn to regression analysis over this same ten-year period. The first regression contains all of the indicators lagged one and two quarters; the index of leading indicators is also included because of the importance of the monetary component.

$$
\begin{aligned}
\%GDPH \\
= 2.46 - 0.012 ^* CCIN(-1) + 0.079 ^* CCIN(-2) + 0.001 ^* NAHB(-1) \\
(0.2) \qquad\qquad (1.5) \qquad\qquad (0.0) \\
+ 0.031 ^* NAHB(-2) + 3.15 ^* LEAD(-1) + 0.68 ^* LEAD(-2) \\
(0.4) \qquad\qquad (2.0) \qquad\qquad (0.4) \\
- 0.24 ^* NAPM(-1) - 0.07 ^* NAPM(-2) \\
(1.4) \qquad\qquad (0.3) \\
RSQ = 0.096; \; DW = 1.94.
\end{aligned}
$$

The equation is estimated for 44 quarters, from 1990.1 through 2000.4. %GDPH is the percentage change in real GDP at annual rates. The other variables are first differences in consumer sentiment, homebuilding sentiment, leading indicators, and the purchasing managers survey.

The results are not very promising. Only the index of leading indicators with a one-quarter lag is significant. The purchasing managers survey has the wrong sign for both quarters, and none of the other terms has a t-ratio greater than 1.5. The monetary component of the leading indicators did provide some warning of the 2001 recession. Yet over an extended period of time, they do not work very well.

We can draw the following conclusions about the use of sentiment and expectational indexes for predicting the overall economy.

1   Over the past decade, neither consumer sentiment or consumer expectations improve forecast accuracy.
2   The NAHB index of homebuilding sentiment is useful in predicting housing starts, but when used in conjunction with other variables, does not improve forecasting accuracy for overall real GDP.
3   The NAPM index did predict the 2000 slowdown, but in the past it has not been accurate. It also predicted a 1999 slowdown that did not occur.

Finally, we can determine how well the simple model with lagged monetary variables would have predicted real GDP in 2000 – even if the actual values of the stock price are used (table 12.4).

Table 12.5 Predictions of change in real GDP using alternative forecasting methods.

	2000.1	2000.2	2000.3	2000.4	2000
Growth rate – actual	4.8	5.6	2.2	1.1	
Growth rate – constant adjustment	4.1	4.9	3.6	4.2	
Growth rate – AR adjustment	2.1	3.6	2.8	4.0	
Growth rate – consensus	3.0	3.2	3.4	3.2	
Growth rate – monetary leading indicators	4.2	3.7	3.4	3.1	
Absolute average errors					
Constant adjustment	0.6	0.6	1.4	3.1	1.4
AR adjustment	2.7	1.9	0.6	2.9	2.0
Consensus	1.8	2.3	1.2	2.1	1.8
Monetary leading indicators	0.6	1.8	1.2	2.0	1.4

Considering that the stock market term is lagged only one quarter and the turnaround was not known in advance, the "monetary" model would not have generated more accurate forecasts at the beginning of the year either, although it would have improved forecast accuracy in 2001.

12.8 CONCLUSION

Ten years ago, Stock and Watson reviewed all the major forecasting methods and found that none of them adequately predicted the 1990–1 recession. In this chapter, we have reviewed all the major methods and found that none of them adequately predicted the 2001 recession, although the economy might have escaped an outright recession had it not been for the terrorist attacks.

Where does this leave the would-be forecaster?

Twenty years ago, much the same question was asked: at that time, the failure of forecasters had been more acute because of the series of unprecedented events during the 1970s. It was claimed that econometric models were the wave of the past, and would be replaced by a variety of forecasting methods. On the technical side, ARIMAs and VARs would take precedence. On the non-technical side, enhanced methods of calculating leading indicators, indexes of consumer and business sentiment, and informed judgment would play a more important role.

None of these promises has been fulfilled. In fact, there is no "magic bullet" that will produce better forecasts. Forecasters would do well to remember the insight of Bischoff et al. that "nothing is really stable; all structures are changing slowly." What works in the past will not necessarily work in the future.

Critics of econometric modeling point to this conclusion as prima facie evidence that structural econometric models cannot be used to generate accurate forecasts. In fact, the argument can be entirely turned around. That dictum serves as prima facie evidence that no method based entirely on the past will work without adjustment, including surveys and consensus forecasts. Furthermore – and this is important – the evidence is even more overwhelming for mechanical methods such as ARIMA and VAR models.

Making accurate forecasts is difficult. However, the alternative, which is not to try at all, hardly seems to be superior. In this author's view, the most fruitful approach remains the one presented throughout this book. Start with a careful use of econometrics, estimate robust structural knowledge, and keep these models up to date, incorporating recent events and changes as they seem appropriate. From time to time, informed judgment may improve the results, but combining forecasts that are all based on the same body of data and information is unlikely to generate superior results.

When previous structural relationships shift, or when unforeseen exogenous events transpire, no forecasting method is likely to give accurate results. Yet when previous relationships remain fairly stable, or change only slowly, it is our conclusion that structural forecasting models can still provide more accurate estimates than mechanical methods of extrapolation, survey methods, or consensus forecasts.

PROBLEMS AND QUESTIONS

1. Near the end of 2000, public opinion polls quoted in the *Wall Street Journal* and elsewhere showed that just as many people expected a recession in 2001 as did not.

(a) Solve the prototype model for 2001 assuming the same constant adjustments as in 2000. For exogenous variables, assume that trend variables, such as government purchases and industrial production Europe, grow at the same rate as in 2000. The price of petroleum products can be assumed to decline linearly from 100 to 80 during the year. All other exogenous variables can hold their average 2000 values. What do the results show for real growth during the year?

(b) Now go back and recalculate the constant adjustments for 2001 based on the residuals for 2000 and re-solve the model. How do the results compare? Which set of forecasts do you think provides a more reliable indicator of economic activity in 2001?

(c) Late in 2000, the FOMC strongly hinted it would be reducing the funds rate early the following year, which indeed turned out to be the case. Assume that the funds rate is cut by 1% in each of the four

continued

quarters, so it declines to $2\frac{1}{2}$% by 2001.4. Adjust the Fed funds rate equation so that it generates these results. (Hint: because of multiplier effects, the final constant adjustments may not be the same as the difference between the simulated values of the funds rate and the expected target rates.) How are the forecasts affected?

(d)   A recession is usually defined as a decline in at least two consecutive quarters of real GDP and a rise in the unemployment rate of at least $1\frac{1}{2}$%. Using this definition, show what constant adjustments and changes in exogenous variables would be necessary to generate a recession forecast with this model. (Hint: there would probably be a major decline in stock prices coupled with no easing by the Fed.)

2. The NAPM index appears to have predicted the 2001 recession better than the recession of 1990–1 or the slowdown of 1995. For many years, the index of leading indicators gave poor results because one of the components was the change in sensitive materials prices. Many years ago, a rise in prices meant stronger economic activity, whereas more recently it has meant Fed tightening and hence weaker economic activity.

(a)   Taking this into account, disaggregate the NAPM index by its price and non-price components (data are available on the website). Recalculate the index without the price terms and determine whether the short-term accuracy of this index has improved.

(b)   Some have claimed the US economy slowed down in the second half of 2000 because of weaker exports stemming from the stronger dollar. Examine the export order component of the NAPM index, and determine whether the predictive accuracy of the index would improve if this component received a greater weight in recent years.

(c)   The components of the NAPM index that are generally thought to be most closely aligned with leading indicators are new orders, new export orders, and supplier deliveries, whereas backlog of orders, production, inventories, prices, and employment are thought to be more closely aligned with coincident indicators. Determine whether the predictive accuracy of the NAPM index can be improved by providing larger weights to the leading indicator components.

(d)   Since manufacturing is the sector of the economy that fluctuates the most, it would seem sensible to look for signs of turning points in that sector; however, the NAPM index has not performed very well. Based on the key elements in the structure of the macro model, explain why you think that has been the case in recent years.

continued

3. The examples given in the text suggest that (i) the NAHB index of homebuilding sentiment improves forecast accuracy for housing, but (ii) is not a useful leading indicator for predicting overall economic activity.

(a) Reestimate the housing start equation using the NAHB index. Since those data are only available since 1985, that will require truncating the sample period, and some of the terms will become insignificant or take on the wrong signs; they should be omitted. It is also possible that a different lag structure for some of the monetary variables will fit the 1985–99 data better, and you should also make those adjustments. Then calculate the constant adjustment, if any, for 2000 based on the 1999 residuals

(b) Insert this equation into the macro model and solve for 2000. How much do the forecasts for housing starts improve? How much does the forecast for real GDP improve?

(c) This might not be a legitimate test because the sharp decline in the NAHB index early in the year may not have been known to forecasters at the end of 1999. Estimate a simple regression between the NAHB index and lagged interest rates to determine whether the dip in the NAHB index in 2000.2 (it actually started in March) could have been foreseen by forecasters.

(d) The Blue Chip Consensus forecast for housing starts in 2000 made at the beginning of the year was 1.54 million, compared to an actual level of 1.67 million in 1999. Determine how much, if any, the forecast of housing starts and real GDP would have been improved by using the consensus forecast compared to (i) the model forecast, and (ii) an equation with the NAHB index. Quarterly consensus forecasts for housing starts are not available, but for this purpose assume that the consensus forecast by quarter was 1.60, 1.55, 1.50, and 1.50 million starts.

4. Assume that your client is reasonably comfortable with the overall structure of the model you use but doubts that you or anyone else can predict the stock market accurately. As a result, you prepare three alternative scenarios: the S&P index declines steadily during 2001, falling 20% from its level at the end of 2000; it remains at its year-end 2000 level throughout 2001; and it rises steadily during 2001, returning to its peak 2000 level by year-end. Use various sets of constant adjustments to achieve these results.

(a) Determine the impact of different stock market forecasts on all the components of real GDP predicted in the model. Which sectors are most sensitive to stock market fluctuations?

continued

(b) Assume that the Fed would ease in reaction to a stock market plunge
     – as it did in 1987 and 1998. Adjust the constant terms in the equa-
     tions for Federal funds and the money supply so that the average
     growth rate during 2001 is the same if (i) the stock market declines
     20% and the Fed eases, and (ii) the stock market rises 20% and Fed
     policy remains unchanged.

(c) In early 2001, President George W. Bush said he wanted to cut per-
     sonal income taxes by an average of 15%. Actually Bush planned to
     phase in the tax cut, but for purposes of this exercise, assume the
     constant term in the personal income tax equation declined by
     $150 billion at the beginning of 2001. Determine the impact on real
     GDP, interest rates, and stock prices for the year. Based on the tax
     cut multipliers given in the text above, what do you think would
     happen to those variables in 2002 and 2003 relative to the baseline
     (it is not necessary to forecast out through 2003 to answer this ques-
     tion; relative simulations can be performed on data from the late
     1990s).

(d) In order for incremental gain in real GDP during the first year of the
     tax cut to remain intact, the Fed would have to accommodate that
     change through easier monetary policy. Approximately how much
     would the constant terms for the Federal funds rate and money
     supply have to be adjusted to achieve this result?

5. Simulating the model using equations estimated with AR(1) transformations results in larger errors during the 1990s, but we have not examined what would happen if some of the equations were adjusted but others
were not.

(a) Two of the key equations with exceptionally low DW statistics
     are the equations for consumer credit and business loans; that is
     because changes in credit conditions are largely governed by long-
     term changes in Fed policy and banking regulations rather than
     short-term changes in economic variables. Reestimate these two
     equations with AR(1) transformations.

(b) Now solve the model for 2000 using all the other equations and their
     previously calculated constant terms, and compare the forecasts with
     actual values. Are the predictions for loans and credit better or worse
     with the AR(1) equations? What about forecasts of the variables that
     depend on these terms, namely motor vehicles, consumption of
     durables, purchases of computers, and non-residential construction?
     What further conclusions can be drawn about the use of AR(1) terms
     in forecasting equations?

continued

(c) Using AR(1) equations for consumer credit and business loans, predict the economy for 2001 and compare it with the answers obtained in problem 1. Explain which forecast you would prefer to present to management or your client.

(d) The other major sector of the model where equations have unusually low DW statistics occurs in the labor sector. Reestimate the equations for employee-hours, household employment, labor force, and productivity with AR(1) terms, dropping out terms that are insignificant or have the wrong sign. Generate forecasts for 2000 and compare these with the baseline forecast, with particularly emphasis on the forecast for the rate of unemployment, which is the critical variable in this sector. Comment on the usefulness of adjusting low DW statistics by using the AR(1) transformation.

(e) Now estimate the change in the unemployment rate directly as a function of the percentage change in employee-hours, labor force, real GDP, and industrial production (use both unlagged and lagged percentage changes in employee-hours). The DW statistic shows no evidence of autocorrelated residuals. Put that equation in the model and solve for the unemployment rate in 2000. Do you think that is a better method of estimating unemployment?

6. Simulate the prototype model from 1980.1 through 1999.4. Note that the model predicts the early 1980s recession and recovery slightly before they happen, whereas it predicts the 1990 recession after it happened.

(a) What does that suggest about lag times for predicting recessions in the future? How would you adjust the lag structure in preparing future forecasts?

(b) Test the hypothesis that if the Fed had eased in a timely fashion in 1981 and 1990, as it did in 2001, the economy would have not actually plunged into recession. Given these results, why do you think the Fed failed to ease quickly in those earlier years?

(c) Due in part to a tripling of oil prices, natural gas price shortages, Fed tightening, and an unprecedented decline in Nasdaq stocks, the US economy was on the verge of recession in 2001, even before the terrorist attacks. What variables in the model would have to be modified to predict an actual recession?

INDEX

Note: page numbers in italics refer to figures; page numbers in bold refer to tables.